# OLD MONEY, NEW WEST

BOOKS BY ROBERT NELSON
*Early Yuma*

BOOKS BY JACK L. AUGUST, JR.
*Vision in the Desert*
*Desert Bloom or Desert Doom?*
*We Call it "Preskit"*
*Senator Dennis DeConcini*
*Dividing Western Waters*
*Adversity is My Angel* (coauthor)
*Play by Play*
*History of Buckeye Canal*
*The Norton Trilogy*

# OLD MONEY, NEW WEST

*Fife Symington and the Uniquely American Landscapes that Made Him, Broke Him, and Made Him Anew*

ROBERT NELSON AND JACK L. AUGUST, JR.

FOREWORD BY BILL CLINTON

Fort Worth, Texas

Library of Congress Cataloging-in-Publication Data

Names: Nelson, Robert, 1967– author. | August, Jack L., Jr., 1954– author.
  | Clinton, Bill, 1946– writer of foreword.
Title: Old money, new West : Fife Symington and the uniquely American
  landscapes that made him, broke him, and made him anew / Robert Nelson
  and Jack L. August, Jr. ; foreword by Bill Clinton.
Description: Fort Worth, Texas : TCU Press, [2021] | Includes
  bibliographical references and index. | Summary: "By 1994, Arizona
  Governor Fife Symington was arguably the hottest young star in the
  Republican Party-a lively, articulate voice for a new breed of
  culturally moderate conservatives perfectly positioned for a US Senate
  run and perhaps a shot at the presidency in 2000. Instead, earlier
  decisions and mistakes he made as his real estate empire collapsed amid
  the Savings and Loan Crisis would torpedo his political career, bankrupt
  him, and place him at the doorstep of federal prison. Then a new
  century-along with a preemptive presidential pardon from President Bill
  Clinton-brought new hope and opportunities as well as international fame
  in the world of UFO research. While unique, Symington's story is also an
  American story. Born into one of the wealthiest families in America,
  Symington could have hunkered down in old-money leisure. Instead, he
  left the country to fight in Southeast Asia and then, like millions of
  Americans before him, went to make his name amid yet another real estate
  boom in the American West. He brought his old-school conservative fiscal
  philosophies with him, but soon found himself at war with the cultural
  conservatives within his own party, particularly on issues of
  immigration and the environment. Symington was an early pioneer in
  successfully navigating what is now an existential threat for moderates
  in the Republican Party: how to govern with conservative-leaning values
  without kowtowing to the worst instincts of the radicalized, nativist
  right"— Provided by publisher.
Identifiers: LCCN 2021036157 | ISBN 9780875657875 (cloth) | ISBN
  9780875657974 (ebook)
Subjects: LCSH: Symington, J. Fife, 1945– | Governors— Arizona— Biography.
  | Arizona— Politics and government— 1951– | BISAC: BIOGRAPHY &
  AUTOBIOGRAPHY / Political | LCGFT: Biographies.
Classification: LCC F815.3.S96 N45 2021 | DDC 979.1/053092 [B]—dc23
LC record available at https://lccn.loc.gov/2021036157

Design by David Timmons

TCU Box 298300
Fort Worth, Texas 76129
To order books: 1.800.826.8911

For Jack, of course.

# CONTENTS

Foreword by Bill Clinton     IX

Preface and Thanksgiving     XI

Prologue     1

Chapter 1: The Star-Spangled Lineage     10

Chapter 2: Monkeys and Mondo Trasho     25

Chapter 3: "Symington is a Fascist!" at Harvard     41

Chapter 4: War     49

Chapter 5: A Second-Class City     53

Chapter 6: How to Get Ahead in Business     58

Chapter 7: A World-Class City     67

Chapter 8: How to Get Ahead in Politics     81

Chapter 9: Boom Time with a Time Bomb     92

Chapter 10: Decisions, Decisions     97

Chapter 11: Debacle and Depression     104

Chapter 12: The Race Is On     110

Chapter 13: "Same Old Ev"     121

Chapter 14: A Blur of Plurality     128

Chapter 15: One More Time     141

Chapter 16: The Rookie     148

Chapter 17: On a Roll     157

Chapter 18: The Devil Is Allegedly in the Details     165

Chapter 19: A Tale of Two 1992s     176

Chapter 20: Big Budget Feud     189

Chapter 21: Back in the Black                              198

Chapter 22: A Right Turn?                                  209

Chapter 23: The Mercado                                    215

Chapter 24: The Bully Pulpit                               224

Chapter 25: The Problem with Polls                         232

Chapter 26: The Big Swing                                  240

Chapter 27: Contract with Arizona                          248

Chapter 28: A Bad Fall                                     258

Chapter 29: Blood in the Water                             268

Chapter 30: Tough Guy                                      278

Chapter 31: "Who Is This Guy?"                             281

Chapter 32: Space Invaders                                 285

Chapter 33: Pre-Trial Diversions                           290

Chapter 34: "Arizona's Trial of the Century"               299

Chapter 35: Dog Days and End Times                         313

Chapter 36: Hard Times                                     327

Chapter 37: The Waiting Game                               336

Chapter 38: New Hope and $8.25 an Hour                     342

Chapter 39: The Remaining Legal Issues                     351

Chapter 40: The Foodie                                     360

Chapter 41: "You Couldn't Make This Stuff Up"              369

Chapter 42: Reefer Sensibleness                            380

Epilogue                                                   387

Notes                                                      393

Index                                                      458

# FOREWORD

I first met Fife Symington in early 1965 when he came down from Harvard to visit a school friend from Baltimore, Tommy Caplan, who was my classmate at the Georgetown University School of Foreign Service. Tommy lived just a few doors down from me in a freshman dorm, and we had become good friends by the time Fife came to visit.

The three of us palled around one chilly afternoon and evening, and I enjoyed the visit, although we were as different in our backgrounds and politics as daylight and dark. I was a Southern Baptist from Arkansas, a strong Democrat, and supporter of President Johnson. Fife was the scion of a well-known Maryland family, an Episcopalian, and a conservative Republican whose maternal great-grandfather was the union-busting tycoon Henry Clay Frick. His father had just run for Congress as a big supporter of Senator Barry Goldwater, who had been a guest in their house. Fife had been to Europe, skied the Alps, and jumped horses in foxhunts. I played the saxophone, enjoyed movies and meals with friends and family, and before coming to Georgetown, had been out of my native state only for trips to Louisiana, Mississippi, and Washington, DC.

In today's culture, where disagreement so often seems to require personal disapproval and distancing, we might not have gotten to know each other. But I liked him. He was neither affected nor arrogant, and seemed as curious about my life as I was about his.

I saw Fife a few more times during college. A couple of years later he helped me out of a real situation. By now, several competing versions of Fife's rescue of me in Nantucket Sound, just off West Beach in Hyannis Port, have made the rounds. All are probably true, up to a point. For what it is worth, my memory is of scraping my hands, arms, and legs badly on a barnacle-covered rock I grasped when I had become exhausted swimming against a strong tide. The rest-stop was a painful nightmare, so I let go, hoping I could make it back to shore. Fife was on the beach, saw what was happening, and rushed out to help me. Luckily, we hit a long, narrow sandbar halfway in and could walk the rest of the way. But Fife hadn't known that sandbar was there or how much trouble I was in when he bolted to my aid. I never forgot his instinctive kindness and courage.

Our terms as governors overlapped briefly, and I had several encounters with him during my first term as president, usually at the twice-yearly National Governors Association meetings. Especially after 1994, as America grew much more polarized, I'm sure more than one Republican told him he should have just let me drown. I used to kid him about it, too.

When Fife's legal troubles derailed his life and led to the loss of his governorship, he applied for a pardon and I decided to grant it. Not because of the long-ago rescue, but because the court of appeals had reversed his conviction due to the improper dismissal of a juror—one who was determined to acquit him—after other jurors complained she was "holding up" a resolution of the case; because he had already paid a heavy price in losing the governor's office and paying millions in legal fees; because he was still facing civil claims he'd be better able to pay out of prison; and because I was told the US attorney was not eager to retry the months-long complicated case.

I'm glad the last twenty years have been happy ones for Fife. He's a decent man who was ambitious and adventurous, served honorably in the Vietnam War, made a new life for himself in Arizona, was a serious, successful governor, had a large family he loves, and kept going in the face of troubles that would have broken many people. It's an interesting American fable. As Robert Browning famously said, "A man's reach should exceed his grasp, or what's a heaven for?"

—BILL CLINTON

# PREFACE AND THANKSGIVING

To extrapolate on a famous line from one of Fife Symington's ideological adversaries: It takes a village to write a biography.

That's especially true when the subject seems intent on living
several lives in a single lifetime, a lifetime itself intertwined with many of
the defining periods and people of the American Century.

Symington's blue blood childhood was shaped by his hard-bitten
great-grandfather, Henry Clay Frick, the notorious robber baron who became the second-richest man in America (behind John D. Rockefeller) as
he helped transform the country into the industrial leader of the world.

Symington's Frick-born free-market conservatism was then galva-
nized by the man credited with reviving the conservative movement
during the early 1960s, US senator Barry Goldwater, who later convinced
Symington to run for governor of Arizona. Symington also found himself in one of the epicenters of civil unrest during the turbulent sixties.
(But unlike most at Harvard College, he marched against the grain of
protests to reach the ROTC classes that prepared him to assist in a conflict he supported.)

Later, he would build a thriving real estate business amid the rise of
the American Sunbelt, then watch his company and fortune dissolve
amid the catastrophic Savings and Loan Crisis that nearly shattered the
US economy. His detractors, among them federal prosecutors, would
suggest Symington's run-and-gun business practices were as much part
of the systemic economic problem as he was a victim of its ravages.

He was one of the poster boys for the neoconservative's "Republican
Revolution" of the mid-1990s. Symington had balanced the budget of
Arizona and even created a budget surplus using supply-sider policies.
Couldn't the same things be done for America? (Plenty of critics, of
course, countered that Arizona's 1990s fiscal renaissance was due more to
the policies of the Democrat running the country than the Republican
running the state.)

Symington helped give birth to the US charter school movement, re-ignited the argument that the rights of US states under the Tenth Amendment were being usurped by federal overreach, and assisted in building new trade corridors with Sonora and other Mexican states during the early days of the North American Free Trade Agreement.

Of course, Symington's decade-plus of personal financial tribulations and legal gymnastics—during which he spent an estimated $15 million on attorneys as the feds and his creditors spent even more—is a tale unto itself.

Beyond policy and financials, Symington's contributions to the nation's culinary scene, the medical marijuana industry in the Southwest, and the body of evidence that humans are not alone in the universe make Symington an even more difficult subject to corral in a single manuscript.

Covering so much ground demands heavy sourcing.

Thank you, first, then, to Fife Symington, for hundreds of hours spent recounting work and personal stories, digging for documents and photos, and fact-checking passages of the manuscript. (All this after several years of refusing to assist in any such project.) Some of the review was uncomfortable—he was and remains a controversial figure. Certainly appreciated was Symington's commitment to the idea that the biographers were obligated to try their best to call balls and strikes, not cheer a home team.

Thank you, too, to his family—Ann, Helen Clay, Fife IV, Scott, Richard, Tom, and Whitney all provided invaluable insight.

This book would not have been possible without the board of the Southwest Center for History and Public Policy: Jim Howard, Richard Mallery, Francie Austin, Dino DeConcini, and Dr. Mindy Clark. Mallery, a longtime business associate of Symington's, and Howard, a longtime political adversary of Symington's, additionally provided invaluable information and perspective.

Helping greatly with interviews, editorial review, and other elements critical to this project were Doug Cole, Tommy Caplan, Tom Zoellner, Kathy August, Bill Clinton, Terry Lynam, Stephanie Mahan, Michele Reagan, Denise Nelson, Andrew Nelson, Molly Spain, Kathy Walton, and the archives staff of the Arizona State Library.

Thank you also to those who agreed to be interviewed for the book, particularly Robert Wilson, Randy Todd, John Dowd, Jay Heiler, David Schindler, Wes Gullett, Maria Baier, Grant Woods, John Waters, Martin

Lowy, Mary Jo Pitzl, Deb Shanahan, Peter Hayes, Andrew Ross, John Dougherty, Art Laffer, Chuck Coughlin, Omer Reed, Skip Rimsza, Greg Stanton, Camilla Strongin, and Linda Valdez.

Thank you, too, to a remarkable cast of Arizona journalists. The reporting and writing of John Kolbe, Howard Fischer, Keven Willey, Steve Wilson, Charles Kelly, Shaun McKinnon, Jerry Kammer, Pat Flannery, Mark Flatten, Dennis Wagner, Terry Greene Sterling, Dolores Tropiano, David Bodney, Rick Barrs, Jeremy Voas, Pitzl, Shanahan, and Dougherty provided details—particularly from Symington's stints as a high-flying developer and two-term governor—that would be impossible to reconstruct without their efforts throughout the 1980s and 1990s.

Finally, certainly the most difficult and awkward acknowledgment: Thank you to the late Jack August, who passed away in 2017 after dedicating countless hours to interviews, document dives, and writing on Symington's life. Jack wrote several nonfiction books that now rest firmly in the canon of Southwestern political and legal history. Jack loved a colorful tale from a sweeping landscape, so he was thrilled to be tackling the story of the ever-contentious, ever-unpredictable Symington and the old blue blood East and new Wild West he inhabited.

This story, along with numerous histories of foundational events in southwestern US history, would not exist without Dr. August. He was a friend, teacher, adviser, and mentor to countless others beyond his coauthor. He is missed every day at the same time he continues to inform every day. Thank you, Jack, for all you did and all the treasures you left behind.

—ROBERT NELSON

# PROLOGUE

Fife Symington had just finished reciting the Lord's Prayer during a Saturday morning prayer breakfast in early 2001 when he felt the quaking of the phone in his pocket.

In front of him on the restaurant table sat an imprudently large wedge of white cake topped with a fondant rose—a gift from a group of already trail-frowzy hikers at a nearby table who were celebrating the tenth birthday of their Camelback Mountain hiking club. Two of the hikers had offered Symington a piece after seeing the former governor of their state walk into the popular North Phoenix diner. "We know you love the mountain, too," one of the hikers said.[1]

During his six-plus years as governor, Symington had made a pre-dawn hike of the iconic Valley landmark part of his daily routine. Often under the faint light of the morning star, the avid outdoorsman would barrel up the Echo Canyon Trail at a pace brisk enough to leave his two-man security detail hundreds of yards behind in the desert.[2] Symington, a lifelong adrenaline junky seemingly happiest reading or relating tales of manly vigor, had long been quick to relate that, in two instances, a state trooper tasked with flanking him had vomited trying to keep up.

The Camelback Mountain preserve was a special place to Symington for another reason: it was Symington's idol-turned-mentor, Barry Goldwater, who had led efforts in 1965 to forever protect the mountain from the sprawl of Phoenix and its suburbs that now surround it.[3]

Next to Symington sat Episcopal priest Frank Williams, Symington's longtime friend and spiritual adviser. Symington was a lifelong Episcopalian, who, after his mother had forgotten to have him baptized as a baby, was baptized hurriedly after his sixteenth birthday at the church in New York where his great-aunt, Helen Clay Frick, was a longtime parishioner. Grauntie, as the Symington children called her, was the daughter of Henry Clay Frick, the pugnacious industrialist and union-buster who

was, according to *Forbes* magazine, the second richest man in America
the year before his death in 1919.[4]

Also at Symington's table was Joe Albo, a former prosecutor and
Democratic political force in the state. The two had met in the 1980s
before Symington ran for governor. Despite their significant political differences, Symington appointed Albo to be the state's top cop as head of
the Arizona Department of Public Safety.

Albo and Symington were talking when the phone buzzed. Symington
pulled the phone from his pocket and looked at the number. Upon seeing who was calling, Symington apologized for the interruption, stepped
away from the table, and put the phone to his ear.

It was his ninety-year-old father, John Fife Symington Jr., who, amid
a career as an executive with Pan American World Airways, had also
served as US ambassador to Trinidad and Tobago and ran unsuccessfully
three times for Congress in Maryland's then heavily Democratic Second
District.[5]

"Fife, is this true?" the elder Symington asked.

"Is what true?"

• • •

That same morning, attorney John Dowd was lounging in his modest
ranch-style home in Northern Virginia watching Bill Clinton and George
W. Bush emerge from the presidential limousine and amble into the east
entrance of the US Capitol. It was just before noon on Inauguration Day,
January 20, 2001, and Dowd, renowned for his successful "Keating Five"
defense of John McCain and his ferocious 252-page betting-scandal report that left Pete Rose banned from baseball for life, was slipping from
antsy to crestfallen as the transfer of power from Clinton to Bush neared.[6]

The likelihood of a "preemptive" presidential pardon for his latest
big-name client, ruined developer and toppled Arizona governor Fife
Symington, seemed to be fading. The pardon petition written hurriedly
a month before by Dowd and his partner, Terry Lynam, must have fallen
on deaf or overly burdened presidential ears. So it goes, he figured. Success is the exception when someone outside an administration's orbit
submits a pardon to the president of the United States, especially when
that outsider is requesting something as exotic as a "preemptive" pardon.
(Beyond Jimmy Carter's 1977 blanket order that draft dodgers could not
be prosecuted for evading military service, only a few individuals—most
notably mega-insiders Richard Nixon and Casper Weinberger—had ever

received a pardon that blocked the government from prosecuting certain past actions.)[7]

Yet Dowd had felt justified to hope. After all, his client's convictions for misstatements on financial documents given to lenders—convictions that forced Symington to resign after more than six years in office—had been overturned by the Ninth Circuit Court of Appeals two years before. Since that time, Alejandro Mayorkas, the new US attorney in Los Angeles who would oversee any reintroduced charges, had seemed reticent about refiling, instead offering increasingly light plea deals that Symington seemed increasingly slow to refuse.[8] Bluffing or not, Symington had said in one meeting with Mayorkas that he wanted the fight, and Mayorkas wasn't showing equal zeal to commit the thousands of hours and millions of dollars it would take for a round two in a federal courtroom in Phoenix.[9]

The trial of Fife Symington in 1997 on twenty-one counts of extortion, making false financial statements, and bank fraud had taken nearly three months. The jury took another three weeks to decide that Symington was guilty on seven of the charges that accused him of deliberately misstating his net worth on loan documents (one of those seven convictions was soon after thrown out by the judge in the case).[10]

The core issue: Prosecutors argued that Symington had intentionally misstated his net worth on legally binding financial documents in an attempt to keep his business afloat during the Phoenix real estate market cataclysm of the late 1980s and early 1990s. Any misstatements, Symington's defense argued, were simple oversights, mistakes made by outside accountants or, in the cases in which Symington was asked to estimate the value of his remaining real estate assets, instances of Symingtonesque optimism that, okay, sometimes perhaps bordered on delusional boosterism.

Dowd even argued Symington sometimes wasn't optimistic—he was just plain correct. After all, Dowd argued, the Symington-built Camelback Esplanade, home to a three-hundred-room Ritz-Carlton Hotel and some of the Valley's highest-priced commercial rental space, was making money again by the mid-1990s. (What Dowd didn't mention, though, was that the Esplanade was arguably viable again only because its new owners had nabbed it at fire sale prices when creditors were liquidating Symington-built properties.)

Fife Symington worked hard to make beautiful things, Dowd had argued. Forget his name. Forget his lineage. The old Eastern money never made it to the New West. In his real estate life in Arizona, Fife Symington was more blue collar than blue blood.

Dowd had worked himself to the edge of burnout while defending Symington through that crazed summer of 1997. He had been mobbed daily by as many as forty newspaper, radio, and television reporters as he emerged from the courtroom at noon and 4:30 p.m. each day, when temperatures regularly topped 110 degrees. He had been pushed and he had pushed back, hurling profanities at questions he found offensive and even slapping the tape recorder from the hand of one of the Valley's most respected investigative reporters who was refusing to take "no comment" as an answer.[11]

When prosecutors argued Symington lied to creditors and lenders about his net worth as his real estate empire melted, Dowd, the retired Marine captain, argued with ever-increasing thunder that Symington was just a victim like everyone else when the distended Valley real estate market burst.

In crafting their pardon petition, Dowd and Lynam only included a CliffsNotes outline of the sprawling financial case. Character-witness testimonials were included. One additional argument was presented: Even if one believed Symington was guilty of knowingly misrepresenting his net worth to creditors and lenders, he had already suffered and paid dearly. For one, he had lost his job as governor of Arizona. He had already paid any debt he might have owed to society, Dowd, Lynam, and Symington's character witnesses argued.

At the end of the day, though, the quality of the petition might not matter at all. Ironically, Symington's attorneys likely had the best chance of winning a pardon if the president viewed the petition only as a formality. Winning likely depended more on what Clinton already knew and how Clinton already felt about Symington.

Dowd knew long before coauthoring the petition that Clinton had strong feelings regarding Symington. Dowd knew Clinton had followed his client's case. Clinton had told him so during a chance meeting a few years before at a Baltimore Orioles game.[12]

At that meeting in the president's box at Camden Yards—as Dowd, Symington, and Clinton watched the game in which Cal Ripken broke Major League Baseball's record for most consecutive games played—

Clinton turned to Dowd and explained the foundation of his obvious fondness for Symington:

"You know Fife saved my life, don't you?"

And after all, it was Clinton himself—relaying instructions through a mutual friend—who had educated Symington and Dowd on exactly how to get a petition into the Oval Office as quickly as possible.[13]

But nearly a month had passed since Dowd's assistant had walked that petition from Dowd's office near DuPont Square to the White House. It must have gotten lost in the shuffle.

Dowd and Lynam would just have to continue their negotiations with federal prosecutors.[14]

But just as Clinton and Bush disappeared into the Capitol, Dowd's phone rang.

• • •

Attorney David Schindler was visiting his mother in Los Angeles on the morning of the presidential inauguration. Schindler wasn't thinking much about the transition of power, in good part because it no longer would impact his life. He had already bounced from his position as an assistant US attorney for a more lucrative private-sector job in which his expertise prosecuting white-collar criminal cases made him a master at defending the accused.[15]

By January of 2000, David Schindler was defending people in Symington-like predicaments, not dedicating his life to putting them behind bars as he did from 1995 through 1997, as lead prosecutor in Symington's case.

Schindler recognized the phone number when the call came that morning. It was a reporter from the *Arizona Republic* in Phoenix who had covered the grueling trial in which Schindler and his team presented 1,400 financial documents in a tired cafeteria-like federal courtroom that felt barely cooler than the Sonoran summer outside. It was the longest trial nearly everyone involved had ever suffered, and most of the key players lost piles of dress clothes to yellow sweat stains. But the "audit in the courtroom" strategy landed seven convictions out of twenty-one charges from the jury. Schindler felt he had done his job.

Then, it was a questionable decision by the judge to dismiss a troublesome juror that allowed Symington's successful appeal to the Ninth Circuit, not any mistake by Schindler.

When Schindler answered the phone, he simply chuckled when he was told that Symington had been given a type of pardon that protected him from any further prosecution in these past financial dealings. It was over.

Smart play by John and Terry, Schindler thought to himself. Well done—they engineered a political avenue. Schindler knew well that Clinton believed the DOJ had a pattern of overreaching. Schindler also guessed Clinton, because of the Whitewater investigation, must have had empathy for Symington. Dowd and Lynam had played every card they had. Schindler would have done the same thing.

That day Schindler told reporters, "I think it's very unfortunate that the President chose to circumvent the process."[16] But Schindler said he had no ill will toward Symington. He even wished him good luck in his future endeavors.

But Schindler still believed, and would continue to believe, that Fife Symington had intentionally misled his investors. For years after, when it came time for Schindler to give an elevator-speech synopsis of the case, he would usually point to just two pages to back his belief that Symington deserved to be punished.

Symington, according to Schindler, was promising creditors—under penalty of law for misrepresentations—that he was too poor to pay them back at the same time he was promising potential lenders he was plenty wealthy to pay them back.

Schindler didn't buy Symington's explanation for the inconsistencies in the numbers he presented to lenders and creditors regarding the values of his properties. (Besides claiming some dates and numbers were simple mistakes, Symington said he had been asked for different types of estimates from different lenders during the volatile real estate market. For example: One lender, Symington argued, wanted him to give them his best estimate of worth *over the long term*, while another lender wanted Symington's estimate of the value of his properties if they were sold *that same day* in the heart of the depressed market.[17] Obviously, Symington argued, those would be very different numbers.)

Schindler accused Symington myriad times of trying to cloud the issue with irrelevant details. Those two financial documents filed in the early 1990s in which Symington valued his property differently, Schindler argued, clearly stated that deception was intended.

Schindler told reporters: "It was pretty simple."

• • •

Tommy Caplan had lingered at the White House until 10:30 p.m. the night before Bush's inauguration. Caplan, a bestselling author and co-founder of the PEN/Faulkner Award for Fiction, had been asked by a friend to give his nine-year-old daughter a tour of the White House. The girl had begged to see the inner sanctum; Caplan had promised to take her; and if he didn't take her that night, there probably wouldn't be another chance.[18] He was a close confidant to President Clinton, his old college roommate at Georgetown and one of his closest friends since, and that Friday evening would probably be the last time Caplan would be free to come and go and roam much of the White House at will.

Caplan and his guest strolled casually from room to room amid the bedlam typical of the White House on an administration's last day. Staffers scurried by with boxes and other personal items while cleaning crews prepared the house for its next inhabitants. Amid the tumult, the famously urbane Caplan mixed his duties as a tour guide with a cavalcade of goodbyes and well-wishes. It was not a melancholy farewell, though, he said later: "Everyone knew it was coming. It was time to go."

Caplan later said he didn't ask anyone if they knew if the president had pardoned Symington. Although Caplan considered Symington a close friend and thought he deserved to be freed from the cloud of potential new charges, Caplan said he felt it improper to insert himself in, or even ask about, the pardon review process or outcome.

Caplan's friendship with Symington predated his friendship with Clinton. Caplan and Symington had been close friends at Gilman School, a private prep school in Baltimore. Symington and Caplan were editors together on the school newspaper: Caplan ran the features department; Symington was his editor-in-chief.[19]

Even in high school, the two had significantly different political opinions. While Symington had already become an acolyte of conservative Arizona senator Barry Goldwater, Caplan was a volunteer for, and eventually president of, the Teen Democrats of Maryland for the Kennedy campaign of 1960.

The two friends did, however, work together to start the "Youth to Youth Pilot Project," through which young people corresponded with contemporaries in underdeveloped countries.

After Gilman, Symington went north to Harvard and Caplan went south to Georgetown, where dorm rooms were assigned alphabetically.

Caplan's was a few doors from Clinton's. The two freshmen quickly bonded over a shared fascination with John F. Kennedy.

When Symington visited Caplan that first winter, Caplan introduced him to Clinton. Through their college years in the mid-1960s, the three occasionally crossed paths at gatherings.

During one get-together on a blustery day at a beach near Hyannis Port, Massachusetts, Caplan approached Symington and asked if he had seen Clinton. Symington said he hadn't, but he had an idea where to look. Scanning the waters, Symington and Caplan spotted Clinton some fifty yards out from land. To Symington, it appeared Clinton was caught in a riptide and was being pulled out to open water. Symington, a gifted swimmer and varsity lacrosse player at Harvard, jumped into a rowboat and hurriedly paddled to position himself between Clinton and the open sea.[20]

Symington grabbed Clinton by the hair, then by his arms, and dragged him into the boat. Symington later remembered asking Clinton: "You need a ride?"

Symington soon forgot about the encounter. But Clinton, lacerated after being raked over shoals and sure he was about to die, never forgot that a guy named Fife Symington had saved his life.

Caplan bristled at the idea that any pardon was a favor returned. Any help for Symington from the president, Caplan told friends and reporters, would be on the merits of whatever Symington's attorneys argued in their petition.

Here is what Caplan had done to help Fife Symington. This is it. Nothing more, he said later:

Symington had called Caplan—the two typically talked every month or so—shortly before Thanksgiving. Symington told Caplan he had heard about the first round of pardons from Clinton. Symington asked Caplan if he knew anything about how the pardon process worked. Caplan told Symington he didn't know, but promised to inquire.

Caplan was quick to tell reporters later that Symington did not ask Caplan to attempt to influence Clinton's decision, nor did Caplan himself attempt to pressure the president to offer the pardon.[21]

At a White House Christmas party December 19, just one month before inauguration day, Caplan said he approached the president and said, "Fife has expressed an interest in whether there will be any pardons and if so, how to seek one."

Clinton told Caplan to tell Symington to apply and then gave Caplan the steps Symington needed to take to get the petition to the Oval Office in time.

Caplan relayed the information to Symington. Symington called Dowd, Dowd and Lynam wrote the petition, and just a few days later, the petition reached the hands of Bruce Lindsey, the deputy White House counsel.[22] As part of the petition application, Caplan also filled out a character affidavit for the DOJ's pardon attorney.

As Caplan sat on his couch in his Baltimore apartment the morning of George Bush's inauguration, he had no confirmation whether or not his old friend Bill Clinton had pardoned his other old friend, Fife Symington.

Yet he had an inkling. He assumed he would have been told if the pardon had been rejected. He imagined he had picked up body language from certain critical staffers that a pardon was possible. It was an awkward little dance. He wasn't going to ask. But he certainly wanted to know the answer.

Watching television that Saturday morning, broadcasters and commentators across the networks were taking issue with the massive number of pardons given by Clinton in the waning hours of his administration.

Caplan watched the final 140 names scroll across his television the morning of the inauguration. Finally, deep in the list, he saw the name John Fife Symington III.[23]

Caplan, believing his friend and his friend's family had suffered much already, was thrilled. The Symingtons, he believed, deserved to be able to move on with their lives.

# Chapter 1

# THE STAR-SPANGLED LINEAGE

owering over young Fife Symington's world was the famous and
infamous god of American capitalism, Henry Clay Frick. Symington's beloved grandfather was Frick's son. Symington's mother
was Frick's granddaughter. The Frick story, the Frick money, the Frick
philosophy, and the Frick lifestyle all sculpted the existence of the fifteen
great-grandchildren of the famed industrialist. In that family, and in a
household in which Henry Clay Frick was framed only as good and great,
Fife Symington came to idolize his great-grandfather.[1]

By 1918, Frick, worth more than $220,000,000 according to *Forbes*
($4.1 billion in 2020 dollars), trailed only John D. Rockefeller in wealth.
Carnegie was third. Henry Ford was eighth. Vanderbilts, Astors, and Du
Ponts appeared farther down the list.[2]

In the Symington household, Henry Clay Frick was a hero in the
bloody Homestead Steel Strike. Frick's business partner, Andrew Carnegie, was a duplicitous scoundrel. In the Symington household, the Johnstown Flood was never discussed because Henry Clay Frick shouldered
no culpability.

Henry Clay Frick was born in 1849. Little in his childhood years suggested he would become a man famous for his iron constitution.

Frick was a sickly child who suffered from chronic indigestion and
a weak heart. Frick contracted rheumatic fever when he was six and remained so frail for the next seven years that he often struggled to walk to
school.[3]

Unable to play outside, he became an avid reader and crack arithme-
tician. By his teens, he already had his future planned, telling classmates
he would learn the intricacies of industry, then, with his gift for numbers
and unmatched drive, get filthy rich.

Frick didn't need to go far to find the source of his wealth.

In the mid-nineteenth century, the Youghiogheny, Monongahela, and
Allegheny rivers—heavy flowing streams that marked the natural envi-

ronment of Frick's youth—served as highways of commerce for goods heading to market in Pittsburgh, which was then a manufacturing mecca. Pittsburgh also served as a critical river port for the expanding country, shipping freight, coal, and settlers to the western frontier.[4]

The coal beneath the Pittsburgh area produced an unusually high grade of coke, an essential ingredient in the manufacture of iron, and in its refined form, steel.

In 1871, Frick secured funding for fifty coke ovens. He then used family connections to seek out Judge Thomas Mellon, arguably the most powerful banker in western Pennsylvania. Mellon approved that loan and a second larger loan after sending a loan agent out to Frick's operations.

The agent reported that Frick was a "young man with a cast-iron nerve." "Give him the money. Lands good, ovens well built; manager on job all day, keeps books evenings, may be a little too enthusiastic about pictures, but knows his business down to the ground."[5]

Frick continued building, including a one hundred-oven project next to the Henry Clay mine. With business robust, Frick paid off loans and reinvested profits in more lands and ovens.

Frick then not only survived the financial collapse of 1873, but used the downturn to buy up distressed properties. By 1878, Frick had one thousand ovens producing one hundred carloads of coke a day. Not yet thirty, he was a millionaire and had earned the title of "King of Coke."

Frick then pursued a partnership with Andrew Carnegie, who had run up considerable debt in his pursuit of competitors' holdings. H.C. Frick Coke Company became the exclusive supplier of coke for all of Carnegie's iron and steel works. In addition, Frick obtained a half interest in Carnegie's Monastery Coke Works. The two went on to build one of the most profitable—and one of the most bitterly contentious—business partnerships in US history.[6]

In the early 1880s, Frick led a group of wealthy Pittsburgh investors in the purchase of an abandoned reservoir and its earthen dam fourteen miles up the south fork of the Little Conemaugh River, above the booming town of Johnstown. The dam and reservoir had been built decades before as part of the region's canal system.

A clubhouse was built, the lake was stocked with exotic fish, and in time, fifty of Pittsburgh's wealthiest citizens had purchased cottages along the lake and become members of the South Fork Fishing and Hunting Club.[7]

As part of the development of the property, the dam was lowered to accommodate a road, and screens were placed in front of the spillway to keep fish in the reservoir. The aging dam was in need of several repairs, according to later civil engineering reports. But those repairs were never completed.

On May 28, 1889, the area was hit by an unprecedented downpour. The dam gave way. The flood that struck Johnstown killed 2,209 people, making it the third-worst loss of life in American history behind the Galveston Flood and the September 11, 2001, terrorist attacks.

To many Gilded Age reformers and members of the struggling working class, the club's wealthy members incarnated the indifference of the nation's rich to the plight of the working man.

As Frick battled in court with Johnstown survivors, he used increasingly Machiavellian tactics to keep workers in line.

In 1888, unionized workers at Carnegie and Frick's Homestead mill had won a favorable three-year contract after a prolonged strike at the Carnegie Steel property. Carnegie and Frick vowed to break the union and restore their full control of their mills once that contract expired at the end of June 1892.

As negotiations with the union floundered through spring, Frick began fortifying the mill in preparation for a lockout. Frick surrounded the mill with an eleven-foot fence topped with barbed wire and installed water cannons and snipers' nests. Frick then hired more than three hundred Pinkerton men to guard the mill, which newspapers of the time began calling "Fort Frick."

On the morning of July 6, the Pinkerton guards were brought by barge to secure the mill and escort strikebreakers. But workers and townspeople learned of the scheme, stormed to the river's shore, and fired on the Pinkertons. Nine strikers and seven Pinkerton men died in the fight.

Six days later, thousands of heavily armed members of the Pennsylvania state militia arrived, took control of the town, and jailed the leaders of the strike.

While public sentiment and newspapers were widely supportive of the union's efforts before July, the mob violence of July 6 dampened sympathy for their plight. Frick's reputation then received another boost through violence when anarchist Alexander Berkman, who had no ties to union leadership, attempted to assassinate Frick to spark an anti-government, anti-capitalist revolution in America.

Two weeks after the state militia took control of the town, Berkman entered Frick's office and shot him twice in the neck. Just as Berkman fired again, he was tackled by Carnegie Steel's vice president, Alexander Leishman. According to Leishman and Frick's account of the incident, Frick then rose and joined Leishman in trying to subdue Berkman. Berkman was able to stab Frick four times in the leg with a homemade knife before the would-be assassin was finally subdued.

What followed—or what was reported to have followed—would become the stuff of legend. Once the doctor arrived, according to reports, Frick refused anesthesia and helped direct the doctor in his two-hour-long struggle to remove the bullets. As the process began, Frick is reported to have said, "Don't make it too bad, doctor, for I must be at the office on Monday."[8]

A week later, Frick was back at work. In the nation's newspapers, he had gone from devil to superman in three weeks. Opinion of him would continue throughout his life along two greatly disparate paths: He was a charitable, heroic ironman leading America toward its destiny as an industrial superpower; or, he was a brutal tyrant willing to crush anyone who stood in his way.

By the time of his death, Frick had built an art collection that included the works of Goya, Monet, Rembrandt, El Greco, Gainsborough, Whistler, and many other masters. In 1914, he completed the sixty-room mansion on Fifth Avenue that remains the home of the famed Frick Collection.

Henry Clay Frick died in late 1919, just a year after B. C. Forbes declared him the second richest person in the United States in a story headlined: "Rockefeller Heads List With $1,200,000,000—Mrs. Harriman Wealthiest Woman—Frick Ahead of Carnegie."

Frick left $117 million of his $145 million estate to charitable endeavors and had given away millions more during his lifetime. Unlike Carnegie, Frick mostly chose to avoid public acclaim for his charitable works. Frick seemed indifferent to the opinion of that segment of America who considered him, as one journalist labeled him, "The Most Hated Man in America."[9]

J. Fife Symington III inherited a portrait of his great-grandfather. Symington hung the portrait near his office desk throughout much of his early business career. It looked to be a message to potential clients that they were in the presence of a young businessman with both a distinctive financial pedigree and a belief that unencumbered markets and private property rights were the backbones of the American dream.[10]

But the man Symington idolized meant something else to many he would encounter later in business and politics. Symington's pedigree could be seen as a stain and be used as a weapon in political battles. He was a Frick, after all, and for both progressives and old-school populists, that name would always represent outlandish wealth built unfairly on the backs of average Americans.

• • •

Henry Clay Frick and Adelaide Howard Childs were married in Pittsburgh on a chilly day in mid-December of 1881.

Two years later, Adelaide gave birth to a boy. The couple agreed that Adelaide's maiden name should be carried on in their new Frick family. The boy was named Childs.

Adelaide bore three more children during her husband's rise to financial and industrial prominence, but only one, Helen Clay, survived childhood.

Childs and his sister grew up amid some of the richest families in the country on the Frick's estate in Pittsburgh's East End.[11] After attending Shady Side Academy, Childs left for Princeton the same year his father became director of U.S. Steel.

Childs, to the increasing consternation of his father, showed little interest in courses related to business, instead gravitating toward biology and the natural sciences. In the years after graduating, the younger Frick increasingly focused his energies on collecting and studying creatures from around the world. In 1910, Childs returned from British East Africa with 126 types of mammals, which he donated to the Carnegie Museum of Natural History. During a second expedition to East Africa two years later, he collected more than five hundred mammals for the Carnegie Museum and more than five thousand birds for the Smithsonian Institution. His collection would go on to play a central role in what became the featured attractions of the Museum of Natural History's "Hall of African Wildlife."

His sister, Helen Clay, later known as "Grauntie" to her grandchildren, found her calling closer to home. Since her youth, Helen had grown increasingly appalled by the plight of the underpaid, malnourished, and overburdened young women who worked in shoe and textile factories in the Boston area. In 1909, acting, she said, on a dream from her childhood, she asked her father for enough money to provide a place for some of these women to rest and recover during the summer months. He obliged, renting her the nearby Stillman Farm.[12]

(Ironically, her father celebrated her progressive actions at the same time he allowed similar working conditions in his own factories.)

A year later, Henry Clay Frick agreed to expand the facility by purchasing a thirty-seven acre farm near Wenham, Massachusetts. The permanent facility was called the Iron Rail for an old iron railing that enclosed the property. The Iron Rail upheld Helen's rules for the women: "Don't flirt. Don't fib. Don't gossip. Don't use slang. Don't wear frills, rats, or puffs."

Childs was smitten by Helen's best friend and assistant, Frances Shoemaker Dixon of Baltimore.[13]

Childs and Frances, known as Dixie to friends, began dating after Childs returned from East Africa in 1912.[14] A year later, they announced their engagement—news that lit up the society pages of the East.

The United States entered the war in Europe four years after the couple's marriage. While many of Childs's friends volunteered for military service, he remained on the margins. During the summers he played polo and golf at Eagle Rock, periodically playing the polo circuit in Georgia and Florida. In 1916, he earned his pilot's license and signed up for a new experimental program, the Civilian Military Training Program. He spent a month in Plattsburg, New York, as part of the program, which prefigured what became the Reserve Officer Training Corps (ROTC).

That same year, Childs, Dixie, and their two girls moved to Redlands, California.

With money from his father, Childs purchased a used airplane for $12,000. The elder Frick hoped that Childs could help in the air war against Germany. Childs wanted the airplane mostly to expedite and expand his scientific research.

In late December of 1917, Dixie gave birth to the couple's third child, another girl, Martha Howard Frick.

According to one of Frick's attorneys, Frick created a will in 1913 that bestowed most of the Frick estate to Childs. Two years later, though, the simmering disappointments with Childs's disinterest in business matters and comparative lack of involvement in the war effort apparently prompted the elder Frick to change his mind. Frick created a new will in which the major portion of the estate not designated for charity would go to Helen.

As a result, upon Henry Clay Frick's death in 1919, Helen Clay Frick became the wealthiest unmarried woman in the United States.

Childs inherited much less, receiving $3 million. Dixie, too, received far less than many anticipated: $2 million in trust.

(Childs couldn't have felt too jilted, though. Just before Frick's death, Frick bought Childs a Georgian Revival mansion and a plot of land outside New York overlooking Roslyn Harbor that, after heavy renovations, the Frick family named "Clayton." The mansion later became the Nassau County Museum of Art.)[15]

Meanwhile, Childs's professional career continued to blossom. During the 1920s he completed a scientific expedition to Mexico, funded an American Museum of Natural History foray to Santa Fe, discovered a new fossil specimen, "Hemicayo" (the dog bear), published a 119-page article on this discovery in the distinguished *Bulletin of the American Museum of Natural History*, and provided hundreds of boxes of fossils discovered from his field work to the American Museum of Natural History.[16]

Adelaide Frick passed away in late 1931. Once again, much to Childs's consternation, Helen inherited a significantly larger portion of the remaining family fortune.[17]

Childs Frick and his descendants, then, although certainly wealthy, were not nearly as wealthy as the outside world assumed.

Late in 1931, as the Frick grandchildren pursued their various interests, Martha, Childs's third child, took a late summer trip to Scandinavia. During this time, Martha, most often referred to as "Marsie" by her family and friends, met a young Pan American Airways employee, J. Fife Symington, Jr., of Baltimore, who was stationed temporarily in nearby Port Washington on Long Island.

Symington's letters to Marsie grew increasingly romantic in the following months. The young couple announced their engagement in early 1939.[18]

Despite misgivings, the Fricks hosted an engagement party for the Symingtons and their friends at the Fricks' mansion in Roslyn Harbor.

The elegant affair prompted a thank-you letter from Fife Jr. to his soon-to-be mother-in-law, Dixie Frick. "Dear Dixie," he wrote, "your

Childs and Frances Frick with their three daughters. From left: Adelaide, Martha, and Frances. Courtesy of the Symington family archives.

lovely party and the whole round of festivities at Clayton were just too marvelous and one and all had a truly superb time. The Baltimoreans as well as the Philadelphians all called me up Monday morning to sing your praises and to comment on the boundless hospitality given them by you and Mr. Frick." A clearly relieved Symington appeared to gain his footing with the iconic family: "You both have certainly been wonderful about Marsie's and my engagement and I do want you to realize how deeply touched and grateful I am for all that you have done."[19]

The couple married in March of that year. Four days later, the newlyweds set sail for England.

• • •

The Symington story begins more than six hundred years earlier with one of the most legendary disembowelments in Scottish history.

The name "Fife" itself is a nod to the Symingtons' notoriously fiery Scottish heritage, one that begins with the first laird of Symington, Thomas of Symington, whose life story is woven into the origin legends

Martha and Fife Symington Jr. on their wedding day on Long Island, New York, 1939. Courtesy of the Symington family archives.

of Scotland and whose death rivaled William Wallace's in valiance and viscera.

In 1306, for his bravery in taking back two Scottish castles from the English, Thomas was made Castellan of Castle Douglas by the legendary Robert the Bruce. (Castle Douglas was the inspiration for Sir Walter Scott's novel, *Castle Dangerous*.) The castle was then retaken by the English, after which Thomas led an attack on Palm Sunday of 1307 to take it back. Thomas was nearly disemboweled during the fighting, yet continued to lead the charge, coaxing his men forward with sword in one hand and intestines in the other.

Truth or grotesquely embellished legend, the story lived on in Scottish lore. According to source documents used by Scott for his book, a sculpture of Thomas of Symington was erected in a churchyard. He was depicted raising a sword in his right hand while using his left arm to support his entrails as one might hold an infant.

Sadly, the statue could not be located when Thomas's descendants went searching for it in the early 1800s.[20]

The American Symington story begins in the late eighteenth century in the Scottish Highlands, where the Earl of Fife arranged a marriage for his daughter, Margaret Leith Fife. The marriage was unsuccessful and Margaret, desperately unhappy, ran away to America to find a new life. With utmost secrecy she boarded a ship for America. During the crossing she captivated two passengers.

One, a Scotsman named James Symington, found Margaret irresistible.

The other passenger was famed American patriot Robert Morris, a wealthy merchant and banker from Philadelphia, a close friend of George Washington and later, one of the signers of the Declaration of Independence.

At the time of the crossing, Morris was sixty-five. He treated Margaret as a daughter.

In 1787, Symington persuaded Margaret to marry him. The wedding took place in Morris's home, and Morris himself gave away the bride.[21] Margaret Leith Fife became the first of many Symingtons to carry the names Leith and Fife. Soon after, James and Margaret moved to a home near Wilmington, Delaware. There, James operated a mill where he ground flint. Soon after, the couple had their first child, Thomas Alexander Symington.[22]

Thomas served as an apprentice to his father in the stone-cutting business. The family then moved to Baltimore in 1803. That city and its environs became the Symington home for the next several generations.

Thomas went to work for William Stuart, who maintained a thriving stone-cutting and marble business in Baltimore. When war broke out in 1812, Stuart became a lieutenant colonel of the US Infantry and as such, was second-in-command at Fort McHenry in Baltimore Harbor during the British fleet's all-night bombardment of the fort. An American negotiator on board a British warship, Francis Scott Key, described the chaos in which Stuart fought in a short poem, *The Star Spangled Banner.*[23]

Stuart, in addition to becoming a war hero, was a successful businessman and active in politics. He served as a member of the Maryland House of Delegates and later served as mayor of Baltimore. Thomas Symington, while working for Stuart, met Stuart's daughter, Angeline, and in 1825 they were married.[24]

Thomas became a wealthy businessman in the Baltimore area. Among his properties were marble quarries in Vermont, Tennessee, and Maryland. Thomas produced much of the marble for the 1850 addition to the Capitol building in Washington, DC, and provided the cornerstone of the Washington Monument and the capstone at its apex.[25] When Thomas died in 1875, at age eighty-two, he left an estate of $100,000.

Thomas and Angeline had six children—two daughters and four sons—before her early death in 1860. They named the oldest son William Stuart after Angeline's father.

The first William Stuart Symington (he dropped the "William" as did subsequent descendants) enlisted in the Virginia militia at age twenty-two to fight for the Confederacy in the Civil War.

Stuart Symington was a second lieutenant and within a year, was appointed first lieutenant in the Confederate army. He became an aide to his first cousin by marriage, General George E. Pickett. Symington served in that capacity throughout the war and fought with Pickett at Five Forks, Drewry's Bluff, Gettysburg, and Petersburg.

Under Pickett, Symington had his horse shot from beneath him during the infamous charge ordered by Robert E. Lee to take Cemetery Ridge at the Battle of Gettysburg. Pickett's Charge, as the ultimately over-audacious assault became forever known, was a valiant but disastrous maneuver afterward referred to as the "high-water mark of the Confederacy," suggesting the battle was the turning point of the Civil War.

The commander of Union troops holding the high ground at Cemetery Ridge was Brigadier General James S. Wadsworth, whose granddaughter, Evelyn, would become Mrs. W. Stuart Symington III.

After marrying Lelia Wayles Skipworth, Symington entered the fertilizer business. He struggled, and the company went out of business in 1885. The family lost their mansion and moved into a small rental house.

Despite financial setback, Stuart and Lelia had eight children—one daughter and seven sons.

Stuart later regained his fiscal footing and served as secretary of the Consolidated Gas Company. During the last years of his life, he was viewed as one of Baltimore's leading citizens, and despite the financial highs and lows, the Symingtons continued to move in the most prestigious social circles of Baltimore society.

Stuart and Lelia's fifth child, John Fife "Jack" Symington, was born in 1877. Jack grew up in Baltimore as the family struggled to regain its social status.

He was one of three Symingtons to attend Lehigh, a school that excelled in engineering education. Jack, Tom, and Harry served apprenticeships with various railroads. In 1901, Tom founded the T. H. Symington Company, a successful manufacturing and sales concern that once employed all six of his brothers. Tom, according to family accounts, was a mechanical genius who designed and built the first compound steam locomotive used in the United States, among several other inventions.

Tom realized he needed an effective sales department. He persuaded Jack and Harry to join him. Soon, the Symington brothers prospered and were welcomed into Baltimore's high society.[26]

In 1910, Jack and Arabella Symington celebrated the birth of the first of their five children, John Fife Symington Jr. Four siblings followed, and all grew up in foxhunting and riding country outside Baltimore.

Fife Symington Jr. entered Princeton in 1929, just as the nation's economy crashed.

When Symington graduated in 1933, he took time out to participate in a family tradition: he rode as a gentleman jockey in the My Lady's Manor and Grand National point-to-point races.

During these years, Symington spent many hours in his parents' library listening to discussions between Juan Terry Trippe and his mother's younger brother, John Hambleton. Hambleton and Trippe were airline pioneers who founded Pan American World Airways. They enthusiastically outlined their dreams and plans for transoceanic and transpolar

Symington Jr. in hunting gear, 1950s. Courtesy of the Symington family archives.

Symington Jr. riding during a Maryland hunting event, 1930s. Courtesy of the
Symington family archives.

flight. Fife Jr.'s participation in these discussions provided a window of
opportunity for his future employment at Pan Am. After graduating
from Princeton, Symington secured a job with the airline.[27]

He started work at the metal bench in the tool and die branch, where
he was tasked with pounding out large chunks of steel secured in a vice.
His Princeton degree helped little. Symington's foreman later told him
that he was the dumbest mechanic he had ever seen on the metal bench.

After his short training period, Symington spent fourteen years in Pan
American operations and sales positions in Brazil, Argentina, Baltimore,
Port Washington, and London. He became Pan Am's first representative
to the British government.

Symington returned to the US in 1937 to run sales and traffic in Baltimore and Port Washington for the inaugural Baltimore to Bermuda four-

engine Clipper flights. These flights were preparation for the planned transatlantic flying boat service. Afterward the Symingtons returned to England, where they lived until May 1940, when German bombers damaged London and France began to fall. They returned stateside and moved into the Duck Cottage on the grounds of Clayton.[28]

During this time, Marsie learned that she was pregnant, which prompted a note from her father, who, although reserved and sophisticated in comportment, was also capable of saucy short poems and limericks.[29] Childs's note read: "When Marsie first heard from the stork, she said, 'I now sway I don't walk, I played too hard on the Fife, Now I'm stuck as a wife, and soon now the infant will squawk.' Love, Father."

In 1941 the young couple celebrated the birth of their first child, Helen Clay Symington, the first great-grandchild of Henry Clay Frick.

Marsie gave birth to two more children over the next three years, both girls. When Marsie became pregnant again in 1944, the couple hoped for a boy. Marsie delivered her youngest child on August 12, 1945, at Presbyterian Hospital in New York City. When nurses brought the infant to her bedside for the first time, she reportedly said, "Oh, God, it's another girl, take her away!" The nurse quickly unwrapped the baby and said, "No, Mrs. Symington, it is a little boy!"[30]

They named the infant John Fife Symington III.

# Chapter 2

# MONKEYS AND MONDO TRASHO

hilds's daughter, Martha, or Marsie, was raised in a home in which creatures of the world roamed freely. Her most beloved pet was a black bear her father brought back from the Canadian wilds as a cub.

In time, as the bear reached full maturity, its fierce protectiveness of Martha became so disquieting her parents felt compelled to donate the bear to the Brooklyn Zoo. It was placed in a cage, loaded in the back of the family station wagon, and driven from Pittsburgh to Brooklyn by the family's chauffeur. As the vehicle crossed the Brooklyn Bridge, the bear broke from its cage, terrifying the driver, who then slammed on the brakes and dashed from the station wagon. The Brooklyn Bridge was closed until police were able to corral the bear and transport it to the zoo.[1]

Distraught about the loss of her friend, Marsie longed for the day when she would own her own home where animals of every sort could run free.

In the late 1940s, Marsie—Mum to her children—and her husband Fife Symington Jr., moved their family from New York to a fine country home outside Baltimore given to them by Childs. That house, Zemlyn Porches, soon inherited that creature-friendly Frick-family terrain of their past homes in New York and Pennsylvania.

The main house was surrounded by 160 acres of gently rolling horse pastures. The young Fife Symington lived among a menagerie of domesticated and barely domesticated animals. Sometimes his mother would surprise him with a new pet.[2]

When he was twelve, Symington was rushed to the hospital for an appendectomy. When he returned home, he was set up in his bed with instructions not to move.

Soon after his arrival, the door to his room burst open. In sashayed a spider monkey chattering with its arms raised over its head. The

Martha Frick Symington in her twenties. Courtesy of the Symington family archives.

Martha Frick Symington and her four children. From left: Helen Clay, Martie, Fife III, and Arabella, 1947. Courtesy of the Symington family archives.

monkey then bound for the television and climbed to its top, inadvertently brushing the on/off switch. The sounds of *Gunsmoke* began blaring from the television, the monkey leaped in terror into the air, then landed on the boy's tender incision. As the agonizing pain subsided, Symington's mother explained that she had purchased the monkey to entertain him while he was bedridden.

In time, a nine-foot-tall chicken wire cage was built in the boy's bathroom, but the monkey only stayed in the cage at night. Symington named the monkey "Lulu," and the two were soon close friends.

A few months after Lulu arrived, Symington walked into his bathroom and found a four-foot-long alligator in his bathtub. The gator was a practical joke gift his mother had received. She thought her son might enjoy having an alligator.

As the alligator (soon after named Ally) grew, it was placed in an aquarium from which it quickly learned to escape. Ally would beeline toward Lulu's cage and thrash against the chicken wire to gain entrance for a quick meal. Lulu retaliated by digging her long fingernails into the alligator's back through the chicken wire. The hissing and screeching would

Fife Symington III, circa 1947. Courtesy of the Symington family archives.

Symington on his horse, Star, along with Symington Jr., at their home in Maryland.
Courtesy of the Symington family archives.

wake the boy, who would then drag the agitated reptile from under Lulu's cage, swing it up into the air by its tail, and drop it into the bathtub.

It was just common knowledge in this home that alligators cannot escape from bathtubs.

The boy would then lie in his bed with Lulu until the monkey was calm enough to return to her cage.

The Symingtons also had a pet raccoon, a gander, several horses, a pet steer named Blacky, and a pet skunk named Chanel No. 5.

Henry Clay Frick had provided the wealth and leisure time for Childs to take a deep dive into the natural world; Childs had passed his love for the world's creatures onto his daughter; and his daughter created a home

Symington during a family vacation to Scotland in the early 1950s. Courtesy of the Symington family archives.

menagerie in which a boy could come both to adore the fauna of the world and have no fear of engaging it.

The 160-acre property served as a working farm with pigs, chickens, and cows, and as a home for several fine horses. Symington fished the creek that ran through the property. He learned to shoot. In particular, he learned to ride horses—a family tradition on both sides of the family. His father was a particularly gifted horseman, winning numerous competitions, and Zemlyn Porches sat in the heart of Maryland hunt country. The boy would sometimes be in the saddle for three or four hours at a time accompanying his father on foxhunts or training for equestrian events.

Seven-year-old
Fife Symington
III with his
basset hound,
Snowball.
Courtesy of
the Symington
family archives.

Symington spent the summers of 1957 and 1958 at a camp in the woods of Ontario. He fished, hiked, and took days-long camping trips. At one point, the twelve-year-old wrote to his mother. "I was surprised to no [sic] that you think I am homesick. Well I'm not," he declared. He took pride that he was "learning to cook meals" and took part in cooking contests. The boy asked about his dog, Snowball, and Lulu the monkey, then complained to his parents that someone put chewing gum on his sleeping bag.[3]

In late summer 1958, camp director Roderick H. Cox wrote a letter to Marsie and Fife Jr. suggesting their son was beginning to mature. Cox concluded Symington was "going places" and that the elder Symington, who had begun his first campaign for Congress in the summer of 1958, "better get him on his campaign team as a young man with ideas and determination."

The glowing report prompted a quick and prideful reply from Symington's father. "Dear Fifie," he wrote. "Happy returns and I hope you receive this on your birthday." He said he had received "a wonderful letter" from Cox "telling me that you are his right hand man and that he depends on you in the pinches."

"Apparently," the elder Symington added, "you are learning to be a little leader and that is what I had always hoped you would be."

Normally, though, the elder Symington was more often autocratic and temperamental than supportive. He was a stern disciplinarian, and he cracked down on his often rambunctious son with harsh words and occasionally, corporal punishment. If things were not exactly as Symington's father wanted, it would, as one family member said, "trigger his harsh side."[4]

When the younger Symington was fourteen, his father came toward him intent on hitting him for some perceived misdeed. Symington, already emerging as a gifted defensive lineman on his school's football team, fought back. The elder Symington swung, and Symington ducked, dropped into a three-point stance, and burst upward toward his father's chest, driving him down onto a dog bed in the home's breakfast room.

The elder Symington never took another swing at his son.[5]

In contrast, Symington's mother was doting and jovial. But her spirit seemed to dim over time, and the number of drinks increased.

Marsie was, as another family member said, "bright, funny, frustrated, and devoted to her children and martinis." Family members suggested her increasingly strained relationship with her domineering husband contributed to the problem. Symington's parents grew apart and would ultimately divorce.

Symington's relationship with his three sisters was often defined by their shared relationships with their parents. While growing up, Symington was particularly close to Martie, the youngest of his three older sisters, perhaps, he would posit later, because they both felt bullied at times by their father. Martie and Fife's relationship soured as years passed, though, as the two took different positions on how to respond to their mother's growing drinking problem.

Arabella was the prankster of the family, once presenting her brother

Symington with his sisters, late 1940s. Courtesy of the Symington family archives.

with a large, beautifully wrapped Christmas present the boy discovered was a box of coal. Unlike Martie, though, Arabella was on her father's good side, but often at odds with her mother.

It was Helen Clay who would become the boy's closest ally in the family beyond childhood. Helen Clay, who would go on to be an accomplished art historian and chairwoman of the Frick Collection, was a brilliant student from her earliest school days. She pushed her younger brother when he strayed from his studies. After she headed off to Radcliffe, she successfully convinced her younger brother that Harvard was the best school for him. He followed her advice then, and would continue to see her as a trusted adviser and cheerleader throughout adulthood.

From 1952 through 1958, Symington attended Calvert School in Baltimore, a top private school that reflected the face of "Establishment Baltimore."[6]

Symington was an indifferent student (much to Helen Clay's dismay at the time), more interested in football, physical activities, and fun. He chafed at the "extremely regimented education system," as he later described it, as well as the coat and tie requirement, and the overall lack of pedagogical innovation. His grades were mediocre, and he found himself taking remedial reading.

And he rebelled. Calvert had a morning ritual in which students lined up to shake the hand of the school's principal. Symington got his hands on a tiny metal "joy buzzer." One morning, with the device concealed against his palm, Symington shook the principal's hand, sending the man reeling in shock. Soon after, Symington received the paddling he knew would come.[7]

Symington's popularity grew after the brave outrage, but Symington still felt stifled by the environment. He longed for an environment in which there was more intellectual interaction with teachers and fellow students in the classroom, and he longed for a place that better appreciated creativity.

While at Calvert, Symington befriended another rebellious spirit named John Waters.

Waters, whom William S. Burroughs dubbed "The Pope of Trash," went on to make movies such as *Mondo Trasho, Pink Flamingos, Polyester, Hairspray,* and *Cecil B. Demented.*

Symington and Waters's families often carpooled to Calvert.

While Symington, the budding conservative, hated Calvert, Waters, the budding face of gonzo filmmaking, loved it. Waters would later say, "It was the only school I ever liked."

Yet the two were close friends. Occasionally, Waters would get a special treat: Marsie would send a limousine to take the boys to school. While Symington was embarrassed by the show of wealth, Waters loved it, later telling people, "I was in a limo in grade school. I thought it was quite glamorous."[8]

Waters's first attempt at entertaining the public involved turning his family's garage into a "horror house." "Kids would enter the pitch dark through spider webs and risk breaking their necks in the little traps I had set throughout the maze," Waters later recalled. Parents of terrorized children complained, and the "horror house" soon closed.[9]

Waters then began staging his own puppet shows after seeing the ornate puppetry of Leslie Caron's 1953 classic, *Lili.* Symington served as his puppet assistant. Area parents began hiring the duo for local birthday parties. Waters and Symington were performing four times a week at the height of the program's popularity.

Symington and Waters parted ways in 1958 when Symington left for Gilman School, and Waters headed to a Baltimore public school.

As Symington entered Gilman, the world around him was changing. White Southerners had come to Baltimore by the thousands during World War II, altering the city's political landscape. These newcomers added upon existing racial restrictions in the city. They mobilized to prevent school integration after the *Brown v. Board of Education* decision of the Supreme Court in 1954.

While many working-class whites supported the candidacy of segregationist George Wallace in the Republican primary season of 1964, the Symington family instead backed the young hardboiled conservative senator from Arizona, Barry Goldwater, who was already an old ally of the family.

The Symingtons first hosted a Goldwater fundraising event at Zemlyn Porches in 1958.

A few months before that event, Goldwater drove out alone from Washington, DC, to Zemlyn Porches to discuss the upcoming event and the elder Symington's first congressional bid. Goldwater didn't arrive as a passenger in a black sedan, as the twelve-year-old Symington expected, but instead climbed out of the driver's seat of a Corvette Stingray. Goldwater wore cowboy boots and a cowboy hat. To the young fan of *Gunsmoke*, it looked as if Marshal Dillon had just come to visit.

Goldwater and Symington's father sat in the library discussing politics as the younger Symington listened. The two discussed nuclear deterrence, the evils of Communism, and the need for resolve, determination, and unyielding strength in dealing with the Soviet Union.

Six years later, the Symingtons hosted a Goldwater fundraiser during the 1964 presidential primary. Former vice president Richard Nixon and Milton Eisenhower, president of Johns Hopkins University and brother of Dwight Eisenhower, attended the event.[10]

It was here that Nixon and Eisenhower met secretly in the home's library to lay out a plan for Gov. William Scranton of Pennsylvania to enter the presidential race. When Marsie discovered the two talking and realized an anti-Goldwater plot was afoot, she scolded both men. With her son at her side, Marsie told Eisenhower to leave the farm and yelled at Nixon, "As for you, Dick Nixon, you should be ashamed of yourself! Go out there and give the Goldwater speech you were supposed to give!"

Symington's parents remained deeply involved in Maryland Repub-

Fife Symington Jr. meeting with President Dwight Eisenhower. Courtesy of the
Symington family archives.

Fife Symington Jr.
during his run for
US Congress in 1958.
Courtesy of the
Symington family
archives.

lican politics throughout Symington's childhood. For one, they played a significant role in the rise of Spiro Agnew, who became governor of Maryland and later, in 1969, vice president under President Richard Nixon. While a student at Gilman School, Symington worked for Agnew in one of his campaign offices.

At Gilman, teachers took a pragmatic approach to the emerging politics of class and race. They discussed the topics openly, often using them as educational opportunities for a student body that reflected a broad political spectrum.[11] Gilman changed Symington's perspective on education. He respected the teachers and began to enjoy being pushed intellectually.

Symington excelled at football and lacrosse while discovering a passion for learning. Redmond "Reddy" Finney, a well-known athletic and intellectual figure in the private school realm, served as Symington's teacher, mentor, and ultimately, surrogate father.

Symington's transcripts show him going from a below-average student to excelling in English and in ancient, modern, and American history.

One of Symington's English and history teachers, Nick Schloeder, served as his adviser. Schloeder, a liberal Democrat who was also a no-nonsense former Golden Gloves boxer (who once threw an unruly Gilman student out a window), challenged the young Republican with progressive opinions. Schloeder, although very different in temperament and politics from Symington, soon became Symington's other favorite teacher along with Finney.

Finney described Schloeder in an interview in 2016:

"Nick was an authentic leftist and he tried to put forward these ideas to challenge the kids, knowing many had come from families with opposite views. While Fife may hold fast to his political point of view, he acknowledges those who differ."[12]

Back home, Symington's father continued to push him toward his own favorite hobbies and sports. The elder Symington was particularly fond of horse racing and foxhunting.

Just sixteen, Symington competed in a major steeplechase event called "My Lady's Manor." Symington felt he was too young and out of his depth, but after being goaded by his father, he entered the race along with nine other competitors.

The horse he was riding, Neddie, stood eighteen hands high and al-

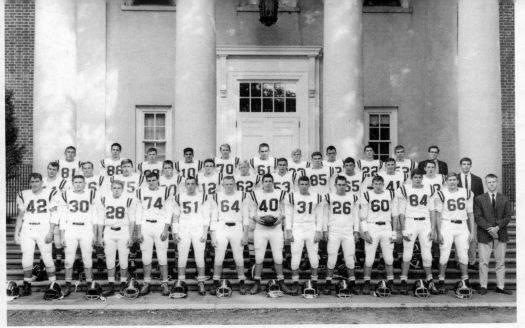

The Gilman School football team, 1962. Symington played right guard and place kicker on the undefeated team. Courtesy of the Symington family archives.

though inexperienced, was a gifted jumper. As the race unfolded, the pair burst from the middle of the pack.[13] Soon Symington found himself in second place. He was pushing the leader as they approached the "In and Out," a spot at which horse and rider jump a fence, cross a road, and jump a second fence. Neddie jumped early. The duo slammed into the first fence, fell to the road, and the horse rolled over Symington.

Symington woke up on the X-ray table at Union Memorial Hospital in Baltimore with his parents hovering over him.[14] The couple was embroiled in a heated argument. "You almost killed our son!" his mother shouted, while the senior Symington told her to "Shut up!"

Symington never fully forgave his father for pushing an inexperienced teen into a race with college-age competition, a potentially deadly move that left Symington with a shattered collarbone and severe concussion. The event, Symington said years later, created an element of distrust with his father that would last for years.

The accident also solidified Symington's growing sense that the lifestyle of a hunt-country gentleman was not for him.

Instead, he dove into activities at school. Besides football and lacrosse, he became editor-in-chief of the *Gilman News*.

In both football and lacrosse, Finney served as his coach. Symington was unusually fast for a big kid, so Finney used him as a defensive guard. "He was so quick he was by the linemen before they could block him," Finney said later.

Symington enjoyed expressing his views as editor of the school newspaper. He soon developed a close friendship with one of the paper's features writers, Tommy Caplan. When Symington became editor of the paper his senior year, he chose Caplan to be the editor of the features section.

As Symington espoused his conservative views, Caplan emerged as a strong young liberal voice, eventually becoming president of the Teen Democrats of Maryland for the Kennedy campaign of 1960.

When President Kennedy launched the Peace Corps in 1961, Caplan's father hatched an idea both the liberal and conservative could back—a companion program with the corps through which teenagers would correspond with their contemporaries in developing nations.

The younger Caplan decided to take action, and Symington jumped on board, starting the "Youth to Youth Pilot Project." The duo soon had several other students writing and receiving letters from teenagers in Senegal, Mali, and other newly independent nations. The project attracted the attention of the Kennedy White House. Caplan, Symington, and several other Gilman students met with Ted Sorensen, President Kennedy's special counsel and author of many of Kennedy's most famous speeches. In 1963, Caplan even appeared on *The Today Show* to explain Youth to Youth.

Throughout these years, Symington, who was boarding at Gilman, regularly wrote his parents. The letters increasingly revolved around political issues and Symington's fascination with the views of Barry Goldwater.

"The next political club meeting is this week. Guess who is going to speak to the club? None other than yours truly, Fife Symington," the Gilman junior wrote proudly. "I'm representing Barry Goldwater's conservative philosophy in the national and international affairs." Symington told his parents he had worked all weekend reading fifteen articles from the Goldwater platform plus the recently published Goldwater primer, *Conscience of a Conservative.*

As graduation neared, Symington's father, with whom the teen still battled frequently, expressed his strong preference for Princeton. But when Symington met with the Princeton University admissions group, he was put off by their arrogance, later claiming he intentionally scuttled the interview to avoid an offer from the school.

Soon after, three Harvard admissions officers arrived at Gilman, and Symington, with prodding by Helen Clay, decided to interview with them. The three stared at him for a few moments and said, "Take thirty minutes to tell us what gives you a kick out of life."

He spoke extemporaneously about his broad experience at Gilman, his love of sports, editing the student newspaper, and his classes. At lunch one of his instructors approached him and whispered, "You had a great interview. You are admitted to Harvard early if that's what you want." Symington readily accepted the offer.[15]

His photo and its caption for his senior yearbook captured much of the future Symington: "Very conservative in his views . . . an artful diplomat . . . Varsity football and Lacrosse star . . . power wielding Editor-in-Chief of the *News* . . . skiing enthusiast . . . bound for Harvard and politics."

Heading to Cambridge, Symington said later, offered something he longed for: some distance from a society in which he would always be perceived to be some hunt-country dandy who was given everything he had.

"I wanted to strike out on my own," he said. "I wasn't comfortable being a Frick." He wanted life more like it was on the football field. "You didn't get the position because your family had money. You got the position because you hit the other guy harder, were faster, were better."

With Gilman in the rearview mirror, Symington, like his grandfather Childs, went into the wilderness to find adventure.

Symington and nine others set off on a canoe trip down the Rupert River from its headwaters in Lake Mistassini, the largest natural lake in Quebec. They hoped to be the first non-whites to canoe the full length of the river. If they succeeded, they'd also be the last to make the full run: The waters of the James Bay Hydroelectric Project were about to flood a stretch of the river, forever burying much of the pristine wilderness.[16]

Two weeks into the trip, Symington wrote his parents, describing the rugged conditions. "My beard is red and itches terribly . . . my clothes are filthy and the bugs are amusingly atrocious," he wrote. He described the slow, deliberate methods required to navigate the sometimes-huge rapids, small victories in catching fish to eat, and the "feeling of accomplishment" at the end of a tiring day. Also, the eighteen-year-old wrote a few lines about the 1964 Republican primary: "I recently heard from some Ohio fisherman that Barry had it made!" He ended the lengthy missive, "Give my love to my three sisters, and tell the Senator (Goldwater) that the Canadian Indians really go for him!"[17]

The Canadian Broadcasting Corporation flew reporters to interview the scraggly young men when they finally reached James Bay after six weeks. *Fur-Fish-Game*, a magazine devoted to outdoor challenges, wrote extensively about adventure.[18]

Later, Childs Frick was excited to hear a full accounting of the historic expedition, and his grandson was even more excited to tell the tale.

Chapter 3

# "SYMINGTON IS A FASCIST!" AT HARVARD

Fife Symington knew he was out of step with most of his fellow students within weeks of reaching Harvard College. As progressives and radicals railed for revolutionary change on the nation's campuses in the 1960s, Symington focused on art, history, political philosophy, being a regular starter on the lacrosse team, and at every turn possible, challenging those he called "long-haired monstrosities" who were challenging the establishment.

Because of those conservative views and surely, his haughtiness in articulating them, Symington once returned to his dorm room to find "Symington is a Fascist!" scrawled on his door.

His freshman year, he frequently wrote to his mother complaining about the tumult and cultural upheaval going on around him.

"Did you know that the University went 83 percent for (Lyndon) Johnson and that the *Harvard Crimson* endorsed him for the presidency?" Symington wrote to his mother his freshman year. "Surprise, eh? Bah, what a bunch of fools." He criticized the college newspaper for this transgression, harping, "They had the impertinence to say that Johnson would make a better father than Goldwater! Bah, again! It just goes to show what kind of fuddy-duddies brought up those ravishing, long-haired monstrosities that live next door."[1]

In an earlier letter his freshman year, the nineteen-year-old congratulated his parents on a successful fundraising event for Goldwater, then expounded on Harvard's political culture. "Around this loony bin" Symington said, he found it difficult to find politically conservative allies.

Symington's conservative political and economic philosophy grew in sophistication, as did his ability to articulate those views with more nuance than dandy bombast, once he discovered the works of Friedrich Hayek in a freshman economics course. Hayek, the Austrian-turned-British economist, social theorist, and political philosopher, championed classical liberalism. His emphasis on free markets and liberty resonated

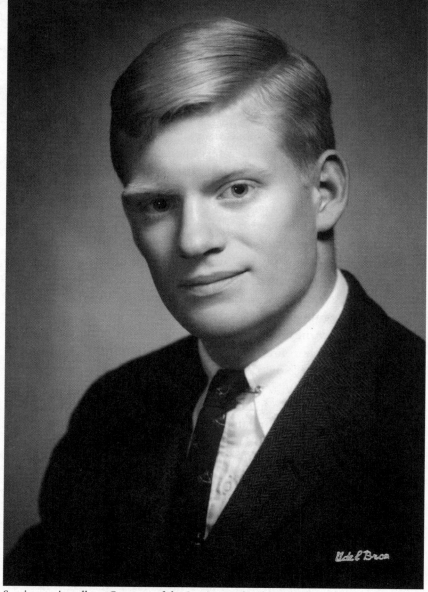

Symington in college. Courtesy of the Symington family archives.

with Symington. Hayek's two important works, *Road to Serfdom* (1944) and *The Constitution of Liberty* (1960), which both ran counter to the tide of mainstream Keynesian economic thought, remained foundational documents for Symington throughout his business and political career.

Symington's professor, whom Symington classified as "a Swedish Marxist economist," wasn't as enamored by Hayek's theories.

"That professor held the virtues of Cuba and Fidel Castro over our heads," Symington complained to his parents. He claimed he had written a compelling paper opposing his professor's views only to receive "a C-minus based on my political views."[2]

Hayek argued that loose monetary policy and "big government" ultimately threaten individual freedoms. In *Road to Serfdom*, Hayek outlined how entitlement programs and nationalized healthcare led to economic instability. When the body politic has no debt restrictions and unlimited access to the income of the citizenry, economic disaster is the inevitable outcome, Hayek argued.[3]

Symington's position on the Vietnam War also transferred almost seamlessly from his conservative, aristocratic Maryland home.

Symington wrote several course papers on the Vietnam conflict, many of which took aim at his fellow students. In one letter to his parents, he wrote, "You know the old story about morality and self-determination in international politics. Well, in this case of South Vietnam those liberal idiots apply all those lovely, hollow and meaningless terms to substantiate their arguments."

He continued with a rhetorical question, "Gosh, Mum, Don't you think Mao Tse Tung, who exterminated the Tibetans, that Ho Chi Minh, who likes to arm guerrillas so they can kill 'capitalists' . . . are the most moral communists in the world?" He proclaimed that there was one answer: "Long Live Edmund Burke," the philosophical founder of modern conservatism.

He regularly condemned the creeping communist threat in Europe and elsewhere. "Communism can crop up in any kind of situation; look how strong it is in France," he argued, "then see how well it thrives in poverty stricken Cuba."

In his second semester at Harvard, the theme of the Vietnam War dominated Symington's letters to his family. In one lengthy communiqué, Symington suggested the conflict in Vietnam held only two alternatives. "One will signify total war and our success or defeat," he argued. "The other is that we will probably bomb the North Vietnamese, so that Russia will come to her aid."

Sprinkled amid the lengthy political rants were well wishes for his parents, his monkey, his alligator, and occasionally, his various other pets.

Antiwar protests and activities at Harvard in the mid-1960s were especially irksome to Symington. Students there became increasingly angry

Symington and two other US Air Force ROTC cadets. Courtesy of the Symington family archives.

that Harvard didn't distance itself from the war (by terminating contracts with ROTC, for example), so the university was deemed complicit.

Protesters saw ROTC as the staffing mechanism for an army used to repress popular movements. During the first semester of 1966, seventy-one Harvard students pledged to refuse the draft. The following year, three hundred students imprisoned a recruiter from Dow Chemical—a manufacturer of napalm used in Vietnam—for several hours.

Unlike many of the hawk-tongued children of the moneyed class, Symington joined ROTC shortly after arriving on campus with plans to enter the Air Force upon graduation. His zeal to serve was also a fiercely countercultural move on a campus that, as he described it, "was gripped by a virulent strain of pacifism."[4]

Symington and other ROTC cadets were heckled as they walked across campus in their ROTC service uniforms. In time, Symington and others began carrying their uniforms from their dorms in paper bags.

When the issue came to Barry Goldwater, though, Symington was still willing to walk the gauntlet. Symington wore a large "Goldwater for President" button on his left breast throughout much of the 1964 presidential campaign. While waiting for a flight at Boston's Logan Airport, a middle-aged man once took such offense to the Goldwater pin that he blurted, "What's the matter with you, son, are you mentally demented?"

As an escape from campus life, Symington decided to begin flying lessons. (He was on an allowance, which allowed him to carve out enough funds to pay for the instruction.) He flew out of Beverly, Massachusetts, about thirty miles from Cambridge, where he stayed at Henry Clay Frick's former second home, the 104-room brick "cottage" known as Eagle Rock.

Symington was already showing a gift for public oratory and inter-party politicking by his sophomore year. He bragged in a letter to his mother in early 1965 that "your fledgling son overcame a challenger for an upper-class office" in the Harvard Young Republicans Club. According to the *Harvard Crimson*, the conservative group with which Symington was involved "managed only one clear-cut victory in the major club offices, electing John F. Symington III '68—a distant relative of US Sen. Stuart Symington (D-Mo.)—as Corresponding Secretary."[5]

Symington was an obvious candidate for Harvard's elite clubs. He found a traditional harbor in the storm of 1960s Harvard when he was selected to the famed Porcellian Club.

The Porcellian is the oldest, most secretive, and arguably most prestigious of Harvard's "Final Clubs." Women are not allowed inside its doors. Distinguished guests of Porcellian members could visit—but only once. (The club once turned down President Dwight Eisenhower's request for a second look.) In a June 1966 article published in the *Harvard Crimson*, the author declared, "The members of the Porcellian thrive on a substitute world of their own. Pictures of famous graduates adorn their walls (Oliver Wendell Holmes is prominently displayed). The members addressed each other as "brother" and refrained from discussing politics."

Theodore Roosevelt was a member. Refused for admission were two undergraduates deemed too socially inadequate: Joseph P. Kennedy and Franklin Delano Roosevelt.

"The riots that broke out because of the Vietnam War, and the break-

Symington with other members of Harvard's Porcellian Club, 1967. Courtesy of the
Symington family archives.

ing of all the store windows . . . reflected a cultural divide in which . . . the
Porcellian members were on one side and the rest of the student population was on the other," Symington's longtime friend and fellow Porcellian
member Terry Considine later reflected. "The Porcellian was a bit of an
anachronism."[6]

Finally, there was the passion that seemed as out-of-character for
Symington as it had for his great-grandfather. Symington loved art.

Symington fell in love with the work of the Dutch masters under the
tutelage of Dr. Seymour Slive, one of the world's leading authorities on
seventeenth-century Dutch painters. Symington wrote his senior essay
for Slive's class on the Dutch landscape painter Jan van Goyen.

Symington also enjoyed the art-restoration seminar taught by Elizabeth "Betty" Jones at the Fogg Museum. She introduced Symington to
X-ray technology, ultraviolet light, and spectrometers to study paint-
ings and trace the evolution of each artist's work. During one class, as
Symington practiced using alcohol-soaked Q-tips to remove a yellow
glaze from a portrait of Abraham Lincoln, the areas he dabbed became

smudged. He was relieved to learn that he had not ruined a masterpiece, but rather uncovered a fake.

As summer approached, the head of Keewaydin Camp offered him a job taking parties on canoeing trips and leading hikes into the Canadian Northwoods. He mused that the job would be fun because he could "boss around" adults and show them how to fish. "But I want to get into another wilderness this summer," he informed his father, "a human wilderness, an environment where I can learn things of value and meet nice people."

Symington issued a proposal to his father. "What do you think if I worked in London for the summer?" he asked. "Would Mr. (John) Phillomore be able to give me a job in a bank where I could learn something and put whatever I've got to offer to use?"

He landed a position at Baring Brothers Merchant Bank, one of Britain's most prestigious financial institutions and the world's second-oldest merchant bank.[7]

Symington learned the inner workings of banking practices and procedures. He worked in the securities department, learning how stocks were bought and sold and how they were transferred and put into trusts. He later moved into the credit department, where he learned much about international trade and the various forms of letters of credit. "I feel like I'm learning something worthwhile for a change," Symington wrote his parents.[8]

Symington maintained a robust social life while in England. During one party at the Savoy in London, he met a young Canadian college student named Leslie Barker. Symington was soon enchanted by Barker, who said she had gone to England for the summer to be "a shepherdess by day, and a barmaid by night."

The relationship continued after the two returned to North America. That fall, Symington took Barker for an event at Eagle Rock, the famous Frick estate. Barker wrote in a letter that she found her date "fun-loving, smart, well-traveled, yet innocent, and a good person."

Symington was equally smitten, writing in a letter to his parents that, "Leslie Barker, that beautiful and very grown up lady from Toronto, who I met in London last summer, came down to see me for three whole days last week. She is a senior at the University of Toronto and quite brilliant."[9]

The two often visited the Frick Collection, ate dinners together, and traveled to "Uncle Clay's" estate at Castle Point in Bermuda.

Symington and Barker became engaged just before his graduation in the spring of 1968. The wedding was scheduled for June 21, 1968, but was moved up three weeks because Symington received his orders to report to Tyndall Air Force Base in Florida for active military duty.

Barker was unsure how a middle-class young woman was expected to act in Eastern high society.[10] One week after the engagement announcement, amid a series of pre-wedding appearances that included a formal ball, Leslie wrote a lengthy letter to her future mother-in-law.

"You must have noticed I looked a little distressed, but I'm renowned for clamming up when there is something on my mind," she wrote.

Leslie said she believed Fife was making a sacrifice in marrying her "whether or not those particular aspects of society are important to him or not." She then surmised that, "You and Mr. Symington have probably always imagined the merger of two great families and you cannot help but be disappointed."

But she concluded with a statement of forbearance: "If I were not so sure of my feelings and my ability to make Fife happy I would never have put you in such a position."[11]

The couple married June 1, 1968, in Toronto. They honeymooned at Castle Point, Bermuda, where Leslie wrote scores of thank-you letters for the wedding presents she had received. After a week in Bermuda, Fife and Leslie moved into a hotel in Mexico Beach, Florida, the community closest to Panama City, where Symington began his three-year stint in the US Air Force.

Gone was the Porcellian Club, and base housing wasn't Eagle Rock. In one day, Symington went from a honeymoon in Bermuda to life as just another one of thousands of second lieutenants entering service as America sent a record number of troops to Southeast Asia.

# Chapter 4

# WAR

L ike many residents of the city, Fife Symington came to Phoenix by way of Luke Air Force Base.

Soon after beginning flying lessons during his freshman year at Harvard, Symington went to Washington, DC, to visit his cousin, US Senator Stuart Symington, who had served as the first secretary of the Air Force from 1947 to 1950. Fife Symington told Stuart he was considering joining the Air Force ROTC program. The senator from Missouri gave a rousing endorsement for all things Air Force. Upon returning to Harvard, Symington joined the ROTC program with dreams of being a fighter pilot.[1]

Symington took the extensive eye test demanded of all potential Air Force pilots not long before receiving orders in 1968 to report to Tyndall Air Force Base in Florida. He was crushed to learn he had flunked the depth perception test. Even though he was a licensed civilian pilot with commercial, multi-engine, and instrument rating, he would not be allowed to be a fighter pilot.

Instead, he spent the summer after graduation training as a weapons controller, a job similar to that of an FAA air traffic controller, but one managing more complicated, multiaircraft missions in fluid, wartime scenarios.

From Tyndall, Symington was sent to the NORAD SAGE Center at Luke Air Force Base in Arizona, where he served as one of thousands of officers around the world tasked with operating NORAD's immense network of computers and other equipment that monitored the skies for Soviet missiles and bombers.

The Symingtons bought their first house in Scottsdale, and Symington began commuting to Luke Air Force Base in the far West Valley. After the initial rush of learning a new skill in his first year job, he settled into the often humdrum and repetitive life of a controller at a training base far from the battlefield.[2]

First Lieutenant Symington at Luke Air Force Base, late 1960s. Courtesy of the Arizona State Library, Archives and Public Records, History and Archives Division, Phoenix, RG1_SG26_S6_B08_F023_I01.

After nearly two years at Luke, Symington knew he would soon be getting orders for his remote assignment, which could take him to any US base in the world. He was bored. He wanted to go to Southeast Asia to be involved with the war effort in Vietnam.

During leave in Maryland Symington again went to Senator Symington's office hoping for guidance. The senator introduced Symington to a colonel serving as the Senate Air Force Liaison. Symington said he didn't want to "serve in some irrelevant post." Two months later, at the height of the conflict in Southeast Asia, Symington received orders to report to Udorn Air Force Base in Thailand.[3]

The Air Force flew about 80 percent of its air strikes on North Vietnam from bases in Thailand, so officers with Symington's skill set were in high demand there. Indeed, by the time Symington landed at Udorn, more airmen and support personnel were operating out of Thailand than out of South Vietnam.

While serving at Udorn, Symington lived in a hut he rented from a Chinese rice trader. A large clay urn on the roof collected rainwater for baths and showers. Leslie and the couple's first child, Fife Symington IV, or "Fifie," came to visit for several months during his deployment.

Symington at Udorn Royal Thai Airbase, 1970. Courtesy of the Arizona State Library, Archives and Public Records, History and Archives Division, Phoenix, RG1_SG26_S6_B26_F039_I01.

Symington and other weapons controllers ran the air war over Laos and parts of North Vietnam from Udorn's Brigham Control, a nondescript building with a roof that leaked with every rain. It was not Symington's dream job in the pilot's seat, but it was intense and important nonetheless. Split-second decisions by levelheaded controllers amid a maelstrom of incoming information could save lives, particularly when a plane went down in jungles teeming with North Vietnamese soldiers.

The newly minted captain guided more than four thousand tanker rendezvous and numerous search and rescue operations during his fourteen months at Udorn, none more intense than when a CIA helicopter with six people onboard was shot down west of Dien Bien Phu on the Laotian border.

As Symington helped guide the pilot toward a drop zone, the helicopter came under heavy fire. Symington heard gunfire followed by screaming followed by the deafening roar of a crash. Then silence. Symington directed the pilot of a nearby F4 Phantom fighter jet to make a low pass over the site to look for life. The pilot spotted movement, then made contact with the helicopter's pilot.

The pilot and several of the agents had survived the crash. As enemy soldiers approached from one side of the helicopter, the survivors slipped away from the other side by scrambling down a steep ravine covered with razor-sharp elephant grass. Once Symington's team knew the CIA team was clear of the helicopter, several jets swooped in toward the downed helicopter as NVA troops swarmed the wreckage. As napalm incinerated the chopper and those nearby, the CIA team slipped deeper into the jungle. It took twenty-four hours for the survivors of the crash, with the help of Symington's crew, to locate a safe location for an extraction.

After the men were safely off the ground, the pilot of the downed helicopter got on the radio and thanked Symington for guiding the CIA team to safety. Symington thought he recognized the pilot's voice, but with the possibility of the enemy listening to the transmission, he didn't ask the pilot's name.

Earlier that day, one of Leslie's close friends came to the door of the couple's hut screaming that her husband might be dead. The helicopter piloted by her husband Capt. Freddie Fromm, had been shot down over enemy territory.

Symington ran out onto the tarmac to greet the survivors as they landed. First to jump off was a bloodied but exuberant Freddie Fromm, who yelled, "Symington, we need a drink!"[4]

Symington was later awarded the Bronze Star for his cool-headed leadership during that extraction and several other complicated missions.

Soon after he arrived back in Arizona in 1971, the Air Force began offering early retirements as the war in Southeast Asia began to wind down. After an intense tour of duty, the prospect of running out the clock with another year of drudgery at Luke was not appealing. Symington decided it was time to try civilian life. He had enjoyed studying the US Constitution and the legal history of the United States. Perhaps he would try law school.

# Chapter 5

# A SECOND-CLASS CITY

To understand Symington's business and political career, it helps to understand the unique crossroads of go-go development, easy financing, limited-government braggadocio, and big-government dependency known as the Valley of the Sun.

By the early 1980s, Phoenix had grown large enough to develop an inferiority complex of world-class proportions. The city had grown from 106,818 in 1960 to 789,704 in 1980.[1] The Valley—including Tempe, Mesa, Glendale, Scottsdale, and Chandler—held over 1.2 million people. It was the ninth largest city in America (up from twentieth in 1970). At its rate of growth during the mid-80s, the city was projected to be one of America's five largest cities by the early 2000s.

But Phoenix's growth up until 1980 had little to do with the qualities of the metropolis itself. Prior to World War II, the "Three Cs" of Arizona—copper, cattle, and cotton—had lured a hardy breed of pioneers and laborers to the scorching landscape of central Arizona. After World War II, with federal reclamation programs such as the Salt River Project and Theodore Roosevelt Dam securing water and electricity for the Valley, most people came for the dry air, cheap houses, low taxes, and interminable sun. Arizona came to be known for two more "Cs"—citrus and climate.[2]

During the winter months, the area's myriad resorts and model homes teemed with a blend of winter-weary Midwesterners as well as Californians longing for more square footage. You went to Phoenix half the year for what was outside, not inside. If you were going to stay, you were going to stay because the price was right.[3]

It was during the stifling heat of the six-month Phoenix summers that locals most became aware that their metropolis was short on many of the cultural and architectural amenities that made America's great cities great.

For prospective homeowners, the Del Webb model of desert home-building—low-density, low-cost tract housing built cheaply and swiftly upon concrete slabs—was made even more attainable for middle-class Americans with Arizona's low taxes and the ready availability of home loans.

People wanted homes, land was cheap and plentiful, loans were easy to come by, and homes could be built quickly. Phoenix grew from 187 square miles in 1960 to more than 300 square miles just a decade later.

Through the 1960s and 1970s, the savings and loan industry boomed in the Valley (it was difficult to find a major community leader who wasn't on the board of an S&L). Numerous local thrifts such as South-west Savings and Loan Association made consistent, healthy profits on various fees by bringing in money through customer savings accounts and sending that money out as thirty-year, fixed-rate housing loans. It was a profitable model as long as federal regulations were favorable to the thrifts and interest rates stayed reasonable.[4]

Fife Symington joined the board of directors of Southwest Savings in 1976.

This record-setting growth was not, as it is often assumed now, inevitable in this particular place. Indeed, in the 1940s and 1950s, several other cities in the region were nearly the size of Phoenix and arguably had more amenities and business heft. El Paso, 50 percent larger than Phoenix in 1940, was also well positioned to be the largest metropolis of the region by the last quarter of the century. Just after World War II, boosters in Albuquerque, Tucson, and even smaller towns such as Yuma could make compelling arguments that their cities were destined to become the biggest beneficiary of America's shift to the Sun Belt and the military-industrial complex's move south and west toward what came to be known as the Gunbelt.[5]

Why did Phoenix rise to the top? The wealth of natural amenities and cheap resources, for one, of course. But strong leadership was also key, as were the sweeping powers granted to those leaders by the public, thanks, in some part, to an outbreak of venereal diseases.

In *Phoenix: The History of a Southwestern Metropolis*, arguably the definitive book on the city's history, historian Brad Luckingham described the overly rollicking wartime era that could have ruined Phoenix's reputation nationally and squelched its ascent to a major metropolitan area.

The year before the Japanese attack on Pearl Harbor, Thunderbird Field was opened north of Glendale and was soon used by the Army Air

Corps to train cadets. Soon after, England's Royal Air Force began training cadets northeast of Mesa as the Battle of Britain raged back home.
The success of those facilities led boosters to begin an all-out push to
make the Valley the aviation capital of America. Members of a municipal
aviation commission argued to federal officials that the region offered
excellent flying weather throughout the year, level surfaces, few rainy
days, little wind, and as one of their pitches stated, "the availability of a
vast, uninhabited territory, near at hand for gunnery range purposes."

At the same time, from inside government, Arizona's senators, Ernest
McFarland and Carl Hayden, used their influence and committee positions to angle for their home state.[6]

The Army Air Corps ultimately selected a site south of Mesa for a $4.7
million facility that became Williams Field. To the northwest, $1.5 million
was spent to build what became Luke Air Force Base, which, like Williams, drew tens of thousands of young American men and women to the
Valley for military training. After their service, many Air Force personnel,
like Captain Fife Symington, decided they wanted to make Phoenix their
home.

Many of those airmen ultimately bought inexpensive tract homes
from the developer of Luke Field—the king of inexpensive tract home
developments in the Southwest, Del Webb.

By the early 1940s, there was only one real obstacle to phenomenal
growth: Phoenix had a national reputation for a laissez-faire attitude toward bad behavior. Not only was the local government widely considered
corrupt and inept, it was woefully incapable or unwilling to crack down
on illicit activity—particularly prostitution, an industry that boomed as
thousands of young men began roaming "Red Light Row" during their
off hours.

Throughout 1940, base medical personnel continued to see a spike in
the number of airmen needing treatment for sexually transmitted diseases. As city officials failed to act, citizens, along with the powerful *Arizona
Republic*, began demanding action.

Mild crackdowns followed, but "Red Light Row" and houses of ill re-
pute elsewhere would reemerge soon after. In late 1942, the commanders
of the Valley's military installations issued orders that personnel were to
stay out of Phoenix. Those orders made national news, and Phoenix's
reputation as a desert Gomorrah went national.

"The action of the military is a distinct blot on Phoenix," *Republic* editors lamented. "The question is: Are the people going to remain passive . . . or are they going to demand that something drastic be done?"[7]

In 1949, reformers, led by a small group of increasingly powerful businessmen and supported by a majority of the population, finally overthrew the old city government political machine. A strong, independent city manager would guide city affairs while being shielded from political operatives in hiring and firing matters. Civic leaders, organized under the name "Charter Government Committee," served as de facto overseers and guardians of the transformation, even naming a slate of CGC-approved candidates for the city council. Newspaper magnate Eugene Pulliam talked a young Barry Goldwater into joining the lineup of CGC candidates that won seats in 1949.[8]

In 1950, Phoenix won the All-America City Award. From then on, CGC candidates won election after election while a wholly growth-oriented CGC leadership, made up of the city's top businessmen, bankers, developers, and lawyers, became the dominant power in the city. With Pulliam, attorney Frank Snell, and banker Walter Bimson in the lead, the group's vision for the future of the city and surrounding cities became the path of the newly christened "Valley of the Sun."[9]

By the time Fife Symington arrived at Luke Air Force Base in the late 1960s, the Valley had a firmly established leadership class and a maturing and increasingly affluent upper crust itching to make Phoenix known for more than just outlandish population growth.

At the same time, though, frustrations were growing among minorities and the working class that they were being left out of the prosperity. Phoenix leadership was absolutely white and overwhelmingly male. Neighborhoods primarily occupied by Latinos increasingly became the homes and dumping grounds for major industries. College students organized in the 1960s, and Mexican American advocacy groups and workers' rights groups blossomed and began demanding social reform. In 1970, enraged and energized by the shootings at Kent State, a group of college-age journalists started the city's alternative newspaper, *Phoenix New Times*, which spent much of its time railing against the city's white elites. Phoenix quickly grew a big-city counterculture.

Traffic and air pollution were getting worse. The term "urban sprawl" found common usage. Stories of developers and industries contorting zoning laws, lining pockets, and fouling or stealing water abounded.

Through the 1970s, discontent about pollution, sprawl, inequality, and seemingly increasing government corruption grew.

When Fife Symington emerged as the face of the $400 million Camelback Esplanade development, he was immediately a divisive figure. He was either another filthy-rich agent of get-rich-quick sprawl, or a visionary at the forefront of Phoenix's push to become a truly "world-class city." Within weeks of first proposing the Esplanade to city leaders, Symington became, depending on your perception of the city's past and hopes for its future, the embodiment of everything right or wrong with Phoenix. He even played both roles in the state's largest newspaper. As *Republic* editorial writers heralded his Esplanade plan, for example, popular *Republic* columnist and Pulitzer winner Tom Fitzpatrick already had a derisive nickname for him—"Mr. Plushbottom IV."[10]

In J. Fife Symington III, it seemed, the people of Phoenix quickly saw either what they aspired to be or what they had always despised.

# Chapter 6

# HOW TO GET AHEAD IN BUSINESS

In the weeks following his early out from the Air Force, Symington increasingly soured on the idea of spending three years getting his law degree at the University of Arizona. Since Gilman, he had spent his life as a cog in an institution.

Except for his time in Thailand he was generally bored during his military career.[1] But even there he had become more acutely aware of his distaste for bureaucracy. When he guided missions, he often had to wait for his Thai compatriots to get clearance to take action as critical seconds ticked by. He was finished waiting for others and being at the mercy of bureaucratic morass. He would set out on his own.

He already had considered investing in real estate during his time in the Air Force. On the verge of one significant investment with friends, though, he was dissuaded by his parents' attorney in Baltimore, a long-time family friend who embodied the conservatism of a man who had weathered the Great Depression. The attorney warned Symington that real estate, especially out in the Desert Southwest, was a risky business.

But Symington embraced that foundational go-west ethic of building a new life on new land. And honestly, he just needed to earn some money. He had a wife, mortgage, and two young children, Fife IV and Scott, to support.

So he signed up for real estate classes, labored eight hours a day through the summer of 1971 to earn twenty-four hours of class credit, then took and passed the state real estate exam. By fall he had a job with Ed Post Realty, bouncing from house to house in residential neighborhoods with couples looking for a new home.

After hosting a few open houses, he decided he would rather pursue the bigger fish in the commercial real estate market.

During his short career as an agent he had already befriended one of the biggest players in up-market Paradise Valley and Scottsdale real estate, Ellie Shapiro. With her help, Symington landed a gig representing

Frank Rand, who was trying to buy a commercial lot on Miller Road.

(As he researched for Rand, Symington realized the greatest potential for high-end development lay along stretches of Camelback Road, which dissected much of the Valley's wealthiest neighborhoods.)

While Symington worked for Rand he was contacted by a representative of Eastern Airlines, Lew Huck, who had gotten Symington's name from another friend of the Symington family, Larry Rockefeller. (The Rockefeller family owned Eastern Airlines.) The airline's ownership group wanted to buy the famed Arizona Biltmore Hotel and the surrounding thousand acres just north of Twenty-Fourth and Camelback, which had been put up for sale by the Wrigley Family. Huck wanted Symington to serve as Eastern's man on the ground in Phoenix—basically the group's gofer tasked with researching and acquiring everything investors would need to determine the value and development opportunities of the property.[2]

Soon, Symington was immersed in the minutia of city, county, and state zoning laws. As he spent twelve-hour days piecing together a potential development plan for the property, two larger players in the real estate world, Lincoln Property Company and Trammell Crow Company, were brought in to assist.

Within a few months, Symington and his partners in Phoenix had a plan. But Eastern officials were hesitant. Again, he felt he was being stymied by indecisive decision-makers above him.

"Sometimes I get quite aggravated with (Eastern officials) because they act like demigods and have very little consideration for other people's time and efforts," Symington wrote to his mother in December 1972. "All the factual research, land comparables and zoning matters, and general valuations were to all intents and purposes taken care of by last June. But when you're dealing with a large corporation like Eastern you are not dealing with independent men who make their minds up quickly; you are dealing with men who have their particular niches of power and they are excruciatingly careful about every decision they make lest they lose their niche.

"I for one could never be part of a corporate structure," he wrote.[3]

After a year, the Rockefeller-led group offered $15 million in cash and Eastern stock for the resort, the Wrigley mansion, and the surrounding thousand acres, which would be subdivided into smaller lots.[4]

But the Wrigleys also received an offer from Talley Industries. The

Talley offer was all cash, and the Wrigleys ultimately took the cash offer.

Symington, working on commission, received nothing for his year of work. He was crestfallen.

He thought his year couldn't get any worse.

In early 1972, as the Symingtons' fortunes seemed to be rising, Ellie Shapiro helped the couple find a house in the desert north of Phoenix that, with remodeling and updating, could be their dream home. Shapiro recommended a well-known architect to handle the remodeling and additions to the house.

One afternoon, Leslie sat her husband down and said she wanted a divorce. She didn't tell him why. Symington suggested the couple go to marriage counseling. He wanted to know what had happened and whether or not their relationship could be fixed.

But unbeknownst to Symington at the time, Leslie had fallen in love with their architect and wanted to move on. After a joint custody agreement was arranged and the divorce was finalized, Symington found himself in uncharted emotional waters.

"This hasn't been a particularly good year," he told his mother in a letter that December.

But by mid-1973, Symington's fortunes were improving.

After several emotionally toxic months, the divorce proceedings increasingly turned civil. The couple went on to share custody amicably in the years that followed.

Although Symington made no money pursuing the Biltmore, he had earned the respect of officials at both Lincoln and Trammell Crow. Symington had proved adroit in pulling a deal together, and the deal was big enough that he caught the eye of some of the city's most influential business people. Soon after the Biltmore deal failed, attorney and civic leader Richard Mallery, who the *Arizona Republic* soon after labeled one of Arizona's most powerful people, asked Symington to invest in, and join the board of, Southwest Savings and Loan Association.

That year, too, Symington—then a newbie member of the Republican Tusk & Trunk Club in Phoenix—accidentally made a splash in Arizona Republican circles during a visit to the city by Vice President Spiro Agnew. As Agnew was being led through a crowd of the state's Republican bigwigs, he spotted Symington deep in the crowd and headed toward him, against the wishes of Agnew's handler, Phoenix power broker and longtime Barry Goldwater pal, Harry Rosenzweig. Agnew reached Symington and asked him, "What the hell are you doing here?" Agnew asked about Symington's parents. The two discussed Symington's stint as an Agnew campaign staffer back in Baltimore years before.[5]

All the while, the area's elite wondered about the identity of the young man who stopped the vice president of the United States in his tracks.

Soon after the failed Biltmore purchase, Lincoln's founder and chairman Mack Pogue and regional partner Preston Butcher offered Symington a position as the company's operating partner representing Arizona. The pay was unimpressive—$14,000 a year. But Symington would earn 25 percent of any commercial building deal he put together. He would finally have a chance to make deals with very little outside interference. He took the job on the spot.

Symington would come to revere both Pogue and Butcher. "They were inspirational entrepreneurs," Symington would say later.

Over the next year, he flourished, putting together deals that resulted in more than 300,000 square feet of warehouse space being built in Phoenix. The space was being leased as quickly as it was being built. By October of 1973, Fife Symington was on his way to being one of the leading warehouse builders in the Valley.

Then in late October, the Organization of Arab Petroleum Exporting Countries (OAPEC) announced an oil embargo. The price of oil quadrupled within six months. Gas prices spiked as the US economy staggered.

As Symington kept building and taking out construction loans, companies crippled by the oil crisis stopped leasing space. Within months of turning healthy profits, Symington and Lincoln were unable to make their payments on many of their bank loans.

In the hobbled economy of late 1974, Symington first learned how companies work with banks to avoid defaulting on loans.

Symington and Lincoln went to Aetna, which had loaned the money for the warehouses and office buildings, and made an argument most any developer with management expertise was making to their lenders at the time:

*Sure, you could take the property. But then you'd be stuck with some empty buildings that aren't worth much in this economy that you have no expertise in managing once companies begin leasing warehouse space again. We've proven we can turn a profit and pay our bills when the economy is stable. Instead of foreclosure, wouldn't it be in your best interest to simply give us a little more time?*

Aetna held off foreclosure, and after a one-year debt-service mora-torium, the economy recovered, warehouse leasing picked back up, and Symington and Lincoln began paying off their debts again.

Debt-service moratoriums have saved countless companies. But this leap of faith by lenders can also be a costly mistake if there's no rebound. Over time, debt-service moratoriums became common practice for many major US lenders. Still, some financial institutions shied away from the practice, especially when there was less certainty of a quick market turnaround.[6]

After three years with Lincoln, Symington decided he had learned all he needed to start his own company. He teamed up with one of his old Lincoln coworkers, Danny Madison. They named the company Inverness after the historic town in Scotland.

Symington had grown bored with developing warehouses. He wanted to make money, but he also wanted to enjoy making money. He decided to focus his energy on developing "garden office buildings," which, in the mid-1970s, were fashion-forward amid the sprawl of strip malls through-out the Valley.

The garden office complexes involved significant landscaping and more tailored architectural designs. In time, heavily softscaped, up-mar-ket office plazas transformed stretches of northern Phoenix and Scotts-dale into shaded, low-density commercial landscapes more akin to Santa Barbara than the rest of suburban Phoenix.[7]

As Inverness grew, Symington was approached by the owners of a small oil and gas company in which Symington had invested. The com-pany, Vega Petroleum, owned by Jerry Nelson, Herb Miller, and Richard Mallery, was in financial peril, and investors were upset with the owner-ship group. Since Symington was a proven entrepreneur who himself was one of the company's investors, Vega's owners thought Symington was a good fit to be the company's new president.

The only problem: Symington didn't know a thing about the oil and gas business.

Still, the money was good and the possibilities seemed endless as the United States pursued energy independence. So Symington handed most of the Inverness work over to Madison and headed to West Texas to take classes explaining the inner workings of the oil business. Symington then went to work with a respected petroleum geologist in an attempt to lo-cate new oil reserves southeast of San Antonio.

In letters sent to friends and relatives at the time, Symington seemed varyingly optimistic and gloomy about his prospects in the oil industry. So it went in the fickle Texas oil business at that time: Prices fluctuated, competition was intense, and production could vary wildly. (Wells producing two hundred barrels one day, for example, could be producing less than five barrels a few days later.)[8]

As Vega's production fluctuated, Symington looked for chances to buy out other companies in the market. In 1978, he identified a small company, Remuda Oil, owned by an old man who wanted out of the business. Symington ran the numbers, put together a deal, and Vega, by then headed by famed Arizona agribusiness tycoon John Norton, bought the small company.

Norton, known in the Southwest as the "Lettuce King," was notoriously gruff, and in particular had little regard for people in business who made money facilitating business rather than producing products.[9] When Symington approached Norton to receive what he believed was the promised commission for putting together the deal, Norton balked at paying. Norton called Symington to his office near Sky Harbor Airport. An argument ensued. Symington felt Norton was bullying him. Symington told Norton to "go screw yourself" and with his dramatic exit from Norton's office, gave notice that he was quitting as president of Vega Petroleum. He would focus his attention on Inverness.[10]

But later the same week, Madison announced he wanted to buy Inverness from Symington. Madison increasingly had been handling and growing the business and felt it was his time to go out on his own (as Symington himself had done with his exit from Lincoln, Madison pointed out). Soon after, Madison bought Symington out and within the course of a few months, both of Symington's jobs were gone.[11]

After a few weeks of sulking and soul searching, Symington decided to simply start up again with a new entity, the Symington Company. He quickly put together a deal in early 1979 on land leased from Bill Levine (who would go on to be one of the Valley's richest men) to build an office building along the Camelback Road corridor. Within two years, the Symington Company was involved in the development of numerous garden office buildings in Scottsdale and along Camelback Road. After a series of structures that were completed within the development world's gold standard of "on time and under budget," the company increasingly added staff as it began to manage the properties it had built.

As Symington's financial prospects rose and fell and rose again through his first few businesses, his star steadily rose in political and social circles in the city. Although some stigma still clouded the reputation of a divorced man in the 1970s, he was—even as a single father of two young boys—considered one of the more interesting eligible bachelors in the Valley.[12]

While Symington was still involved with Vega Petroleum with Jerry Nelson and Richard Mallery, Mallery invited him to an art opening in Tucson hosted by Michael Pulitzer, whose famed media family owned the Tucson paper.[13]

Symington agreed to go. He hitched a ride to Tucson with another friend who would be attending the event.

Near the midpoint of the soiree, Symington met John Pritzlaff, who was serving as the US ambassador to Malta at the time. Symington's father was ambassador to Trinidad and Tobago and like Pritzlaff, a graduate of Princeton, so the two had much to discuss.

Soon after Symington met Pritzlaff, Pritzlaff's wife came over and introduced herself. Mary Dell Pritzlaff was arguably the leading lady of the Valley's social scene and, like her husband, a major player in the state's Republican hierarchy. Both came from well-to-do Midwestern families, especially Mary Dell, whose father, Spencer Truman Olin, was an executive and a leading stockholder in the massive Olin Corporation, which owned numerous companies, including Winchester, the legendary maker of rifles and ammunition. Mary Dell's grandfather was the company's founder, Franklin Olin.

Symington spent much of the remainder of the evening talking with the Pritzlaffs. Afterward, the couple asked Symington if he'd like to ride back to Phoenix with them. Symington agreed and spent much of the next ninety minutes being grilled by Mary Dell about his political beliefs. Symington apparently passed the test.

As the three approached Phoenix, the Pritzlaffs asked Symington if he would mind if the couple stopped at their home before dropping Symington off at his house. Symington again agreed.

As he waited in the Pritzlaffs' kitchen, their daughter, Ann, walked in. Ann and Symington chatted for a few minutes as Symington waited for his ride. Both had just enough time to find the other interesting enough to consider meeting again.

A week later, Symington called Ann, who was a second-grade teacher at the time. Ann said, "I was wondering when you were going to call." The couple went to dinner, and as they talked, they realized they had experienced very similar upbringings in households with very similar politics. (They also realized that her parents had clearly engineered that first meeting.) The couple began dating regularly. Within only a few months, in mid-1975, Symington had gone from describing Ann in letters home as "a nice young lady I just met" to inviting her to meet his parents.

"I'm really so happy about everything and so pleased that you like Ann," Symington wrote to his parents in late October. "I know John and Mary Dell P. are looking forward to meeting you."[14]

Ann and Fife were married the next year. After the birth of their first child, Whitney, Fife's constant commuting to Midland in his Beechcraft Bonanza became more tedious than exciting. With three young children, a return to developing garden office complexes within miles of home became much more appealing.

By the early 1980s, the Symington Company had developed, and was managing, several hundred thousand feet of office space. A series of office buildings along Fortieth Street and Camelback Road arguably became the benchmark for upscale, low-density office space in the Valley. One of the more prominent structures was the gleaming "5080 Building," most notable for the creative civil engineering that allowed the structure to straddle the sometimes gully-washed Cudia City Wash.

Soon after the 5080 Building was completed, what was deemed a one-hundred-year flood pounded the Valley. As Symington and his lead architect and partner, Randy Todd, stood on a bridge beneath the structure watching the water rise, Todd was unnerved, while Symington seemed unfazed. Soon the water rose to within a few feet of the base of the bridge. A mattress floated by, along with other chunks of debris. Still, Todd would say later, Symington seemed sure that nothing bad would happen. "I guess we'll see if we have a good engineer," Symington quipped as it appeared the water was about to rise into the building's parking garage.[15]

The rain stopped just in time, the water receded just in time, and the 5080 Building went on to quickly turn a profit for the company. Soon Symington was arguably the leading builder of garden office buildings in Arizona and with that, one of the most aggressive developers along Camelback Road and Scottsdale Road. By 1981, even though short-term interest rates for construction loans were approaching 20 percent, the Symington Company was growing.

Symington decided it was time to go after a piece of undeveloped land that he had coveted since he first began his development career.

Not long before Symington started the Symington Company, billionaire Daniel Ludwig bought Southwest Savings from a group of investors led by an Indiana bank, which hoped to convince federal regulators to allow it to merge their banking activities with the Arizona savings and loan. Their argument: with the bank's ability to tap major money markets, Arizona would benefit from having an entity capable of plugging hundreds of millions of dollars in mortgage funding into a fast-growing area starving for capital.[16]

Federal regulators shot down the merger in late 1974, and Southwest stayed locked into the low orbit of providing residential mortgages from money placed in the thrift by individuals looking for a safe place to earn a steady return on what, for many, was their life savings.

As the 1980s began, Ludwig called Symington to his New York office to discuss the future of the thrift. The famed shipping magnate—elderly and confined to a wheelchair by that time—told Symington he "only wanted big deals." Ludwig said he didn't buy Southwest Savings and Loan to try to survive off home loans in a brutal interest-rate and regulatory environment. Ludwig said he wanted to expand into the financing of substantial commercial developments.

Symington told Ludwig about a grand idea he had for the southeast corner of Twenty-Fourth Street and Camelback Road.[17]

Ludwig loved the idea.

Soon after, Randy Todd and others at the Symington Company began hearing their boss make cryptic references to a new project in the works.

Symington didn't want competitors getting wind of the plan, so he figured he'd just refer to the budding project with grand nonsensical names.

Sometimes it was called "Project Z." At other times, it was called "Mission Mars."[18]

# A WORLD-CLASS CITY

U p to 1982, Fife Symington was an unknown beyond the Valley nobility, business community, and the inner circles of the Republican Party.

By 1985, though, Symington was such a household name that Tom Fitzpatrick, the Pulitzer-winning populist metro columnist for the state's largest paper, had created his own nickname for a Symingtonesque character, Mr. Plushbottom IV. In a March 1985 column, Fitzpatrick set a scene in the year 2035 in which Plushbottom sat in the library of his fifty thousand-acre oceanside estate in Maryland telling a young reporter the story of how he hoodwinked the people of Arizona and why they were so easily hoodwinked.[1]

"Actually, (the people of Phoenix) were little more advanced than the native Indians at the time," Fitzpatrick's Plushbottom character told the writer. "What were they really but a motley group of transplants from places like New Jersey and Indiana? What did they really know about anything?"

The fight over Symington's then-$400 million Camelback Esplanade project, which, at a planned twenty-one stories, would tower over a neighborhood with a building height-limit of four stories, catapulted Symington into statewide celebrity and infamy. To some, he was a bold and brilliant self-made millionaire leading Phoenix toward a world-class future; to others like Fitzpatrick, he was a slick silver-spoon carpetbagger pushing a cash-cow monstrosity by dazzling them with a deceptive, million-dollar ad campaign.

The Esplanade itself became a vessel into which both supporters and detractors poured their disparate perceptions of the Valley's history and predictions for its future.

The worst opinions of the Valley of the 1970s and 1980s echoed similar themes: Phoenix was little more than a haphazard sprawl of fouled air and water boomed by a small, elite club of greedy white businessmen.

Nonsense, said the counter-argument: Phoenix was a city saved from obscurity and ignominy by a group of visionary civic leaders who had placed the region on the doorstep of greatness. If the Valley was so bad, why did so many people want to leave their homes elsewhere in the United States to live here? And if those people want affordable, single-family homes, how can you blame someone for giving them what they want? As with any metropolis, sure, there were some problems that needed to be solved. But they could be solved.[2]

Throughout the 1970s, an increasingly broad swath of the citizenry of Phoenix began clamoring for stricter limits on growth patterns in the city. In an effort to limit sprawl and all its deleterious impacts on living conditions, the city council in 1979 enacted the Concept 2000 urban village plan as the foundational guide for future development.

The idea was basically this: The city would be divided into nine urban villages in which residents would have easy access to employment, shopping, educational opportunities, and leisure activities. Not only would Valley residents spend less time in their cars, they would be given the opportunity to create the type of civic connections typical of small towns.[3]

With this bold plan, the City of Phoenix quickly became viewed as one of America's most innovative combatants of sprawl.[4] The city and its planning department won several national awards and for years after would be credited with being an international pioneer—at least in theory—in the creation and implementation of smart-growth policies.

The Urban Village Concept, though, made for a somewhat conflicted city stance. Downtown Phoenix was dying; the city's center was hollowing out. How could the downtown be saved if employers and retail businesses were being driven toward urban villages mostly located many miles from downtown?

For the most part, the solution was simple: Large structures and major civic projects would be limited to downtown and the Central corridor running north from downtown, whereas medium-sized and smaller, lower-density structures and developments would be allowed, even promoted, for the core of the Urban Villages.

During this same time, the structure of the Phoenix city council was overhauled in a way intended to diversify representation in the city. Instead of the city council members being elected without regard for where they lived, the council would consist of representatives elected by voters in the districts in which the council member lived.[5]

In Phoenix's Sixth District, which included the tony Biltmore area and several of Fife Symington's garden office complexes, Democrat Ed Korrick was elected in part due to his promises that he would protect the quiet, low-density residential feel of the area.

Within Korrick's district sat a vacant twenty-acre lot at the southeast corner of Camelback Road and Twenty-Fourth Street that many of the state's commercial real estate developers considered the most desirable piece of land in the entire city.

The lot, known as the "Friedman parcel," had sat undeveloped primarily because the land was owned by savvy trustees of the estate of David Friedman, the longtime owner of the land who died in 1974. They believed the property was only going to increase in value with time, so they were in no hurry to sell.

Fife Symington would often drive to the empty lot and dream of a series of gleaming towers full of major businesses, restaurants, fine retailers, and a luxury hotel that were at the heart of his "Mission Mars" project. He believed it would be a spectacular example of the Urban Village Concept in action and a message to the world that Phoenix was now a player.

Standing in the way of his dream was a difficult landowner, a more difficult councilman, a few thousand potentially angry homeowners, and a mayor who was a political foe. He also would have to find someone who could design a uniquely monumental structure as well as find investors willing to drop nearly half a billion dollars into a project with no legitimate comparables in a market known as much for its volatility as its possibilities.

But Daniel Ludwig wanted big deals in the newly deregulated S&L landscape and liked this big deal, so Symington did have one thing going for him: Southwest Savings and Loan, although it could never afford to finance the whole project, did have enough money—and Ludwig's willingness to gamble—to make a spirited run at acquiring the land that would surely need a controversial rezoning to make it profitable.

By 1982, the Symington Company had about forty employees, six project managers, and numerous structures in various stages of development that were redefining the Camelback Road and Scottsdale Road corridors. That year, Symington hired an architect who had been contracted for several of his projects, Randy Todd, to be his second in command. Soon after, Todd was made privy to details of "Mission Mars."

Fife Symington, early 1980s. Courtesy of the Symington family archives.

After Symington's meeting with Ludwig, Symington got the ball rolling on "Mission Mars." He approached Jerry (Jerome) Hirsch, with whom he had partnered on the rezoning effort for the successful Scottsdale Seville Center development. When the pair decided to join together again, Symington suggested they go after "the Holy Grail" of vacant lots, the southeast corner of Twenty-Fourth and Camelback.[6]

The battle plan was simple in its general elements, but arguably the most complicated in Arizona history in its particulars:

1. Get the Friedman land with no delusions that it would be cheap or be sold without strings attached. (They agreed there was only one way to get it: Symington would make a $25 million, all-cash offer with no contingencies and promise a closing within thirty days.)

2. Find a world-renowned architect to create a plan so impressive that few could deny the project was "world class."

3. Get Ed Korrick out of office.

4. If Korrick remained in office, begin a public relations blitz to go around Korrick and others on the city council who were sure to question putting a skyscraper on a corner far from the city's core.

5. Find a few hundred million dollars.

Symington seemed undaunted—arguably invigorated—by the herculean challenge, several of his partners and employees said later. "He was a man possessed by the idea," Todd said years later.[7]

The Philadelphia attorney representing the Friedmans was tough and cagey, but after about a year of negotiations, Southwest acquired the land.

Symington and his team approached Eberhard Zeidler, the architect responsible for Toronto's spectacular mixed-use shopping mall and office tower, the Eaton Centre, among several other innovative structures in North America. Zeidler was given some basic height, use, and size guidelines. He was limited to about twenty stories and around three million square feet. The ideal project would have a footprint of about fourteen acres and some open space between towers through which the surrounding landscape could still be viewed. The hope was for a visually arresting structure that would complement the desert and the nearby mountains and of course, command with its world-classiness the highest dollar-per-square-foot rental prices in the Valley.[8]

Symington himself dreamed of a structure with several relatively narrow towers separated by ample space or "view corridors." He imagined an ultra-modern take on the Gothic cathedrals of Europe.

Zeidler was energized by the prospect of building a major structure nearly unbound by cost in the iconic Sonoran desert. For inspiration, both Zeidler and the developers looked toward two similarly grand successful projects, the Galleria in Houston and the Embarcadero Center in San Francisco.[9]

Zeidler returned to Phoenix with an audacious plan that featured two twenty-story office towers, two fifteen-story office towers, two nineteen-story condo towers, and a ten-story hotel. The structure looked like a crystalline mirror image of the desert mountain that ran west-to-east just a few miles north of Camelback Road.

It was a breathtaking structure that thrilled Symington as much as it convinced him that the city would never allow it. He would fight for it, though. Who knows? he thought. Maybe with enough convincing, the people of Phoenix would rally behind the project with such vigor the city council would have to fall in line.

So, with a plan in place, it was time for the really tough part.

Working within a planning budget of $3 million (the Symington Co. would make around $700,000 in development fees for shepherding the project from dream to shovels-in-the-ground), Symington went to work on getting the zoning and support for the massive structure he needed.

Symington and his partners first pushed to get a more pro-growth representative for the Sixth District. Symington donated $15,000 to the campaign of Ed Korrick's opponent in the 1984 election. Symington's father-in-law, John Pritzlaff, donated $10,000, then penned a scathing letter printed in the *Republic* depicting Korrick as an obstructionist, union-owned liberal Democrat who was out of touch with his constituency.[10]

Several editorial and column writers throughout the state weighed in on a city council race that otherwise would have drawn little attention. For chamber-of-commerce types it was a battle between big thinkers building a great city and shortsighted NIMBYs (acronym for "Not In My Back Yard"). For those who liked the area the way it was and who distrusted developers, it was a battle between big money and the little guy. It was during this city council race that the populist columnist Fitzpatrick first cast Symington in the role of a wily, blue blood puppetmaster.

"The single most fascinating figure in the Phoenix City Council runoff campaign hasn't deigned to step on stage so the rest of us can get a good look at him," Fitzpatrick wrote in the *Republic*. "J. Fife III is not only the brains but a substantial part of the financial muscle behind the candidacy of Jim Gardiner in the silk-stocking Sixth District."[11]

The race was so heated that Korrick once drove his Mercedes-Benz over three of Gardiner's campaign signs. Korrick defended his actions by saying that several of his own signs "have been mutilated."[12]

Still, Korrick won, arguably in part because he accused Gardiner of being in the pocket of developers such as Fife Symington.

Having made an even bigger enemy in Korrick, Symington realized his project needed significant outside help to overcome Korrick and his allies, one of whom was the city's Democratic mayor, Terry Goddard. Symington believed his only chance was to build an unstoppable wave of public support. For that he would need a major public relations campaign.

(Over the next eighteen months, $4 million would be spent on the campaign to sell the Esplanade idea to the people of Phoenix. The campaign dwarfed the efforts of many statewide political races.)

In 1984, Symington brought on a team of public relations officials who helped organize a multipronged assault on the opposition. The project would need an enticing name, so pollster Earl de Berge was hired to test potential names. Giralda, Camelback Center, Zacatecas, Promenade, Aldea, Aldea Center, and Century Center failed to suggest merriment and pedestrian activity and a sense of place like the winning name, the Camelback Esplanade.[13]

By the end of 1984, Symington had towed Zeidler's nine-foot-long polystyrene model of the Esplanade to more than seventy speaking engagements. A public relations team helped craft a barrage of primetime radio and television advertising. The development's marketing team recruited labor organizations to walk nearby neighborhoods soliciting petition signatures, mailed thousands of glossy four-color brochures, and even hosted a Mexican fiesta on the old Friedman lot that drew several hundred people.

Deborah (Deb) Shanahan, who covered the Esplanade battle for the *Republic*, would later describe the Esplanade campaign as "one of the rowdiest periods of my career. It was an all-out blitz. Some people bought in, and others were really put off by it."[14]

Symington's development team even offered $1 million to neighboring residents to finance projects in their own neighborhoods. Mayor Terry Goddard called the offer "a bribe."

Symington countered that he was simply trying to address concerns by neighbors that the Esplanade would impact their neighborhoods. Symington also offered to spend several million dollars to create various traffic-calming areas around the Esplanade to alleviate congestion, a major concern of neighbors trying to grasp the impact of 2.4 million square feet of commercial space packed in a twenty-story high-rise.

While surveys suggested that the majority of Phoenix residents thought the Esplanade was an impressive structure that deserved to be built, far fewer believed it fit into the Urban Village Concept, nor belonged outside the already established locations for Phoenix's towering structures. Members of the Camelback East Village Planning Committee suggested that the Esplanade was too high and offered too few significant open spaces.[15] Symington argued that any reduction in size would be like "taking a meat cleaver" to Zeidler's masterpiece.

Even with the millions spent, the investment group Symington led had difficulty getting traction with the people. The Camelback High Neighborhood Association board split 5–5 on accepting Symington's $1 million, which, by board rules, was a rejection.[16] Vice Mayor Howard Adams damned the tactic with faint praise, telling Shanahan, "We have been insisting that developers go out and talk to the neighbors about their projects. We never dreamed that suggestion would be carried to such a grand extreme."

It was, as another council member noted, as if Symington "was trying to get the Esplanade elected governor."

A consulting team hired by the city suggested that the Esplanade's 2.4 million square feet would, along with other proposed development in the fast-growing area, overload the area with traffic.[17]

The Esplanade's designers, of course, disagreed. In a study commissioned by the Symington team, researchers estimated that the impacts of the additional traffic brought by the Esplanade would be mitigated by the $5 million added to the project design to install traffic-calming and traffic-rerouting features.

Symington's response to all those who questioned his tactics: his team was going far beyond any other previous developer, and spending far more than any other developer, to make the Esplanade a good neighbor.

Several of Symington's development team would later regret this tactic of, essentially, trying to circumvent members of the city council by creating an overwhelming public groundswell that would force council members to vote for the Esplanade. (Indeed, several council members said in interviews that year that Symington had offended them with the move, with one saying, "If he had just worked with us instead of against us, I think things wouldn't have become so contentious.")

Symington wasn't alone in believing the citywide campaign was the right play, though: "This may be the new way of doing business under the district council system," one well-known Arizona political operative told the *Republic.* "You may need to have constituents in every district telling their representative that they support something that's a value to the city that's sitting in some other district."

Regardless, the battle created heated exchanges and increasingly spirited verbal attacks on Symington. Although measured and urbane in his tone, Symington struck back with sharp insults of his own. In private, he often described the campaign for the Esplanade in sports and war tactics clichés.[18]

He knew detractors would confront him, but he was blindsided by the intensity of the attacks, most of which had ancient class-conflict issues at their core. It was as if Henry Clay Frick himself was trying to build the Camelback Esplanade.

Korrick and Fitzpatrick were the most virulent of his critics and arguably were the two most responsible for turning the Esplanade debate into a class war.

"A world-class shark circles in for the kill; will the City Council harpoon it?" a headline on one of Fitzpatrick's columns read. The column ended with a tirade that perhaps best encompasses the visceral, seemingly immovable contempt some class-conscious Arizonans felt for J. Fife Symington III:

"Symington's entire advertising and public relations thrust has been that the rest of us shouldn't care what happens to the neighborhood around 24th and Camelback," Fitzpatrick wrote.

"I am not surprised that J. Fife Symington III thinks like this. His roots are not in Phoenix. He is, after all, a man of inherited wealth who has never had to do a serious day's work in his life.

"He is a developer. What a developer does with a piece of property is fill it to the rim with shops, offices, stores and parking places until he gets so rich he can go buy another vacant lot or perhaps a whole block of residential homes and tear them down.

"A developer, in his own way, is like a shark. You can no more hold him responsible for destroying neighbors and families than you can hold a shark responsible for tearing the bodies of swimmers to pieces."[19]

Symington received several death threats during the Esplanade fight. He even felt compelled to hire a bodyguard to accompany him during his last few public appearances.

It was in this environment that Symington's public relations director, Joanne Ralston, suggested Symington and his wife enroll in an intensive media-training class in which people new to the public arena learned how to negotiate hardball interviews and calmly weather public ridicule.

Ralston had heard that Arch Lustberg, already a nationally respected trainer for people entering public life, had just started his own company. He was offering an immersive three-day, one-on-one training course (using the set of a local television station) on how to stay on message and avoid emotional reactions when confronted with challenging or even hostile interviews or interactions.

After giving a brief outline of the contents of the course, Lustberg sat Fife Symington on the mock set of a television interview program, turned on studio lights and a camera, and began conducting an interview.

At first, the interaction was chatty and casual, with Lustberg asking harmless questions about Symington's life and work. But soon, Lustberg began pelting Symington with a barrage of pointed questions about his project and his motives. Lustberg even unleashed personal attacks in an accusatory tone (Lustberg had interviewed Symington's cohorts, probing for ways to formulate questions that would fluster or anger him). Symington floundered. He began to sweat, his light skin turned red, he began shifting positions in his chair and grabbing near his crotch to adjust his pants.

Lustberg then replayed the videotaped interchange, stopping the tape to discuss each mistake. It was a humbling, disquieting experience for Symington, who had to that moment believed his own life experiences had fully prepared him for public life. He told his wife later that day that the interview combined with its postmortem was one of the most embarrassing moments of his life.

At the end of the third day of training, Lustberg sat Symington down in the same studio format and peppered him with a new round of increasingly nasty questions. What Symington had learned to do (and what Lustberg would go on to teach hundreds of national public figures) was to distance himself emotionally from the exchange, focus on speaking to the audience rather than the interviewer, and calmly redirect any questions asked toward an answer that advanced his mission.

In his final interview, Lustberg even began making accusations out of whole cloth: "Fife," Lustberg said, "there was an article written yesterday in which several people were interviewed that asserted that you beat your wife."

Symington had learned that you avoid the instinctual, "I don't beat my wife!" because, Lustberg argued, a public official should never "repeat the negative" when asked an accusatory question. Symington chuckled at Lustberg's accusation, paused, and said with a smile, "I love my wife, we have so many beautiful children together, we love our time together. We're always amused by the extent some people will go to when they disagree with you."

Symington learned a few more tricks: Always pause when asked a tough question (Lustberg argued that long pauses make interviewers uncomfortable.) Also, don't squint and don't frown. Be prepared. Be genuine. Don't be defensive.

It was a transformative three days for both Fife and Ann Symington that would impact how they presented themselves to the public throughout the remainder of their public life.[20]

By late January of 1985, the Camelback Esplanade fight was watercooler talk across the Valley. In the days leading up to a late-January planning commission meeting—the first major hurdle for the Esplanade—Symington and the Esplanade were the leading evening news piece on Valley television news stations and commanded above-the-fold headlines in papers in Phoenix, Mesa, Tucson, Flagstaff, and Yuma. The pages of the *Republic* were filled with dissections of the project, profiles of Symington, impassioned opinions from both sides, and even some inside-baseball bits such as a feature based on gossip about how both planning commission and city council members might be voting.

More than 1,500 people attended the planning commission meeting during which the Esplanade was debated. Zeidler's polystyrene model was placed before the commissioners as a parade of supporters and opponents spoke to them from behind a podium located near the front of a packed auditorium.[21]

Esplanade supporters argued that the Esplanade was an embodiment

of the Urban Village Concept. They argued the project would employ
five thousand people and pump $400 million into the local economy.
As always, there was the emotional plea that the Esplanade was "world
class," and that if Phoenix hoped to be a world-class city, it needed the
Esplanade.

Several opponents mentioned that the project was spectacular. It was
just too big for Twenty-Fourth and Camelback. Neighborhood groups
argued their streets would become gridlocked.

Arguably the biggest obstacle standing in the way of the twenty-story
Esplanade was the city's own planners, who, after their own research, suggested there be a twelve-story limit on the structures. Planners believed
the construction should be conducted in phases to allow for proper planning of transportation improvements.

The 2.4 million-square-foot complex with eight buildings ranging
from eight to twenty stories tall was voted down. Symington and his
group would have to come back with something smaller.

Soon after, Symington came back with a design with a fifteen-story
limit.

The planning commission and its staff again recommended the project have a twelve-story limit. The mayor and his backers were pushing for
a limit of six stories with the possibility of expanding to nine stories. The
Camelback East Village Planning Committee was suggesting six stories
with a total usable space of 1.3 million square feet.

Symington's team believed they needed ten to twelve stories to make
the Esplanade profitable. In private, Symington actually didn't expect to
get fifteen stories and had designs in place for something in line with the
planning commission's recommendations.[22] But he wanted to argue for
fifteen stories so he had room to compromise while still making a development that had both a chance of being profitable and just as important,
had the numbers that larger investors would find attractive.

In March, the day before the Phoenix City Council hearing that would
decide the project's fate, Symington announced that the Ritz-Carlton
Hotel Co. would be running the Esplanade's hotel—as long as the building was ten stories high.

Mayor Goddard, who favored a nine-story limit, knew what was up:
"This is an effort to exert pressure on the council before the hearing."

Six hundred people attended the hearing the next day. Thousands
more watched KAET-TV's live coverage of the five-hour event, which

was then reviewed the next day by the *Republic*'s Bud Wilkinson, who wrote about the meeting as if he was reviewing a new television show:

"Goddard conducted himself in a manner that translated well on the small screen," Wilkinson wrote.

"Councilwoman Mary Rose Wilcox, meanwhile, seemed to be hurt by the cameras' presence. She appeared whiny and unprepared."[23]

A Tucson journalist said that Goddard and Symington both made for "very compelling television."

In the end, Symington lost—for the most part. The council voted unanimously to limit the height of the project to nine stories and 1.5 million square feet. Symington announced that "The Esplanade as we know it has been killed."

The council set a hearing on a rescaled project for late April.

Todd, Symington's right-hand man, was devastated. Symington, though, acted as if nothing had happened.[24] Soon after Zeidler's super structure was nixed, Symington chartered a jet and took the company's top staffers on a trip to Santa Barbara. His idea: Get his staff to a beautiful place, let them vent, then, amid Santa Barbara's famed architecture, have them brainstorm.

Within weeks, the Symington Company had a new design. Zeidler was let go. Todd was charged with quickly taking the team's ideas and turning them into a more modest structure. Mission Mars was gone. But Symington kept reminding his team that they had, in great part, won. He announced: "Sometimes you have to lose to win." After all, he noted, nobody was proposing a structure limited to the location's current zoning limitation of four stories.

Symington had succeeded in shifting the debate. Opponents no longer argued for four stories because Symington said that, at four stories, only a low-cost, high-density office building could make money on that property. He basically threatened to make the corner a low-rent district.

Todd and Symington returned to the city council in April of 1985 with their new polystyrene model. With only two hundred people in attendance and no television coverage, the council voted unanimously to approve a 1.5 million square foot project, which was 35 percent smaller than the Esplanade first proposed eighteen months before, with eight buildings that would range from two to eleven stories.[25]

Symington's group would pay $10 million for traffic studies and improvements and put one percent of the cost of the project into public art.

Symington called it "a victory for everybody"; Korrick and Goddard did the same. The Esplanade finally had its green light, and Arizona had a new local celebrity.

With the city's approval, the Symington Company could, as Todd later joked, "start the really hard part"—getting the money and doing the arduous prep work needed to get the "shovels in the ground."

# Chapter 8

# HOW TO GET AHEAD IN POLITICS

S oon after touching down in Arizona in the late 1960s, Symington went searching for like-minded young men. He soon found the lo-cal chapter of the Republican social group, the Tusk & Trunk Club, which hosted Republican speakers, organized events and fundraisers for candidates in area races, and of course, provided an opportunity for net-working for young businessmen and political aspirants.

Symington was committed to supporting Republican candidates, but his aspirations were economic, not political. Still, he was tabbed by the Republican ruling class of the 1970s as a potential player among the next generation of Arizona conservatives.[1]

Symington was in charge of bringing speakers to the Tusk & Trunk meetings and events, and in so doing, established relationships with an increasing number of Republican leaders throughout the state.

Symington was known in political circles as one of the most effec-tive fundraisers in the state by the early 1980s.[2] While many found go-ing door-to-door asking for money uncomfortable, it was, as Symington himself would suggest later, "second nature for a developer."

In the early 1980s, he became finance chairman for the state Repub-lican Party, a position that occasionally landed his name in the local papers.

Just as Symington and Southwest Savings were beginning their plans to purchase the lot at Twenty-Fourth and Camelback, a recently retired Navy captain named John McCain moved to Phoenix with his new wife, Cindy, the daughter of Jim Hensley, the owner of a major Arizona beer distributorship. After John McCain became vice president of Hensley & Co., he quickly announced an interest in entering politics. In February 1982, not long after arriving in Arizona, McCain announced his intent to run as a Republican candidate for Congress.[3] He hoped to replace an Arizona political icon, Republican Representative John Rhodes, who was retiring after thirty years in the House. (Rhodes, who served as Minority

Leader for seven years during the 1970s, might be most famous for being one of three Republican leaders, along with Goldwater and Senate Minority Leader Hugh Scott, who met with President Richard Nixon two days before his resignation in 1974. The three informed Nixon he didn't have the support in the House or Senate to survive impeachment proceedings.)[4]

McCain was widely welcomed as a future star of the next generation of Arizona Republicans. For one: he had a compelling, heroic personal story, having spent five horrific years as a prisoner of war in North Vietnam.

McCain began the rounds of service-group speaking engagements, early on hitting the Scottsdale Sunrise Rotary Club, of which Symington was a member. After the Scottsdale meeting at which McCain spoke, Symington approached McCain, introduced himself, handed him his business card, and explained how the two men had a connection.

Symington first explained his controller position at Brigham Control at Udorn Royal Thai Air Force Base. In that capacity, Symington remotely guided several air rescue missions into North Vietnam.[5]

"Did you ever know that when you were a prisoner of war, we tried to get you out?" Symington asked McCain.

Symington had helped guide an aerial armada to the North Vietnamese prison camp at which McCain had spent much of his time in captivity. When the rescue party arrived, though, they discovered the American prisoners had been moved to another camp.[6]

McCain didn't know about the rescue attempt, but the connection made for an unusual conversation-starting tale the two would relate to others for years after. Not long after the Rotary luncheon, McCain called Symington, and along with Grant Woods and Jay Smith (both of whom would soon become political forces in the state), Symington joined McCain's first campaign staff as a volunteer.

Symington handled fundraising, McCain won, and Symington's own star rose higher in the Republican political world.

As the Esplanade battle raged, Symington shifted focus back on McCain, who, after just two terms in Congress, had decided to seek the Senate seat of the retiring titan of Arizona Republican politics, Barry Goldwater. With Goldwater's backing, an unusually unified party behind him, and a platform and background appealing to many moderates, McCain crushed former state legislator and Arizona Corporation Commissioner Richard Kimball by 20 percentage points in November 1986.[7]

With McCain's win and Symington's own high-profile semi-win with the Esplanade, Symington was poised to have a viable shot at public office.

Which he claimed, at least at that moment, was of no interest to him. He needed to find the investors for the Esplanade and get shovels in the ground as quickly as possible. If he was successful, the Symington Company would be firmly established in the big leagues of the region's developers. If he failed, his company could be ruined, or at least lose its treasured reputation for always being "on time and under budget."

So, too, if he kept Southwest Savings sitting on dirt with no return for too many years, the thrift, already riding downward with the majority of the nation's other savings and loans, would collapse. Politics would have to be a side passion.[8]

In 1986, popular Democratic governor Bruce Babbitt announced he would not seek a third term. After twelve years of Democrat governors, Republicans were hungry to take back the top state office.

The Republican primary looked to be a cakewalk for longtime state legislative leader and Republican power broker Burton Barr. Barr's only competition in the primary was an archconservative populist Pontiac dealership owner named Evan Mecham, who had lost three previous statewide races dating back to 1962. Mecham had a loyal following among Arizona's far-right and conservative Christians, but was seen as far too impolitic, unsophisticated, and anti-party-mainstream to be a viable candidate.[9]

But Mecham, who also owned a small publishing company, pounded Barr with the pen, distributing copies of his conservative newspaper that painted Barr as a corrupt pawn of the "good-ole-boy Phoenix 40." While Barr and his supporters didn't treat Mecham like a serious threat, "Mecham threw mud that stuck," political pollster Earl de Berge said after the race.

Like many in the business community, Symington, a longtime Barr supporter, had to quickly become a Mecham supporter. Symington donated a relatively modest $2,000 to Mecham's campaign.

Mecham faced off against Democrat Carolyn Warner and Independent Bill Schulz. Polls had Warner ahead for much of the time leading up to the November 4 election, but Mecham attracted a surprisingly high number of undecided voters to win. In election postmortems, political analysts deemed the race a "change election" in which voters were ready to try Republican state leadership after twelve years with a Democrat. Also, it became clear that the presence of an Independent candidate who had long been a Democrat pulled voters more from Warner than from Mecham.[10]

Mainstream Republicans, for the most part, announced their support for Mecham in hedged language, voicing confidence that Mecham would drop some of his incendiary right-wing rhetoric and bigoted policy ideas once he encountered the reality of governing a diverse population and trying to navigate a legislature with strong Democratic leadership.

Evan Mecham instead continued to be Evan Mecham. As 1987 dragged on, Mecham became increasingly bitter as criticism intensified of his policies, staff choices, inability to work with legislators, offensive off-the-cuff pronouncements, and inability to govern. Increasingly, too, he became an embarrassment to the state.

As he vetoed a series of high-profile pieces of legislation, he proclaimed he didn't have to work with state legislators because he was bound only to the US Constitution, which, he proclaimed numerous times in his writings, was revealed by God to its authors. Several of his appointees had no experience related to their new positions. He once used the word "pickaninny" to describe African American children. He claimed he wasn't racist because he had hired black people who, he said, he didn't hire because of their color, but because "they are the best people for the cotton-picking job."[11]

As Arizona's business community increasingly formed ties with Japanese businesses and banks (and at the same time Symington was wooing Japanese investors), Mecham pronounced that a group of Japanese businessmen "got round eyes" after seeing the number of world-class golf courses in the Valley.

Most famously, Mecham followed through on his campaign promise to cancel Martin Luther King Jr. Day as a holiday for state employees, a policy enacted the year before with an executive order by Governor Bruce Babbitt. Babbitt had acted after the state legislature voted against a paid holiday, a move that placed the legality of the paid holiday in question. Mecham's words quickly overshadowed any legitimate legal debate when

Former Arizona governor Evan Mecham. Courtesy of the Archives of Jack L. August Jr.

he stated to black leaders, "You don't need another holiday. What you folks need are jobs."

In Public Enemy's video for their song "By the Time I Get to Arizona," the rappers are seen faux-assassinating Mecham by detonating a bomb they attached to his limousine. Musicians such as Stevie Wonder refused to play in Arizona, and Bono announced during a U2 concert at Sun Devil Stadium that he was donating money to impeach Mecham. Protests became common around the city, and perhaps most jarring to the business community, the NFL announced they would move Super

Bowl XXVII to Pasadena, California. With the move, NFL officials vowed Arizona wouldn't be considered for another Super Bowl until the holiday was restored.

Mecham, beyond just an embarrassment, had become extremely bad for business.

One month after Mecham was elected—three weeks before he had even taken office—a self-described retired businessman named Ed Buck began what appeared to be a mostly facetious recall campaign against Mecham. Buck began giving out "Recall Ev" bumper stickers. Buck told *Republic* political writer Sam Stanton, "If nothing else, hopefully we can send a message to Ev that says, 'Ev, straighten up.'"

As the outrages and alleged misdeeds quickly piled up, the call for a recall vote gained steam, particularly after Mecham's six-month mark in office, the time after which the Arizona Constitution allows for any recall effort to begin.

By early July, Buck, himself a controversial figure (he was an openly gay, part-time fashion model who was awaiting trial on a charge of attempting to illegally obtain narcotic pain killers), was gaining local stardom as his effort gained momentum and behind the scenes, piled up bills he couldn't pay.

In October, Barry Goldwater suggested Mecham should resign. Symington then gave the recall movement a much-needed boost, a $2,000 donation that was more valuable in its message that Arizona's business elite—even those like Symington who had donated to Mecham's campaign—were willing to go public with their belief that Mecham had to go.

For Symington watchers—perhaps most notably, Barry Goldwater—the fact that Symington's modest donation was a major news event showed he was still viewed as a significant statewide public figure whose political opinions were considered newsworthy.

The move warranted comment from state senator Bob Usdane, the Republican Senate Majority Leader, who scolded Symington for the move. Responding to Symington's comment that Republican Party leaders were "prepared to take the Republican Party over the cliff wrapped in a blanket of Mecham loyalty," Usdane said, "If the Republican Party is going over the cliff, then (Symington) is helping it."[12]

At the time of Symington's donation, Buck's drive had accumulated 386,000 signatures. But he also had collected his own growing list of de-

tractors, including many in his group's leadership team and staff who
had become disgusted by Buck's own tactics. Buck was described by
those who had worked with him, and then quit, as being "totally self-
consumed," a man "stuck in the 'terrible 2s,'" and as another fellow coordinator said, "perhaps a sociopath."[13]

A few weeks after Symington donated to the Buck-led campaign,
Symington and a small group of business leaders created the Coalition
for Effective State Leadership. The group would reenergize the recall
effort increasingly being damaged by Buck's shortcomings. Although
just one of several organizers, Symington was quoted first in the story
about the Coalition by three of the state's major newspapers. The group
collected a list of major figures in the business community calling for
Mecham's resignation or his ouster by recall, an unprecedented step for
business figures because, as Symington pointed out at the time, "these are
people who deal with everybody and anybody. They don't like to make
enemies."[14]

A grand jury was convened to investigate allegations that Mecham
had loaned his own auto dealership $80,000 in public funds. As the re-
call effort reached its needed number of signatures, the *Republic* broke
a story that Mecham likely broke campaign finance laws by failing to
report a $350,000 loan to his campaign by an Arizona real estate devel-
oper. Another scandal erupted when Mecham was accused of instructing
the state's top law-enforcement official to bury a report detailing death
threats made by a Mecham appointee to a government employee. A few
days before his one-year anniversary in office, Mecham—along with his
brother and campaign finance manager—was indicted on charges of
perjury, fraud, and failing to report a campaign contribution.[15]

One week later, the Arizona house of representatives began discussing
the possibility of impeachment. Less than a month later, the house voted
for impeachment, which sent the issue to the Arizona state senate for one
of the most unusual government proceedings in Arizona history. Essentially, the senate chamber became a courtroom, Arizona's state senators
became the jury, and Mecham came before them arguing against his impeachment. After a five-week "trial," the senate voted to convict Mecham
for obstruction of justice and misusing government funds. Because of
these convictions, he would be removed from office.

The Arizona secretary of state, longtime high-level civil servant Rose
Mofford, became Arizona's first female governor.

As Mecham's impeachment proceedings ground on in early 1988, Fife Symington was hard at work building support for his old friend, retired US Representative John Rhodes, who had filed to run for governor against Mecham in the recall election set for May 17. In a span of two weeks after Rhodes announced his candidacy, Symington led a fundraising effort that raised $500,000 for Rhodes's campaign.[16]

Through the spring, a strange rift began to divide those who believed Mecham needed to be removed from office. Symington and many other Mecham opponents believed that Mecham was not guilty of the charges that were brought against him by the legislature. (Indeed, Mecham was acquitted of actual criminal charges two months after his impeachment.) Mecham found strange bedfellows in Symington and major civic leaders, who argued that the issue should be decided directly by the people of Arizona, not, as they saw it, in murky, politically charged proceedings in front of a biased "jury."[17]

Nonetheless, Mofford, a moderate Democrat, became governor, and after a challenge to the legality of canceling the upcoming election, the mighty war chest Symington had filled for Rhodes had to be returned to donors.

Mainstream Republicans would have to wait another three years to take back the governor's office.

Within months of the recall-election-that-wasn't, Symington was back in the news, this time as the voice of a group of businessmen who opposed a proposition going before Arizonans that would make English the official language of the state.

The "English Only" movement had come to Arizona, and for many in the state, it was seen as a racist attack on the state's Hispanic community.

That a Republican developer with deep conservative roots was out fighting such a measure was met with welcome surprise, but also, suspicion that it was a financial and political move, not a moral one.

Symington would argue that one need not be limited to one motive for taking action.

By the time the proposition emerged, Symington had developed a strong relationship with several powerful Latino labor and business leaders. As the Esplanade debate heated up, Symington had made a friend in Patrick Emmett Cantelme, the head of the 33,000-member Central Arizona Labor Council. The two fought together for the Esplanade project because Symington had agreed to use union labor. In return, Cantelme

From left: Former Arizona governor Rose Mofford, Fife Symington, and Ann
Symington, 1991. Courtesy of the Arizona State Library, Archives and Public Records,
History and Archives Division, Phoenix, RG1_SG26_S6_B13_F06_I06.

promised to get the job done on time and on budget with no work stop-
pages.

(At the same time, Symington was beginning work on a smaller development in downtown Phoenix involving several leading Latino leaders and civic groups. "The Mercado" would be a celebration of the city's
often-overlooked Hispanic heritage.)

Symington held a press conference outside the state capitol building
with three other businessmen arguing that an "English Only" law would
jeopardize the state's $25 billion in exports and the 139,000 jobs that sup-
ported those exports. In his announcement, Symington sounded both
like a sophisticated free-market economist and a person who, although
claiming otherwise, was prepping for a candidacy.[18]

Speaking about Japanese investors in particular, who he argued were
particularly wary of investing in unstable or unfriendly locations, he said,

"When you create inhibitions to international business, then those capital markets will start going to other states that don't have those inhibitions. And so, basically, what we do is we throw ourselves into an uncompetitive posture in relation to the broader market."

Symington called out the proponents of Proposition 106, saying that it wasn't just wrong for business; it was "clearly intended to strike a blow to minorities."

(While writing about the new anti-English Only group, the *Mesa Tribune* mentioned Symington was then seeking $30 million in investments from a Japanese company for the Esplanade project.)

With polls showing a majority of Arizonans supporting Prop. 106, Symington was accusing a large number of Arizona Republicans of being racists, a stance that associates noted could damage any chance at higher office.[19]

Symington spoke on the issue throughout the state. He supported his arguments regarding the proposition's economic impact with detailed references to Hayek and other economic luminaries.[20] He argued the proposition was not only racist, but an anti-American move displaying shocking ignorance of both the founding documents and the history of the country.

The anti-Prop. 106 forces seemed to gain ground in the weeks before the November vote, but the "English Only" proposition ultimately squeaked by.

Symington's leadership role in the Mecham recall effort and the anti-English Only group seemed to boost Symington's image among centrists and business leaders. His stances appeared to position him as a moderate pro-business Republican willing to break party ranks when the good of the state was at stake. He angered the far right, but introduced himself to suburban independents and moderates who, if they knew him at all, knew him only as the guy who had made news trying to build a bunch of giant towers.

Symington, while claiming his advocacy was not mixed with political aspirations, had just put himself on the shortlist of much-needed new faces in the state's Republican Party.

As Symington's star was rising, the party's aging leadership, led by Barry Goldwater, was looking toward a new decade after one in which no mainstream Republican had served as governor. Not only had the party struggled in gubernatorial races, it was now tarnished with the legacy of Evan Mecham.

It was in this environment that, in early 1989, Barry Goldwater called Symington and others he considered party up-and-comers to his home overlooking Paradise Valley. Something had to be done, he believed, to energize the party and bring a new face to the fight for the governor's office.

# Chapter 9

# BOOM TIME WITH A TIME BOMB

The Esplanade was no easy sell to big money. It was, as the spirited battle had shown, a new and unproven business model, particularly for that region of Phoenix. Although Symington had an impressive streak of successes with his garden office complexes and other structures, none were near the size of the Esplanade. Finding the more than $100 million needed to finance the Esplanade's first phase would be a challenge.

Symington landed two big tenants early in the development process that strengthened his argument to major investors. As the Esplanade was still facing scrutiny by city officials, executives of the Ritz-Carlton Hotel Company, who were seeking a Valley location, agreed with Symington that the Esplanade's up-market project fit with Ritz-Carlton's market niche.[1]

Symington and Randy Todd flew to Atlanta to meet the hotel chain's owner, William Johnson, who, as lunchtime approached, suggested they dine together at a nearby restaurant, Houston's. As they ate, Johnson suggested Houston's was a restaurant worthy of the Esplanade. Symington and the owners of the restaurant agreed—Houston's would expand to Phoenix, becoming the first Houston's in the western United States. Another piece was in place.[2]

Symington also bagged an early commitment from planned-community builder and management company Del E. Webb Corp., which agreed in late 1985 to lease 65,000 square feet for its new headquarters. The proposed Del Webb headquarters would fill about a third of one of two first-phase towers (then projected to cost nearly $120 million to build).

As Todd and Symington traveled, attempting to bag tenants and investment, they also canvassed the world for the finest materials for their structures. They made several trips hunting for the perfect glass for the Esplanade's façade. Symington also flew to Italy shopping for marble, set-

Slabs of marble on display at the Italian quarry from which the marble was purchased for the Camelback Esplanade. Courtesy of the Symington family archives.

tling on a type from a quarry once mined to build many of the most famed structures of ancient Rome.

Working against Symington was increasing evidence that the market for office space in the Valley was softening.

Through the spring of 1986, Symington several times mentioned to friends and associates that he was close to getting an investor to commit. But after initial excitement and interest, one potential investor after another declined. His team grew increasingly anxious.

In late July, some six months after the project was first slated to break ground, Symington missed another target for a start date. With that, Del Webb executives decided to search for another location for their headquarters.

During this time, Symington had been working with investment bank

Salomon Brothers on a comprehensive financing package for the Esplanade. After months of negotiations, Symington and his team thought they had a deal. But at the last minute, Salomon Brothers' executives demanded personal financial guarantees from Symington and others in the Southwest Savings leadership team. Led by Southwest's CEO Don Lewis, the development group decided they could not take such a potentially crippling gamble. Angry at Salomon Brothers for the eleventh-hour rearrangement of terms, Southwest's board and Symington's development partners decided to look elsewhere for loans.[3]

As bulldozers sat ready to break ground, the future of the Esplanade looked grim. In the eighteen months after the project's approval, the only stories appearing in newspapers detailed how little progress had been made. Throughout the community—especially among the project's detractors—Symington was starting to pick up a reputation as an "all show, no go" guy. All Valley residents saw was an empty lot.[4]

By the time another big player entered the arena, Symington and his team, while trying never to look desperate, were desperate for a deal.

William Cochrane Turner, US ambassador to the Organization for Economic Cooperation and Development (OECD), had orchestrated the first meeting between the development group and Salomon's leadership. After that deal imploded, Turner called Symington and asked him out to lunch. As they ate, Turner asked Symington, "How would you like to try working with the Japanese?" Turner had connections with the leaders of Shimizu, the largest construction company in Japan at the time.

Turner warned Symington, though, that even though the company was hungry for large projects in the United States, any decision coming from Shimizu would likely come slowly. Shimizu's leadership, like leaders of many of Japan's most powerful companies, adhered to the "ringi" decision-making process that values consensus-building and laborious research. Symington needed decisiveness, but he needed major players involved even more.

On Christmas Day of 1986, Symington finally received word that Shimizu's board had approved the project.

Along with Shimizu came their leading finance partner, the largest bank in Japan at the time, the Dai-Ichi Kangyo Bank, or DKB. By the beginning of 1987, teams of lawyers and financial and construction experts were hard at work creating the mountain of paperwork needed to launch such a massive and complex project.

"The closing was like a lawyers' convention," Symington would tell friends after the deal was completed.

Shimizu's US lawyers were based in New York. The development group was represented by Snell & Wilmer, one of the largest firms in Arizona. For several weeks, Symington, Todd, and a cavalcade of attorneys bounced back and forth between Phoenix and New York signing papers. As the final closing day approached, conference tables in law offices in both Phoenix and New York were covered in documents needing to be signed. Finally, closing day came. Symington, Todd, and the team's lawyers flew to New York for the final round of signings.

Symington's writing hand began to tingle and numb as the final day wore on. Members of the ownership group and representatives for Shimizu played a sort of musical chairs; moving around the table, stopping at one document, signing, then moving on to the next document.

Finally, Symington sat down across from two top executives from Shimizu and DKB and looked down at what he believed would be the last collection of documents he would have to sign to get the bulldozers moving.

Before he began signing, though, one of Shimizu's top executives slid a document over to Symington for him to sign. Here it was again: A personal guarantee from Symington to back the construction loan.

Even though all parties had initially agreed that Symington would not be personally liable in the deal, Shimizu and DKB's directors rethought their position. They decided, without telling Symington, that they wanted the peace of mind of knowing that Symington had some of his own skin in the game.

Symington, though, didn't have much skin to give. He wasn't as wealthy as the world seemed to assume he was. Again, he was mostly the "sweat-equity" guy, the guy who put the deals together, not the rich guy laying down all the money. If the real estate market dipped, which it always did, the big players had the reserves to weather the downturn. It was the little guys—especially little guys with most of their portfolio in real estate like Symington—who got bankrupted if they were carrying too many loans when the revenue stopped streaming.

But by that point, the whole project likely would implode if the deal didn't go through. Sneaky ploy, Symington thought to himself. He had to do it, but he knew he was in deep trouble if something went wrong.[5]

But Symington believed in his project, so much so, he later admitted, that he didn't fully think through the devastating potential implications to his personal finances if his creditors came for his personal assets. He was certain industry giants like his new partners wouldn't let the project fail. They had the money to weather storms, after all.

And so the documents were signed, handshakes were exchanged, and the bulldozers began moving dirt. The media flocked back to the story and Symington was the city's can-do guy again. Symington was thrilled. Those around him saw the bounce back in his step—the frenetic swash-buckler returned. He was free from begging and signing, he was back to what he loved: designing and building.

Within months, the Esplanade began rising from the ground near the southeast corner of Twenty-Fourth and Camelback. The momentum grew and Symington's name regained its sizzle. Symington felt like he was finally truly playing in the big leagues.

# Chapter 10

# DECISIONS, DECISIONS

On February 5, 1988, as per Arizona law, Arizona Secretary of State Rose Mofford became acting governor after the Arizona House of Representatives voted to impeach Evan Mecham.

Mofford was the perfect placeholder for a state rattled by the tempestuous embarrassment who came before her. Mofford, a moderate Democrat (the state's governor and secretary of state are elected separately), had served honorably and effectively for forty-seven years in state government. She was generally liked and respected by the mainstreams of both parties, and for a large swath of Arizonans outside the political spheres, she struck a calming, affable, engaging tone. She was the anti-Evan.[1]

Friends and detractors alike, though, viewed her as a placeholder. She certainly wasn't the new face of either party. Straddled by the lack of mandate in her ascension, even if she was bent on revolution, she would have been in a weak position to reform.

Also, she literally was a placeholder in the months after Mecham was impeached by the house. If the peculiar trial the state's constitution demanded of Arizona's state senators exonerated Mecham, he would return immediately to the governorship.

Then, even if Mecham was found guilty by the senate, the state's judiciary would have to figure out if Mofford was supposed to serve out Mecham's term, or if a special election needed to be held as soon as possible to elect a new governor.[2]

Simply, this whole impeachment process was new to the state and when the state was created only seventy-six years prior, its founding fathers didn't provide a terribly clear roadmap for either the impeachment or the gubernatorial succession process.

Two months after she stepped in as acting governor, the Arizona State Senate "convicted" Mecham, which allowed Mofford to move forward with her own agenda.

During those two months of the senate trial, Fife Symington had
helped elevate John Rhodes (with the quick $500,000 in campaign con-
tributions) into a position to be the Republican challenger to Mofford in
a recall election that was planned for May. Just weeks before the planned
election, though, the Arizona Supreme Court ruled that Mofford should
serve out Mecham's full term. The special election was canceled.

Rhodes and his supporters were stunned. The ruling seemed an odd
interpretation of the Arizona State Constitution, they felt, and certainly
went against the spirit of the law. Simply: when at all possible, they argued, the people should decide who leads their state, not some obscure
law regarding succession in cases of impeachment that gives the reins of
the state to someone not elected to that position, especially since, in this
case, it was a member of the opposing party who would hold the office
for more than two years.

As Arizona returned to business-as-usual during the summer of 1988,
Barry Goldwater began discussing the future of the Republican Party in
Arizona with his fellow members of the old guard. Goldwater believed
Republicans needed fresh faces to represent the party in the post-Me-
cham era. Others, though, believed the party's support should begin
to coalesce behind a sturdy, proven moderate, a face Arizonans already
knew and trusted. Goldwater soon found he was outside the mainstream
of thought within Arizona's Republican leadership.

No matter. Goldwater summoned Symington and four other young
Republicans who had led Rhodes's blitzkrieg gubernatorial campaign to
his home.

By this time, Goldwater was retired from politics and to some extent,
had already been put out to pasture by many in the party. But sitting in
his library, surrounded by warm leathers and much of his collection of
Native American art and his own black-and-white photography of his
native state, Goldwater still looked to the young men like the great chieftain of Arizona.[3]

The conversation began with gripes and commiserations about the
Arizona Supreme Court's ruling that canceled the special election. John
Rhodes would have been governor if the people had been allowed to
speak, the partisan crowd (and some polls and political commentators)
agreed. They had been robbed—the state had been denied the chance to
restart and move forward in earnest.

Goldwater let the youngsters vent, then quieted the room. He had brought this group up to his perch just west of Camelback Mountain to make an announcement.

"This is the time for the new generation to step up to the plate," he told the group.

Then Goldwater looked at Symington.

In the silence, the other four in the room turned their heads toward Symington.

"Barry, I'm a developer," Symington responded to the stare. "I couldn't get elected dog catcher."

Goldwater said he believed otherwise. Symington essentially had already run a statewide campaign during his fight for the Esplanade. Republicans, particularly business Republicans, had generally rallied around him in his fight against city hall and the anti-growth forces.

Symington certainly knew how to raise money. Sure, he hadn't run for state office, but he had been involved with numerous state campaigns and also, Goldwater noted, he had grown up with a father who was very often running for office.

Goldwater argued Symington was gifted at articulating the reasoning behind the policies and beliefs of the Republican Party. He looked good at the podium. He was certainly a fiscal conservative, but beyond his economics, he had shown contempt for exclusionary social-conservative causes while expressing many center-leaning views at a time the state needed moderation. (Goldwater himself had moderated greatly since his 1964 presidential bid.)

"But guys. I'm a real estate developer," he said again.

"Relax," Symington remembers Goldwater telling him. "You come from the outside. That's a good thing."

Goldwater then offered to be his campaign chairman.

Symington said he was happy with his current life. The Esplanade was finally rising from Twenty-Fourth and Camelback. The Symington Company had fifty employees and several projects lined up beyond the Esplanade.

"I'll talk to Ann," Symington remembers saying to Goldwater as Goldwater escorted him to the front door. "She would have to be on board with this."

The Symingtons already had been considering a trip to a resort up the coast from Santa Barbara on Big Sur. They decided to go and use the time to ruminate on the pros and cons of a run for governor, which both knew would greatly impact the whole family.

The pros:

*It would be an adventure.* This argument perhaps had the most visceral appeal. Although the Esplanade was far from complete, the monumental struggle for approval, money, and design elements was mostly over. Fife Symington missed the adrenaline rush of the hunt. The children were out of diapers and in school. Ann was interested in the idea of getting out and campaigning.

*Symington believed he could be helpful.* He had long felt his brand of business-savvy fiscal conservatism mixed with moderate social views would give Arizona what it needed—financial stability with a modern social and cultural sensibility.

*Politics were in their blood.* With Pritzlaffs and Symingtons for parents, both had grown up with the buzz of campaigns around them. For them, it would be something like returning to a sport you had played as a kid.[4]

*They had the financial ability to run a good campaign.* Both Symingtons knew they would take flack for infusing their own money into a race, but they felt it would be necessary to seed their long-shot campaign until it gained enough traction to draw significant donors. A long shot would be no shot, they agreed, without the ability to pull on personal and family coffers.

The cons, were, however, seemingly equal in gravity.

*The children.* A campaign for governor, even if it died in the primary, would mean time away from the kids. The children would be exposed to people who dislike their parents and perhaps, children who dislike them because of their parents. But the assumption that it would be a negative experience was hypothetical. The kids might also gain an education about public life and the inner workings of politics and government that few children would ever get.[5]

*Symington was barely known outside of Phoenix.* He would be going against well-known political incumbents. He would have to build a state-wide organization from scratch.

*It would be a huge financial burden.* Yes, they had money. Yes, they had access to money. But while fairly wealthy themselves and a phone call away from additional family wealth, dumping $500,000, certainly dumping a million dollars, into a campaign could strain their budget and endanger their future, especially if the real estate market on which their finances partially depended crashed.

*Symington had absolutely no governing experience.* He'd been driving campaigns for more than fifteen years. He'd been running a company. But he had never been elected to any position. How would he run a government with thousands of employees serving a state of more than four million people?

*He had made enemies.* His Esplanade tactics had left scars and he knew those he had angered would show up louder than ever if he ran for governor.

*It might impact his business.* He knew he would have to spend significant amounts of time away from his company if he ran for governor. But he was confident that Randy Todd would be capable of running the operation during any campaign, and capable, too, of taking over the operation if he was elected governor. (Symington wrongly believed, though, that he could still partially run the company in major matters even if he became governor of the state.)

(Both Symingtons denied in later interviews that they ever discussed the idea that a gubernatorial run might help Symington's business, a motive often suggested later by opposing attorneys in both civil and criminal court.)

During lunch the day before they left the resort, the conversation came back to politics. They each said they had noticed their spouse had become more animated as they spoke about the adventure of a political campaign. Fife Symington remembers saying to Ann, "I don't think there's any way this is going to be a fact-based decision. It's a gut thing."

She remembers agreeing. They should go with their gut. "Let's do it," she said.

When the couple returned home, they explained to their children how their life was about to change. Only twelve-year-old Whitney had substantial concerns. She was worried about the change to her family and school life. But she said later, she ultimately agreed that the ride could be interesting.

Symington wrote to the leadership team of Shimizu telling them (while asking for their blessing, essentially) that he had been asked by Barry Goldwater to run for governor, and that he had said yes.

Symington said later that he knew that Shimizu's leadership—and a broad swath of Japan's business community—had deep respect for

Goldwater. Symington assumed Shimizu's leadership team would view the request from Goldwater as an honor for Symington and a directive that shouldn't be denied. He assumed Shimizu's leadership would likely welcome the chance to potentially make a new friend in Barry Goldwater.

Symington explained that Randy Todd, with whom they had already been working closely, would become their primary point of contact.[6]

Symington then began assembling a campaign team. Towering over the fledgling campaign was its chairman, Barry Goldwater. With Goldwater on board, Symington ran to friend Jay Smith, who had managed John McCain's campaigns throughout his meteoric rise from Arizona outsider to US congressman and then US senator.

Peter Hayes, with whom Symington had worked on the Rhodes campaign, also agreed to jump on board.

Then things slowed down. It was still more than two years before anyone was going to be elected governor.

Potential Republican candidates were exploring candidacies much earlier in the election cycle than usual, due to the Mecham upheaval and the installation of a Democrat as governor two years before the next election. Indeed, by the summer of 1988—two years before the primaries—the likely candidates were already broadly known.[7]

None of them knew if they'd be facing a vulnerable or invincible Rose Mofford.[8]

After the court's decision that Mofford would serve out the remainder of Mecham's term, she began appointing moderates from both parties to positions within government and on state boards. Many state employees who had quit under Mecham were brought back into government.

After six months, a quiet order had been restored. But while Mofford did have a few substantial legislative victories—among them a hard-fought victory to enact legislation aimed at lowering carbon-monoxide levels 22 percent in the Valley—she also slowly seemed to lose some of her reputation as the friendly face of calm competence.[9] She became more combative with the press and increasingly seemed worn down by the pressures and long hours of the job. By late 1988, many Republicans were beginning to feel they could win back the governor's office.

In January of 1989, the Phoenix-based Behavior Research Center released a poll showing Mofford was still popular with Democrats, with 53 percent saying she should be the Democratic nominee for governor in the next race.[10] The pollsters presented the group of likely voters with a

list of potential candidates from both parties. Phoenix Mayor Terry Goddard trailed Mofford by 30 percentage points among Democratic voters,
with Arizona Chief Justice Frank X. Gordon Jr. coming in third.

Republican voters broadly rejected the potential candidates presented
to them. Forty-nine percent of the respondents said "none-of-the-above"
to the four names mentioned. Of those polled who would commit, 27
percent said they'd want US representative Jim Kolbe to be the Republican gubernatorial nominee, while 18 percent said they hoped that Evan
Mecham would return and represent the party. Maricopa County Supervisor Fred Koory, a longtime insider in Arizona Republican political
circles, received the nod from only 4 percent of those polled, while Phoenix developer Fife Symington brought up the rear with just 2 percent of
the vote.

Not a single Republican living in Tucson said that Symington should
be the Republicans' nominee.

There was a lot of work to be done if Fife Symington was going to be
the next governor of Arizona.

# Chapter 11

# DEBACLE AND DEPRESSION

A
s Fife Symington's political star and signature project rose, financial institutions were collapsing.

Eight major Arizona savings and loan institutions would be
in government hands by the time Symington began his gubernatorial bid
in earnest. Southwest Savings and Loan, for which Symington served as
a director until 1984, was declared insolvent and taken over by federal
regulators on February 17, 1989.[1]

In his book *High Rollers: Inside the Savings and Loan Debacle*, Martin
Lowy, arguably the nation's foremost expert on the S&L crash, laid out
a history of key events in US economic fortunes and policymaking that
doomed hundreds of thrifts.

Lowy, formerly a Federal Deposit Insurance Corporation attorney, argued that public opinion regarding the reasons for the S&L crash didn't
always meet reality:

"There's this easy idea that there were a bunch of greedy scammers
everywhere intent on fraud," Lowy said in a 2018 interview. "There was
Charles Keating, sure. Speculators and fraud artists really did flourish.
But it was federal policy that truly created the disaster and destroyed
most of the thrifts."

"At the end of the day, the vast majority of the savings and loans were
operated by honest people who may have made mistakes, but who were
mostly just caught up in a system that by the early 1980s was doomed by
policy and circumstances to fail."[2]

Southwest Savings and Loan was started for the same reason as most
other Arizona thrifts—to benefit from the housing boom in the Valley in
the 1950s and 1960s. During that time, better highways and the emerging
interstate system began connecting Arizona to the overpopulated West
and the over-chilly Midwest. At the same time, air conditioners became
affordable, World War II and Korean War vets needed larger homes for
their booming number of babies, interest rates were reasonable, and the

US government offered incentives designed to help Americans who aspired to homeownership.

The S&Ls, commonly referred to as "thrifts," needed money to lend for residential loans. Amid the housing boom of the 1950s and early 1960s, S&Ls began competing for peoples' savings by offering ever-higher interest return rates on savings accounts, along with myriad gifts and other incentives. That battle continued well into the 1980s.[3]

In 1966, in response to the rate wars, Congress put a cap on interest rates that thrifts could pay out.

That cap, Lowy said, began a slow rot at the core of the nation's S&L industry. Amid the slow growth, high interest rates, and inflation of the 1970s, the cap on the interest rate thrifts could offer led people to invest their money elsewhere. At the same time, high interest rates for home loans amid a sluggish economy meant fewer Americans were able to qualify for loans. The number of failing S&Ls began to skyrocket by the end of the 1970s.

Exacerbating the problem: Most thrifts held countless long-term home loans made at the low interest rates of the past. When interest rates skyrocketed, thrifts were forced to pay high interest rates to obtain money to loan at the same time they were contractually obligated to the long-term home loans they had given when interest rates were much lower.

By 1979, there were so many failed thrifts that the federal agency tasked with insuring deposits had only about a fourth of the money it would need to pay the investors in the failed thrifts. To deal with the shortage of money to cover failures, the government allowed many struggling S&Ls to remain open with expectations they would become profitable again when the real estate market improved.

In many ways, federal policy began to mirror the informal lending policy in the Valley of the Sun, where many lenders believed they were often better off restructuring loans than foreclosing on properties during downturns.

In October of 1979, the federal government changed its monetary policy in an attempt to slow rampant inflation. Interest rates rose even higher.

In early 1980, Congress passed the Depository Institutions Deregulation and Monetary Control Act, which deregulated interest rates, expanded S&L's ability to invest outside of the single-home residential market, and raised the federal deposit insurance amount to $100,000.

Finally, S&Ls could offer loans for commercial real estate projects, which, especially in the case of large construction loans, could generate substantial interest payments and fees.

It was during this time that billionaire Daniel Ludwig bought Southwest Savings and Loan and not only kept Fife Symington on his board, but summoned him to New York to tell him, "I only want big deals."

In 1983, the S&L industry reported record growth and the number of failed thrifts declined. Yet 50 percent of thrifts still lost money. It was boom time for thrifts that could drum up capital, and a continued period of decline for those that couldn't.

Two years later, amid growing concerns that growth was coming from unsafe investing, the federal government began to implement a series of regulations intended to protect consumers. The Federal Home Loan Bank Board adopted new capital rules to slow growth in the S&L industry while also moving to protect investors by limiting direct investments by S&Ls to 10 percent of the thrift's total assets.[4]

Those protections, Lowy and others argue, had the opposite effect by further destabilizing an unstable industry.

This was the same year that Phoenix city leaders approved the revamped Esplanade and Symington—with land design plans, and his own fees paid for by Southwest Savings—went out looking for a massive construction loan.

The next year, more capital rules were enacted to reduce growth. Another law limited the fees S&Ls could collect on loans. Then, in August of 1986, federal tax reforms were put into place that, in the process of simplifying the tax code, removed several tax shelters favorable to developers, lenders, and investors.

Real estate immediately became a less attractive investment. Some estimates suggest the Tax Reform Act of 1986 was responsible for a 25 percent decrease in commercial real estate values within three years.

In 1985, real estate-limited partnerships in the United States generated $16 billion in new capital investments. By 1989, according to federal data, real estate partnerships landed only $1.5 billion in new investments— about one-tenth as much as just four years before.

As Symington and his partners struggled to find a major investor to begin construction on the land owned by Southwest Savings, the thrift and hundreds like it found themselves in an economic environment in which survival would be nearly impossible. Only a turnaround in an increasingly stagnant real estate market in the Valley could right the ship.

As S&Ls began toppling around the country—particularly in the Sun Belt—the Federal Savings and Loan Insurance Corporation was itself declared insolvent. A law was then passed giving the FSLIC the authority to borrow $10.8 billion to continue its payouts.[5]

Investors and homebuyers became skittish in an arguably overbuilt market. In 1987, for the first time in years, the value of real estate began to decline in the Phoenix metro area.[6]

Southwest Savings and Loan limped on through 1988. But its biggest investment, the land and all the costs and fees associated with trying to get development started on the Esplanade, had yet to begin paying off because of the unforeseen length of acquiring approval and construction financing.

After Southwest was declared insolvent in early 1989, Congress, facing arguably the greatest financial catastrophe since the Great Depression, overhauled the nation's regulatory structure for S&Ls. Among other moves, the FSLIC was dissolved, and S&Ls were put under the Office of Thrift Supervision and the FDIC. More money was appropriated to help cover the losses of tens of thousands of Americans.

That year, too, the Resolution Trust Corporation was created not only to liquidate failed S&Ls and their remaining holdings, but also to identify wrongdoing or negligence by S&L managers and directors.

The RTC and the agencies supporting it were not only a federally run and subsidized property owner and quasi-realty company, they were also an investigating entity tasked with recovering as much of the losses as possible through lawsuits against S&L leadership.

In the Valley, where S&Ls seemed to sit at every major intersection, 1989 was a time of deep uncertainty. With that uncertainty came even more uncertainty and decline in the real estate market.

Once the RTC was fully organized, it began selling off property. It quickly became clear that RTC leadership wasn't operating like the real estate business owners with whom they were essentially competing. RTC policy dictated that property be moved quickly. Unlike other private owners of Valley real estate, the RTC didn't let property sit on the market until the right buyer arrived, or until the market improved. RTC officials were directed to liquidate quickly, which led them to quickly slash sales and leasing prices on the buildings the government had acquired.[7]

The RTC's quick-turnaround policy quickly impacted the Symington

Company. After acquiring a garden office building next to one of Symington's largest garden office complexes, for example, the RTC offered leasing rates at less than half the market value at the time. Those leasing space from Symington and other Valley companies moved to the cheaper space. Valley companies slashed prices to meet RTC prices. Even if companies were able to keep their buildings leased, though, the revenue generated by the slashed rates often wasn't enough to pay bills and service debt, especially if the real estate company was, like the Symington Company, heavily in debt.

Ultimately, only a small percentage of the 1,043 S&Ls failures were found to be the result of fraudulent practices. But amid that small percentage, there were some infuriating cases of average Americans being ruined by the greed and dishonesty of S&L owners. Perhaps most notorious among them was a Valley multimillionaire named Charles Keating.[8]

In 1984, the same year Fife Symington stepped off the Southwest Savings board, Keating, a wealthy Phoenix developer, bought the California-based Lincoln Savings and Loan. He paid $51 million—double the thrift's estimated net worth.

Keating badly wanted the thrift because of those changes in banking laws that allowed S&Ls to branch out from making small-dollar home loans to making much larger investments.

Lincoln's assets more than tripled in three years under Keating. Keating paid himself handsomely for his perceived success, setting aside $34 million for himself and family members as well as more than a million dollars to donate to political campaigns.

Regulators began investigating Keating's investment and bookkeeping practices in 1987, but arguably with the help of five US senators, including Dennis DeConcini and John McCain of Arizona, the investigation was scrapped. About the same time, the federal bank board slightly relaxed lending regulations.

(Although McCain—aided by Symington's future attorney John Dowd—navigated the resulting "Keating Five" scandal with little damage to his reputation, DeConcini, who arguably had the most tangential involvement in the matter of all five, would struggle more than McCain to clear his name.)[9]

After Lincoln and its parent company, American Continental, went bankrupt in 1989 (the same year as Southwest), the full picture of Keating's financial deceptions became clear. Keating was convicted of conspiracy, fraud, and racketeering. He was sent to prison, then had those charges overturned on appeal, after which he pleaded guilty to lesser charges. (Keating did not return to prison. The judge overseeing the plea agreement ruled Keating had served enough time for the original charges.)

Charles Keating's high-profile case and his conviction set into the public's mind a perceived modus operandi of all those involved with S&Ls during the 1980s. Keating's case, and the assumptions that emanated from it, would have major implications for Symington in the years to come.

Indeed, one of the lead investigators in the Keating case was attorney Mike Manning, who would later hound Symington for more than a decade with accusations he had misrepresented his net worth to those who financed the Mercado development in downtown Phoenix.

Throughout the 1990s, Manning rarely missed an opportunity to draw parallels between his high-profile criminal case against Keating and Manning's own high-profile civil case against Symington.

# Chapter 12

# THE RACE IS ON

E van Mecham was the first to enter the race for governor, announcing in early 1989 that he expected to easily regain the office he was
forced to leave.

Potentially more threatening to Symington was former state senator and Maricopa County Supervisor Fred Koory. Koory had significant
name recognition in the state. He was a moderate on many issues. And
after decades as a party stalwart in the state, he was the favored candidate
of Republican leadership.

Both Symington and Koory, though, would likely be trounced by US
Representative Jim Kolbe, a popular moderate who many believed would
vacate his seat in Congress to run for governor. Kolbe announced early in
1989 that he would make a decision on running by that summer.

By the first week of April 1989, the worst-kept secret in Arizona political circles was whether or not Fife Symington would run for governor. It
was widely known that Symington had hired Jay Smith, who had orchestrated McCain's successful congressional and senatorial races. Symington
already had a full speaking schedule around the state. He already had
significant money lined up for a campaign.

Standing in his way, though, were party officials concerned Symington would pull voters away from Koory or potential candidates Kolbe or
Representative Jon Kyl. If the moderate vote was split among more mainstream candidates, the party might once again end up with Mecham.

John McCain told Symington he wasn't ready for a statewide race
even though McCain's star campaign manager already had signed on to
Symington's campaign. Several other high-profile Republicans visited
him in his new office in the Esplanade to ask him to wait another four
years. It was Fred Koory's turn, Symington was told.[1]

Koory himself even came to the Esplanade to ask Symington to stay
out of the race. Koory's demeanor—that of a father scolding a callow

son—angered the headstrong Symington, who later told friends that any reservations about running disappeared after that discussion with Koory.

But Symington played coy to the end. When newspapers reported on April 11, 1989, that Symington would be announcing his candidacy, Symington claimed he was actually still debating whether he would run.

The next day, Symington did what everyone knew he was going to do. In his announcement, he said one of his biggest reasons for running was to save the Republican Party and Arizona from the only other official candidate at the time—Evan Mecham.

"There is no avoiding the fact that Evan Mecham was a terrible governor and created havoc in this state and in the Republican Party," Symington announced on a talk radio show that day. "I'm in the race to be an alternative to Evan Mecham." Earlier that day, Symington called Mecham "a schoolyard bully" who needed "a punch in the nose."[2]

Symington—with the help of Smith and Salt River Project lobbyist Peter Hayes, among others—articulated his battle plan to win in his inaugural press release: He would offer a positive alternative to Mecham for "sensible Republicans." He would be the candidate offering a clear, detailed, moderate policy path that would pull Arizona from the doldrums caused by the leadership prior to Mecham, the destructive leadership of Mecham himself, and the placeholder leadership of Mofford.

His youth (he was forty-three) was not a disadvantage, Symington argued: "I hope that my campaign can be a catalyst for younger voters." His lack of political experience was not a negative: "I know that I begin this campaign as an underdog. I have never run for political office. I have a lot to learn about campaigning.

"All my working life I have been involved in enterprise. I have learned that to get things accomplished one must bring people together, inspire them with purpose and pursue objectives with unrelenting determination. That's the kind of leadership I intend to offer voters."

He quoted Thomas Wolfe, then finished with a clear mission statement: "From this day forward, Republican voters will know there is an alternative to Mecham. And they will also be asked to judge me not as an alternative to Mecham, but as a businessman, manager, and fiscal conservative who can return Arizona toward a path of progress and pride."[3]

Symington was out of the blocks in solid fashion, most of the state's political analysts reported the next day. The general reaction: Symington, although a near-unknown outside the Valley, had succeeded at catching the imagination of voters and the media. He had succeeded at forcing himself into the conversation.

One week later, the Symington camp announced in a press release that Barry Goldwater had announced his support for Symington "after reviewing news coverage of Symington's announcement," which was certainly stretching the truth to give the appearance that the old chieftain wasn't a Symington team insider, but rather a convert swayed by the new candidate's trajectory and public reception.

With Symington's announcement, though, came many of the same criticisms that had haunted him during the fight for the Esplanade. He was a carpetbagger. He was a snooty silver-spooned, old-money Easterner who probably looked down on, and knew nothing about, the people he hoped to govern.

It was a perception Symington and his team needed to dispel if he had any chance to win. For starters: He wouldn't be bandying about his full name. He wasn't J. Fife Symington III anymore. He was just Fife Symington.

Which still wasn't plain enough for some. Since his first name was actually John, a few friends suggested he should go as "Jack" instead of "Fife." Symington refused to go that far to convince Arizona he was one of them.[4]

Symington touted his success as a developer and promised to run the state, which was a few hundred million dollars in debt at the time, more like a business. He promised to identify waste and perhaps implement some innovative revenue generators such as selling off some government buildings that state agencies would then lease back.

Yet in those early days and weeks of his campaign, the media and much of the public were more interested in talking about his pedigree than his policies. E. J. Montini, the popular young metro columnist for the *Arizona Republic*, spent one paragraph of his column following Symington's announcement talking about Symington policy positions, a few paragraphs about the enemies the developer had made getting approval for the Esplanade, and then fourteen paragraphs on Symington's air of privilege and unique first name.

"Even Fife Symington sounds haughty, as if he needs a nickname. Something people can relate to. Something manly, yet not presumptuous. Something like—'Bubba.'"[5]

Symington in his Esplanade office with painting of Henry Clay Frick behind him. *PHOENIX* magazine, 1989. Courtesy of *PHOENIX* magazine.

Symington, though, had what he felt was a strong argument against the outsider label. For one: He could honestly claim that, with two decades living in the Valley under his belt, he was more of a native than hundreds of thousands of Arizona residents. His home life with small children running every which way in a fairly modest home was relatable for vast swaths of suburbanites. Ideally, he would be seen as urbane and wonk-smart on a broad range of issues, but still wholly accessible and relatable.

And most seemed to agree, he had—perhaps thanks to the strong jaw, still-athletic build, and confident demeanor—*the look*.

Within weeks of his announcement, Symington had a statewide organization taking shape.

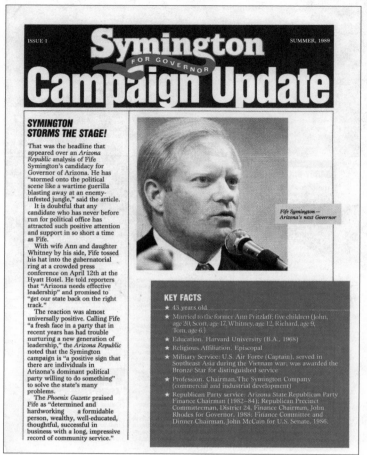

Early first campaign literature. Courtesy of the Symington family archives.

ISSUE 1     **Symington**     SUMMER, 1989
FOR GOVERNOR
# Campaign Update

## SYMINGTON STORMS THE STAGE!

That was the headline that appeared over an *Arizona Republic* analysis of Fife Symington's candidacy for Governor of Arizona. He has "stormed onto the political scene like a wartime guerilla blasting away at an enemy-infested jungle," said the article.

It is doubtful that any candidate who has never before run for political office has attracted such positive attention and support in so short a time as Fife.

With wife Ann and daughter Whitney by his side, Fife tossed his hat into the gubernatorial ring at a crowded press conference on April 12th at the Hyatt Hotel. He told reporters that "Arizona needs effective leadership" and promised to "get our state back on the right track."

The reaction was almost universally positive. Calling Fife "a fresh face in a party that in recent years has had trouble nurturing a new generation of leadership," the *Arizona Republic* noted that the Symington campaign is "a positive sign that there are individuals in Arizona's dominant political party willing to do something" to solve the state's many problems.

The *Phoenix Gazette* praised Fife as "determined and hardworking      a formidable person, wealthy, well-educated, thoughtful, successful in business with a long, impressive record of community service."

*Fife Symington—
Arizona's next Governor*

### KEY FACTS
★ 43 years old.
★ Married to the former Ann Pritzlaff; five children (John, age 20, Scott, age 17, Whitney, age 12, Richard, age 9, Tom, age 6.)
★ Education. Harvard University (B.A., 1968)
★ Religious Affiliation. Episcopal
★ Military Service. U.S. Air Force (Captain), served in Southeast Asia during the Vietnam war; was awarded the Bronze Star for distinguished service
★ Profession. Chairman, The Symington Company (commercial and industrial development)
★ Republican Party service: Arizona State Republican Party Finance Chairman (1982–84); Republican Precinct Committeeman, District 24, Finance Chairman, John Rhodes for Governor, 1988; Finance Committee and Dinner Chairman, John McCain for U.S. Senate, 1986.

With his plan to cut government spending, enhance law enforcement efforts against a growing crime problem, and review the necessity of many of the state's regulations and tax structures, Symington could be appealing both to conservatives and Arizona moderates. His plans to improve public schools, protect Arizona's environment, and fight the growing prejudice against Mexican immigrants would also appeal to moderates and perhaps, even right-leaning Democrats.

By early May, Symington, albeit with little competition yet in the race, seemed to be gaining traction. His candidacy's posture presenting him as a dignified, fresh-faced, moderate outsider seemed to be appealing in the dreary political climate after Mecham's impeachment.

Not everyone agreed with that assessment, though. In mid-May, the

Republican National Committee, led by Lee Atwater, conducted a secret study of the electability of the current and likely Republican candidates in the Arizona gubernatorial race. The study, conducted by Roger Stone, a young conservative operative who already had developed a reputation for political skullduggery, was then leaked, likely by Stone, to the media in Arizona.[6]

Stone's study argued that Evan Mecham was seen as too divisive to win in a hypothetical race against Mofford. Stone also concluded that Symington lacked a sufficient political base to win.[7]

The study, and the leaking of the study, seemed to be a calculated play by national party figures to push Jim Kolbe or Jon Kyl into the race. However, the study's primary impact was to enrage Republicans in a state known for its century-old contempt for Eastern meddling.

Symington and Smith agreed they had been given a political gift. The pair held a press conference on the steps of the RNC building on Capitol Hill. Symington argued the Republican National Committee should stay out of Arizona politics and stop trying to derail Symington's candidacy. Arizonans were fully capable of making their own decisions, Symington argued.

It was a grand act of political theater. For the most part, Arizona Republicans seemed to agree with Symington, including Barry Goldwater, who penned a scathing letter to the RNC that was published in the state's newspapers.

In the days after the Stone report was leaked, the editorial boards of each of the state's major newspapers weighed in on the issue. The *Republic*'s lead editorial read: "To the RNC: Stay Out."[8]

The story made headlines in several of the nation's leading papers, too. Nationally syndicated political columnist Robert Novak, for one, shredded the RNC for its bald-face attempt to influence the Arizona election.[9]

The RNC had inadvertently created a big argument against one of the big arguments against Symington: He wasn't the fancy bigwig from the East. He was the candidate to pick if you wanted to snub the fancy bigwigs in the East.

A week later, Kolbe, arguably the Republican most likely to win the primary and biggest Republican threat to Mofford, announced he would not be a candidate. He decided to stay in Congress. Some reporters and political insiders said the fact that Symington was gaining traction so quickly (and picking up the state's top Republican organizers around the state so quickly) had led Kolbe to rethink a run. He was no longer a shoo-in to win.

Symington told a reporter for the *Arizona Daily Star* the next day that "this is undoubtedly a major boost for my campaign. Jim Kolbe and I were drawing from the same well."

For the same story, Jay Smith, the master political consultant and wordsmith, was clearly excited about the state of his candidate's campaign: "People have been clamoring after us during the last 24 hours like we're the Love Boat pulling out of port," Smith said. "All the gangplanks are extended, and the political activists are scampering on board."

Symington's momentum in the center didn't faze those on the far right.

A former Mecham top aide and out-state populist rabble-rouser, Sam Steiger, who had a strong resume (having served five terms in the US House of Representatives), jumped in. But Steiger's tough-talking, hard-right libertarian ideas (he authored a book called *Kill the Lawyers!*, after all) not only limited his appeal, but made it likely he would be splitting the vote of Arizona's far right with Mecham.

Also announcing later in the Republican primary was Bob Barnes, another Mecham supporter who had little money, few new ideas, and few supporters. Many politicos in Arizona believed Barnes ran only to be Mecham's attack dog during the campaign. Barnes would go negative on candidates other than Mecham in the crowded field while Mecham angled for broader appeal by staying positive.

Ann quickly grew into her role as aspiring first lady and political heavyweight in her own mold. She both toured with her husband and gave speeches on her own articulating their shared vision for the state. If Symington looked too much like a slick real estate developer from back east, Ann's personal stories about growing up in Arizona, being a schoolteacher, and herding the couple's five children softened, humanized, and localized her husband's public persona. She was invaluable in helping transform her husband's image for those Arizonans who held a negative, two-dimensional perception of Symington from the Esplanade fight four years earlier.[10]

The Symington team began building their statewide organization and the Symingtons began hitting the service-group luncheon circuit. They spoke anywhere they were granted airtime. Increasingly, the couple found themselves in the farthest reaches of the state, where, except for in the expanse of the Navajo Nation, Evan Mecham was the candidate to beat.

The summer of 1989 passed with little news from the gubernatorial horse race. After all, it was still more than a year away from even the Republican primary.

The Symington team continued to intensify their political schedule through the fall. In October, Symington found an opportunity to show he was committed to fighting the increasing movement of drugs from Mexico through southern Arizona. In a press release, his staff announced that Symington had asked Arizona's congressional delegation to lobby drug czar William Bennett to select the southwest border of the country as one of two "Drug Enforcement Areas," along with Florida.

Symington pointed to language in the Anti-Drug Abuse Act of 1988 that would open the door for increased federal spending to fight the influx of drugs into the state.[11]

It was a sophisticated political move. Symington looked influential—even in charge—and so aware of state and federal illegal drug issues that he was giving the state's congressional delegation a roadmap for increasing federal money to the state.

Symington was bouncing around the state giving his opinion on myriad issues, occasionally even federal issues that were, unbeknownst to his audiences, causing great distress in his business and personal life.

In September of 1989, Symington chatted with Howard Fischer, then a reporter at *Phoenix New Times,* about the growing S&L crisis, which Symington blamed on Congress and their 1986 Tax Reform Act.

"Inherent in the law were some things that made life very difficult for financial institutions and how they handle real estate," Symington told Fischer. "In addition you have a market which is significantly overbuilt across the country" that was also burdened with "relatively high interest rates."[12]

By the spring of 1990, the campaign was fully organized and prepared to canvass the state. Symington began peppering the media with statements and story ideas.

As the campaign and its growing support network of volunteers readied to launch in earnest, Symington released "The Symington Plan," a deeply detailed fifty-five-page document outlining the candidate's proposed policies, which covered more than a dozen aspects of state government.[13]

Reporters joked that Symington himself might be the only person to read the whole document. But for some, it was proof this newbie was not only serious, but was prepared once in office to launch an aggressive activist agenda aimed at righting Arizona's governmental woes.

That he had sought so much sage advice to build his platform and written such a detailed policy plan positioned him in contrast to Mecham and Steiger—both shoot-from-the-hip cowboys—as well as Koory, who struggled to define his candidacy and shake a reputation as a boring, status-quo pick.

Perhaps most notable, or surprising, was the space and thought dedicated to environmental issues threatening Arizona. On environmental issues, Symington looked like a moderate Democrat.

Polls showed that frustration with the growing brown cloud over Phoenix, as well as anger that city leaders had long sat silent as polluters poisoned the Salt River Valley, had crossed party lines by 1989. It wasn't unsafe for a Republican to talk of environmental regulation. A business Republican like Symington could also argue that filthy air and fouled groundwater were bad for business, particularly homebuilders. If Arizona was going to balance its growing deficit, it needed cuts, yes, but also a healthy influx of taxpayers. Arizona's reputation as a haven depended on clean air.[14]

Symington, who had spent much of his free time in the ocean or wilderness, claimed his environmentalism was personal and heartfelt. He was not unlike Goldwater, who mixed both a passion for conservative values with a passion for the natural world and an awareness and empathy for the plight of the state's native peoples.[15]

The "Symington Plan," which Symington wrote with the help of several well-respected experts in various fields, listed ninety-two actions Symington would take as governor in nine major areas.

In the economic sphere, Symington would bring his business-world expertise to the governor's office with a slew of major changes:

- He would cut 6 percent from operating and administrative budgets, except for K-12 education budgets.
- He would support a budget reform bill instituting private-sector budgetary practices.
- A task force of business leaders would be created to identify state

functions that he believed could be better handled by the private sector.

- A Purchase and Lease-Back Plan, whereby the state would sell off assets and then lease them back, would be created to help balance the budget and even create a "rainy day fund" to help the state weather the inevitable downturns.

For the environment, he promised to push for stronger sentences for polluters, create incentives for the recycling industry, study trash-to-energy plants, raise hazardous waste dumping fees, promote the feasibility study of the creation of a light-rail system, purchase electric vehicles for the state, promote solar research, and encourage state employees to use mass transit. In all, he proposed sixteen relatively progressive environmental protection actions.

Even his state education priorities, besides his strong support for parental choice and charter schools, were unusually moderate if not center-left: He proposed expanding Head Start Programs, creating teen pregnancy prevention programs, supporting bilingual programs in schools, and strengthening the state's financial aid programs for higher education.

He promised to be tough on crime—a must for candidates in a state increasingly plagued by gang and cartel violence as it became a drug corridor to the nation. But he also stressed he would increase drug education in schools and create programs to help keep kids away from drugs. At the same time he was being tough, he was also promoting substance-abuse rehabilitation programs in the state's prisons.

His prison reforms also included the controversial businessman's solution for prison overcrowding and skyrocketing spending: he would privatize Arizona's prison system.

He would "attack the problem of the uninsured," create rural health-care funds, push for tort reform to help lower insurance and medical costs, and create an independent Department of Mental Health.

By early 1990, the Symington team was in place. Jay Smith was publicly listed as the head of advertising and other media outreach but also continued to be the chief strategist for the campaign. Bunny Badertscher, then chief of staff for Representative Kolbe and a respected campaign manager in area politics since 1965, was "loaned" by Kolbe to Symington to manage his campaign.[16]

The "Symington 1990" campaign had by far the largest war chest of any of the candidacies for governor by the start of 1990. Symington began the year with $273,342 compared to less than $59,000 for Mecham. The three other candidates combined had less money than Mecham.[17]

Beyond the Symingtons' own money, the rest of the quarter-million dollars had come mostly from $550 checks (the maximum legal amount that could be donated). Opponents noted often that many of those checks came from Maryland. Fred Koory said several times in campaign speeches that he "wasn't trying to buy the election"—a clear stab at Symington. Steiger, Mecham, and Barnes all quickly pointed to Symington's comparatively massive campaign bank account as proof that Symington was a rich Easterner who wasn't in tune with the people of Arizona.

The money, then, was both a blessing and a curse, but as one political observer noted, "it was much more of a blessing than a curse."

At the beginning of 1990, with more than seven months left before the September 11, 1990, primary, Symington was already approaching Mecham in the polls. Symington's name recognition had skyrocketed.[18]

But Symington and all of his opponents still were facing an uphill battle to win Arizona Republicans. The electorate was clearly worn out by the chaotic political landscape in the state. Pollsters generally found little enthusiasm for candidates and ample skepticism.

Indeed, the most consistent winner when Arizonans were asked whom they'd vote for in September wasn't even a candidate in the race. The most popular pick for much of the race was "undecided."

# Chapter 13

# "SAME OLD EV"

B y the early summer of 1990, there were five Republicans and one Democrat in the race for governor.

Once Democrat Rose Mofford announced she would retire from politics rather than run for governor, Phoenix Mayor Terry Goddard, the articulate young superstar among Arizona Democrats, would run unopposed by any serious candidacy.

With less than three months from the beginning of that summer, Fife Symington, Evan Mecham, Fred Koory, and Sam Steiger all arguably still had a chance to win the Republican primary.

Mecham's best chance to win, pundits argued, was if Arizona's moderate Republicans, unexcited by their choices, stayed home. Mecham's base was a minority within the party, but they punched above their weight because the vast majority of them actually went to the polls. Mecham still had strong support in rural Arizona and within his brethren in the large LDS community in the state.[1] His supporters believed the impeachment proceedings were a political hit (even some of Mecham's enemies agreed he didn't deserve impeachment) and that his financial dealings were completely legal (Mecham was not convicted of fraud in his criminal case).[2] He was an ideological purist to his fans who, unlike other state leaders, actually succeeded at blocking tax increases. Sure, he sometimes misspoke. That's what normal folks do, his supporters argued.

Steiger, whose campaign chairman was John Norton, Symington's notoriously disagreeable boss from West Texas oil days, believed he could win if he could get real money to help him sell his modified cowboy libertarianism (he was a rancher from the proudly rural town of Prescott one hundred miles north of Phoenix). Many moderates and business Republicans considered him a blowhard loose cannon, but he was entertaining, articulate, and engaging on the stump. He also was well known in the state; he had both outsider populist cred and insider experience as a US congressman; and as the primary approached, he seemed to either move toward the center or successfully articulate that his brand of conservative libertarianism was far from the rigid bigoted ideology of his former boss, Evan Mecham.

Steiger didn't want regulation on guns, and he didn't want laws blocking abortions. He was for limited government regarding nearly all issues.

Steiger became both a rural and a man-of-the-people choice. Columnist Tom Fitzpatrick, the anti-Symington muckraker who had left the state's largest daily since the Esplanade days to be the lead columnist for *Phoenix New Times*, wrote a column so supportive of Steiger that Steiger used it in full-page advertisements in other papers. Fitzpatrick noted that Steiger had not received "one favorable mention in the *Republic*," which would be a badge of honor for antiestablishment voters. Even the *Wall Street Journal* did a glowing piece on Steiger during the primary. The article's author clearly was enchanted by Steiger's quick-witted cowboy groove.

In that same column, Fitzpatrick took his usual stabs at Symington as well as the polls that showed Symington in the lead that summer.

"J. Fife Symington III has been labeled the front runner by pollsters who talk mostly to themselves," Fitzpatrick wrote, making sure to include both the "J" and the "III" that had gone missing for the campaign.

Steiger, while calling for money in the opinion-piece-turned-ad, made a very clear statement whose fault it would be if Evan Mecham was reelected. They were the same people who were to blame for the state's high percentage of far right-wing political figures in elected positions:

"The Republicans who stay home must get to the polls," Steiger said, suggesting that if he wasn't going to win, he'd rather have Symington than Mecham. "In this primary election, if the Republicans vote as lightly as they have in the last four state elections, they are going to end up with a candidate who can't win the general election."[3]

Pollsters and political analysts agreed with Steiger. Mecham's base made up about 15 to 18 percent of Republican voters. But nearly all of them voted. In the 1986 primary, only 35 percent of Republicans voted, which allowed Mecham's small but engaged band of supporters to win the day.

Mecham would have his base, but no one else. Symington and Steiger (or Koory if he could somehow burst from the single digits) not only had to grab the attention of that vast mass of unengaged residents of the suburban Valley, they needed to get a much higher percentage of them to the polls.

What seemed to become quickly clear to newer Arizonans was that the state's public schools were underfunded. Suburban moderates certainly enjoyed Arizona's low taxes, but they were generally supportive of better funding for the schools, polls showed. Moderates wanted to fight the brown cloud and they worried that gangs and drugs were overtaking much of the Valley.

Fife Symington had a plan for these visceral issues of the generally disconnected suburbanites. And when he started showing up on their televisions, he appeared to be, and comported himself in a manner that suggested him to be, the exact opposite of the frumpy little used-car salesman who had caused moderate Arizonans so much embarrassment.

As the months passed, Symington's strong stance on private property rights and his ability to articulate those beliefs through the lens of the US Constitution's Tenth Amendment seemed to pull rural voters to his camp. Out among ranchers and miners feeling besieged by federal land management regulations, he quickly became a serious contender against Mecham and Steiger.

Perhaps even more important: Symington had the support of Barry Goldwater. "People in rural Arizona have such an intense respect for Barry," he told a campaign staffer at the time. "You mention his name, it's instant respect."[4]

Symington got another boost in late April when his proposal to sell off state buildings—and then lease them back to save money—became the talk of the town. Newspaper editorials landed on both sides of the issue, and letters-to-the-editor and talk-show callers obsessed on the concept. "Republican Fife Symington's wacky proposal to sell 3,000 state structures built and owned by Arizona's taxpayers just proves there are kooks aplenty in both political parties," one letter to the *Republic* started. The other letter on the issue appearing that day applauded the plan in theory, but suggested the state only allow twenty-year leases on buildings under construction or still in the planning stages.[5]

At least on this issue, it seemed all press was good press. Symington's plans were being discussed broadly during that time (perhaps because people already had chewed on Mecham and Steiger's ideas in past elections), which was the same period a poll showed Symington passing Steiger and Mecham among Maricopa County Republican voters. Still, the largest vote-getter was "undecided."

June 1990, though, was a decisive month. Symington, working with hundreds of thousands of dollars more than his closest opponent, began ad campaigns at the same time he increased his speaking schedule.

Other candidates struggled to raise money in the collapsing economy and accused Symington of "buying the governor's office," as Steiger put it.

But Symington also was the candidate covering the most ground and the only candidate going door-to-door in the summer heat in Phoenix and Tucson. He not only was meeting thousands of voters one-on-one, he was countering accusations that he was a disconnected rich boy who was buying the election.[6]

Symington was leading his closest opponent by 12 percentage points by the end of June. Just as he began to pull away, his campaign sent videotapes to every undecided Republican in the state that showed Symington speaking for more than eight minutes about why he should be governor. The video-cassette campaign, which cost about two dollars per tape, was one of only four such efforts by candidates in the nation. Steiger and Mecham tried to paint the expensive video campaign as another sign that Symington was leading only because of money, but polls continued to suggest voters didn't care about Symington's financial advantage.

Koory, even though he put more than $100,000 of his own money in his campaign in June, was a non-issue by July. Steiger and Mecham seemed unable to pull support from the state's vast pool of nonvoting moderate Republicans, while Symington's centrist-leaning, environmentally friendly brand of conservatism seemed to win over undecideds.

By mid-July, the dynamic of the race had changed. Koory and Steiger were fading fast as Mecham gained little traction beyond his base. Smith and Symington decided he should begin focusing more of his time on the stump talking about the Democratic sure-thing, Terry Goddard. Goddard himself had started to take shots at Symington, which, political analysts noted, was likely helpful to Symington because it suggested Symington was the likely primary winner, and perhaps the Republican that Democrats feared most in the general election.

As Symington appeared to be pulling away, Goddard began suggesting that Symington was not as successful in business as he claimed. And

Steiger and Mecham, as the state's political reporters had predicted, began aiming more cutting language at the frontrunner.[7]

The state's media outlets began looking deeper into Symington's life, particularly his arguably opaque finances.

Candidates increased their speaking schedules and engaged in a series of debates as the primary neared. Increasingly, Symington's speeches would be infiltrated by Mecham supporters, who would arrive early and place literature on the chairs in which Republican audience members would soon sit.

In debates, Symington did his best to stay calm and focused under the barrage of insults from Mecham and to a lesser extent, Steiger. ("Best to stay away from Steiger," Symington said at the time. "He's like a porcupine. Let him fire his insults. Get a good laugh. Then let it go.")

Mecham's attacks remained consistent throughout the race: *Symington is not a real Arizonan. He's a lackey for the business elite. He's a developer. He doesn't mind homosexuality. He's soft on abortion.* Symington honed responses that seemed to effectively deflect Mecham's attacks while increasingly drawing laughs at Mecham's expense.

Symington's campaign generally avoided mud fights with opponents. But two weeks before the primary, Symington and Smith agreed it was time to hit Mecham hard. All of Symington's "staying on message" might cause voters to forget the embarrassing nonsense of Evan Mecham. Symington and Smith crafted a blistering press release to help Arizonans remember life under Evan Mecham.

"One thing about Ev—he's consistent," the release started. "Here it is two weeks to go in the campaign and he's out there slinging his mud.

"The fact is by now everyone knows his tactics. He's untruthful; he distorts the few facts he has been able to absorb; and he jumps to wild conclusions."[8]

Symington went on to explain that he has a plan, that Mecham didn't, and that it was time for change. Symington explained why Mecham had been unusually rambunctious in previous weeks as he set the stage for the bigger battle to come:

"Ev Mecham is feeling the heat. It's no surprise that he's coming at me like a cornered animal."

The primary race was called early the evening of September 11. Symington's victory speech was a mix of thank-yous, restatements of policy goals, and calls for party unity.

The next morning, *Arizona Republic* editorial writers described his victory as "astonishing." *Arizona Daily Star* editors said Symington had "scored a convincing victory for reasonableness and competence" under the headline, "Oh happy day!"[9] Symington had taken 43 percent of the vote in a five-candidate race and had handily beaten Mecham, who took 24 percent. Mecham had succeeded at holding his base, but had failed to expand it.

A headline in the *Chicago Tribune* read: "Results in Arizona delight Republican leaders." "We nominated our strongest candidate," the party's national spokesperson, Charles Black, said in the story.[10]

In Arizona, even staunch Democrats cheered the defeat of Mecham in the primary. Symington probably was the tougher fight for Goddard, but the fight would be between two articulate moderates. With either candidate, editorials throughout the state argued, it would now be possible to heal the state's reputation.

Mecham promised to support Symington in the general election because, as he said, "Goddard will be a total disaster. Symington would only be an 80 percent disaster." But within days of Mecham's primary loss, his supporters began collecting signatures to get Mecham on the general election ballot as a third-party candidate.

A Mecham candidacy would likely be disastrous for Symington in his battle against a competent foe with unified Democratic support.

In less than a week, Mecham supporters had collected the names of twelve thousand people who said they would write in Mecham's name on their November ballot.

Republicans and Democrats both dreaded the idea of a replay of the 1986 election, which Mecham won with only 40 percent of the vote because a third-party candidate had drawn votes from the moderate Democrat.

Money began flowing into both major campaigns, with Symington outdistancing Goddard. But for several reasons, political observers placed Symington at a big disadvantage against Goddard, who began a new round of attacks on Symington at his own victory speech after a decisive victory over a nearly nonexistent opponent:

Arizona Democrats were united, while Republicans had just gone through a divisive primary that alienated a large percentage of the party. The Democrats were hungry, too, to erase the embarrassment of their 1986 loss to Mecham.

Two weeks after the primary, the *Arizona Republic* released the first poll of voters regarding the upcoming general election. Of likely voters, 49 percent were leaning toward Goddard, while only 32 percent were considering Symington.

Symington publicly blamed the discrepancy on Goddard's much higher name recognition. The gap would close, Symington promised. People already knew Goddard. They were quickly getting to know Fife Symington.

But internally, campaign staffers were concerned by one particular aspect of the survey: While more than 70 percent said Goddard had "a well-defined program for moving the state forward," only 33 percent believed Symington had a plan.[11]

The gigantic "Symington Plan" clearly wasn't reaching voters.

Symington was in trouble. He had just seven weeks to close a seventeen-point gap.

Symington joked to Ann in September: "I don't think we'll be sleeping much in the weeks to come."[12]

# Chapter 14

# A BLUR OF PLURALITY

As Arizona's good name was dragged through the mud in 1987 and 1988, non-Mechamites looked for solutions, not only to end his hold on the state, but to make sure something like Mecham didn't happen in the future.

Infuriating to most Arizonans was the idea that the state had become a laughingstock thanks to a man who only won 40 percent of the vote. It seemed undemocratic that the majority of Arizonans didn't want Evan Mecham, but got him anyway.

In the fall of 1988, amid the chaos caused by Mecham, the Arizona legislature voted to place a proposition on the November 1988 ballot saying that anyone running for statewide office must get more than 50 percent of the total number of votes. If no candidate got a majority, a runoff election would be held between the top two vote-getters.

Proposition 105 was something of an afterthought on the 1988 ballot. Most Arizonans and the region's media outlets focused on Proposition 106, the aggressive "English Only" proposition that not only inflamed racial tensions in the state, but made Arizona the testing ground for such ideas in other states. Liberals and many moderate Republicans—Symington included—thought it was an unnecessary act meant only to alienate and subjugate immigrant communities. For many nationally, the tales coming from Arizona of Mecham's nonsense and the "English Only" push fit the narrative that the state was a bastion of far-right-wing intolerance.

Indeed, the *Arizona Republic*'s editorial board only gave the election-reform issue four paragraphs in its 1988 pre-election endorsements.

"Normally we would not favor an amendment to the Constitution in reaction to an isolated political event, but the upheaval of the past year involving Evan Mecham's impeachment and removal from office was anything but normal.

"It is unlikely that the added costs of an infrequent runoff election would be too burdensome, nor is it likely that the measure would spur a proliferation of third-party and independent candidacies," the editorial continued. "What this amendment would do would be to give the voters and elected officials the confidence that public servants hold their position of trust with the support of a majority of the electorate."

Editors of the *Arizona Daily Star* appeared to give the issue more thought. Under the subheadline, "Change to runoff only seems like a good idea," the editorial's author laid out several ways the proposition, as stated, could cause significant problems in the future:

Arizona had a strong libertarian bent, for one. Any Libertarian or other third-party candidate getting even 10 percent of the vote could easily throw any of the five statewide races into a runoff.

How many people would show up to vote in these runoff elections? When would they be held? (Imagine trying to hold an election during the holiday season, the editors posited. If the state waited until after the holidays, a governor might not be in place until after the legislative session had begun in mid-January.)

"The election procedure outlined in the state Constitution has worked since 1912," the editorial argued. "Fear of Mecham is no reason for rewriting it."[1]

Regardless, Arizonans did approve Proposition 105. Henceforth, the governor, secretary of state, attorney general, treasurer, and superintendent of public instruction would need at least one more vote than 50 percent of the total number of votes to win.

The next day, none of the papers in Yuma, Tucson, Phoenix, or Flagstaff gave the proposition's victory more than a few paragraphs. It seemed like little more than a cathartic act for voters—a jab at Mecham in the realm of the hypothetical.

Symington, as he fought the "English Only" proposition, also had much more tepid feelings about the majority-vote push. To him, it seemed unnecessary and potentially problematic. Unlike the proposition's supporters, he saw nothing undemocratic about an election being won by the candidate who garnered the *most* votes, not the *majority* of votes. Around the United States, plurality wins were common. Around the world, dozens of democracies had multiple viable parties. Elections in those democracies would be shuttered en masse as large numbers of offices went unfilled until an additional election was held, Symington argued at the time.

But Symington also wasn't passionate about Prop. 105. He thought little of it as the first few months of 1989 brought much bigger news events—the fall of Mecham, the candidacy of Rhodes, the supreme court decision keeping Mofford in place, and in his personal life, the meeting on the mount with Goldwater and the skyward climb of the Camelback Esplanade.[2]

Even in the days and weeks following Symington's primary victory, the potential impact of the new law didn't enter conversation. Symington was quickly deemed the underdog by pollsters and political observers, so getting ahead of Terry Goddard was the only issue that mattered.

And after all, Evan Mecham had promised to support Symington. The Symington team quickly focused on getting Mechamites out to vote for Symington, not on hypotheticals of a write-in candidacy throwing the election into a runoff.

Terry Goddard's big lead looked like the only issue that mattered.

For one, beyond name recognition, Goddard seemed to be well liked by the majority of civic leaders throughout the state. As mayor of Phoenix for six years, he had been a leading figure in countless statewide events and organizations, perhaps most notably, the state's League of Cities and Towns.[3]

After the primary, Goddard and Symington faced off for the first time in front of the attendees of the annual meeting of the League of Cities and Towns in northwest Tucson. This was a gathering of opinion makers from every population center in the state. It was a room in which Symington had to do well if he was going to mount a serious attack on the frontrunner.[4]

Goddard, his staff, and supporters were confident they would win the day. Unlike Goddard, Symington was mostly unknown to the mayors, city council members, and leaders of cities outside Phoenix.[5] Or he was known among city leaders for how he had tormented Phoenix's city leaders during the Esplanade fight. Symington was, to some, just some famously disruptive developer that city leaders around the state hoped never darkened their doors.

Symington and Jay Smith agreed that Goddard would likely spend most of his time in front of fellow city leaders attacking Symington as an out-of-touch, elitist developer. Assuming Goddard would quickly go negative in a room favorable to the mayor and wary of the developer,

Symington gambled that cheeky playfulness was his only chance to win the day. He would disarm critics and disorient Goddard by being silly.

The league's executive director, Jack DeBolske, had been the popular voice of the group since 1960. Symington, the student of ancient Greek culture, suggested giving DeBolske an award that played off the man's seemingly timeless stature as the leader of the group. After ideas were tossed around in a pre-event staff meeting, Symington suggested awarding DeBolske a scroll celebrating "The Great Zeus" for "his fatherly hand in guiding the leaders of the state since the beginning of time."

Symington and Smith wrote up a parody decree and sent a staffer to a nearby print shop to design an embossed scroll.

Symington was chosen to speak first at the event. He stood up before the audience, paused in silence for effect, then unrolled the scroll and began reading the satirically regal tribute.

A large cross-section of the power-packed audience laughed through the announcement and cheered DeBolske as he gamely accepted the honor. Once the ruckus calmed, Symington spoke about his policy plans, focusing on how they would benefit communities throughout the state, not just the large cities. He avoided broadsides at Goddard, and when finished, received applause arguably more robust than would be expected for a fairly unknown developer speaking to an audience often infuriated by such people.

Goddard stood, gave a speech similar to his primary speeches but sprinkled with more swipes at Symington's blue blood background and lack of government experience. Goddard argued he was the candidate with the relevant experience, not Symington. It is "fixing roads, it's stretching resources, it's forming public-private partnerships, it's fighting for new jobs," Goddard told the audience. "It's not choosing new chandeliers for the Ritz-Carlton Hotel." Goddard was met with solid applause.[6]

Media coverage the next day made only passing reference to the Zeus scroll gag amid light coverage of the event. But for Symington and his staff, his spirited showing in front of a tough crowd suggested their campaign had a chance.

Their optimism put them in the minority of race prognosticators.

One problem: Terry Goddard was not the perfect foil for Symington like Evan Mecham had been. Indeed, a common argument was that the two candidates were barely indistinguishable in their moderate policy

stances (beyond Symington's slightly tougher talk on state financial issues and criminal sentencing guidelines).

Even Symington's strongest conservative views seemed hedged with
moderate caveats. For example: He said he wanted better schools and
better early-childhood care and education while he lambasted a major
school-funding proposition. He wanted better treatment programs for
low-level drug offenders at the same time he wanted to execute drug
kingpins.

Goddard mixed in fiscal conservatism and tough-on-crime rhetoric
as he pushed for more significant funding for public schools and expanded treatment programs for low-level offenders.

Even their maturation backstories were similar.

"Two peas in a pod," one woman wrote to the *Arizona Daily Star*.

Soon after the primaries, *Republic* columnist E. J. Montini presented
readers with a ten-question quiz testing to see if readers knew their candidates. "Which candidate supports a woman's right to have an abortion?
A. Goddard. B. Symington." "Which candidate says he better understands
working stiffs? A. Goddard. B. Symington."

The joke: You could answer Symington or Goddard to all ten questions and be correct on every question.[7]

Goddard painted Symington as an out-of-touch Eastern rich boy trying to buy himself an office, but journalists and the Symington crew were
quick to point out that Goddard's own origin story was also one of privilege and private schools.

After all, Goddard was, like Symington, a Harvard man in the late
1960s who came from a long-respected, wealthy family.

*Republic* reporter Peter Aleshire wrote a lengthy profile exploring the
parallel paths of the candidates.[8] In Aleshire's story, Terry Goddard's father, former governor Samuel Pearson Goddard Jr. (who had beat Har-
vard-educated Richard Kleindienst in Arizona's 1964 Arizona gubernatorial race), took offense at the idea that the Goddard bloodline was similar
to the Symington-Frick line:

"The fact we went to Harvard is irrelevant," the elder Goddard argued. "Our people were merchants, farmers, and sailors. Add together
Fife's family, and you've got American royalty."

Terry Considine, Symington's close friend from Harvard days, responded: "It has intrigued me that people make an issue that Fife was a
patrician. Goddard has as patrician a background as anyone else."

Goddards had been going to Harvard since the 1600s, several news-paper features over the years had pointed out. Like Symington, Goddard was also a product of private schools aimed at prepping students for the Ivy League.

Goddard's story, though, was quieter than Symingtons. Goddard was a westerner at heart struggling to fit in with a landscape with which Symington was familiar. Goddard dated little, saying "I was really pretty monastic" as he tried to mix academics with the rigors of his crew team. In several stories and interviews leading up to the race, Goddard described himself as a sort of tepid, overly moderate fringe member of the radicalized Young Democrats at Harvard.

Since their Harvard days, the story noted, the right-winger and the left-winger both became more moderate and nuanced in their thinking as they navigated "the real world."

One significant issue on which Symington and Goddard differed was Proposition 103—better known as ACE—which would have significantly raised the amount of money the state could spend on education (Arizona's Constitution set a cap on that spending). The proposed funding increases and the taxes needed to support them were estimated to pump more than $5 billion into Arizona's notoriously underfunded public schools during the 1980s.

The Arizona Citizens for Education initiative was polling well as the primaries ended, but against the wishes of some more fiscally centrist staffers and supporters, Symington vigorously opposed the proposition. The large tax increase combined with what he argued was a lack of accountability and metrics for success made ACE untenable to the long-time fiscal conservative.

It was widely believed that Symington would be crippled in his attempt to close on Goddard if he continued to attack the seemingly popular plan. But as October ground on, Symington and anti-ACE forces were able to produce data and precedent from other states suggesting ACE would be difficult to manage and hard on the economy while offering limited, if any, benefit to Arizona's children.[9]

ACE offered Symington the opportunity to effectively brand Goddard with one of the most popular conservative attack labels of the time: "Terry Goddard is a tax-and-spend liberal," Symington announced in his first post-primary speech. He then repeated the catchy jab countless times throughout the month of October. (It was a label that two years earlier arguably sank the candidacy of Democratic presidential nominee Michael Dukakis.)

Symington also seemed to succeed at flipping Goddard's attacks regarding Symington's lack of experience. Symington argued that Goddard, mayor of Phoenix for six years, was a "professional politician," something inferior, Symington inferred, to a successful veteran from the crucible of the free market.

While Symington touted the two million square feet of office and warehousing space he had developed in the Valley, Goddard worked to link Symington to S&L bad boy Charles Keating and other S&L scammers who, by 1990, had become the bogeymen of American finance.

The two candidates undertook grueling statewide travel schedules through October. Goddard had reason to feel confident he would take Tucson and much of Phoenix, Flagstaff, and the Navajo Nation. Symington needed to gain ground in the greater Phoenix metro area, make strides into the Democratic stronghold of Tucson, and build on his surprisingly strong support in rural areas, a support bolstered by the oft-mentioned backing from Barry Goldwater as well as Symington's staunch support for private property rights.

Symington even attacked Goddard for the fact that Phoenix compiled $300,000 in fines from the Environmental Protection Agency. Goddard pointed out that the industrial source of those pollutants and fines had been closed four years prior to him taking office.

Ann, meanwhile, accompanied her husband on many of the most exhausting campaign runs around the state. Articulate in the language of compassionate conservatism and in her support of her husband's candidacy, Ann, the teacher and mother, made a compelling sidekick. She was especially appealing to suburban moms, something Goddard, a bachelor, couldn't counter. Along with Ann and the couple's brood of energetic children, the Symingtons painted an attractive picture of a family values-oriented couple whose home life mirrored those of hundreds of thousands of parents in a state brimming with young families.[10]

Symington appeared to be proving he was a competent challenger with a viable statewide machine, several strong debate showings, and a knack for fundraising and political advertising. Still, surveys conducted by local pollsters suggested Goddard's double-digit lead was holding. Indeed, a poll taken just days before the general election suggested Goddard would win easily.

Whitney, Fife IV, Richard, and Tom with Fife and Ann Symington, 1990. Courtesy of the Symington family archives.

However, Symington and his staff had good reason to believe the polls being cited in the public arena were wrong. When Jay Smith joined Symington's campaign, he had pushed Symington to spend extra money to hire the noted national pollster, Bill McInturff of Wirthlin Partners and Public Opinion Strategies.[11] Smith argued that McInturff's methodology and larger samples helped his studies track closer to eventual outcomes than the average local polling companies.

McInturff had Symington running a few points behind Goddard, but Symington was, by McInturff's measure, easily within reach.

On the morning of November 6, 1990, Symington went to a nearby polling location and while voting (for himself), was hit with the realization that by the next day, the grinding race toward the primary and general elections would be over. He would either be returning to a previous chapter of his life in the business community or he'd be diving into the turbulent unknown world of the governor's office.[12]

Determined to have a relaxing afternoon before a hectic evening, Symington went to an afternoon matinee before a short rest at home.

Ronald Reagan campaigning for Symington in 1990. Courtesy of the Arizona State Library, Archives and Public Records, History and Archives Division, Phoenix, RG1_SG26_S6_B10_F06_I1.

Fife Symington and Vice President Dan Quayle during a Symington campaign event, 1990. Courtesy of the Arizona State Library, Archives and Public Records, History and Archives Division, Phoenix, RG1_SG26_S6_B05_F023_I01.

Senate Minority Leader Bob Dole speaking to Arizona CEOs and Republican political leaders in the Ritz-Carlton during Symington's run-off campaign, 1991. Courtesy of the Arizona State Library, Archives and Public Records, History and Archives Division, Phoenix, RG1_SG26_S6_B07_F010_I02.

The Symingtons with California governor Arnold Schwarzenegger. Courtesy of the Symington family archives.

Upon rejoining his staff and close friends and family in a hotel suite in the Hyatt Regency Phoenix, he learned that exit polling was leaning against him.

Within an hour of the polls closing, Valley television stations began reporting early returns. Goddard was leading comfortably. As the hours passed, Symington never pulled ahead as the percentage of votes counted passed 50 percent.

The only thing known for sure by 9 p.m. was that the ACE initiative to bolster school funding was going to lose badly. Since Symington was ACE's highest profile opponent, the strong vote against ACE suggested voters were listening, and liking, what he had to say. That had to be a good sign, he imagined.

Still, prognosticators on television increasingly predicted a Goddard victory.

Between 9 p.m. and 10 p.m., though, the gap began to close. As Symington supporters began to draw toward televisions in the Hyatt ballroom, Sam Mardian, a Symington friend and a wiz with numbers and political calculus, came to Symington in the election suite with a prediction: Symington was going to win because the heavily Republican Green Valley and Foothills areas of Tucson had not yet reported. With Republicans outnumbering Democrats by several thousand in the precincts yet to report, Symington, he predicted, would end up a few thousand votes ahead.

By 1 a.m., it appeared that Mardian's predictions were correct. Symington had slipped ahead and had continued to build on his lead. Supporters in the Hyatt ballroom began chanting for Symington to emerge and give a speech, but he knew the race wasn't over. Between 1 a.m. and 4 a.m., results drifted back toward Goddard several times, but he was never again in the lead.

Just before 4 a.m., Symington went from the election suite down to the Hyatt ballroom and told the fifty or so remaining supporters to go home and get some sleep. Although the numbers were promising, nothing would be known for sure until the next day.

At the same time, over in the Sheraton Adams Hotel, Goddard gave an upbeat speech to his supporters, and also told them to go home and get a few hours of sleep.

When Symington awoke later that morning, he was greeted with more good news. He was stretching his lead over Goddard. As votes from the last precincts were counted, Symington led by more than four thousand votes. At that point, there was no way Goddard could catch him.

That was the good news.

Lost in the frenzy of the ever-shifting toe-to-toe bout was the fact that there was a third candidate, Max Hawkins, a little-known Mecham crony running a write-in candidacy primarily to provide a staunchly pro-life candidate in a race in which the leading candidates supported abortion rights.

Hawkins received 10,864 votes from conservatives who very likely would have voted for Symington.

When all the votes were in from rural precincts (some of which had been besieged by a blizzard), Symington had received 522,348 votes compared to Goddard's 518,128. That gave Symington 49.7 percent of the vote compared to Goddard's 49.2 percent.[13]

Meaning, because of the write-in candidacy of a former Mecham staffer, there would have to be a runoff race. Neither candidate had crossed the 50-percent threshold mandated by the law put in place after Mecham's win by plurality.

Fife Symington hadn't considered the possibility of a runoff election.[14] He was focused solely on Goddard, and so the governorship seemed contingent only on beating Goddard.

What had been euphoria for Symington slipped slowly into the depressing reality that he could be campaigning for weeks, if not months, depending on when the runoff voting would take place.

Ann hadn't considered the possibility of a runoff, either. Exhausted from the endless campaigning, she cried upon learning that the race would continue.

Symington channeled some of that frustration into a thirty-minute press conference that, while maintaining the tone of a victor and a fighter ready for more, also more than hinted to his family's weariness—and the state's weariness—with seemingly endless political turmoil.

"My family is sick of it, the people are sick of hearing from us, so you're not going to hear from us again until January 1," he told reporters. He then retreated to his home with his family and made good on his promise. Mostly.[15]

Goddard decided to stay in the public eye through the holidays.

In the days after Symington's announcement of his nearly two-month retreat from politics, he was on the phone with staffers already mapping out their path to victory. Symington would lay low, but sure, there would be numerous discussions and small gatherings to generate the money needed to launch a major media campaign through January and February. Fundraising, though, would likely be much easier and quicker for the runoff, his staff figured. Republicans could taste victory.

For the most part, the Symington campaign would just keep doing what it had successfully been doing.

With momentum in Symington's favor, Goddard badly needed some good news for him, or bad news for Symington, to recharge his campaign.

# Chapter 15

# ONE MORE TIME

Political analysts and campaign organizers offered numerous theories about Symington's surprising come-from-behind near-victory. Jim Howard, Goddard's campaign manager, gave Symington credit for effectively using the "tax-and-spend" and "professional politician" labels to weaken Goddard's standing among undecided voters and for making an effective plea for Republicans to "come home" to the party.

Howard also said Symington was helped by the infusion of more than a million dollars from his mother and wife. That money helped finance a relentless media campaign that included a radio ad featuring by-then-beloved Ronald Reagan.

What Howard didn't mention in his postmortems to reporters was the shock to morale the almost-loss sent through the Goddard campaign. Besides continuing frustration with Goddard's inability to connect on a personal level with many voters, staffers, and potential donors, Howard and others knew well that candidates who were the leaders in a race prior to a runoff almost always win the runoffs. As long as there wasn't some major scandal or other defining event between the election and the runoff, Symington would be the favorite.[1]

On November 11, an *Arizona Republic* sub-headline made a prediction: "Gloves likely to come off for runoff."

Democratic consultant Rick DeGraw argued that Goddard would need to be much more aggressive in attacking Symington's financial record. Symington's "private record should be as open as his public record because he wants to be governor."

Democratic strategists were well aware that, by the end of 1990, Symington's development and real estate management company was floundering as federal investigators continued to dig through the financial records of the Valley's S&Ls, including those of Southwest Savings and Loan.

"I think Terry Goddard will return to his political roots, which is a populist-attack politician," the Republican political analyst Robert Robb added.

With the runoff election more than two months off, Goddard and his supporters would have ample time to mine for dirt and pound on the theme that Symington was not the remarkable business success he was said to be.

A paragraph from one of Symington's October campaign fliers, written by Jay Smith, soon would be quoted extensively, and questioned extensively:

Under the subheading "Fife Symington's Impressive Business Record," Smith wrote, "Fife Symington is more than a survivor in today's negative business climate; his business is thriving amidst a real estate depression. That's because Fife is a good businessman with a strong business ethic. In a slowing economy, Fife has taken a cautious, steady approach and has known how to cut budgets and where to trim fat."[2]

It wasn't very hard by early 1991 to find evidence that contradicted the campaign's claim that, "His business is thriving amidst a real estate depression."

Goddard's staff built their book. Symington, meanwhile, mostly continued with the strategy that had brought him to within a couple thousand votes of victory: Promise, as he said often, "to take Arizonans to the mountaintop"; stay with the soft but effective jabs that Goddard was a "tax-and-spend liberal" and a "career politician"; and use his campaign's ample war chest to continue his national-caliber media campaign.

That strategy had to change immediately one morning in early February.[3]

Two weeks before the runoff election, two stories related to Arizona made front-page headlines in the nation's newspapers.

One story announced that the US Senate Ethics Committee was divided along partisan lines on whether or not to discipline the five senators who had intervened with RTC regulators on behalf of Arizona developer Charles Keating. Three Republicans on the six-member committee favored dismissing Republican senator John McCain and Democrat senator John Glenn from the case, saying evidence showed they had broken no ethics rules. Three Democrats, however, wanted Senators McCain, Glenn, Don Riegle of Michigan, and Dennis DeConcini of Arizona to receive the same treatment—they would all receive a letter criticizing them for their questionable tactics helping Keating dodge federal investigators.[4]

Since the committee felt the evidence was stronger against the fifth senator involved, Senator Alan Cranston, a Democrat from California, Cranston would likely receive a punishment more severe than the proposed letter.

The five senators became known as the "Keating Five." They were accused of meeting with both bank board chairman Edwin J. Gray in 1987 and a group of California-based regulators who were in charge of the investigation into Lincoln Savings and Loan owned by Keating, who, along with associates, had donated more than $1.3 million to the campaigns of the five senators.

McCain, the only Republican among the five, had the closest personal relationship with Keating. McCain and his family took vacation trips to the Bahamas on Keating's corporate airplanes in 1983 and 1986. Although McCain did not pay Keating back for the trips until 1989—a year in which Keating emerged as the face of greed in America—the House Committee on Standards of Official Conduct decided McCain's repayment ended the issue. The Senate ethics committee ruled the issue of the Bahamas flights was closed when the issue was ruled on by the House of Representatives (since McCain was a US Congressman at the time of the alleged infraction).[5]

Many saw that as a mere technicality that saved McCain from a much larger hit to his political career.[6]

The S&L crisis was at its height, and Americans and their elected officials were hunting for heads.

The second Arizona-related story also involved a thrift—the much smaller Southwest Savings and Loan—and the decision by the head of the Senate's Judiciary Committee, Ohio Democratic senator Howard Metzenbaum, to release a thirty-page report just two weeks before the Arizona gubernatorial runoff accusing Fife Symington of violating federal conflict-of-interest laws.

Metzenbaum released the report the morning of February 7 and announced he would hold a hearing on this issue in his Senate Judiciary subcommittee later that day.

Ann and Fife Symington were in New York City that morning pursuing donations to finance the remainder of the runoff campaign. The

Symingtons planned to leave that afternoon for Washington, DC, for a fundraiser hosted by President George H. W. Bush.

Around 8:30 that morning, Jay Smith, who was tipped off by another political client, Senator Bob Dole, called Symington to alert him that Metzenbaum had called for the hearing to be held at 1 p.m. that afternoon. Symington immediately called to book a flight to Washington, DC, but all planes were grounded that day due to heavy rain and lightning along the East Coast.

Symington then looked at his watch and having made the drive from New York to Washington before, called a limousine service explaining he had an emergency and needed to be driven to Washington in four hours. It could be done, the dispatcher told him. Within fifteen minutes, the Symingtons were picked up from the curb of their New York hotel and headed southwest down I-95 through heavy storms toward a hearing room inside the US Capitol.[7]

The limousine ride, aided by the limousine's car phone, gave Symington the opportunity to strategize with Smith and the attorney Smith had invited to advise Symington during the financial investigations, John Dowd, who had served as Senator McCain's attorney during the "Keating Five" investigation. Dowd and Smith reviewed the accusations with Symington and suggested approaches to answer the questions.[8]

Dowd, Smith, and Symington arrived in the hearing room about five minutes before Metzenbaum started the hearing.

Jack Landers, a former examiner for the Federal Home Loan Bank Board, told Metzenbaum's subcommittee that Southwest's board of directors twice violated conflict-of-interest regulations while agreeing to finance the first stages of the Esplanade project, a project that ultimately resulted in what regulators estimated was a $21 million loss to the thrift.

The report concluded that Symington was involved to an inappropriate degree in Southwest's 1984 decision to finance the Esplanade project, a claim Symington, who officially left the Southwest board on January 30, 1984, strongly denied.[9]

After addressing the specific accusations, Symington went on the offensive.

"I resent this attempt to denigrate my achievements and to call into question my judgment and even my integrity," he said while looking at Metzenbaum.

Symington wasn't alone in feeling he had been ambushed. Senate Minority Leader, Republican Bob Dole, immediately called foul:

"I smell politics, and it stinks," the usually reserved Dole told an Associated Press reporter. "What we see today is a vicious attack, a blind-side hit without fair notice or fair play."[10]

Besides Dole's explosive accusations, Symington and his attorneys fired back at Metzenbaum, sending a letter to the US Attorney General requesting an investigation to determine if there had been any communication between Metzenbaum and Goddard prior to the release of the report.

Metzenbaum denied that politics were involved, saying he swiftly released the report and conducted the hearing simply because "we were ready to go at this time."[11]

The Metzenbaum report said it would cost taxpayers $250 million to bail out Southwest Savings, which was seized by regulators two years earlier. Symington was targeted in the report, Metzenbaum said, because Southwest's $30 million loan to back his project was the largest in the thrift's history. Metzenbaum accused Symington of violating conflict-of-interest laws by receiving the loan for the Esplanade while he still sat on the board. Symington said he hadn't participated in any board vote related to the Esplanade project. He argued the money didn't go to him, saying the thrift in fact had made a "direct investment" in the property. He also argued that the Southwest loan already had been paid back and that Southwest still stood to receive more income as new phases of the Esplanade were built.[12]

As for Metzenbaum's claim that the Esplanade deal itself would cost taxpayers more than $21 million, Symington said the government would only lose money if it sold the property before the real estate market bounced back and the project was fully developed.

Symington, Smith, and Dowd appeared to have succeeded at partially recasting the news of the day. Headlines around the country the next morning generally mixed the news of the accusations against Symington with Symington's accusations against Metzenbaum. "S&L probe touches off Arizona political spat," read a typical headline that appeared in the *Journal Star* in Lincoln, Nebraska.[13]

What could have been a crippling blow to Symington's campaign was further neutralized by seemingly similar allegations against Terry

Goddard.[14] Indeed, while dismissing the allegations against Symington, an editorial in the conservative-leaning *Republic* opinion section went after Metzenbaum and Goddard much more than Symington: "Far more intriguing than the innuendo about Mr. Symington and Southwest Savings are Mr. Goddard's dealings with MeraBank, whose loans to Mr. Goddard greatly exceeded standard lending guidelines—this at a time when Mr. Goddard, as mayor of Phoenix, was in a position to accommodate MeraBank in a variety of ways."

MeraBank, like Southwest Savings, had also been taken over by the RTC, but the editorial noted, "Mr. Metzenbaum has expressed no interest in Mr. Goddard's relationship with this bankrupt thrift."

Two days earlier, several news outlets also reported that Goddard's Phoenix home had been assessed at nearly half its actual value. The discrepancy was dismissed as a computer error by the county assessor's office, which it surely was, but the issue, combined with Goddard's relationship with MeraBank, seemed to nullify the impact on voters of the Metzenbaum hearing.

Arizonans went to the polls again on February 26. Early returns suggested a Goddard victory. "Euphoria swept through the Terry Goddard campaign early Tuesday night as preliminary election results gave the Democrat a solid lead," wrote Jeff Herr of the *Arizona Daily Star* the next day. "Campaign manager Jim Howard's eyes sparkled as he reviewed incoming results showing a sizable Democratic turnout in Pima County, a stronghold of Democrats."

But "as in the general election," Herr noted, "it turned out that the ballots of conservative voters in Mesa and Sun City were among the last to be tabulated."[15]

Around midnight, the numbers surged in Symington's favor. Conservative voters for write-in candidates in the general election seemed to come home to Symington. Symington gained significantly among absentee voters, perhaps, suggested *Republic* writer Mary Jo Pitzl, thanks to "a glossy, laser-printed card mailed to more than 600,000 Republicans' homes statewide. The cards were request forms for absentee ballots, and unofficial results Wednesday showed they were put to good use."

Symington also flipped several thousand voters from Goddard,[16] which ultimately gave Symington a 52 percent to 48 percent victory.[17]

After a muted late-night celebration at the downtown Hyatt Regency, Symington returned to his room to grab a few hours of sleep. He was up around 8 a.m. and already beginning to field calls from well-wishers such as Vice President Dan Quayle, Senator Dole, and Jack Kemp, the Secretary of Housing and Urban Development, who was already considering a 1994 presidential bid.[18]

After two years on the campaign trail, Fife Symington was finally going to be governor.

But much had changed since he first decided to run.

State employees and private contractors who depended on state funding were bracing for widespread layoffs in the face of a $200 million budget deficit. The economy was still hobbled and the state's reputation remained in tatters, even more so after several state lawmakers were indicted for taking bribes and Arizona voters rejected a Martin Luther King Jr. holiday. As Symington entered office, the NFL was threatening to move the 1993 Super Bowl from Arizona and take away tens of millions of dollars in revenue with it.[19]

As the number of problems grew, the upheaval and lack of leadership in state government had left it struggling to keep up.

An editorial in the *Tucson Citizen* the day after the election captured the mood in the state at the time:

"Now it's time for (Symington) to get to work. It's not too late to salvage the 1991 session of the scandal-shocked Legislature and push through bills to address the neglected issues and restore confidence in government. . . . Never has leadership been more desperately needed. It's time for all of Arizona to work together to put the problems of the last few years behind us."[20]

Fife Symington, the candidate who bragged about the fact he had never held political office, was now tasked with running a state in crisis.

# Chapter 16

# THE ROOKIE

Fife Symington was inaugurated on the blustery late morning of March 6, 1991, two months after the governor of Arizona was supposed to take office and two months after state legislators had begun crafting a budget amid a financial crisis.

No matter. Symington and the dignitaries who spoke that day hit themes of new beginnings, new directions, and working together to, as one speaker said, "make Arizonans proud to be Arizonans again."[1]

After an invocation by a Phoenix rabbi and a blessing by a Hopi elder, the Symingtons walked to the balcony at the front of the old Arizona Capitol to be sworn in.[2]

Symington himself spoke only ten minutes, choosing to focus on broad themes centered on family, good business sense, and bipartisanship rather than any specific policy plans.

Barry Goldwater said Symington "would do a lot of good for the state"; President Bush said in a note read by an assistant that "the people of Arizona have wisely invested their confidence in his leadership"; and John Rhodes, Symington's longtime friend and mentor, playfully tied Symington's election to what he called "two good omens"—the end of the Persian Gulf War and a recent downpour that had brought Arizona's reservoirs and the state back from the brink of drought.

"You have a mandate the likes of which I don't think anybody has ever seen in this state," he added. "You've been elected twice in the past four months."

Another good omen was the speech by former governor and respected national figure Bruce Babbitt, who had campaigned for Terry Goddard.

Symington's inauguration, he said, is a "new beginning for Arizona." "The first thing to do is get together, lower our voices, and start talking to each other and see if we can get some things done.

"I really think we've bounced off the bottom," Babbitt said, speaking

Symington's inauguration in 1991. Courtesy of the Arizona State Library, Archives and Public Records, History and Archives Division, Phoenix, RG1_SG26_S6_B004_F025_I06.

before a crowd that included Arizona's living former governors, most notably Evan Mecham.

That Babbitt, a moderate Democrat, spoke so fondly of the moderate Republican entering office suggested bipartisanship might be returning to Arizona government.

Goddard's loss stung Democrats who, just a few months before, expected their candidate to cruise to a win and give the party a strong mandate in state government. But most seemed accepting of Symington as a consolation prize of sorts: Although the vein of aggressive fiscal conservatism that ran though his beliefs and policies was concerning, they believed he was much more likely than Mecham to listen to and understand their positions.

Indeed, state Democrats who spoke in near-apocalyptic language after Evan Mecham's election generally echoed Babbitt's optimism in interviews following the inauguration. Symington would be someone with whom they could work, several Democratic state legislators said.[3]

That would be a necessity for Symington: Democrats held the majority in the Arizona State Senate.

After moving into his office on the Ninth Floor of Arizona's capitol building (without the potentially off-putting portrait of his famous great-grandfather), Symington's most pressing issue was the state budget, which legislators had been negotiating, and in some cases finalizing, for several weeks before Symington's arrival. For House and Senate leadership, the newbie governor was someone to be quickly courted and, through wise counsel, guided and perhaps manipulated.

Symington invited several legislators to his office in his first days. Instead of finding a rookie underwater enough to agree to most anything, they found someone who already had a detailed budget proposal and his own battle plan for getting it approved.

One Republican house leader told Symington during her visit that, in regard to the budget, "the train has already left the station." "Well it hasn't left *my* station," Symington responded. "I campaigned on a pledge of no new taxes." The house leader lectured Symington on parliamentary procedure and how things *actually* get done in Arizona state government. Symington was told there was no way he would be tampering with the emerging budget. "We'll have to agree to disagree," he said as the legislator walked from his office.[4]

"No way was I going to get rolled," he said afterward to a staffer as he recalled his uneasy first meeting with House Speaker Jane Hull.

To have any success, though, he would have to negotiate, and particularly with senate Democrats, schmooze and disarm. Shortly after Symington unveiled his budget proposal, which reconfigured and expanded state funding cuts proposed by Republican legislators, Senate Appropriations Committee Chairman Jaime Gutierrez called Symington a budgetary "Edward Scissorhands."

A week later, Gutierrez entered his senate office and found a gift on his desk with a note attached. "Dear Jaime: This is a personal gift from me to you. I hope it will make your job of cutting the budget easier. Sincerely, Fife 'Scissorhands' Symington, Governor."

Gutierrez admitted to reporters that he laughed upon opening the gift—a new pair of scissors. Gutierrez disagreed vehemently with

Symington with Speaker of the House Jane Hull in 1992. Hull succeeded Symington as governor of Arizona. Courtesy of the Arizona State Library, Archives and Public Records, History and Archives Division, Phoenix, RG1_SG26_S6_B06_F016_I03.

Symington's deep cuts, but he said he had no ill will toward the man himself.[5]

Symington's demeanor and willingness to meet with Democrats to argue his position were generally commended and deemed effective, at least in maintaining civil discourse that had been lacking in the previous years.

Keven Willey, the *Republic*'s respected political reporter and columnist who labeled herself a "radical centrist," wrote an uncharacteristically pro-Symington column several weeks into the new governor's tenure that arguably captured the mood in state government at the time.[6]

Republicans were widely supportive of the Symington budget, even with its proposed deviations from numbers already on the table, she noted. Republicans were so united in their delight in Symington's budget, Willey posited, that "we may be witnessing the reunification of the Arizona GOP, if such a thing is possible."

Symington's budget was hard to lambast because it was based on a necessity with which nobody disagreed: The state budget had to be balanced. Symington's plan balanced the budget without raising taxes.[7]

Beyond the balanced budget, Symington's plan would, theoretically, create a $72 million reserve—a rainy day fund the state could tap in a crisis rather than make last-minute cuts to programs or violate constitutional debt limits.

To cut millions from the $3.47 billion budget initially proposed by legislative staffers, Symington cut public education funding more than the proposed budget, but nearly negated the blow by adding more than $4 million for school districts experiencing unusually high growth and adding more than $11 million for a variety of programs for underprivileged children. While trimming allocations to the state's Department of Environmental Quality, his plan would give more to tourism promotions, children's programs, and the Arizona Department of Corrections.[8]

Critics focused what criticism they could on the budget's assumption that $11.5 million would come from federal coffers to pay for health care programs long paid for by the state. Also, the Symington budget assumed state agencies wouldn't spend about $35 million of the money allocated to them for the next year, which critics labeled the "smoke and mirrors" Symington had promised not to use.

Still, Willey summed up the general Democratic response to the budget with a quote from Senate Majority Leader Alan Stephens. Symington's budget, he said, "isn't irrational, draconian or Mecham-like in its approach."

Again, Symington was receiving a huge boost by simply not being Evan Mecham.

Besides crafting and battling for his budget, Symington quickly began pursuing money to purchase the land on which an unpopular hazardous-waste plant was planned twenty miles southwest of Phoenix. The state needed $44 million to buy the land from the hazardous waste disposal company, ENSCO. It would be Symington's first chance to execute on his promise to bring business practices to government solutions—the state would sell a building owned by the state, then lease that building back from the owner.[9]

The plan was judged to be either brilliant for unlocking trapped capital or an example of real estate-developer voodoo economics that would cost the state much more in the long run.

Besides starting a collection of task forces to address lingering problems in the state, Symington also unveiled his plan to streamline government to reduce wasteful spending. Called the State Long-Term Improved Management Plan, or Project SLIM, Symington proposed to spend $2.5 million for an in-depth analysis of thirteen state agencies, which employed 19,500 people, to identify positions or programs that could be streamlined without harming state services. Project SLIM was the manifestation of one of Symington's biggest campaign promises—to maintain the same level or a higher level of service from state agencies without raising taxes on the people the state serves.

As Memorial Day neared, though, a budget had still not been approved as Republicans and Democrats struggled in the Joint Legislative Budget Committee to reconcile differences between the proposals from the Republican-led house and Democrat-led senate.

Democrats pounded Symington and Republicans for their efforts to freeze teacher salaries and cut funding to several programs for the needy. Senator Jaime Gutierrez, to whom Symington had earlier playfully given the scissors, was increasingly vocal in his criticism of the Symington plan. He railed on the budget's $6 million cut for Children's Rehabilitative Services and the Republicans' fight against Democrats' push to redistribute $8 million from the general fund for programs for the mentally ill.

Another sticking point: Symington's budget, Dems argued, would cripple an expansion of Arizona State University that educators argued was critical to the health of the university system.

The Democrats criticized Symington for adding money for tourism, but not bending on cuts to some state services for the underprivileged.

Ultimately, the committee split for the Memorial Day break in a huff, with both sides arguing the other side was negotiating in bad faith.

But in fact, the distance between the two sides in total dollars was, by state budget standards, fairly small—$22 million, or less than one percent of the previous year's allocation. Neither side thought it prudent to raise taxes. It mostly came down to priorities.

In the end, it mainly was Symington's line-in-the-sand—the creation of a $72 million pot of money to pay for inevitable expenses later in the year—that would have to budge.

Finally, in the third week of June, Symington agreed not to veto a budget that created only a $50.2 million surplus.

Although he had given ground, Symington came away with a state budget that mostly met his campaign's conservative fiscal promises while meeting the seemingly incongruent promise of returning comity to state government.

While the budget deal of July 1991 received most of the press, Symington had also approved a bill banning the importation and incineration of hazardous waste at facilities owned by the state while both increasing oversight of privately owned incinerators and starting a program to cut down the amount of waste produced by the state.

Along with those Sierra Club-supported laws, Symington also signed into law the appropriation of $300,000 to pay for staff and utilities to keep recreation centers in gang-ridden neighborhoods open at night through the remainder of the summer.

Symington's "CEO approach," as political historian Thad Beyle labeled it, seemed to have more appreciation for the societal safety nets sometimes abandoned in fully supply-sider plans.[10]

At his one hundred-day mark, which encompassed most of the lengthy budget brawl, Symington was seen in a favorable light by more than 60 percent of Arizonans, according to polls. At the same time, though, most of those polled said it was too early in his administration for them to feel firm in their opinions.

Fife and Ann Symington taking part in the Martin Luther King Day march early in Symington's first term. Courtesy of the Arizona State Library, Archives and Public Records, History and Archives Division, Phoenix, RG1_SG26_S6_B08_F024_I01.

"People generally are still in a wait-and-see mode," pollster Bruce Merrill said.[11]

The *Republic*'s Mary Jo Pitzl, tasked with reporting on the governor's office at a time when Arizona papers still assigned multiple reporters to cover state government, wrote at Symington's one hundred-day mark that he "has maintained a pace that even his critics say is impressive."[12]

Pitzl listed off the fruits of Symington's aggressive push to make good on promises. Besides establishing the budget surplus, he "was being hailed as a savior of the Valley's hopes for the Super Bowl" by endorsing a paid state holiday honoring Martin Luther King Jr. At the end of his first month, he created—and then made himself the leader of—a task force aimed at reforming Arizona's education system.

Pitzl continued: Symington had begun work to ban hazardous waste burning in the state, which hinged on the negotiations he had started to buy the ENSCO property, the site of the hazardous waste plant threatening Phoenix's southern suburbs.

He had made trips to Mexico and New York City to work on trade deals for Arizona businesses,[13] kept his promise to take "government on the road" by making several visits to outstate communities and in line with his promise to be more accessible to the press, made regular

California governor Arnold Schwarzenegger visited Arizona while heading the President's Health Commission. Courtesy of the Arizona State Library, Archives and Public Records, History and Archives Division, Phoenix, RG1_SG26_S6_B11_F37_I01.

appearances on radio talk shows, and talked often and extensively with print reporters.

In May, after accusations by Latino leaders that Symington had been insensitive in comments made about the reasons for the Valley's high-crime rates, he accepted an offer to spend a day and night in one of the areas of South Phoenix most impacted by violent crime. As depicted by his detractors—that he was simply spending a day in a different part of his hometown protected by his security detail—the act seemed insignificant. But to others, the optics were positive: He had accepted a challenge meant to help him better understand the plight of inner-city families.

Pitzl's story, mirrored generally in tone and content by similar stories from around the state, quoted several Democrats who, while disagreeing—sometimes vehemently—with some of Symington's ideas, gave him credit for his tone, energy, and willingness to negotiate in good faith:

"He certainly hasn't made the profound and fundamental mistakes that Governor Mecham did," the senate's minority whip told Pitzl.

And to top it off, Pitzl wrote: "His brushes with controversy have been few."

# Chapter 17

# ON A ROLL

W ith only one week to transition from candidate to governor, Fife Symington moved many of his campaign staffers—"the people who got me there," as he called them later—into top positions in the governor's office.[1]

He was advised that people gifted at campaigning are not always gifted at administrating. But he trusted his staff of two years. With little or no time for a thorough search for seasoned state managers, he decided to place most of his campaign staff into significant executive-office positions.[2]

He then began to expand his staff with both compatriots from his political sphere and experienced career civil servants. He also created new positions intended to expand markets for Arizona businesses. Besides creating a position for a "special assistant for federal relations," he appointed his former campaign press secretary, Annette Alvarez, to be "executive assistant for international development." Alvarez's primary job was to improve and expand relations with the Mexican government and the Mexican state of Sonora, which borders Arizona.

To address another one of his major campaign promises, he brought in Rita Pearson, an attorney experienced in environmental law, whose first task involved tackling the uniquely complicated effort to close the ENSCO hazardous-waste facility. As "executive assistant for the environment and natural resources," Pearson would also be leading other efforts to safeguard and expand Arizona's protected lands. As Symington seemingly followed through on his environmental protection promises, he appeared poised to be one of the most environmentally friendly Republican governors in the United States.[3]

While negotiations with Environmental Systems Co., parent company of ENSCO, were at first smooth, Democrats in the legislature had balked during budget negotiations at the leaseback concept, which they argued would, over twenty years, cost the state twice the $44 million tab. They favored a cash buyout.

But House Republicans ultimately succeeded at luring votes to pass Symington's financing plan. With the senate on board, the state moved to sell two newly built prison units at the massive state prison south of Phoenix for $44 million, after which the state would lease those facilities from the investor group that had signed on for the deal.

By not paying the $44 million up front, Symington's promised rainy day fund was preserved.

As the budget debate—and the priorities represented in it—arguably drew the most attention through Symington's first months, it was the governor's efforts to begin reforming the state's education system that likely impacted more average Arizonans over the coming years. During his campaign, Symington had promised to hold administrators accountable if students didn't meet clearly defined academic metrics. At the same time, local school administrators would be given more independence to react to needs specific to their districts. More specifically, Symington would push for open enrollment in public schools (meaning students could attend schools outside those serving state-drawn attendance boundaries). He also wanted to create a system in which parents would receive vouchers to offset costs at private schools if they chose not to use the public school system (which they paid into with their tax dollars).

He argued that the bureaucracy of the Arizona Department of Education was "bleeding resources away from the classrooms."

On the same day the state budget was approved, Symington convened a meeting of the "Governor's Task Force on Educational Reform." Forty-two administrators, education experts, business leaders, parents, and representatives of other interest groups peppered Symington with questions and advice on how to improve education in the state.

The *Republic* staff polled each member of the task force on several education-related questions.[4] Thirty-one of the forty-two members believed funding of school districts was not equitable, which echoed the sentiments driving a lawsuit filed against the state the month before by the Center for Law in the Public Interest and Southern Arizona Legal Aid Inc. That same month, federal authorities demanded state education officials allocate $47 million they argued had been withheld illegally from poorer school districts in the state.

A majority of those polled didn't believe the problems of Arizona's school system could be solved if school funding "was significantly boost-ed." The group was split nearly evenly on Symington's idea allowing parents to send their children to the school of their choice as well as his plan to create a school voucher program. The majority agreed that the state should consolidate many school districts, which, in line with Symington's ideas, would likely make the state system more efficient and cost-effective.

Advocates for poorer districts argued the task force's findings likely would be scuttled if they went against the governor's already stated desire to cut taxes, reduce bureaucracy, open school borders, and create a school voucher program.

Backing Symington's plan were the powerful members of the Arizona Business Leadership for Education, known as ABLE. As ABLE pushed for reforms matching Symington's ideas, another powerful group, Parents Advocating Choice in Education, had begun a petition drive to place the issue of open enrollment on the ballot the next year.

Robert Donofrio, a superintendent of schools in one of Phoenix's poorer neighborhoods, wrote on his survey: "I'm afraid that the hidden agenda may be to promote choice and private schooling at the expense of the poor children."

The same month the state budget was approved, America West, one of Arizona's major employers and a key player in plans to expand the state's trade with Mexico and other countries, filed for Chapter 11 bankruptcy. The airline would go under if it could not restructure successfully. Loss of a leading employer would not only torpedo the Valley's already strug-gling economy, it likely would cause rate hikes at Sky Harbor Interna-tional Airport and damage the credit rating of Arizona's largest airport and transportation hub.[5]

The death of America West would even impact the stock portfolios of many Arizonans, an inordinate amount of whom had invested heavily in their home airline.

As Phoenix officials, legislators, and top businesspeople scrambled to help save the airline, Symington announced he might be willing to pro-vide state financial aid for a bailout as long as there "is a definable pay-back for the citizens of the state." Symington, along with other leading political and business leaders, intensified their pursuit of a plan to some-how lift America West out of bankruptcy and return it to profitability, a community-wide effort that would be a rare feat if accomplished.

Arizona Cardinals owner Bill Bidwill with Symington's longtime attorney and business partner, Richard Mallery. Courtesy of the Arizona State Library, Archives and Public Records, History and Archives Division, Phoenix, RG1_SG26_S6_B02_F025_I08.

Such talk about state money potentially going to bail out a corporation certainly didn't mix with Symington's pronounced philosophy of limited government. But Symington and other legislators suggested America West was, to echo an infamous phrase from later corporate bailouts, *too big to fail*. Also, as Symington said, since that state contribution would come from lottery revenues, it was "just gambling money anyway."

Over the next several months, Symington and business leaders such as Symington's old business partner, Richard Mallery, assembled the money and management team to pull America West from bankruptcy and restructure it as a budget airline.[6] Symington promised $1 million from lottery proceeds to bolster the effort. Symington and others prodded John Teets, who had restructured both the Greyhound and Dial corporations in Arizona, into investing the largest chunk of the $15 million needed to pay the Debtor in Possession in the America West bankruptcy case. Phoenix-based corporations were also asked to promise to buy two years' worth of airline tickets from a restructured airline to give it a strong base of income as it rebuilt. Another Arizona business leader skilled at company restructuring, Bill Franke, took the helm of the ailing airline, and as Franke guided the airline back to viability, the controversial loan from the state was paid back in full. Symington and Phoenix's unusually tight circle of business leaders had succeeded at keeping America West solvent at the same time the group was increasingly maligned by average Arizonans as an antiquated, elitist "good-ol'-boy network."[7]

Symington's push to greatly expand trade with Mexico, Japan, and Europe didn't make as much news as most of his early policy moves. To him, though, greatly expanding trade was critical toward his goal of increasing state revenues at the same time taxes were cut.[8] Simply, he wanted to bring in more money through tourism (he called for a three-fold increase in tourism spending amid the budget crisis) while increasing the revenues of Arizona businesses—and thus state tax revenues—by negotiating trade pacts with foreign countries. Symington also proposed opening international trade offices in Mexico, Japan, and perhaps other countries, expanding greatly on Arizona's single trade office in Taiwan.[9]

The first trade office was opened in Mexico City with businessman David Clay as its director. The opening of the Mexico office came several months into a multipronged push by Symington to improve trade relations between foreign countries and the state.[10] While a flurry of trips by Symington, key staffers, and representatives of the business community were mostly greeted favorably by business leaders, Democrats increasingly portrayed the trade missions as junkets for Symington and his staff and friends. The media increasingly followed with criticism when the prices of the trips were revealed.[11]

Soon after the Mexico City trade office was opened, Symington traveled to Mexico City himself as five state senators traveled to Hermosillo in Arizona's Mexican neighbor state of Sonora.[12] A few weeks after Symington's trip, those same five senators joined a larger delegation of Latino lawmakers, businesspeople, and Symington staffer Annette Alvarez on a trip back to Mexico City, which included a meeting with Mexican President Carlos Salinas de Gortari and the country's secretary of commerce and industrial development.

One major goal of the bipartisan group: promote a proposal by America West to offer nonstop flights from Phoenix to Mexico City, a move that business leaders believed would not only boost the struggling airline but boost tourism and business relationships with Mexico.

The aggressive strategy, which throughout involved ongoing discussions between Mexican and Arizonan officials, was arguably a significant

Symington with Mexican president Carlos Salinas de Gortari at Los Pinos, the official residence of the president of Mexico until 2018. Courtesy of the Arizona State Library, Archives and Public Records, History and Archives Division, Phoenix, RG1_SG26_S6_ B22_F016_I01.

part of an economic boon for the state: According to US Department of Commerce numbers, Arizona's exports to Mexico doubled from 1991 to 1992, from $930 million to $1.8 billion.

While the trade negotiations with Mexico took place amid improving relations between the two countries on the national level (the North American Free Trade Agreement was being negotiated at the time), the people and political figures in the United States were becoming much less friendly toward the Japanese.

At the time, the Japanese auto industry seemed on the verge of destroying the US auto industry. Americans blamed the domestic auto industry problems on unfair trade policies while the Japanese blamed the trade imbalance on inferior American cars.

As "Buy American!" stickers appeared on cars and trucks throughout the United States, Symington and Arizona business leaders began their effort to convince the Japanese to buy Arizonan and perhaps, move more of their operations to facilities in the ever-sunny desert Southwest.[13] Both Toyota and Nissan already had test facilities in the desert outside Phoenix, and at the time, Arizona already was exporting nearly $400 million a year to Japan, making it the third largest buyer of Arizona goods behind Mexico and Canada.[14]

Symington and Arizona's business leaders knew there was an even bigger fish to catch: Arizona was in a unique position directly north of Mexico's west coast, a position that, if NAFTA would be approved in a way favorable to Arizona, could make Arizona an ideal location for Pacific Rim countries hoping to access the Mexican market.

Soon after Symington took office, his staff began negotiating with a business organization tied to Japan's Ministry of International Trade and Industry to locate a trade adviser in Phoenix. The adviser, who was sent to Phoenix the following year, was seen as a critical step to create inroads for small and midsized Arizona businesses. Essentially, the adviser for the group, known as JETRO, would inform and work as a liaison for companies hoping to expand into Japan.

At the same time, Symington began reaching out to dozens of Japanese companies to measure interest in developing ties to the state.[15] In September, Symington announced a major trip for an Arizona trade delegation to Japan to meet with business leaders.[16] Symington was confident he could succeed at building a uniquely lucrative relationship with the country.[17] After all, he was not just a businessman who had traveled internationally seeking investors for his projects; the major investor and the construction company building the Camelback Esplanade were two of Japan's largest and most influential companies.

Symington and eight others left for Japan on September 20. The group met with the leadership of nineteen major Japanese companies as well as government and tourism officials.

The delegation then spent two days at a resort in Hawaii on the return trip, which was billed as an opportunity to discuss the results of the trip and discuss what actions would be needed moving forward.[18] Upon the group's return, reporters were informed the trip's estimated cost was $20,000.

The trip received little attention outside the upper echelons of Arizona's business world, where Symington's aggressive trade overtures were generally supported and deemed productive.

Indeed, as 1991 came to a close, focus seemed to steer from Symington's policy initiatives toward a series of gaffes and questionable actions by him and his top administrators.

For one: the Japan trip and several other trade-delegation excursions were widely deemed unnecessary junkets.

Along with complaints about extravagant expenditures, several members of Symington's hastily assembled staff didn't appear up to the challenge of their new jobs.

Perhaps most damaging was the barrage of stories emerging from the RTC about Symington's financial dealings, particularly in the financing of the Camelback Esplanade and a much smaller development downtown called the Mercado.[19]

Reporters, columnists, radio hosts, cartoonists, and Democrats in the state began to throttle Symington and his administration for perceived miscues.

While Symington arguably achieved or put in motion the majority of his campaign promises within his first six months, polls began to show what was most important to Arizonans: they wanted drama-free state governance.

In one poll taken in October of his first year, 30 percent of respondents said Symington was doing a "good or excellent job," down from 40 percent in July. His job performance by October was rated as "poor" by 17 percent of those polled, a disturbing jump from only 12 percent in July. Another poll conducted by the *Republic* that month showed that, for the first time during his administration, less than 50 percent of respondents said they approved of his job performance.[20]

Symington and his supporters seemed baffled by the sagging poll numbers and increased focus on what they viewed as trifling matters. He arguably was doing what he promised; yet he was being viewed unfavorably by a majority of those he represented.

While Symington publicly blamed Democrats, the media, and the RTC for his dipping numbers, he also knew staff changes were needed.[21] He knew, too, that he had to regain control of his own narrative or he would, as one staffer later described it, "suffer political death by a thousand cuts."[22]

# Chapter 18

# THE DEVIL IS ALLEGEDLY IN THE DETAILS

Throughout Fife Symington's first year in office, rumors swirled that the Resolution Trust Corporation planned to bring a lawsuit against Symington and other past and present board members of Southwest Savings and Loan.

Stoking those rumors were repeated leaks from RTC officials to reporters about the RTC's ongoing investigation.

Particularly damaging (and infuriating to Symington and his attorney, John Dowd): On September 13, 1991, the *Washington Post* published excerpts of an internal memorandum written by RTC senior attorney Suzanne Rigby in which she stated, "Symington spent Southwest's funds with reckless abandon." Rigby said in the memo, which was marked "confidential," that Symington had "reaped a huge financial benefit and then walked away from the project virtually untouched."[1]

In October, a former RTC attorney gave a lengthy interview to a *Phoenix New Times* reporter suggesting he and other investigators were thwarted by top FDIC officials in their investigation of Southwest. The extensive *New Times* story also included passages of several letters written between banking regulators and Southwest officials in which regulators voiced concerned about the Esplanade deal. The story included quotes from a 1984 report from the Federal Home Loan Bank Board accusing Southwest directors of twice violating federal law in their dealings with Symington's project, claiming Southwest leadership failed to get written approval before entering into the Symington transaction and failed to obtain "a formal appraisal prior to the purchase."[2]

Dowd and Jay Smith fired numerous letters to newspaper editors in the Valley accusing them of imbalanced reporting,[3] but the drip-drip-drip of negative headlines continued to take a toll.[4] Symington's poll numbers slid at the same time Democrats felt emboldened—even amid a series of Symington wins—to finally bring out their long blades.

Dowd had begun preparing for any potential RTC case in the frantic hours prior to Senator Metzenbaum's S&L subcommittee hearing just before the gubernatorial election. Symington turned over troves of documents to Dowd and his partners, as did Symington's associates and accountants, and the Dowd team constructed what they felt was a strong defense against the RTC's claims.[5]

As the months passed after the Metzenbaum hearing, Symington's attorneys waited for requests for documents and interviews from RTC investigators that never came. The staff and attorneys at Dowd's law firm, Akin Gump, only communicated with RTC officials once between February and December of 1991. In that late September meeting, Symington's attorneys and Smith met with Alfred Byrne, general counsel of the FDIC, and a representative of the Inspector General's Office, regarding the leaking of the confidential material to the *Post* reporter.[6]

On December 17, 1991, as carolers and musicians performed Christmas songs in the finally bustling Esplanade, the RTC filed suit in federal court in Phoenix claiming that Symington and Southwest's other directors had caused tens of millions in losses by making unsafe loans, the largest of which paid for the land for the Esplanade and the expenses incurred by Symington during his years working to make the project a reality.[7]

Symington, Dowd, and one of Symington's real estate attorneys, Bill Shore, again brought out evidence that they claimed refuted the RTC allegations while, again, accusing the RTC of pursuing the Southwest case as a political hit on Symington, or to target Southwest officials because they were wealthier (at least billionaire owner Daniel Ludwig) and more vulnerable to lawsuits than most of the country's S&L directors. (Besides the relative wealth of Southwest's leadership team, the company had no liability insurance in place to shield members of its board from claims. Instead, Ludwig promised to absorb any claims against the thrift himself.)[8]

"Unlike most suits filed by the RTC against officers and directors of defunct S&Ls," a *Washington Post* article suggested, "the action against Southwest carries the potential for a huge recovery, since some of the former directors of the institution, including Symington, are wealthy. Others were insured against damage claims by one of the richest men in the world—reclusive billionaire shipping magnate Daniel K. Ludwig."[9]

RTC attorneys and officials countered by saying on several occasions that their legal complaint "spoke for itself."

That complaint said that Southwest directors had shirked their duties as outlined in federal bank law by taking part in risky investments that weren't properly vetted with federal officials. The biggest of the bad investments was Southwest's purchase and rezoning of the Friedman land on which the Esplanade was being built, a deal regulators claimed was also riddled with instances of conflicts of interest by Symington.

Specifically, the fifty-four-page suit, which sought $140 million from Symington and a dozen other former directors and officers, alleged that Southwest lost more than $236 million as a result of "negligent, imprudent decisions" and double dealing. The RTC alleged that $140 million of the losses came from just two developments—the La Paloma in Tucson in addition to the Camelback Esplanade. Resolving the Southwest collapse, the RTC estimated, would cost the government $941.4 million. In all, about seven pages of the suit related to Symington.[10]

By the time the lawsuit was filed in late 1991, the Esplanade encompassed the three hundred-room Ritz-Carlton, a pair of eleven-story office buildings, three restaurants, and a small upscale mall. According to a Phoenix leasing specialist familiar with the project, the first Esplanade office building was 93 percent full with several national companies for tenants. The newer tower was 50 percent occupied.[11]

The combined lease rate of the two towers was about average for commercial real estate properties in Phoenix at the time, two real estate experts told the *Republic*. Both said they considered the Esplanade "one of the top five" developments in the Valley.[12]

But even the biggest boosters admitted the Esplanade was feeling the recession. In stories in the *Republic, Gazette,* and the *Daily Star*, Symington and his company's success in shepherding the landmark development was always mitigated by lukewarm comments from tenants and economic prognosticators. The general manager of the Ritz-Carlton told the *Republic*'s Don Harris, "I think we're all doing fine," but would say little else because, he said, "articles tend to be looking at what's wrong rather than what's right."

A representative of the Greater Phoenix Convention and Visitors Bureau said the hotel was "holding its own." "It had a decent summer and a good fall" considering the languishing economy, the rep said.

"Just give it a little time, though," the Visitors Bureau spokesperson said. "It's set to take off once (the economy) gets going again."

While media outlets explored the long-term viability of the Esplanade, though, the current or future health of the Esplanade was not considered relevant in the RTC lawsuit, which focused primarily on the legality of the loan acquisition process for the project six years earlier.

So, by the end of 1991, the Camelback Esplanade was a bizarre Valley real estate dichotomy: It was being described as one of Arizona's finest developments at one of the most desired locations in the state at the same time it was lambasted as a disastrous white elephant, so poorly conceived that it crippled or sank most of the investors involved.

Symington had succeeded in getting the project mostly completed, but he had piled up debt that couldn't be serviced by the collapsing rate for high-end commercial lease space.

The Symington Company itself was still alive in late 1991, but it certainly wasn't thriving. During this time, Symington had to divorce himself from daily operations of his company as it tried to navigate the depths of the recession. Symington had incorrectly believed he could run his business while he ran the state, an idea that the state's newly minted attorney general, Grant Woods, had been quick to dismiss. It was left to Randy Todd, Symington's former second-in-command, to run the foundering company.[13]

After the RTC announced the suit, Symington, Dowd, and Shore held a ninety-minute press conference at the Esplanade during which the group presented detailed rebuttals to each RTC allegation. Then Symington went on the offensive, unleashing a chain of accusations and insults at the RTC's leadership and the investigators responsible for the lawsuit.[14]

"I will confront the RTC aggressively and do my best to expose their Gestapo-like tactics and bungling mismanagement of Arizona assets," he said.

"It's definitely what I could call a one-way Salem witch-burning," he added.

He then read the RTC's allegations one-by-one and responded in detail to each.[15]

Dowd held his own press conference afterward in which he reiterated Symington's points (with a bit less fire and more legalese) and then attacked the RTC's long list of claims with his own long list of detailed retorts.

For example, the RTC argued in the lawsuit that Symington and Southwest's vice president had deceived the thrift's board of directors by claiming the land for the Esplanade would cost $25.9 million while failing to notify the board of a $5 million line of credit promised to the land's seller—the Friedman Family Trust—as part of the deal.

Symington and Dowd provided documents they argued proved that the line of credit had been disclosed to the board and to state and federal regulators.[16] The RTC investigators, they said, didn't have the document because "they never asked for any documents," Dowd said.

Symington said that although he had eighty boxes of documents related to Southwest and the Esplanade's financial dealings, the RTC's investigators never asked to see those documents nor any others before making their accusations. The only contact Symington or his attorneys had with RTC investigators, Dowd said, was when Dowd and other attorneys met with RTC and other government officials in late September to discuss the leaked confidential document to the *Post*.[17]

Symington and Dowd offered copies of board minutes that appeared to confirm Symington had abstained from voting on the project on September 21, 1983. Symington offered his letter of resignation to the Southwest board on January 30, 1984, which, according to Symington and Dowd, meant that Symington was not involved with, and therefore not liable for, any Southwest actions after January of 1984.

The RTC complaint argued that Symington resigned months later, on March 22, 1984. That was the date the Southwest board of directors accepted Symington's resignation at their March 1984 meeting. Besides producing Symington's letter of resignation, Dowd also cited a Federal Home Loan Bank Board examiners report that stated "Mr. J. Fife Symington resigned as a Director on 1/30/84."

Symington had given Southwest board members a presentation regarding the Esplanade on September 20, 1983, while he was still a board member. The board voted unanimously to approve spending $25.9 million to purchase the land as well as spending an additional $5,450,000 to secure a line of credit for the Friedman Trust. Symington and Dowd produced the board meeting notes from the September meeting confirming that Symington abstained from the vote.

The RTC argued Symington was still in violation of conflict-of-interest laws regardless of his abstention from the vote.

According to board notes from the meeting, some board members worried about a potential conflict of interest as they discussed what Symington would be paid to get the land rezoned and prepared for construction. For investigators, a passage from the Southwest board minutes from

the meeting got to the heart of the issue: "The development fee of ap-
proximately $7.8 million for Director Symington was also discussed," the
minutes read. "The Chairman reported there was concern that Director
Symington had a conflict of interest in this project and informed the
directors this question would be addressed by the Federal Home Loan
Bank in the next few weeks. Director Lewis stated it was management's
recommendation that the Association proceed with this project."

To prove Southwest officials had properly sought approval from federal officials, Dowd produced a letter dated December 2, 1983, in which
Southwest President Donald Lewis requested a ruling regarding Symington's involvement from Charles Deardorff, a vice president within
the Federal Home Loan Bank who was in charge of S&L supervision.[18]
(A significant bone of contention moving forward: Southwest officials
claimed they got the necessary approval from Deardorff's office; RTC
officials said Southwest moved forward with the deal without official approval from Deardorff's office.)

Another key accusation: The RTC suit claimed Southwest's directors
and officials failed to properly oversee expenditures incurred during the
development of the Esplanade property and accused directors of allowing Symington to collect fees far beyond what was originally stated. In the
original agreement, Symington's estimated pre-development costs were
set at $2 million, of which he would receive a percentage of the money for
his work. (In the September 1983 meeting, $7.8 million was suggested as
a total payment to Symington over the planned ten years of the project.)
The costs, the RTC claimed, ended up being $13 million, $2.2 million of
which went to Symington and his team. Symington's group also received
$5.8 million once Esplanade construction began, the RTC contended.

RTC investigators, Symington and Dowd claimed, hadn't done their
research about the historically contentious and lengthy fight to gain approval from the city for rezoning and the final plan for the Esplanade's
height and design. Getting the Esplanade approved cost Southwest more
because much more work had to be done than initially projected. Symington contended that $13 million was spent during the two rounds of
the Esplanade zoning battle.

Also, at least according to figures presented by Symington and Dowd,
Southwest was doing well on their investment and would do better as
more Esplanade parcels sold.

Here are the key numbers as Symington and Dowd saw it:

Southwest spent about $31 million for the property (that's including the $5.4 million line of credit purchased for the Friedman Trust). The thrift then advanced "another $10-$13 million for development costs fees, etc.," according to Symington. Since the land was appraised at $31 million before zoning and then $64 million after it received approval for the Esplanade, Southwest had spent about $45 million for a $64 million piece of property.[19] Southwest received a total of $30 million in two payments as construction began on two pieces of the property. "Southwest thus is only $17 million short," Symington and Dowd argued in their written responses, an amount the thrift (meaning the RTC) would easily recover if the remaining three parcels of the property were sold once the Phoenix real estate market rebounded.

Symington argued that he personally only collected $1.4 million for his pre-development work, while the rest went to partners and subcontractors in the project. He argued that he and the Symington Company had earned that $1.4 million, saying to reporters, "I spent two years of my life and significant resources of my company on that zoning battle."

The RTC claimed that Southwest's management was negligent in assuming nearly all the risks related to the Friedman land purchase while Symington, who put up nearly nothing, looked to received nearly 40 percent of profits from the improved property. The land deal was "inherently unsafe and unfair to Southwest," the RTC contended. Symington countered that, in his agreement with Southwest, Southwest assumed the risk related only to the purchasing and rezoning of the undeveloped land. Symington's exposure—primarily that $9.2 million personal guarantee on the $169 million construction loan—was related to the Esplanade construction projects on the land.

"I did not, unlike the RTC bureaucrats, have a crystal ball," he was quoted as saying in a *Republic* story the next day. "In 1983, I could not foresee the crash in land values caused by the stupidity of the United States Congress."

Symington then accused the RTC of attempting to sully his wife's name. Ann was named in the lawsuit. The wives of many directors of failed thrifts in Arizona were being named in RTC lawsuits because Arizona was a "community property" state, meaning the government theoretically could have access to a spouse's property to pay back S&L losses even if the spouse wasn't involved in the thrift. Symington argued that not only was Ann not involved with Southwest, he and his wife had no community property together because they had signed a prenuptial agreement stating that their personal finances would remain separate.[20]

As the RTC's case against Southwest clouded Symington's new administration, he was also hounded by accusations of excessive patronage in his hiring and favoritism toward old business associates in state contracting.[21]

Particularly aggressive in deconstructing Symington's hirings was David Bodney, then editor of *New Times*, who nearly weekly wrote heavily reported pieces about Symington's finances or questionable hires. In September 1991, Bodney wrote a pair of cutting articles quoting a collection of business leaders complaining about the job former campaign staffer Annette Alvarez was doing as "international relations aide."

Particularly critical of Alvarez's work was Japan's consul general, Tom Kadomoto, who, according to Bodney, claimed Alvarez "ruined a golden opportunity to have a senior trade representative of the Japanese External Trade Organization placed at the Capitol—an exorbitant gaffe that has deeply offended Japanese government officials."[22]

In several cases, daily newspapers in the state then used the muckraking newsweekly's stories as sources for stories daily editors seemed reticent to report themselves.[23]

"Symington aide called unqualified," a *Tucson Citizen* headline read in October. The story's second paragraph read: "The *New Times*, a Phoenix-based weekly newspaper, said Annette Alvarez was appointed to her $60,000 job as a top aide to Symington only because of her close friendship with the governor."

The *Los Angeles Times* also did a story that extensively quoted *New Times*. Symington told the *Times* reporter that Alvarez "is here to stay and she is terrific and that *New Times* stuff is total baloney, and we realize that we're just going to have to put up with it."

Symington was also accused of traveling from the state too much. A September 3, 1991, Associated Press story noted he had spent nearly two of his first six months in office outside of Arizona, with six trips to California and two to Mexico in the mix.[24] Press Secretary Doug Cole argued that Arizonans should want their governor traveling to explore trade opportunities: "We have a very activist governor who is going, going, going. He sees an opportunity, and he goes after it," Cole told the AP.

(In a later interview, Cole described the second half of 1991 as "one of the most difficult periods of the administration. It never seemed like we could get any momentum.")[25]

But the frustration building in the governor's office didn't seem to impact the governor himself. Even his heated responses to accusations, particularly those from the RTC, were calm and urbane in tone. "He just went about his business," Cole said later.

• • •

Occasionally, the new job provided Symington with some reinvigorating, once-in-a-lifetime highs, often in the form of some event that made being Arizona governor the challenge and adventure Symington had imagined it being.

Amid the tumultuous fall of 1991, for example, Symington was asked to hike into the Grand Canyon with then president George H. W. Bush.

The president, who had been pushing a clean-air initiative, decided he wanted to see for himself the air pollution from California that was increasingly fouling the air over the Grand Canyon. Bush, who had hosted a fundraiser for Symington earlier that year, wanted Symington to join him for a tour of the canyon. On a clear September day, Air Force One landed at the tiny airport at Tusayan, Arizona. From there, Bush, Symington, and Secretary of the Interior Manuel Lujan rode together to the canyon's South Rim in the presidential limousine.

During the ride, Symington said in a later interview, Bush told him: "Fife, I want you to stay close to me when we hike into the canyon. You know these press people: they're not in very good shape and I want to have some fun with them."[26]

At the time, soon after the end of the successful Gulf War, President Bush was at the height of his popularity. In front of a hoard of cameras and local and national journalists, Symington was given the opportunity to pal around with a president sporting a nearly 90 percent approval rating.

Bush, a former college baseball star who exercised daily, was itching for a hike when he reached the South Rim. Soon Bush, Symington, and Lujan, followed by a gaggle of US Secret Service agents and reporters, were bounding down the trail from Mather Point.[27]

After about thirty minutes, the group found a suitable location for a photo op and Bush gave a short speech about the importance of a clean-air program to protect national treasures like the Grand Canyon.

Symington with George Bush, Secretary of the Interior Manny Lujan (far left), EPA Administrator William K. Reilly (far right), and a NPS ranger during the president's visit to the Grand Canyon, 1991. Courtesy of the Arizona State Library, Archives and Public Records, History and Archives Division, Phoenix, RG1_SG26_S6_B11_F36_I05.

Then, according to Symington, Bush grabbed his shoulder and said: "Now, stay close. We're going to have some fun."

Bush set a brisk pace up the switchback trail to the South Rim.[28] Symington, who exercised regularly, stayed at his side. Within a few hundred yards, though, most in the press corps began to struggle to keep up. Near the halfway mark Bush and Symington turned around to see a long, spread-out line of hunched figures struggling up the trail.

Bush, Symington, and Bush's Secret Service agents reached the end of the trail alone. From there the group watched the long line of stragglers struggling up the last several hundred yards of the trail.

But the joy of exhausting journalists soon turned to a serious medical emergency: Interior Secretary Lujan also wasn't terribly fit. As the trailing group approached the rim, Lujan sat down on a rock complaining of chest pains. He was carried the remainder of the way on a stretcher and taken to a nearby hospital.

Lujan recovered quickly, and the day was ultimately an invigorating success for Symington. He had spent the day at the president's side amid one of the world's greatest backdrops for photo ops. And by being able to stay at Bush's side, he had hours to build a relationship and discuss issues.

"If only every day could be like that day," Symington mused later.[29]

That good news day quickly faded from public memory. Such one-and-done events don't need media follow-ups. The news cycle was soon fed again by new angles on the plot lines of staff dysfunction and personal financial duress.

His poll numbers continued to slip. By early 1992—within half a year of being broadly heralded for his successes—he was, outside his Republican base, a very unpopular governor.

# Chapter 19

# A TALE OF TWO 1992s

The New Year began for the Symington administration with a *Time* magazine story describing Symington as the "latest candidate for rogue in Arizona's political gallery." The existence of a national story on Symington became a local story. The main thrust of the criticism: Symington promised a return to normalcy. Arizona was being mocked once again on the national stage for a newsworthy lack of normalcy.

Symington's RTC scrum and staff blunders likely wouldn't have shown up on *Time*'s radar if not for Mecham, the Keating Five, and AzScam before them. Unfair or not, though, Symington was being bundled with three recent generators of bad local press on the national stage.

In late March, a cabinetmaker named Michael McNally announced he would begin a petition drive to have Symington recalled.[1] Within two months, McNally claimed to have seven hundred volunteers canvassing the state who had collected nearly 200,000 signatures (those numbers were never independently confirmed because the drive fell short of the necessary signatures).[2]

Arizona State pollster Bruce Merrill had Symington's approval rating below 25 percent by late spring, which, he pointed out, was a "lower percentage than we ever measured for Evan Mecham."

As Merrill pointed out, Mecham had a right-wing base that stayed with him no matter what he said or did. But when more moderate Republicans like Symington struggled, Merrill argued, there was no immovable ideological base of supporters that would stick around through tough times.[3]

(To be fair, no statewide political figure was faring well amid the S&L scandal and sickly economy in early 1992. Indeed, it was a significant news story when Symington's poll numbers got so bad they dropped below those of US Senator Dennis DeConcini, a Democrat, and Republican Senator John McCain.)[4]

Democrats in the state legislature had gone from complimenting Symington's style to engineering a lawsuit in which the legislature accused Symington of abusing his line-item veto powers (the first such suit in Arizona history). The RTC case loomed. In a few cases, as Merrill pointed out, Symington had appeared to handle criticism and calls for changes in his administration with a "public be damned" attitude. Speaking of Symington's refusal to shake up a staff that often was drawing headlines for questionable behavior, Merrill suggested: "There's a certain arrogance there that these people and these relationships are more important than the people of Arizona."

Merrill did predict Symington's poor numbers could easily reverse if he could get the press and people looking again at policy and governing successes rather than financial woes and staff blunders.

That would be difficult. Extra reporters from the five largest newspapers in the state—the *Republic* and the afternoon *Phoenix Gazette*, the *Mesa Tribune*, the *Tucson Citizen*, and the *Arizona Daily Star*—had been assigned to cover the increasing number of story threads emerging throughout Symington's first year. *Phoenix New Times* and *Tucson Weekly*, the major weeklies in the state, had former daily investigative reporters focused on the Symington administration. Television reporters increasingly dug for new leads from within a government that had become the top story in the state. Perceived administration gaffes were becoming punch lines on morning radio, and even the *Republic*'s right-leaning editorial writers seemed to focus more on missteps than policy.

Several spheres of influence quickly formed within the governor's office, two top Symington staffers said later. Throughout the first year of Symington's administrations, a power struggle within the office sometimes created mixed messages to legislators and the public. A few staffers became favorite sources for area reporters as they leaked dirt on their adversaries in the office.[5]

Two of Symington's appointed staffers, George Leckie and for a shorter period, Annette Alvarez, drew much of the accusations of questionable behavior.[6] In the years to come, as most of the palace intrigues of 1991 and early 1992 faded, it would be Leckie's actions as a Symington staffer that would most dog Symington's administration throughout his tenure.

After Leckie's successful stint as Symington's campaign finance chairman (he raised more than $2 million), Symington rolled him into the

position of deputy chief of staff, first under chief of staff Bunny Badertscher, then under her replacement in early 1992, Chris Herstam. As
such, Leckie was in charge of the office budget and personnel issues.

Leckie was blamed for hefty over-expenditures in the governor's office that led to a projected $271,000 shortfall for the administration's first
year. One of the problems: Seven staffers received $10,000 pay increases
in their first year.[7] To stave off busting his budget, Symington drastically
cut his staff and the pay of those who remained. Three staff members
were laid off, five were transferred to other state departments, and all
remaining staff members were forced to take an 11.2 percent pay cut.

As reporters began digging into state financial records, more stories about Leckie's dealings came to light. Leckie had once erroneously
claimed he was working during a week he was on vacation. He billed a
state fund more than a thousand dollars for a vacation with his girlfriend,
which he didn't repay until after a reporter questioned him about the
expenditure. He continued to pay two aides out of the governor's budget
after they had quit their jobs. Under his watch, more than $200,000 was
paid to a Florida lottery consultant without seeking competitive bids.

Leckie argued that most of the issues were rookie mistakes or, in the
case of the consultant, simply the going price for the best consultant to
help turn around the state's struggling lottery. Symington vehemently defended Leckie, but ultimately moved him from financial oversight of the
governor's office to oversight of Project SLIM, Symington's ambitious,
multimillion-dollar project to identify wasteful spending and streamline
state government.

Leckie was then accused of funneling Project SLIM contracts to
friends and business associates, most notably to the accounting firm that
handled Symington's business accounts, Coopers & Lybrand.

As reporters dug for more Leckie-related news, they found a police report in the Paradise Valley Justice Court showing that, one evening three
years earlier, Leckie had hit a car and a bicyclist while making a U-turn,
then hit the driver of the car as she emerged from her car to look for any
damage.

Leckie told police he had had "four or five glasses" of wine during
a business-related dinner. He told police he wasn't intoxicated and the
police did not do sobriety tests. Neither the bicyclist nor the car's driver
were seriously injured. Ultimately, Leckie pleaded guilty to two minor

traffic-related misdemeanors, paid a $215 fine, and was ordered to take driving classes.

Morning radio personalities and newspaper columnists spent days joking about the bizarre traffic incident. For Symington and his staff, it felt like a cheap shot from the media regarding a trivial traffic matter.[8]

But many others saw it as even more proof that Leckie was a major liability for Symington. Yet Symington stood behind Leckie, which drew more fire on Symington.[9]

While Symington enumerated Annette Alvarez's successes as a trade liaison, others downplayed her accomplishments and instead focused on a series of problematic financial issues. In March of 1992, it was reported that the Symington campaign had paid the federal government $9,000 that Alvarez had owed in back taxes. Symington staffers said they simply signed over to the government consulting fees and salary owed to Alvarez.

*Republic* reporter Mary Jo Pitzl then found that Alvarez had failed to pay the state back for more than $1,000 she had spent during a trade-related trip to New York. Symington had put the price of a hotel and other expenses on his credit card. Alvarez claimed to Pitzl that she had repaid Symington, but Pitzl's reporting showed that she hadn't. The money was finally paid back.

Alvarez said the issue was nothing more than an oversight, but it was yet another small story that became another of a growing number of embarrassments for Symington.

Even more disruptive: rumors spread that Symington and Alvarez were romantically involved, a notion sparked in large part by the amount of time they spent together on trade missions and the appearance of financial favoritism. Those rumors were fueled by a note Alvarez wrote during the gubernatorial campaign that was leaked to the press. In the note, Alvarez seemed to allude to a romantic relationship with Symington in passages such as "I do know I love you." "And it will be forever, but I don't think it's the kind of love I'm looking for." Symington vehemently denied the accusations; Alvarez described her feelings for Symington as "nothing more than an inappropriate crush." No proof of an affair emerged, but the innuendos had a long and colorful shelf life for Symington's detractors.[10]

In an interview years later, Pitzl summed up the media response to the Alvarez allegations this way: "We looked at it, but nothing significant came of it. I was gathering a lot of material but there was a wariness that we needed to have absolute, bullet-proof evidence, and my editors were definitely not comfortable with what we had."[11]

Neither Alvarez nor Leckie quit as the revelations mounted.[12] By mid-March of 1992, Symington, increasingly protective of his staffers and furious at members of the media, was looking more and more like a besieged leader at the helm of an administration adrift.

By June, though, the media spotlight on Symington's underlings began to dim. The governor, with considerable nudging from numerous leading Republicans and Republican strategists, had begun to overhaul his top staff.[13]

Alvarez resigned at the end of March.[14] Responding to her resignation, Symington thanked her for what he described as her tireless and effective work establishing new trade relations for the state.

George Leckie resigned in late May. In a written response to Leckie's resignation, Symington thanked Leckie for "revitalizing" Project SLIM, contributing to economic development in the state, and for correcting "a seriously deteriorating situation" with the long-floundering state lottery.

Perhaps even more important for stability in the Symington administration was the resignation of chief-of-staff Chris Herstam. Herstam, a respected former legislator, had often been opposed to the governor's policies and decisions during Herstam's four-month tenure as chief of staff. Herstam, politically more centrist than Symington, quickly became a favorite off-the-record source for reporters who had known him from his time in the state legislature. It was Herstam, Symington and many others in the administration believed, who was the source of many of the leaks and news tips coming out of the governor's office.[15]

Herstam resigned in late May.

Symington needed someone he could trust in that job, someone respected in the community, and someone with significant government administrative experience. He needed someone to help bring order back to his administration.

Jay Smith suggested their mutual friend and longtime political ally, Peter Hayes, who, at the time, was manager of government relations for the powerful statewide utility, the Salt River Project. Prior to his work with SRP, Hayes was a staffer for US Representative John Rhodes, with whom Symington had long worked closely. Symington approached

Symington's chief of staff, Peter Hayes, in 1992. Courtesy of the Arizona State Library, Archives and Public Records, History and Archives Division, Phoenix, RG1_SG26_S6_B05_F05_I21.

Hayes. Hayes argued he didn't have the right experience for the job; Symington explained why he was wrong. Hayes reluctantly agreed to take the job on one condition—that he could quit after one year and return to his old job.[16]

Political and business insiders broadly agreed Hayes was an inspired choice, considering the situation. Not only did Hayes have administrative experience, as a lobbyist for one of Arizona's most powerful and respected entities, he had a wealth of goodwill stored up with business and state leaders. He carried no baggage. And he was nearly legendary in the region for his charismatic wine-and-dine ways of getting what he needed without burning bridges.

Just the appearance of Hayes seemed to re-grant Symington a honeymoon phase.

Arguably more significant over the long term was the quiet hire of a "special assistant for policy development." Two months earlier, a top Republican, who like others was concerned about the governor's staff issues, suggested Symington meet with a young attorney and conservative policy wonk named Jay Heiler, who had worked in the state attorney general's office in the late 1980s. Heiler had left Arizona to become an editorial writer for the *Richmond Times-Dispatch* but was interested in returning home. Symington agreed to meet with Heiler.

Heiler, though, had little interest in meeting Symington.[17] Heiler, known as a conservative firebrand since his days editing Arizona State University's college newspaper, felt Symington was, as he later said, "a bored business guy." Heiler felt Symington's struggling administration would be a bad place for him to land back in Arizona, and Heiler felt he had no ideological kinship with Arizona's leader. "I thought he was a sort of Great Gatsby figure who decided to get himself elected to office and then tried to be a warm fuzzy figure and make everybody love him," Heiler said later.

Heiler changed his mind as the two discussed politics and political philosophy. Heiler said he came to believe that Symington was an engaged, natural leader who had a strong understanding of policy and a core appreciation for, and knowledge of, the mechanisms of fiscal conservatism.

Heiler quickly saw his calling: He would help the impressive Fife Symington he had just met replace the rudderless Gatsby caricature of Fife Symington he believed he would meet.

Symington said he needed help getting back on track, so Heiler offered his thoughts on what needed to be done.

"You've been put in a weakened position," Heiler argued. "You've tried a little too much to attempt to try to be all things to all people.

"You know what happens to politicians who are determined to walk a moderate path while they're in office?" Heiler asked rhetorically. "You have to be very adept at it. If you aren't, you end up looking squishy and irresolute and you end up with no real firm support from anybody anywhere on the political spectrum."

Besides restructuring the office, Heiler argued Symington needed to create a clear policy strategy, what Heiler later described as "a strong activist agenda."[18]

Heiler would become Symington's Cardinal Richelieu and more than

Top Symington aide Jay Heiler during a school visit in 1993. Courtesy of the Arizona State Library, Archives and Public Records, History and Archives Division, Phoenix, RG1_SG26_S6_B02_F023_I01.

anyone beyond the governor, the person who shaped Symington's policy through the remaining five years of his tenure.

Along the way, Heiler often would be accused of, or credited with, pushing Symington into hard right positions that seemed at odds with the moderate Republican Arizonans elected in 1991.[19]

Along with the staff shakeup and the addition of Hayes and Heiler, Symington had a series of small victories and bursts of good optics through the late spring and summer of 1992.

In late February, prior to the arrival of Hayes and Heiler, Symington went before a congressional subcommittee in Washington to answer
questions about the Southwest Savings affair. Symington forcefully attacked the RTC investigation as a political hit job and belittled the competency of investigators after errors in the RTC claims were identified.[20]
He said he had no intention of settling with the RTC, claiming, "I want
unconditional surrender."[21]

Few cared locally, but on the national stage, Symington's performance
in front of the subcommittee drew broad praise from top Republicans.

The state budget Symington proposed in January of 1992 was still
holding its form in spring as budget negotiations crawled along in the
legislature. "The Symington Plan" was still leading the discussion even
when it was under attack.

Also that spring, the governor was faced with a unique emergency, the
handling of which would either support the recent public portrait of an
ineffectual blunderer or the earlier one of a decisive, world-wise leader
uniquely qualified to solve the problems of the troubled state.

For years leading up to early 1992, Arizona's Native American tribes
had argued they had the right to operate full casino-style gambling operations on their reservation lands. As a series of legal challenges by the
tribes failed, five Arizona tribes had continued to operate casino-style
slot machines. In early 1992, the US Attorney for Arizona sent the five
tribes letters ordering them to stop operation of those slot machines.
Tribal leaders ignored the letter. In early April, the US Attorney, Linda
Akers, sent another letter threatening that FBI agents would be sent to
confiscate the slot machines if the tribes continued operating them.

The five tribes ignored the US Attorney again.

At the heart of the escalating tensions was this: Although casino-
style gambling was legal on reservations within the United States, the
gambling was only legal within states that had agreed to allow gambling
within their borders. Simply: Arizonans and their leaders had not agreed,
so by federal law, the tribes within Arizona were in violation of federal
law by operating gaming halls without an agreement with the state.

On May 12, 1992, FBI agents raided the gambling operations of all five
tribes. The largest and most contentious raid took place at the bingo hall
on the Fort McDowell Indian Gaming Center. There, agents with guns
drawn entered the building at 6 a.m., then directed the loading of the

video poker and slot machines onto moving vans rented from Mayflower Transit.

In response, casino workers and other Fort McDowell Mohave-Apache Indian Community members used their cars, pickup trucks, and several massive green dump trucks to block the eight moving vans full of 350 video gaming machines from leaving the parking lot.[22] By about 8:30 a.m., dozens of tribal members were in a standoff with the forty FBI agents and US Marshals who had raided the gambling hall. "I will stand and fight for these machines to come back so our children can have something for their future," tribal member Kimberly Williams told an Associated Press reporter during the standoff.[23]

The governor's office wasn't notified until around noon. It was newspaper reporter Mark Flatten, not any public official, who alerted the state's leadership with a call to Symington's press secretary, Doug Cole, from a phone booth near the standoff.[24]

When the governor's office was notified of the raid and standoff, Symington and his top staffers rushed to a waiting helicopter at Sky Harbor for the ten-minute flight to the Fort McDowell site.[25]

The governor's helicopter landed near a parking lot where protesters were blocking the moving vans. Symington rushed from the helicopter toward the center of the standoff and began attempting to defuse the situation.

It was, at the very least, an impressive entrance.

Previous to the standoff, both Symington and Arizona Attorney General Grant Woods had been supportive of a move by federal authorities to confiscate the slot machines if the tribes continued to defy the court orders. It was the state that had argued successfully that such gambling machines were illegal in Arizona, and thus on reservations within the state, but Arizona state agencies had no authority on reservation lands.[26]

As Arizona's governor stood on reservation land amid federal agents and tribal members, he technically had less say in the issue than any other person in the group.

Still, Symington was able to talk federal officials into allowing a ten-day moratorium on the removal of the gaming machines so the issue could be discussed further, a deal that was accepted by Tribal President Clinton Pattea after a twenty-five-minute, closed-door meeting with Symington. The Mayflower trailers full of gambling machines were unhitched and left to sit as federal authorities drove away and the protesters mostly disbursed (the makeshift barricades, however, remained, and about two dozen tribal members spent the night in the parking lot).[27]

A paragraph in a *Republic* story the following day summed it up this way: "Fearing violence, Symington persuaded both sides to let the machines remain in the gaming-center parking lot for ten days under private guard."

It was a good day for the governor, even though all involved knew the issue of gambling on Arizona's reservations was far from over.[28]

During that ten-day "cooling off" time, Symington, his staff, and several outside advisers created a thirty-two-page proposal outlining new parameters for gambling on tribal lands within Arizona.[29]

At the same time, Republican Attorney General Grant Woods pressed his case that it was his job—not the governor's—to speak for the state in negotiations with tribes.[30]

Symington and Woods traded stern letters accusing each other of overstepping their legal authority. "Arizona law is clear and unambiguous," Woods wrote. "I, not you, am the one to resolve claims against the state of Arizona; your role is one of consent, nothing more."[31]

Symington argued: "Because of your apparent confusion as to whether you represent the tribe, the governor, or the attorney general without a client, I believe it is important for us to discuss your role as legal counsel to the governor."

Woods took particular offense at this statement. He had stated on several occasions since Symington had taken office that the state attorney general represents the state of Arizona, not the sitting governor. "My 'client' is the state of Arizona, not you."[32]

To many observers, the spat looked like little more than political posturing for a Republican primary still two years away. Woods, a charismatic young centrist Republican, would be a serious challenge to Symington in 1994, especially if Symington floundered as he did in the fall of 1991 and the early months of 1992.

After discussions with Woods that more clearly laid out responsibilities in the negotiations, Symington presented the proposal to tribal leaders. Symington had clearly softened his stance on gaming on tribal lands in the state. Tribal leaders were frustrated by the number of gaming restrictions in the proposal and worried that agreeing to state restrictions impinged on their sovereignty. But with the deal, they could have casino-style gambling without relentless litigations and the constant threat of raids.

Symington's draft gaming compact included one major concession to the tribes: Slot machines and video games of chance would be authorized. More expansive gaming would be dependent on the outcome of a lawsuit that five tribes had filed against the state.

With that authorization, though, came restrictions. There could be only one gaming operation on each reservation, and no more than 250 slot machines at those locations. Payment for wagers could not exceed $250. The tribes would give the state jurisdiction to enforce the gaming laws agreed upon with the state.[33]

The first Arizona tribe signed a compact with the state in early July. While several other tribes signed compacts in the second half of the year, several more continued to haggle for looser regulations into the next year.[34]

Although the battle over the size of casinos and what types of games would be legal was far from settled by the end of the year, Symington emerged from the Indian gaming intrigues of 1992 with broadly positive reviews from the public.

"Throughout the affair," one *Republic* editorial stated in late May, "Gov. Symington has displayed decisive leadership."[35]

Symington also began ramping up efforts to get the issue of a state-recognized Martin Luther King Jr. Day onto the next ballot. Symington's argument for both the moral imperative of the move and yes, the economic value of making up with the NFL, quickly seemed to impact public sentiment on the issue. By the summer of 1992, the majority of Arizonans being polled were in favor of creating the holiday.

Commenting on Symington's support for the increasingly popular holiday, pollster Bruce Merrill suggested, "It's possible to be conservative in one area and liberal in another."[36]

With the resignation of most of the staffers and those feeding stories to the press made unwanted headlines, Symington increasingly made headlines only for his actions and decisions made in the normal course of governing. Peter Hayes, the new chief of staff, appeared to be successfully guiding the administration into quieter waters. (For Hayes, no news was good news.)[37] The RTC case loomed, but little new came from investigators in the second half of 1992.[38]

Symington increasingly felt like he was surrounded by a loyal crew of

Symington staffer Doug Cole outside his office on the ninth floor of the Arizona State
Capitol Executive Tower, 1993. Courtesy of the Arizona State Library, Archives and
Public Records, History and Archives Division, Phoenix, RG1_SG26_S6_B004_F023_I68.

seasoned professionals.[39] It became, as Doug Cole would say later, more
of a military-like environment with chain-of-command. Policies and
courses of action were debated "heatedly," Cole said, "but in the end, Fife
was the guy people elected to be governor and it was his decision and
when he made his decision, we all charged in that direction."[40]

Symington's poll numbers slowly improved through the year. As one
pollster said, the basic message from Arizonans was becoming clear: Take
away the nonsense and Symington could be a popular leader.

# Chapter 20

# BIG BUDGET FEUD

Fife Symington had been governor for nine months before he gave his first State of the State address. The January before, when he should have been giving his first address to the people of Arizona, he was instead scrambling to raise money for his runoff election against Terry Goddard.

Symington clearly could have used the policy bully pulpit and feel-good boost that comes with that first grand-opening speech.

Cheated of that proper introduction, Symington needed his first State of the State in January of 1992 to get right to the point. He needed to talk cold, hard policy to get back on schedule with the sweeping "Symington Plan."

He wanted $60 million in tax cuts for Arizonans. He wouldn't take less. Government, he said, was going to be put "on a severe diet" in an effort to lower the tax bills of Arizonans, with the largest proportional cuts to those in the middle and lower income brackets.

Symington and the Symington Plan were channeling the ideas of one of the most prominent fiscal conservatives of the time—Art Laffer, the famed inventor of the supply-sider's hallowed "Laffer Curve."[1]

Laffer had been an economic adviser to Ronald Reagan during the 1980s. After 1988, he began serving as a consultant for mostly Republican government officials throughout the country.[2] Laffer used his simple curve (which he often literally drew out for his bosses and clients) to illustrate the idea that somewhere between taxation of zero percent—which obviously produces no government income—and a tax rate of 100 percent—which obviously leaves no income for taxpayers—there is an ideal tax rate at which the economy will reach its fullest potential while fully funding government. That theoretical sweet spot, Laffer argued, leads to a supply-side conclusion in which lower taxes, particularly for top earners and generators of wealth, will actually generate enough increased government revenue, thanks to a more robust economy that

Symington giving his first State of the State Address. To his right: Senate President Pete Rios and Speaker of the House Jane Hull. Courtesy of the Arizona State Library, Archives and Public Records, History and Archives Division, Phoenix, RG1_SG26_S6_ B004_F007_I23.

offsets any potential deficit caused by reducing upper-income tax rates.

"Nonsense justification for tax cuts for the rich," is what one top Democrat called Laffer's supply-side ideas just as Symington was pitching those ideas to Arizonans.[3]

During his first term, Symington invited Laffer to speak to his staff to explain the economic philosophy that, for Symington, was an accessible Americanized incarnation of the ideas of his economic lodestar, Friedrich Hayek. (Not coincidentally, Hayek was the economist who most influenced Great Britain's conservative legend, Margaret Thatcher; he was later presented the Presidential Medal of Freedom by George H. W. Bush.)

In a later interview, one of Symington's chiefs of staff, Wes Gullett, described the Laffer sessions this way:

"Ours was a supply-side philosophy and it was a supply-side philosophy to the point where Fife would have Art Laffer come to staff meetings and we would be required—the entire staff would be required—to spend the day with Art Laffer so that he could . . . educate us on why we believed what we believed."[4]

Symington was itching to overhaul Arizona's tax policies to reflect the concepts of Laffer and other fiscal conservatives he respected. But while the proposed $60 million tax cut drew cheers and widespread support, it only equated to an extra dinner and a movie for the bottom half of earners. Although he announced tens of millions in tax and budget cuts, he believed most of the savings would come from acting on the findings of Project SLIM.[5]

With the cuts came a bit of "compassionate conservative" expenses. He wanted a small inflation-countering raise for state workers, $10 million for programs for the profoundly mentally ill, and another $1 million for at-risk preschool children.

Obviously, something had to give in the Symington-proposed budget. His budget didn't include the usual extra funding for public schools to offset inflation increases, a move that would save the state about $80 million.

Another $80 million would be saved by slashing the budget of the state's medically needy, medically indigent program (MNMI), a move that would impact an estimated 45,000 people in Arizona without health care.[6]

Arizona's three universities would receive no funding hikes. Community colleges would lose $10 million.

Once state government was "lean and mean," he would push for deeper tax cuts.[7]

Although his education and healthcare cuts drew sharp criticism and seemed to go against public opinion, polls also showed that Arizonans were still broadly on board with Symington's tough-love fiscal trajectory.[8]

Fewer people seemed on board with his idea to bring charter schools to Arizona. Fewer still seemed to support his plan to offer vouchers to parents who chose to send their children to charter schools.

Under the overarching goal of expanding "borderless educational opportunities for Arizona students" (and in theory, forcing free-market competition that would force all schools to improve to keep students), plans were put in motion to allow charter schools to operate in the state.

If Symington had his way, Arizona would be close on the heels of Minnesota, which had just become the first state to sanction a charter-school system.[9]

Minnesota would be the template for proposals and programs that would soon be pitched in nearly every state in the nation with greatly varying success.

"The idea behind this revolution is simple," wrote educator and historian Jon Schroeder in his history of Minnesota's charter schools. "Grant parents, teachers and others in the community the opportunity to start and run new public schools outside the direct control of local school districts."[10]

Schroeder continued: "They would be less regulated, but would have to abide by the underlying principles of public education: open to all, publicly funded, no discrimination, no tuition, no teaching religion. They would be judged on the results they achieved."

In Minnesota, the new schools were granted a "charter" by the state that would define academic success and outline the scope of the school's mandate. The charters were similar to those used by early state legislatures to begin operation of state colleges and universities.

For each student enrolled, the schools received the state's per-pupil education expenditure.

Symington had hoped Arizona could beat Minnesota to the punch, or at least achieve a tie. But more so than in Minnesota (a state well known for being game for pioneering ideas), the idea was problematic to many educators and wholly alien to a public raised in public schools.

In Arizona, charter school opponents worried that charter schools would undermine existing schools. If most of the students who migrated to charter schools were higher-achieving learners from underperforming public schools in underserved neighborhoods, they asked, how would those underperforming schools ever improve to serve those who stayed behind?[11]

Also, how would an underfunded state education department (already struggling to oversee its districts) properly monitor a loose confederacy of new schools?

Arizona is not Minnesota. But Arizonans increasingly seemed ready to try new ideas for old problems in its public schools. Symington and the pro-charter school blocks in the education and business community were ready in 1992 with detailed legislation to make Arizona the second state that allowed charter schools.

Symington's first State of the State drew mixed reviews.[12] "State of the State addresses by previous governors have been interrupted frequently by applause," Mary K. Reinhart of the *Daily Star* wrote. "Symington drew applause just five times, once when he mentioned his support for a holiday honoring the Rev. Martin Luther King Jr. and four times during his proposal to cut taxes by $60 million."

"It may not last as long as an ice cube on a Gila Bend sidewalk in July," a *Tucson Citizen* editorial began the following day. "But Gov. Fife Symington's State of the State speech proposal to cut taxes was as refreshing as, well, ice on a 110-degree day."[13]

Like his ideas or not, several editorial writers concluded that he had articulated clear goals and a solid plan of action, qualities often lacking in such addresses.

It was then time to dive into the trenches of the legislative session. Budget and legislative negotiations that year were likely to be a brawl. As the session started, the majority Democrats in the senate knew they were dealing with a weakened Republican in the governor's office. With the 28 percent approval rating Symington charted in January, they could be more forceful in opposing his more traditionally conservative initiatives.[14]

At the same time, Democrats still knew that budget sacrifices would have to be made amid a recession. And much of Symington's plan was still moderate if not, as in some of his environmental and at-risk children initiatives, downright left-leaning.

By late March, Symington was already frustrated enough at senate Democrats to write them a line-in-the-sand letter: He would not sign any budget that didn't include several of his key demands.

He was willing to close down the government unless the 1992-93 budget included $60 million in tax cuts and $4.5 million for his waste-hunting Project SLIM. He also wanted his clean-air measures approved.

The letter sent to each Democrat in the senate did not go over well.

"If you want something done, the least effective thing you can do is a mass postcard mailing," the *Republic* quoted Democratic senator David Bartlett as saying. "If you really care about these bills, you could . . . call us on the phone."

Republican John Greene stabbed back: "If the governor had enough time to come and sit down with all the prima donnas in the body, we'd have a governor that wasn't doing his job."[15]

By early May, Symington and members of the legislature of both parties were in an unusual position. In the dismal economy, tax revenue projections were dire enough that Democrats and Republicans alike were resigned to painful cuts in state spending. Looking at a $100 million shortfall to maintain state services, Senator Gutierrez, the Senate Appropriations Committee Chairman, sounded like a Symington conservative when he announced, "I don't see how we can get away from a real potential for layoffs" of state government employees.

Everyone had their knives out, but Symington was still at odds with legislators on where to cut and how deeply. He had struggled, too, to push his signature policy initiatives of education reform and tax deductions, as well as environmental protection actions that went too far for some Republicans and not far enough for some Democrats.

In the second week of May, Symington sent a letter to the heads of state agencies instructing them to have protocols in place to allow an orderly shutdown of the government on June 30 if a budget deal hadn't been reached. It was a warning to legislators as much as a directive to agencies: He would shut down government before he would watch his policy babies die.

Pete Rios, the senate's president who had spoken somewhat fondly of Symington the year before, brought up the fact that Symington had taken a vacation amid the grinding budget negotiations.

"My position is the governor should be part of the process. Be available. Don't go skiing," he said.

The same day as he was chastised for the March vacation, Symington was meeting with thirty-five members of minority groups from around Arizona to discuss the need to create jobs in areas of the city with high unemployment, particularly summer jobs for at-risk teens. Several leaders suggested creating urban enterprise zones, after which Symington asked for more specific proposals to be brought to another meeting with him in two weeks.

That meeting came days after the riots in Los Angeles in the spring of 1992. Along with Phoenix Mayor Paul Johnson, Symington began meeting regularly with minority groups in the region.

Like other state leaders, Symington was desperate to alleviate growing racial tensions in the state. In May of 1992, with the MLK Day not yet on the ballot, let alone passed, Arizona arguably still had the worst reputation for racial sensitivity outside the former Confederate states. That had to change or, as many leaders suggested, Arizona would not only be a state left behind, but one increasingly ostracized as it had been by the NFL.

The fear of being left behind also pervaded the languishing budget debates. Arizona would keep adding people, but if the state's leaders couldn't ensure a good education, safe streets, a clean environment, and good-paying jobs, the state would continue to grow primarily from an influx of retirees looking for cheap houses, low taxes, and sunshine. The state's modest momentum from the 1980s in diversifying the economy would stall, and the tax base would continue to be one dimensional through the 1990s and beyond.

Symington said he refused to budge from his education, environmental, public safety, and tax-reduction goals because he saw them as a way out of mediocrity. The fiscal conservative needed to rectify major government inefficiencies to pull off seemingly conflicting goals. His opponents refused to budge because they said Symington's cuts would ensure the mediocrity Symington claimed to be fighting.

So, by late June, Symington was still entrenched fighting for his special recipe of cuts and increases that Democrats argued were little more than a shell game.[16]

Project SLIM, and the cuts identified during its first year, were the key to the "Symington Plan" being something more than "voodoo economics," the term George H. W. Bush had slapped on Reaganomics.

But Project SLIM, what Symington had called his "pet project," was generating more bad headlines than good ideas early in the budget process. Besides the cloud over George Leckie, respected members of the project's steering committee were resigning in protest. One top education official left the committee after he came to believe a target amount for cuts had been set prior to the creation of the committee. "If you start out your deliberations with your conclusions already drawn, that is a sham," the official argued.

Project SLIM's credibility took another blow within a day when the steering committee's chairman, the respected retired general manager of SRP, stepped down, saying only that the effort "had strayed from its original purpose."

Nonetheless, by late June, significant cuts proposed by Symington and the sixteen-member steering committee were still alive in the proposed state budget.

After a flurry of eleventh-hour haggling, though, Symington signed the core appropriations bill, thereby avoiding the chaos state workers feared as the July 1 deadline neared.

After the dust settled from the third-longest legislative session in state history—one so tortuous that a representative passed out while arguing in its final hours[17]—the governor walked away with a collection of trophies:

He succeeded at getting Arizonans the first major tax cut in more than a decade. But the cut was only one-fifth of the $60 million he wanted.

He got the allocation for Project SLIM to continue, but one-third of the money would have to come from savings made by the program.

State air quality regulations would be brought up to match federal requirements. There would also be a strengthening of programs aimed at reducing air and water pollution in the state.

He landed a slightly larger budget for the lottery. The agriculture-inspection stations would disappear. The state would add more than 1,400 prison beds within the coming year. Programs for the seriously mentally ill would receive $10 million more than they did the year before. Preschool programs for at-risk children would get another $1 million.

Teachers and schools received only a 0.5 percent inflation raise, which didn't match inflation, but that was better than Symington's plan for no inflation raise.

His hoped-for $80 million cut in state health care benefits for uninsured Arizona adults was reduced to $22.5 million. (When possible, patients without insurance would have their costs covered by federally subsidized programs, not state ones.)

State employees received the slight raise he wanted and none would be furloughed; universities would receive the same money as the year before; and there would be no growth in most social services.[18]

Other Symington ideas would have to be revisited in 1993:

He didn't get the protections he wanted for wildlife habitats and only a few hundred thousand dollars were cut from community-college budgets, far less than the $10 million he had wanted.[19]

Perhaps the toughest loss of the session: Legislators shot down a host of school reform ideas, including open enrollment. Arizona would not be chartering K-12 schools for at least another year.

Even with those losses, though, Symington's first full session was broadly labeled a success.

The *Phoenix Gazette*'s veteran political reporter John Kolbe summed Symington's legislative record up this way: "Symington's klutzy, condescending style in dealing with his political peers often obscures one of the best-kept secrets of his 16-month tenure—that he has been remarkably successful in the legislative wars."

# Chapter 21

# BACK IN THE BLACK

In early November 1992, likely for the first time in several years, a national political story coming out of Arizona shined a positive light on the state. More than 60 percent of voters supported an initiative to create a paid Martin Luther King Jr. holiday in Arizona, removing the state's ignominious place as the only state in the country without a King holiday at the same time it became the only state that approved the holiday with a statewide vote, not an act of the state legislature and governor.[1]

"Arizona Restores King Day, Image" a headline in one Ohio paper read.[2]

A spokesperson for the NFL, which had canceled plans to hold the 1993 Super Bowl in Arizona because of the state's rejection of the holiday, announced that Tempe (where the Cardinals played at the time) immediately would be a top contender for the 1996 Super Bowl. Four months later, NFL owners voted to site the 1996 title game at Sun Devil Stadium on the campus of Arizona State University.

Symington himself had negotiated many of the major details of the deal directly with the NFL's commissioner at the time, Paul Tagliabue.

Along with the estimated $300 million boost to the economy, Arizona would get a massive public relations boost. This state once so repugnant that it merited sanctions would now be hosting a multi-day, sunbaked celebration of its beauty and vitality. Implicit in the successful execution of the logistical behemoth would be a clear message that the state's major metropolitan area was capable of remarkable feats, not just remarkable population growth.

Fife Symington had aggressively championed the creation of the holiday both on moral and economic grounds. Courting high rollers and pitching big projects had long been his day job, so Symington's look, language, and bearing were ideally suited for any dealings around the Super Bowl.

Politically, Symington's MLK Day fight wasn't necessarily a boost for his reelection chances. He was alienating the Mechamites and others to the far right who had succeeded at making Arizona the last state to adopt the holiday. If he was going to win reelection in 1994 amid the relentless coverage of his personal financial woes, he would likely need a large percentage of the party's right wing in his camp.

At least he would only need a plurality in 1994. In the 1992 midterm election, Arizonans voted to jettison the majority-vote requirements that had caused the chaotic runoff election two years before, meaning a third-party candidate or write-in Mechamite wouldn't so easily trigger another painful runoff.[3]

Arizonans also rejected what would have been the most restrictive abortion laws in the country. Looking at this decision along with the MLK Day vote, it appeared that a large number of the typically disengaged suburbanites had become tired of being defined by the state's ultra-engaged far right.

Republicans took back the state senate that November, something Symington could also claim as a big midterm win, especially since he raised $500,000 for Republican candidates and vocally opposed several Democrats who lost their races. Republicans would control both chambers and the governor's office in 1993.

Arizonans also backed an effort to limit the legislature's power to raise taxes. Any proposed state tax increase would need a two-thirds majority of votes, not just a simple majority, to pass.

Voter turnout that November was high even for a presidential-election year, likely because the ballot proposals at the state level were numerous, consequential, and controversial. (On the national level, voters wanted change, choosing Democrat Bill Clinton to be president over incumbent George H. W. Bush.)

The biggest message sent by Arizona voters: Arizonans were still fiscally conservative, but increasingly forward-thinking and tolerant in social issues.[4]

Although Symington's poll numbers still languished (along with those of every other political figure in the state), he had a good argument that the midterm had been a vote of confidence for the core values of his administration.

With a seemingly renewed mandate, as well as an increase in wins and a decrease in drama in the second half of 1992, Symington and his staff

The Great Salt River Cleanup, 1993. Courtesy of the Arizona State Library, Archives and Public Records, History and Archives Division, Phoenix, RG1_SG26_S6_B25_F020_I02.

Symington dons the gorilla suit during the celebration of the Twenty-fifth Anniversary of the Phoenix Suns in 1993. Symington's left gorilla hand is blocking Phoenix Suns owner Jerry Colangelo. Courtesy of the Arizona State Library, Archives and Public Records, History and Archives Division, Phoenix, RG1_SG26_S6_B10_F01_I8.

felt energized and confident as they entered their third year of governance.[5]

In late January of 1993, Symington was given another opportunity to look like a man in charge: After historic rainfalls in January, the Salt River flooded, causing tens of millions of dollars in damage.[6] Symington successfully lobbied President Bush (just days before Bill Clinton's inauguration) to declare the area a federal disaster area. Symington then moved quickly to begin cleaning up the mess left behind, which culminated later that year when Ann Symington led a massive effort to clean up debris from a landfill that had been partially washed away by the swollen river.

Symington's State of the State address in early 1993 reflected his growing confidence. Feeling he was carrying a mandate from the people as he began work with a Republican-dominated legislature, he laid out more aggressive tax cuts, government spending cuts, and policy goals that he had good reason to believe would become state law with limited opposition.[7]

He pushed for a decrease in state personal income taxes for all Arizonans while he increased the tax exemption for retirees by more than 20 percent. The increase in the exemption amount would cost the state an estimated $30 million, meaning that money would have to be made up through either government cuts or an increase in revenue from, primarily, the federal government.

For example, Symington called for the end of the fully state-funded indigent health care plan in place at the time. The program, which cost the state roughly $82 million, served to protect the working poor without insurance. That job, Symington argued, was for the federal government, not the state of Arizona. Serving the emergency medical needs of illegal immigrants was also something for which the state should not be paying, he argued.

Symington also called for a crackdown on parents who were behind on child support payments.

To foster economic growth, Symington pushed for an acceleration in the depreciation schedule for property owned by businesses in the state. He argued companies would reinvest those savings in expanding their businesses, and that it would serve as a draw from companies considering a move to Arizona.

He also proposed to phase out a .25 percent commercial lease tax. He proposed to phase the tax out over eighteen years, while other

Republicans hoped to eliminate the tax more quickly.[8] He also wanted $5 million for job training. All these pro-business moves would be critical, he said, for Arizona to benefit from the coming North American Free Trade Agreement. (At the same time, he also advocated for a significant expansion of Interstate 17 to facilitate the movement of goods between Mexico and the United States via Arizona.)

Amid rising crime rates and gang-related violence in the state, Symington pushed for "truth in sentencing" laws popular around the country at the time. He believed convicted criminals should be barred from parole and other devices that reduced the time they were actually spending in jail or prison.

(Jay Heiler, Symington's conservative policy wonk who had worked in the state attorney general's office, was the lead architect of Symington's criminal code reforms.)

Also, teens would be prohibited from carrying guns without parental permission.

The 1993 version of the Symington Plan did less than previous years to address the state's environmental woes. His most significant idea: to spend $1.7 million to install more energy-efficient HVAC units and lighting in the state's buildings. He also hoped to create "environmental enterprise zones" to draw companies that manufactured products using recycled materials.

As in his State of the State address the year before, Symington spent ample time discussing the merits of education reform (after he announced cuts to public universities).[9] He again pushed for open enrollment as well as legislation allowing the creation of charter schools.

It was the Republican-held house, not the Democrat-held senate, which had sunk Symington's aggressive education reform package the previous two years. Unlike most of his agenda, his education reforms would still be facing majority opposition in at least one of two state legislative bodies.

But Republican legislators had extra incentive to roll with Symington. If Republicans wanted a Republican governor in office past 1994, they would want their kindred candidate to collect as many wins as possible.

For all the wind in his political sails, though, Symington continued to be dogged by the RTC's investigation into his dealings with Southwest Savings and Loan. In February, as the legislature advanced swiftly in a pro-Symington direction, Symington found himself running out of

Fife and Ann Symington greeting Bill and Hillary Clinton at the National Governors Association dinner at the White House in the mid-1990s. Courtesy of the Symington family archives.

money. As legal fees mounted (star attorney John Dowd was not cheap), Symington announced he would be creating a "legal defense fund" to help him fend off investigators and perhaps seek some sort of settlement.

With one announcement, Symington exposed himself to criticism on two fronts: Was such a move legal, and even if so, ethical? And just by floating the idea of a legal defense fund, Symington was announcing that he was likely approaching a dire financial situation.

Detractors labeled any such fund to be unethical while mocking Symington for continuing to tout his business acumen even as his business was obviously in trouble.[10]

Symington's interest and need for a legal defense fund "hit the state Capitol like a one-two punch," wrote the *Republic*'s Keven Willey. "Everyone, it seems, is wondering how politically significant it will be.

"Here's betting very," she wrote.

Like several other political commentators, Willey predicted that Symington could overcome this new controversy for one simple reason: "One thing Symington has going for him in 1994 that he didn't in 1990 is a record as governor. So far, it's a pretty solid one—at least on issues like cutting taxes and reducing state spending."

Symington abandoned the legal defense fund idea in early February, shortly after a three-day trip to Washington, DC, during which he met with the new Interior Secretary, former Arizona governor Bruce Babbitt, and the newly minted president, former Arkansas governor Bill Clinton. "I've come to the conclusion that, ethically and perceptually, it would be a mistake," Symington told reporters.[11]

While the personal financial issues continued to surface as they had in Symington's first year, Willey, John Kolbe, and other political analysts noted that, with the help of his revamped staff leadership, Symington had become more adept at refocusing the narrative back on his aggressive agenda. Heiler, spokesman Doug Cole, Hayes, and then Hayes's replacement Wes Gullett battled much more successfully than past staff lineups to limit the number of distractions within the administration.

State Republican legislators could help Symington out greatly, Willey argued: "You can bet GOP lawmakers will try extra hard to deliver on many of Symington's biggest proposals."

The legislative session ended in mid-March, more than three months earlier than the 1992 session. Although Symington's education reform would have to wait, the laws and budget that emerged closely reflected Symington's wish list from his State of the State speech in January.

As bills and budgets meandered through the house and senate, Symington was continuing his attempt to reform state government. The goal: cut enough waste and generate enough new revenue streams that his proposed cuts in funding would not result in a decrease in services.[12]

At the same time, he pursued his other avenue for cutting costs: get the federal government to foot the bill. Besides meeting with Babbitt and Clinton, Symington spent much of his three-day trip to Washington suggesting to legislators and federal officials that Arizona was paying for indigent care that was supposed to be covered by the federal government.[13]

Symington also announced a sweeping plan to overhaul the process used to collect child-support payments. Nearly half a billion dollars in payments were past due in cases handled by the state, according to statistics from the state Department of Economic Security. Payments had not been regularly paid on time in 97 percent of the nearly 300,000 child-support cases.

"This is a human tragedy," Symington said when announcing his plan. "The collection process is in shambles. Arizona's families and children cannot wait any longer for a solution."[14]

Administrative law judges would be added to the DES process so that delinquent payment issues could be addressed more quickly. Private collection agencies would then aggressively pursue the unpaid money.

Symington said the new program would increase collections by $50 million in the coming year and by $150 million in fiscal 1995. His revenue predictions were tagged by some as wildly speculative, but few could argue that Symington was wrong in trying to overhaul the DES collection process.[15]

Beyond the moral imperative, the overhaul was also good business. The more delinquent payments the state could collect, the less the state would have to pay to support those who were not receiving those payments.

The week after Symington announced his DES reform plan, a local poll of more than seven hundred registered voters had Symington's favorable rating more than 50 percent higher than a year before. Voters generally supported his plans to reform state government.

Nationally, Symington was making headlines as the chairman of the influential Western Governors' Association.[16] He was a leader in national discussions about NAFTA, and was often serving as the spokesperson for western states on federal land management issues. It was during this time that Symington's name began being dropped when Republican leaders and political commentators discussed who might lead the next generation of Republicans on the national stage.

The increasingly confident and focused Symington, along with his effective, low-drama new crew, seemed to truly be hitting their stride.

One problem, though: Arizonans were noticing, but they weren't noticing enough. Symington was still only viewed in a favorable light by 38 percent of those questioned in one early 1993 poll. His huge jump in popularity had only taken him "from terrible to below average numbers," one commentator said.[17]

Beginning in 1993, local pollsters began including polling questions regarding potential challengers in the next gubernatorial election. One of Symington's potential opponents, Phoenix mayor Paul Johnson, received a 67 percent positive rating for his work as mayor of the state's largest

From left: Symington staffer Ken Burgess, Symington, and former chief of staff and longtime Arizona political operative Wes Gullett. Courtesy of the Arizona State Library, Archives and Public Records, History and Archives Division, Phoenix, RG1_SG26_S6_B004_F025_I06.

Staffer Cindy Grogan with Symington's longtime secretary, Joyce Riebel. Courtesy of the Arizona State Library, Archives and Public Records, History and Archives Division, Phoenix, RG1_SG26_S6_B004_F025_I07.

Maria Baier, special assistant to Symington, 1994. Courtesy of the Arizona State Library, Archives and Public Records, History and Archives Division, Phoenix, RG1_SG26_S6_B004_F008_I22.

From left: Arizona Department of Revenue director Paul Waddell, Symington, and Joe Albo, director of the Arizona Department of Public Safety, 1993. Courtesy of the Arizona State Library, Archives and Public Records, History and Archives Division, Phoenix, RG1_SG26_S6_B13_F01_I01.

city. Another poll suggested Terry Goddard would beat Symington by more than 20 percentage points if the gubernatorial election was held at the time of the poll.[18]

In quotes to the *Republic*, press secretary Doug Cole addressed the good news/bad news nature of the poll, basically arguing that the good news was the only valid news:

"This is proof that the people of Arizona are behind the governor's policies," Cole said. As for the still sub-average popularity issue, "All governors are lightning rods," he said. "They are the focal point of all politicians in this state."

If Symington was hoping for a second term, it was clear he needed to continue having his agenda drive the conversation about him, not his personal finances or any staff dramas. Both his friends and opponents agreed that if he could maintain momentum and then stand before voters with a long list of accomplishments and a short list of fresh scandals, he still could be harder to beat than polling hypotheticals predicted.

# Chapter 22

# A RIGHT TURN?

As Jay Heiler had said the summer before, if Symington was going to win in 1994, "he would have to get ahead of the bad press by becoming a strong activist executive around a clear policy agenda." As 1993 wore on, it appeared Symington was having some success following that game plan.[1]

In particular, Symington found traction as a crime fighter. As the juvenile crime rate in the state spiked in 1992 amid a flurry of high-profile crimes in which gangs and drugs were involved, Symington presented the Heiler-designed outline for tough-on-crime state criminal-code reform.

By 1992, labeling Democrats as "soft-on-crime liberals" who created the "revolving door" prison system had become as effective politically as painting them as "tax-and-spend liberals."[2]

With the Republican-controlled state chambers, numerous changes were made to the state's criminal code.

A law was expanded that allowed anyone involved in certain felonies that resulted in a death to be charged with murder.[3] The 1993 revisions widened the felony-murder rule to include deaths involving marijuana offenses. Maximum sentences for sex crimes against children increased 50 percent. Symington also wanted an end to parole for felons. "Truth in sentencing" was the buzzword at the time for Americans sick of violent criminals getting released after only serving a fraction of their original sentence.[4]

Symington fired the head of the state parole board that summer after what Symington perceived to be a string of overly generous paroles given to violent criminals and a lack of respect for the opinions of victims.[5] In one case, Symington met with the victim of a convicted rapist after the victim was barred from speaking at the parole hearing of her attacker. "When you listen to how her life was basically ruined by this man, I believe in justice," Symington told the media. He removed the parole board chief because he "was insensitive to victims," Symington said, and "obsessed with criminals' rights."[6]

For Republicans, "victim's rights," like "truth in sentencing," increasingly became effective policy initiatives in the early and mid-1990s.[7]

That fall, soon after his spat with parole board members, Symington announced a $32 million program to combat juvenile crime, which had become an even bigger issue through the spring and summer of 1993 after a string of especially violent assaults and murders by teen offenders.[8] Symington mixed in several added prevention measures to his plan—additional programs for at-risk preschoolers, parent training, curfews for young people, police in schools, and boot camp for juvenile offenders—but it was his ideas on punishment that drew the most press.

He supported the death penalty for any murder committed by gang members, including those committed during a drive-by shooting. When asked if the death sentence included teen killers, Symington answered: "That's perfectly possible." He even proposed calling on the Arizona National Guard to help fight crime.

Symington's sweeping anti-gang initiative, coming on the heels of his proposals to revamp the state's criminal code, was welcomed statewide by prosecutors, police, and sheriffs, including the newly elected sheriff of Maricopa County, Joe Arpaio, who had won his seat on a similarly aggressive anti-crime stance. (Arpaio started his famed "posse" in November 1993. Symington was quickly a member.)[9]

While winning traditional tough-on-crime voters, Symington's plan—except for the ideas of executing teens and calling out the National Guard—appeared to be widely supported by moderates. The *Mesa Tribune*'s editorial page heralded it as, "Indisputably the most balanced and comprehensive proposal offered by an Arizona leader to date." A *Phoenix Gazette* editorial writer called it a "tour de force proposal."

*Republic* columnist Steve Wilson facetiously asked Jay Heiler if the governor was "suffering from liberal fever" with his proposal to spend the majority of the $31 million in the plan on prevention.[10] Heiler, the former conservative editorial writer, was happy to play: "What you see here is not an all-out embrace of the idea that massive redistribution of wealth is the right thing to do," Heiler shot back.

He continued more on point: "I don't think there is any disagreement between conservatives and liberals that many children growing up now

Symington with Maricopa County Sheriff Joe Arpaio in 1993. Courtesy of the Arizona State Library, Archives and Public Records, History and Archives Division, Phoenix, RG1_SG26_S6_B11_F38_I05.

are not receiving the socialization they need to have a chance to succeed in life."

The *Republic*'s E. J. Montini suggested one problem with Symington's plan, or at least his tough-on-crime rhetoric: it was hypocritical. Montini broke out statistics from the Department of Corrections and other sources suggesting that, prior to being tough on crime, Symington was quite soft on it. DOC data, for example, showed that the thirty-three sex offenders paroled during Symington's term had only served an average of five years (Symington had recently chastised the DOC's parole board for releasing a sex offender after twenty years). "What about all the others?" Montini asked. "Where was the governor then?"[11]

That summer and fall, Symington also came out forcefully against a resolution in the US House of Representatives pushing for mining industries to pay an 8 percent royalty on gross sales from minerals taken from federal lands.

Secretary of the Interior Bruce Babbitt, the former Arizona governor, had long pushed for reforms to the 120-year-old federal mining laws that allowed companies to buy federal lands—taxpayer-owned lands, he often pointed out—for as little as $2.50 an acre, while also paying no royalties for ore removed.[12]

In Arizona's vast mining country, though, a reform that looked like fair play to many was certain death to the state's mining industry.

Mining-industry officials estimated the bill, proposed by West Virginia Democrat Nick Rahall, would kill off more than forty thousand jobs nationally, with hundreds of those coming from Arizona's copper-mining communities.

In late August, Symington attended and spoke at a rally of more than two thousand people in the Arizona mining town of Globe.[13]

To broad applause, Symington went all-in in his condemnation of any change to the law:

"There's been some confusion in Washington as to who the endangered species is," Symington announced. "I don't believe it's the spotted owl."

The bill "is an example of out-of-control bureaucracy in Washington."

Symington was arguably just a state leader out protecting jobs in his state, but he was doing so in language that mocked environmentalists and federal-land reform measures with red-meat right-wing populist rhetoric. When his speech was dissected the next day in the media in Phoenix and Tucson, some wondered if he was making a deliberate move to grab the hard-right vote as too many moderates focused on his personal problems rather than his leadership successes.

Symington denied that he had changed. He had long complained about federal overreach, for one. Regarding crime, he said he had a long record of supporting programs for the young and the innocent while pushing for severe punishments for violent felons.

One other minor event that year played into this idea that Symington was reaching right for the anti-government, culture-warrior crowd. On the Wednesday before Christmas 1993, Symington sent a letter to Northern Arizona University interim president Patsy Reed calling for her to cancel a second-semester class titled "Transsexualism and Society." In his letter, Symington called the "obscene" class an "insult to taxpayers" who are paying for much of NAU's classes with their tax dollars.[14]

Heiler, who then held the title of "communication director," said Symington wanted the class canceled. The following day, though, Heiler better reflected the governor's limited power in university curriculum matters: "Whether they cancel the class is up to them," he told a *Republic* reporter. "The governor has no power, nor does he wish to exert any."

What Symington wanted, nearly every opinion writer in Phoenix and Tucson argued, was to score political points with the cultural conservative block of his party.

Keven Willey posited that, had Symington been "truly concerned about the appropriateness of such a course, he might have picked up the telephone and queried the president of Northern Arizona University" rather than send her a five-paragraph letter at the same time he sent the letter to media outlets.[15]

"So upon examination, what we have here is not so much a governor concerned about the educational value of a certain sociology class, but a governor desperately searching for popular-sounding, headline-grabbing, incendiary issues on which to construct himself a cause for re-election.

"The bad news is that Symington has 11 more months in which to ply his trade," she wrote.

By December of 1993, Symington felt like anything he did would be labeled a cynical political move by the Phoenix and Tucson media.[16]

Whatever his intentions, though, likely voters agreed that the transsexualism class wasn't appropriate, according to polls. They agreed that crime was a major problem, that the court system was too lenient on violent criminals, and that the governor was taking appropriate steps to prevent and fight crime. Rural Arizona generally also seemed to appreciate his states' rights rhetoric.

"Never has a governor been so active trying to better the state while having those accomplishments either ignored or labeled as cynical, or lambasted for being either too little or too much," one letter writer to the *Mesa Tribune* argued.

"I get it," another letter-writer complained. "Criticism is more fun than complimenting. But when you're just criticizing for the fun of it, you're being dishonest. It's especially unbecoming of those who fancy themselves journalists."

In a statewide poll of eight hundred Republicans in December 1993, Symington was eleven percentage points ahead of Phoenix mayor Paul Johnson. The problem: Johnson was a Democrat (although a very centrist one).

In Maricopa County, where a higher percentage of voters knew who Johnson was, Symington trailed Johnson by six points among likely Republican voters.[17]

But that was still another improvement for Symington compared to polls that summer.

Goddard's massive lead in popularity had shrunk, and Symington's own numbers had inched up from a low point a few months earlier.

By December, Symington knew he likely would be facing one of three popular Democrats and possibly two Republican primary challengers (Grant Woods was still considering a run along with a Republican stalwart named Barbara Barrett). And Symington likely would be doing so with considerably less money in his war chest than in 1990, when he had significant family money involved. Whatever was to blame for Symington's unimpressive numbers amid what arguably was a successful record, he would need to have a good 1994—absent of any palace intrigue or RTC drama—to win reelection.

"The common thinking seems to be that the incumbent governor, Republican Fife Symington, has already rolled over and died," Willey wrote in an October column headlined "Self-centered Dems underestimating opponents."

"I think they've lost touch with reality," Willey wrote. "Symington, for all his faults, has, after all, demonstrated an ability rare among politicians: keeping campaign promises."[18]

# Chapter 23

# THE MERCADO

B y the early 1980s, downtown Phoenix became a dismal landscape
once corporate and government workers abandoned the area after
a day's work. Like other city cores throughout the United States,
downtown Phoenix went dead after business hours, save for the movements of people on the margins. Dilapidation continued to creep into
downtown as people and the businesses and cultural amenities they demanded moved outward toward suburbs such as Glendale, Ahwatukee,
and Chandler.[1]

By 1985, civic-minded Phoenix residents wanted few things more than
a rebirth of the city's heart.

Such a dream could never come true, though, if every new development—especially those that included major retail and lodging—kept
gravitating toward hot spots far from the downtown like Twenty-Fourth
Street and Camelback Road.

In the early 1980s, city planners and leaders of the Phoenix social-
service agency, Chicanos por la Causa, began envisioning a multiblock
downtown revitalization project called the Mercado, designed to repli-
cate the bustling markets of Mexico's major cities. Along with mostly
small retail shops, the Mercado would offer ample retail office space as
well as something the city arguably should have had decades before—a
first-rate, downtown-based, Latino cultural center.[2]

Leaders in a city widely criticized for burying the region's Latino heritage were thrilled by the idea of a Latino-led development leading the
revitalization of downtown Phoenix. From the first mention of a potential "mercado-like" project by Pete Garcia, president of Chicanos por la
Causa, city leaders and members of the city council were quick to offer
financial incentives to help the nonprofit.[3]

City officials were presented with the Mercado plan as well as another
significant downtown development, Square One, just as big dreamers
in government and the business community were convinced that

downtown redevelopment was the pathway to becoming a "real" American metropolis. San Francisco, Chicago, Dallas, Houston, Denver, and many other more mature metro areas had thriving art scenes, major sports arenas, and grand music venues in or near their core. Americans were excited to come to the Valley in winter. But they were not at all interested, and likely a bit afraid, to go into the center of the biggest city in the Southwest.

In a study by urban development expert Neal Peirce completed in early 1987, the downtown was both the city's biggest problem and its best hope for a bright future.[4]

Residents of neighboring cities, he wrote, think of downtown Phoenix as "a dumping ground and a dangerous place. It has slums and winos and soup kitchens; small wonder the homeless congregate there.

"There is no question that downtown Phoenix, among major US cities, presents a most curious case," Peirce wrote in his report, which was commissioned by the *Arizona Republic* and its afternoon sister paper, the *Phoenix Gazette.*

"Because, to put it bluntly, there is so little downtown there. Incredible amounts of land in the central area are simply vacant."

Phoenix, Peirce said, had "the most deserted downtown" of any major city in the country.

But advances are being made, he said. The first example of visionary planning he listed was "the Mercado—a traditional Mexican market."

"Phoenix needs much more of that kind of vision," he wrote.

A few companies, with the help of major tax breaks and other incentives, stepped into the void. In 1987, the twenty-six-story One Renaissance Square opened. It was the first new downtown high rise in a decade.[5] Near the same time, Phoenix voters approved nearly $110 million in bonds to be used to build cultural and recreation projects downtown.

That same year, Rouse Company began development downtown on the Arizona Center. At 800,000 square feet with 150,000 feet planned for retail on an 18.5-acre site, the behemoth would hopefully serve as a major anchor around which a vibrant retail shopping area would emerge.

At the same time, another group of investors was struggling to get Square One off the ground. That project had been stalled since 1983 because of a breakdown in negotiations with existing businesses in the area.

Indeed, Square One, which its developers had hoped would win the race to be the first new downtown retail store in decades, looked to be dead. Some other project might have to take its place.

As the plan for a downtown Mercado began to gel in city hall,[6] Chicanos por la Causa leaders realized they would need a level of financing and management acumen the nonprofit didn't have. What they needed to do, Garcia and others agreed, was create a for-profit entity that could partner with someone who could land more than $10 million, and perhaps, a few major long-term tenants that could secure the Mercado's future.

In late 1985, outside the emerging plans for downtown, the highest profile development in Arizona was the planned Camelback Esplanade, and one of the hottest developers was Fife Symington. He was the guy who most looked positioned to land financing for a project with worthy goals but arguably questionable financial viability. Like the Esplanade, the Mercado would be a first.

As the Camelback Esplanade was beginning to materialize, Symington decided to attend an event in the southern Arizona town of Rio Rico sponsored by the community-development nonprofit Arizona Town Hall. After the event, Garcia and fellow Chicanos por la Causa leader Tommy Espinoza approached Symington with a proposal.[7]

They laid out their plan to build a mercado-styled retail, office, and lodging complex in downtown Phoenix. They had a guarantee from the city to provide the land. They had promises for more support from the city.[8] There was a significant urban-development grant waiting for a worthy cause. All they needed was someone who had clout in the development and financial community who was an expert at bringing large commercial developments in "on time and under budget."

Symington loved the idea.

While others in the development and business community saw a bad bet, Symington saw the birthplace of the new downtown. Even if tenants and shoppers were slow to come to the new project, he believed that civic leaders would provide additional support for the project as it worked toward viability.

Soon after the Symington Company teamed up with the for-profit offshoot of CPLC, Garcia, Symington, Randy Todd, and Mary Hughes, the Symington Company public relations director, along with several architects, traveled to various Mexican cities to study Spanish colonial architecture. They visited Aztec and Mayan ruins and the markets of several Mexican cities, which are most often large permanent buildings owned by, and regulated by, the local municipal government.[9] There they found every manner of food or item sold out of small vendor stalls. There was music and the aroma of countless meats, vegetables, and spices in the air. Vivid color adorned walls. And very often, there was something downtown Phoenix lacked: that magical bustle of a community collected in a communal core involved in all manner of commerce and play.

In the mountains northwest of Mexico City, the men found their prime inspiration in the quaint village of Guanajuato, where colorful and sometimes eccentric buildings dotted the hillside.[10]

But truth was, some Mexican mercados were already beginning to crumble under the same pressures that drove American retail from downtowns. As communities had grown, strip malls closer to residents' suburban homes sapped income from traditional business centers.[11]

The most forward-thinking community leaders in Mexico were scrambling to revitalize their urban cores. A viable mercado would be critical to any such efforts.

Even if the Phoenix Mercado was a high-risk, moderate-reward development as many predicted, there were other advantages beyond profit for Symington. It was a chance for him to work with the city and a respected nonprofit on friendly terms. It was a chance for him to build bridges within the Latino community.

Pulling off such a project would be good for business and politics, sure. But Symington was adamant that he believed a revitalized urban core was critical for any bright future for Phoenix. At the same time, he argued, it was time for a major Latino cultural presence in the downtown of a city at the heart of a state famously ignorant of, and even hostile to, its own origin story and a large percentage of the state's population.[12]

Another good indicator that he was acting on impulses beyond good business: after difficult lending negotiations in a difficult market, he unwisely agreed to make himself personally liable if the loans for the project went into default. As with his personal guarantee on the Esplanade construction loan, Symington was putting his personal financial stability in jeopardy.

"He definitely has the heart of a gambler," his longtime attorney and business partner Richard Mallery said later.

But Symington argued he wasn't gambling. For one, the developers had those assurances from the city.

The Phoenix City Council unanimously approved the Mercado in 1986. It would be built on two blocks of city land between Van Buren, Washington, Fifth, and Seventh Streets. It was "a different kind of reception (from city officials) than the type that one of the developers, J. Fife Symington III, received over his last proposal, the Camelback Esplanade," wrote Deborah Shanahan of the *Republic*.

"I want this project to happen," one councilman announced. "I'm excited about it and very happy to support it."

The city agreed to a sixty-year lease of the land with no rent payments in the project's first years. Rent would rise to 25 percent of the net cash flow once a $1 million loan CPLC made to the project was repaid. The city offered to install trees, benches, and walkways around the two blocks, a project estimated to cost about $1.3 million.

The city council also offered the city's "best efforts" to construct a $9 million parking garage near the Mercado to address a severe shortage of parking in the area. (Such a parking garage, though, would have to be approved by voters, council members noted.)

As approved by the council that day, the Mercado was planned to house 82,000 square feet that would provide space for a courtyard surrounded by small specialty shops (the most mercado-ish part of the Mercado), as well as 35,000 square feet of office space, a 125-plus-room hotel, and a 10,000-square-foot Latino cultural center.[13]

It was then time for Symington and Todd to once again scour the landscape for financing. Beyond a total of $3.7 million in grants secured by the nonprofit, they would need $10 million.

The Symington Company had ten projects at the time that, at some point, would need both short-term construction loans and long-term loans. Nearly all of those projects, though, were along the fast-growing "Camelback Corridor" east of the Esplanade and far from the urban core. They were retail or office developments that the Symington Company had a history of successfully building and managing. For those projects, lenders were relatively easy to secure.

The Mercado was a different animal, though, and lenders were skeptical.[14] They were especially concerned because the real estate market in the Valley had softened considerably.[15] Also concerning was the potential competition from other projects.

In late 1986, Ramada Inc. pulled out of the project, which, Symington said then, prompted him and the Mercado's other development partners to drop the idea of a hotel.

A year after the city's approval of the project, Symington finally secured a loan from First Interstate Bank, which had loaned $2.3 million to a Symington partnership to build a shopping center in Mesa.

But First Interstate Bank officials wanted two significant concessions from Symington, one of which he and Todd had never been subject to:

Symington would need to sign the personal guarantee. And to even get the construction loan, Symington first would have to secure the long-term loan for the project, which then would be used to pay off the construction loan from the bank.[16]

This meant that, for one, Symington potentially would be liable for any cost overruns that drove the estimated construction costs higher than the amount of the long-term loan.

As the Mercado took shape through 1989, it was celebrated as a major triumph for the city, a feel-good mash-up of multicultural beacon, innovative small-business incubator, and urban renewal flintstone. Media feature stories—even from the ever-skeptical *Phoenix New Times*—raved about the vibrancy of the space and the creators' willingness to take bold and beautiful risks in design and décor. The Mercado, one writer said, "may be the most interesting and exciting project ever to be built in downtown Phoenix."

Jean Novotny's September 1989 story in the *Republic* captured the excitement in the weeks leading up to the Mercado's official opening:[17]

"If you think the outside of the Mercado is intriguing, just wait until you get inside and start wandering the cobblestone streets. It's in the interior of the development where the magic begins and you get a chance to meet the characters of the Mercado, a playful takeoff on Spanish colonial architecture.

"One of those characters is Palenque, a member of Mayan royalty. He's made of carved and painted wood and serves as a screen for a pay phone. Look also for the Running Man as he carries a plate of food on his journey through Las Delicias, the food court and one of five neighborhoods in the village. Then check out the stone cat perched atop a wall and the three monkeys who double as musicians. Watch out for the 60-foot featured serpent, also a stone carving, that slithers along the wall of Case

Symington and company staffer Olga Soto. Courtesy of the Arizona State Library, Archives and Public Records, History and Archives Division, Phoenix, RG1_SG26_S6_B08_F023_I02.

De Xochipilli, the cultural neighborhood. That's the bright blue neighborhood in the northeastern sector of the village."

R. Steven Bassett, the lead architect on the Mercado, offered up three quotes that collectively defined the beauty of the Mercado and the dangers inherent in the endeavor. They summed up the feeling of joy and pride among the project's creators, but also an underlying anxiety.

Bassett said his team occasionally had to stand back and critique their work to ensure they weren't "having a bit too much fun with the project," he said. "It's one of the few times when a client will tell you to be as creative as you can but with the directive we stay in the budget. They encouraged us to be creative but that it also be leasable and a financial success." The project's creative designer added, "Few developers have the courage to be as creative as the Symington Co. and Chicanos por la Causa were with the Mercado." They knew they had to be "out there," he said, because they knew "they would have to make a huge statement" to be successful as "the first major retail development in downtown Phoenix."

Business stories about the Mercado ended with a sentiment rarely seen in the dry analytical pages of business sections: They, too, most often referenced the "hope" of city and other leaders that the project would succeed.

Everyone but Symington seemed to see the project as a noble gamble.

Many of the Mercado's tenants were small upstart businesses taking advantage of subsidized rents that were one-third what other retailers were paying. Established businesspeople such as Carol Steele opened a sort of mercado-within-the-Mercado with a bakery, tortilla factory, flower shop, and gallery. City Councilman Howard Adams was one of the first to rent the Mercado's community room, Xochicalli, for a reception.

In late September 1989, the Mercado hosted a massive fiesta celebrating Mexican Independence Day. The space teemed with a mix of leaders, artisans, and area dignitaries as diverse as any the city had seen before. Democrats mixed with Republicans and celebrated their collective success. People who may never have voted for a Republican congratulated Fife Symington as a visionary and a hero. It was a kumbaya moment like few others in the so-often-divided Valley.

Within a year, though, the reviews of the beloved and celebrated Mercado were already growing darker.

Whatever the reasons, the Mercado was languishing in 1990 as Fife

Symington quickly gained ground on his political opponents.[18] Along with the Camelback Esplanade, the Mercado quickly was becoming yet another albatross from Symington's business life waiting to enter his public life.[19]

# Chapter 24

# THE BULLY PULPIT

If anyone doubted Fife Symington was serious about serving a second term, an advertisement appearing in the February 27, 1994, *Arizona Daily Star* should have allayed any uncertainty:

"EXTRA, EXTRA, EXTRA!" boomed the headline for the ad. "Please Help Us Return $10.2 Million To The People On This List!" To the side of the sensational pronouncement was a letter from the "State of Arizona EXECUTIVE OFFICE." It was from "Fife Symington, Governor," and it pronounced that the state's unclaimed property unit had been working overtime to locate and return unclaimed property to thousands of "rightful owners."

The proclamation continued: "In this new, never-before published list of unclaimed property of more than $50 in value, there is at least one that could result in a check of more than $50,000. Recently, some individuals have been rewarded handsomely for checking the list for their name." For one: "An elderly woman living on a fixed income received over $8,500 from the sale of stocks and bonds her husband never told her about."

Symington's team effectively took an existing, little-known government program and made it a vehicle to look as if Symington, from the "EXECUTIVE OFFICE," was involving the people of Arizona in some sort of high-dollar, good-government sweepstakes that could even help little old ladies.

Symington's numbers weren't that good, but he had the bully pulpit, and he knew how to use it. A Democratic legislator quoted in an early-1994 *Republic* story granted that Symington was "really on a roll."

There's no better bully pulpit for a governor than the State of the State address in a reelection year.

The governor's address to the legislature that January, as one House Democrat said, was "pretty dang good across the board. It certainly was a master's class in how to use your office to help you win back that office."[1]

Symington's 1994 State of the State Address was the first to incorporate a video teleprompter. Courtesy of the Arizona State Library, Archives and Public Records, History and Archives Division, Phoenix, RG1_SG26_S6_B12_F11_I21.

Friends and non-friends generally agreed that Symington looked calm and confident. He was forceful in an amiable way, generally, and albeit in broad strokes, described with significant craft the needs and philosophies that would be driving his agenda for the coming year. And he looked in charge without the haughty and arrogant air detractors sometimes saw. As another usually critical Democratic legislator said: "When Symington first came in, he acted like a chief executive officer who looked at the legislature as an ineffective board of directors. After he found our egos were too big to be satisfied with that role, his relationship with the legislature improved."

Certainly, not all onlookers were impressed as much by the content of the speech. An *Arizona Daily Star* editorial savaged Symington's address, attacking its core ideology by saying it was thick with "outmoded hatred of government, a simplistic individualism, a retreat from leadership. . . . The point here is that while it was 1985 in Fife Symington's head Monday, or perhaps the middle of George Bush's disastrous single presidential term, it remains steadfastly, complexly, and confusingly 1994 here amid the dysfunctional classrooms, impoverished trailer parks and neglected neighborhoods of Arizona."[2]

The precision of the speech, along with the increasing discipline in Symington's outlining of his goals and his reasoning behind those goals, was not just a product of a maturing politician. Jay Heiler was regularly pushing Symington to stay on point. Symington listened to Heiler, and Heiler became increasingly adamant in urging Symington to use pre-pared speeches—the ones that Heiler and his hand-picked speechwriter, attorney, and journalist Maria Baier always composed or helped com-pose. Heiler would later say: "People liked it when (Symington) would speak off the cuff. And I got there and said, 'Well, I'm sorry. That's just bullshit. He can give an informal quality to the prepared messages but we've got to prepare messages. We have to start bringing some discipline to what we're saying in the community and how we're framing these issues.'"[3]

Symington agreed with Heiler—to a point.[4] The governor had been elected by the people on a platform crafted by him long before his dream staff was put in place, he reminded his dream staff. He would be more disciplined and focused, Symington promised, but he wasn't going to be a robotic, focus-group-fashioned façade of himself.

In that critical election-year State of the State speech, Symington not only laid out another ambitious agenda, he loaded it with lists of what he argued were promises kept and data suggesting the Symington Plan was working. Most notably, perhaps, was the fact that the state had built up a hefty budget surplus, a goal that would have seemed laughably optimistic when Symington took office.

Yes, state coffers were benefitting from an economic upswing that gen-erated more tax revenue for the state, but Symington believed he had the ammunition to argue that Project SLIM, although too-often shrouded in controversy, had resulted in cost-cutting efficiencies in state government that greatly amplified the rosy financial picture for the state.

(Arizona legislators would be facing a bizarre budget battle in 1994: They would be debating how best to utilize an estimated $200 million in surplus dollars in the 1995 fiscal year, not fighting over what cuts or tax increases would be needed to properly fund the government without incurring debt.)[5]

Symington again promised to push for more savings through the state's indigent care program, suggesting that the state could save $270

Symington unveiling his Middle Income Tax Relief Act in 1994. Courtesy of the Arizona State Library, Archives and Public Records, History and Archives Division, Phoenix, RG1_SG26_S6_B01_F013_I08.

million by shifting some 183,000 people from state-subsidized care to care from the entity that he believed was legally mandated to provide the funding—the US Department of Health and Human Services. If his gargantuan program reached its goal, the state could both decrease taxes and, for one, better fund education. If the idea's supporters could navigate a labyrinth of bureaucratic, legal, and political challenges, the plan could be the single largest win-win for the state budget.

But that was the future. With more than $200 million already sitting in reserve, he proposed an across-the-board personal income tax cut that would keep $100 million in Arizonans' pockets.

Polls showed that Arizonans liked the idea of paying less in taxes through Symington's Middle Income Tax Reduction Act, as one could imagine. Polls also showed that Arizonans weren't terribly impressed with their windfalls from the 1992 reduction, which became known as the "hamburger" tax cut because the average $4 savings in taxes paid for a hamburger (in theory). They also weren't much impressed with the slightly larger cuts in 1993, which became known as the "chicken dinner" savings.

The other big economic news: The unemployment rate was half what it was when he took office, a fact he noted without overtly taking credit for.

Symington also seemed in tune with the majority of Arizonans regarding crime. Teen violence and the ferocity of gang violence had again appeared to increase in the previous year, and the Valley had experienced two more crimes that shook average Arizonans—the murder of a couple in their driveway in a car-jacking gone wrong and the killing of a young child in a drive-by shooting. Arizonans wanted to fight back. Polls taken in late 1993 and throughout 1994 consistently showed that Arizonans were more concerned about the rising crime rate than any other single issue. As for the likelihood of crime and punishment being a major issue in the coming election, pollster Bruce Merrill quipped: "You know right away there isn't anybody in Arizona who is for *more* crime."

One of Symington's comments made it into a national AP story on how states were ratcheting up their fights against crime. Amid a confident speech littered with snappy tidbits of intellectual peacocking, Symington said: "I was not sent here to sit meditating on Freud or on the latest 'root causes' of criminal behavior. The criminal law deals not with theories, but with thugs." (Keven Willey joked the next day: "I suspect it was one of Symington's favorite passages.")[6]

With that, Symington rattled off the details of the $31.7 million crime-fighting plan he had introduced two months before.

(Which was announced just a month after a lesser-known elected official, Maricopa County Sheriff Joe Arpaio, had announced the creation of a four hundred-member volunteer "sheriff's posse" to assist his deputies in increasing the law-enforcement presence in the Valley. Symington quickly became a member of the posse and asked Arpaio to dispatch posse members to area malls.)[7]

Symington wanted mandatory prison sentences for anyone convicted of using a deadly weapon in the commission of a crime. That reform would build on his success in "truth in sentencing" efforts the year before. Also, Symington referenced his push to send juveniles accused of violent crimes to adult court and putting in place an "impact education plan" making parents responsible if juveniles in their care committed a crime. Parents had to pay court costs and were required to work with their children when sentencing included community-service projects. (Symington received significant national press for his criminal justice positions after he spoke at the Republican Governors' Association meeting in Phoenix in the days before his State of the State speech.)

As Symington talked tougher, though, he also pushed for early education programs aimed at at-risk children and teens. He supported what was called the "Success by Six" initiative, which would invest more than $22 million throughout the remainder of the century on programs targeting an estimated 14,000 children. "Success by Six" was arguably the Symington-backed initiative with the strongest bipartisan support.

He heralded the success of his education reforms but said the state had "unfinished business." He would once again be fighting for a school-choice program that included payments from the state to aid parents who wished to send their children to charter, private, or parochial schools beyond the boundaries of their closest public school.

That proposal arguably had the least bipartisan support.

Symington's last major talking point probably best illuminated his core constitutional conservative values:

Mining and timber industry frustration with federal land-use restrictions fit perfectly with Symington's belief that the rights of the states defined in the US Constitution had been trampled by an ever-expanding federal government, especially in western states made up of massive swaths of federal land. (Symington was quick to quote verbatim the Tenth Amendment, which states that "powers not delegated to the United States by the Constitution, nor prohibited by it to the States, are reserved to the States respectively, or to the people.")

Once he became Arizona's governor, Symington quickly became one of the most quoted voices for western states regarding federal laws regulating federal lands.[8]

Symington's ardent states' rights beliefs didn't much concern urban Arizonans. But for those whose towns, homes, and workplaces were surrounded by Arizona's massive swaths of federal land (and for those less impacted by drive-by shootings), a state's right to make decisions on land within its boundaries was considered a fundamental issue.

Symington pronounced in his speech: "Sometimes, Washington forgets that the states created the federal government and not the other way around.

"On every front—mining, timber, ranching, agriculture—the communities of Arizona have found themselves under increasing pressure."

Symington then announced the creation of the "Constitutional Defense Council," and asked the legislature to fund it.[9]

"We will remind the federal government from this chamber and in federal court that just because they reside on the Potomac, they do not have a divine right to dictate to the Salt and the Gila."

The idea: to create a fund to pay for the state to challenge federal mandates deemed to be overreach.

Part of that overreach, Symington had long argued, was the federal environmental laws that dictated how federal lands could be used as well as the amount of money the government wanted for use of that land. He stood with miners, loggers, and ranchers in their fight to lessen federal restrictions and put more governance of lands within Arizona into the hands of the people of Arizona.

But at the same time Symington seemed on the side of the state's most conservative Republicans in some environmental issues, he was also at war with them over a collection of bills aimed at draining state environmental funds for the benefit of those leasing federal and state lands for business purposes.

Arizona voters had approved the creation of two funds that would funnel lottery proceeds toward the creation of parks and better preservation of critical wildlife habitat. Quickly after the creation of the Heritage Fund and the State Lake Improvement Fund, though, a group of Republican state legislators began pitching bills that would channel that money into private hands. One bill, for example, would allow those funds to be used to pay federal land lease holders in Arizona who claimed to have lost money due to federal regulations.

Symington promised to veto any bill that threatened the Heritage and SLIF funds. Soon after Symington's address, the *Republic*'s Outdoor Editor, Barry Burkhart, wrote: "Symington has always been a champion of Heritage. I can't imagine why conservatives are opposing a governor of their party. This has to disturb him."[10]

It didn't, though, because it was nothing new.[11] Symington had long been at odds with many to the right of him regarding land use.

For him, he said, the Heritage Fund and SLIF were untouchables. The people of the state of Arizona voted to use their tax dollars to preserve the beauty and natural habitat of the state, he argued. That's a funded mandate from the people of Arizona.

In this case, considering Symington's philosophical underpinnings, it made sense for a states' rights proponent who railed against unfunded mandates to be a friend of the environment pushing $20 million towards conservation projects.

While Symington's language by 1994 often sounded as if he had moved considerably to the right, his actual policy positions, as a whole, still were those of a moderate business-centric Republican with occasional left-leaning environmental or social safety-net tendencies. As such, analysts generally agreed, he was in a strong position to corral both those to his right and those in the vast Arizona center in the coming election if—and this was always the big "if"—he could keep the personal financial intrigues to a minimum.

Chapter 25

# THE PROBLEM WITH POLLS

Political consultant and *Republic* contributor Steve Tuttle started his 1994 New Year's Day prognostication column with a sentiment that seems to be aired at the beginning of every election year in America.

Basically, he mourned the decline of Western Civilization during the year past, then announced a not wholly sarcastic hope for the year to come:

"We might as well admit it," he wrote. "Any year in which the most popular books contain the deviant ramblings of Rush Limbaugh and Howard Stern, not to mention the excretory drivel of Robert James Waller, can't have been all that good.

"But 1994 will be better, if for no other reason than we get to enjoy the amusements of an election year."[1]

Directing Symington's 1994 campaign would be Chuck Coughlin, the cigar-chomping political operative who first made his name as financial director for Senator John McCain's 1986 senatorial race. Coughlin and Symington later worked together when Coughlin ran the statewide campaign promoting a state-supported Martin Luther King Jr. Day.

Symington and his staff quickly coalesced around the theme for his reelection campaign.[2] The quick, catchy slogan "Promises Made, Promises Kept," hit print, radio, and television early and often after Memorial Day.

This round, Symington would be squaring off against the winner among an eclectic collection of Democrats who felt Symington was easy pickings. Before the general election, though, Symington would have to dispatch a surprise entry into what was assumed to be an uncontested primary.

Coming after Symington was Barbara Barrett, a former FAA deputy administrator, local attorney, and Republican Party insider with a Reaganite pedigree, a gift for playing both insider and outsider, and a deep war chest thanks to her own success and the success of her husband, Craig Barrett, then chief operating officer (and four years later, CEO) of computer giant Intel.[3]

(Her candidacy was a surprise to Symington. Barrett had met with him and his chief of staff, Wes Gullett, in the governor's office months before she announced her candidacy. At that time she promised Symington and Gullett she would not run for governor.)

Barrett had an unusually charming and inspiring backstory, which, when coupled with her rise to high posts in the Civil Aeronautics Board and the FAA, made her a compelling speaker in most any venue in Arizona.[4]

But Barrett seemed stranded in a sort of political DMZ. She said she stood for change, but she floundered trying to articulate how she would be different from Symington. If she stood any chance of winning, she would have to either effectively pitch a different conservative vision for Arizona or attack Symington about perceived moral lapses throughout his first tenure.

Barrett plugged $750,000 into her own campaign, leased a plane, and began canvassing the state at a breakneck pace. She was well received, reporters noted, but even admirers seemed to struggle articulating reasons to vote for her in the coming primary.

Symington's team decided the best way to engage their opponent was to not engage (except to occasionally mention she had broken a promise not to run).[5] As Barrett pushed for a series of debates with Symington, Symington's four top voices—Chuck Coughlin, Doug Cole, Jay Heiler, and Wes Gullett—seemed to take turns telling the media that the governor was too busy running the state to engage in debates.

It was a strategy that even Barrett's handlers admitted they would have used: Don't give an underdog opponent legitimacy by acting as if they're a serious contender.[6]

Having spent the spring and summer of 1994 gaining little or no traction,[7] the increasingly frustrated Barrett (and certainly her high-powered consultant, Reagan-election-henchman Richard Wirthlin) decided she had no choice but to go negative. In a full-page ad in the August 21 *Republic*, she went about as negative as a candidate can.

"Hey Governor, come out and fight like a . . . person."[8]

"Why did Fife Symington refuse to debate Barbara Barrett? What is he hiding from us?"

Besides some claims that Symington was responsible for out-of-control growth in state government, the lengthy ad primarily focused on the allegations of bid-rigging in the awarding of Project SLIM contracts and the grand jury and FBI probes into his business dealings.

Democrats delighted in the free print and television advertising. Polls suggested some Republicans and undecideds, particularly women, seemed to appreciate her willingness to violate party decorum.

Senator John McCain took the lead among Republicans in chastising Barrett for her new ad strategy. In an August 23 letter to Barrett, McCain, in the cutting tone he was more known for in the 1990s, wrote: "Your mean-spirited and inaccurate attack ads in the *Arizona Republic* and on television not only contradict the kind of campaign you told me and others that you would run; they also violate the pledge you signed to 'not participate in nor condone political attacks' and 'do nothing that in any way jeopardizes the candidacy of the successful Republican gubernatorial nominee.'"

Barrett was undeterred, though. Three days after she received McCain's letter, she once again publicly called for Arizona Attorney General Grant Woods to convene a grand jury to investigate the accusations that George Leckie had illegally steered a $1.5 million Project SLIM contract to Symington's personal accountant three years earlier. (Woods was already investigating possible antitrust and procurement violations at the time. The month before, four county attorneys presented a report stating that although they found the procurement procedures of the early Symington administration to be "extremely lax," they found no wrongdoing.)[9]

Symington countered that Barrett was well aware that Project SLIM issues had nothing to do with him. The governor, by statute, had no involvement in procurement contracting, he argued when the two finally met in a late-August question-and-answer session with the *Mesa Tribune*'s editorial board.[10]

Polls through the summer generally showed Barrett behind Symington by a two-to-one margin. Barrett's late aggressiveness didn't seem to help. In the September 13 primary, Symington won 68 percent of the vote to Barrett's 32 percent.[11]

It was a rout, but it was unclear if Symington had been helped or hurt by facing an aggressive challenger. Winning by greater than a two-to-one margin showed support for Symington was strong and galvanizing; on the other hand, losing one-third of voters in the primary as a sitting gov-

# Senator John McCain

WASHINGTON, D.C. 20510

August 23, 1994

Mrs. Barbara Barrett
P.O. Box 45394
Phoenix, AZ 85064

Dear Barbara:

I am deeply disappointed and puzzled by your recent decision to launch a negative attack against Governor Fife Symington; a move that has all the hallmarks of the kind of desperation tactics often associated with losing campaigns late in an election. Having spent years in the political arena, I am not easily surprised by the depths to which candidates can sink when their aspirations for elected office are fading. In your case, however, I had taken you at your word that your ambition would never overcome your sense of fair play and that your campaign would avoid the low road upon which you are now so eagerly embarked.

Your mean-spirited and inaccurate attack ads in the Arizona Republic and on television not only contradict the kind of campaign you told me and others that you would run; they also violate the pledge you signed to "not participate in nor condone political attacks" and "do nothing that in any way jeopardizes the candidacy of the successful Republican gubernatorial nominee."

You will recall your letter to me in April asking my help in keeping the Governor's campaign "on a higher track." Its ironic that the advice you asked me to give the Governor was unwelcome in your own campaign.

Again, I am seldom surprised when troubled campaigns "go negative," but I am annoyed when they expose the degree of hypocrisy apparent in your decision to abandon your self proclaimed commitment to run a positive, issues-oriented campaign. I had not previously attributed to you that level of cynicism.

I am obliged to remind you, Barbara, that your new found enthusiasm for cheap shots and character attacks may only serve to handicap our Party's chances in November while simultaneously tarnishing your own reputation among Arizona Republicans. It will do nothing to improve your own prospects in September. On the contrary, I expect it will remind many voters that Fife Symington, unlike his opponent, is a candidate and a governor who can be relied upon to keep his word.

Sincerely,

John McCain

John McCain
United States Senator
NOT PRINTED AT GOVERNMENT EXPENSE

Sen. McCain's letter to candidate Barrett chastising her for anti-Symington campaign.
Courtesy of the Symington family archives.

ernor suggested there were enough registered Republicans disenchanted by Symington that they could tilt the general election to the Democratic candidate. Symington certainly didn't benefit from the ferocious attack on his ethics.

As the primary approached, it appeared Symington was in a precarious position against any of the three Democrats.[12]

As 1994 began, Terry Goddard was already squared up for a rematch and deemed by several polls to be the frontrunner in any lineup of potential Democratic challengers. He had high name recognition statewide, experience running statewide campaigns, and he had kept himself relevant in state politics since his gubernatorial loss three years earlier. Despite being upset by Symington—twice—Goddard still had widespread support and was still the same guy *Time* magazine said "had presidential hopeful written all over him."[13]

He was a known quantity with plenty of competency, but he was also a known quantity with little sizzle and, according to the majority of analysts, little new to say. And at least according to Keven Willey's sources in the Democratic National Committee, Goddard was no longer the "it guy" in Arizona.[14]

In his speech announcing his candidacy in mid-February, it appeared Goddard and his staff were well aware they could not parrot their 1990 talking points. They would need to get ahead on the hot topics of 1994. And there was no hotter topic that year than crime and punishment.

Goddard spent so much of his candidacy announcement talking tough on crime that the *Republic*'s editorial writers opined: "Gosh. Have crime and violence in Arizona flipped so far out of control that other matters on the minds of people pale in comparison?"[15]

The editorial essentially chastised Goddard for not talking enough about the things he talked about in 1990: "This discussion (about crime) ought not to come at the virtual exclusion of thoughts and ideas on fiscal policy, education reform, building prisons, university budgets, water policy and the like. Goodness knows that there is no shortage of problems that will confront the next governor."

In March, Paul Johnson, the thirty-four-year-old mayor of Phoenix, entered the race with a long speech covering a much broader swath of state issues than Goddard. More than Goddard, too, Johnson took direct aim at Symington on numerous topics, from the usual ethics and personal finance shots to several detailed policy criticisms delivered with

Symington with Phoenix mayor Paul Johnson in the early 1990s. Courtesy of the
Arizona State Library, Archives and Public Records, History and Archives Division,
Phoenix, RG1_SG26_S6_B09_F029_I24.

long-blade wit. He lambasted Symington for letting the proposed youth
program, "Success by Six," get upended by a few far-right legislators. "If
a governor isn't creative enough to stop Bob Burns, one legislator out of
90, from frustrating the will of the majority of both parties . . . then I say
Arizona can't wait to send them both down the road," Johnson said.[16]

On guns, he accused Symington of "preaching about street crime
while his own Department of Public Safety puts seized weapons back
on the streets. Next January, I'm melting those guns." Unlike Goddard,
Johnson had a recent resume in crime-fighting: he had pushed a city or-
dinance requiring parental consent for anyone under the age of eighteen
to carry a gun, a rule that the NRA was challenging in court.

He was, in the parlance of the 1990s, a "New Democrat," meaning
he was a few policy-position tweaks from being a moderate 1980s
Republican.[17]

Johnson received an early boost when George Will wrote about him
in the days after announcing his candidacy. In his nationally syndicated

*Washington Post* column, Will quoted Johnson's policy ideas extensively, especially his juvenile-crime deterrents, while arguing Johnson had been a model in showing how a new generation of Democrats with new ideas of city governance were modernizing big-city government.[18] The third Democratic candidate was Eddie Basha, owner of the ubiquitous Arizona grocery chain, Bashas'. Bashas' was the family-owned grocery store that had grown as Arizona had grown and succeeded as giant national chains flooded Arizona hoping to feed the sprawl. Everybody knew Eddie Basha, even the non-natives of the city suburbs, because the Basha name blared from the retail centers every few miles throughout the urban centers of the state. Many people shopped at Bashas' simply because they wanted to "buy local." Eddie Basha was pretty much a local hero.

Besides being a longtime stalwart within the Democratic Party, he was, as his advertisements everywhere in every medium said, "your friendly neighborhood grocer."

Meaning, he was precisely the kind of candidate that wins primaries.

Basha considered skipping college to work in the family grocery store, but his father pushed him to get a degree. After attending Stanford, Basha returned to Arizona and eventually began running the small company. As other local grocery stores were squeezed out by increasing competition, Bashas' expanded to seventy stores by 1994.

Basha had long been a significant contributor to local causes and charities (including returning 25 percent of the company's profits to the eight tribal communities that had allowed him to build stores on their land), while serving on numerous local and state boards. His primary passion was education: after serving on the Chandler School Board and the State Board of Education, he became a member of the Arizona Board of Regents in 1990.

In his speech announcing his candidacy, Basha focused much of his time railing on the state's treatment of its public schools, so much so that he was quickly labeled a one-issue candidate.[19] And a very liberal one, at least by Arizona standards. At the same time he was widely admired, analysts questioned whether he could convince the state's notoriously tight-pursed taxpayers to embrace the idea of increasing funding for languishing programs.

No matter how liked Basha was, Symington would have little problem tagging Basha with that ever-effective label of "tax-and-spend liberal."[20]

The last major poll—taken by Earl de Berge ten days before the Democratic primary—had Johnson in first with 26 percent, Goddard next with 25 percent, and Basha in last with 15 percent. To his credit, de Berge did note there was an unusually large percentage of undecided voters. He predicted the race would be closer.[21]

Ten days later, it was the often-last-placed Eddie Basha who eked out the victory, pushing past Goddard late Tuesday as votes rolled in from rural precincts. Johnson came in third.[22]

The race, as generally predicted in the days before September 13, was close. Basha totaled more than 93,000 votes, just four thousand more than Goddard. Johnson, though, had faded badly, garnering just over 70,793 votes.

In the post-mortem, pollsters and commentators tried to make sense of what appeared to be an unlikely win. Basha had pulled an unusual amount of Republicans over to the Democratic Party to vote for him. He did very well among groups not adequately represented in polls, particularly Hispanics and Native Americans, who heavily supported Basha over his opponents. He had looked his best in a late ad in which he defended himself against the Johnson attack. That seemed to have pulled undecideds who, as Steve Wilson wrote, liked Basha's "underdog status, his small-town folksiness and the straightforward style of his TV ads."

So, it would be "your friendly neighborhood grocer" versus the controversial but arguably effective sitting governor.

Early polling suggested it would be a blowout.

An Arizona Republic/Channel 10 News poll conducted days after the primary showed Basha leading Symington 42 percent to 36 percent. Just two weeks later, an Arizona State University polls showed Basha had a comfortable sixteen-point lead over Symington.

Indeed, Eddie Basha would go on to lead in every public poll prior to the November election, a fact that, for reasons made obvious after the primary, neither comforted Eddie Basha nor disheartened Fife Symington.[23]

More ominously for Symington's team, the campaign's internal polling—extensive polling that had more often proved to be accurate—had Symington down by twenty-three points.

*Chapter 26*

# THE BIG SWING

One of Fife Symington's signature accomplishments had been his successful guidance of Arizona's Indian gaming issues from near-shootout to a unanimously agreed-upon pact, which went into effect in 1993.

Mission accomplished.

Except that, in fact, the gaming issue never seemed to get put to rest, with somebody somewhere—whether from the tribal, federal, state, or public arena—questioning, or testing the limits of, the language of the agreement.[1]

As the 1994 primary entered its final week, for example, news broke that a tribe-run casino near Tucson was running five blackjack tables, a game that was supposed to be illegal under the federal Indian Gaming Regulatory Act and not permitted under the state agreement. Pascua Yaqui Tribe members argued, however, that they were offering a hybrid version of blackjack that was legal due to a loophole in the federal act. Three other tribes were considering adding the game to their casinos.

An *Arizona Daily Star* story suggested the issue could become a problem for Symington in the coming election. "Symington's political quandary is that opponents could accuse him of backing down . . . from his previous position if he doesn't take action against the blackjack tables."

But if he does move against the tribes, "he could alienate Indian voters. His past opposition to a wider operation tribes sought and his successful pressure on state lawmakers to back his hand incurred a strong outcry not only from various tribal leaders," the story continued, "but from Arizona political and elected officials who supported the tribes."[2]

The news suggested two things: The Indian gaming issue wasn't going away anytime soon, and most every significant move Symington made until November was going to be probed by political analysts to determine its political intent and likely election impacts. The race was on.

As the general election fight began, Democrats accused Symington of a bait-and-switch in the previous election, saying he won pretending to be more of a centrist than he truly was (or had become in the hands of Jay Heiler). They sold Basha, basically, as the centrist Symington had claimed to be.

For example, they argued that by 1994, Symington had become a leader in a campaign to get millions of acres of federal land transferred to state ownership. Symington's increasingly heated states' rights rhetoric in opposition to the Endangered Species Act was proof, Democrats said, that he was desperate for votes and money from rural voters and the major employers who felt impeded by federal red tape, especially federal environmental laws.

The editors of the *Daily Star* in Tucson reflected that city's more environmentally conscious population: "Imagine the consequences (of such a transfer) in owl-bashing, business-coddling Arizona. Even now, state land efforts are famously chaotic, under-budgeted and anti-environmental. Under the contemplated transfer, disaster might befall lands that environmental groups already declare to be Arizona's most poorly managed, over-grazed territories."

In the Republican-leaning state, Basha would have to pull the suburban moderates into his camp by energizing them with the idea he was the protector of Arizona's air, land, and, with his education programs, children. (Amazingly, Basha had won the Democratic primary without winning Maricopa or Pima Counties. He couldn't win a general election without a stronger show in the urban areas.)

One thing Basha had to do, as the *Republic*'s Keven Willey pointed out, was to remind moderates of, as she described it, "Symington's abandonment of his education and environmental pledges." Also, Basha would want to "remind voters that Symington campaigned in 1990 on the importance of having a successful businessman in the governor's chair."

"The operative word here is 'successful,'" Willey wrote, referring, of course, to Symington's financial troubles.

Basha would have to stay positive, most agreed. He was a passionate champion for his causes, but his passion would need to be channeled through his beliefs, not at his adversary. He still was your friendly neighborhood grocer, after all. Basha would need to avoid the types of snarky jabs and direct attacks that ricocheted back to wound Barbara Barrett in the primary.

To counter Basha's immense war chest of goodwill, Symington needed to tout his fiscal successes while arguing he improved schools, state government, and the environment without spending money. Several of his stances, particularly those on property rights and limited government, had strengthened his hold on his party's right side, but he needed to grab those moderates that either felt he had drifted too far right or who believed his administration had ethical issues.

In the days after the primary, Symington turned quickly to the tactic that had worked so well against Terry Goddard: Symington simply called his opponent a "tax and spend liberal" and "bleeding-heart liberal" as much as possible. Indeed, Symington went on KTAR Radio the day after his primary win and used those exact words to describe Basha.

But Symington avoided being nasty and did not impugn Basha's character. Even when describing Basha's "tax-and-spend" and "bleeding-heart" tendencies, those beliefs were couched only as wrong-headed ideas coming from a well-meaning, upstanding Arizonan.

Symington and his team definitely agreed on one thing: They had to be nice to Eddie Basha.

The dynamic of the 1994 general election race, then, was considerably different from that of the 1990 race or the 1994 Republican primary. With Basha not wanting to damage his own image and Symington knowing his own image would be damaged if he tried to damage Basha's,[3] the 1994 general election was a much more civil affair than it would have been had anyone other than Eddie Basha been Symington's challenger.[4]

Symington no doubt benefitted from a race in which the negative headlines he had made would not be a major issue.

Symington also benefitted from the national political scene, where polls showed Americans turning against Democratic President Bill Clinton as well as those in the Democrat-held House and Senate. Indeed, as often as Symington called Basha a "tax-and-spend liberal," Symington also called him a "Clinton tax-and-spend liberal."

To be sure, though, the gray area between "teasing" and "attacking" was explored, particularly early in the campaign when Symington's team released the first chapter of a "book" titled *The Book on Basha: Chronicles of a Liberal.*[5]

Amid the fun, the Symington team's book, along with an inspired retaliatory parody book from Basha's team, actually gave a fairly detailed roadmap of the critical election issues of the day.

The first chapter of *Chronicles of a Liberal* lampooned Basha's idea that, if need be, the budgets of various state government departments could be cut 5 percent to increase spending for education and youth-centered crime-prevention programs. Symington argued such a plan would impede the state's crime-fighting abilities by making the state unable to pay for 950 new beds needed by the Department of Corrections.

The authors of *Chronicles of a Liberal* were more emboldened than deterred. If the first chapter was any indicator, the strategically timed release of each chapter could set Basha in a perpetually defensive posture.

After setting up the book's premise in "Chapter One," "Chapter Two" argued why Basha's opposition to Proposition 300, the aggressive plan to strengthen private property rights against perceived government overreach, was proof that Basha valued big government over the rights of the people. (The measure was mainly supported by realtors concerned about the impact of eminent-domain grabs in the city, as well as the cattlemen, farmers, and miners who felt unnecessary federal government regulations were threatening their livelihood.)

"Why has Eddie Basha joined the liberals on the environmental left in opposing such a law?" the book asked.

Basha and his team, knowing that they couldn't spend their campaign playing defense against chapters of some imaginary book, fired back with an imaginary collection of children's books titled *Symington: Four Short Tragic Stories*. Basha's farcical retort also mixed jokes with hard policy.[6]

"It's a bad law that will cost uncounted millions," Basha said of Prop. 300, throwing the "tax-and-spend" label back at Symington.

One "Tragic" story had only four words: "George Leckie. The end."

After Basha's parody book appeared, Symington said, "you will not hear personal insults from the Symington campaign," a comment that came just after he said, "Besides being a liberal, it turns out the self-described 'chubby grocer' can be a little mean."

Symington released another installment of *Chronicles* at a press conference a few days later. "Chapter Three" detailed how Basha's plan for a state tax to fund education would drive up taxes on homeowners around the state while doing little to improve education or balance inequities in the funding of Arizona's school districts.

Basha countered that Symington had ignored the funding and inequity problems during his first term and would likely do so again if given a second term.

By mid-October, *Chronicles of a Liberal* had faded from view, replaced instead by a flurry of advertisements by both candidates and more head-to-head debates. In one Symington ad, Arizona superintendent of public education, Democrat C. Diane Bishop, sharply criticized Basha's ideas on education reforms.

In an *Arizona Daily Star* story in mid-October, pollster Bruce Merrill cautioned the Symington staff about doing exactly what the Symington staff knew they shouldn't do: "The more (Symington) attacks Basha, the more it helps Eddie," he said.

Symington's campaign manager, Chuck Coughlin, suggested Merrill and Basha didn't know what "negative" really looked like. "I totally reject that idea," Coughlin told the *Daily Star* reporter.[7]

While Symington spent $220,000 during his primary race, Basha had pumped $1.2 million into his much more competitive primary campaign. Still, Basha had more fundraising power than most, allowing him to match Symington in spending for the general election. Both candidates spent more than $700,000 for political consultants and advertising after the middle of September.

Soon after the primaries, Symington dropped his policy of disengagement and agreed to at least four face-to-face debates. Besides Basha, Symington would also have to face off against Libertarian John Buttrick, who, for an Arizona Libertarian, was atypically appealing and aware of the functions of the state government he wanted to chop. He was, therefore, an actual threat to pull off several thousand voters from Symington.[8]

Ultimately, among the meetings of the candidates, only one was televised statewide. As such, the candidates' October 23 face-off was the biggest stage for them to be seen by Arizonans.[9]

The candidates hammered their usual themes. "We brought Arizona back to prosperity," Symington said, touting his role in helping spark the booming economy of the time. He pointed to his success in working with the legislature to bring about criminal justice reform, school choice, and tax cuts.

Basha and Buttrick then worked to dismantle that appearance of resounding success.

Buttrick labeled Symington's plan to abolish the state income tax as "Esplanade economics." He followed that clever line that didn't quite make sense with another shot, accusing Symington of allowing hundreds of new "useless" laws that, among other things, "regulated ostrich ranches" and "outlawed the growing of certain colors of cotton." "This is not the record of a governor who downsized government," the Libertarian said. (Buttrick's quote-worthy insults to Symington made up about a third of the following day story in the *Arizona Daily Star*.)

Symington and Basha ignored Buttrick, returning to similar themes and fairly genial rules of engagement in their presentations.

Basha returned frequently to his idea that better schools and youth programs were the path to a better Arizona.

Symington said the coming charter schools were the key to real improvement in Arizona's schools. He pushed for a pilot program offering four thousand school vouchers to low-income Arizonans. Basha strongly opposed vouchers.

Symington gained broadly favorable reviews for the outing and would later say the debate was a "turning point in the race."[10] Still, as with much of the race, the debate was pretty ho-hum political fare. Throughout September and October, nobody landed a knockout blow.

But throughout those two months, Symington, if polls could be believed, kept generally gaining ground on Basha. As the reality of the election grew near, it appeared average Arizonans began to settle back into their normal groove in which "liberal" was still a dirty word.[11]

Still, as November began, it appeared Basha continued to transcend his opponent's branding efforts. Although internal polls conducted by Symington consultants showed Symington moving ahead, Basha was still considered the favorite by most polls in the week before the election.[12]

But on October 31, Basha said something that Symington's team could very easily suggest made Basha far too liberal to represent Arizonans.[13]

Symington, Basha, and Buttrick agreed to field callers' questions together on a Phoenix radio station program. One caller simply asked if the candidates would sign a bill approving same-sex marriages.

Symington said he would veto any such bill. Buttrick and Basha said they would sign it. As talk show host Barry Young moved to another question, Symington interjected, arguing that Basha should fully explain his position on the issue. Basha took the bait, saying, he "supported civil rights for all minorities, including homosexuals." Basha then repeated his pledge to sign a bill recognizing same-sex marriages.[14]

Depending on your perspective, Basha either hedged or clarified his position the next day. He said he did not advocate same-sex marriages.

However, if the people of Arizona said through their representatives that they wanted same-sex marriages to be legal, Basha said he would not attempt to block the move.[15]

The exchange on same-sex marriage allowed Symington a huge opportunity: He could repeat something he knew most Arizonans agreed upon: "I believe same-sex marriages demean the institution of marriage," Symington repeated several times in the days after the radio debate. The "liberal" label was now easily affixed to Basha.[16]

Basha's campaign chairman offered a compelling but perhaps unhelpful defense: "Eddie doesn't believe in discrimination, he never has and he never will. If you're a bigot, you should not support him."

Jay Heiler, Symington's top aide, looked less compassionate following Basha's comments. After hearing Basha's admission that he would support a same-sex marriage law, an excited Heiler jokingly asked one of the male reporters covering the statehouse if he wanted to marry him. Heiler, seemingly forgetting he was joking with reporters, also referred to homosexuals as "queers" during the off-the-cuff exchange.[17]

Heiler apologized for the comments once they were made public. The incident incited a flurry of condemnations, but it ultimately seemed to do little damage to Symington's campaign.[18]

As Arizonans headed to the polls the morning of November 8, Democrats were cautiously optimistic that they would dethrone the governor by day's end.[19]

By nightfall, though, that optimism was already gone. Symington, along with just about every other Republican running for high office, was going to win.

Few if anyone, though, predicted the size of Symington's victory—52 percent to 44 percent, with Buttrick grabbing 3 percent. It was a twenty-plus-point swing from polls taken at the beginning of the general election race.

Symington won by a large margin in Republican-heavy Maricopa County, which encompassed Phoenix and its suburbs, and did better than many predicted in rural Arizona and in the more Democratic-leaning Tucson area.

Perhaps Symington's win, as *Daily Star* columnist Tom Beal suggested, was just a reflection of a fundamental change in the political makeup of Arizona: "The 50-year trend is now complete," Beal argued. "This historically Democratic state (90 percent in the '40s) is now solidly a Republican one. The GOP has the numbers. It inflates its majority by getting more of its voters to the polls."[20]

Symington's financial and legal woes had minimal impact on voters' decisions, according to an exit poll of more than 1,500 voters sponsored by the Associated Press and several television networks. The extensive exit poll offered an unusually precise window into public opinion on Symington that was difficult for local pollsters to match.[21]

Symington, the poll suggested, successfully linked Basha to Clinton, whose unpopularity as of 1994 helped bring about the so-called "Gingrich Revolution" or "The Revolution of 1994."

Basha overwhelmingly won with minority voters and those who considered education to be the top priority for state government.

Besides grabbing much of the moderate vote, Symington successfully energized the conservative wing of his party. Numerous conservative-leaning voters said Basha's comment that he supported same-sex marriage legislation pushed them to vote for Symington.

Arguably the most intriguing bit of information from the large poll: about half of the voters polled said they believed Symington was honest. Of those, nearly eight out of ten voted for Symington.

Meaning, conversely, that thousands of Arizonans voted for Symington even though they didn't fully trust him.

Symington's campaign slogan "Promises Made, Promises Kept" apparently resonated with the majority of voters. Republicans across the country used many of the same themes in the 1994 elections that brought a majority of voters nationally into the Republican camp.

That Symington could draw 80 percent of the vote from those who didn't believe the ethics accusations or care that his business was in tatters, suggested something else, too:

If Symington's early mistakes and his personal financial problems would fade from the headlines, he likely would be a very popular governor.

The Symington team had one paramount hope for his second term: Please, let the past stay in the past.

# Chapter 27

# CONTRACT WITH ARIZONA

A s his second term began, Symington had a seasoned, unified staff that worked well together, a far cry from the post-1991 runoff emergency assemblage of former campaign staffers sometimes both ill-prepared for, and sometimes unaware of the parameters of, their positions.[1] With a wave of pro-Republican sentiment sweeping the landscape around them, even detractors were admitting the administration was in a groove.[2]

When giving the Republican response to President Clinton's State of the Union address that year, New Jersey governor Christine Todd Whitman gave Symington a shout-out for his "innovative tax-cutting policies" that she claimed had spurred growth in Arizona while balancing a budget and cutting taxes. She basically was suggesting that, with their "Contract with America," her party could do for America what Symington was doing for Arizona.[3]

In the first year of his second term, for better or worse, Symington arguably was pitching more aggressive changes to Arizona law and its relationship with the federal government than any governor in the state's history. (He was also, to the chagrin of those in his way, pitching laws that would consolidate power under the executive branch. Symington proposed moves that would pull responsibilities from the attorney general, the Corporation Commission, and the Game and Fish Commission, among others.) With a fresh mandate and Republicans running most everything in the state, Symington was more likely to get output from the legislative process that better resembled his input.[4]

*Republic* contributor Steve Tuttle wrote with a caveat on New Year's Day of 1995: "Fife Symington may become the most active and powerful governor in recent memory because there is simply no one to stop him."[5]

(In his piece, Tuttle also poked fun at a Symington administration hypocrisy: "Symington will continue to flail away at the evils of federal spending, while his chief mouthpiece, Doug Cole, continues to brag about how much federal grant money the governor has obtained.")

Such end-of-year debriefings and beginning-of-year prognostications were (and still are) common copy in the slow-news holiday season. Some common themes and snapshots of the Zeitgeist usually emerge, and the media mood of early 1995 was generally positive in that it was less apocalyptic than in the previous few years.

"The overwhelming majority of Arizonans will have another pretty good year," Tuttle predicted. "Look around, folks. Things aren't nearly so bad as columnists and commentators like to claim."

After Symington's State of the State address, the *Republic*'s lead editorial raved, "For four years, Symington's fiscal policies have been more than a beacon for the rest of the country, wooing new companies and spurring the state's economic growth. They have allowed Arizonans to keep more of their hard-earned money, meaning that government spends less. It's an enviable record, to be sure, but Symington wants to take it to new heights with the down payment on an eventual phase-out of the state's income tax."[6]

The editorial predicted that Symington's "ambitious set of proposals to build upon his administration's achievements—decidedly of the meat-and-potatoes variety—would for the most part breeze through a largely sympathetic Legislature" that would "likely find it difficult, if not impossible, to find fault with the governor's tilt toward more tax cuts, reforms in the juvenile justice system and his quest to push the cause of states' rights in the face of mandates from Big Brother."

The editorial even repeated Symington's playful homage to Spiro Agnew's alliterative stab at inside-the-beltway politicos: "No issue has seemed to galvanize Western states quite like the clarion call to rise up against what the governor called 'the little potentates of the Potomac.' Symington is on the cutting edge of the states' rights bandwagon, and he wants to build upon last year's creation of the Constitutional Defense Council by waging aggressive legal warfare against federal mandates that flout the Tenth Amendment and cloud the future of our state."

Although the machinations of Symington's personal financial case and the George Leckie/John Yeoman alleged $1.5 million bid-rigging scheme ground on,[7] those issues—compared to years past and years to come, at least—seemed to be background noise in the months after Symington's reelection.

In January of 1995, perhaps for the first time during his tenure, the majority of analysis pieces on Symington mentioned only policy and performance issues.

That certainly didn't mean all loved all his ideas. As he became more confident, it was widely argued that he became a more confident champion of causes farther to the right than prudent or representative of most Arizonans.

The *Republic* editorial noted, "As we said, the Symington agenda is ambitious, so much so that controversy will be right around the corner. Environmentalists certainly won't like him going out after the Clean Air Act, despite his contention that a lawsuit against the Clean Air Act does not mean that we will abandon cleaning our air. The education establishment is sure to object to another run at a pilot voucher program enabling 2,000 low-income children to use $1,500 grants to attend the private, parochial or public school of their choices. And there will be opposition to the Symington plan to remove all limits on personal campaign donations."

The *Arizona Daily Star* editors were more pointed in their critique of Symington's anti-federal rhetoric.[8]

"Gov. J. Fife Symington III makes for an unpersuasive rebel," the *Daily Star's* editorial read the following day. "However, rebellion now burns across the land, and so there Symington was yesterday, turning his fifth State of the State address into a mostly irresponsible and irrelevant attack on the federal government."

Mark Kimble of the *Tucson Citizen* likened Symington's lengthy anti-federal attacks to those made by leaders of the Confederacy in 1861.[9] "It didn't work the first time when shots were fired at Fort Sumter on April 12, 1861," Kimble wrote. "And you have to wonder whether Civil War II has any chance of success after its opening barrage was fired here on Jan. 9, 1995."

Symington's $200 million tax-cut plan did benefit low- and middle-income Arizonans (at least percentage-wise) and his voucher program would start with breaks only for low-income children. But his battles against federal environmental regulations and his idea to pull the cap from campaign donations were ideas that were widely pegged as pro-big money and anti-environment. The left and pockets of the center sharpened their rhetoric against some of his policies as it appeared he was drifting from moderation.

His support of a plan to fashion a sort of waste-trimming, back-to-work-oriented Arizona version of welfare seemed, as one federal report suggested, "punitive."[10] The plan, named the Employing and Moving People Off Welfare and Encouraging Responsibility (so it would have the acronym "EMPOWER"), would cap funding for welfare mothers after two years, would limit the number of children eligible for money, and would require teen mothers who were unwed to live with their parents. More job training programs and employment opportunities would be available under the new program, all to incentivize the movement of jobless Arizonans off welfare and into the then-booming job market.[11]

Conservation-minded experts in the state were also concerned that Symington's plan to reorganize state departments overseeing wildlife and land management would reduce public input on conservation issues in the state. Less public input, they argued, meant more corporate influence over decisions.[12]

Symington's audacious solution for the Valley's floundering freeway plans wasn't to everyone's liking, either. Besides shelving mass-transit plans, the West Valley would lose proposed freeway miles—for the time being at least—while East Valley road projects would get moving again thanks to a boost of existing state revenues. Even in the East Valley, though, local leaders felt Symington had failed to properly consult them and with that, failed to make the Red Mountain Freeway wide enough and the Santan Freeway long enough.[13]

*Arizona Daily Star* editors argued he had also backed away from campaign promises to strengthen the state's health-care programs for the poor.

At the same time, Symington proposed spreading a bit of the new-found state wealth to state workers. The $35.2 million in pay raises was too little considering past freezes, critics argued, but yes, it was something, at least.

(In arguing for the pay raises for state employees, Symington displayed his ever-increasing comfort with, and enjoyment in, playful intellectual strutting. This time, he quoted Alaric, the Visigoth who laid siege to Rome in the fifth century: "If you want me to sack Rome, you have to give me the troops." "You sometimes had to run to the dictionary or encyclopedia during the speech," a member of the capitol press pool said later.)[14]

The legislature's budget announced that month mirrored Symington's in the push for a $200 million tax cut, but proposed spreading the cuts over more than one state tax, not just from the state income tax as Symington proposed.

The budget from the Joint Legislative Budget Committee didn't have a pay increase for state employees while adding nearly $100 million to help offset the expenses incurred due to the growth in the state's public schools. There was no mention in the legislature's budget regarding money Symington wanted to start the "Arizona Military Institute," a planned two thousand-student 7–12 school for problem teens. Also, the legislature's budget called for the establishment of an $87 million "rainy day fund"—a stash of cash set aside in case of a budget emergency in the future.

Republicans to Symington's right wanted the rainy day fund rather than the state-employee pay raises, so, while he'd be wrangling with Democrats for the extra school financing, he'd be facing off with many in his own party to get the pay raise.[15]

As for school vouchers: leaders of both the Senate and the House Education Committees were presenting alternative proposals. "As good Republicans they won't announce it dead," the *Daily Star*'s legislative reporter wrote. "Their new plans are tacit admission the Symington plan is fatally wounded."

And conservatives in his party were not at all interested in the return of Symington's plan to add nearly 150,000 low-income people to the state's federally subsidized health-care program. Although the plan was estimated to save the state more than $100 million a year by moving those needing financial assistance to a program funded by the federal government, conservatives feared the move would add to the number of people on welfare rolls while increasing federal control over Arizona's state government.

Symington saw no hypocrisy considering his states' rights position, nor did he agree the plan would increase the number of people receiving welfare benefits.[16]

"It is giving health care, preventing these people from going onto welfare and it saves the taxpayers of the state a lot of money," he said. "That, to me, is not expanding welfare."

Symington also saw no hypocrisy in his calls for a smaller federal government at the same time he was leading a charge to have the federal government bail out the crumbling Mexican economy.

Indeed, at the same time he was becoming a national darling of the

Republican Party, he was one of the most aggressive proponents of a proposed multibillion-dollar aid package to Mexico that most Republicans believed would be, as Republican presidential candidate Pat Buchanan put it, "daylight robbery of the nation's wealth."[17]

But Arizona badly needed its next-door neighbor and leading international trade partner to stay solvent.[18]

In late January 1995, Symington left Phoenix on a flight to Washington, DC, for the winter meeting of the National Governors' Association. The hot topic that year: Welfare reform. A majority of governors—primarily the thirty Republican governors—supported a plan in which states would be given significantly more control over how the federal money they received for welfare programs was spent.[19]

While Symington awaited his connecting flight in a snow-shrouded terminal at Indianapolis International Airport, he heard his name announced over the terminal's public address system. He was being paged. He was directed to pick up the nearest airport courtesy phone.

"Fife, this is Ernesto," he heard when he answered the call. "I have a big problem."[20]

It was the newly elected president of Mexico, Ernesto Zedillo, with whom Symington had already begun discussions to ease trade barriers as part of the North American Free Trade Agreement.

Zedillo explained that, without help from either the US Congress or President Clinton, the Mexican banking system would collapse within days. Zedillo knew Symington would be meeting with Representative Newt Gingrich, the new Speaker of the US House of Representatives, and other Republican congressional leaders during the coming three days of meetings. He knew, also, that Symington would have access to Clinton, who would be speaking at the governor's convention as well as attending a lengthy work session with governors regarding welfare reform.[21]

Zedillo asked Symington to do everything he could to push for a US loan to Mexico. Symington promised to do "everything I can do to help," then asked if Zedillo had talked yet with the new governor of Texas, George W. Bush. Zedillo hadn't. Symington suggested that Zedillo ask Bush, as governor of Mexico's largest US state trading partner, to join Symington in lobbying Gingrich and others to approve the bailout. Zedillo then called Bush and Bush agreed to join Symington in his lobbying efforts in Washington that weekend.

Once in Washington, Symington and Bush met with Gingrich and other House and Senate Republican leaders. Bush and Symington explained the potentially devastating impact of a Mexico financial meltdown on the economies of their states. But after two spirited meetings, it became very clear, Symington said later, "Republicans in Congress would not be supporting a loan."

What Bush and Symington arguably succeeded at doing, though, was convincing Gingrich and other Republicans not to use the issue as a political football if Clinton used his executive powers to approve a loan from the US Treasury to Mexico. Gingrich, Bush, and Symington went to the White House for a brief meeting with Clinton. According to Symington, Gingrich told Clinton, "Leadership will support your efforts, but you have to take the lead."[22]

Two days later, Clinton gave a speech at the governors' meeting in which he announced he would use an executive order to send up to $20 billion to the Mexican government as part of a larger worldwide effort.[23]

The package, which totaled $48.8 billion, succeeded at stabilizing Mexico's currency and helped restore worldwide confidence in Mexico's economy. Mexico paid back all of the money it borrowed from the United States—along with interest—by early 1997.[24]

Symington later received an award from the Organization of American States for his role in helping pave the political path for the loan.[25] In his award acceptance speech, Symington noted that Clinton was willing to take the lead on the bailout even though it was a broadly unpopular plan in the United States. "It took a lot of courage by the President," Symington said in his speech.

Back in Arizona, by mid-March, Symington and the legislature had pushed through a $4.5 billion budget, which arguably included the most sweeping expression of Symington's fiscal beliefs during his tenure. Legislators had broadly supported a $231 million income-tax reduction. Another $200 million in cuts were promised for the next year, a move that was less palatable to Democrats who were concerned that essential state programs would get cut in the coming year if the economy slowed.

With the cut and the promised cut, Arizonans would be paying nearly a billion dollars less in state taxes since Symington first took office.[26]

Critics of the tax cuts pointed to the final version of the tax-reduction plan (which was reshaped several times in the final day of negotiations) as less the promised relief to low- and middle-income Arizonans and more of another gift to the richest Arizonans.

The equity debate was one as old as taxes themselves: Supporters pointed out that everyone was getting a 21 percent tax decrease and that those earning under $20,000 with a family of four wouldn't pay any state income taxes. Detractors pointed out that although the across-the-board percentage cut sounded egalitarian, it in fact meant that more than 50 percent of the billion dollars in cuts would go to the wealthiest 4 percent of Arizonans.

Even with the late flurry of modifications, Symington praised the final version of the tax-cut plan, saying it brought the state's tax code much closer to his ultimate goal—a true flat tax by which all state taxpayers (other than the working poor) pay the same percent of their income with no deductions.

Supporters of flat, or flatter, taxes focused on the simplicity and equality of everyone paying the same percentage of their earnings. Detractors focused on the inequality of the total amount of money taken from each pocket.

"In simple economic terms," wrote Symington foil E. J. Montini, "the rich get richer." Montini then blamed Democrats as much as Republicans for the inequities he saw in the tax cuts: "I understand, finally, why Democrats lose elections in Arizona. It's simple. There are no Democrats in Arizona. There can't be. Otherwise they'd be trying to break down the palace gate."

Those who questioned the wisdom of promising a similar cut the following year pointed to several potential problems on the horizon. One issue dripped with irony: As Republicans on the federal level began mirroring Arizona's tax-cutting successes, they would be chopping federal aid to the states. One DC think tank argued the Republicans' proposed federal tax cuts would reduce funding to Arizona by $146 million in the coming year. If the "Contract with America"-based budgets stayed around until 2002, the estimated cost to Arizona would be $1.3 billion.

Arizona's leaders were also accused of using some voodoo math by having two of the tax cuts phase in over several years, meaning the full impact of the loss of revenue wouldn't be realized fully until the late 1990s.

Of course, supply-siders and trickle-down believers said the growth and spending spurred by the cuts would more than make up for the initial cuts.

A Rocky Mountain Poll released in late January showed Symington's job-approval ratings hitting 47 percent, the highest numbers he had ever garnered in the Earl de Berge poll.[27]

A KAET-TV statewide poll in late March showed that Symington's approval ratings had leapt to 64 percent, while only 28 percent disapproved of the job he was doing.[28]

If the polls were to be believed, he was the most popular he had ever been in his four years of running the state.

That same poll checked the public pulse regarding yet another major Republican move supported by Symington: with budget issues out of the way, the legislature was still debating some of its more controversial bills, one of which involved giving the governor's office and other agencies independent attorneys rather than ones assigned to them from the office of the Arizona Attorney General.

Most everyone saw the bill as a Symington vendetta against his sometimes-ally, often arch rival Attorney General Grant Woods, the popular centrist who always seemed to be looming or working to foil Symington either politically or legally. On this issue, most Arizonans sided with Woods—they wanted legal representation of state agencies to stay in Woods's office.

In the same poll, though, even though people generally saw the move as more of a shot directed at Woods than good policy, Arizonans still gave Symington a higher approval rating than Woods, which was unusual if not unique during the prior four years.

Symington's plan to refuse several federal crime-fighting and welfare grants, which Symington argued limited the state's latitude in decision-making, was shot down. However, Symington did get backing for one of his high-profile, anti-federal-meddling stances: legislators agreed to forbid the use of state tax dollars to pay the federal officials tasked with overseeing state prisons.

In eleventh-hour negotiations, legislators agreed to move Arizona's presidential primary up to February 27 so the state could be a player in the national conversation about presidential candidates.[29]

(The early Arizona primary was the brainchild and pet project of Senator John McCain. According to one Symington staffer, McCain wanted to use an early Arizona primary to launch the candidacy of his close political ally, Phil Gramm.)[30]

Symington's first veto that year came on a Woods-backed plan regulating the use of DNA blood tests in criminal cases.

Symington followed that little jab with two major moves involving environmental policy in the state. One Republican-backed bill he vetoed would have effectively undone the Endangered Species Act in the state by giving jurisdiction over the act's application process to the legislature.[31] His veto was cheered by environmentalists, but his motives, his critics argued, weren't to save the environment: The veto was "about power and the governor's relentless accumulation of it," wrote Keven Willey. "The governor vetoed the bill to protect his authority, not the environment."

He argued he wanted to protect both.

He also vetoed what had become labeled the "Polluter Protection Act," a plan that would have granted immunity to companies if they voluntarily disclosed their illegal polluting to the state. More odious to critics was a provision of the bill that would allow companies to keep their environmental records secret regardless of whether they self-reported or not. The plan was sold as a way to encourage businesses to clean up their messes voluntarily without fearing backlash, but as Arizona Department of Environmental Quality Director Ed Fox noted, it more likely would lead polluters to hide any violation.

Willey suggested Symington's motives for that veto were to "avoid a referendum" by Arizona voters.

In mid-March, Symington signed into law a $431 million tax cut as part of a $4.5 billion budget. It was the largest tax cut in state history.[32]

While reporting her column on Symington's vetoes, Willey overheard an intriguing inside-baseball exchange between Coughlin and Heiler. Heiler, who urged the governor to sign the bill, admitted, "It's never going to hit the books" (because it would be challenged by referendum). "Coughlin turned to Heiler," Willey wrote, "and said, 'We're not worried about your 25 percent,'" referring to the hardest right of the party who mostly favored the bill. "'What the governor needs to do is court,' as Symington's chief of staff called it, 'the moderate squish vote.'"[33]

If the polls were right, though, Symington didn't need to court the "squish vote," he just needed to hold onto it. For the first time since he took office, polling showed he was generally popular with both the right and left side of his party along with a large swath of the state's independent voters.

# Chapter 28

# A BAD FALL

Phoenix experienced the second hottest day in its history on July 28, 1995, when the temperature reached 121 degrees. People ran to the streets attempting to fry eggs on the pavement. Some airplanes were grounded at Sky Harbor out of concern the planes couldn't gain lift in the super-heated air.[1]

Deep in more projects than ever before and on the cusp of having a remodeled governor's office, Fife Symington wasn't much bothered by the horrendous summer heat.[2]

The Super Bowl was coming. Another large company had announced a major expansion in Arizona. Symington had just teamed with Sonora's governor Manlio Fabio Beltrones to create the first major tourism-based agreement between border states in the history of either country. (A new joint tourism board would push for border improvements and stream-lined travel regulations to promote what the governors termed a "two-nation vacation.")[3]

A federal judge sided with a Symington-supported, lower-court decision to ban slot machines on tribal lands.[4] He started a widely lauded program to focus the efforts of sixty Department of Public Safety officers on the troubled neighborhoods of South Phoenix. Symington's regular trip with his staff to meet-the-governor town halls around the state seemed to be building an ever-strengthening rural base of support for his agenda.

With the good feelings came speculation that Symington was poised for higher office. When Senator John McCain became presidential candidate Phil Gramm's national campaign chairman, Symington took charge of Gramm's state campaign (the only other governor backing Gramm was the governor of Texas, George W. Bush). Speculation followed that, if Gramm won, McCain would take a cabinet position and Symington would replace McCain.[5]

When Gramm's campaign fizzled, speculation still remained that the

Symington with Sonoran Governor Manlio Fabio Beltrones in Hermosillo in the early 1990s. Courtesy of the Arizona State Library, Archives and Public Records, History and Archives Division, Phoenix, RG1_SG26_S6_B01_F008_I03.

Arizona power shift would happen no matter which Republican won against Bill Clinton in 1996.

Symington was even drawing kudos from conservation-minded Arizonans with his plan to protect nearly 700,000 acres of state trust land from development. In announcing the plan, Symington expounded on the importance of protecting Arizona's open spaces "for current and future Arizonans."

About the same time, the Sierra Club released its environmental "grade card" for Arizona political figures. Democrats did considerably better in the assessment, of course, but Symington received a passing grade.[6] The club's statehouse lobbyist, Raena Honan, thanked Symington for "standing up against extremist bills" from his party's far right. (Honan, however, didn't thank many of Symington's top staffers: "They are mean-spirited bullies and proud of it," she told a *Republic* reporter.)

Symington's seemingly dichotomist attitude toward the environment (being anti-Endangered Species Act while proposing massive conservation plans, for example) confused Arizonans of all political persuasions.

If anyone understood Symington's environmental stances—and generally mirrored his policy stances—it was Ed Fox, Symington's director of the state's Department of Environmental Quality. Fox, previously an environmental law attorney for the powerful Phoenix firm Snell & Wilmer, was viewed, particularly by moderates, as one of Symington's most effective, and least political, department-head appointments.

But in late July of that year, Fox resigned. In a farewell interview with Willey, Fox voiced concerns about the state of Arizona politics ("This year was the worst," he said. "People just shout at one another."), and also explained how he could be a strong advocate for Arizona's air, water, and land while standing beside a governor who was leading a national revolt against the Endangered Species Act.[7]

"As word of Fox's resignation leaked Tuesday," Willey wrote, "speculation abounded that it was triggered by disagreements with Gov. Fife Symington, whose administration has marched so steadily rightward in the last three years as to risk falling off the edge of the Earth-is-flat movement."

Not so, Fox said. Not at all. "In four years, there has been only one issue where he went against me."

"His rhetoric about states' rights doesn't automatically equate to opposition to environmental regulation," Fox continued. "Most people don't appreciate that."

Fox "enjoys the kind of debates over public policy that Symington provides," Willey wrote, "but not the kind of grenade-lobbing warfare that the Legislature provides."

As Symington cruised at work, though, his personal finances continued to collapse.

Throughout August, out of public view, Symington and his attorneys worked feverishly with the loan-holders of the Mercado to renegotiate terms.[8] The Mercado, by then flanked by a much-larger retail development (something the city allowed after city council member promises to protect the risky but "important" Mercado),[9] had been a money pit since it opened. The project had already been sold at auction in 1993 for a fraction of its original cost after Symington failed to talk city officials into a $5.2 million bailout plan. The loan holders wanted more—they wanted Symington's personally guaranteed millions with interest, and they wanted it quickly.

In July, the legal dispute went to a judge, who ruled that Symington needed to pay the Mercado lenders $8.8 million. The judge amended the ruling a month later to include interest accrued. The grand total: Symington was to pay $11.5 million. The ruling was a significant win for the pension funds at the same time it all but doomed Symington's chances of financial recovery.[10]

Symington countered that the recession had caused his real estate company to lose too much of its holdings and management work to rebound. Symington offered $500,000 (some close friends had offered money to help him out, he said). No deal.

On September 20, Symington filed for bankruptcy in the US Bankruptcy Court in Phoenix, listing some $24 million in debts versus about $62,000 in assets.[11]

Symington announced the filing in a Wednesday morning press conference in which he called the trip to the US Bankruptcy Court "the most traumatic moment in my life." He then spent the rest of the day telling his side of the story through any media available (including his own Wednesday radio show). He was unusually humble and self-effacing as he rolled out the details of his financial collapse, even saying to a room full of Arizona realtors at a Tucson conference: "Don't worry. I'm not going to give you any advice about real estate."[12]

He then argued: "When people say Fife Symington has walked away from financial responsibilities, they've missed the point. I have lost absolutely everything I created through the years of hard labor in real estate."

His major remaining assets were ASU season football tickets, $1,500 in clothing, $1,000 worth of scuba equipment, and a watch valued at about $100.

Legally out of creditors' grasps and not listed as assets—and one reason the negative press regarding Symington's bankruptcy was amplified—was his family trusts dispensing $38,000 a year, the $16,000 in his retirement plan, and a $30,000 life insurance policy. Ann's substantial inherited wealth wasn't included. The couple had signed a prenuptial agreement in 1976 stating they would keep their finances and property— including property acquired during the marriage—separate.

An Associated Press story quoted bankruptcy attorney Robin Leonard about how the average Arizonan would likely perceive Symington's bankruptcy case: "I'm sure that to a lot of people, it's going to seem fundamentally unfair," she said.[13]

The lead of William F. Rawson's AP story that ran in papers nationwide identified why the bankruptcy mattered more than most: It appeared to suggest hypocrisy and a campaign promise based on a false premise. "Gov. Fife Symington, a real estate developer who was elected on a promise to apply his business acumen to state government, filed for bankruptcy yesterday," Rawson wrote.

The media swarmed the bankruptcy documents and found plenty of fodder. In the days and weeks following the filing, Symington's failed finances were by far the biggest story in the state.

Each day seemed to bring some new angle on the story. The state's major news outlets dissected Symington's chances of politically surviving his bankruptcy.

Symington "is wounded and bloody, but he has tremendous recuperation powers," the top Democrat in the state house of representatives said.[14]

Still, Democrats seemed reinvigorated by Symington's bankruptcy.[15]

"It sickens me to think that Symington will continue to have all the trappings of respectability when he has literally been stealing from the retirement funds of working men and women," said Assistant Senate Minority Leader Sandra Kennedy. "He was caught and won't pay it back."

Through the remainder of 1995, commentators and Symington opponents seemed to paint most any new announcement by the governor as an attempt to draw attention from his financial woes. (Symington didn't always help his case. One major public-relations gaffe was his decision to vacation in Europe with his family just before declaring bankruptcy.)

In the same month as his bankruptcy, Symington told the directors of state departments to begin identifying programs to be eliminated so the governor and the legislature could keep their promise of a $200 million tax cut. As he made that announcement, Symington was touring the state holding town halls in which he asked citizens to identify programs they felt they could live without.[16]

He was accused of being willing to cut jobs and services to make headlines that weren't about his finances.

On October 3, Charles Schwab & Co. announced they would be adding 2,300 employees to their operations. Symington and Jim Marsh, director of the Arizona Department of Commerce, had personally negotiated the deal with Schwab executives. Several other companies soon after announced intentions to grow their businesses in Arizona.

With every bit of potentially good news, it seemed, came some embarrassing news related to his personal finances. When his ASU season football tickets were put up for auction to help cover his debt, for example, the editor and co-owner of the *Phoenix New Times* (the hard-charging alt-weekly Symington refused to acknowledge existed) bought them for $2,200 and gave them to members of the six union pension funds involved in the Mercado loans. The paper's ticket purchase made national news; Symington's statewide tour didn't.[17]

Symington pitched a plan to eliminate the state department of education as well as the practice of collective bargaining by teachers. Symington argued he wanted to streamline and consolidate in a way that would improve schools. Dems said, again, that he was just trying to make headlines, and that he was being increasingly mean-hearted in the process.

He created a new high-level government position to lead the fight against drugs, particularly the growing movement of Mexican methamphetamine into the state.[18] During the same time, he outlined his newest plan to overhaul the juvenile justice system. Most notable was his push to have any fifteen-year-old accused of a violent crime tried as an adult.

One response by several Democratic leaders embodied the near-jubilant mood of the opposition. In mid-October, Phoenix representatives Art Hamilton and Ken Cheuvront unveiled a parody rock-concert T-shirt emblazoned: "Symington Diversion Tour: 1995." The T-shirt's reverse side listed the Democrats' interpretation of Symington's post-bankruptcy moves:

"Destroy Arizona's Public Schools." "Attack the Juvenile Justice System." "Appoint a 'Meth Czar.'" The list ended with a blank space accompanied with the line: "Fill in the blank. He's not done yet."[19]

In November, an AP story accused the governor of failing to disclose his legal debts on the yearly financial statements he was required to file with the state to expose potential conflicts of interest. Cole, Symington's spokesman, cited an exemption in the disclosure law for debts "resulting from the ordinary conduct of business."[20]

Symington and his first gubernatorial campaign staff were also accused of falsifying documents in an effort to hide questionable campaign contributions and expenditures.[21]

Anytime some financial move by Symington was questioned in the press, it was combined with speculation on whether he could, or should, remain in office. Regarding the reporting of attorney fees, for example, Mike Evans of Arizona Common Cause argued that not reporting such debt "could very well be a violation—a Class 1 misdemeanor." Rob Carey from the AG's office then said, "If a violation did occur, a misdemeanor could provide grounds for impeachment."

Symington's poll numbers went from stellar to abysmal within the span of a few months.

A November Behavior Research Center survey suggested that half as many Arizonans believed Symington was doing a "good or excellent" job as did at the beginning of the year.[22] Other local polls showed similar precipitous declines in his popularity between the beginning and end of fall. A poll conducted for KAET-TV and ASU showed the number of Arizonans who gave Symington favorable or very favorable ratings had dropped from 61 percent to 37 percent by the end of October.[23]

Whether politically motivated or heartfelt, Symington's fight with what he deemed "federal overreach" intensified throughout the first year of his second term. The fight came to a symbolic head just before Thanksgiving in a showdown between state and federal officials at the Grand Canyon.

On the morning of November 16, just after eating breakfast with Ann, Symington hopped into his waiting car and began perusing his stack of morning newspapers. As he opened the *Republic*, he was greeted with the headline "Grand Canyon Closes."[24]

A federal budget impasse had closed down much of the federal government. With that, all the nation's national parks were shuttered.

Symington was furious, saying later: "Did I get a call from Bruce Babbitt, the secretary of the interior and former governor of the state? Did I get a call from anyone at the Grand Canyon, the state's largest tourist destination? To say I was pissed is an understatement.

"I made my mind up right then: I was going to open the Grand Canyon."[25]

Once he reached the Capitol, Symington announced his intentions to Chief of Staff Wes Gullett, who asked Symington if he "was being serious," then to Doug Cole, who also asked if he was being serious. Symington wanted to meet immediately with the heads of Arizona's Department of Public Safety and the Arizona National Guard, as well as the leaders of both the state house and senate.[26]

An audacious plan took form: Dozens of DPS officers, state parks personnel, and fifty unarmed Arizona National Guard troops based in Flagstaff would mobilize and travel the next morning to the Grand Canyon and await the arrival of Symington and other state leaders at the Grand Canyon Airport.

Symington and state leadership crafted a letter to Clinton and Babbitt demanding that the park be reopened. The state would pay furloughed federal employees to work if necessary. If that wasn't possible, Symington offered up Guard troops, state parks employees, and DPS officers to provide basic services.[27]

(Several state leaders quickly agreed to seek private donations if necessary to finance the operation. Two of Arizona's leading developers, John F. Long and the Del Webb Corporation, ultimately donated several million dollars to create a fund to front money for park operations during shutdowns.)[28]

Symington hoped to keep the operation secret until everyone arrived at the Grand Canyon the next morning, but Pentagon officials got wind of the planned troop movement from Flagstaff and called Cole, who had to explain the troops were being sent by the governor—unarmed—to open the Grand Canyon to visitors.

Pentagon officials didn't welcome the news. US Attorney Janet Napolitano was directed to have a federal judge on call to approve a restraining order to rein in the governor. Soon, Cole was getting calls from media outlets around the world as domestic reporters rushed to reach the Grand Canyon's tiny airport by the next morning.

Symington flew to the Grand Canyon the following morning and emerged from his plane into a throng of Interior Department and state staffers, DPS officers, Guard members, curious onlookers who couldn't get into the park, and a mass of reporters, microphones, and cameras.[29]

After stepping from the plane, Symington walked over to the park's top official, held out his hand and said, "You might not believe this, but I've come in peace."[30] The superintendent then handed Symington a letter from federal officials rejecting his plan for reopening the park using the state employees Symington had gathered at the airport.[31]

Although Symington described the congregation of state employees as a show of "human resources," the presence of the state police and the state's National Guard troops (who remained under state authority until "federalized," which they could have been at any time during the confrontation) certainly added to a sense that Symington's threats might be backed by some sort of force. He fueled concern that an altercation might ensue with his heated rhetoric: "If the response (to the letter from state officials) is not satisfactory and it looks like they are going into an extended closure of the park, then I would get together with leadership and plan our strategy to reopen the park immediately."

His suggestion that he was willing to direct DPS officers to remove barricades and use what he termed "special military police" for other functions only intensified the sense that a fight was imminent between a US state and the US government.

At least he described the gambit as "a *bloodless* coup."

Symington and state Speaker of the House Mark Killian met with Interior Department officials for about an hour in the Grand Canyon Airways building at the airport.[32] He failed to convince officials to put his plan for opening the park into motion. But Symington took away one small prize from the discussions: Officials agreed to continue the discussions.

And also, one big prize: Lots of press. An AP photo of Symington emerging from discussions flanked by two Arizona DPS officers appeared in dozens—if not hundreds—of newspapers around the world. Symington likely got more national and international press on November 18, 1995, than on any other day of his life.

Coverage of the standoff by a newspaper in Santa Rosa, California, revealed one of the public's takeaways from this unprecedented move: next to the paper's Symington/Grand Canyon story was a story more pressing to Californians headlined: "Rangers shoo visitors away from Yosemite."[33]

In Arizona, the move—beyond those directly impacted by the lost tourism dollars—was viewed mostly from pre-established perspectives.[34] Symington was either mounting a courageous stand against a federal government with too much power, or he was shooting from the hip as he sought any press that didn't involve his bankruptcy.

The buildup to the standoff was much more thrilling than the aftermath. After Symington was informed by federal officials that his demands would not be heeded, the governor sent everyone home, held another blustery press conference, and then headed back to Phoenix. He promised, though, to pursue the issue aggressively until the park was opened.

A temporary federal budget deal (a continuing resolution) was reached that weekend, so the issue faded quickly from the national stage as the park reopened. But although the park was open, there still was no safeguard that it wouldn't close again amid another budget feud. Indeed, another closure could come quickly. The stopgap budget measure only funded the government for another month, not the full fiscal year.[35]

In the weeks following, Symington and federal officials agreed on a deal that would allow the park to stay open using state money during any future shutdowns. In mid-December, the federal government once again shut down when the stopgap budget measure expired. This time, though, the state of Arizona immediately began paying $17,625 a day for stripped-down operations at the Grand Canyon. Arizona was then reimbursed when the budget impasse ended.[36]

(Arizona became the first state to successfully open a national park during a government shutdown. That mechanism to keep the gates of the Grand Canyon from never closing was activated several times in the following years.)

Although he was turned away from the Canyon, Symington arguably succeeded at focusing attention on the real-world impacts of budget intransigence. And no matter one's opinion on the wisdom of his acts, he certainly had the look of a decisive leader, particularly among those Americans who agreed with him that the federal government had accumulated more power than the Founding Fathers had intended.

Back home, though, the news cycle quickly returned to the normal rhythms of late 1995—for every action Symington took as governor, there seemed to be an equal and opposite amount of negative news or commentary. It was like early 1992 all over again.[37]

If Symington was going to get back his winning ways, he needed to settle the bankruptcy issue quickly and he needed federal investigators to finish their probe.

# Chapter 29

# BLOOD IN THE WATER

The Super Bowl was coming January 28, 1996. With a collection of other major sporting events early that year, the Valley would announce to the world that it was, yes, world-class, at least at hosting athletic events. And everyone would be wealthier for it (the Super Bowl alone would bring an estimated $300 million to the region).

With his fight for a Martin Luther King Jr. Day and his leadership in planning the state's role in the Super Bowl events, Fife Symington arguably deserved significant credit for the celebratory mood in the Valley.

When the predicted second government shutdown hit in January 1996, Symington's plan to finance Grand Canyon operations with state and private funds kicked in immediately. The mechanism created by Arizonans made national news, with one newspaper headline calling the deal "A National Success Story."[1]

That same month, he gave a State of the State address in which he bragged about giving Arizonans a significant tax cut while still keeping the state out of debt and the economy humming.

From one perspective, it would seem that things couldn't get much better for a governor.

From another perspective, though, it would seem things couldn't get much worse for a governor.

On New Year's Day 1996, Arizonans learned that a fund had been set up to help Symington pay his legal bills (he owed John Dowd and his firm more than $600,000, for one).[2] Mary Jo Pitzl of the *Republic* framed the issue as two watchdog groups and many Arizonans saw it: "The law may permit it, but Gov. Fife Symington's resurrected legal-defense fund still raises ethical and moral questions."

That same day, papers across the state published the yearly Top Ten story list compiled by members of the state Associated Press. The connection of Arizona right-wing extremists to the Oklahoma City bombing took the top spot. Symington's bankruptcy took third behind another story involving Arizona's increasingly dangerous anti-government fringe groups.[3]

A week into the new year, Symington's old partner in the Esplanade project filed a lawsuit claiming Symington owed him $1 million. Jerome Hirsch's accusations that Symington hid money owed to him from the Esplanade deal drew another unflattering front-page banner headline in the *Republic*: "Ex-partner accuses governor of fraud."[4]

Symington and his team finally got to move into their remodeled offices on the eighth and ninth floors of the state Executive Tower.

Which brought back the issue of the price tag for the remodeling. Symington was broadly lambasted for spending $2 million to make his office nice while schools and other government entities were targets of significant budget cuts.

Another story broke that Symington had yet to pay off $2 million in tax liens on his failed properties.[5] Those taxes were corporate obligations from the death-spiral days of the Symington Company that he would work to settle, he said. But the similarity in the price of the office and the amount Symington's business entity owed the state made an easy target for critics.

*Republic* reporter Jerry Kammer noted in his January 26 story on the tax liens that the information was "unearthed during research into the governor's bankruptcy."

Indeed, once Symington announced he was bankrupt, nearly every fiscally conservative move he made was greeted with widespread sarcasm from critics claiming hypocrisy. The news cycle, whether driven by a policy or personal story, became a negative feedback loop in which his personal financial problems drove or seeped into most every story.

Symington and his staff became increasingly angry at reporters, even announcing at one point that Symington would only take questions from television reporters,[6] who he said were more objective and focused on his job of running the state. (Newspaper writers said he liked the softer questions from television reporters.)[7]

After the tax-lien story, state Democrats called for a joint legislative committee to review Symington's conduct related to the unpaid corporate taxes. House Minority Whip George Cunningham was quoted in the *Republic* as saying, "I think, where the public's confidence in the chief executive officer reaches such a low point, perhaps we should offer a public forum in which he can defend himself. The public has a right to know."[8]

Two days after the Super Bowl, a statewide poll showed that 42 percent of Arizonans said Symington should quit. Perhaps more surprising: nearly half of rural Arizonans thought it was time for him to step down.[9]

"The only poll that matters is the one taken on election day," Cole said, which, since polls had failed to predict both of Symington's wins, had become their standard response to negative numbers.

"The positive that I saw in the polls is that 58 percent of the people in this state want me on the job," Symington himself said.

Another poll showed that only 24 percent of Arizonans believed he was doing a good or excellent job.

Assuming the polls were close to correct, Symington, no matter how well he was doing in his day job, was being judged by the stories regarding his failed finances.

And he was being judged on his reaction to questions regarding his failed finances, others theorized. Pollster Mike O'Neil suggested Symington's crashing poll numbers in rural Arizona might be a product of Symington's attitude, not his finances: Rural Arizonans, he said, "see a double standard. They know that if they get behind on the electric bill, their power will be shut off. Symington, on the other hand, stands behind his lawyers and accountants and seems indifferent to owing millions."

Legislators already had a good idea what Symington would be proposing when he presented his State of the State address to open the 1996 regular session of the state legislature.

Even with Republican majorities still in both chambers, some analysts suggested Symington would struggle more than the previous year to get his way. Symington's likely problem: He had already received what the current legislature was going to accept of the Symington Plan. Many of his remaining pet projects—like school vouchers—were retreads that had already met opposition across party lines.[10]

Or his ideas, especially those stemming from his increasingly aggressive push to wrestle power out of federal hands, were just too far right—or perhaps just too fanciful—to pull a majority vote even with both chambers again controlled by Republicans.

His idea to have the state take over management of the Grand Canyon wasn't well received.[11]

He wanted $50 million in income tax reductions toward his goal of abolishing the state income tax, which, according to Republican leadership quoted in the following day's papers, wasn't going to be a priority for them. Symington wanted violent teens to automatically go to adult court while broad opinion seemed to favor leaving some discretion to prosecutors and judges.

He even joked about the tepid response he once again received when mentioning vouchers.

Besides crime, education remained the hottest issue in the state. Arizona was still struggling to oblige the Arizona Supreme Court's order directing legislators to equalize spending in the state's school districts.

Under state law at the time, districts depended solely on property taxes collected within the district, leaving districts in which property was less valuable with less money than those in high-rent districts. Symington said the state needed "a responsible means" of increasing access to equal funding, but no concrete plans were offered.[12]

He promised to continue his fight for the protection of Arizona's open spaces, a sentiment that drew a standing ovation from legislators from both parties.

Those who didn't mind him taking a perceived victory lap deemed the speech a success. Those who wanted specifics regarding the major issues still plaguing Arizona, though, found the speech wanting.

Editors of the *Arizona Daily Star* argued the speech lacked the specifics common in Symington's previous State of the State addresses. "In all it was a curious speech, with few concrete proposals and many already lost causes."[13]

Symington's budget proposal in early 1996 increased spending $130 million over the prior year while still cutting $250 million in taxes.[14]

The Arizona economy was still strong in early 1996; companies were moving into the state; and trade was accelerating with Mexico as barriers fell both as part of the North American Free Trade Agreement and new agreements between Symington and his counterpart in Sonora.[15]

His emboldened detractors found little traction questioning his handling of the economy. His opponents, and many of his usual friends, did, however, find fault with his unwillingness to pass more of that growing revenue to programs that had worked with static or reduced funding since Symington took office.[16]

As the budget battle heated up, Symington did push for state workers to get a raise, saying they had been treated "shabbily." At the same time, though, he argued that the state's three public universities didn't deserve increased funding beyond an adjustment for increases in enrollment because they already had "fat" budgets.

Although Arizonans certainly were frustrated by a seemingly inordinate increase in university tuition, fees, and budget-increase requests, university leaders countered that Arizona's universities spent only $7,500 a year to instruct each student, less than the national average of $11,000 at the time. While Symington wanted university officials to focus on streamlining as state agencies had, he soon found a growing opposition to his opinion on the state's schools within the business community that had been one of his strongest bases of support.

The powerful business group Greater Phoenix Leadership wrote lawmakers imploring them to boost university spending more than four times more than Symington had proposed. If the state's universities are underfunded, they argued, they would fall behind other states in the ability to provide a highly educated workforce.[17]

Symington took his first major anti-abortion stand, supporting and signing into law a statute that banned minors from having abortions without parental permission. "A lot of youngsters are very ill-informed about the choices they make," Symington argued. He also supported pro-life advocates in their push requiring women to be educated on the risks of abortion and informed about other options available.

An important note, though: Symington said he would not have approved the statute if it had not allowed a "right of judicial bypass" for the young mother, which allowed her to go to a judge to seek relief if her family opposed her decision.

Throughout the newsworthy legislative session, though, Symington's actions as governor were routinely eclipsed by stories related to his finances or former employees.

On February 8, news broke that Symington's longtime accountant, John Yeoman, had been put on leave by his employer, Coopers & Lybrand. That set off a series of stories revisiting the alleged bid rigging of Project SLIM contracts by George Leckie and Yeoman five years earlier.

An increasing amount of evidence suggested that Leckie illegally communicated with Yeoman in late 1991 to help Yeoman land a major state contract for his accounting firm, Coopers & Lybrand.

The Leckie/Yeoman bid-rigging tale had become headlines again after a story in 1994 by *Arizona Republic* investigative reporter Jon Sidener detailed evidence that "Gov. Fife Symington's representative on a committee to award a $1.5 million state contract improperly telephoned a bidder with close ties to the governor. . . .Soon after, the firm cut its bid by more than $400,000 and won the contract." A series of investigations followed, which included a deposition of Yeoman's former secretary, Margaret Kendall, in which she told state investigators that Yeoman and his firm had inside information on competing Project SLIM bids before Coopers made its final, heavily reduced bid. "I think everyone who worked there knew because of the contacts that Yeoman had with the governor that it was going to be a done deal and no one was surprised," Kendall told investigators. In July of 1995, Coopers & Lybrand paid the state $725,000 to settle claims of impropriety. Leckie soon after agreed to pay $25,000 to the state.

But while the Leckie and Yeoman affairs seemed to be settled with state investigators, federal investigators continued to gather evidence. On March 14, 1996, prosecutors were able to get a federal grand jury to indict Leckie and Yeoman.[18]

Leckie was indicted on seven counts related to the bid-rigging allegations. Yeoman was additionally accused of perjuring himself in sworn testimony before a grand jury. That story consumed the news cycle for days, with new details from the case drawing headlines for months to come.

Republican leadership downplayed the Yeoman and Leckie tale. Michael Hellon, the Republican national committee representative for Arizona, called the indictments "just another two-day story."

Symington said he felt "great sadness" when he heard the news of the indictments of his two close friends. Symington was not accused of wrongdoing himself, but he was accused of not working hard enough to investigate if Leckie and Yeoman—both old friends—had improperly communicated prior to Coopers & Lybrand winning the contract.

Within days of the indictments, Symington signed a bill that would require members of state committees evaluating bids to sign a statement in which they promised to have no conflicts of interest and promised to restrain from any contact with bidders during the process. A committee member could be fined up to $10,000 for violating the law.

The legislation was known widely as the "Leckie Bill."[19]

In early April, two days after Leckie and Yeoman both entered pleas of not guilty to the charges against them, Yeoman died of injuries suffered in a horrific car accident. Yeoman was turning left from the southbound lane of North Seventh Street in Phoenix when a pickup truck traveling seventy-five miles an hour struck the side of his vehicle. The pickup driver, who was traveling an estimated thirty miles an hour over the speed limit, admitted to police that he had used methamphetamine shortly before the crash.

Symington's responded to the accident in a written statement for the press:

"All those who knew him knew his many qualities as a person, his kindness toward others and his love for his family," Symington wrote. "He was a faithful husband and a devoted father. That is how we will remember him."

Yeoman later was found to have a blood alcohol level of 0.11, slightly above the then 0.10 legal limit. Friends suggested he had been drinking more in the months prior to the accident due to the stress of losing his job and being indicted.[20]

Those involved in proving Symington's guilt or innocence agreed that losing the man who knew Symington's finances better than anyone—including possibly Symington himself—would complicate and slow any courtroom resolutions. Losing such a pivotal witness, too, would cast further doubt on any decisions made in court. Indeed, both Mike Manning and John Dowd argued soon after Yeoman's death that they had lost an important asset in proving their case.[21]

Two weeks after Yeoman's death, the federal grand jury that had been investigating Symington since 1991 sent subpoenas to three state agencies requesting documents related to Symington and Project SLIM. Dowd said the subpoenas were of "no concern" and noted that Symington was "the one who asked for an investigation."

What was known for sure regarding Symington and the bid-rigging accusations: he had dismissed warnings early in his tenure from his own staff that, as a *Daily Star* reporter put it, "the bid process might be tainted."[22]

In early April, Wes Gullett stepped down as Symington's chief of staff. He was replaced by Heiler, who the *Arizona Republic* described as "a conservative ideologue who is credited with scripting Symington's shift to the right in recent years."[23]

Amid it all, Symington kept working. As daytime temperatures began topping 100 degrees after a dry winter, several fires broke out across the state. More than three thousand acres burned around Four Peaks northeast of Phoenix while another forest fire torched several thousand more acres and cost $3.5 million to fight. Symington declared a state of emergency and stayed in close contact with firefighters.[24]

Through the same period, Symington and the business leaders he had assembled were making national headlines with their efforts to help Arizona benefit from the new North American Free Trade Agreement. During a four-day summit in the Mexican state of Sonora, Arizonan and Sonoran members of a joint trade commission proposed several ground-breaking measures to make the adjoining states a leading trade corridor between Mexico, the United States, and Canada. Among several other initiatives, the group members drew up plans to remove beef-exportation barriers and to create a joint center for manufacturing development to attract international manufacturing investment to the two-state region.

"The more business we can take away from California, the better," Symington joked to loud applause at the summit.[25]

Following that trade summit, Symington then sat down for two days as Mike Manning grilled him under oath. As the attorney for the pensioners who had lost money in the Mercado deal, Manning was looking for both hidden money and any evidence of wrongdoing that would void bankruptcy protection for Symington.

The stories about the deposition occupied multiple pages in at least three newspapers, far more space than was devoted to the results of the trade summit. Which was more important? Symington's staff and supporters had a diametrically opposed opinion on that issue compared to editors and his critics.

Manning announced that, from the information gleaned in that deposition, he believed he had reason to file suit in US Bankruptcy Court to prevent the Mercado debt from being discharged.

On May 20, Ann Symington spent a day being deposed by Manning, who hoped to bolster his argument that "the wealthy heiress," as she was several times referred to in newspaper stories, held liability for her husband's $25 million in business debts. Manning argued that "They had a substantial business relationship as well as being wedded."

Phoenix decided not to challenge Symington's efforts to have his tax debts to the city forgiven. Critics questioned whether Symington had received special treatment because he was governor of the state.

State business continued in the background. By May 2, Symington had vetoed seventeen bills, a personal record. Most notably: he vetoed the legislature's tax-cut plan because homeowners in nineteen school districts would see an increase in their property taxes. (Those Arizonans had been paying less than a newly mandated school tax of $4.72 per $100 of assessed value. His argument: the state should absorb the $60 million cost rather than put it on a segment of the state's taxpayers.)

As fires raged around the state, the infamous, emissions-based "Brown Cloud" that hovered over the Valley continued to grow. Symington announced he was considering holding a special legislative session to address the growing menace.[26]

That story, and any other state government story, was quickly overshadowed by arguably the biggest news in the state since the Mecham impeachment:

On June 13, federal prosecutors announced they were indicting Symington on twenty-three counts accusing him of defrauding First Interstate Bank, Valley National Bank of Arizona, Dai-Ichi Kangyo Bank, and the union pension funds. Also included in the thirty-nine-page indictment was one count alleging Symington attempted to "extort concessions" from the pension funds and one count alleging he perjured himself when he told Manning he believed a December 31, 1989, financial statement "represented an accurate picture of my financial condition."[27]

The news of criminal indictments seemed to be the last straw for many Arizonans. The editorial boards of the *Republic* and several other newspapers in the state called for Symington's resignation.[28] In polls taken after the indictment, the majority of those questioned also believed he should resign.[29]

Democratic leadership generally stood with their Republican brethren: while some Democrats argued Symington should be impeached or should, as Eddie Basha suggested, "take a leave of absence," the general consensus appeared to be that Symington should only resign if he was found guilty on the charges, or if he clearly showed signs that he no longer could fulfill his duties as governor with such a weighty distraction.[30]

Symington was clearly shaken by the news of the indictments. His voice cracked during a press conference after the announcement, which *Republic* writer Martin Van Der Werf called "a rare indication that Symington is beginning to feel the pain of his bankruptcy and monumental legal troubles." When Symington called Senate Majority Leader Tom Patterson to inform him of the indictments, Symington was "for the first time, quiet and concerned," Patterson told Van Der Werf.[31]

Two days later, Symington said on his KFYI-AM radio show that he had called former governor Evan Mecham to apologize for raising money for the effort to recall him.

"I told him the Fife Symington of those years is very different from the Fife Symington of 1996, that very few people have kind of walked the walk and endured the kind of public process that he went through and that I'm now going through."[32]

Republican leaders from around the state gathered in Phoenix to hold what was essentially a pick-me-up rally for the governor. Symington spoke to the group, outlining the indictments while spending most of his time talking policy. "There were testimonials given on what a great job he had done," then senator Jan Brewer said. "People said they were willing to do anything and everything to help him."[33]

Supporters even broke out dozens of "I Like Fife" stickers from the 1990 and 1994 campaign.

Ann also spoke and fielded questions about how she and her children were doing. Several media outlets reported on the impacts the sprawling federal investigation and legal morass were having on the personal lives of those around the governor.

While Symington did show some emotional vulnerability, he also seemed less capable of containing his contempt for the federal investigators. A *Republic* banner headline suggested a coming storm: "Indictments likely to fuel Symington's intensity."

"Today, after seven years, they are finally making their accusations," Symington sniped. "If there's anything good in this event, that is it. After all this time, the people of Arizona are entitled to hear the facts and reach their own judgment."

Symington also barked at media members for what he saw as a reporting double standard: "The dominant media culture, which is so keen for cynical portrayals of elected officials, is mysteriously childlike and uncritical before the boldest exercises of judicial power."

Within days of the indictment, Symington and his staff began more aggressively rebuffing questions about his finances and legal troubles. Symington, Cole, and Heiler regrouped and made a plan for the coming months.[34]

Focus on your jobs and our goals, and ignore everything else.

# Chapter 30

# TOUGH GUY

B efore the 1994 election, a word of praise from Governor Fife Symington was valuable currency.

As the November 1996 elections approached, small-fry politicians went courting for big-name endorsements. This time, though, it appeared the constant trickle of bad news from the bankruptcy and criminal court pre-trial proceedings truly were eroding his base of support.

Symington spokesman Doug Cole said Symington was still getting numerous requests for endorsements, but admitted that Joe Arpaio, along with Senator John McCain, were that year's Republican golden boys.[1]

Representative Scott Bundgaard of Glendale got Symington's endorsement in 1994, but didn't get it, or seek it, in 1996. Bundgaard instead went to Arpaio. "Joe Arpaio's endorsement carries a lot of weight in any district, but especially in the more conservative parts of The Valley," Bundgaard said. "He appeals to people's get-tough-on-crime attitude."

This while Symington was leading the campaign for Proposition 102, a sweeping tough-on-crime plan that sought a constitutional amendment to shift control of the juvenile justice system from the courts to the legislature and, in the process, increasingly to the executive branch.

While Proposition 102 appeared to be popular with a majority of Arizonans frustrated with growing juvenile crime and the courts' inability to curb it, Symington was opposed by a broad swath of respected leaders. Indeed, every living governor opposed the move, and five of them were even willing to pose for a photo together for a story detailing their unified opposition.[2]

In the accompanying story, Evan Mecham urged "Caution and restraint."

Symington, seemingly more entrenched and combative than at any time in his time as governor, ignored the warnings—and the accusations of a power grab—and sharpened his insults at judges and the media members he saw as unquestioning cheerleaders of his opposition. At an Arizona Town Hall event in Grand Canyon Village, Symington veered from the primary topics of the Town Hall—education and health care—and unloaded on the news media, university leadership, and judges, saying they promoted "anti-values" that destroy public trust in their elected officials. "They have galloped off to a Brave New World," he said, "dragging a confused and divided society behind them."[3]

E. J. Montini's *Republic* column the following day carried the headline, "J. Fife Paranoia at the helm."[4]

Countering arguments that he was drifting even farther right, Symington contended that Proposition 102 and several other major issues of 1996 involved two core beliefs that he had held since Barry Goldwater first walked into his home when Fife was a boy:

One, that judges at all levels had abused the limited powers offered them by the US Constitution.

"As Hamilton put it," Symington said at a Goldwater Institute event the year before, "the essential role of the federal judicature was to settle those relatively few court cases that the Constitution assigned to federal jurisdiction."[5]

And two: that all three branches of the federal government had strayed unconstitutional distances from the Tenth Amendment. Leading the charge against the rights of the states, he said in his Goldwater Institute speech, had been an activist judiciary led by judges "who today sit on life-tenured thrones where they rule over the nation like so many philosopher kings."

Symington suggested he was on the verge of a lifelong dream and a legacy-level achievement—to help reorient the relationship between the judiciary and the American people back to how the framers of the Constitution had envisioned that relationship.[6]

Republican Maricopa County Attorney Rick Romley summed up the darkening opinion of Symington after the governor's Grand Canyon Town Hall speech: "It's absolutely insane. He is supposed to be a consensus builder, and all he did there was divide us." That particular speech amid a seemingly changing tone from the governor had, as a *Republic* writer phrased it, "the political upper crust abuzz." "That's all people are talking about right now," Romley said.[7]

Voters ultimately supported Prop. 102, giving Symington the go-ahead for his signature gambit—to move oversight of the juvenile system away from the courts and to move older juveniles to adult court automatically for a yet-to-be-stipulated collection of violent crimes.

But initiatives that would have directed the legislature to expand state indigent care, allow medical marijuana, lighten drug-related punishments, and allow casino gambling on the Salt River Reservation—all ideas Symington opposed—all passed by wide margins.

Symington told reporters he likely would veto any legislation that came to him legalizing certain drugs, immediately releasing state prisoners, or giving the Salt River Community carte blanche on placing a major casino anywhere on their land.[8]

State law was unclear on whether or not the governor had the power to veto the results of a state referendum. Symington's view was that the results of a statewide initiative vote were essentially the same as a bill approved by the legislature, which he obviously could veto. (State law was later changed to clarify that the governor must sign the results of a statewide initiative into law. Also, as part of that 1998 "Voter Protection Act," legislators could no longer gut voter-passed initiatives as they had after the passage of the controversial 1996 propositions.)

The headline for Keven Willey's column the next day reflected the resoundingly negative reaction to Symington's legal theory: "Governor May Be Losing It."[9]

Indeed, Symington seemed to be at war with much of the state in the weeks after the 1996 midterm election.

# Chapter 31

# "WHO IS THIS GUY?"

Fife Symington's mother, Martha Frick Symington, passed away in late November 1996 due to complications from pneumonia.[1] Symington had been visiting his mother daily at a Scottsdale hospital during the three weeks before her death. After his mother passed away, Symington spent much of the following two weeks with family as they came together to prepare her funeral and celebrate her life.

A few days after returning to work after his mother's funeral, Symington traveled to Vermilion Cliffs on the Arizona/Utah border to witness one of the country's great endangered species recovery stories. The California condor had been extinct in the wild since 1987. Standing with Senator John McCain and Interior Secretary Bruce Babbitt, Symington looked on as six giant California condor fledglings took flight. The six birds, raised in zoos in Los Angeles and Idaho, were the first captive condors released outside of California.[2]

After watching the birds soar away from the cliffs, Symington told reporters: "I used to be of the mind that we should repeal the Endangered Species Act. This particular experience leads me to believe that we just need to modify it, and that it is possible to work in a spirit of partnership to resolve these very important natural resource and wildlife issues."[3]

After a quiet holiday season spent with his family, Symington crafted his State of the State address to launch 1997. Beyond his usual calls for tax cuts, vouchers, and criminal-justice reform, the speech was arguably the most introspective and philosophical of any speech he had given during his time in office.

He used his pre-dawn hikes up Camelback Mountain as the foundational metaphor for his address.

"No matter how many mountains life puts before us, or how steep, the essential thing is to keep climbing," he said. "Worry is a waste of time; bitterness is a loss of ground."

In the weeks following the speech, as he began responding to the

legislation and issues coming his way, he continued to confuse the left
and anger the hard right.

"Like Night and Day," one headline barked. "Who is this Guy?" another one asked.[4]

Columnist John Kolbe wrote, "Last week, a new governor emerged,
surprisingly introspective, conciliatory and even a bit humble."

Kolbe suggested that Symington's change in tone was due more to
his political instincts than some epiphany. Symington, he theorized,
was changing his rhetoric to match the Zeitgeist. "For a guy with such
well-chiseled political views, what's interesting is how accurately those
annual speeches mirror the shifting nuances of their times. While the
basic themes have remained mostly unchanged (efficient government,
lower taxes, more academic rigor, tougher crime penalties, etc.), the *tone*
in which they've been wrapped always reflected the changing environment around him."

Symington said he hadn't changed. He promised he wasn't trying
to soften his image in preparation for the coming court battles. But the
list of issues he all of a sudden was championing in early 1997 suggested
some sort of change of heart: in a matter of months, he had begun a series of battles for hate-crime laws, sweeping clean air initiatives, cutting-
edge mass-transit projects, sprawling swaths of unmolested state wilderness lands, significant raises for universities and state workers, and tens
of millions of extra dollars for remodeling and construction of public
schools in the state's poorest districts.

If you were one of the many analysts who believed Symington needed
Mecham voters to hit positive poll numbers (or election numbers) ever
again, his actions in late 1996 and early 1997 seemed, from a political perspective, exceptionally unwise.

As the 1997 legislative session began, economic numbers from the pri-
or year began to trickle in. The state once again brought in more money
than projected—$100 million this time. Record numbers of people were
moving to the Valley, and both residential and commercial real estate sales
were healthy. The region's high-tech sector—and with it the number of
higher-paying jobs—showed double-digit job-numbers growth.[5]

(The Camelback Esplanade sold again, too, for $174 per square foot,
making it, according to a *Republic* story, "one of the most expensive office
deals since Arizona's real estate bust of the late 1980s." A pension fund,
the Oregon Public Employees Retirement Fund, bought the complex for

$87 million. The company that bought the distressed Esplanade property from Shimizu Land Corp., AEW, made an estimated $55 million profit in the deal.)[6]

Arizona's exports grew 18 percent in 1996, hitting almost $10 billion—more than double what they were shortly after Symington took office.[7] Soon after those numbers were released, Symington again met with Sonoran governor Manlio Beltrones to further reduce barriers to trade and tourism.[8] After overseeing the weeklong meeting of the joint Arizona-Sonora commission, the two men announced plans to spend millions to improve sanitary landfills and water and sewage systems along the border while also working together to protect sensitive wildlife habitat in the region. Beltrones and Symington also agreed to create a pilot program to help Arizona become a major supplier for Mexico's "twin plants" in which American products are assembled or processed and re-exported back to the United States. For their efforts, Beltrones and Symington made national headlines in Mexico and the United States for being leaders in the NAFTA-era push to improve cooperation between the two countries.

"So much for the naysayers who warned that the North American Trade Agreement would be a bad deal for the US," Symington said after the announcements.

(But even successes negotiating with Beltrones were overshadowed by charges of wrongdoing. A *New York Times* investigative report in February suggested Beltrones was aiding Mexican drug cartels, charges Beltrones denied.)[9]

As Symington pushed to abolish the state income tax—one of his signature goals since taking office—much of the legislature and public seemed less interested in tax cuts than in spending the boom-time windfalls on upgrading the state's decaying public schools.[10]

Symington emerged from the legislative session that spring with much of his agenda intact.[11] He signed off on a $110 million tax cut, an extra $50 million for school maintenance, and $43 million in pay raises for state workers. He got his "Arizona Preserve Initiative" (although he didn't get the $1 million appropriation for it), and perhaps most central to his long-term agenda, he signed into law his years-old proposal that would send minors fifteen and older to adult court for violent offenses.[12]

He was also successful in lobbying legislators to avoid passing any legislation that legalized marijuana or would lead to the immediate release of state prisoners.

He even landed a sort of school-vouchers-light program that allowed Arizonans to get a tax credit for donations of up to $500 for private school tuitions.

Symington and most news outlets ranked it as one of his most successful.

"I think it's really been an extraordinarily fruitful session," he said.[13]

He signed a measure blocking insurance companies from denying health-care coverage based on the results of genetic testing. Two insurance companies had threatened to stop offering their health care and disability insurance to state employees if the bill passed, to which Symington responded, "I'm genetically indisposed to threats."

The *Republic* editorial board lauded Symington for "defying insurance companies."[14]

Even the *Daily Star* editorial board, one of his strongest critics in the state, gave begrudging kudos to Symington that spring. "Whatever the inspiration, this governor—the one who chooses to take care of the state's people—is much more attractive than the other one."[15]

Symington's apparent move toward the center, and his increased interest in spending state money on progressive projects, arguably was most pronounced when he announced he would be creating a task force to study the possibility of creating a high-speed train service between Phoenix and Tucson. As he announced the plan to an Arizona Town Hall meeting focused on transportation, Symington mused about the future of transportation in the Valley and the world.

"Surely I'm not the only one who has sat in traffic jams, imagining that my car had a special helicopter feature," he said. "In the future, high above those old roads in lanes but at different altitudes, people will be zipping to and from work, from city to city and state to state."

He ended his speech with a quote from his favorite character from his favorite television program, *Star Trek: The Next Generation*: "As Capt. Picard might say, 'Make it so,'" he told the town hall audience in May.

*Daily Star* columnist Tom Beal suggested Symington's comments were an effort to build evidence so Symington could cop "an insanity plea" in the federal criminal case.[16]

More likely, though, Symington's newfound fascination with futuristic modes of travel was triggered by a bizarre event two months earlier.

# Chapter 32

# SPACE INVADERS

At around 7:30 p.m. on the night of March 13, 1997, people in southern Nevada began reporting a massive V-shaped object in the sky flying slowly toward the south. Over the next three hours, thousands of people from Nevada through Arizona and into Sonora reported seeing something similar.

Most of the sightings came from Phoenix residents around 8 p.m., where hundreds of people reported seeing a black, V-shaped craft lined with several spherical lights passing over Squaw Peak in north Phoenix and heading in the direction of Tucson. Numerous people described it as being the size "of a football field" or an "aircraft carrier."

About two hours later, another set of lights was reported to be, as one observer said, "hovering over the city."

The straight line of lights seen and widely videotaped at around 10 p.m. were proven within days to be a series of flares dropped by four A-10 Warthogs during a training run from Barry Goldwater Range southwest of the Valley.

However, no such easy explanation emerged explaining the first object or objects.[1]

As Symington arrived at the governor's office the morning after the sightings, he learned that law enforcement entities throughout the state had received multiple calls from people reporting having seen the strange lights in the Arizona sky. As the number of reported sightings grew, Symington called the director of the state's Department of Public Safety, the commander of Luke Air Force Base, and the commanding officer of the Arizona National Guard. None of them could explain the first set of lights. Symington asked the National Guard's commanding officer to contact officials at the Pentagon, but he, too, received no explanation.

There was minimal media coverage in the first days following the sightings. The lead story in the following day's *Republic* was Symington's announcement that he would run for a third term.[2] There was no mention of the sightings in the paper.

As stories of strange lights continued to be reported to government and media outlets in the following days, the *Republic*'s Susie Steckner went searching for answers. Her story five days later in the *Republic* stated "reports poured in Thursday to Luke Air Force Base, the National Weather Service and the National UFO Reporting Center in Seattle." The first call to the UFO Center, Steckner wrote, "came from a former police officer who spotted the strange cluster of lights" north of Prescott, Arizona.[3] The UFO Center, according to the story, quickly received a series of calls from Kingman, Prescott, Prescott Valley, Dewey, Chino Valley, Glendale, Mesa, and Phoenix. Steckner's short story ended with the observations of an eleven-year-old boy, Tim MacDonald, who said he saw the object while leaving a Cub Scout meeting in Phoenix. "It looked like a stealth bomber," the boy told Steckner. "It was moving very slowly. It was there for two or three minutes."

In the following days and weeks, stories about the two events continued to pour into print, radio, and television news outlets, particularly to the morning and afternoon talk radio shows.[4]

National interest in what became known as the "Phoenix Lights" skyrocketed after a story appeared three months later in *USA Today* that called the event "the most confounding UFO report in 50 years."[5] "The army of people demanding answers has grown to the point that a Phoenix city council-woman has launched an inquiry," wrote *USA Today*'s Richard Price. Price suggested that because of the number of reports involved and the consistency of the claims (related to the first sighting), "the events of March 13 may add up to the most contentious and confounding UFO report since the so-called UFO age was launched 50 years ago by the legendary crash of a 'spaceship' outside Roswell, N.M."

A flurry of other national stories followed, which Jonathan Wald, a producer with NBC Nightly News, told a *Republic* reporter was a result of June being "a slow news time."[6]

As the interest grew, Symington was increasingly pressured to find answers.

A week after the *USA Today* story, Symington held a presser to announce that the source of the lights had been determined.

Symington announced from his press conference podium that DPS officers had captured an alien. Two DPS officers then escorted the perpetrator toward the podium. The towering, oblong-headed creature suspiciously matched the height of the towering Jay Heiler.

After Symington's chief of staff removed the giant head of his space-alien costume, Symington teased the press corps: "This just goes to show you guys are entirely too serious."[7]

The stunt drew laughter from those who hadn't seen the lights, and cries of foul from those who had.

Symington then said he had no intention of ridiculing those who said they had seen an alien craft. He simply wanted to have a bit of fun amid the continued worldwide coverage of what was being called the largest mass UFO sighting in US history.

"I don't discount . . . there may well be life out there," he said following his unveiling of Heiler. "But if this event was truly significant, I think you would probably have national security involved, the Air Force, and everybody else working on it."

Behind the scenes, though, Symington and several other Arizona leaders—including John McCain—were continuing to press US Air Force and Pentagon officials for an explanation of the first lights seen that evening. While some were ultimately satisfied with claims that all the lights that evening were flares or high-flying military jets, others felt they weren't getting the full story.[8]

At a Phoenix City Council meeting a few weeks after the sighting, Councilwoman Frances Barwood asked if anyone was investigating the sightings.[9] "I was met by a whole bunch of stares," she said later, then "a whole bunch of ridicule" along with more than a hundred calls from people claiming to have seen the same V-shaped object.[10]

She continued to seek answers long after Symington's press conference, as did Symington.

Many of those who believed they had seen an alien spacecraft didn't expect to hear honest answers from their leaders. "He wouldn't tell even if he had learned something," one Phoenix Lights witness said of Symington. "They wouldn't want people to freak out."

And the negative reaction to Frances Barwood's curiosity would certainly keep other public officials quiet on this issue. Giving credence to UFO sightings, Barwood would suggest later, is how you get your political legacy defined by giving credence to UFO sightings.

• • •

A few months before the Phoenix Lights episode, Candice St. Jacques

Symington with stars of *Guv: The Musical*, a 1991 spoof of Evan Mecham's troubled tenure as governor of the state. Courtesy of the Arizona State Library, Archives and Public Records, History and Archives Division, Phoenix, RG1_SG26_S6_B26_F031_I04.

Miles premiered her sequel to her 1991 local hit musical review, *Guv: The Musical*, which centered on a barely fictionalized Evan Mecham. The highly anticipated sequel, *Guv: The Emperor Strikes Back,* had an imperious Fife Symington as its new star, supported by satirical versions of the current big newsmakers of the time such as Joe Arpaio, Rick Romley, Grant Woods, recently departed Phoenix Suns player Charles Barkley, and Ann Symington.[11]

The sequel received solid reviews, but it wasn't the unhitched romp of the Evan Mecham-based lampoon. The biggest problem, two reviewers and the director herself said, was that for all the rowdiness of his tenure, Fife Symington wasn't nearly as easy to spoof.

"I didn't feel (Symington) was quite as funny as Ev," St. Jacques Miles said before the premiere of the show, which the real Symington attended. "He's more intelligent, for one thing. Much of the humor in the first *Guv* came straight out of the record: We just quoted Ev's remarks.

"People viewed Mecham as kind of a goof. But a lot of people think Fife got caught in the downturn of the economy. A lot of people see him as beleaguered.

"There's just more ambiguity there," St. Jacques Miles told another reporter. "He's a harder character to pin down."

In early May, the grounds of the state capitol and legislative buildings grew quiet. Things always slowed as first-quarter, budget-and-bill wrangling subsided, but 1997 was different, many legislators said. "It appears to me that the business at the Legislature has virtually shut down," Glendale Republican senator Scott Bundgaard said.[12]

No interim committee meetings were planned until the heart of summer. No special sessions were planned until fall.

"Everybody knows that, for the next three months, this place will be taken over by the O.J. (Simpson trial) phenomenon," Democratic state representative Ken Cheuvront told the *Republic*. "Everyone will be transfixed on finding out what happened during those years (Symington) was a developer."

# Chapter 33

# PRE-TRIAL DIVERSIONS

B y the fall of 1996, the drumbeat of non-gubernatorial governor stories had returned to its 1991 and 1992 levels. Much of the unfavorable press emanated from the offices of the media-savvy giant-slayer in the civil case, Mike Manning. His job: to stop the bankruptcy court judge from discharging Symington's debts, which would leave the pension funds he represented with pennies on the dollar. As he had been in the Charles Keating case, Manning was relentless in his legal acrobatics to find any money that might have been illegally hidden from creditors.

To his supporters, he was the wiz-kid Boy Scout from Kansas who had battled crooked rich guys for the good of the average American.

One of Arizona's most respected authors, Charles Bowden, cowrote a national bestseller about Keating in which Manning played a leading role. In Bowden and Michael Binstein's book, *Trust Me: Charles Keating and the Missing Billions*, Manning was the citizen-lawyer personified.[1] "He has an unwavering moral compass," Jeff Gaia, then president and CEO of Banc One Mortgage, said in a profile of Manning in the *Republic* in late 1996.[2]

Others, particularly those whose reputations were damaged under Manning's microscope, described him as a legal Tasmanian Devil. Sam Daily, who was convicted and then acquitted of charges stemming from Manning's work for the FDIC, described Manning this way to Charles Kelly of the *Republic*: "He will go out and destroy people just to enhance his reputation." Daily's partner, Fred Figge, was diagnosed with cancer while in prison, and then, after being released after acquittal, won a $400,000 settlement for ineffective medical treatment by the Bureau of Prisons. Terminally ill, Figge wanted to leave a message behind for federal investigators and, in particular, Mike Manning. Figge's tombstone reads: "Murdered in cold blood by the US Government."

Squared off against Manning was Symington's bankruptcy attorney, Robert Shull, a low-key veteran Phoenix attorney well respected among

September 2, 1997, Phoenix, AZ, USA: Prosecutor David Schindler is at the center of a media storm after a day of testimony at Arizona Governor Fife Symington's trial. © The Arizona Republic, USA Today Network.

the Valley's business uppercrust, but certainly not the charismatic public showman with famous scalps like Manning or Symington's lead attorney against the government, John Dowd. Shull would ultimately spend more than six years battling Manning, with most of his time spent blocking and deflecting a flurry of attacks he most often termed "frivolous, "irrelevant," or "fishing expeditions."[3]

And for six years, US Bankruptcy Court Judge George Nielsen served as referee for a very close, high-scoring match.

Assistant US Attorney David Schindler, one of what *Republic* columnist John Kolbe called "US Attorney Nora Minella's minions,"[4] became the face of the criminal case against Symington. Still in his midthirties, Schindler had built a reputation as a relentless prosecutor and one of the most adept in the US attorney's office in Los Angeles at deciphering deeply technical cases and then describing them in layman's terms to a jury. Schindler's other major cases at the time involved two of the higher-profile computer-hacking investigations in the country.[5]

Prosecuting a sitting governor, though, was by far the biggest and most complicated case of Schindler's career. Fellow prosecutors said Schindler was obsessed with the case, with one attorney later saying: "He wouldn't let the case go, even for an hour." Schindler, his partners at the time said, "had trouble delegating things. . . . He was absolutely relentless."[6]

Young and hungry, Schindler would spend his weekends studying financial records in Los Angeles, then board a Southwest Airlines plane to Phoenix during the week for depositions, hearings, and finally, the trial.

Schindler would be joined in the courtroom by George Cardona, a brilliant numbers wiz in the Central District office who had worked as a systems engineer in Westinghouse's Defense Electronics division before getting his law degree at Yale.[7]

Then there was John Dowd, the cigar-smoking, ex-Marine-who-acted-like-it, Washington insider who, among a long list of headline-grabbing cases, successfully defended Senator John McCain in Senate Ethics Committee hearings in the Keating Five scandal and helped Major League Baseball root out gambling misdeeds by Pete Rose and Yankees owner George Steinbrenner.[8]

There was more to Dowd than the Dowd persona, friends argued. They described him as a teddy bear outside of the legal sphere—a doting father of five, three of whom were adopted by him and his wife, Carole—and as one friend said, a "man capable of great charity."

Squared off against prosecutors, hostile witnesses, or members of the press corps, Dowd's demeanor ranged from fairly amicable to vicious. Probing reporters were met with profanities and fierce verbal punches that looked likely to precede real punches. He famously (in local media lore, at least) swatted a tape recorder from investigative reporter John Dougherty's hand. After a newspaper story Dowd felt was slanted against Symington, he roared, "Why don't you . . . get a rope and string his ass up?"

That comment may have said more about Dowd than people realized: He was raised in Alabama by a civil rights-crusading father so hated by segregationists that they once placed dynamite in the family's backyard (the explosives were removed before anyone was hurt). Dowd adopted three African American children. He had often quietly donated time to cases in which he saw racially tinged injustice.

His detractors saw only a blustery, overrated, high-priced pit bull who might not have spent enough of his career—at least recent career—in a criminal courtroom to give bite to his famous bark.

No matter the deeper-waters backstory or current competency, for most onlookers, Dowd was a much-appreciated dab of color in an otherwise drab, seemingly endless desert of documents and inscrutable legal machinations.

Dowd wouldn't be facing the federal government alone. Joining him was Terry Lynam, a partner at the DC law firm Akin Gump, who had spent much of his early career as a top fraud investigator with the Department of Justice. Lynam arguably understood the intricacies of the case better than anyone, including the prosecutors now trying to do his old job.

Lynam was the quiet brain behind Dowd's brains, brawn, and occasional bluster.[9]

Even quieter was Symington's third defender, Luis Mejia, a well-respected Phoenix native who had also assisted Dowd and Lynam in the investigation of Pete Rose and the defense of John McCain. Prior to heading to Washington in 1989, Mejia had worked at the powerhouse Phoenix legal firm of Lewis and Roca, the former employer of Janet Napolitano, then US attorney for the District of Arizona. Mejia definitely knew the lay of the corporate and legal land in Arizona.[10]

After the comparatively calm summer of 1996 (Dowd had asked Symington to keep a low profile),[11] banner headlines announced in mid-September 1996 that the accounting firm of Coopers & Lybrand would be paying the federal government $2.275 million to avoid potential charges for its work related to Project SLIM and/or the governor's business finances (Coopers & Lybrand had already settled with the state for $725,000 a year earlier).[12] As part of the deal with federal prosecutors, the firm released a statement in which the company laid most of the blame on John Yeoman, Symington's longtime accountant who had recently died, and Symington himself.[13]

The company had determined that Yeoman had received "confidential information regarding competitors' bids and deliberations" during meetings with George Leckie. Regarding Symington directly, the company's executives blamed Symington for failing to report debts and for exaggerating property values when he submitted his financial information to Yeoman, whose role was only to review "the consistency of Symington's methodology."

For Manning and prosecutors in Symington's criminal case, it was a massive coup. Both of Symington's accusers were now able to hold up

in court a letter from a "Big Six" accounting firm saying they believed
Symington had given them false financial information that they then
passed on, without proper review, to Symington's creditors. And as per
the agreement, prosecutors would have access to any Coopers & Lybrand
employee to testify against Symington. Also, federal investigators and
prosecutors had a judgment and some stunning admissions to show
those accusing them of conducting nothing more than a taxpayer-fund-
ed witch hunt.

Dowd responded with a ferocious denunciation of prosecutors and
the leadership of Coopers & Lybrand.

Dowd's take was basically this: Federal prosecutors threatened felony
charges against the company, and the company's executives, who were
facing a public relations disaster, decided to throw a dead man under the
bus and pay a small amount (for a multibillion-dollar company) to wash
themselves of liability.

(Dowd's argument later would be bolstered by a decision rendered by
the Arizona Board of Accountancy, as well as subsequent admissions by
Coopers & Lybrand officials, that federal prosecutors had put excessive
pressure on the accounting firm to say what prosecutors needed them
to say.)

There was another issue with how prosecutors and Coopers & Lybrand presented the settlement to the public, Dowd argued:

"The fact that this (agreement) information was released during the
pendency of this important criminal litigation will be brought to the attention of the court," Dowd wrote.

In the following months, any legal actions in either case made headlines, and there were plenty of legal actions being taken.

In February 1997, Nielsen, the civil court judge, approved a deal with
several creditors through which Ann Symington could avoid any future
liability for her husband's debts. Ann was to turn over a cache of Symington family heirlooms valued at nearly $65,000 that Fife Symington had
given her after she paid a portion of his legal bills in 1993. The governor
himself agreed to pay $31,250 to settle the remaining outstanding claims
against him.[14]

That left two creditors: the pension funds and Symington's old business partner, Jerome Hirsch, who had showed up in the second half of
1996 saying Symington still owed him $1.8 million from the days of their
Esplanade partnership.

Symington and Hirsch soon settled for an undisclosed amount, leaving only Manning fighting Symington in bankruptcy court.[15]

Manning announced he believed Symington would be receiving as much as $2.5 million after his mother's death from a trust established by his grandmother, Helen Frick. Shull accused Manning of once again releasing confidential documents to reporters. Manning argued that any trust disbursements to Fife Symington serving as evidence in the case were public documents.

In late April of 1997, after Manning deposed Symington for more than four hours, both sides filed motions against each other. Shull, while asking for the judge to stop Manning's "harassment and disrespect," also requested that any further questioning be delayed until after Symington's criminal trial just weeks away.[16]

The bankruptcy issue then went quiet except for a lawsuit filed by a separate creditor in late May seeking $500,000. The creditor argued Symington had paid his mother $500,000 in an attempt to shield the money.[17]

Three months before the criminal trial began—far from Phoenix and related to a different case—the US Supreme Court ruled that people could be convicted for fraud for making false statements to a lender even if the lender didn't rely on those statements to make the loan. Meaning, back in Arizona, Fife Symington could go to prison for his bad numbers even if they weren't used by the lenders in their decision to loan him money.[18]

Even before the criminal trial, the number of indictments began to vacillate. In January, two fraud charges were dropped, but Symington was indicted on two new charges of defrauding a Baltimore bank and his longtime lender, Valley National Bank.

Two months earlier, officials with the Baltimore bank agreed to write a letter to Dowd and prosecutors confirming they had not based their decision to loan Symington money on Symington's reports. "While Mr. Symington was required to provide a financial statement, it was not relied on in any way in the decision to issue the line of credit." The $300,000 line of credit was secured by Martha (Symington), who had a long financial relationship with the bank. Since the loan was already secured, the statement from Fife Symington was a formality in the process of opening the line of credit."

Symington had signed a document in dealings with Mercantile Bank that stated the person receiving the loan "understands and acknowledges that in complying with the foregoing request, Mercantile is relying exclusively upon the integrity and financial strength of the undersigned." Symington placed his net worth at $5.3 million at that time. That he had signed that document at nearly the same time he told a different creditor he had a negative net worth of $4.1 million proved that he intended to deceive, prosecutors argued, and that's all that mattered legally since the US Supreme Court decision months earlier.

Dowd called the new charges nothing more than a "pathetic publicity stunt" aimed at "prejudicing Governor Symington's right to a fair trial."[19]

Dowd stayed on message throughout the spring of 1997: His client, he claimed, was the victim of a politically motivated hit job by an enormous cabal of bureaucrats with limitless money who were allowed to wander far beyond the scope of their original investigation to find anything to justify their existence and further their careers.

Prosecutors just kept arguing that Symington had kept two sets of books.

In late January, US District Court Judge Roger Strand began the process of whittling five hundred potential jurors down to the twelve people—along with a few alternates—who could be impartial regarding a well-known public figure with strong political views.

Those people also needed to be able to spend an estimated three months in a courtroom.[20]

Strand, described as a "capable and well-organized but not a towering intellect" in a *Republic* profile of the judge,[21] told the opposing attorneys that he didn't believe familiarity with the case was a reason to automatically exclude people from serving on the jury.

Dowd began working to exclude anyone who might have a political bias against the governor. He wanted potential jurors to be asked a series of questions that would expose any pre-existing negative perception of his client.

Schindler worked equally hard to make sure there weren't any jurors who thought Symington could do no wrong.

Throughout the spring, Dowd peppered Strand with other requests. Strand agreed with him that the financial managers for the pension funds should be required to give Dowd any documents that he sought to defend Symington in the criminal case. Manning and the government both wanted Dowd's access limited to the amount the firm had to turn over in the bankruptcy case.

Print, radio, and television reporters struggled to boil down the arcane machinations from both the civil and criminal courtrooms for an Arizona audience that, in large part, thought there was only one case—the one involving prison time—emanating lots of noise leading to a simple binary choice, guilty or not guilty.

Howard Fischer, a veteran reporter whose work for Capitol Media Services appeared in papers throughout the state, arguably was the lead disseminator from the two federal courts. As Dowd and Schindler filed motion after motion and Strand made judgments based on laws nobody but lawyers knew existed, reporters like Fischer strove to explain in layman's terms what it all meant and why it mattered.

"What do federal prosecutors know about Gov. Fife Symington that they don't want to share?" Fischer led one story. "That's the question the governor's lawyers are asking. And they want US District Judge Roger Strand to tell them—or, at least, give them a chance to argue why the information should not be kept secret.

"Government lawyers are asking Strand for permission not to disclose some statements made by the governor, according to documents filed yesterday."[22]

Later in the story: "Terence Lynam, another of the governor's lawyers, said he had no idea what sort of statements by Symington the government attorneys might have, or why prosecutors think they don't have to turn them over."

"Kafkaesque" became a popular word in Arizona in the spring of 1997.

Amid it all, Dowd and Symington ferociously denied that they were seeking, or would take, a plea deal. In fact, Symington, Dowd said, "was looking forward" to sitting under oath on the stand to "finally let the people of Arizona see the truth."

Sides fought to have evidence deemed relevant or irrelevant. The jury pool dwindled. Dowd filed several motions to have the charges dismissed.

Strand finally did dismiss one charge on May 6, saying the charge based on prosecutors' claim that Symington didn't disclose "unfavorable change" in his financial health to Valley National Bank was "unconstitutionally vague."[23]

Perhaps the only thing prosecutors and Symington's defense ever agreed on: "No question the jury was fairly picked," Dowd said of the twelve jurors and five alternates selected after a three-day process, mirroring comments by Schindler.

The jury first met May 15, at which time Strand read to them the government's forty-three-page argument for the remaining twenty-two counts against Symington.[24] Then Strand dismissed the jury for the day, instructing them to be back the next day to hear David Schindler explain in the morning why failed businessman Fife Symington was a crook, then hear John Dowd in the afternoon explain why the honorable governor of Arizona was an innocent man.

# Chapter 34

# "ARIZONA'S TRIAL OF THE CENTURY"

W hatever experience federal judge Roger Strand might have
lacked in wrangling intricate and nuanced bank-law proceedings, he was inarguably a national star in the push to modernize the American courtroom.[1]

Fife Symington would be tried in what became dubbed "The Courtroom of the Future."

The federal courthouse in Phoenix was still a sweaty dinosaur. But
inside Strand's courtroom, everyone involved—judge, jurors, witnesses,
attorneys, and the public in both the main and overflow rooms—would
be able to see each of the ten thousand documents entered into evidence
on a monitor as the attorneys presented them. Prosecutors and defense
attorneys would even be treated to a near-instantaneous video feed of
the court reporter's transcript that, thanks to cutting-edge software, had
been translated back into English from the reporter's masterful gobble-
dygook.

"It's a dramatic departure from the past, when attorneys grappled
with file cabinets full of hard-to-index documents, passing them around,
seemingly for days on end," a *Republic* story explained.[2]

Meaning, even though the three-month trial would be mentally and
physically tortuous, it would have been even worse in almost any other
courtroom in America.

(For the attorneys involved, though, there was one catch: Strand ordered that anyone inputting into the system had to take, and pass, a test
on how to use the equipment.)

More than one hundred media credentials were issued for the trial,
but the interest from the national media outlets, at least at the trial's beginning, was limited. Only six non-Arizona outlets sought credentials.[3]

"Locally, there will be lots of trial coverage," *Republic* reporter Eric
Miller predicted, "and at times it will surely seem as though broadcast
and print media are giving it more attention than it deserves. On the

other hand, some local reporters are concerned that the tedious trial . . . has the potential to put readers and viewers to sleep."

Attorneys for both sides worried about the impacts of bedlam and boredom on jurors. They also contemplated how both might work in their favor.

The majority of onlookers seemed to agree the media circus would likely hurt Symington's chances of a fair trial. Boredom arguably worked against him, too: although prosecutors would numb jurors with many more documents and tangential witnesses than the defense, the sheer amount of stuff—relevant or not—might suggest guilt to a juror. The prosecutors had another advantage: saying somebody kept "two sets of books," a term most any layman understands, is a simpler argument than that of the defense.

Both sides worried that preconceived notions might be the determining factor.

Among Symington's most aggressive detractors, a more sinister narrative emerged: "I'd guess that the overwhelming evidence against Symington would convince an average well-informed, socially conscious and civic-minded citizen of the state that the governor is guilty," the *Republic's* E. J. Montini surmised. But "this isn't about politics. This isn't about evidence. This isn't about justice. This is about reality. . . .He'll win. You know it."[4]

From a spectator's perspective in Strand's courtroom, the jury was seated along the wall to the left, and Symington and his defense attorneys sat near the jury on the left side while prosecutors sat to the right near the court clerk. Between both attorneys and the judge stood a lectern from which arguments would be made and—thanks to the new visual-aid tech—from where attorneys would load document files from their CD-ROMs for display on courtroom monitors.

The seven seats directly behind Symington, Dowd, and Lynam were reserved for Symington's family and closest friends. Those seats were most often occupied by Ann, one or more of the Symington children, and Ann's parents, John and Mary Dell Pritzlaff.

Members of the media were packed into the two rows behind Symington's family, which put reporters within a whisper's distance of the family.[5]

Only twenty-four seats remained for the public, so another room in the courthouse was turned into the "overflow room." From there, several dozen citizens could watch the proceedings and see exhibits close up on closed-circuit television monitors, thereby giving the room the feeling of a small keno hall.

That room was empty during the tedious process of jury selection. Indeed, it seemed only Symington's family and reporters were interested in those first uneventful days of the trial.

The jury was finalized late Thursday of the first week. It was finally time for the main event. Opening statements would be given the next morning, Strand announced. On the morning of May 16, 1997, the Symington/Pritzlaff clan was joined by John and Cindy McCain. Even Dowd's wife and son attended, as did Schindler's wife of four weeks. (Schindler introduced Dowd to his new wife. "You're a saint for marrying him," Dowd quipped).[6]

The full media blitz was on. The *Republic,* for one, began dedicating multiple pages to daily courtroom dramas, with a main story often penned by multiple A-list reporters and accompanied by transcripts and more than one piece of staff-penned analysis, numerous quick-hit highlight lists, and gossip column-style standing features such as "The Court Observer," which included subcategories like "Overheard" (saucy quotes from players or onlookers) and "Spotted" (the McCains joining the Symingtons was a big deal). The graphics department created sophisticated, sometimes half-page schematics identifying and explaining key numbers in key documents. Gifted sketch artists provided glimpses inside the courtroom from which cameras had been banned. (Dowd and his frumpiness received the least-flattering treatment.)[7]

Most every day of the summer, the state's media outlets dedicated time and resources akin to that later expended on Arizona Cardinals playoff games.

(Nationally, though, another ongoing trial overshadowed Symington's: Timothy McVeigh was facing first-degree murder charges for his role in the bombing of the federal building in Oklahoma City.)

Schindler started his presentation with a two-hour breakdown of Symington's alleged crimes (at times augmented by unwieldy placards like those used by street-corner pizza hustlers) while working to simplify issues and make friends with jurors by implementing a tone akin to a kindly lecturing elementary school teacher: "We're going to ask you to tell the defendant to quit lying, to start playing by the same set of rules we all play by."[8]

Schindler made a series of promises to jurors:

"You will see that on December 31, 1989, and May 4, 1990, when he said he had a net worth of millions of dollars, he was basically flat broke."[9] "We will show the defendant lied while under oath in order to conceal the fact that the statement he submitted to a lender was blatantly false." And related to perhaps the most serious charge in the eyes of many Arizonans, Schindler predicted: "We will show that as part of the cover-up, he abused his office of governor of Arizona."[10]

That afternoon, Dowd worked to let jurors meet that nice guy his friends described in the earlier *Republic* profile. Yes, Dowd admitted, Symington was sometimes bad with details and numbers and had been "too optimistic and too aggressive" during his business career. But "crimes of optimism," Dowd reminded jurors, are not actual crimes. "The evidence will show that these statements were not material to lending decisions," Dowd claimed. "They didn't influence the banks."[11]

Like Symington, Dowd framed the trial not as a frightening day-of-reckoning for the governor, but rather "the beginning of the end of a long journey . . . a painful journey."

"It is," Dowd said, "in a sense, a relief." Symington, Dowd suggested, would finally be allowed to tell his side of the story. Symington, Dowd said, considered the courtroom the first "level playing field" he had been given since the federal investigation began seven years earlier.[12]

Dowd suggested in his opening statement that prosecutors neither understood the documents on which their case was based nor cared that the documents were not the reason Symington received any of the loans.

Regarding the accusation of extortion, Dowd bragged that he would prove that charge to be a politically motivated fantasy.

Dowd also would attempt to use the acquittal of George Leckie of bid-rigging charges a week earlier as ammunition to suggest the case against Symington was equally undeserving of convictions.[13] Indeed, Leckie attended Symington's trial, and Dowd seemed happy to have him there. (A *Republic* reporter overheard Dowd chatting with Leckie at the trial about Leckie's recent acquittal and Leckie's ongoing battle with cancer. "Every time I feel sorry for myself, I think of you," Dowd was quoted as telling Leckie.)[14]

Dowd needed jurors to empathize with Symington. In his opening statement, he described the case against Symington as a form of persecution that, he argued, could befall anyone on the jury if they were unlucky enough to draw the eye of federal investigators.

At the end of the day, the players emerged from the courtroom to a throng of reporters. Some weary courtroom observers scurried away, some engaged.

With the Phoenix summer taking grip, chances seemed particularly high that three months of daily scrums would test the civility of everyone involved.

The following Monday, Symington spent much of his hour-long, bi-weekly radio show on KFYI being asked about the trial. He did get a bit of time to explain why he opposed environmentalist-backed plans to lower the water level of Lake Mead to protect the endangered Southwestern willow flycatcher, but that certainly wasn't the paramount interest of callers.[15]

Many callers were simply interested to hear how he was holding up:

"I remember my dad telling me years ago a little Scottish proverb: You might as well be happy while you're living, for you're a long time dead," Symington responded to one caller.[16]

"We're in full cry, we're in battle, which is exactly what I hoped would happen," Symington claimed to another listener.

That week, Joyce Riebel, Symington's longtime former secretary, was the uneasy star of the show and, because of her close proximity to Symington and his financials throughout his life as a developer, one of the biggest stars of the trial.[17] Prosecutors led with nearly three days of direct questioning of Riebel even though, she said, she personally believed that Symington never intended to deceive investors. It wasn't what Riebel believed that mattered, though. What mattered was what prosecutors could get from her mouth when they showed her critical details of several hundred Symington loan-related documents generated since she began working for him in 1982.

It was Riebel's testimony that, when guided by a prosecutor's questioning, suggested Symington kept two sets of books to deceive lenders and creditors whether Riebel knew it—or would admit knowing it—or not. She would be used by prosecutors to, as one *Republic* writer put it, "paint a picture of a developer who was cunningly selective in the financial information he provided to lenders."

Once prosecutors had what they wanted from Riebel, they worked to

suggest her loyalty to him was simply a financial transaction.[18] Symington had paid Riebel's legal bills during the years of the federal investigation, Schindler point out. (As an employee of his company, Symington's
team argued on cross-examination, it was his company's obligation to
pay for legal counseling for an employee being interrogated regarding
company business.)

Riebel's four days of examination and cross-examination would set
a rhythm that defined the tone of the trial: Every time prosecutors unveiled documents that seem to confirm Symington was intentionally lying about his available net worth when he signed loan documents under
penalty of law, Dowd and Lynam countered that Symington either simply made mistakes or was having legal actions mischaracterized.

On Thursday, Schindler focused on evidence suggesting Symington
knew by 1987—two years after the Esplanade was approved at Southwest
and three years before he secured loans for the Mercado—that he was
in financial trouble. Schindler produced a note written by Symington
in 1987 that appeared to show he knew the value of his real estate assets
would, under scrutiny by a CPA, be deemed too low for him to qualify for
certain bank loans critical to the survival of his company.

Prosecutors also revisited a theory that Symington employed a color-
coding system on financial documents to ensure that lenders received the
particular information he wanted particular lenders or creditors to have.
Riebel said she knew of the coding system, but believed Symington was
using it to snare the employees who were responsible for leaking company documents to political rivals and journalists.

Schindler portrayed Symington as being secretive about his financial
documents because he kept them in a locked cabinet. Talking to Lynam,
Riebel explained that Symington kept childhood photos, a marriage cer-
tificate, and his Bronze Star in that locked cabinet. She said she believed
that he was simply locking up things he didn't want to lose or have stolen.

Schindler dug deep into the financing history of several of Symington's projects with Riebel. When Symington needed credit from Valley
National Bank, the document submitted to Valley bankers showed Symington was worth $5.3 million at the end of 1990. Schindler contended
that, at nearly the exact same time, Symington told First Interstate Bank
(the Mercado lender) that he needed to renegotiate terms of a loan because he was $4.1 million in the hole.[19]

Although the documents had similar dates on them, Riebel said, they were simply carelessly dated, in-office-generated financial assessments that, in some cases, were older assessments quickly re-dated and sent out the door amid a flurry of activity. She also argued they were estimations based on a different set of metrics than assumed by prosecutors, or the same metrics open to different interpretations.

The concept Riebel suggested and that Dowd and Lynam needed jurors to buy: Symington was being asked to provide estimates based on varying criteria at a time that values and occupancy rates and lease rates were oscillating wildly. For one, Symington's buildings generated money based on the number of tenants they held and what prices those tenants were paying per square foot. Tenants were always coming, tenants were always going. New buildings were filling up with tenants. Some weren't, but then seemed to be, but then, within months, weren't again. Determining values (and making money) became especially difficult once the Resolution Trust Corporation began selling off office buildings at fire-sale prices, which forced competitors to match the lower lease rates of those buildings or lose tenants.[20]

Once Valley businesses had to match RTC-driven leasing rates, Dowd and Lynam argued, even fully leased buildings became incapable of servicing their own debt. But that decline was a slow process and one only fully predictable in hindsight. Prosecutors, Dowd and Lynam argued again and again, expected Symington to have "20/20 hindsight."[21]

On cross-examination, Riebel told Dowd she believed Symington's accountants at Coopers & Lybrand were the actual experts in Symington's finances and the point-people on lender issues.

If things were amiss, she suggested, why didn't Symington's million-dollar accountants fix the errors?

Schindler was clearly frustrated by Riebel's take on why the numbers coming out of Symington's office were suspect. "Would your opinion change if you knew (Symington) overstated the value of his real estate projects?" Schindler asked her pointedly during her fourth day of testimony. "Not unless I knew he did it on purpose." Minutes later, when Riebel failed to answer a question regarding liquidation value of real estate, Schindler cut in. "You didn't seem to have a problem explaining liquidation value to Mr. Lynam."

Schindler had suggested earlier that Coopers & Lybrand actually did their job, keeping estimated values of properties current, but that Symington, through Riebel, chose in several instances to give the accountants updated assessments only when it met Symington's financial needs.

Schindler also showed Riebel a statement sent to Valley National Bank in April 1986 that put Symington's net worth at nearly $9 million. Another financial statement sent to Mellon Bank of Pittsburgh with the exact same "as of" date showed his net worth to be nearly a million dollars less. Riebel said the larger number included an extra million dollars in "readily marketable securities" while the second did not. Schindler then provided evidence he said proved those "marketable securities" were, in fact, the four family trusts in the Mellon Bank that were controlled by a trustee who did not have to agree to release money to Symington beyond a normal yearly disbursement. So, in fact, they weren't "readily marketable securities," Schindler argued.

But, Riebel said, Mellon Bank, the bank used by the Symingtons and Fricks for decades, already knew about that trust fund. "Mr. Symington and I discussed the fact that Mellon Bank knew this information and we didn't need to put it on the schedule," Riebel said dryly.

Schindler often accused Riebel of changing her testimony between the trial and her grand jury appearance years earlier. Riebel said that since she had more time to review her records this time—and had more records collected by investigators and Symington's attorneys to review—she had a more detailed, and thus accurate, recollection of the events of the prior twelve years.

As the week of testimony drew to a close, Dowd asked jurors, "Did everybody take their NoDoz?"

The public didn't show up for the trial in the numbers expected, perhaps, as one reporter suggested, since "they'd already suffered through accounting classes in school." The open seating in the main courtroom wasn't often filled, and sometimes, the only people in the overflow courtroom were reporters hoping to hear and see the proceedings better.[22]

After a palpable "wow-this-is-actually-happening" buzz around the state the week before, it seemed like much of Arizona treated the trial like a championship game in a sport they didn't like: They didn't want to watch the actual event; they just wanted to know the final score.

Reporters, particularly those in television, struggled not to lead their trial updates with the antics of fifty-year-old Quinny Reynolds, a self-described professional drummer of Jamaican-Haitian descent who attended the trial because he wanted "to be here to watch Symington." "I always liked him," Reynolds told a reporter after one session. "I value him more than any governor. He tried. I don't believe he's a criminal."

By the afternoon of the second Friday, Reynolds, who wore a neck brace, was struggling with pain and boredom from his seat in the fourth row. He stood and began, as a *Republic* reporter described, "making swirling hand gestures, pulling on his ponytail and pressing the brass, dog-head-shaped handle of his cane to one temple as if in pain."

He apparently was doing some sort of hybrid *tai chi* to help his back. During the afternoon break, a federal marshal asked Reynolds if he'd like to go to the more relaxing overflow room. Reynolds said he'd be able to tough it out in the main courtroom.

Reynolds was "good television," but beyond a few Dowd or Mary Dell Pritzlaff brawls with the press, the trial was decidedly not.

Riebel was followed by Citibank executive Noel Thompson, a witness Schindler suggested proved that lenders actually did depend on Symington's personal finances, not just the value of his projects. Dowd countered with evidence suggesting, of course, otherwise.

The Citibank executive dove deep into bank law. Guided by Schindler, Thompson explained "contingent liability" this way: *Your son wants to get a car. He needs a loan. He's not worth much and isn't making money, so the lender wants you to guarantee to pay off the loan if your son can't. If you agree to the deal, you're on the hook for some, or all, of the loan.*

In this analogy, Symington was mom and dad. And yes, banks expected mom and dad to pay off that loan if their child couldn't.

That's an oversimplification and an analogy that didn't fit the realities of real estate lending in the Valley at the time, Dowd and Lynam argued, which was a common rebuttal by both sides when simplicity tilted the scales the other way. Both sides knew this: if they could make things simple to their advantage, they were likely to hit jurors with "I think I get it!" moments, and the side that got more of those moments probably would win the battle.

The wife of a former partner of Symington's testified Symington was slow in paying interest on one promissory note and never paid on another.

A former Symington contractor said he loaned Symington $100,000.

The contractor said he received a few payments on the loan's interest, but nothing else. The contractor said he never pursued the loan and had no plans to.

Occasionally, testimony wove in with Symington's political life. Symington's former partner in the Scottsdale Centre, Timothy Boyce, described under prosecutors' questioning that the project was a money pit from the day the partnership purchased it in 1985. The Centre, which Boyce characterized as a "trophy building" and a "premier Class A" mixed-use project, "generally . . . ran in the red because the partners struggled to get the space rented out." They found themselves struggling to compete with lower-priced options in the area, Boyce said. The amount of cheap space available skyrocketed in the second half of the 1980s because of a market decline that escalated as the Resolution Trust Corporation sold off properties below market value, he explained.

From Boyce's testimony, prosecutors, and then the media, pounded Symington for what looked to be a clear lie to the public as he was running for governor. After the story appeared in late 1990 suggesting Symington was $200 million in debt, Symington said the numbers were bogus. He said only one of his projects, the office building at 1515 E. Missouri Street, was in trouble. "I think everything else is OK," he said in response to the story at the time. That was the same time, though, that Boyce said members of the Scottsdale Centre partnership were discussing throwing their project into bankruptcy.

Symington didn't participate in the bankruptcy discussion, Boyce said, but he knew about it. Boyce said Symington told him to "do what you think is in the best interests of the limited partners.

"Don't worry about the campaign," Boyce said Symington told him. "One bankruptcy isn't going to change" the course of the campaign. Boyce said Symington told him that he had "taken his lumps" on other issues throughout the campaign and predicted he could survive a partnership bankruptcy if it had to happen.

The takeaway from Boyce's testimony: Symington had been a standup guy with his partners in the project—even contributing money to the project he had no hope of recouping—but was mischaracterizing the health of the project to both lenders and voters. After Travelers Insurance Co. sued the partnership for defaulting on a $23.5 million loan for the project, Symington told reporters his initial investment in the Scottsdale

Centre was only $25,000 at the same time he was telling lenders he had a $1 million equity interest in the project.

Which might sound bad, Dowd conceded. But then again: what if Symington was expecting to recoup that money he pumped into the project without formal conditions? Symington, Dowd said, "believed in the long-term viability of the project." What is one thing everyone knows about Fife Symington? "He had no quit in him," Dowd argued.

Dowd noted that as of 1997, the Scottsdale Centre, like the Esplanade, was making money. It just wasn't Fife Symington making the money, because he was forced to sell years earlier when the market was at its lowest point.

It would greatly help Dowd if jurors could look beyond the specific allegations to instead judge his client on the positive, present state of his once-failed creations such as the Camelback Esplanade. Schindler needed jurors to keep their minds in the time period Symington's properties were failing. Schindler's pitch: Whether or not Symington's properties were profitable at the time of the trial in 1997 was irrelevant to the accusations of fraud committed years earlier.

Other Scottsdale Centre partners and lenders testified, but the issue always reduced to this: prosecutors said the new evidence provided was proof Symington knowingly misrepresented his wealth to both lenders and voters. The defense cast the Centre as the perfect example of Symington's strong commitment to financial partners and his non-criminal "crimes of optimism," which, if you consider that his projects were again successful by 1997, weren't even technically optimistic. As of 1997, Symington, Dowd argued, was just *correct*.

Generally speaking, by the end of the trial's third week, it was clear how both sides were framing their arguments. The foundations were built. It was just a matter of spending a couple more months getting their cases built out.

Donald Lewis, former president of Southwest Savings and Loan, testified about Southwest's relationship with Symington and the Esplanade. He outlined how a project that appeared to be a big moneymaker in 1983 turned into a crippling $40 million money pit when it was still unbuilt in 1987. Prosecutors wanted Lewis's testimony to set the table for their argument that Symington lied on financial statements to keep the Esplanade project alive.[23]

Lewis, Shaun McKinnon of the *Arizona Daily Star* wrote, "helped government prosecutors set the stage for Symington's later dealings with the
Esplanade, a $200 million project that ultimately ruined Southwest and
finally sold for $70 million at auction."

Lewis was replaced on the stand by one of Symington's former personal accountants, who testified that debts she had documented in her
records never appeared on the final financial statements given to Coopers & Lybrand.[24]

One of those loans came from the general contractor on the Esplanade project, who gave Symington $2.25 million in 1985 hoping it would
help expedite actual construction on the site. Symington offered half his
share in the Esplanade as collateral, which, at the time, "was worth more
than the loan," Robert Hunt testified. But as the Esplanade floundered
and was ultimately sold for a fraction of its original cost, that collateral
became worthless.

Prosecutors said Symington tried to deceive other potential lenders by
not including the debt to Hunt on loan documents.[25] Dowd and Lynam
argued Symington didn't need to report the debt because it was secured
by shares of the project.

Another witness said he purchased all of Symington's remaining share
of the Esplanade in 1987 (after which Symington allegedly still told lenders he owned it), while the next witness, the Symington Company chief
financial officer, James Cockerham, said he believed Symington kept his
personal financial documents in sealed envelopes to keep uncomfortable
truths hidden.[26]

He admitted that Symington's financial documents could be difficult
to locate at times: "I can recall going from person to person trying to find
them."

Schindler had difficult witnesses in both Riebel and Cockerham. Both
still considered themselves friends with Symington and were using the
same attorney provided by their former employer.

Perhaps Cockerham's most damning testimony suggested that Symington was claiming on loan documents that he owned larger percentag-
es of certain properties than he actually did, and that he perhaps knowingly inflated the value of those properties on documents sent to lenders.
In particular, Cockerham seemed to confirm prosecutors' assertions that
Symington claimed he owned 15 percent of a $4 million property at near-

ly the same time tax documents showed he owned only 7.5 percent of the property that had failed to sell months before at an asking price of $2.8 million.

On cross-examination, though, Dowd arguably turned the comptroller's appearance into a defense win: Cockerham said it was his job to draw up documents for Symington to confirm to Esplanade investor Dai-Ichi Kangyo that Symington was still worth more than $4 million (a requirement for Symington to draw more money from the construction loan). Cockerham testified he never referred to the original agreement to be sure Symington was making accurate financial statements. "Did you ever give any thought to the fact that Mr. Symington may no longer have a $4 million net worth when he signed the draw request?" Lynam asked. "No sir," Cockerham responded. "I didn't put a note or memo on the draw request to ask Mr. Symington if that was still correct. I should have. I just didn't make the connection."

A pattern began to appear. Sometimes, it seemed, Symington would sign anything put on his desk and sometimes, those putting the documents on his desk weren't fully sure why the documents needed to be signed. More broadly, Cockerham suggested that he and Symington's accounting firm, Coopers & Lybrand, may have been to blame for some of the errors that became criminal in the eyes of prosecutors once Symington signed documents under penalty of law.

Cockerham's testimony was critical to both sides. But because it involved copious amounts of document reviews, it was long and exceptionally tedious.

Luckily for members of the media, Reynolds, the Jamaican-Haitian drummer, stayed around.[27] During Lewis's testimony, according to the *Republic's* daily feature "The Court Observer," Reynolds gyrated and made spastic, sweeping motions with his hands and arms as he held a piece of paper with Lewis's name on it.

He denied to reporters that he was casting a spell. He was just trying to channel a good vibe to Symington. He didn't believe in witchcraft; he "believed in God, Jesus Christ, and Fife Symington."

As June rolled into July, the oppressive heat outside began to raise the temperature in the old federal courthouse. Dowd's suit jackets were doused in sweat by the end of most days. As the government witnesses from the worlds of business and accounting told similar stories about similar loans for similar projects, their collective testimony began to run together and run on.

By July, one reporter noted, it seemed as if Reynolds was the only person involved in the trial who was happy to be there.

# Chapter 35

# DOG DAYS AND END TIMES

K even Willey mused in a column in mid-June that the trial tedium, created by the government's strategy of "death by a thousand paper cuts," could be mitigated by replacing the real players in the trial with famous actors.[1]

Dowd? Maybe Ned Beatty or some mashup of Bruce Dern and Andy Griffith. Lynam? Bruce Dern. Schindler? Sam Waterson. George Cardona? Woody Allen.

She suggested a title based on Samuel Beckett's absurdist play, *Waiting for Godot,* with its famously pared-down set. Perhaps *Waiting for a Verdict,* she suggested, not taking into account that Strand's techno-courtroom was the opposite of a spare set.

By mid-June, the attorneys had figured out the computer system, which, while speeding up the dissemination of information, removed the only consistent source of entertainment—slapstick computer incompetence—beyond whatever Reynolds was doing that day.

Sometimes, though, the net result of a day's tedium did energize coverage if testimony seemed to significantly tip the scales.

A former Coopers & Lybrand accountant, Katherine Wrigley, testified that she was asked to compile a report in 1991 that she was told would be used to, as she said, "help establish that Mr. Symington didn't have the net worth to honor" several loan agreements. The numbers she was given to compile the report, she confirmed to prosecutors, didn't include Symington assets and property valuations she had seen in the prior financial reports she had prepared.

Perhaps most fascinating in Wrigley's testimony: she confirmed that her partner at the firm, the since deceased John Yeoman, had "coded" confidential copies of Symington's statements to be used as a method to help discover who was leaking documents, as she said, to "the press or others" during Symington's first gubernatorial campaign. (At the time,

Yeoman was also Symington's political campaign treasurer and personal accountant.)

Under cross-examination, Lynam used Wrigley's testimony suggesting lax oversight by Coopers & Lybrand and Yeoman as proof that it was Symington's million-dollar accountants, not Symington, who were ultimately to blame for faulty financial documents reaching creditors and potential new lenders.[2]

A Valley National Bank official testified that Symington never told her about the Mercado's long-term loan in 1989. Another banker, Douglas Hawes, testified that, based on the dates on a series of documents, he believed it was fair to say Symington had denied the accuracy of a financial statement on the exact day that he used that statement to obtain a loan at a different bank. (Hawes was discussing the documents Symington and his secretary said were misdated by accident: Basically, Symington and Riebel claimed, financial documents compiled from months earlier were accidentally sent out stamped with the date they were compiled, not the date they were sent to a lender.) Another Valley loan officer, Kendall Milhon, testified he would not have approved loans to Symington had he been told Symington's financial statements were inaccurate.

Martha Frick Symington's lawyer said he knew of her son's financial troubles by 1992.[3]

A managing director for Citicorp's real estate division suggested Symington repeatedly, from his company's perspective, over-reported the value of his properties. David Feingold said he only found out later about several of Symington's debts. He also was unaware that Symington's trusts would potentially be off-limits if Citicorp needed to collect. Feingold said that, yes, such information was an important component in their decisions to loan money.[4]

Feingold also testified that he believed Citicorp didn't foreclose on a $10 million loan to Symington in part because executives were concerned there would be repercussions from the sitting governor or his supporters.[5]

That admission was likely a big win for prosecutors in their attempts to paint Symington as an unsympathetic character. Here was a bank official confirming that bank executives feared getting into a public scrape with a sitting governor. It suggested that Symington was more likely than the average person—like the members of the jury—to get bailed out by his debtors.

The *Republic*'s front-page story led with Feingold's comment regarding the mindset of Citicorp executives.

The *Mesa Tribune*'s lead story, though, didn't mention the comment. The *Tribune* story, "Official: Governor disclosed finances to lender," led with testimony much more favorable to the governor.

The *Republic*'s Steve Wilson wrote about the significant difference in coverage of the trial in the Valley's two largest print media companies. "You might think there are two Fife Symington trials going on in US District Court," Wilson wrote. "The stories are often slanted differently, and at times, dramatically so." He didn't suggest bias was at work in the two different media takeaways, just two very different interpretations of what issues were most important amid the day's events. Wilson argued that this disconnect in media coverage of the trial could be a window into jurors' perceptions: "If reporters can evaluate the testimony so differently, so can jurors."[6]

In mid-July, among a series of secondary players that gave similar testimony, prosecutors brought in Donald Eaton, the investment adviser to the labor unions that invested in the Mercado.[7] Eaton was key to the outlier extortion charge claiming Symington had threatened to use his power to drive away potential state-government leases from the Mercado if the investors forced him to fully honor the terms of his personal guarantee.

It looked like any other hot boring day in court.

But a bit of early palace intrigue quickly suggested otherwise. Before Eaton took the stand for a second day, Schindler approached Judge Strand and asked him to force Dowd to reveal his sources for a line of questioning Schindler knew Dowd would be pursuing later in the day. Schindler also asked that Dowd's questions to Eaton regarding the mysterious issue and Eaton's answers to the questions be stricken from the court record.[8]

Strand denied Schindler's requests as the courtroom buzzed in anticipation of potential intrigue.

Schindler then questioned Eaton, who testified that, during an October 1991 telephone conversation, Symington said he would steer Arizona State University and Maricopa County government agencies away from renting Mercado space if the pension funds filed a default notice on the loan.[9]

(As an executive with McMorgan & Co., Eaton signed off on the

Mercado loan in 1990, then led negotiations as the loan fell into default the following year. Eaton was then fired by McMorgan the next year.)

Eaton testified that Symington had begun approaching him for concessions within a year of the finalization of the Mercado loan.[10] McMorgan, though, refused to modify the loan.[11]

Then came the cross-examination. Dowd began his questioning by asking Eaton about his state of mind at the time investigators came asking him about his involvement with the Mercado. "You were out of a job and you were not happy about that, were you?" Dowd asked.

"I can't say I was thrilled," Eaton responded.

Dowd suggested Eaton blamed his firing on Symington. Then Dowd dropped his bomb:

"You told your neighbors in San Carlos, California, that you'd get even with Fife Symington, didn't you?" Dowd asked. "In fact, you told them you'd pay your way to Arizona to get even, didn't you?"

Eaton paused, then denied the allegations. Dowd dropped the issue and moved on.

Dowd moved on quickly because he believed he had already quickly made his point:[12] The specificity of the questioning—and the alien nature of the accusation—surely suggested to the jury that Dowd held evidence that Eaton had a vendetta.

"Eaton's credibility crumbled under Dowd's sharp cross-examination," a *Republic* editorial writer suggested. "Dowd alleged that Eaton blamed Symington for his subsequent dismissal from McMorgan and swore revenge. Eaton denied this, but his voice-cracking nervousness during Dowd's cross drew his believability into question."[13]

Since the single extortion charge against Symington was based primarily on Eaton's interpretations of undocumented conversations, Dowd and Lynam felt that an admission by Eaton of malice toward Symington would very likely torpedo that count.

(In a later interview, Dowd said he wasn't bluffing with Eaton. Dowd had hired a private investigator to follow Eaton. The investigator, Dowd said, had interviewed Eaton's neighbors, who readily passed along Eaton's quotes regarding Symington.)[14]

Prosecutors concluded their case with testimony from Jean Wong, a former employee, who testified that Symington was actually a detail-oriented math wiz, an unwanted compliment since Symington's attorneys were arguing otherwise.[15]

Under examination by Schindler, Wong portrayed herself as a tireless lieutenant whom Symington had under-compensated and skipped over for promotions she deserved. During her seventy- and eighty-hour workweeks, she said, she watched Symington obsess over every detail of his projects and finances, which prosecutors argued showed Symington was surely aware of the substantial misstatements in his financial documents.

On cross-examination, Dowd worked to portray Wong as a very well-compensated, disgruntled employee who was bending reality to get back at Symington for promoting Randy Todd over her to be the Symington Company's second-in-command. Dowd pointed to transcripts of Wong's FBI interviews in which she said Symington was, in fact, "not detail-oriented."

"Well, it really would depend on the circumstances," Wong told Dowd.

After presenting ten thousand documents and testimony from more than thirty witnesses over eight weeks, the prosecution rested.

Analysts treated the moment as a sort of halftime break. The *Republic*'s editorial board even provided a loose ranking of witnesses from damning to least damning.

The editors ranked the testimony of the Symington Company's former controller, James Cockerham, as the most useful for the government's argument. Cockerham spent more than a week on the stand reluctantly speaking on details suggesting Symington was bending reality with his reported property valuation. Cockerham was deep inside Symington's numbers, perhaps as much as anyone other than deceased accountant John Yeoman.

Second place went to Wong. Runners-up in the *Republic*'s rankings were Feingold and Thompson from Citicorp; attorney Paul Meyer, who said Symington told him his interest in the Esplanade was worth $2 million near the time Symington told others he was penniless; and Katherine Wrigley, who said she was bothered enough by inconsistencies in Symington's financial statements to write a memo to coworkers saying she felt she shouldn't perform a financial review requested by Symington.

During that pause, the Department of Economic Security reported that the state's jobless rate hit a thirteen-year low.[16] With staff coffers full, Symington continued to promise more for state programs, including $9 million for the ever-struggling Child Protective Services.[17]

Other tidbits of governing happened during the trial. For one: In mid-July, Symington held a press conference to promote cleaner-burning fuels to help clean the Valley's brown air.

Regardless, Symington's poll numbers remained at record lows.[18] The trial was dictating public perception of the governor. The support and money for CPS and environmental programs was greeted cynically: Symington, his detractors said, was acting moderate and socially conscious to enhance, as one commentator described it, "his jury appeal."

Dowd and Lynam would be relatively quick. They felt they had already established much of their case in cross-examination.[19]

As the defense began their questioning, Dowd said he still hadn't decided if he'd present the one witness everyone wanted to see—Symington himself.

Dowd and Lynam picked Randy Todd for their opening scene. Symington's right-hand man arguably knew the Symington Company better than Symington himself. Indeed, it had been Todd who managed the company as Symington drifted into politics, and it was Todd who took over the company once Symington left. He was the witness who could best describe the inner workings of a heavily leveraged real estate company trying to survive a historic market downturn.

Todd had spent much of Symington's first year in office struggling to save the Mercado.[20] Todd explained to the jury how McMorgan & Co. made a difficult task impossible. Todd testified that McMorgan was denying leasing offers, a practice that would only make sense, the defense argued, if McMorgan and the pension funds stood to gain from a quick death for the Mercado.

McMorgan & Co. rejected numerous potential renters, documents showed, including a Phoenix restaurateur with a history of success and a US congressman with a history of paying his bills.

Todd also cast doubt on the earlier testimony of Jean Wong, the longtime employee that suggested Symington, among other things, was an exceptionally detail-oriented micromanager. Todd described Wong as a disgruntled employee who became particularly bitter when Symington promoted Todd to be his top assistant and then president of the Symington Company.

In cross-examination of Todd, Cardona painted Symington's top lieutenant as an extremely biased witness. Todd, Cardona argued, was paid well by Symington and had built his own successful company from the remains of Symington's failed one.[21]

As Todd finished his testimony, Dowd and Lynam won a significant concession from Judge Strand: against the wishes of prosecutors, the defense could put on the stand a respected accountant whom the defense asked to review the accounting work of Coopers & Lybrand.

With the death of John Yeoman, the defense argued they had lost their key witness and their ability to expose the mistakes made within Coopers & Lybrand. No expert witness could replace John Yeoman, they argued, but they deserved to have someone speak to the quality of Coopers' work for Symington.

CPA Lawrence Field, who often served as an investigator for the State Board of Accountancy, spent three hours detailing how, in his opinion, Coopers & Lybrand failed on several occasions to warn Symington regarding inaccurate information in the personal financial statements that were then sent to lenders.[22]

In particular, Field said Coopers & Lybrand had not fulfilled its obligation to make sure critical information from its own tax department had been given to the firm's audit department, which Symington had hired to perform reviews of his 1987, 1988, and 1989 financial statements. Field said that Coopers & Lybrand had copious amounts of information about Symington's real estate holdings and debts that did not reach the auditing department. The point Dowd and Lynam hoped to make: Symington had paid Coopers & Lybrand to be the details people—to make sure he was providing accurate information to lenders—and the "Big Six" accounting firm had failed him.

Prosecutors countered by painting Field as yet another biased witness. Schindler pointed out that he had received more than $250,000 from state contracts and had been paid $75,000 by the defense to review the work of Coopers & Lybrand. Prosecutors argued Symington worked to keep the tax and audit departments from sharing potentially damaging information. Field said that it was clear that both departments had the information needed that, had they communicated, would have corrected many of the bad numbers at the heart of the majority of indictments.[23]

Field's testimony was overshadowed by two other stories that day. Mary Dell Pritzlaff, Ann's famously cantankerous mother, gave Channel 12 reporter Lew Ruggiero two elbow shots to the back as Pritzlaff tried to assist Symington's elderly father through the crowd outside the courtroom. *Republic* photographer Michael Chow captured Pritzlaff's second shot to Ruggiero, which produced an image for the next day's

July 23, 1997, Phoenix, Arizona: Mary Dell Pritzlaff, Arizona Governor Fife Symington's mother-in-law, shows her displeasure with the media on Wednesday, July 23, 1997, after the day's proceedings at the federal courthouse in Phoenix. Pritzlaff also gave media members a couple of elbows. © The Arizona Republic-USA Today Network.

paper akin to the moment Jack Ruby shot Lee Harvey Oswald. Pritzlaff then kicked Chow in the shins and stuck her tongue out at him. (A *Republic* writer quipped the next day regarding the irony of Pritzlaff's warring demeanor while in the process of escorting Fife Symington Jr., a former US diplomat.)[24]

Overshadowing Pritzlaff's outburst was the announcement for which everyone had been hoping:

The governor would be taking the stand in his own defense.

Behind the scenes, before he ever announced he'd put Symington on the stand, Dowd had already begun prepping Symington for an appearance.[25] Dowd peppered Symington with the defense's line of questioning, making sure Symington could make clear for the jury the context of details in their questions. Then, friendly Dowd would step away and return to Symington pretending to be the toughest version of David Schindler. Amid Dowd's questions he throttled Symington with snide insults and repetitive insinuations intended to fluster and anger witnesses (Dowd had plenty of experience with that tactic). Dowd was on his worst behavior so his client was prepared to remain at his best in the courtroom.

More than forty journalists, about twenty of them lugging television cameras, congregated at the courthouse steps the morning of Symington's testimony—about double the usual number during the trial's dog days. The forty seats in the overflow room were finally filled. In the packed seventy-three-seat courtroom, Symington's posse was nearly fully in attendance: Ann was there with their five children, along with the Pritzlaffs and Fife Symington's father.[26]

Quinny Reynolds was seated in the overflow room, eyes closed—seemingly in deep meditation or prayer—with his hands alternately placed on his thighs or chest.

Symington's appearance in court was so newsworthy that most news outlets commented on his appearance: "A classic look," one news-turned-fashion reporter noted, "worthy of his East Coast patrician origins." No detail was overlooked. Symington, several noted, was wearing a small lapel pin signifying the Bronze Star he had been awarded for his service in Thailand during the Vietnam War.

Symington said little that Dowd and Lynam hadn't already said for him during the previous forty days of deliberations. But here was the man himself saying it. He appeared calm, speaking in a measured, quietly confident, sometimes almost "I-can't-believe-you-guys-think-I-did-something-wrong" tone, as Dowd methodically asked him if he did any of the things alleged in the criminal counts.

"Did you try to fool any of your lenders with your financial statements?" Dowd asked. "I certainly did not," Symington responded. "Did you try to take advantage of any lending institution with your financial statement?" "No," Symington answered. "Did you gain any advantage by the errors and omissions in your financial statement?" Symington fired back: "I did not."

Dowd asked Symington to explain away the discrepancies.

"The financial statement just wasn't a big priority for me," Symington said near the end of the first day. "My head was in other things—visiting construction sites, meeting with architects and engineers. I was really busy, really on the go."

Then, Symington showed contrition, not for bad intentions, but for bad mistakes: "The financial statements—I just didn't pay attention the way I should have. That's what happened."

ion to those all-im-
portant personal guarantees: In the real world of real estate loans, he
explained, those personal guarantees aren't there so the borrower pays
all the money back from their own pocket if a project fails. The personal
guarantee, Symington argued, is given because banks want those personal guarantees more as an assurance that the projects will be finished
on time and on budget.

(This last concept arguably would be the most alien to jurors who
likely believed the personal guarantee meant what it sounded like it
meant.)

The jurors had to grasp a few more esoteric concepts to acquit. They
needed to gain a full appreciation for, and understanding of, the heavy
risk/healthy reward world of Arizona commercial real estate (If a developer succeeds in the crucible, he or she gets—and should get because of
the huge risk—those six- and seven-figure payoffs you see in those documents). Jurors needed to understand the forces beyond Symington's control that laid waste to the Arizona real estate landscape nearly a decade
before. And they needed to also appreciate (this was Dowd's idea more
than Symington's) how the governor's own psychological makeup—
particularly the sort of jump-over-the-cliff-before-looking optimism—
made him a sucker for big risky adventures like "Project Mars."

But jurors also needed to be reminded that the biggest of those risky
adventures—the Camelback Esplanade—was actually successful again in
the 1997 market.

Symington and Dowd spent hours reviewing documents already reviewed by numerous other witnesses. The discrepancies in every document at the heart of the indictments were explained away as mistakes or
misunderstandings.

Much of Symington's remaining conversation with Dowd was, essentially, a collection of charges against the lead prosecutor in the case.
Dowd and Symington suggested that Schindler was a wildly ambitious
man with unlimited resources whose defining skill was his ability to
make the utterly mundane sound scandalous.

Reviews of Symington's two days of testimony guided by Dowd were
generally favorable, focusing as much on Symington's chutzpah for taking the stand as on anything said.

But chatting for two days in court with Dowd's pussycat side was the
easy part. Cross-examination by Schindler, who, amid Dowd's softball

questions sometimes stewed like an all-star wrestler begging to tap in, would be another.

Finally, on the third day, Arizona's "trial-of-the-century" might live up to its billing.

But according to reviews, it didn't. For three more days, Schindler grilled Symington regarding every number the prosecution believed showed an attempt to deceive.[27] Symington then explained how each instance of alleged fraud was a mistake, or a hastily handled bureaucratic technicality that mattered to no one in the financial transactions or, very often, again, something Schindler just didn't understand.

Dowd occasionally would interject to suggest Schindler wasn't ignorant, but rather was intentionally leaving out key details that supported Symington's explanation. Dowd needed jurors to believe prosecutors were lying by omission.[28]

On the fourth day, both Schindler and Symington looked withered from the document dump. Their exchanges remained cordial but increasingly dour.[29]

One detailed, lengthy exchange late on the fourth day arguably took jurors closest to the matter at hand in the case—was there willful deception, or simply mistakes made and common practices followed? It was a moment in the trial that, like several other key moments, pitted the simple "two-sets-of-books" argument against the complicated "this is the reality of the business" counter-argument.[30]

Schindler asked: "Now, the same day that you provided this financial statement to First Interstate Bank, you also submitted a copy of it to Valley National Bank, right?"

Symington responded, "That may well be the case. . . . I believe that my secretary, Joyce Riebel, testified to the $3,348,000 error in her testimony that she had made other corrections on the schedule, but somehow this particular uncorrected number appeared in the 1988 schedule."

"Now, on that same date," Schindler continued, "you provided another copy of this December 31, 1987, financial statement to Valley, right? . . . If you could turn to page two, tell us what date you signed this one."

"5-19-88," Symington responded.

"Same day as the one from First Interstate Bank, right?"

"That's correct," Symington answered.

"And again, you certified it was correct?"

"Yes, this is the same certification," Symington answered.

Schindler then asked: "And you submitted your personal financial statement to Valley National Bank in order to renew your personal line of credit and to renew the Symington Company's line of credit, right?"

"All I know is that Valley Bank asked for my financial statement," Symington responded to this pivotal question. "Why they renewed the line of credit, is, I think, a separate issue. But they were periodically asking for an update of my financial statement. They would ask . . . Joyce to send it and we would send it."

"These were unsecured lines of credit, right?" Schindler asked.

"That's correct."

"And you knew," Schindler continued, "from your days at Southwest Savings and Loan that when you have an unsecured loan or a line of credit, you're looking to the borrower alone, right, because there is no security as you just said?"

Symington then took on the tone of an economics professor: "Well, actually, Mr. Schindler, that's incorrect. When I was on the loan committee at Southwest, we were a real estate lender. The loans that we made were against real estate assets. Someone's financial statement and even guarantee was really of minor interest to us in our lending policies. We wanted to make sure that we lent against the real estate asset and that we could recover our investment out of that real estate investment should the developer be wiped out. That's how we approached our lending."

Later in the exchange, Schindler brought in another financial statement signed near the time as those given to both First Interstate Bank and Valley National Bank.

"Mr. Symington, this financial statement (to Valley) and the one that you provided to First Interstate Bank were both signed on May 19, 1988, right?"

"That's correct."

"And that's one month after you provided your December 31, 1987, statement to (Dai-Ichi Kangyo Bank), right?"

"That's correct."

"Well, why didn't you just give First Interstate Bank and Valley National Bank the same December 31, 1987, financial statement that you'd given to (Dai-Ichi Kangyo) on April 1?"

Symington responded: "Well, I thought I had. I mean that's the whole point here. That, you know, people make mistakes, Mr. Schindler. And

Joyce would bring me a financial statement and I would sign it and it would go out the door. And I wouldn't necessarily review it. And it was under the assumption that I was giving the same statement. So a mistake was made. Those things happen."

Schindler ended his cross-examination after five days. Dowd asked Symington a few more questions in his redirect to clarify points, and the governor then returned to the governor's office. He would have no more say in the matter.[31]

On August 5, attorneys gave their suggestions to Judge Strand about the language to be used in Strand's instructions to the jury prior to deliberations. Key for Symington: that jurors needed to be able to consider "good faith" when judging his actions.

That same day, Strand decided to dismiss one of the twenty-two counts against Symington, saying there was insufficient evidence supporting the bank-fraud charge related to the Baltimore bank.[32]

Attorneys then gave their closing statements.[33]

Although Schindler was expected to give the closing arguments for the government, George Cardona was the prosecutor tasked with summarizing the government's case. Cardona described Symington as a guy too smart and too experienced to be the naïve, mistake-prone character portrayed by the defense.[34]

"Look at who Mr. Symington is," Cardona said. "This is a highly educated man, who is highly intelligent, who ran his own development company for ten years."

Cardona paced between his exhibits and the jury box, speaking, as one reporter put it the next day, "in the energetic tone of a college professor laying out the results of his research."

After reviewing the collection of incidences in which Symington overstated the current market value of his properties, Cardona asked jurors to dismiss Symington's claims that he was only guilty of being overly optimistic. Cardona used an analogy he knew jurors—nine of whom owned homes—would appreciate: He asked jurors to imagine themselves telling a bank their house was worth $150,000 when a recent appraisal had placed its value at $75,000. "If you went and did that, the bank would laugh at you if they knew what you were doing," Cardona said.

In his closing arguments, Dowd reasserted that beyond a few oversights (that should have been caught by his well-paid accountants),

Symington never lied while always doing what he was asked to do by lenders.

After an overarching assault on the government's case, Dowd attacked each of the criminal counts.

After more than four hours, Dowd, visibly drained, finished with a personal appeal: "The last five years we've been entrusted with Fife Symington's life and reputation. And now, we entrust them to you. I know you'll do justice."[35]

The jury then disappeared from public view to determine Symington's fate.[36]

In the news vacuum during those private deliberations, members of the media went hunting for legal experts to draw up the odds.

*Republic* columnist Steve Wilson, after interviewing a collection of judges and trial experts, suggested that the length and nature of the trial alone would likely lead to at least one conviction. (Wilson himself, like many in the press corps and beyond, had been predicting a hung jury simply because of the complexity of a case.)[37] One judge interviewed for the column pointed to a study that showed juries actually rarely deadlock, especially in lengthy trials. Long trials, another judge suggested to Wilson, "bring people together" with a collective sense of duty that they need to produce results.

Another legal expert suggested that some idea of fair play can sneak into discussions when numerous counts are involved: *It was close, so the score should be close.*

Trial consultant Hale Starr argued the Symington trial, by its nature, could easily go either way. And it might be Lady Luck, not Lady Justice, making the call.

"We do a lot of mock trials," Starr told Wilson. "It's not all that common to present the same evidence to three groups of people, and one comes back unanimous guilty, one comes back unanimous not guilty and the third group ends up hung."

*Arizona Daily Star* reporters surveyed twenty-two Tucson legal experts, politicians, and real estate professionals. Eleven believed Symington likely would be convicted on at least one charge.[38] Of the remaining half, five said he would be acquitted, while six said they felt it was impossible for them to predict the outcome of the trial.

Most observers agreed on one thing: It might take awhile for the jury to reach a verdict.

# Chapter 36

# HARD TIMES

S ymington stayed in his office, and away from the media, during the
jury's first week of deliberations. He needed to be close to the federal courthouse, Doug Cole told reporters, in case the jury reached
a verdict.

It was a tense week in the governor's suite. For the first time in three
months, Symington could stay at work and focus on work. He tried, but
still. Staff knew, too, that their lives could be upended at any moment.[1]

Secretary of State Jane Hull told friends she felt fully briefed and prepared to take over as governor as she continued to pretend that everything was business as usual.[2]

State schools superintendent Lisa Graham Keegan intensified her
mostly one-sided war of words with Symington, her onetime ally. Keegan
announced she would begin a petition drive to get a half-cent sales-tax
hike for school funding onto the 1998 ballot. The plan, she argued (along
with a fairly broad coalition of Republicans and Democrats), would
more equitably fund the state's schools than local property taxes, which
raised more money in districts with the highest property values, meaning
wealthier Arizonans got better-funded schools.

Keegan was willing to use the language of race warfare to argue her
case, saying this of those who sided with Symington against her plan: "At
least the Klan people wear sheets."[3]

Amid Symington's troubles, the Republican Party really didn't need
one Republican comparing other Republicans to members of the Ku
Klux Klan.

Numbers released that week suggested ozone pollution was on the
rise again, bringing fresh speculation that EPA officials would slap potentially growth-slowing restrictions on the Valley.[4]

Symington brought together a panel of doctors, educators, and spe-
cialists in law, religion, and elder care to compile, as Symington said,

"recommendations for quality medical care at the end of life and for preservation of Arizona's legal and cultural disfavor of assisted suicide."[5]

And tribal gaming issues continued to smolder. Tribes showed no intention of complying with an order from the director of the Arizona Department of Gaming to cease the playing of poker in casinos. Some worried another standoff might be on the horizon.[6]

After a week behind closed doors, jurors emerged from the court-house and climbed into two white vans. As reporters scrambled towards the vehicles, David Schindler yelled to reporters: "They're just going to lunch!"[7]

The twelve jurors were already tired of the deli sandwiches being de-livered to the courtroom, so Strand let them lunch at a nearby Mexican restaurant, where, reporters noted, the jurors laughed and joked and ap-peared to broadly enjoy each other.

That was pretty much the big trial news from the first week of delib-erations.[8]

Beyond the jury's festive lunch mood, though, reports leaked that one juror had increasingly been at odds with the other eleven.

Then, on Tuesday of the second week, Judge Strand dismissed a seven-ty-four-year-old woman from the jury, saying only that it was "for good and sufficient legal cause." As the woman—known then only as "juror No. 161"—pushed through reporters to leave the building, she barked at the throng: "I'm not going to tell you anything." When asked if it was dis-appointing to be released, she said: "Of course it is. I worked hard at it."[9]

She told a reporter the next day that she felt "railroaded."[10]

Dowd and Lynam pounced.

Transcripts of conversations between court officials, jurors, and the dismissed juror weren't released until the following day. The transcripts showed Strand had acted on the complaints of other jurors who said the woman had proven incapable of understanding the intricacies of the case. In a special hearing with the judge, jurors said they repeatedly at-tempted to explain, among other things, each point of discussion and each straw vote taken by her fellow jurors as they pushed toward a deci-sion. The woman seemed perpetually baffled, they testified, sometimes even forgetting how she had voted just minutes before.[11]

Dowd said the dismissed juror was simply a holdout—someone who refused to go along with the crowd that, apparently, was moving toward one or more convictions.

Transcripts of a discussion between Strand and the woman (by then identified as Mary Jane Cotey), suggested Dowd might have an argument. When Strand asked Cotey about her concerns regarding her fellow jurors, she said: "They are all talking about a complete unanimous vote. They don't seem to want to put it off for a while because we've been through it enough. A lot of them have to go back to work. A lot of them have families—things like that."

Dowd framed it this way: Cotey believed Symington was innocent on all counts; her opinion was inconvenient for the other jurors, so she was booted so the other jurors could wrap things up quickly. Dowd argued that by dismissing the juror instead of declaring a hung jury, Strand had violated Symington's constitutional right to a fair trial in which all members of an impartial jury agree that, beyond a reasonable doubt, a crime had been committed.

Schindler simply pointed to the numerous comments of Cotey's fellow jurors to suggest she legitimately wasn't up to the task.

Judge Strand sided with Schindler, saying, "It is fundamental that no juror should yield a thoughtfully held position simply to arrive at a verdict. But there has been nothing stated by any of the jurors that would indicate that this is the situation here."[12]

Symington was in his office when Dowd called with the news about Cotey. After Symington hung up the phone, he walked from his office down to the long hallway linking the Executive Tower and the old state capitol building and began pacing back and forth.[13]

Symington said later that he had always believed he was going to be acquitted. He was fighting and he was going to win and that's how he kept his brain straight through all the static.

But in his mind, he would say later, the removal of a juror who would have hung the jury on all counts surely meant the road was close to clear for convictions. It was the first time he became sure he soon would be forced to resign as governor of Arizona.

Symington's unyielding confidence—what his detractors called unyielding arrogance—had vanished. His mind raced and he could imagine the resignation and the isolation afterward and the unknown of an appeal (no matter how confident Dowd was), and for the first time he could visualize spending real time in prison.

Symington walked back to his office and sat down and stared at the wall. His mind continued to race. He stared at the wall with his mouth slightly agape and a confused look on his face until he heard a voice that said:

"Everything will be okay."

He would say later he had never been "a particularly spiritual person." He wouldn't conclusively attribute the words to a source beyond a desperate brain seeking firm ground. But whatever the source, the words calmed him. He said later that a sense of peace "washed over him" and that he would repeat the mystically delivered phrase (*or it would be repeated to him*) whenever he felt like he was drowning.

Then he went about his business, doing his best to act as if nothing of consequence had happened in the proceedings or in his mind.

Two days after Cotey's dismissal, Dowd submitted a mistrial motion. Earlier that day, Strand had rejected Dowd's request for a hearing in which he could interview the dismissed juror.

Strand said he might allow such an interview "following the discharge of the jury," a move that would potentially create even more legal and political conundrums.

Dowd's request for a mistrial faced what some judged to be an impossible hurdle: Strand would have to admit that, by dismissing Cotey, he made a mistake so profound that the previous three months of agony would have to be repeated in front of a new jury.

Strand denied the motion.[14]

Back at the Executive Tower, Symington continued acting as if nothing was bothering him.[15] In a bet with Iowa's governor, he agreed to pony up an eleven-foot-long burrito if Arizona's arena football team lost to a team from Iowa in ArenaBowl XI. Iowa's governor would have to give Symington eleven pounds of Iowa pork chops if the Iowa team lost.[16]

Symington was delighted to have anything to do that didn't have to do with his trial.

As Symington governed, Dowd appealed. Prosecutors sought to lower the burden of proof in the case to reflect the US Supreme Court ruling earlier that year which upheld a law stating that knowingly making false claims is a crime whether the claims impacted decisions or not. Dowd attacked prosecutors for trying to violate Symington's constitutional right to a fair trial. Strand ruled that the Supreme Court decision came too late to be applied in the Symington case.

The jury continued to deliberate through the end of August. Reporters struggled to provide trial copy.[17] Howard Fischer of Capitol Media

Services wrote a piece appearing in several Sunday papers in which real estate agents pondered if Symington's earning potential in the real estate world would be impacted if he was convicted. The verdict: It might be, it might not be.[18]

The *Republic*'s Catherine Reagor wrote a piece in early September in which several Phoenix developers admitted to basically doing what Symington was accused of doing as the Valley real estate market crashed in the late 1980s. Reagor talked to numerous developers and her sources, unsurprisingly requesting anonymity, described the myriad ways they tried to survive through the downturn by courting lenders as they held off creditors.[19]

"The question the trial didn't answer," Reagor wrote, "is whether any developer's financial statement was to be believed in the 1980s?"

"A lot of small developers probably did move around numbers on their financial sheets in the late 1980s," a prominent real estate analyst said.

"Prosecutions were rare," Reagor continued, "probably because, even when banks discovered phony entries, they preferred to work with developers to get what money they could on the debts rather than toss them to authorities."

And every developer in Arizona in the late 1980s and early 1990s, several sources told her, believed their projects would rebound if they could hold off their lenders just a little bit longer.

Reagor wrote: "Some people thus saw the Symington jury's dilemma as a commentary on the times: To acquit was to say that Symington was just part of that ambitious and fragile era, guilty of heady self-promotion but not a crime. Why single him out because he had the stature of the governor's chair?

"To convict was to say he was more flagrant than most in his deeds, or at least to say that enough was enough and that the hammer needed to fall on at least one cagey developer."

Just before 10 a.m. on the Wednesday after Labor Day, Judge Strand summoned both Schindler and Dowd to the federal courthouse. Strand told them he had just received a note from the presiding juror saying their decisions had been reached.

Dowd called Symington, who stood from his desk, slipped on his suit jacket, and began telling others in his office that a verdict had been reached. After lunch, Symington met up with Dowd and Lynam at the defense table as Ann and their two oldest sons, Scott and Fife IV, filed into their normal seats behind the governor.[20]

At 1:19 p.m., the counts and verdicts were read:

Count One: Deadlocked. Count Two: Deadlocked. Count Three: Deadlocked. Count Four: Not guilty. Count Six: Deadlocked. Count Seven: Deadlocked. Count Eight: Deadlocked.

With the previous dismissals, the prosecution was zero for nine with their stack of charges related to Symington's dealings with First Interstate Bank and Valley National Bank.

The defense had reason to feel good.

But then, on Count Ten—the fifth of the indictments accusing Symington of defrauding Valley: Guilty.

That was it. Symington's time as governor was over.

Both Fife and Ann Symington leaned forward in their seats and looked downward. Lynam shifted in his chair with a look of bewilderment. Dowd remained stoic.

Symington was found guilty on the final charge related to his dealings with Valley, then was found guilty on all four of the charges related to his dealings with Dai-Ichi Kangyo Bank (which, like Valley, had never sought legal recourse against Symington). The jury deadlocked or found him not guilty on the Citicorp-related charges and deadlocked on the accusation that he perjured himself in bankruptcy court. Finally, he was found guilty of attempting to defraud the union pension funds at the same time he was found not guilty of attempting to extort money from those pension funds.[21]

It was Symington's attempts to fend off lenders in the Mercado and the Esplanade projects that ended his political career and left him one sentencing hearing from federal prison.

Symington walked from the courtroom with his family—all of whom looked dazed by the news—into a quickly growing mass of reporters and onlookers.

Lynam had tears in his eyes after the verdict. He was confident he had made a strong case for acquittal and devastated, he said later, by the feeling he had let Symington down. For his part, Dowd scowled and vowed to fight.[22]

Symington pushed through the crowd with his DPS detail and slipped into the governor's Lincoln Town Car, which was filmed from Channel

Governor Fife Symington waves goodbye after resigning in 1997 following his conviction on bank fraud. © Michael Chow, USA Today Network.

12's helicopter, à la O. J. Simpson's lowspeed case, as it drove slowly to the Executive Tower.

As he entered his office, Symington was greeted by a gauntlet of supporters, staffers, agency heads, and legislators. He then pushed into his office, called Jane Hull, and offered to "be fully cooperative in ensuring a smooth transition." Then he wrote his resignation speech. He had promised to make quick work of the transition of power if it was needed, so he rushed to have his speech prepared by the end of that day.[23]

At 5 p.m., Symington and his wife entered the governor's formal reception room on the second floor of the Executive Tower to say goodbye and, they hoped, to guide to the extent possible the narrative of his legacy:

"I leave this office knowing that I have done my best," he said. "I have done the things that I promised I would. . . . We know that whatever has been built well, will stand even after the builders have gone."

Ann remained somber through the announcement. Symington's voice cracked several times. He paused several times as certain pronouncements punched him with the magnitude and finality of the moment.[24]

Symington left the building eighteen minutes later with his family, retreating to solitude as the rest of Arizona scrambled to make sense of the events.

For the state's media outlets, it was the biggest story in years. The *Republic* published its first "Extra" since President Kennedy's assassination, and its three-year-old website crashed the evening of the resignation after more than 400,000 visits.

In his ever-meta media column, the *Republic*'s Dave Walker even provided a post-game-like review of the quality of every news outlet's coverage.[25] (Channel 12 won, he decided, thanks to both Lew Ruggiero's reporting and the fact the station had busted out their helicopter to tail the governor.)

Within moments of the verdicts, political friends and enemies leaped toward microphones to offer their take on Symington's legacy.[26] Comments were predictable. State Senator Tom Patterson, a Republican who represented part of Phoenix, said, "While the jury has spoken, we must remember Fife Symington's leadership has made Arizona a better place to live, to work, and to raise a family.

"No matter what a federal prosecutor who spent millions of taxpayer dollars and years to get a verdict against Fife Symington says, this is a legacy that Fife Symington can be proud of the rest of his life."[27]

Patterson's fellow senator, Democrat George Cunningham, went after Symington with his Dowd-like wit, comparing the concept that Symington could take credit for the 18 percent tax cuts and economic prosperity to "the rooster taking credit for the dawn."

Several of Symington's most capable and notable foes, Lisa Graham Keegan, Grant Woods, and House Minority Leader Art Hamilton, all chose muted blows with comments about looking more toward the future than the past. "I look forward to working with the new governor," Keegan said. Woods stabbed with a bit more gusto, saying he looked forward to working with an administration less guided by "politics or narrow ideology."[28]

As talk and debate about Symington reached record levels, the man himself recoiled from the public eye.

Amid the turmoil of the previous years, Symington always had an all-consuming job into which he could dive. He always had a stage and a support crew to argue his side of the story. He had his successes to lean on and those bursts of adoration and positive energy that come from public appearances.

He had gone from the leader of the state to a guy with no prospects in a matter of hours. He found himself facing waves of anger most every hour of every day. Now, all of sudden, he was a guy helplessly waiting for the dreaded knock at the door.[29]

After Symington was found guilty on the seven charges, Judge Strand set Symington's sentencing date for early November—about two months in the future.

Best estimates had Symington looking at three years in a federal prison, likely at Nellis Prison Camp located on Nellis Air Force Base several hours north of Phoenix in Nevada.[30]

Symington would officially hand over power to Hull at 5 p.m. on Friday of the week following the verdict. However, at 11 a.m. on the day of the verdict, Symington called Hull to tell her he was leaving for a vacation with Ann. Therefore, Hull actually became the head executive of the state at that moment.

(One of Hull's first public comments was to announce that she planned to "continue the policies of Fife Symington.")[31]

When reporters asked where the Symingtons were headed, Cole gave them an answer liberating for him in tone but heartbreaking in content: "He's a private citizen now and he doesn't have to tell anybody."

One of Symington's last tasks on his last day was to clear his personal items out of his office. He loaded boxes full of family letters, campaign correspondences, and campaign mementos into small moving vans and had many of the boxes hauled to a small locker in a nearby storage facility. Those documents would sit untouched—forgotten or abandoned—for nearly twenty years.

# Chapter 37

# THE WAITING GAME

It was unlikely Fife Symington truly would be sentenced two months after his trial ended. Just three weeks after the verdicts, both Dowd and Schindler requested the sentencing hearing be pushed back until February 1998. Schindler wanted more time to prepare reports based on the advice of federal probation officers. Dowd wanted time to prepare his arguments to have the convictions overturned.[1]

During those same months, Mike Manning continued to push for more time to question Symington. Shull, Symington's bankruptcy attorney, argued Manning had plenty of information from two days of deposing Symington and Symington's two weeks on the stand in the criminal trial, but Judge George Nielsen ultimately gave Manning another shot at Symington.

Except for news that Manning and the pensioners had filed a $14 million suit against Coopers & Lybrand,[2] the bankruptcy proceedings mostly disappeared from the news cycle, as did the ongoing battle between Schindler and Dowd before Judge Strand. There was only one last issue that Arizonans generally cared about: How long would the former governor of their state have to spend in prison?

The public debate did continue, however, on whether or not Fife Symington deserved what might be coming to him. Particularly on radio, callers' opinions varied wildly, from those who believed Symington was the victim of a decade-long conspiracy to those who not only believed he deserved his convictions, but that he should receive the maximum sentence possible because of his tough-on-crime laws while governor.[3]

This last idea involved "poetic justice," as two opinion writers called it, although one suggested a tough sentence wasn't perfectly poetic because Symington, they believed, had been the victim of his "mad-dog advisors" regarding criminal justice policy. In essence, Symington shouldn't do harder time just because he hired Jay Heiler.[4]

Ironically, Symington potentially was looking at a shorter sentence because of his push for longer sentences for some crimes. In their pre-sentencing maneuvers, Dowd and Lynam argued that Symington should be kept out of prison, or at least have a shortened sentence in a prison with only white-collar criminals, because he might be a target for his policies. The defense team actually surveyed current and former federal prison inmates to see if a potentially dangerous bias existed. Several inmates admitted they thought Symington deserved harsh treatment and that he had made their lives worse, but no inmates made specific threats.

Dowd also argued that Symington was the victim of "financial bigotry." "By attacking Mr. Symington and his family for skiing, attending private schools, and belonging to various clubs, the government reflects a financial bigotry which has no place in the sentencing process," Dowd wrote to Strand.[5]

Throughout the delay, Strand received letters suggesting he should go light on Symington. Among those asking for leniency was Michael Welborn, chairman of Bank One, an institution that had already forgiven $780,000 in defaulted Symington loans.[6]

Art Laffer, the famed economist who had called Symington his "favorite governor," wrote Strand suggesting the judge might not be seeing the real Fife Symington. Laffer made this extraordinary psychosocial observation in an attempt to soften Strand's view of Laffer's acolyte and former employer: "Fife also by the very nature of his background was loath to admit to others his errors or his self doubts," Laffer wrote to Strand. "But in truth he was introspective, self-doubting and critical of his own behavior. In private with me he often questioned his own actions and sought perspective on himself. And while his external demeanor may or may not show remorse and humility I know he feels both and feels both deeply. His upbringing mandated that any display of remorse or contrition was a sign of character weakness. But in all seriousness he feels as much remorse and contrition as anyone."[7]

Laffer admitted, though, "I know nothing about Fife's business dealings that were the subject of this trial."

As the February sentencing date grew closer, media outlets began running stories describing what Symington's life would likely look like at a minimum-security prison like Nellis. A basic theme was this: whoever told you Nellis Prison Camp in Nevada was like a country club ("Club Fed" was the term for America's lowest-level prisons) definitely had not been in prison at Nellis.[8]

Prisoners received a strip search upon arrival, then received a bed as-signment in a room consisting of between ten and twenty-five bunks. Breakfast was served at 5:30 a.m., after which inmates prepared for the day in bathrooms that, for the most part, had no doors, toilet stalls, or shower curtains.

Nellis was categorized as a "work camp," meaning the inmates' days were spent at assigned jobs at the camp. After dressing in standard khaki uniforms and steel-toed work boots, inmates worked until late after-noon at any number of menial jobs. They were directed in their duties by armed officers who, as one former Nellis inmate said, "aren't always having a wonderful day."

Preparing food in the kitchen was widely considered the most coveted job of myriad uncoveted jobs.

There was very little difference between the meals being prepared at the prison camp and the ones offered to the Air Force personnel next door at the base. Most meals included a meat of some sort along with rice or potatoes, a beverage, and what was often the highlight after a long day of tedious work, a dessert.

As the new year arrived, Dowd and Lynam scrambled on two fronts, preparing their appeal for the panel of three appeals-court judges in San Francisco while collecting character witnesses and combing case law to argue for the shortest sentence possible. They were swinging for the fences in California, where they argued Cotey's dismissal violated Sym-ington's Sixth Amendment rights, while working to chip away at a prison sentence some legal analysts predicted could reach five to six years of actual time served without an aggressive defense.[9]

Prosecutors wanted ten years.[10]

In late January, Symington's assigned probation officer, who was tasked with calculating an appropriate sentence based on federal guidelines, sug-gested six to eight years in his written statement to Judge Strand.[11]

At the same time Strand weighed sentencing opinions, he also was re-evaluating the strength of the seven convictions. While he continued to rebuff Dowd's argument that Symington deserved a new trial because of the dismissal of the juror, Strand did toss out one of the convictions, agreeing that it could not be determined that Symington lied about his financial situation when he asked for a loan extension from Valley Na-tional Bank.[12]

It was very good news that might not impact Symington's life one bit.

As Symington found his days too long and empty in the weeks before sentencing, he devised a plan to address both idle hands and the quality of life if he did go to Nellis. He would go to culinary school.[13]

He wasn't a particularly good cook. He didn't necessarily like cooking. But he was an aficionado of fine foods, he was familiar with the restaurant business (he had co-owned one for a time), and he liked the idea of someday being a restaurateur who knew both the business and the food-alchemy side of his trade.

The Symingtons had dined several times at a restaurant run by the students of the Scottsdale Culinary Institute, one of the most respected culinary schools in the country. Guided by veteran chefs, the student-run restaurant offered some of the finest food in the Valley and, in particular, arguably the best pastries and baked goods around.

While Symington didn't care for cooking, he loved to bake. Even while governor, he later said he sometimes imagined a post-politics life in which he owned a few restaurants where he could personally assist with the dessert menu.

The intense eighteen-month program at the Scottsdale Culinary Institute seemed like a chance to bury his mind and body in a new project and, perhaps, if the appeals didn't work out, make himself a top candidate for the prized job of cook.

But the next culinary school year didn't start until late that summer. He would only be attending if either Strand or the judges of the Ninth Circuit allowed him to remain free during the appeal process.

In late January, Strand announced that Symington's sentencing hearing would take place at 9 a.m. on the first Monday of February 1998 in the same courtroom in which he was convicted.

Unlike most of the many days of the trial, media outlets and interested citizens had plenty of lead time to plan for this major news event.[14]

As Ann, Tom, Whitney, and Fife Symington emerged from their home that morning, several helicopters circled overhead. As they drove through the gates blocking the entrance to their North Phoenix neighborhood, they were met by cameramen and reporters. As they walked from their car into the courthouse, they were met by the most reporters and onlookers they had ever faced. And this time, since Symington was no longer governor, there were no DPS officers protecting them as they careened toward the courthouse steps.

Symington and his family then passed through a mass of supporters and a collection of his top staffers, many of whom he hadn't seen since he left office. After hugs with dozens of friends and family members, an already emotionally spent Symington entered the courtroom and joined Dowd and Lynam at the defense table. Behind him, his father, the Pritzlaffs, Fife IV, Helen Clay, and several other family members and close friends took their seats.[15]

It would be a short hearing. Character witnesses wouldn't be speaking. Cardona and Schindler would make their argument for a long sentence, Dowd would argue toward probation and Symington would give his first public statement since he left office.

Symington, speaking in a voice quivering from a mix of dread and anger, said he was sorry for his mistakes as he detailed the damage already done to him and his family:[16]

"I certainly did not pay close enough attention to the accuracy of my personal financial statements, and I bear responsibility for that. . . .

"Throughout the lengthy investigation and during the trial," he continued, "I cooperated fully and testified truthfully. If I had to do it all over again, I would never have touched my personal financial statements, but simply turned them over to others and spent the additional money to have them done. What is important today did not appear to be important then.

"The pain and upheaval for me and my family is indescribable and ongoing. It's sometimes hard to believe that from such stupid mistakes a nightmare was born and flourished."

Schindler then attacked Symington for continuing to say he had not intended to hide his true financial condition from lenders and creditors under penalty of law. "What we have here, your honor, is a complete lack of remorse, dare I say arrogance," Schindler said.[17]

Strand then explained his reasoning behind the size of the sentence he was about to announce. He mentioned the law that allows reductions in sentences for inmates who could face abuse for their positions and opinions prior to their incarceration. He also stated that statutes allowed him to reduce sentences if the losses incurred by the defendant's activity were not in line with the length of the suggested sentences.

Symington walked to the podium in front of Strand, and the judge announced Symington would begin serving a sentence of thirty months at Nellis beginning in seven weeks.

Symington left the podium wide-eyed but composed. As he passed his oldest son, Fife IV, he whispered, "Could have been worse." He then hugged his son, Tom, whispering in his ear, "It will turn out OK."[18]

Fourteen-year-old Tom Symington was inconsolable. As he wept, Ann and Whitney, both stunned by the reality of the moment, began hugging family members. Dowd walked over and hugged Tom and told him, "We're fighting this. This isn't over."

Outside, the throng of reporters pressed against the family as they pushed toward their cars. A member of a group supporting full gaming on the Salt River tribal lands (the group apparently had shown up outside the courthouse to celebrate the sentencing of their nemesis in the issue), stepped in front of Symington and wiped dirt across his shirt. Former staffers, led by Chuck Coughlin, stepped forward to serve as lineman to continue through the crowd.[19]

Ironically, Strand, while suggesting Symington could be in danger in prison for his political stances, didn't order adequate security for the family as they left the building.[20]

Reporters tailed the family, but were stopped by a security guard at the entrance to the gated community in which the Symingtons lived. The helicopters began circling as the family entered the house. There was little conversation in the home in the hours that followed. Everyone, it seemed, was trying to process what life might look like moving forward.

After the media retreated, things quieted down into a new, uncomfortable normal. Dowd and Lynam began pushing for Symington to remain free during his appeals. But any decision by Strand on that issue wouldn't come for weeks, and who knew if, or how quickly, the Ninth Circuit judges might respond to the request to keep Symington free. Confident words aside, nothing was actually known for sure in the weeks after sentencing.

It was during this time that Symington began to pack a massive yellow duffle bag with everything he believed he would need—and experts in such things told him he would want and need—during a stint in prison.

# Chapter 38

# NEW HOPE AND $8.25 AN HOUR

T
erry Lynam and John Dowd filed an appeal to Judge Roger Strand
on March 9, 1998, asking that Symington be allowed to stay free
while his Ninth Circuit appeal was being reviewed.[1]
To allow Symington to remain free past his March 20 prison report
date, Strand would have to concede that an appeal of his decision to remove the juror had merit. That meant, once again, that Strand would
have to question his own judgment on an issue critical to maintaining
the convictions.

Strand ruled that Symington's appeal had no merit the next day and
therefore, Symington would still need to report to prison in Nevada just
over a week later.[2]

As Symington began packing his duffle bag, he also immersed himself
in a passion project that allowed him to stay involved with public policy.
Since the beginning of the year, he had been guiding a campaign to collect 170,000 signatures to put an income-tax-repeal initiative on the November ballot. Republican US Representative Matt Salmon, a longtime
ally of Symington who appeared to be polishing his statewide resume
for the 2002 gubernatorial race, had become the more public champion
of the cause after Symington's resignation. But Symington used his still-
considerable clout in Republican circles to raise money and organize the
campaign.[3]

As Symington worked to keep busy, Dowd and Lynam crafted and
then submitted their appeal to the Ninth Circuit. They were angling toward a trifecta of wins: First, they needed the judges in San Francisco to
agree their case had merit. That would trigger a hearing before a panel of
three judges in San Francisco several months out, a time during which
the Ninth Circuit judges would likely allow Symington to remain free
pending a decision. Then they just needed to convince two of the three
judges that Symington had been denied his right to a fair trial when
Cotey was dismissed from the jury.

Symington would then remain free until the full Ninth Circuit Appellate Court ruled if they would hear Schindler's arguments seeking to overturn any decision made by the three-judge panel in Symington's favor.

If Schindler failed there (and then, perhaps, if he persisted, was later rebuffed by the US Supreme Court), the US attorney in Los Angeles would be forced to bring new indictments against Symington, something Dowd and Lynam knew prosecutors wanted to avoid.[4]

Essentially, Dowd and Lynam, who would write the appeal, had to go on a major winning streak to keep Symington out of Nellis.

Besides their appeal of Cotey's removal from the jury, Lynam and Dowd would argue that Judge Strand had given improper instructions to the jury and that prosecutors had revealed in their closing arguments evidence deemed inadmissible earlier in the trial.

Dowd and Lynam also wanted two convictions overturned related to Symington's dealings with Dai-Ichi Kangyo Bank in the Esplanade deal, saying the government only proved that Symington submitted incorrect statements to DKB, not that he did so intentionally.

In broad strokes, Lynam's appeal was fairly simple: The Sixth Amendment states, "In all criminal prosecutions, the accused shall enjoy the right to a speedy and public trial, by an impartial jury."

The challenge for Lynam: he needed to find case law that established precedent clearly outlining situations in which a judge can legally dismiss a juror without violating the Sixth Amendment rights of the accused. And of course, he needed to craft an argument that Cotey had been dismissed incorrectly in relation to those established guidelines.

Lynam found two cases that provided the foundation for their argument: In *United States v. Brown*, judges in another federal appeals court argued that "a court may not dismiss a juror during deliberations if the request for discharge stems from doubts the juror harbors about the sufficiency of the evidence." In *United States v. Ross*, which was ruled on in the Ninth Circuit in 1989, the judge writing the majority opinion stated, "To remove a juror because he is unpersuaded by the Government's case is to deny the defendant his right to a unanimous verdict." A judge in another key case in the Second Circuit Court of Appeals in 1997 argued, "If a court could discharge a juror on the basis of such a request, then the right to a unanimous verdict would be illusory."

Lynam zeroed in on several quotes by jurors during the arguments for Cotey's dismissal. Amid the thousands of hours of depositions and testimony during the investigation and trial, a few words by a few jurors could be the only ones that ultimately mattered.

Because of Cotey, "we are blocked and blocked and blocked," said one juror. "And I don't want to be blocked anymore."

Another juror asked Strand to dismiss Cotey because, if he didn't, the result would be "an undecided vote, a hung jury."

Lynam also quoted Cotey saying, "I can't agree with the majority all of the time, at least temporarily," stating also that Cotey admitted to feeling "bullied."

As to Cotey's competence as a juror, he noted that several of the jurors had actually spoken highly of Cotey's intelligence and commitment to the process.

Schindler and Cardona countered with their own ammunition of case law girded with numerous quotes from jurors regarding Cotey's alleged incompetence as a juror. One juror, Cardona wrote, "stated that Juror Cotey would ask questions unrelated to the discussion, would be uncertain about which count they were discussing, would go off on tangents unrelated to the discussion, and would mumble about 'something else' and 'go off on her own.'"[5]

Ninth Circuit judges in San Francisco agreed a few days later that Symington's case deserved their attention. With that, the judges ordered that Symington was to remain free until they made a ruling.[6]

He would get to go to culinary school, and he would get to continue fighting to get the state income tax abolished.

A re-energized Symington quickly bounced back into the public sphere.[7] He granted several media interviews and agreed to make his first appearance on radio since his conviction. Symington even floated the idea that he might run for office again—if his convictions were overturned, or if his convictions were expunged after he served his time. "I have a good record," he told the *Republic*'s David Leibowitz. "All the things I've been tagged on occurred well before I became governor."

Newspapers were flooded in the following days with letters from readers outraged that Symington was unrepentant. One *Daily Star* reader quipped under the headline "Fife's no hero" that: "Obviously, with so much time on his hands, Symington has become a legend in his own mind."

The push to abolish the state income tax struggled to gain traction in the building heat of late spring. In June, Symington announced the effort had only received half of the number of signatures needed, which put the effort hopelessly behind schedule. The main problem, he told the *Republic*: "We just couldn't get enough people out getting signatures."[8]

When asked what he would do next: "I'm doing all kinds of things . . . all of them private," he said.

Symington entered the Scottsdale Culinary Institute in August, committing to forty hours a week of classes for the full year.[9]

He knew he would get through at least half of his training. Dowd and Lynam would argue their case before the three-judge panel in San Francisco in late fall, which almost surely would push any ruling beyond the holidays into 1999.

The Symingtons were able to celebrate Thanksgiving, Christmas, and the New Year together (although the yellow bag was always waiting just in case the three judges ruled quickly). Symington savored the time with family. He knew he might not have a normal holiday season again until 2002.

In February, Symington wrote a letter to the *Arizona Republic* in which he mourned the recent death of political writer John Kolbe. Symington took one stab at Kolbe's contemporaries—"Journalism today is becoming more about the naked exercise of power or perhaps worse, mere spectacle"—but otherwise focused on his respect for Kolbe and his work even though Kolbe often wrote scathing pieces about him. The tone of the letter suggested Symington was perhaps more self-aware and more respectful of the duties of working journalists than he sometimes appeared to be during his tenure: "Perceived deviations from avowed principle, or else obvious lapses into sheer political stupidity, were sure to bring you withering fire from the headmaster of the old school," Symington wrote. "When John was with you, he could give support without being fulsome; and when he was against you, he could criticize you forcefully, but never venomously."[10]

While Judge Strand had allowed prosecutors three months to make their criminal case against Symington, both sides would have only twenty minutes before federal appellate judges.

On a cool late fall day in downtown San Francisco, Dowd and Lynam faced off against Schindler and Cardona in front of three federal district court judges in the city's historic US Court of Appeals Building.[11]

Lynam argued that comments from jurors proved Cotey had been railroaded off the jury because she had refused to budge from her position that Symington was innocent of the charges on which he was found guilty. He repeated several times one more damning comment made in the first note sent by jurors to the judge after the first full week of their deliberations: "Your honor, we respectfully request direction. One juror has stated their final opinion prior to a review of all of the counts."

Schindler and Cardona repeated their argument made at the end of the first week of jury deliberations: It was clear from the majority of comments from Cotey's fellow jurors that she was, by the standards set by previous case law, unfit to continue as part of the jury.

Prosecutors and defense attorneys both emerged from the hearing unsure which way the panel was leaning.

However, it seemed clear that one judge, Betty Fletcher, was sympathetic to Symington's position. Cotey, she said, had "every right" to emerge from the trial believing the government had failed to prove guilt. And, Fletcher continued, Cotey had every right not to give her reasons for her decision to her peers.

"If she had been agreeing (with the other eleven jurors), do you think they would have made her state her reasons?" Fletcher asked Cardona. "Are they entitled to do that? This is a very disturbing dialogue here."

Judge James Fitzgerald, though, seemed to side with the prosecution. He said he believed that jurors "seemed sincere" in their concern that Cotey was not capable of understanding critical aspects of the case.

The third judge, A. Wallace Tashima, was a closed book in his questioning. If a decision could be predicted from the direction of the judges' questioning, it seemed Symington's fate would be decided in a two-to-one decision in which Tashima was an unknowable deciding vote.

Symington sat through the hearing with Ann. He would get points knocked off his culinary-school grade for the absence, his teachers told him, but he felt it was important to show his face to the judges. Like his attorneys, though, he saw no confirmation that he would be free or imprisoned when their decision was released.[12]

December passed without word from the court. In January, Arizona made history when five women stepped into the state's top five government positions. Jane Hull was sworn in as governor by US Supreme Court Justice Sandra Day O'Connor, the Arizonan who became the court's first female juror, while Betsey Bayless became secretary of state, Carol Springer became treasurer, Lisa Graham Keegan remained as superintendent of schools, and Janet Napolitano, the one Democrat, became the state's attorney general. Hull did not invite Symington to the inauguration events. He spent the day instead at culinary school, where he had begun to learn the business side of restauranteering.

February came and went. March came and went. Dowd and Lynam worked on new cases from their Washington, DC, office. In late March, a *Republic* food writer asked one of the Culinary Institute's instructors, Will Getchell, how Symington was doing in his class work. (Several columnists had commented in the previous months that Symington surely wasn't serious about becoming a chef.)

"He's a very serious chef," Getchell said. "And he's good. Right now he's taking the business courses. Rumor has it that he might open a restaurant with Ann."

On the afternoon of June 22, Lynam received a call from a *Republic* reporter who had been tasked with checking the Ninth Circuit's docket several times a day for the previous six months.[13] The reporter told Lynam the three-judge panel had ruled two to one in Symington's favor. They agreed that Symington's rights to a fair trial had been violated. All convictions were voided. Fife Symington was no longer a felon.[14]

Lynam called Dowd, who had left the Akin Gump offices for the day feeling ill. Dowd immediately returned from Virginia to DC for a round of high-fives and celebratory phone calls and press interviews.

Judge Fletcher, as seemed likely from her line of questioning, wrote in the majority opinion that Symington's rights had been violated by the dismissal of Cotey. In his dissenting opinion, Judge Fitzgerald, as his questioning seven months before suggested, decided that Strand had ample reason to dismiss Cotey.

The wild card, Judge Tashima, argued that although the complaints regarding Cotey were numerous and compelling, jurors had also too clearly articulated a hope that the proceedings would be hastened by getting rid of Cotey's dissenting voice.

Symington and his family were jubilant. For the first time in two years, Symington himself saw a future without prison and the stain and severe professional restrictions that come with a felony conviction. He could have a relatively normal life.[15]

He could get his passport back. He could get his real estate license back. He was no longer prohibited from making major purchases or entering into any financial contracts without approval by his supervising officer.

But in fact, the issue was far from settled. The full Ninth Circuit panel of judges could overturn the three-judge ruling. There was still an even worse scenario: Prosecutors could come back with the charges (perhaps with a few new ones based on additional evidence revealed during the criminal or civil trial), there could be another trial, and the trial could end with convictions that might draw a tougher sentence.[16]

No matter. At a press conference following word of the court's ruling, Symington looked happy to be in front of cameras. Although he had earlier floated the idea of returning to politics, he claimed he and Ann most wanted life to remain the same.

"Ann has been senior warden at our church and is doing a great job, finding a new rector and helping run the largest fiscal parish in the state," Symington told reporters. "All of our kids have been in school. You just get right back into living life and you try not to be too sad . . . and sort of dwell on 'Oh gosh, this happened.' That's just not a constructive way to operate."

Symington was also free again to run for office. His oft nemesis, Grant Woods, suggested he probably would. "It would not surprise me a bit to see him run for governor," Woods said, adding that he thought Symington, still popular with Arizona conservatives, could win a primary but likely would struggle in a general election.[17]

Secondary to conversations about Symington's new life was the fact that Schindler still wanted him in prison.[18] Schindler said he would appeal to an eleven-judge circuit court panel to overturn the ruling of the three-judge panel. If they wouldn't hear the case, he said the US attorney's office in Los Angeles would look to file new charges.

Working against Schindler, though, the full court rarely reviewed cases, let alone overturned cases, from its three-judge panels.[19]

Working against the US attorney's office in Los Angeles, Schindler, the successful prosecutor who knew the most about the Symington case, was about to go into private practice.[20]

Also, there was a new US attorney in Southern California since Symington's conviction, and it didn't appear Alejandro Mayorkas (another emerging legal star who twenty years later would become Joe Biden's Secretary of Homeland Security) had much appetite for relitigating one of the longest and most expensive cases in the office's history.

Symington decisively addressed what they knew Mayorkas hoped for: A plea deal.[21] "I know I'm innocent, and I don't think you ever compromise your principles," he said.

"We will fight," Dowd said defiantly to reporters. "And we will win."

Soon after the overturning of his convictions, Symington agreed to pay $100,000 to settle with the creditor seeking $500,000, claiming Symington had illegally moved that amount to his mother shortly before declaring bankruptcy. With that settlement, only the Mercado-based pension-fund case remained.

Schindler and Cardona petitioned the eleven-judge panel in the Ninth Circuit in early August, a week before Schindler announced he was joining the prestigious Los Angeles law firm Latham & Watkins.[22]

Six months later, the panel declined to overturn the decision by the three-judge panel.[23] Mayorkas would either have to mount a costly new attack on Symington sans Schindler, get a plea agreement out of an emboldened Symington, or simply move on.

Before the eleven-judge-panel snub to prosecutors, the Arizona Court of Appeals overturned a ruling in Maricopa County Superior Court that Symington was liable for $11 million in debt for the Mercado debacle.[24] The decision would give Symington a chance to argue in a later court case that none of his actions caused lenders to lose money in the deal, which could lead to him having his debts cleared in bankruptcy court. (That superior court decision, though, was immediately appealed to the Arizona Supreme Court, and even if the lower court decision was upheld, the decision wouldn't stop a civil trial planned for early 2000.)

With the series of court wins, most onlookers expected Symington to abandon the grueling menial labor of a working restaurant kitchen and return to real estate development.

Instead, Symington approached master chef Franco Fazzuoli, owner of Franco's Trattoria in Scottsdale, asking for a kitchen job. Symington needed several months of real on-the-job training to complete the final stage of his culinary training. He considered Fazzuoli one of the top chefs in the Valley, so Symington told Fazzuoli he would take any beginning kitchen job that opened up at any salary. Symington just asked that Fazzuoli be liberal with both advice and frank criticism.

Fazzuoli agreed to hire Symington.[25] On Monday, August 23, 1999, while attorney Robert Shull worked up a new round of arguments against the pension fund's $18 million Mercado claim, Symington went to work in the kitchen of Franco's Trattoria for $8.25 an hour.

# Chapter 39

# THE REMAINING LEGAL ISSUES

B y the spring of 2000, only two major legal issues remained in Fife Symington's life. If he could resolve those, he would be, financially and literally, a free man.

The six union pension funds represented by Mike Manning still wanted about $18 million (that was the $10 million Mercado loan from more than a decade before with an ever-growing amount of interest tacked on). The civil trial would finally begin mid-March of that year, with a resolution likely not coming until late summer or fall.[1]

As the bankruptcy trial began, Symington continued to refuse to negotiate with Alejandro Mayorkas in Los Angeles. Mayorkas, although showing no sign of preparing his office to refile charges, refused to completely drop the issue. He still wanted Symington on at least one count.

Mayorkas chose to delay. In early 2000, he said he would not bring any new charges until after the bankruptcy case was settled.[2]

The trial in US Bankruptcy Judge George Nielsen's courtroom followed a familiar script.[3] Symington's attorney, Robert Shull, would contend that Symington provided accurate information about his financial condition to McMorgan & Company and the pension funds to secure the construction loan to build the Mercado in 1987, and by successfully building the Mercado and leasing much of its office and retail space, met his obligations to receive that money in 1990.

Manning would work to show Symington exaggerated his worth to secure the Mercado loans and that loan managers relied on fraudulent numbers to make the loan. This point was key to a Manning win: US bankruptcy law requires fund advisers to prove they depended on false financial documents when making the loan in question.

This requirement in bankruptcy law created awkward strategies for the combatants. For one, Shull would argue Symington not only gave defensible estimates of the value of the sixteen properties in which he had an interest, but that, perhaps even more important, McMorgan executives failed in their duties to the pension funds to check if Symington was worth what he said he was worth.[4]

The argument, at its heart, was that fund managers led by Donald Eaton were negligent by trusting Symington too much. Also, Shull would argue, whether Symington's financial statements were "correct" at any given time had no practical significance. McMorgan officers, the argument went, had signed a commitment letter obligating them to make the construction loan unless Symington was insolvent at the time.

In his testimony, Eaton said that after talking with other developers and property managers in the Phoenix area, he found "nothing that would contradict" Symington's financial statement or personal guarantee. Symington had a "very good reputation" in the development community. Eaton admitted he might have felt overly confident in Symington's numbers after learning of Symington's reputation.

Under Shull's cross-examination, Eaton confirmed he did not call Symington's other lenders to find out if he was having trouble repaying his other loans. Shull said Eaton would have discovered Symington was having financial trouble if he had done due diligence.

So, in one of the stranger moments in Symington's long legal journey, Eaton provided testimony unfavorable to Symington's case by explaining that Symington had a stellar reputation. Symington's own attorney argued that Eaton didn't work hard enough to find out Symington was not nearly as successful as Eaton believed him to be.

The *Republic*'s Steve Wilson noted the peculiarity of the argument, then added: "The ex-governor said it was the fault of the union pension funds for loaning him $10 million without doing their homework. That's a fascinating thing to say, because when someone else looked into his finances and raised questions in 1990, Symington was outraged. The inquisitor was Terry Goddard, ex-mayor of Phoenix and Democratic candidate for governor."[5]

James Cockerham, Symington's former chief financial officer, gave testimony suggesting Symington was well aware of the fact his company was struggling at the time he received the loan for the Mercado.[6]

Symington took the stand himself on the last day of March.

One early exchange between Symington and Manning seemed to sum up in a few words the usually sprawling and esoteric debate regarding Symington's net worth as the Phoenix real estate market crashed.

Manning said Symington had told pension fund managers in May 1990 that the Ritz-Carlton Hotel at the Camelback Esplanade was worth $62 million. Symington's own estimate, though, was nearly $5 million more than an outside appraiser had estimated the property to be worth a year earlier.

"I stuck with the $62 million figure because I thought the Ritz-Carlton was worth more than that," Symington protested. "I built the project. I was better able to judge its value."[7]

Shull told reporters outside the courtroom that day: "It's just someone else's opinion of value." He noted that Symington and the appraisers' numbers were still less than 10 percent apart at a time when property values were swinging wildly.

Manning landed cleaner blows questioning Symington about a series of statements about his finances between late 1987 and 1991 that seemed to shift depending on his needs. For one, Symington told pension fund lenders he was worth $12 million in November 1987, then continued to claim through 1991 that he was worth more than $10 million at the same time he was telling his employees and creditors that the market crash had left his company barely solvent.

Again and again, as during the decade prior, Symington countered that he knew more about his properties' value, and especially their long-term value, than hired appraisers making estimates in a volatile bear market.

Fine, Manning would respond. But why did those estimates fluctuate so greatly between the big numbers he showed lenders and the small numbers he showed creditors?

Manning and Symington faced off for a week. Near the end of Manning's questioning, Symington asked the judge if he could stand because his back was hurting.[8] After being allowed to stand, Symington placed his hands on his hips and began answering questions in a more pointed tone. To onlookers, it looked like Symington, the high school football and college lacrosse star, was about to jump Manning, who had played linebacker while in college. The tense moment led to a new line of debate among reporters and commentators—who would win a cage match between Mike Manning and Fife Symington?

Symington's testimony ended with a ten-minute grilling from Judge Nielsen himself. In response to questions, Symington agreed that it was his duty to prepare his financial statements carefully. He acknowledged that pension funds had the right to rely on Symington's claim that his net worth was $12 million.[9]

Media coverage of the bankruptcy trial was a fraction of that for the criminal trial. There was no daily coverage in the national press. Besides having the feeling of a rerun, Nielsen allowed several lengthy breaks in the trial, effectively upending any potential for narrative tension. (In mid-April, the trial went on hiatus until July 10, 2000, then, after two weeks, the trial paused for a month, then, after a few days of testimony, stopped until late August.)

In late July, as Manning wrapped up his questioning, Judge Nielsen offered unusually frank public comments on his perception of the worthiness of the case. He said he believed the pension funds had proven that Symington gave false financial statements to them, but offered insufficient evidence that loan officials relied on those statements when approving the loan.[10]

That was good news for Symington. But Nielsen made it clear those were only "preliminary leanings."

On August 30, the trial resumed again (reaching its twenty-ninth day in a span of five months) with testimony from a lending expert who sided with Shull and Symington's argument that the pension funds' loan officers had failed to do their jobs. Again, a case was made that Symington's own numbers shouldn't have been trusted.[11]

A good lender must "confirm the accuracy of a financial statement" provided by anyone, but especially a real estate developer like Fife Symington.

"They tend to be more optimistic than other individuals in society," the witness testified.

Shull presented his final witnesses on September 6. Nielsen scheduled closing arguments for November 16—nearly eight months after the trial began.

On November 17, Mike Manning told Judge Nielsen that Symington "lied to the pension funds" and "lied to the people of Arizona and the press." Besides arguing that Symington didn't intentionally mislead pension fund managers who failed to do due diligence for their clients, Shull said it would be "draconian" for Nielsen to stick Symington with an $18 million debt. He would "go to the grave with this debt," Shull told Nielsen.

Nielsen didn't say when he would release his ruling.

In the weeks surrounding the final argument in the trial, Dowd remained in contact with the federal prosecutor's office in Los Angeles.[12] While Mayorkas's actions, or inactions, suggested he didn't want another trial, he also refused to agree not to pursue new indictments.[13] Symington himself seemed to drift toward the possibility of some sort of plea agreement. Soon after those closing arguments were heard, Symington admitted he was considering a plea in the criminal case to "spare my family the financial and emotional toll of another trial."[14]

By early December, Symington had piled up about $6 million in legal fees, which were draining away much of his remaining investments and inheritances.[15]

Three days after the bankruptcy trial ended, the White House announced that President Clinton had granted presidential pardons and sentence commutations to eleven convicted felons. Earlier in the year, Clinton had granted several other pardons, primarily to applicants he believed had been overcharged during the get-tough 1990s.

How Clinton would use his pardoning powers had become a major national news story. In mid-December, a *New York Times* Sunday edition included a series of articles and op-eds examining them.[16]

As Symington sat at his kitchen table reading the story in the Sunday paper, it dawned on him that he might have a shot at ending his fight with the federal government without firing another shot.[17]

Symington joked to Ann that with so many pardons seemingly going to Democrats, President Clinton might find it in his heart to forgive an innocent Republican.[18]

The pardon idea lingered, especially once Symington researched and discovered that, yes, the president has the power to block the government from pursuing indictments that did not yet exist. That evening, Symington discussed the issue further with Ann. The conclusion wasn't hard to reach: Why not just give Tommy Caplan a call and test the waters?

Symington knew that Caplan, although holding no official title in the White House, seemed often to be there. (Not only did Caplan help Clinton polish some of his writings, Clinton considered him one of his most trusted confidantes.)

Symington called Caplan after dinner. Caplan said he'd be happy to ask Clinton if Symington might be eligible for a pardon. It would be easy: Caplan was to attend a Christmas party at the White House the following night.[19]

Caplan called Symington the next morning. Good news. "I'd like to help Fife," Caplan said Clinton told him. "But," Clinton stressed to Caplan, Symington needed to "get a Petition for Pardon on my desk ASAP."

It was only a month before Clinton would leave office, after all. And that month included the holidays.

When Symington called Dowd to pass along Clinton's instructions, Dowd thought Symington was joking.[20] Even as Symington related more specifics of how the unusual opportunity came to be, Dowd still was skeptical. Symington became irritated: "This is not a joke, John!" Symington told Dowd. Symington gave Dowd the phone number for Clinton's aide in the Oval Office. "Call the damn number. They are awaiting your call."

Dowd called back twenty minutes later "astonished and breathing heavily," as Symington described events years later. "My God, this is for real!" Dowd told Symington.

Dowd and Lynam immediately found the petition form online, printed it out, and began researching. Then Lynam, the wordsmith of the duo, began to write.

As Lynam wrote, Lynam and Dowd also contacted several people close to Symington to write character affidavits to be included in the petition. The petition had to include at least three.[21]

The White House press office released Clinton's final round of pardons a few hours before Bush's inauguration. That list immediately became a major national story.[22]

Lynam, a news-radio junky when suffering DC's famous gridlock, was out running errands when, amid a rapid-fire succession of better- and lesser-known names, he heard "J. Fife Symington III."

Lynam immediately pulled to the side of a street in Arlington, Virginia, and called Dowd at his home fifteen miles to the west in Northern Virginia.

Before Dowd or Lynam could reach Symington, ninety-year-old Fife Symington Jr. saw the pardon list scroll across the bottom of his television screen while watching Fox News. The elder Symington jumped to his feet to phone his son.

Symington called Ann. Ann told the children and her parents. Members of the media began calling Dowd, Symington, and David Schindler.

Justice had been done, Dowd said. Clinton made a mistake, Schindler said.[23] "I have my life back," Symington said.

Public responses that afternoon and the next day fell into several camps:

The rich and powerful had ducked justice once again, some argued.

Assuming he was guilty of some amount of financial chicanery, others argued, Symington had already paid his debt to society.

Or, assuming he was innocent and a victim of government over-reach—an argument from which Symington himself never wavered—Symington had suffered a grave injustice for far too long.[24]

Editorial writers at the *Republic* suggested Clinton erred in giving the pardon because "likely lost forever is the chance that Arizona will ever hear from Symington an admission of wrongdoing."[25]

Everyone agreed that Symington was a very lucky man.[26]

Symington unpacked his yellow duffle bag and stuffed it deep in the back of a bedroom closet.

Now, only the ruling in bankruptcy court stood between him and a life without courtrooms.

Three weeks after Symington was pardoned in relation to the criminal case, Judge Nielsen finally released his decision in the bankruptcy case. Nielsen upheld the claim of the pension funds that Symington had given McMorgan false financial statements and that McMorgan had depended on that information to loan money to Symington, a ruling that kept Symington on the hook for the whole of the Mercado loan.[27]

It was a huge loss right on the heels of a huge win.

However, the amount owed by Symington was still in question. Manning wanted the $10 million plus $8 million in interest. Shull told the *Arizona Republic* the amount should be "substantially less." It was up to Nielsen to find a number, or up to the two parties to settle.

Members of the pension funds involved were happy with the ruling, but far from happy with the process that led to the ruling.[28] The pension funds had already spent nearly $5 million during the five years of litigation, retired operating engineer Dave Helm told the Associated Press, and "I'm sure (Symington's lawyers) are going to appeal, and we'll spend another $20 million out of the pension fund." Several pensioners voiced another frustration: considering Symington's financial situation since the early 1990s, where did Manning expect to get enough money to even cover his own legal fees?

(In fact, Manning later recovered those legal fees from someone else.

In another Symington/Mercado-related case, a judge ruled one of Symington's lenders owed the pension funds up to $12 million, a number that included $1.9 million in legal fees.)[29]

After Nielsen's ruling, Manning began combing Symington's finances for potential revenues while Shull continued to whittle away at Manning's lofty numbers.[30] The two quietly negotiated through the late spring, through the summer, and through early fall.

On September 25, six years after the litigation began, the parties reached an agreement:

In a hearing attended only by attorneys, Symington, and a few of his family members, Nielsen approved a plan in which Symington would pay about $2 million to the pension funds.[31] Manning had found a pot of money. Upon the death of Symington's uncle and scuba-diving partner, Henry Clay Frick II (who was in his mideighties), Symington was poised to inherit nearly $4 million. According to the agreement, Symington would pay the pension funds 40 percent of his inheritance, or, pay exactly $2 million if that 40 percent of the inheritance was less than $2 million. As part of the deal, Symington agreed to drop his appeal of Nielsen's February ruling against him.

Everyone declared victory. Manning had a favorable court ruling and a bag of money to show the press, and Shull had protected his client from coughing up a much larger bag of money. Symington, Shull said in a press conference after the announcement of the agreement, was "just thrilled it's all over."

Symington estimated that the entirety of his legal problems had cost him and his family more than $15 million.

The Symingtons then took a short celebratory weekend trip together.

Soon after they returned, Symington met with a few of his old political advisers to discuss an idea he had been mulling for several months: He thought he'd make a good Speaker of the Arizona House of Representatives. He might just run for the house seat in his district, then make a run for the Speaker position once he was elected.[32]

Some allies were shocked that he wanted to return to any level of politics. Many onlookers just thought he wouldn't stand much of a chance, considering the baggage from the previous four years ("I don't think Arizona voters have such short memories," joked the former publisher of the *Scottsdale Progress*, Jonathan Marshall).[33] People who cared about his health argued he should enjoy his thriving private life.

The idea soon melted away. The waters had been tested. The response was tepid at best. Symington chose to stick with his budding culinary career.

# Chapter 40

# THE FOODIE

T here was a year-long waiting list when Symington enrolled in the
Scottsdale Culinary Institute. Symington asked to meet with SCI's
president, Darren Leite (son of the school's famed founder, Elizabeth Leite), to ask that he be allowed to start with the fall class of 1998.
Symington explained that he might not be able to attend a year later because he might be in prison. Even if his convictions were overturned, he
added, life circumstances likely would make full-time schooling difficult
a year later.[1]

Leite not only agreed to let Ann and Fife Symington enroll that fall,
but he also promised to aggressively shield Symington from the press or
over-curious onlookers. Neither Leite nor the Symingtons wanted his attendance to disrupt education at the school.

Ann quit after six weeks. The rigorous, full-day class schedule at SCI
was undermining her church duties and other endeavors.

The dozen or so instructors at SCI were surprised when Ann bowed
out. They had started a betting pool regarding the Symingtons' commitment to the endeavor: Of the Symingtons, it was Fife who several instructors predicted would quit first.

Symington also outlasted the nineteen-year-old from Nebraska with
whom he was paired for cooking and cleaning duties. Almost a third of
the class of thirty-five didn't make it through the first month-and-a-
half—an intense period in which students learned the foundations of
the French Method while experiencing the frenetic pace (and sometimes
stomach-curdling chores like cleaning out the deep fryers) of a genuine
high-end restaurant.[2]

But by the end of SCI's "boot camp," Symington's passion for the culinary arts had only grown.[3] The frenzied tempo was fuel for an adrenaline
junkie at the same time it kept his mind away from what had been and
what might be.

He had eaten in plenty of fine restaurants in his life—he knew the names and flavors of the five mother sauces of French cuisine well—but the flavors he loved had always seemed like works of alchemy by hidden wizards. After a few weeks, he was beginning to make sauces and dishes that weren't half bad. He was feeling the rush, he said later, of blossoming as a craftsman. It was thrilling to be, however humbly, on the creation rather than consumption side of fineness.[4]

Detractors argued it was all an act.[5] As time passed, they conceded it was at least a good act.

As Symington entered SCI, the institute itself was in upheaval. In the months before Symington started classes, the Leite family sold SCI for $10 million to Career Education Corporation, which was gobbling up culinary schools around the country. Elizabeth Leite stepped down as president and was replaced by her son, Darren, who had agreed to stay on to help in the transition.

Near the end of Symington's first six weeks, Darren Leite, already frustrated with the new corporate owners of the Leite family business, resigned as president.

After completing those first six weeks, Symington moved on to a basic baking class taught by chef Robert Wilson, one of the school's most accomplished chefs prior to coming to SCI.

Symington proved a quick hand at baking techniques, and Wilson and Symington were fast friends. Symington learned that, like Leite, Wilson was concerned about the direction of SCI in the hands of a company known for fast expansions of what had been small, often family-owned operations. There would be pressure to recruit and graduate more and more students. Quality control on all ends was likely to slip.

If SCI (soon after named Le Cordon Bleu College of Culinary Arts-Scottsdale) was going big, maybe there was room in the market for something small.

Symington, Wilson, and SCI chef Warren Blim brainstormed at dinner one evening. What if the best of SCI—the small classes, the clear focus on quality rather than quantity—could be maintained in a school that would shed what was wrong about SCI? The SCI degree took too long to acquire and was too expensive. Symington, Wilson, and Blim agreed that too much time was spent in classrooms learning superfluous information (they agreed one nutrition class was particularly mind-numbing). If the fat could be trimmed from the curriculum and more talking and teaching could be integrated into the students' kitchen time, a student could learn as much as they currently were at SCI in, perhaps, half or two-thirds the time. By shortening the time, then, they could charge significantly less than SCI's $35,000 tuition.

In initial discussions, they imagined starting this new kind of culinary school in San Diego. Over the coming year, though, they increasingly believed their model would work best in Scottsdale in the shadow of Le Cordon Bleu. (At the least, they knew they could easily poach from the increasingly unhappy staff there.)[6]

Darren Leite, seemingly waffling between enjoying his freedom and seeking a new challenge, joined in conversations about creating the new school. He would be the obvious choice to run the culinary school, but his ambivalence regarding the project worried Symington and Wilson. This would be a major undertaking. Would Leite be committed enough to guide it to success?

As Symington was finishing his in-class work at SCI, he began his externship with Franco Fazzuoli.[7]

Soon, Fife Symington was laboring away in a hot kitchen while Franco's dining room swelled with diners often rubbernecking in the direction of the kitchen. Again, television cameras were kept outside the door to avoid disrupting the dining experience and the stream of fine Italian entrees and desserts from the kitchen. In one of the few interviews he gave during his externship, Symington described the experience:

"I'm just getting my sea legs, doing a bunch of different things," he told the *Republic*'s Dolores Tropiano. The day of the interview, he told the reporter, "I'm learning how to make bouillabaisse sauce with fresh vegetables."[8]

"I love walking into the kitchen in the morning when it's quiet and the preparation begins," he continued. "New color is introduced into the room, the fresh aromas, and then the kitchen develops a steady crescendo as the day wears on. It's the process that I love."

Fazzuoli labeled Symington "a natural." "He's paid for what he's done, even with what he's doing now," Fazzuoli told Tropiano, with no specifics regarding what he believed Symington had "done," or whether payment was just. "He used to be governor of Arizona and now he's an apprentice in my place. He's learning how to cut meat and fish. I think that shows a lot of character. He really humbled himself."

When asked if he planned to open a new restaurant, Symington said,

"That's a possibility." He wasn't asked, nor would he have revealed at the time, that he was most interested in opening a culinary school.

In the months following the completion of his externship and his graduation from SCI, Symington and Wilson started looking for potential locations for their school. They initially scouted old grocery stores, but settled on an unfinished shell of a building at Mirage Crossings in North Scottsdale. Symington would bring in his old development partner, Randy Todd, to finish the construction.[9]

The old team was back together again.

And stuck in an old position. They needed an investor. They estimated they needed $1.2 million to get the school off the ground.

So Symington approached billionaire Jerry Moyes, owner of Swift Transportation, one of the largest trucking companies in the country.[10] (Symington and Moyes had become acquaintances during efforts in the 1990s to streamline the state's regulations on the trucking industry.)

Symington later described the second of two brief trips to Moyes's office to pitch his business model.

Symington said that at the end of the fifteen-minute meeting, Moyes said, "'Okay, what do you need me to do?' I said it will cost you $1.2 million," Symington related. "Jerry pulled out his checkbook, wrote out a check and slid it across the desk to me. It was written out for the whole $1.2 million. As he slid it to me, Jerry says, 'Fife, I want you to keep this quiet. I'm a trucker. It would appear pretty strange to my fellow truckers if they knew I was helping start a culinary school.'"

Moyes was joking, thankfully. It was important for the school's future that people knew serious money was behind the endeavor.

After Arizona Culinary Institute LLC was formed with Ann and Fife Symington, Moyes, Wilson, and Leite as founders and owners, a lease was signed on the new building.

Construction work began just before September 11, 2001.

The group had no idea how the catastrophic terrorist attacks of that day might impact a fledgling culinary school. It couldn't be good, but they pressed on.

Also weighing on Symington: in late October, he was diagnosed with prostate cancer. During a routine exam, Dr. Larry Bans noted that Symington's PSA (Prostate Specific Antigen test) numbers were rising—an indication of the presence of cancer cells. Bans ordered a biopsy, but the tests came back negative for cancer. However, Bans wasn't satisfied that Symington was cancer-free and order a second biopsy, which came back positive.

A month later, Symington had his prostate removed. It took several months for him to recover. That spring, he was tested again and shown to be cancer free.

Construction of the Culinary Institute was completed January 21, 2002. The next day, the Arizona State Board for Private Postsecondary Education approved ACI's license, and three weeks later, six students—one of whom was Symington's daughter-in-law, Marci—became the first class of the Arizona Culinary Institute.

(Marci would later become a prominent food critic with her blog TEXAZ TASTE.)

At the same time ACI was under construction, Symington was also, as he described it, serving as "an informal adviser" in the development and opening of "Thaifoon" in Scottsdale. Thaifoon would be run by Desert Island Restaurants, which was building three other Thaifoon restaurants in the region. Desert Island also managed two Roy's Pacific Rim restaurants in the Valley and three Ruth's Chris Steak House locations in Hawaii.

In a *Republic* story about Symington's emergence on several culinary fronts, Randy Schoch, Desert Island's CEO, said he and Symington talked daily about the operations of Desert Island. "He has great business acumen," Schoch said. "So the state's loss is my gain."

Thaifoon brandished an impressive list of high-profile investors, including Jerry Colangelo, University of Arizona football coach Dick Tomey, and Ann Symington. Ann, through her company, Fleur de LLC, also held a small interest in the new culinary school.

"I guess I'm really looking after Ann's interests," Fife Symington said.

The subtext here: with Mike Manning still chasing the money, Fife Symington couldn't have money, especially extra money to invest. Even more so than in the 1980s, Symington was the "sweat-equity guy" in any deal.

Which, since he was never an operating partner stuck with daily chores, left him free not only to focus on the nurturing of the culinary school, but also to build his own culinary career.

After his externship with Franco Fazzuoli, Symington left and focused on building his business interests. The hiatus from the kitchen didn't last long, though. Fazzuoli fired his pastry chef at Franco's Trattoria after a string of arguments. He called Symington and offered the job, and Symington agreed as long as he could tailor his pastry preparations around his business commitments. Soon, Symington was in the kitchen early in the morning, then, with his desserts prepared by midday, off to the culinary institute or one of his new ventures. He told friends and family that he may have finally found "the perfect life balance."

But as celebrated as Franco's Trattoria was in the food pages, it was making very little money at its location in North Scottsdale. Fazzuoli closed that restaurant in early 2001 with intentions to open a new one in a more affordable space that would better accommodate his type of restaurant.[11]

It took eighteen months for a new Franco's to open. Two locations fell through. In early 2002, restaurant space opened in the Camelback Esplanade.[12] Roy's was moving out, even though the restaurant's parent company, Desert Island, was locked into a lease there for another five years. Symington, both pastry chef at Franco's and "informal adviser" to Desert Island, came up with a plan that helped both his boss and his business partner.

That fall, Franco's Italian Caffe opened in the Esplanade. The food would be more Americanized and less expensive than at his previous restaurant, which would hopefully fill more seats in the larger space. Franco's longtime lead chef, Steve Martin, would head the kitchen, and Symington would oversee the pastry department.

Although the space was arguably too large for a new local restaurant, Franco's was buoyed by its relationship with Desert Island. Even if Franco's didn't generate enough to pay for the expensive lease in Arizona's most expensive space, the restaurant was still generating income to cut Desert Island's losses as they paid off the rest of the lease for Roy's.

By the time of Franco's Italian Caffe's grand opening, Symington had also started the Symington Group, a political consultant company, as well as the Symington Private Equity Group, which connected investors with entrepreneurs seeking seed money. He needed quality office space from which he could easily commute to his morning pastry-chef job at the Esplanade. So he leased office space at the Esplanade.[13]

Yes, it was a bit expensive for a pastry chef with a couple of fledgling businesses. But it was too perfect, he figured. He could live his two business lives without getting in his car and of course, there would be no more appropriate place from which to relaunch his business career than from the building that made him both famous and infamous.

For more than four years, Symington's workday most often began around 8 a.m. He would go to the ninth floor of one of the Esplanade towers, check emails and hold a quick morning meeting with partner Camilla Strongin and their small staff, then grab one of the white chef smocks hanging from his office door and head down to Franco's. Once in the kitchen, Symington spent several hours preparing the desserts that would be served that day. Besides an arsenal of Italian classics, Symington would prepare his signature "Governor's Cake," also known as "The Governor." The ultra-rich two-layer chocolate cake, topped with two kinds of icing, drew positive reviews from food writers and most diners with no animus toward its creator. The dessert was billed as "high taste, low taxes" fare on the Franco's menu.[14]

By the beginning of 2005, Fife Symington seemed to have built the perfect professional life. The Arizona Culinary Institute was growing; he was involved in several fairly successful business ventures (and yes, a few unsuccessful ones); he was able to work alongside his family; he was still championing pet causes through his consulting firm; and he was still indulging his culinary passion at Franco's.

Yet Symington, "being Fife Symington and all," as a former staffer later put it,[15] couldn't help himself. Emboldened by his success and the goading of his supporters, he did the unthinkable:

In early February of 2005, Symington announced he was officially a candidate for governor.[16]

Of course, the idea of a return to the governor's office had hit Symington years earlier. Indeed, he had been seriously contemplating a run since 2002, the year he found himself free of both criminal and civil litigation at the same time the person who replaced him, Jane Hull, was struggling as she approached her second election.

Hull had been elected governor in 1998 after she replaced Symington the year before. By the time of her State of the State address in early 2002, a consensus seemed to have formed on her administration and its likely legacy:

The former Speaker of the Arizona House of Representatives and Secretary of State was competent, played well with others, and had made real progress along with the legislature in strengthening the state's ever-struggling education and health-care programs.

Her subdued, genial style was refreshing for many after more than a decade of turmoil and national headlines. Hull's apparent fade toward a centrist position generally seemed to be appreciated early on. But as the end of her first term neared, her numbers were slowly but consistently falling. Her biggest problem as she delivered her State of the State in January of 2002: Arizona, after a streak of lackluster economic years and increasing expenditures, was approaching $1 billion in debt, and increasingly, Arizonans were blaming her for the shortfall.[17]

Her approval ratings reached 65 percent in the months after replacing Symington. By early 2002, one poll had her approval rating at 43 percent. She was not doing very well with Arizona's fickle middle. Worse perhaps for any reelection prospects: she had conservatives feeling like they had been hit with a bait and switch.

Hull's early post-Symington agendas—and the bold language she used to define them—heavily echoed the bold language of the fiscally conservative Symington Plan. Increasingly, though, as conservative *Republic* columnist Robert Robb argued, Hull had waffled.[18] Hull had initially "proposed what she claimed as the largest tax cut in state history," Robb pointed out. "Since then, she has presided over the greatest expansion of state government since the 1960s, when its modern structure was first erected."

A month later, while contrasting Hull and Symington, Robb deemed Symington "one of the most effective governors in state history."[19] "Arizona cut personal income tax rates by 25 percent," Robb continued, "adopted welfare reform two years before the national government, created certainty in criminal sentences and launched the most progressive charter school program in the country."

(Robb, who interviewed a group of generally centrist business leaders for the column, wasn't suggesting a Symington, return, though. "Among those fretting over the lack of leadership in the state," Robb wrote of the business leaders he interviewed, "Symington is dismissed as a leader. In part, for good reason: Someone indicted for cooking his business books isn't exactly a role model. But also because Symington had been 'leading' the state in a different direction than those calling for greater leadership desired. . . . There is a clear ideological bias in the current calls for leadership," Robb argued. "Conservatives need not apply.")

Still, by 2002, many Arizona conservatives were longing for the forceful, articulate conservative words and acts of a Fife Symington-like governor while all Arizonans, one can assume, longed for the days of budget surpluses and yearly tax declines.

With a cleaned-up record, his financial chaos nearly in the past, and a good number of his accomplishments aging well, Symington's old base, which had largely shunned him in the few years after his resignation, began to sound like it could be the foundation for a new candidacy.

Symington himself yearned for a very public and prolonged vindication. He also believed he had solutions to the state's new problems. He had loved being governor. And by 2002, he was hearing a growing chorus again singing his praises.

But even the hopeless optimist realized that 2002 was probably too early for a gubernatorial return. In an April 2001 interview with a *Republic* reporter, he floated the idea of running for some other state-level office, but that idea, too, fizzled quickly.[20]

By 2005, though, the landscape, at least to his eyes, looked ready for the return of Fife Symington.

# Chapter 41

# "YOU COULDN'T MAKE THIS STUFF UP"

S ymington's announcement in early 2005 to run for governor, unlike his earlier hints of various candidacies, was taken, for the most
part, pretty seriously.

Democrat Janet Napolitano, who had narrowly beaten Republican
Matt Salmon for the job in 2002, continued to poll well with Arizonans
as she approached a potential second term.[1] "So Napolitano would be
hard to beat. This is not news," the *Republic*'s Doug MacEachern argued.
"Regardless, the prospect of a Symington candidacy is not insane."[2]

Republicans argued Arizona still clearly was a red state. After all, those
on the right contended, the Arizona legislature had remained in Republican hands since 1992, suggesting Arizona still generally favored the Republican agenda and conservative voices, particularly fiscally conservative voices.

In a February spread exploring a Symington candidacy, the *Republic* included a series of short editorials from political analysts and Symington friends and foes. Public affairs consultant and former Symington
aide Chuck Coughlin noted, "Symington never shrank from a public
policy debate." "It would be nice to have that kind of leadership again."

Mike Manning wrote that, "I would urge Fife not to run for governor
far more for the sake of his family than for the sake of the Republican
Party or our state."[3]

Top Republicans such as former Maricopa County Attorney Rick
Romley were waffling on running, and stars in the next generation of
Republicans such as Representative J. D. Hayworth also seemed to balk at
the challenge.

The party needed a player to step forward. So, citing duty-to-party as
a major impetus, Symington tiptoed into the void.

Jack Jewett, a former moderate Republican state lawmaker and top
political voice in the state, told a Tucson reporter: "I can imagine (Symington) would find the current political climate to his liking." With

explosive growth in the state, Jewett suggested, many voters wouldn't have lived through the daily negative headlines during swaths of the 1990s. Longtime Arizonans turned off by the scandals also may instead focus on the fact that Symington's criminal convictions were overturned and that he had since engineered an engaging comeback story. Also, his activist agenda with a long list of wins, along with some policies and programs that were arguably faring well in the rearview mirror, could lure the state's center to vote with Republicans for a return of the Symington Plan.

Alfredo Gutierrez, a former Democratic state lawmaker and, like Jewett, a popular and savvy political voice in the state, simply marveled at the potential storyline of a Symington run:

"You couldn't make this stuff up," he told a *Daily Star* reporter, of course adding that he didn't want such a wonder to actually come to pass. "This is one of the great scenarios of our time." Gutierrez added this nuanced argument in a *Republic* editorial: "A campaign between Gov. Symington and Gov. Napolitano would be one of ideas and vision. I readily admit that I consider (Symington's) ideas and vision empty and exclusionary. I nonetheless recognize that he is intellectually compelling and philosophically deeply grounded. He rarely compromised his beliefs."

A host of other leaders and politicos chimed in on the issue as most every media outlet in the state sought out experts in such things to prognosticate. Opinion seemed to lean slightly in favor of this scenario: Symington, seemingly rejuvenated and increasingly likable, truly was poised to make a serious run. He could win in a Republican primary if the opposition was unimpressive. (Or, he could just win, as one pundit framed it, because he always won when he wasn't supposed to.) But even with all his wins as a conservative-leaning governor in a conservative-leaning state, he was still simply too easy a target to actually win in the general election, especially against a consistently popular governor like Janet Napolitano.[4]

The 2005 Fife Symington sounded like the bulldog of the 1990s, not the humble, self-aware craftsman Arizonans had come to know since he left office.

"I'll match my record against hers any day," he repeated to several news outlets. To the *Daily Star*, he chided: "I don't think (Napolitano) has really done much as governor except ride the political wave. I can't think

Former governor Fife Symington is flanked by former governors Raul Castro, Rose Mofford, and Jane Hull as then governor Jan Brewer was inaugurated, January 3, 2011. © Nick Oza, USA Today Network.

of any major accomplishments. We have very different visions of the role of government in our lives. There would be quite a contrast for the voters."

Symington had actually brashly re-entered the political game the year before when he and his consulting partner, Camilla Strongin, took the job of fighting Proposition 400, which asked voters to approve a sales tax hike to finance public transportation projects, including the long-controversial financing of a light-rail project connecting downtown Phoenix to populated points east and north. Symington tried to keep the spotlight on the NoOn400 campaign and its public face, Gilbert businessman Dave Thompson. But a late October story by the *Republic*'s Pat Flannery outed Symington as the "man behind the curtain staging the production." Subsequent print, radio, and television stories similarly painted Symington as the Cardinal Richelieu of the conservative-tuned campaign.

News that Symington was behind the NoOn400 campaign drew an explosive reaction from the leader of the pro-light-rail side, Chuck

Coughlin, Symington's old staffer and longtime friend. Coughlin raged in Flannery's story that Symington had promised to stay out of the fight, then had jumped whole-heartedly into the fray by engineering a campaign that turned increasingly negative. (Symington and close associates, along with longtime politicos, were surprised by the rancor from Coughlin toward Symington in the waning days of the fight. Their relationship, however, did survive the encounter.)

Symington's anti-light-rail campaign included a satirical black-and-white television ad featuring scenes from a silent-movie train robbery. The voiceover artist likened those government officials promoting the project to the cartoonish train robbers in the film clip.

Proposition 400 ultimately passed easily. Nearly $8.5 billion of sales-tax revenue would cover half the cost of a twenty-year plan to build the Loop 303 freeway, widen Interstate 17, and expand US Highway 60 and Loop 101. About 15 percent of the money would be used to build the light-rail system.

But while seeming all-in for a rowdy gubernatorial fight with Napolitano, Symington also consistently offered himself an easy out. He would "gladly step aside" in favor of Hayworth or Rick Romley. Symington sounded as if he was running only to ensure a strong Republican voice was in the conversation, or to boost and perhaps prod his ideological compatriots, Romley and Hayworth.

Hayworth announced in March he would rather be a US congressman than a governor. By early May, Romley, US Representative Rick Renzi, and former Arizona Attorney General Grant Woods had all decided not to run.[5]

The field had opened up. No matter. On May 5, Symington announced he was bowing out, saying he wanted to focus his attention on his new political consulting firm, the Symington Group.

Not surprisingly, Symington got accused of announcing a candidacy simply to generate press for his company, a motive Symington vehemently denied.[6]

The following year, the Symington Company made headlines again when Strongin agreed to fashion a public relations campaign for Covance, a biotech company hoping to expand to the Phoenix suburb of Chandler that used animals in its testing of new drugs awaiting approval by the Food and Drug Administration.

Strongin, Symington, and their other partner, John Ragan, came under attack by Covance opponents, most notably People for the Ethical Treatment of Animals.[7] Covance ultimately was given government approval to build a facility in Chandler.

When Symington and Strongin weren't consulting, they were searching for opportunities to connect investors with promising projects that needed capital. Strongin would later describe some days in the Symington offices as "pretty much exactly like *Shark Tank*." Entrepreneurs would come pitching ideas; Symington and his staff would ruminate over the viability of the idea in the market and potential ownership positions. Most projects were turned away, but Symington and crew did buy into a small collection of new ventures. One, a company that built rooftop solar arrays, was particularly successful, landing a contract to build solar arrays on rooftops across the Arizona State University campuses toward the goal of converting ASU to renewable energies.

Some projects weren't so successful. In the early days of Symington's return to business, the Symington Private Equity Group sank money into a high-tech security system that, after securing promising contracts with airports and even the Maricopa County Sheriff's Office, ultimately imploded. The viability and reputation of Hummingbird Defense Systems was not helped when it was discovered that the company's leading spokesperson, a boisterous retired Army major general named Daniel Biondi (who often dressed in uniform with a pistol strapped to his waist), wasn't actually a retired Army general.

Symington and his partners, looking for a spokesman with strong military credentials, had hired Biondi on the advice of a Valley software developer whom the man had befriended. Months after joining the company, Biondi spoke to a group of Maricopa County deputies that included several former members of the US Army's elite special operations team, Delta Force. Those deputies reported to Joe Arpaio that Biondi had made several references to his Army career in black ops that clearly showed he had never had an Army career in black ops.[8] Deputies quickly investigated Biondi and discovered that no such general ever existed. Arpaio then called Symington to alert him that the spokesman for one of the companies financed by the Symington Group was actually a con man. Symington said later that he confronted the man and told him he'd be visited by FBI agents if he didn't leave the state immediately. The man disappeared before any investigation began. His real name remains unknown to this day.[9]

Greenhouses in Mexico proved to be more profitable.[10] Some of Symington's most cherished memories would come from flying his son, Fife IV, to the younger Symington's greenhouses near Culiacán in western Mexico in Symington's single-engine Cirrus. The pair flew over the Sierra Madre Mountains several times, often landing on countryside landing strips so bumpy, thin, and tree-lined that they tested the limits of the father's skill and the son's nerve. Flying over the landscape of Sinaloa, Fife IV would emphasize the importance of not flying too low. "Druggies will shoot at you!" Fife IV once yelled at his father.[11]

The infamous Sinaloa Cartel had been known to shoot down unidentified aircraft flying low over their operations.

• • •

In late 2006, Symington received a package from filmmaker and UFO researcher James Fox. In it was a copy of Fox's 2003 documentary, *Out of the Blue*, which included a segment on the "Phoenix Lights" along with other alleged UFO encounters Fox considered some of the most well-documented cases in world history.[12]

Fox was updating his documentary with new footage. He had spoken with several Arizonans who reported seeing a massive, V-shaped craft slowly flying over Maricopa County. Those people told Fox they felt Symington had mocked them with his 1997 press conference in which Jay Heiler starred as the towering alien visitor.[13] Fox hoped to interview Symington on camera about the stunt. Symington, to Fox's surprise, agreed to sit down and answer Fox's questions.

After a few minutes of small talk to start the interview, Fox confronted Symington with a taped audio recording of a question to Symington from one of those Arizonans who reported seeing the UFO. The woman described seeing a giant V-shaped object in the sky as she drove into Maricopa County from the south on Interstate 10. Then she posed her question: "Is this still a matter of ridicule to (Symington) after he came out with his alien and made us all look pretty foolish? We've all remained unwavering on our description. A lot of evidence has been provided since then. . . . I just wondered if he has taken a new stance on this."[14]

Symington, as he had done back in 1997, apologized to Phoenix Lights believers for any hurt the stunt caused. He said he actually took the reports seriously and had told his DPS chief and the general of the Arizona National Guard to seek out answers.

Another bit of news was mixed almost off-handedly into his response:

"It's a good question. . . . I never felt like the overall situation was a matter of ridicule. We certainly took advantage of it, no question about that. But no, I don't consider it a matter of ridicule at all. I think it was a legitimate occurrence of an unknown craft of some sort. Who knows where it came from. Inexplicable. Probably one of the major sightings in modern history in the country because a lot of people in Maricopa County saw it and I saw it, too. So I . . . See I used to work, when I was with the Air Force, I worked in the SAGE Center there at Luke (Air Force Base). Something like that would go up the chain of command immediately to NORAD in Colorado and then go to the Pentagon. So certainly the military chain of command knew what was going on. So they must have a record of it."

Fox said later to journalist Leslie Kean, "It took me a moment to process it. I was thinking, 'Did I really hear what I think I just heard?' My immediate impulse was to make sure the cameras had been running, and they were. I didn't want to press the point right away, but wanted (Symington) to feel at ease. I left and reviewed the tape. It took a day or two for this to really sink in, and for me to realize I had something huge here."[15]

Fox returned for a second interview and asked the obvious question: In the last interview, "you said you saw the UFO yourself. Could you please describe what you saw?"

The evening of March 13, Symington said, he was at home watching local news when he received a phone call regarding a rash of reported UFO sightings in northern Maricopa County. Symington said he told Ann he was going outside to check if he could see anything in the sky. Trees blocked a clear view from his front yard, so he then got into his personal car (thus sidestepping his DPS security detail) and drove toward a park in north Phoenix, just west of Highway 51 at the base of Squaw Peak (later renamed Piestewa Peak). Once he arrived, he walked to an open space in the park and looked west, expecting that anything in the sky that civilians deemed unexplainable was coming from Luke Air Force Base. "There was a bunch of people there," Symington said. "Somebody said 'look at that!' We turned around, and there was this thing coming from the northwest traveling to the southeast."

It was, in his estimation, nearly the size of a modern aircraft carrier. It was shaped somewhat like a boomerang with a series of five embedded lights. It was "absolutely silent," he said, as it moved slowly overhead.

Symington said he then returned home. When he walked in the door,

Ann said, "Oh my God. You look like a ghost," Symington said, a scene
Ann later confirmed. "It was much bigger than a B-2 bomber," Symington told Fox.

"The lights weren't flares. No flares have the ability to move, hold their
position in the sky, move, and hold their position in the sky," Symington
argued.[16]

On March 18, 2007, the *Prescott Courier* ran a story about Symington's
revelation that was written by Kean (also a UFO researcher and a friend
of Fox's) shortly before the release of the updated version of Fox's *Out of
the Blue*.[17] The story was quickly picked up by news outlets around the
country. Symington agreed to accompany a young CNN reporter, Anderson Cooper, to the park from which Symington claimed he witnessed the
UFO.[18] He also talked to John Hook with the local Fox affiliate, then went
silent on the issue for several months.

James Fox, though, was able to convince Symington to serve as a mod-
erator for an event that November at the National Press Club at which
fourteen other former high-ranking military and government officials
discussed their experiences with unexplained phenomenon in the sky.[19]

Symington appeared on *Larry King Live* on CNN a few days prior to
the panel discussion to retell his story.[20]

Symington was accused by some of making up his UFO story to gar-
ner free press for his business or, perhaps, for another run for office. Symington countered that claiming to see a UFO had already been proven to
be unwise. He also argued he was more likely to damage future business
relationships than help them with his admission. "It doesn't help if people think you're crazy," he noted.

• • •

After its initial class of six, the Arizona Culinary Institute graduated
nearly two hundred students the next year. ACI was David versus the
Goliath of Le Cordon Bleu, but ACI offered a degree that cost less while
taking less time to get what, at least ACI staffers believed, was more of the
essential information to be a top-shelf chef or restaurant manager.

The chefs teaching the classes had long resumes, the school's facilities
were new and modern, and the class sizes remained small while Le Cordon Bleu's class sizes were growing.[21] And unlike most schools across the
country, ACI students graduated with expertise not only in baking and
culinary arts, but also in restaurant operations and finances.[22]

The ACI team didn't make that much money, though, because they

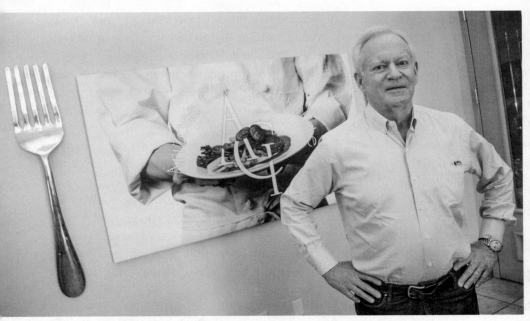

Former Arizona governor Fife Symington is a cofounder of the Arizona Culinary
Institute in Scottsdale. He poses in the lobby, February 27, 2019.
© Tom Tingle, USA Today Network.

charged less, had significant overhead with the new facility (rent was
$45,000 a month, for one), and early on, took everyone who applied,
with students only having to provide a few thousand dollars for a down
payment. And early on too many students lacked commitment and
washed out, and too many students didn't end up paying off the full tuition price.[23]

ACI needed a stamp of approval from the Accrediting Commission
of Career Schools and Colleges, as well as approval from the Department
of Education, to receive federally funded student loans, which was key
to ACI's long-term viability. Robert Wilson, Darren Leite, and Symington started the grueling, likely two-year process of receiving the ACCSC
stamp of approval, which would then allow them to start the similarly
grueling process with the Department of Education.

By 2004, though, Leite, the star former head of the Scottsdale Culinary Institute who was the face of ACI during its precorporate days,
became increasingly removed from the daily operations of the school.
Wilson and Symington believed Leite was suffering from drug and

alcohol addiction. They decided to confront Leite and convince him to enter a rehab program (Wilson and Symington had already secured Leite a slot at the Betty Ford Center in California).

The intervention went poorly. According to Symington and Wilson, what started as a quiet plea that Leite get helped turned into a raging argument in which Leite threatened to punch both men. Leite stormed from the ACI building.[24]

Two months later, Leite was arrested for driving under the influence. Six months later, his father found him dead in his apartment, the victim of a heart attack.[25]

Wilson and Symington pressed on, though, with Wilson taking the helm of the school and Symington devoting more of his workdays to ACI business. In late 2006, the school received its accreditation from the national career-colleges board. Eighteen months later, ACI was deemed a school sturdy and reputable enough to receive money from federally funded student loans.[26]

Just as Wilson and Symington appeared to secure the keys to success, though, the Arizona economy began to tank. Real estate prices collapsed at late-1980s rates, and the broader economy sank as the real estate balloon burst.

By late 2008, people were losing their jobs, which, at first, actually helped buoy the culinary school's numbers. ACI's enrollment bumped up as some newly unemployed Americans pursued a new career in the culinary arts.

But in time, the school began to suffer along with the rest of the country. At the same time ACI was deemed a "School of Excellence" for the 2009-2010 school year, Symington and Wilson were seeking ways to cut costs to stay afloat.

Symington knew one cost-cutting method well because it had been a factor in the collapse of his own company in the previous major recession: He would have to convince ACI's landlord to lower the lease.[27]

Symington and Wilson sought a lease reduction from FirstBank Holding Co. officials, arguing that the rent they were paying was far above what was being paid for similar properties in the real estate market of the time. FirstBank officials refused the proposal.

Symington decided it was time to bring in his old partner from the Symington Company days, Randy Todd.

It was Todd who, after reading the lease agreement ACI's owners had signed more than a decade before, discovered that Symington, Wilson, and the other ACI owners had been promised significantly more parking slots for their facility than ultimately had been provided.

A strategy was then formulated: The culinary school stopped paying rent. FirstBank served a Notice of Default (the first step in a foreclosure process) to the school. Then Symington and Wilson played their trump card: They filed legal papers saying it was FirstBank who had actually broken the lease agreement by failing to provide the contractually agreed-upon amount of parking in the contractually agreed-upon time.

FirstBank swiftly came to the table and a lease reduction was negotiated.

Meaning some thirty years after Symington's own development company imploded due in part to falling rental-space prices that gave tenants leverage to renegotiate, Fife Symington was finally on the winning end of a lease-reduction deal.

# REEFER SENSIBLENESS

In late 1996, Arizona voters approved an initiative legalizing medical marijuana by a two-to-one margin.[1]

Fife Symington had campaigned aggressively against Proposition 200. After learning the initiative had passed, he suggested the Arizona Constitution gave him the right to veto propositions if a majority of registered voters hadn't approved the measure (a majority of those *who voted* passed the measure, not the majority of *everyone who legally could vote*).

Suggesting he might try to veto a vote by the people angered a broad swath of voters.

*Republic* columnist Keven Willey, who commended Symington as often as she condemned him, unleashed a broadside: "True to form," she wrote, "when the rules of the game don't fit his purpose, Symington simply changes the rules."[2]

Symington's opposition to Prop. 200 was more nuanced than simple Never Pot political expediency. He wasn't alone in arguing the proposition's language was deeply flawed.

Over the following days, Doug Cole, then Symington's chief spokesman, walked back Symington's election-night pronouncement. Then, within months, no veto would be needed. The conservative-leaning Arizona legislature had gutted the initiative in bills Symington was happy to sign into law. Medical marijuana would be a dead issue for years to come.

Arizona voters retaliated in 1998 by passing the Voter Protection Act, which not only blocked the legislature from undermining a voter-approved initiative, but mandated that legislators could only "further the intent" of voter-approved legislation.[3]

Fast forward eighteen years to 2016.

Symington's son, Fife Symington IV, approached his father with an audacious idea: He wanted to start a medical marijuana growhouse in Arizona.

Four generations of Symingtons. Courtesy of the Symington family archives.

The younger Symington had found success over the prior two decades building more than eight hundred acres of greenhouses in Mexico in which tomatoes, peppers, and other vegetables were grown primarily for the US market.

For years, Fife IV dreamed of building greenhouses to grow vegetables in his home state of Arizona. For one, he was tiring of all the travel and extended time away from his wife and children (as his father had as president of Vega Petroleum in Texas). But the numbers never added up in Arizona. Any greenhouse in the United States would struggle to make a profit competing with facilities like the ones he and his business parter operated in Mexico.

Indeed, one of the largest greenhouses in Arizona had just closed again after several failed attempts by multinational corporations to make a go of it. In 2015, NatureSweet stepped away from their forty-acre greenhouse in Snowflake, Arizona, 170 miles northeast of Phoenix. The predominately LDS town of six thousand had lost its largest employer.[4]

NatureSweet still couldn't make a profit even though it paid minimum wage to half its employees, then used laborers from a nearby prison for the remainder of the work. They were a terrible corporate citizen in Snowflake, but at least the sprawling state-of-the-art facility was in use. Considering the string of failures, it was likely the greenhouse would stay shuttered forever.

In 2010, Arizona voters again approved medical marijuana. Because of the Voter Protection Act, which was arguably inspired by the actions of Fife Symington III and the Forty-Third Arizona State Legislature, the heavily Republican Fiftieth Arizona Legislature couldn't do a thing about it.

By early 2016, a cannabis supply that legally had to be grown in Arizona was struggling to keep up with demand in Arizona.

Fife IV immediately saw opportunity when he heard of forty acres of greenhouse sitting empty in one of the best spots in the United States for greenhouses (Snowflake basks in 272 days of sun a year with the boosted light intensity at 5,600 feet above sea level).

One major problem, though: That perfect greenhouse was sitting within the city limits of a town in which the majority of citizens were members of a faith that frowned upon alcohol, tobacco, and even coffee and tea.

Prophet Joseph Smith didn't write specifically on the evils of marijuana, but according to the official LDS website, church leaders "have taught Church members to avoid substances that impair judgment." More important, perhaps: LDS leadership in Arizona had been almost universally anti-pot since the idea of medical marijuana first sprouted in the state.

Getting forty acres of marijuana growing in Snowflake sounded about as likely as getting a twenty-one story development at Twenty-Fourth Street and Camelback Road in Phoenix.

The Symingtons knew the argument had to be about good-paying jobs, not about marijuana. For his part, besides offering to invest, the elder Symington promised to wield whatever clout he still carried to calm nerves.

Dad made one other key suggestion: His son would need consultants to help him navigate the difficult road ahead. He suggested "getting the gang at HighGround," the lobbying firm run by former Symington staffers Chuck Coughlin and Doug Cole.

Fife IV approached Cole.

"I just started laughing," Cole said in early 2021. "I mean, I can remember like it was yesterday his dad standing there with a gaggle of reporters saying he might veto the cannabis initiative just passed two to one by voters.[5]

"I said, 'oooookay,'" Cole added. "Then we got to work."

"It was an audacious plan—kind of the Esplanade of Snowflake," Cole continued. "But in the end, from a pragmatic view, it made perfect sense."

Cole, a fourth-generation Arizonan and Arizona history buff, pitched the name Copperstate Farms.

First, a critical measurement was needed. Under Arizona law, no marijuana-related facility can sit within one mile of a church or school.

The LDS temple in Snowflake, one of only five Church of Jesus Christ of Latter-day Saints temples in Arizona at the time, sat 1.1 miles away from the abandoned NatureSweet greenhouse.

It's like it was meant to be.

Cole orchestrated what he called "a first contact" strategy. Fife IV and Cole needed to know who was on their side, and who wasn't, before officially presenting their plan to Snowflake officials in hopes of receiving a permit. Symington also hired an economist to calculate the potential economic impact of the project. Symington and Cole knew they needed hard numbers to back their pitch.

At the heart of the argument: Copperstate Farms would bring two-hundred-plus new jobs with medical benefits and a starting pay of $15 an hour to an abandoned industrial facility in a town struggling after losing its largest employer.

Cole, who had long before developed relationships with many of the key players, then called Brian Richards, the town manager of Snowflake. Richards called back twenty minutes later, first alerting Cole and Fife IV that Snowflake Mayor Tom Poscharsky also would be on the call.

Maybe the economic argument really did have legs.

The Copperstate Farms project faced a long summer of public hearings and often impassioned opposition.

Strange bedfellows emerged. Economy-first conservatives embraced the idea while most cultural conservatives remained anti-cannabis on any terms. Non-LDS Arizonans generally saw the issue in economic and humanitarian terms. Educators and many parents—Republicans and Democrats alike—saw a slippery slope approaching. Business owners—Republicans and Democrats alike—saw the one viable solution to an unemployment and revenue crisis in Snowflake and Navajo County.

Old friends of Cole and his old boss generally offered support or civilized opposition.

"It helped that the Symington name carried a lot weight in that area," Cole said.

During the first week of August, Fife IV called his father explaining he would miss the August 12 celebration of his dad's seventy-first birthday. Fife IV, who had moved to Snowflake that summer to work on the project and knock on doors, said he needed to stay for the town council vote on Copperstate the day after his father's birthday.

Fife IV had a solution, though. His father could pick up Fife IV's wife and three children—one of the children had a birthday near the same time—and bring them up from the smoldering Valley to celebrate in Snowflake.

Sure, there was a bit of an ulterior motive, Fife IV admitted later: "I told him, 'I could really use a cameo from the former governor.'"

The two Fifes met with the mayor, the town council, town officials, and anyone else they could find. The mayor even made a formal proclamation from the town celebrating the event.

"People were thrilled to see him," Fife IV said. "He was still a star there."

Copperstate's public hearings were moved to the spacious Taylor-Snowflake firehouse to accommodate overflow audiences. Early polls showed the majority of Snowflake residents opposed the project. Local opposition was joined by anti-marijuana groups from outside the area. The most aggressive detractors were backed by a group of established Arizona growers who would struggle to compete if Copperstate was approved.

Mayor Poscharsky was the only non-LDS member of the seven-member town council.

The LDS members of the council split 3-3 on Copperstate. Poscharsky placed the deciding vote in favor of the project. The council had to revote four more times after detractors successfully argued the permit language was flawed. The vote remained 4-3 throughout. The empty greenhouse would become a cannabis growhouse.[6]

Knowing the massive one-of-a-kind project would draw statewide attention, the former governor felt he could assist in one other way.

Republican governor Doug Ducey was the strongest anti-cannabis voice in the state (as Symington was in 1996). The elder Symington called Ducey requesting a meeting. Symington told the governor he didn't expect to change his position. He and his son just wanted to explain what they wanted to do, why Fife IV was the right person to do it, and why the plan was a good deal for Arizona.

"My hope was that the project wouldn't become a political piñata," the former governor said in a 2021 interview. "We certainly understood where Ducey was coming from. He held his cards close to his chest. Ducey didn't agree to anything. But it was cordial, and the disagreements tended to remain cordial."[7]

(Two decades earlier, Symington had used a similar maneuver to quell dissent from House Speaker Newt Gingrich for President Clinton's bailout plan for Mexico.)

"That's where my involvement basically ended," the elder Symington said. "This was all my son's deal. I'm just a proud dad at this point."

Symington IV and his partners quickly retrofitted ten acres of the greenhouse. Copperstate produced its first harvest in 2017. Within a year, Copperstate had 230 employees.

Since then, the remaining thirty acres of greenhouse have been retrofitted and put into production. By the end of 2020, the facility had more than four hundred employees.

"The company has become a valuable and intrinsic part of our community," Richards said in early 2021. Copperstate, he said, is "revitalizing our town."

In November 2020, Arizona voters approved the use and production of recreational marijuana by another two-to-one margin.

With the largest growhouse in the nation and four retail dispensaries in Arizona, Copperstate Farms was uniquely positioned to benefit from the new law.

In early March 2021, Snowflake approved Copperstate's plan to double the size of their greenhouse cultivation space to eighty acres.[8]

The company will dominate a statewide recreational marijuana market predicted to reach three billion dollars in sales by 2023.

Indeed, cannabis soon could be generating more revenue than citrus and cotton, two of the original "Five Cs" of Arizona along with copper, climate, and cattle.

All meaning that after helping torpedo medical marijuana in Arizona in the 1990s, the former governor played a key role in helping his son make cannabis the sixth "C" of the state's economy.

A torch was passed. History repeated itself. Irony got a good workout.

As for any idea of hypocrisy: "Yes, I was opposed to marijuana in the 1990s," said Symington, who, due to chronic back pain, now carries a medical marijuana card. But the legalization of cannabis "had been voted on by the public," he said, "and the public has continued to be very clear in its opinion on the issue since then."

"The world has changed," he said. "People change their opinions with new information, and I'm one of those people who changed their opinion."

# EPILOGUE

The Covid-19 pandemic had raged for ten months in Arizona before it caught up with Fife Symington. He had socially distanced, worn masks in public, and mostly limited excursions to quick runs to the pharmacy or grocery store. The only lengthy outings were his two annual fishing trips to Alaska. Before one of those trips, he and his travel partners—old friends Doug Cole, Chuck Coughlin, and Andy Kunasek—all sheltered-in-place and got tested prior to flying out.

During that trip in late August—ostensibly a celebration of Symington's seventy-fifth birthday—Symington injured his lower back during a twenty-minute battle with what fishing partners confirmed was a thirty-inch trout. "It was epic," he said upon return. "Within a blink of an eye, my reel was running red hot. I was having trouble keeping my footing on the rocky river bottom. It was thrilling. But I paid for it later."

He had back surgery in late November of 2020, which laid him up at home for four weeks. He was still mending when his housekeeper called: She had tested positive for Covid-19 just after being in his home.

He never had a fever. But for two weeks, "it felt like I had a horrible flu," he said. His doctor told him to go to the hospital if his oxygen levels sank below 92 percent. His oximeter reading plummeted to 94 percent one day, but never went lower. By early spring his nagging cough was gone, and he was walking without pain. He was ready to get on with his life.

Which would be profoundly different than his pre-Covid life in one monumental way: In the first week of February 2021—after eighteen months of sometimes acrimonious negotiations—he received word that Ann was ready to finalize the terms of their divorce.

The Symingtons refused to discuss the issue in any depth. What was clear, though: They had been growing apart for years. Fife Symington had kept his permanent address in Arizona and had spent the majority of his time in Arizona for the last two decades, while Ann spent most of her

A thirty-inch trout from the Kvichak River in Alaska, 2016. Courtesy of the Symington family archives.

time at their home in Santa Barbara, California. Fife Symington would fly to Santa Barbara most weekends after a work week in Phoenix. Those trips ended two years ago. By the time a "notice of settlement" was logged in Maricopa County Superior Court in February, the couple hadn't spoken directly since Fife Symington filed for divorce in August 2019.

All Fife Symington would say on the matter: "We grew apart—we became increasingly incapable of being together. . . . It's still terribly difficult. There's deep emotional pain—we were together for forty-three years."

"Emotions ran pretty high for awhile during the proceedings," he continued. "Figuring out the fair division of assets can be problematical.

Then the process tends to take a turn toward practicality. We're at the point now we can move on with our lives."

In 2014, Symington's dermatologist suggested he undergo a new treatment for people with badly damaged skin ("I can't count how many pre-cancerous lesions have been cut off me," he said in an early 2021 interview).

Symington went to a plastic surgeon's office, where a physician's assistant covered his face with a light-sensitizing chemical solution before exposing the skin to blue light. (The blue light reacts with the chemical to activate a process that destroys potentially cancerous skin cells.)

"It felt like my face had been set on fire," Symington said. "Then you look like those people blasted by the Ark of the Covenant in the first Indiana Jones movie. It just peels the skin right off your face."

Physician's assistant Rebecca Jirov guided him through the process. Symington would have several more procedures. During one of his follow-up visits, Symington asked Jirov to lunch.

"She's extraordinary. I fell in love with her," Symington said. "It's as simple as that."

Rebecca Jirov during a fishing trip to Alaska. Fife Symington collection.

Symington now lives with Jirov and her two sons. All four tested positive for Covid in January 2021. One of Jirov's boys, Jacob, felt ill for two weeks. His brother, Nicholas, had mild systems. Rebecca was asymptomatic after testing positive. But Symington felt awful for two weeks.

"When we were up for it, we played games, cooked, watched movies," Symington said.

As Symington laid low through most of 2020, he watched intently as Arizona's political landscape made national news.

To Symington, it felt as if Donald Trump wasn't running against Joe Biden. Instead, Trump was running against the late John McCain, who famously rejected Trumpism in scathing language prior to his death in 2018.

Trump had retaliated with vitriol intolerable to many McCain moderates in the state. In November, Republicans did well on the local and state level. But Democrats took both US Senate seats and Arizonans voted for a Democratic president for the first time since 1996.

Symington believes it was Donald Trump who gave those wins to Democrats.

"I sensed his character flaws would bring him down," Symington said of Trump. "Attacking John McCain was just senseless. John and I ran together many times—he always won handily. He was a hero, a gentleman, and was deeply respected by so many people.

"Trump lost Arizona because of the way he treated John McCain."

Yet Symington still didn't break ranks with his party. His business background and lifelong commitment to fiscal conservatism in government wouldn't let him. "I don't agree with Biden's policies," he said. "There's a big mandate toward socialism. I voted for Trump on policy, not personality. And I still believe America does better with a president from the private sector. You need someone who understands fundamental economics—who has lived it."

Symington continues to serve as the head of Arizona Culinary Institute's executive committee while Robert Wilson continues to run day-to-day operations.

Symington also is managing partner of Franco's Italian Caffe, the latest iteration of a Franco Fazzuoli-run, Symington-backed restaurant.

After Fazzuoli's restaurant in the Esplanade closed, he moved to New York to start a restaurant and be closer to family. That venture fizzled.

Fazzuoli needed a new place and was willing to return to Arizona, so Symington brought together nine friends and Fazzuoli fans to raise a quarter million dollars ($25,000 from each investor including himself) to get a Franco's in Scottsdale up and running.

The pandemic stressed both businesses, but both survived thanks to some belt tightening, a couple federal Paycheck Protection Project loans, and Symington-style lease payment renegotiations.

"There were heated conversations," Symington admitted. "I had to call up the landlord of Franco's one weekend and tell him we couldn't pay him on time." Revenue had been down 40 percent through the Valley's high season. "Our landlord justifiably wasn't happy. He has financial obligations he has to meet. I totally understand where he was coming from. Luckily he understood where we were coming from."

Luckily, too, the following weekend was one of the most profitable in months. After busy evenings Thursday, Friday, and Saturday (even with social distancing guidelines still in place), the landlord got his rent on Monday.

For Symington, although the numbers were smaller, the economic downturn of 2020 and early 2021 felt like the late-1980s all over again. But this time: no defaults, no bankruptcies, and no lawsuits. By spring of 2021, both ACI and Franco's were on solid footing again.

Symington and Wilson were even back to considering expansion: "Dallas or Austin," Symington said. "Those markets look like the best fits if we decide to branch out."

"It's been kind of crazy," he said. "I'm supposed to be semi-retired. It doesn't feel that way a lot of the time."

One thing is for sure, he said: He won't be running for public office again.

That idea, though, was still lingering just a few years earlier. Symington announced in 2018 that he *might* enter the 2020 race to fill John McCain's US Senate seat.

The announcement made Arizona's news cycle for a couple days. Then, silence.

"My heart wasn't really in it," Symington said. "I like my life."

He's doing business, but he's not tied to an office. He's involved with food, but he's not tied to a kitchen. He can offer sage political advice to emerging Republicans without the withering fire from opponents both to his left and right. He can fish when he chooses. He'll be returning to Alaska twice each year, he said, "until my last breath."

"I loved being governor," he said. "It was unquestionably the best job in the world. But I've never been fond of *Groundhog Day*. To go back into that world would be repetitive.

"I want to blaze new paths, not revisit the past."

# NOTES

PROLOGUE

1. Fife Symington, in discussion with Robert Nelson, June 6, 2018, author's files.

2. Doug Cole, in discussion with Jack L. August Jr., March 20, 2015, author's files.

3. Charlotte Buchen, "Goldwater to Head Camelback Group," *Arizona Republic*, May 18, 1965.

4. Chase Peterson-Withorn, "From Rockefeller to Ford, See Forbes' 1918 Ranking of the Richest People in America," forbes.com, September 19, 2017. John D. Rockefeller was first. Andrew Carnegie was third.

5. Fife Symington Jr., *A Personal Collection*, 73.

6. John Dowd, in discussion with Robert Nelson, April 2, 2017, author's files.

7. Robert Nelson, "Trump's Lawyer is an Expert at Securing Presidential Pardons," *Washington Post*, January 2, 2018.

8. Jolyn Oklmoto, "Report of Symington retrial denied," Associated Press, May 26, 2000. Rumors swirled of new indictments coming in the months after Symington's convictions were overturned. Mayorkas (who in 2021 would become Secretary of Homeland Security under President Joe Biden) agreed in May of 2000 to postpone any prosecution or grand jury proceedings for six months, which would allow time for Symington's civil trial in US Bankruptcy Court to wrap up.

9. Fife Symington, in discussion with Robert Nelson, June 26, 2017, author's files.

10. "Timeline," *Arizona Daily Star*, June 23, 1999. The *Daily Star* compiled one of the most detailed timelines of Symington's complicated history of legal entanglements during their coverage of the Ninth Circuit's decision to overturn Symington's six convictions.

11. "The Court Observer: Dowd left speechless after incident," *Arizona Republic*, July 12, 1997; see Paul Rubin, "Fife's Fishing Trip," *Phoenix New Times*, February 26, 1992. Rubin arguably provided the most detailed and best-sourced replay of an equally robust tussle between Dougherty, Dowd, and Symington political consultant Jay Smith in the offices of the *Mesa Tribune* in the early 1990s.

12. Dowd, discussion, April 2, 2017.

13. Terry Lynam, in discussion with Robert Nelson, April 20, 2019, author's files.

14. Rick Barrs, "Criminal with an asterisk," *Phoenix New Times*, May 15, 2003. The newsweekly's editor was primarily taking Dowd to task for demanding that *New Times* remove from its website an otherwise glowing food review involving Symington's pastries. "Your article falsely and maliciously stated that Governor Symington is a 'criminal' and that he 'finagled millions of dollars in loans by using false financial statements,'" Dowd wrote regarding the food review. In the letter, Dowd wrote, "Your repeated statements referring to Governor Symington as a 'criminal' and a 'crook' and accusing him of false financial statements are patently false. The jury verdicts on the remaining counts against Governor Symington were reversed and vacated by the Ninth Circuit Court of Appeals in 1999. The United States chose not to pursue the charges. Moreover, Governor Symington received a presidential pardon in 2001. Thus, as a matter of law and fact, he is completely innocent of the charges and not a criminal.'" As part of his column, Barrs, a two-time Pulitzer winner as a reporter for the *Los Angeles Times*, questioned Dowd on the status of plea negotiations with prosecutors at the time of the pardon two years earlier. Dowd denied a newspaper story claim

suggesting Symington was set to accept a plea deal involving a single count of bank fraud. Dowd said, "We never signed anything." "The correct way to say it is, we were in discussions (with federal attorneys) about a plea agreement . . . but we hadn't accepted the (government's) offer."

15. David Schindler, in discussion with Robert Nelson, March 18, 2017, author's files.

16. Pat Flannery, "The most elegant way to end this saga," *Arizona Republic*, January 21, 2001.

17. Lynam, discussion, April 20, 2019.

18. Tommy Caplan, in discussion with Robert Nelson, June 20, 2017, author's files.

19. Tommy Caplan, in discussion with Jack L. August Jr., July 12, 2015, author's files.

20. Jack L. August, Jr., "Two Lives Altered: The Pardon of Fife Symington and the Saving of Bill Clinton's Life," *Arizona Food Marketing Journal*, March 2015; Bill Clinton, *My Life* (New York: Knopf, 2004); Fife Symington, oral history interview by Jack L. August Jr., June 8, 2014, Paradise Valley, Arizona, author's files; Tommy Caplan, oral history interview by Jack L. August Jr., June 12, 2013.

21. Stephanie Shapiro, "Helping a school chum who needed a pardon," *Baltimore Sun*, March 3, 2001.

22. Lynam, discussion, April 20, 2019.

23. Kelly Wiese, "Clinton's pardons give McDougal, others 'fresh start,'" Associated Press, January 22, 2001.

CHAPTER 1: THE STAR-SPANGLED LINEAGE

1. Fife Symington, in discussion with Robert Nelson, February 2, 2018, author's files.

2. Martha Frick Symington Sanger, *The Henry Clay Frick Houses: Architecture, Interiors, Landscapes in the Golden Era* (New York: Monacelli Press, 2001); Samuel Agnew Schreiner, *Henry Clay Frick: The Gospel of Greed* (New York: St. Martin's Press, 1995); Quentin R. Skrabec, *Henry Clay Frick: The Life of the Perfect Capitalist* (Jefferson, NC: McFarland Press, 2010); Kenneth Warren, *Triumphant Capitalism: Henry Clay Frick and the Industrial Transformation of America* (Pittsburg: University of Pittsburg Press, 1996). See also, James C. Olson, *Stuart Symington: A Life*, Missouri Biography Series Book 1(Columbia: University of Missouri Press, 2003).

3. George Harvey, *Henry Clay Frick: The Man* (New York: Charles Scribner & Sons, 1928).

4. The standard account of this period in the creation of urban and industrial America is Robert Wiebe, *The Search for Order, 1870–1920* (New York: Hill and Wang, 1966).

5. Harvey, *Henry Clay Frick*, 69.

6. Les Standiford, *Meet You in Hell: Andrew Carnegie, Henry Frick, and the Bitter Partnership that Transformed America* (New York: Three Rivers Press, 2005).

7. Harvey, *Henry Clay Frick*. See also, William S. Dietrich, "Henry Clay Frick: Blood Pact," *Pittsburgh Quarterly* (*PQ*) (Spring 2009).

8. Tony Michels, ed., "The Attempted Assassination of Henry Clay Frick," in *Jewish Radicals: A Documentary History* (New York: NYU Press, 2012), 95–96; Arthur G. Burgoyne, *The Homestead Strike of 1892* (Pittsburgh, PA: University of Pittsburgh Press, 2006), 146–48.

9. James Nevius, "The Controversial Origins of New York City's Frick Collection," curbed.com, July 29, 2014.

10. Symington, discussion with Nelson.

11. Childs Frick to Mama [Adelaide Frick], June 6, 1896, J. Fife Symington III Personal Papers, Arizona State Archives, Phoenix, Arizona.

12. Martha Frick Symington Sanger, *Helen Clay Frick: Bittersweet Heiress* (University of Pittsburgh Press, 2007).

13. Sanger, *Helen Clay Frick*.

14. Childs Frick to Helen Clay Frick, January 13, 1912, J. Fife Symington III Personal Papers, Arizona State Archives, Phoenix, Arizona; Childs Frick to Helen Frick, March 3, 13, April 14, 1912, Personal Papers of J. Fife Symington III, 1912 File, Arizona State Archives, Phoenix, Arizona.

15. Kaitlyn Leidl, "A Guide to Long Island's Gold Coast Mansions," thirteen.org, retrieved June 19, 2000.

16. *Childs Frick Abyssinian Expedition: Carnegie Museum of Natural History*, www.arcgis.com/home/; Barbara Klein, "Call of the Wild: How Childs Frick, son of Pittsburgh industrialist Henry Clay Frick, provided the foundation for Carnegie Museum of Natural History's world-class collection of African Mammals," *Carnegie Magazine*, Spring 2015, 4–5; Duane Schlitter and Janis Sacco, "Childs Frick and the Santens Brothers: Creating a Superb Collection of African Mammals," *Carnegie Magazine*, May/June 1993.

17. *New York Times*, December 3, 1919. The *Times* wrote an extensive front-page biography on Frick; Sanger, *Helen Clay Frick*, 122, 123.

18. Fife Symington, Jr. to Miss Martha Frick, June 7, 1938, File 1938–1947, Fife Symington, Jr., Personal and Political Papers of J. Fife Symington III (Symington Collection), State Archives, Phoenix, Arizona. The envelope, on Hotel Bethlehem stationery, is addressed to: Miss Martha Frick, c/o Childs Frick, Roslyn, Long Island, New York.

19. Symington, Jr. to Martha Frick, July 21, 1938, File 1938–1947, Fife Symington, Jr., Symington Collection.

20. Charles J. Symington, *Scotch and Soda: A Family History Covering Twenty-Six Generations* (Rochester, New York: Charles J. Symington, 1984); *Arizona Republic*, October 29, 1995; Charles J. Symington, *Skippin' the Details* (New York: Clark & Way, 1966).

21. Charles Rappleye, *Robert Morris: Financier of the American Revolution* (New York: Simon & Shuster, 2011).

22. James C. Olson, *Stuart Symington: A Life* (Columbia: University of Missouri Press, 2003).

23. Fife Symington Jr., *A Personal Collection*.

24. Melvin G. Holli and Peter d'A Jones, *Biographical Dictionary of American Mayors, 1820–1980: Big City Mayors* (Westport, Connecticut: Greenwood Press, 1981), 344.

25. Symington, *Skippin' the Details*, 6. See also, Frederick R. Loviad, *History of the Washington National Monument and Washington National Monument Society* (Washington, DC: Government Printing Office, 1903).

26. Olson, *Stuart Symington*, 3.

27. Helen Clay Chace, in discussion with Jack L. August Jr., October 9, 2016, author's files.

28. For a full history of the Roslyn mansion, visit https://nassaumuseum.org/history/.

29. Symington, *A Personal Collection*, 20–26.

30. Fife Symington, in discussion with Jack L. August Jr., April 20, 2016 and October 13, 2016, author's files.

CHAPTER 2: MONKEYS AND MONDO TRASHO

1. Fife Symington, in discussion with Jack L. August Jr., April 20, 2016 and November 2, 2016, author's files.

2. Fife Symington, oral history interview by Jack L. August Jr., November 2, 2016, author's files.

3. Fife Symington to Martha Frick Symington, August 5, 6, 1953, Frick-Symington Letters.

4. Helen Clay Chace, oral history interview by Jack L. August Jr., January 10, 2015, New York, New York, author's files.

5. Scott Symington, oral history interview by Jack L. August Jr., December 20, 2015, Pasadena, California, author's files.

6. *Baltimore Sun*, November 26, 2010; www.calvertschoolmd.org.

7. Symington, interview by August, December 22, 2014.

8. John Waters and Fife Symington, oral history interview by Jack L. August Jr., July 8, 2014. See also, John Lewis, "100 Years: John Waters Meets Divine," *Baltimore Magazine* (February 2007).

9. Robert L. Pela, *Filthy: The Weird World of John Waters* (New York: Alyson Books, 2002). As Pela wrote, "Waters turned the family garage into a haunted house . . . but his first attempt at entertaining the public fell flat."

10. See Former Governor Fife Symington III, "Sharing Personal Memories of Barry Goldwater,"

Barry Goldwater Lecture Series, September 16, 2007, Scottsdale, Arizona, www.azpbs.org/Goldwater/2007/Symington/html.

11. Tommy Caplan, "Gilman in the Kennedy Years," *Gilman Voices.*

12. Redmond Finney, oral history interview by Jack L. August Jr., November 9, 2014, Baltimore, Maryland, author's files.

13. Neddie belonged to Symington III's older sister. He was a thoroughbred chestnut gelding with four white socks. Helen Clay Chace, in discussion with Jack L. August Jr., November 20, 2016, author's files.

14. Fife Symington Jr., *A Personal Collection*, 55. A snippet of a newspaper account in this brief pictorial memoir reads, "The only casualty in the 10-horse field was Neddie, owned by J. Fife Symington Jr., with his rider J. Fife Symington III at the next to last jump. Young Symington was taken to the Union Memorial hospital by ambulance and was admitted with a possible fracture of the shoulder."

15. Fife Symington, oral history interview by Jack L. August Jr., March 3, 2015, author's files.

16. A detailed account of Symington's 1964 summer canoe trip can be found in G. Heberton Evans III, *The Rupert That Was* (Cobalt, Ontario: Highway Book Shop, 1978). The Rupert had been important to the Cree and major tributaries include the Natastan, Lemare, Marten, and Nemiscau Rivers.

17. Fife Symington III to Fife Symington Jr., July 15, 1964, File 1964, Frick-Symington Letters.

18. A detailed account of Symington's 1964 summer canoe trip can be found in G. Heberton Evans III, *The Rupert That Was* (Cobalt, Ontario: Highway Book Shop, 1978).

CHAPTER 3: "SYMINGTON IS A FASCIST!" AT HARVARD

1. Fife Symington III to Martha Frick Symington, September 9, 21, 1964, File 1964–65, Frick-Symington Letters, Arizona State Archives, Phoenix, Arizona.

2. Fife Symington III to Martha Frick Symington, n.d., 1964, File 1964–1966, Frick-Symington Letters, Arizona State Archives, Phoenix, Arizona.

3. See, for example, Andrew Heywood, *Political Ideologies: An Introduction* (London: Palgrave MacMillan, 2003), 74; F. P. Lock, *Edmund Burke, Volume II: 1784–1797* (Gloucestershire: Clarendon Press, 2006), 585; Jesse Norman: *Edmund Burke: The First Conservative* (New York: Basic Books, 2013); Russel Burke, *The Conservative Mind: From Burke to Eliot* (Washington, DC: Regnery Publishing, 2001); Symington III to Martha Frick Symington, March 1965, File 1961–1965, Frick-Symington Letters.

4. Deborah Laake, "Fife Symington," *New Times*, October 3, 1990; "Remembering 1964–1968 at Harvard." This document was a handout in the 35th Reunion package. It has been edited. Sources for this document are as follows: Harvard University Archives, Harvard University President's Reports, Class Reports, Yearbooks, the *Harvard Crimson, The Harvard Century*, by Richard Norton Smith, *Timetables of History*, 3rd. rev ed., by Bernard Grun.

5. Symington III to Martha Frick Symington and Symington Jr., June 13, 1967, Folder 1967–1968, Frick-Symington Letters.

6. Terry Considine, oral history interview by Jack L. August Jr., July 24, 2013, author's files.

7. Elliot Smith, "The Barings collapse 25 years on," cnbc.com, February 26, 2020.

8. Symington III to Symington Jr., January 1965, Folder 1961–1965, Frick-Symington Letters.

9. Fife Symington III, in discussion with Jack L. August Jr., December 6, 2016, author's files; Symington III to Martha Frick Symington and Symington Jr., June 1965, Frick-Symington Letters.

10. Leslie Jones, oral history interview by Jack L. August Jr., January 6, 2016, Carefree, Arizona, author's files.

11. Leslie Barker Symington [Jones] to Martha Frick Symington and Fife Symington Jr., June 2, 1968, Leslie Barker Folder, 1968–1969, Frick-Symington Letters.

CHAPTER 4: WAR

1. Fife Symington III to Martha Frick Symington, September 9, 21, 1964, File 1964–65, Frick-Symington Letters, Arizona State Archives, Phoenix, Arizona.

2. Symington III to Martha Frick Symington and Symington Jr., July 13, 1969, Folder 1969–1971, Frick-Symington Letters.

3. Fife Symington, in discussion with Robert Nelson, June 12, 2018.

4. Fife Symington, in discussion with Jack L. August Jr., March 13, 2015; Symington, discussion with Nelson, June 12, 2018; Symington III to Martha Frick Symington and Symington Jr., July 13, 1969, Folder 1969–1971, Frick-Symington Letters.

CHAPTER 5: A SECOND-CLASS CITY

1. Bradford Luckingham, *The Urban Southwest: A Profile History of Albuquerque, El Paso, Phoenix and Tucson* (El Paso: Texas Western Press, University of Texas, El Paso, 1982).

2. On Southwestern development, see Bradford Luckingham, *Phoenix: The History of a Southwestern Metropolis* (Tucson, Arizona: University of Arizona Press, 1989); Andrew Ross, *Bird on Fire: Lessons from the World's Least Sustainable City* (New York, New York: Oxford University Press, 2011).

3. Andrew Ross, in discussion with Robert Nelson, October 12, 2018.

4. Martin Lowy, in discussion with Robert Nelson, September 22, 2017; Martin Lowy, *High Rollers: Inside the Savings and Loan Debacle* (New York, New York: Greenwood Publishing Group, 1991).

5. Peter Wiley and Robert Gottlieb, *Empires of the Sun: The Rise of the New American West* (Toronto: General Publishing Co. Limited, 1982).

6. Jack L. August, Jr., *Vision in the Desert: Carl Hayden and Hydropolitics in the American Southwest* (Fort Worth, Texas: TCU Press, 1999).

7. Earl Zarbin, *All the Time a Newspaper: The First 100 years of the Arizona Republic* (Phoenix, Arizona: Phoenix Newspapers, Inc., 1990).

8. Luckingham, *The Urban Southwest*.

9. Richard Mallery, *Loving Life: A Memoir* (Phoenix, Arizona: Legacy West Media, 2018).

10. Tom Fitzpatrick, "The Esplanade: How world class was bestowed on bumpkins of Phoenix," *Arizona Republic*, March 4, 1985.

CHAPTER 6: HOW TO GET AHEAD IN BUSINESS

1. Fife Symington III to Fife Symington Jr., October 25, 1971, Frick-Symington Letters; Fife Symington III to Martha Frick Symington, December 16, 1971, Frick-Symington Letters.

2. Fife Symington, in discussion with Robert Nelson, June 26, 2017; Fife Symington, in discussion with Jack L. August Jr., July 8, 2016.

3. Symington III to Martha Frick Symington, December 20, 1972. Frick-Symington Letters.

4. *Arizona Republic*, June 8, 1973; *Arizona Daily Star*, June 9, 1973.

5. Symington, discussion with August, March 13, 2015; *Arizona Republic*, August 4, 1972; *Arizona Republic*, August 5, 1972.

6. Martin Lowy, in discussion with Robert Nelson, September 22, 2017, author's files.

7. See American Institute of Architects, Central Arizona Chapter, *A Guide to the architecture of Metro Phoenix* (Phoenix: Phoenix Pub., 1983).

8. Walter Rundell, *Oil in West Texas and New Mexico: A Pictorial History of the Permian Basin* (College Station, Texas: Texas A&M University Press, 1982).

9. Jack L. August Jr., *The Norton Trilogy* (Fort Worth, Texas: TCU Press, 2013).

10. Symington, discussion with Nelson, June 26, 2017, author's files.

11. Symington, discussion with Nelson, September 12, 2017; Symington, discussion with August, April 12, 2015, author's files.

12. Ann Symington, in discussion with Robert Nelson, April 18, 2018, author's files.

13. Richard Mallery, in discussion with Robert Nelson, November 9, 2018, author's files.

14. Symington III to Martha Frick Symington and Symington Jr., October 29, 1975, File 1970–1980, Frick-Symington Letters.

15. Randy Todd, in discussion with Robert Nelson, September 25, 2017; Symington, discussion with Nelson, September 27, 2017.

16. See Lowy, *High Rollers: Inside the Savings and Loan Debacle;* Jerry Shields, *The Invisible Billionaire: Daniel Ludwig* (New York, New York: Houghton Mifflin, 1986).

17. Symington, discussion with Nelson, September 12, 2017, author's files.

18. Symington, discussion with Nelson, February 16, 2018, author's files.

## Chapter 7: A World-Class City

1. Tom Fitzpatrick, "The Esplanade: How world class was bestowed on bumpkins of Phoenix," *Arizona Republic*, March 4, 1985.

2. See Andrew Ross, *Bird on Fire: Lessons from the World's Least Sustainable City* (New York, New York: Oxford University Press, 2011).

3. Bradford Luckingham, *Phoenix: The History of a Southwestern Metropolis* (Tucson, Arizona: University of Arizona Press, 1989); *Phoenix Gazette*, August 6, 1980, October 25, 1985, November 14, 1986; *Arizona Republic*, December 19, 1984; City of Phoenix, *Phoenix Planning Issues* (Phoenix: City of Phoenix, 1982), passim; *Phoenix Concept Plan 2000* (Phoenix: City of Phoenix, 1979).

4. Andrew Ross, in discussion with Robert Nelson, October 12, 2018, author's files.

5. *Arizona Republic*, August 19, 1979, January 7, May 22, and November 4, 1981; *Phoenix Gazette*, October 9 and November 4, 1981; *Phoenix New Times*, October 23 and November 10, 1981.

6. Fife Symington, in discussion with Robert Nelson, September 12, 2017, author's files; Randy Todd, in discussion with Robert Nelson, September 25, 2017, author's files.

7. Randy Todd, in discussion with Jack L. August Jr., May 15, 2016, author's files.

8. See *Los Angeles Times*, "Mixed-use Project Planned," September 30, 1984.

9. *Arizona Republic*, September 28, 1984, and November 11, 1984; *Phoenix Gazette*, October 2, 1984; *Tucson Daily Star*, October 1, 1984.

10. *Arizona Republic*, December 7, 1983, and December 8, 1983; *Mesa Tribune*, December 7, 1983.

11. Tom Fitzpatrick, "Real star of council-runoff campaign shines in the shadows," *Arizona Republic*, December 7, 1983. "Last week, one of the Republican Party's heavyweights, former state Sen. John Pritzlaff, entered the lists on Gardiner's side," Fitzpatrick wrote. "That shouldn't be too surprising. Pritzlaff is the father-in-law of J. Fife Symington III. He also is a former Republican finance chairman."

12. Pat Sallen, "Mercedes bends: Korrick admits driving car over foe's campaign signs," *Arizona Republic*, December 10, 1983. Korrick's actions were uncovered by Gardiner himself. "Gardiner, a retired police lieutenant who owns a security firm, said he sent his assistant security manager to Korrick's office to check the underside of the car and found remnants of the signs," according to the *Republic* story.

13. *Mesa Tribune*, June 10, 1984.

14. Deborah Shanahan, in discussion with Robert Nelson, September 26, 2017, author's files. See Deborah Shanahan, "Esplanade: $400 million 'world class' behemoth inspires praise, fear on the eve of hearing," *Arizona Republic*, January 28, 1985.

15. *Arizona Republic*, January 27 and January 28, 1985.

16. *Mesa Tribune*, January 31, 1985.

17. *Arizona Republic*, February 9, 1985.

18. Todd, discussion with Nelson, September 25, 2017, author's files.

19. Tom Fitzpatrick, "J. Fife Sharkington circles in for the kill; will the City Council harpoon him?" *Arizona Republic*, March 6, 1985.

20. Symington, discussion with Nelson, June 26, 2017, October 7, 2018; Ann Symington, in

discussion with Robert Nelson, April 18, 2018; see "The Arch Lustberg communicator collection" (Bloomington, Indiana: Library Video Network, Indiana University, Bloomington, 2004); see also Arch Lustberg, *How to Sell Yourself: Winning Techniques for Selling Yourself . . . Your Ideas . . . Your Message* (Franklin Lakes, New Jersey: The Career Press, Inc., 2002).

21. *Arizona Republic*, January 31, 1985; *Mesa Tribune*, January 31, 1985, and February 1, 1985.

22. Symington, discussion with Nelson, September 12, 2017, author's files; Todd, discussion with Nelson, September 25, 2017, author's files.

23. Bud Wilkinson, "Esplanade showdown proves 'world-class' viewing," *Arizona Republic*, March 11, 1985. Wilkinson led his story with, "As weekly prime-time entertainment, 'Terry and the City Fathers' would never be a ratings sensation, but KAET-TV's live coverage of last week's world-class Phoenix City Council meeting from Symphony Hall offered sensational viewing in spite of the sporadic technical glitches and outages."

24. Todd, discussion with August, May 12, 2015, author's files; Todd, discussion with Nelson, September 27, 2017, author's files.

25. *Arizona Republic*, April 18, 1985. "Not all of the 200 people attending the hearing favored the new design," according to the story. "Some neighbors said it still is too big, but most of the complaints involved having two stories of parking above ground at the southern end of the project."

CHAPTER 8: HOW TO GET AHEAD IN POLITICS

1. Richard Mallery, in discussion with Robert Nelson, January 6, 2018, author's files.

2. Grant Woods, in discussion with Jack L. August Jr., March 19, 2014, author's files.

3. Gail Reid, "Rep. Carlson West seeking Rhodes' seat; 3-way race possible," *Arizona Republic*, February 17, 1982.

4. "John J. Rhodes, 86, Helped Persuade Nixon to Resign," *Washington Post*, August 26, 2003.

5. See Jeffrey D. Glasser, *The Secret Vietnam War: The United States Air Force in Thailand, 1961–1975* (Jefferson, North Carolina: McFarland & Company, 1998).

6. Fife Symington, in discussion with Robert Nelson, September 12, 2018 , author's files; Fife Symington, in discussion with Jack L. August Jr., February 12, 2016, author's files.

7. *Arizona Daily Star*, November 5, 1986; *Arizona Republic*, November 5, 1986. According to the *Republic* story: "Not once during the campaign did Kimball pull any closer to McCain in the polls than 13 percentage points. Most of the time, McCain's margin was in the neighborhood of 25 to 30 points."

8. Symington, discussion with Nelson, September 12, 2017, author's files.

9. Jack L. August, "Upset of the Century: Evan Mecham and the Arizona Gubernatorial Campaign of 1986," 42nd Annual Arizona Historical Convention, Pinetop, Arizona, April 27, 2001.

10. Bruce Merrill, in discussion with Jack L. August Jr., February 2, 2015; *Arizona Daily Star*, November 6, 1986. Glenn Davis, executive director of the Arizona Democratic Party, told the *Daily Star* that Schulz's presence in the race made the Mecham win possible: "The majority of the state is politically moderate," Davis said. "But if you take that majority and split it, the conservative is going to win."

11. See Ronald Watkins, *High Crimes and Misdemeanors: The Term and Trials of Former Governor Evan Mecham* (New York, New York: William Morrow and Company, 1990); Richard Kleindeinst, oral history interview by Jack L. August Jr., Prescott, Arizona, October 22, 1999, author's files; Evan Mecham, oral history interview by Jack L. August Jr., Glendale, Arizona, January 8, 2000, author's files; Bob Corbin, oral history interview by Jack L. August Jr., Prescott, Arizona, April 2, 2001, author's files; Symington, discussion with Nelson, May 12, 2019, author's files.

12. *Arizona Republic*, October 15, 1987; *Arizona Daily Star*, October 15, 1987; *Scottsdale Tribune*, October 15, 1987.

13. *Arizona Republic*, November 29, 1987.

14. *Arizona Republic*, October 29, 1987.

15. Ronald Watkins, *High Crimes and Misdemeanors: The Term and Trials of Former Governor*

*Evan Mecham* (New York, New York: William Morrow and Company, 1990); *Arizona Republic,* January 9–11, 1988; *Arizona Daily Star,* January 9, 1988.

16. Symington, discussion with Nelson, February 16, 2018.

17. Mallery, discussion with Nelson, April 6, 2019, author's files; Symington, discussion with Nelson, June 4, 2019, author's files.

18. Susan R. Carson, "Group set up in Phoenix to aid recall," *Arizona Daily Star,* October 30, 1987; *Arizona Republic,* October 29, 1987.

19. Symington, discussion with Nelson, February 16, 2018, author's files.

20. Fife Symington speeches, Folder 1986–88, Symington Papers.

CHAPTER 9: BOOM TIME WITH A TIME BOMB

1. Deborah Shanahan, "Ritz Hotel vowed for Esplanade," *Arizona Republic,* March 6, 1985; Deborah Shanahan, in discussion with Robert Nelson, September 26, 2017.

2. Fife Symington, in discussion with Robert Nelson, February 16, 2018, author's files; Randy Todd, in discussion with Robert Nelson, September 25, 2017, author's files; Barbara Rose, "Webb to move into Esplanade," *Arizona Republic,* November 21, 1985.

3. Fife Symington, in discussion with Jack L. August Jr., March 12, 2015, author's files; Todd, discussion with Nelson, September 25, 2017, author's files; Barbara Rose, "Camelback Esplanade's big tenant backs out; delay in project blamed," *Arizona Republic,* July 30, 1986.

4. Barbara Rose, "J. Fife Symington's War Games: Man and machine poised to charge," *Arizona Republic,* August 1, 1986. "You think you know what the major issues are that could blow a deal apart, but you never know what is going to boil to the top at the bitter end of the deal," Symington told Rose.

5. Symington, discussion with Nelson, September 12, 2017, author's files.

CHAPTER 10: DECISIONS, DECISIONS

1. Susan Carson, "Mofford takes over governor's office role: Ousts Hawkins; Mecham says he'll be back," *Arizona Daily Star,* February 9, 1988; Walt Nett, "House passes impeachment articles, 42–18," *Arizona Daily Star,* February 9, 1988; Tom Shields, "Mofford plans to flex some muscle," *Tucson Citizen,* February 11, 1988; see Ronald Watkins, *High Crimes and Misdemeanors: The Term and Trials of Former Governor Evan Mecham* (New York, New York: William Morrow and Company, 1990); Bob Corbin, in discussion with Jack L. August Jr., April 2, 2001, author's files.

2. Arizona legislature, Legislative Council. *Report on Impeachment of Public Officers* (Phoenix, Arizona. State of Arizona, 1987).

3. Fife Symington, in discussion with Jack L. August Jr., March 13, 2015, author's files; Fife Symington, in discussion with Robert Nelson, June 26, 2017, author's files; Grant Woods, in discussion with Jack L. August Jr., March 19, 2014, author's files; Peter Hayes, in discussion with Robert Nelson, July 25, 2018, author's files; Richard Mallery, in discussion with Robert Nelson, January 12, 2018, author's files; Fife Symington letter to Barry Goldwater, April 2, 1988, Folder 1988–1990, Symington Papers; *Tucson Citizen,* April 13, 1989; *Arizona Daily Star,* April 13, 1989; *Arizona Republic,* April 20, 1989; Wes Gullett, oral history interview by Jack L. August Jr., Phoenix, Arizona, February 19, 2014, author's files.

4. Ann Symington, in discussion with Robert Nelson, April 18, 2018, author's files; Sam Stanton, "Developer Symington may seek governorship," *Arizona Republic,* April 12, 1989; Whitney Morgan, oral history interview by Jack L. August Jr., December 11, 2015, Pasadena, California, author's files.

5. Ann Symington, discussion with Nelson, April 18, 2018, author's files; Fife Symington, in discussion with Robert Nelson, February 16, 2018, author's files; Morgan, oral history interview by August, December 11, 2015, author's files; Fife Symington IV, in discussion with Jack L. August Jr., November 29, 2015, author's files.

6. Fife Symington letter to Shimizu Land Development Corporation, Folder 1988–1989, Symington Papers.

7. Don Harris, "Symington enters governor's race, attacks Mecham: Foe deserves 'poke in nose,' developer says," *Arizona Republic*, April 13, 1989.

8. Bruce Merrill, in discussion with Jack L. August Jr., June 12, 2014, author's files.

9. Steve Meissner, "Rep. Noland criticizes Mofford, both parties," *Arizona Daily Star*, June 21, 1989.

10. Steve Meissner, "Mofford tops '90 Demo poll; GOP favorite isn't clear-cut," *Arizona Daily Star*, January 25, 1989.

## CHAPTER 11: DEBACLE AND DEPRESSION

1. See Terry Greene Sterling, "The Loan Wolf," *Phoenix New Times*, October 9, 1991; Nathaniel C. Nash, "Arizona is Lost, Next is San Francisco," *New York Times*, May 7, 1989; Tom Furlong, "Westwood Savings Among 25 S&Ls Taken Over by Regulators," *Los Angeles Times*, February 18, 1989.

2. Martin Lowy, in discussion with Robert Nelson, September 22, 2017, author's files; see Martin Lowy, *High Rollers: Inside the Savings and Loan Debacle* (New York, New York: Greenwood Publishing Group, 1991).

3. See Walter Mattern, "Key Circle Ks to offer automatic tellers: S&Ls and stores foresee benefits with offerings of food and finance," *Arizona Republic*, April 25, 1982. Mattern's story describes a novel high-tech method for S&Ls and convenience stores to boost revenues—ATMs. That same issue of the *Republic* included several half- and full-page ads in which Arizona thrifts attempted to lure customers with favorable interest rates and exciting benefits.

4. Lowy, *High Rollers*, 191–96.

5. Rose Kushmeider, "The U.S. Federal Financial Regulatory System," a publication of the Federal Deposit Insurance Corporation, January 1, 2006; see also Michael Dotsey and Anatoli Kuprianov, "Reforming Deposit Insurance: Lessons from the Savings and Loan Crisis," *Economic Review*, March/April 1990.

6. *Arizona Republic*, October 22, 1988; *Arizona Daily Star*, October 21, 1988. The *Daily Star* story noted that Pinnacle West Capital Corp., one of the largest holding companies in the Valley, reported a 38 percent decrease in net earnings in the third quarter of 1988 compared to the same period in 1987, mostly due, according to company officials, "to the downturn in the Phoenix real estate market."

7. See Norman Strunk, *Where Deregulation went Wrong: A Look at the Causes behind Savings and Loan Failures in the 1980s* (Chicago: United States League of Savings Institutions, 1988); see also David Mason, *From Building and Loans to Bail-Outs: A History of the American Savings and Loan Industry, 1831–1989*, PhD dissertation, Ohio State University, 2001.

8. See David Holland, *When Regulation Was Too Successful: The Sixth Decade of Deposit Insurance* (Westport, Connecticut: Greenwood Publishing Group, 1998).

9. Jack L. August Jr., *Senator Dennis DeConcini: From the Center of the Aisle* (Tucson, Arizona: University of Arizona Press, 2006).

## CHAPTER 12: THE RACE IS ON

1. Fife Symington, in discussion with Robert Nelson, May 9, 2019, author's files; Peter Hayes, in discussion with Robert Nelson, July 25, 2018, author's files; Grant Woods, in discussion with Jack L. August Jr., March 19, 2014, author's files; Mary Jo Pitzl, in discussion with Jack L. August Jr., February 22, 2014, author's files.

2. *Arizona Republic*, April 20, 1989. The story noted that Kolbe still planned to wait several weeks to announce a candidacy, which one political observer described as "the longest political striptease" in Arizona history.

3. "Symington blasts Mecham, vows to offer an option for 'normal, decent' GOP voters," *Arizona Daily Star*, June 18, 1989.

4. Symington, discussion with Nelson, February 16, 2018, author's files.

5. E. J. Montini, "A red-blooded tag for a blue blood: J.F. 'Bubba' Symington," *Arizona Republic*, April 14, 1989.

6. Stephanie Mansfield, "The Rise and Gall of Roger Stone," *Washington Post*, June 16, 1986; see Janet Reitman, "Roger Stone Opens Up About Russia, Mueller, Trump and What's Next," *Rolling Stone*, May 22, 2018. Reitman's story documents Stone's notorious career up through his involvement in the campaign of President Donald Trump.

7. Anne Q. Hoy and Don Harris, "State GOP to insist study be dropped: Gloomy prediction on gubernatorial race angers Arizona Party," *Arizona Republic*, May 4, 1989. In the story, Burt Kruglick, the state Republican Party Chairman, admitted that he had agreed to allow Stone to survey the state's political landscape if the finding would be discussed privately. "The remarks in Wednesday's *Republic* broke that agreement," Kruglick said.

8. The *Republic* editorial on May 15, 1989, went on to quote a story in the *New Republic* in which Stone was described as a "state-of-the-art sleazeball." The editorial says RNC officials were considering replacing Stone because of the Arizona incident.

9. See also Jeffrey Toobin, "The Dirty Trickster," *The New Yorker*, June 2, 2008. "For nearly forty years," Toobin wrote in 2008, "Stone has hovered around Republican and national politics, both near the center and at the periphery. At times, mostly during the Reagan years, he was a political consultant and lobbyist who, in conventional terms, was highly successful, working for such politicians as Bob Dole and Tom Kean. Even then, though, Stone regularly crossed the line between respectability and ignominy, and he has become better known for leading a colorful personal life than for landing big-time clients."

10. Whitney Morgan, in discussion with Jack L. August Jr., December 11, 2015, author's files; Ann Symington, in discussion with Robert Nelson, April 18, 2018, author's files; Angelica Pence and Alisa Wabnik, "Scandal takes toll on Ann Symington," *Arizona Daily Star*, June 16, 1996; Campaign flier titled "For Arizona's Families and Our Children's Future," Folder 1989–1991, Symington Papers.

11. Folder 1989–1991, Symington Papers; "Symington urges drug-use designation for state," *Arizona Daily Star*, October 11, 1989.

12. Howard Fischer, "Fife Symington Has a Welfare Plan for Keith Turley," *Phoenix New Times*, September 6, 1989. Two years later, Fischer started Capitol Media Services, which continues to provide state government news content to many of the state's newspapers. Fischer has long carried the unofficial title of "Dean of the Arizona Press Corps." Symington's relationship with *New Times* would become uniquely acrimonious in the years to follow.

13. "The Symington Plan," Folder 1989–1991, Symington Papers; Doug Cole, in discussion with Robert Nelson, June 18, 2020. In the interview, the veteran Arizona political consultant and former Symington press secretary argued that the Symington Plan may still be the "most comprehensive policy-rich statement of a candidate's position" in the state's political history. "It's still used as a template when we develop campaigns today," said Cole, now chief operating officer of HighGround Public Affairs Consultants. "That document defines Symington's whole governorship," Cole said.

14. See Andrew Ross, *Bird on Fire: Lessons from the World's Least Sustainable City* (New York, New York: Oxford University Press, 2011).

15. Symington, discussion with Nelson, February 16, 2018, author's files; Hayes, discussion with Nelson, July 25, 2018, author's files.

16. Symington, discussion with Nelson, June 26, 2017, author's files; Hayes, discussion with Nelson, July 25, 2018, author's files; Pitzl, discussion with August, February 22, 2014, author's files.

17. *Tucson Citizen*, January 19, 1990.

18. "Poll says Symington ahead in race," *Tucson Citizen*, January 26, 1990. The Behavior Research Center poll found that 20 percent of the Republican voters questioned would vote for Symington compared to 12 percent for Mecham. "However," the story continued, "among voters considered most likely to go to the polls, the race appears tighter, with Symington supported by 22 percent and Mecham supported by 18 percent." Fifty-six percent of those polled said they were undecided.

CHAPTER 13: "SAME OLD EV"

1. Martin Van Der Werf, "Meet candidate Fred 'Cory': GOP's Koory struggling in governor race," *Arizona Republic*, June 23, 1990.
2. Evan Mecham, *Wrongful Impeachment* (Phoenix, Arizona: Prime News Press, 1999); Ronald Watkins, *High Crimes and Misdemeanors: The Term and Trials of Evan Mecham* (Phoenix: Amazon Digital Books, 2011).
3. "The One Sure Thing About Steiger," *Arizona Republic*, August 30, 1990.
4. Peter Hayes, in discussion with Robert Nelson, July 25, 2018, author's files.
5. Mike Ullery, "Symington plan another form of debt," *Arizona Republic*, May 1, 1990; Sue Ciulla, "Another wacky idea from another developer," *Arizona Republic*, May 1, 1990.
6. Mary Jo Pitzl, "Symington aims at new target," *Arizona Republic*, July 3, 1990. A paragraph in Pitzl's piece noted a campaign gaffe that contradicted the image Symington was working to project: "One political observer," Pitzl wrote, "said Symington mistakenly reinforced his blue-blood image when the press packet accompanying his gubernatorial announcement included a *Phoenix Magazine* article describing him as 'one of Arizona's wealthiest developers.'"
7. Mary Jo Pitzl, "Symington aims at new target: Goddard now key opponent, not Mecham," *Arizona Republic*, July 3, 1990; Joseph Garcia, "GOP candidates for governor wallow in the mud," *Tucson Citizen*, July 6, 1990.
8. Symington for Governor campaign press release, "Remarks by Fife Symington," August 23, 1990, Folder 1989–1991, Symington Papers.
9. *Arizona Daily Star*, September 13, 1990; *Arizona Republic*, September 13, 1990.
10. *Chicago Tribune*, September 13, 1990.
11. Hayes, discussion with Nelson, July 25, 2018; Folder 1989–1991, Symington Papers; Fife Symington, in discussion with Jack L. August Jr., October 13, 2016, author's files.
12. Ann Symington, in discussion with Robert Nelson, April 18, 2018, author's files; Fife Symington, in discussion with Robert Nelson, June 26, 2017, author's files.

CHAPTER 14: A BLUR OF PLURALITY

1. "Proposition 105: Change to runoff only seems like a good idea," *Arizona Daily Star*, November 5, 1988. "On reflection," the editorial writer suggested, "the measure does not guarantee a mandate for those offices and could actually promote independent candidacies."
2. Fife Symington, in discussion with Robert Nelson, author's files, February 16, 2018.
3. Jim Howard, in discussion with Robert Nelson, author's files, February 26, 2018.
4. *Arizona Republic*, September 15, 1990; "Goddard, Symington showing differences," *Arizona Daily Sun*, September 23, 1990.
5. Howard, discussion with Nelson, February 26, 2018; Symington, discussion with Nelson, February 28, 2018; Peter Hayes, in discussion with Robert Nelson, July 25, 2018; Grant Woods, in discussion with Jack L. August Jr., March 19, 2014. All author's files.
6. Martin Van Der Werf, "Goddard, Symington draw distinctions," *Arizona Republic*, September 21, 1990.
7. E. J. Montini, "Candidates have voters seeing double," *Arizona Republic*, September 19, 1990. Montini set up his satirical quiz with this intro: "It has come to my attention that, in the minds of some Arizona residents, a few minor questions remain to be answered before voters . . . will be able to choose between the two major candidates for governor: Mr Goddard and Mr. Symington. Questions such as, 'Which one is which?'"
8. Peter Aleshire, "Governor hopefuls have Harvard ties of different stripes," *Arizona Republic*, October 7, 1990. The *Republic* sent Aleshire to Harvard to report the story. Aleshire led his piece with a Cambridge scene from many years prior: "J. Fife Symington III clutched the brown paper bag in which he was hiding his Air Force ROTC uniform and hurried, furtive, frustrated and fuming, past the ivy-choked halls of Harvard. He brushed through swirls of liberals, like drifts of New

England leaves. Just across the way, on the sparkling meander of the Charles River, Samuel Pearson Goddard III stroked his heart out in what may have been the world's second-fastest rowboat."

9. *Arizona Republic*, September 30, 1990. The *Republic*'s editorial page echoed Symington's sentiments regarding Proposition 103. "Where is the money coming from? No one has the foggiest idea, and neither the proposition nor its proponents offer any clues," the editorial claimed.

10. *Arizona Daily Star*, September 30, 1990. "On Monday," the *Star* story on a recent campaign event noted, "Symington's charge that Goddard, a bachelor, has no understanding of family values was . . . poorly received by the audience." "The candidate may have crossed the razor-thin line between acceptable attack and mean-spirited smear."

11. Symington, discussion with Nelson, February 16, 2018, author's files; Symington for Governor '90 campaign literature, Folder 1989–1991, Symington Papers.

12. Symington, discussion with Nelson, June 4, 2019, author's files.

13. *Tucson Citizen*, November 7, 1990; *Arizona Republic*, November 10, 1990.

14. Symington, discussion with Nelson, June 26, 2017; Ann Symington, in discussion with Robert Nelson, April 18, 2018. All author's files.

15. Mary Jo Pitzl, "Symington seeking to cut 'noise' of race," *Arizona Republic*, November 20, 1990. Goddard didn't think much of Symington's pause, telling Pitzl, "I think it's absurd for somebody to stand up and say the issues of Arizona stop just because he wants to go on vacation."

CHAPTER 15: ONE MORE TIME

1. Jim Howard, in discussion with Robert Nelson, July 2, 2018, author's files.

2. "Arizona Needs a Governor with Strong Business Skills," Symington For Governor '90 campaign flier, Folder 1989–1991, Symington Papers.

3. Fife Symington, in discussion with Jack L. August Jr., October 13, 2016; Fife Symington, in discussion with Robert Nelson, February 16, 2018; Peter Hayes, in discussion with Robert Nelson, July 25, 2018.

4. See Norman Strunk, *Where Deregulation went Wrong: A Look at the Causes behind Savings and Loan Failures in the 1980s* (Chicago: United States League of Savings Institutions, 1988); see also David Mason, *From Building and Loans to Bail-Outs: A History of the American Savings and Loan Industry, 1831–1989*, PhD dissertation, Ohio State University, 2001; see also David Holland, *When Regulation Was Too Successful: The Sixth Decade of Deposit Insurance* (Westport, Connecticut: Greenwood Publishing Group, 1998); Michael Binstein and Charles Bowden, *Trust Me: Charles Keating and the Missing Billions* (New York, New York: Random House, 1993).

5. Helen Dewar, "Cranston Accepts Reprimand: 'Keating 5' Senator Angers Colleagues by Denying Misconduct," *Washington Post*, November 21, 1991; Robert Rosenblatt and Sara Fritz, "McCain Probed Over Traveling to Keating Spa Thrifts," *Los Angeles Times*, January 5, 1991.

6. "Walter Robinson, "Pluck, leaks help McCain to overcome S&L scandal," *The Boston Globe*, February 29, 2000.

7. Symington, discussion with August, April 20, 2016, author's files; Symington, discussion with Nelson, June 26, 2017; John Dowd, in discussion with Robert Nelson, March 2, 2017.

8. Symington, discussion with August, October 16, 2016, author's files; Symington, discussion with Nelson, June 26, 2017 and February 16, 2018; Dowd, discussion with Nelson, March 2, 2017, author's files.

9. See "Failed Savings and Loan Investigation: Members of the General Oversight and Investigations Panel convened to look at the relationship of Arizona Governor Fife Symington with the Southwest Savings and Loan Association," C-Span Video Library, https://www.c-span.org/video/?24555-1/failed-savings-loan-investigation, February 20, 1992. This five-hour-plus hearing included more than two and a half hours of testimony under oath by Symington. The hearing offers a uniquely detailed look into the allegations against Southwest and Symington and the response of Symington and others accused of improper dealings.

10. Martin Van Der Werf, "Symington accused of loan conflict," *Arizona Republic*, February

8, 1991. Van Der Werf's story was accompanied by a photo of Metzenbaum pointing his finger at Symington during the Senate Judiciary Committee hearing in Washington, DC.

11. See William J. Eaton, "Personality in the News: Hearings put Metzenbaum in Spotlight: Senate: The lawmaker has been aggressive in his questioning of Thomas and Gates. As the liberal point man, he has drawn protests from the GOP," *Los Angeles Times*, September 19, 1991.

12. See "Relationship of Arizona Governor J. Fife Symington III with Southwest Savings and Loan Association: hearing before the Subcommittee on General Oversight and Investigations of the Committee on Banking, Finance, and Urban Affairs, House of Representatives, 102nd Congress, second session, February 20, 1992," U.S. G.P.O.: For sale by the U.S. G.P.O., Supt. of Docs., Congressional Sales Office 1992.

13. See also Lee Davidson, "Hatch wants probe of S&Ls that are linked to Democrats," *Deseret News*, March 10, 1991. The story explains how Sen. Orrin Hatch of Utah joined Sen. Robert Dole in pushing the Metzenbaum-led Senate Judiciary subcommittee on antitrust, monopolies, and business rights to investigate two failed S&Ls tied to prominent Democrats. "They are especially bitter about a Feb. 7 hearing on Southwest Savings & Loan of Phoenix," Davidson wrote, "which Republicans felt was an attempt to wound Republican Fife Symington."

14. See "Finances dogging Goddard," *Arizona Republic*, February 23, 1991. The *Republic* story provides extensive detail regarding Goddard's bank and thrift dealings, which primarily involved relatively modest home loans. In the story, Goddard vehemently denied any wrongdoing.

15. Howard, discussion with Nelson, September 12, 2018, author's files; Jeff Herr, "Late returns crush Goddard hopes, again," *Arizona Daily Star*, February 28, 1991. Goddard told Herr the reason he believed he had lost. "Arizona politics are dominated by the retirement communities. I clearly couldn't break through with them."

16. Mary Jo Pitzl, "Pima, rural and Valley vote keyed Symington win," *Arizona Republic*, February 28, 1991.

17. Laura Laughlin, "Rich GOP Developer Symington Wins Arizona Governor Runoff," *Los Angeles Times*, February 28, 1991.

18. Symington, discussion with Nelson, June 26, 2017, author's files; Doug Cole, in discussion with Robert Nelson, December 5, 2018, author's files; Douglas Kreutz, "Symington, Goddard wheeze to the finish line after long, grueling race," *Arizona Daily Star*, February 27, 1991.

19. Brent Whiting, "NFL celebrates King Day," *Arizona Republic*, February 19, 1991.

20. "Arizona finally gets a governor: Symington wins," *Tucson Citizen*, February 27, 1991.

CHAPTER 16: THE ROOKIE

1. Arizona State University Library, Fife Symington, "The Inaugural Address," High Density Storage Collection, Stacks GV 1.2:I 51 S 95.

2. Mary K. Reinhart, "Symington becomes governor: Promises to reduce government, aid kids," *Arizona Daily Star*, March 7, 1991; Keven Willey, "Sun shines for Symington's 10-minute honeymoon," *Arizona Republic*, March 7, 1991; "The inauguration: A new beginning," *Arizona Republic*, March 7, 1991. KTAR, the leading news radio station in Arizona, broadcast the entire inauguration ceremony. The day of the inauguration, the station ran a promotional advertisement for their extended coverage in the *Republic* that read "Inaugu-radio: Hear Fife Symington's 'Golden Plan' for the 'Copper State' today at 11 on KTAR!"

3. *Arizona Daily Star*, March 7, 1991. The *Star* ran lengthy excerpts of the inauguration speeches, including former Gov. Bruce Babbitt's advice to Symington: "The time goes by very quickly. You'll be remembered only for one or two things. Figure out what those are early on, pursue them and keep after them. Because you're not governor for very long."

4. Doug Cole, in discussion with Robert Nelson, December 5, 2018, author's files; Fife Symington, in discussion with Jack L. August Jr., October 13, 2016, author's files; Fife Symington, in discussion with Robert Nelson, June 26, 2017, author's files.

5. Ed Foster and Mary Jo Pitzl, "Governor aims knife at colleges: Also announces study to 'slim'

406

13 agencies," *Arizona Republic,* April 5, 1991; Keven Willey, "Cutting remarks get budget party off to a good start," *Arizona Republic,* April 9, 1991.

6. Keven Willey, "Symington's moves so far make it hard for Democrats to hate him," *Arizona Republic,* May 7, 1991; Keven Willey, "House budget vote may be beginning of end of session," *Arizona Republic,* April 18, 1991.

7. Howard Fischer, "New Legislature faces tough budget choices," *The Business Journal,* January 7, 1991; see Robert James Esse, *The Budget Process in Arizona State Government: A Layman's Handbook of Budgeting Procedures, with a Glossary of Related Terminology* (Tempe, Arizona: Arizona State University, 1977). This little book has been a primer for citizens, journalists, and numerous freshman members of the Arizona house and senate.

8. "House of Representatives. Summary of Appropriations and Legislation," Arizona State University Library, available in the High Density Collection Stacks (LG 3.3:S 85).

9. Keith Bagwell, "State to buy Ensco plant," *Arizona Daily Star,* May 4, 1991. Bagwell described this scene: "Environmentalists opposed to the facility were jubilant after Symington's Capitol-tower news conference, jumping up and down, and hugging each other. 'We're very shocked, but exalted, pleased,' said Marlene Stephens of Don't Waste Arizona, a group formed to oppose the Ensco facility and the company's plans to import and incinerate wastes."

10. See Thad L. Beyle, *Governors and Hard Times* (Washington, DC: C.Q. Press, 1992). In his book, Beyle analyzes the efforts of several governors as they attempted to tackle budget shortfalls in their state, including, as Beyle called it, "the CEO approach of J. Fife Symington III."

11. Bruce Merrill, a professor at Arizona State University, was the longtime director of the Media Research Center at ASU's Walter Cronkite School of Journalism. KAET-TV (Channel 8) provided funding for many of Merrill's telephone polls throughout Symington's tenure. Jack L. August Jr. conducted an extensive oral history interview with Merrill, who conducted polls of Arizonans for nearly forty years, shortly before Merrill's death in 2016.

12. Mary Jo Pitzl, "100 days: Symington in command: Pace impresses even critics," *Arizona Republic,* June 9, 1991; Mary Jo Pitzl, in discussion with Jack L. August Jr., February 22, 2014, author's files.

13. Ken Western, "Trade-pact hearings spur pros, cons: Arizona state big in U.S.-Mexican plan," *Arizona Republic,* April 9, 1991.

Chapter 17: On a Roll

1. Fife Symington, in discussion with Jack L. August Jr., September 12, 2015, author's files; Fife Symington, in discussion with Robert Nelson, September 12, 2017, author's files.

2. Mary Jo Pitzl, in discussion with Jack L. August Jr., February 22, 2014, author's files; Symington, discussion with Nelson, February 16, 2018, author's files; Doug Cole, in discussion with Robert Nelson, December 5, 2018, author's files; Peter Hayes, in discussion with Robert Nelson, July 25, 2018, author's files; "Symington's Inner Circle," *Arizona Republic,* February 28, 1991. The day after his election win, Symington had the following campaign staffers moving to government staff positions, according to the *Republic:* Bunny Badertscher, George Leckie, Douglas Cole, Susan Marler, Gerard Tobin, Kala Pearson, Annette Alvarez, Chris Herstam, Jacqueline Vieh, James Marsh, Lt. Col. Gary S. Phelps, Dennis O'Connor, Charline Franz, Bruce Mayberry, and Elliot Hibbs. Six of the staffers had their new job listed as "undefined position."

3. "Symington fills three administration posts," *Tucson Citizen,* March 9, 1991. Pearson came to Symington's staff from the powerful law firm of Snell & Wilmer, taking the title of "executive assistant for environment and natural resources."

4. "Governor's Task Force on Education Reform," *Arizona Republic,* June 23, 1991.

5. "Arizonans rush to aid America West," Associated Press, June 29, 1991. When filing for Chapter 11 protection from creditors, America West listed $1.7 billion in assets and $1.3 billion in liabilities.

6. Richard Mallery, in discussion with Jack L. August Jr., December 9, 2015; Richard Mallery, in

discussion with Robert Nelson, March 21, 2018; Symington, discussion with August, April 20, 2016; Symington, discussion with Nelson, May 9, 2019. All author's files.

7. Dawn Gilbertson and Kerry Fehr, "America West gets breathing room," *Phoenix Gazette*, August 19, 1992; Symington, discussion with August, April 20, 2016, author's files; Symington, discussion with Nelson, February 16, 2018, author's files; Mallery, discussion with August, December 9, 2015, author's files; Mallery, discussion with Nelson, March 19, 2019, author's files; Richard Mallery, *Loving Life: A Memoir* (Phoenix, Legacy West Media, 2018).

8. Barbara Deters, "Symington touts trade," *Arizona Republic*, March 9, 1991.

9. See Jon Talton's *Phoenix 101: The Nineties*, https://www.roguecolumnist.com/rogue_columnist/2018/01/phoenix-101-the-nineties.html. The longtime business journalist and author of twelve books extensively explores the history and politics of Phoenix on his website, roguecolumnist.com.

10. "Office to help business with trade in Mexico," *Arizona Republic*, June 29, 1991; Steve Meissner, "Trade pact viewed as boon for Tucson," *Arizona Daily Star*, October 5, 1991.

11. "Symington's aid: Nobody is shocked, but everyone is interested," *Arizona Daily Star*, October 25, 1991.

12. "Symington supports free trade accord with visit to Mexico City," Associated Press, *Arizona Daily Star*, June 20, 1991.

13. See James Amedeo, "Lessons from the America-Japan Trade War of the 1980s," *The National Interest*, July 2, 2018; Tracey Samuelson, "How the U.S. outgrew 1980s trade anxiety of Japan," *Marketplace*, November 29, 2018; Ken Western, "Japanese need to see 'real' state, study says: Key to tourism is awareness," *Arizona Republic*, September 15, 1991.

14. According to the Arizona Department of Commerce, Mexico was Arizona's top international trade partner, followed by Canada, Japan, United Kingdom, Malaysia, Germany, Taiwan, France, Korea, and The Netherlands.

15. "Trade office in Japan sought," Associated Press, October 4, 1991.

16. Jeff Herr, "Symington to lead trade delegation to 'priority' Japan," *Arizona Daily Star*, September 18, 1991.

17. Symington, discussion with Nelson, May 9, 2019, author's files; Mallery, discussion with August, December 9, 2015, author's files.

18. See John Dougherty, "The Governor and the Lawyer," *Phoenix New Times*, June 20, 1996. Longtime Valley investigative reporter John Dougherty produced many of the most detailed newspaper pieces on Symington's business and other dealings throughout his administration. Dougherty's June 1996 article is one of the few stories detailing Symington and Mallery's long business relationship. Dougherty would later develop a famously testy relationship with Symington's attorney, John Dowd; see Paul Rubin, "Governor Fife Symington's onetime Criminal Attorney, Blowhardian John Dowd, Loses Cool on Camera," *Phoenix New Times*, May 12, 2011. Rubin details a contentious meeting at the *Mesa Tribune* offices in which Dowd and Dougherty almost came to blows (or almost didn't, depending on who describes the scene). Dougherty left the *Tribune* soon after the contentious meeting and began writing for the *Phoenix New Times*.

19. "Symington failing to repay loan, may lose Mercado," *Arizona Republic*, September 19, 1991; "Loan default could cost governor 3 Phoenix projects," Associated Press, September 20, 1991. In the story, then press secretary Doug Cole and Symington's development attorney, Richard Mallery, said they expected "the financial problems plaguing The Mercado and two Symington-developed office buildings to be resolved soon." Cole told reporters, "These three properties are very vulnerable. The governor stands a good chance of losing all of them. But three of 12 or 13 (properties) is a very good track record in this market."

20. "Polls show public losing confidence," *Tucson Citizen*, October 21, 1991. According to the story, "Arizonans, who had been giving Gov. Fife Symington high marks for his performance, now are becoming less enthused about his performance as Arizona's chief executive, according to two polls released over the weekend."

21. Symington, discussion with Nelson, June 26, 2017, author's files.

22. Cole, discussion with Nelson, December 5, 2018, author's files.

CHAPTER 18: THE DEVIL IS ALLEGEDLY IN THE DETAILS

1. See *Resolution Trust Corp. v. Dean*, 813 F. Supp. 1426 (United States District Court, D. Ariz., 1993); see also *History of the Eighties—Lessons for the Future: An Examination of the Banking Crises of the 1980s and Early 1990s* (Washington, DC: Federal Deposit Insurance Corporation, 1997).

2. Terry Greene Sterling, "The Loan Wolf," *Phoenix New Times*, October 9, 1991. Key to the story was an interview with a young former FDIC attorney, Mark Hollander, who claimed he had been told not to pursue the case against Southwest by his superiors. Beyond Hollander's accusations, Greene Sterling's long-form piece offered extensive detail on the history of Southwest and Symington's relationship with the thrift, as well as lengthy verbatim passages from letters between Southwest officials and regulators as they discussed the loan regarding the Friedman land. (Sterling later became a Writer-in-Residence and frequent lecturer in ASU's Walter Cronkite School of Journalism and Mass Communications.) See story at https://www.phoenixnewtimes.com/news/the-loan-wolf-6429906.

3. John Dowd to Jeff Bruce and John Dougherty of the *Mesa Tribune*, December 27, 1991, Folder 1989–1991, Symington Papers; Jay Smith to Doug MacEachern, the *Mesa Tribune*, March 13, 1992, Folder 1992–1994, Symington Papers; John Dowd to Jeff Bruce and John Dougherty, January 27, 1992, Folder 1992–1994, Symington Papers; John Dowd to Hal DeKeyser, the *Mesa Tribune*, September 28, 1992, Folder 1992–1994, Symington Papers; Daniel Barr, Brown & Bain (the attorneys for the *Mesa Tribune*) to John Dowd, March 20, 1992, Folder 1992–1994, Symington Papers. This collection of letters offers a fascinating glimpse into Dowd and Smith's aggressive response to newspaper stories regarding the RTC suit and the September 1991 document leak. Smith's letter, on Smith & Harroff letterhead, accuses writers at the newspaper of misstating details of the case, then ends with a reference to the heated meeting at the *Tribune* offices in which Smith, Dowd, and Dougherty argued and, by some accounts, nearly came to blows. At issue: Who first suggested to "step outside" to fight. "Regarding the meeting you (MacEachern) describe at the Tribune involving John Dougherty," Smith wrote, "you state that I 'leaped' to my feet and challenged Dougherty to 'walk outside.' Next you state that 'Smith has publicly contended since then that it was the reporter who challenged him.' When did I say publicly that it was Dougherty who challenged me? The *New Times* article (which to my knowledge, is the only published account of the meeting) suggests that it was I who challenged Dougherty to 'go outside.' I am not quoted in that story disputing their version. In fact, the *New Times* quotes me as saying, 'I certainly don't want to take shots at Mr. Dougherty, verbal or otherwise.'"

4. Ronald Glover, "In Arizona, The Scandals Keep On Coming," Bloomberg News, October 14, 1991; see John Dougherty, "Fife's New Tune: Governor's Jihad Against the RTC has Become a Technical Defense," *Phoenix New Times*, March 24, 1993. This is one of Dougherty's earlier pieces for *New Times* after leaving the *Mesa Tribune* following the fracas with Smith and Dowd in the *Tribune* offices.

5. Fife Symington, in discussion with Robert Nelson, February 16, 2017; Randy Todd, in discussion with Robert Nelson, September 25, 2017, all author's files.

6. Letter from Jay Smith to Doug MacEachern, March 13, 1992, Folder 1992–1994, Symington Papers.

7. "U.S. to file S&L Lawsuit Against Arizona Governor," *New York Times*, December 16, 1991.

8. "Governor of Arizona, 11 Others Sued," *Los Angeles Times*, December 17, 1991; see "Relationship of Arizona Governor J. Fife Symington III with Southwest Savings and Loan Association: Hearing Before the Subcommittee on General Oversight and Investigations of the Committee on Banking, Finance and Urban Affairs, House of Representatives, One Hundred Second Congress, Second Session, February 20, 1992" (Washington, DC: US Government Printing Office, 1992). In this hearing, FDIC and RTC top officials lay out the claims against Symington. Symington and

Dowd then appear before the committee to refute the claims. This report contains a collection of Southwest Symington-related documents that Dowd asked be included in the record of the hearing; Also see James T. Pitts, Eric W. Bloom, and Monique M. Vasilchick, "FDIC/RTC Suits Against Bank and Thrift Officers and Directors: Why Now, What's Left," *Fordham Law Review*, Issue 6, 1995. Available at: https://ir.lawnet.fordham.edu/flr/vol63/iss6/4.

9. Susan Schmidt, "The Governor Vs. RTC," *Washington Post*, February 1, 1992. "If it wins, Uncle Sam hopes to reach into some very deep pockets to recover money for taxpayers," Schmidt wrote. "And one of those pockets belongs to the governor of Arizona."

10. See "Resolution Trust Corporation 1991 Annual Report. Available at https://fraser.stlouisfed.org/files/docs/publications/rtc/ar_rtc_1991.pdf.

11. Folder 1989–1991, Symington Papers; Todd, discussion with Nelson, September 25, 2017.

12. Don Harris, "Esplanade: World class or albatross?" *Arizona Republic*, December 20, 1991. Harris's story offered an in-depth look at the Phoenix commercial real estate market at the time, as well as numerous opinions on the financial viability of the Camelback Esplanade and its Ritz-Carlton hotel.

13. Todd, discussion with Nelson, September 25, 2017; Symington, discussion with Nelson, September 25, 2017, both author's files; Symington Company internal memos, Folder 1989–1991, Symington Papers.

14. "Response of Governor Fife Symington to RTC Allegations," Folder 1989–1991, Symington Papers. This fourteen-page document was read to reporters before copies were given out to all print, radio, and television reporters. Symington closely followed the points in this response when speaking before a US House of Representatives subcommittee three months later.

15. See "Relationship of Arizona Governor J. Fife Symington III with Southwest Savings and Loan Association: Hearing Before the Subcommittee on General Oversight and Investigations of the Committee on Banking, Finance and Urban Affairs, House of Representatives, One Hundred Second Congress, Second Session, February 20, 1992" (Washington, DC: US Government Printing Office, 1992).

16. "Minutes of the Board Meeting, Southwest Savings and Loan Association," September 21, 1983, Folder 1989–1991, Symington Papers; "Certified Resolution, Regular Board of Directors," Southwest Savings and Loan Association, December 29, 1983, Folder 1991–1993, Symington Papers. The Certified Resolution, a notarized document required by federal regulators, includes, albeit in vague language, reference to "a Letter of Credit in the amount of $5,450,000 from the Arizona Bank as required in the transaction." In the document to regulators, the line of credit is only referred to as "other considerations" in addition to land purchase price of $25.9 million. The property, according to this document, had an "MAI Appraisal of $31,575,000." The resolution, wrote secretary Karen Bateman, was approved at a "September 21, 1983" meeting "at which all directors except Mr. Symington voted."

17. See https://www.c-span.org/video/?24555-1/failed-savings-loan-investigation. In this five-hour hearing, the major complaints of both the RTC and Symington are aired before the US House subcommittee tasked with overseeing the FDIC and RTC investigation. This hearing, available in its entirety from CSPAN's website, is a unique opportunity to see Symington, Dowd, and RTC officials state their cases in detail. A side note: The subcommittee's chairman, Rep. Carroll Hubbard, was embroiled in the House banking scandal known as "Rubbergate" at the time of the Symington hearing. Hubbard, a Democrat from Kentucky, spent nearly three years in federal prison after pleading guilty to campaign finance law violations. At the time of the Symington hearing, Hubbard claimed years later, he was serving as an informant for the FBI in their attempt to obtain evidence against other House members. In several cases, Hubbard claimed, he wore a hidden recorder strapped to his body while talking to fellow House members as part of the FBI's investigation of abuses of the House Bank. In 2019, Hubbard switched parties in a failed attempt to win a state legislative seat as a Republican.

18. Donald Lewis, president and CEO of Southwest Savings, letter to Charles Deardorff, vice

president, Supervision Department, Federal Home Loan Bank, San Francisco regarding "Southwest Savings' Director J. Fife Symington, III," Folder 1989–1991, Symington Papers. In the five-page letter, dated December 2, 1983, Lewis, after describing the Esplanade project and Symington's role on the board of directors and as the project's manager, asks for Deardorff's opinion whether Symington could remain in both roles as a Southwest director and Esplanade project manager. Lewis stated that Southwest officials had debated in recent meetings whether Symington's involvement in Southwest's dealings regarding the Esplanade project were a conflict of interest as described in Section 571.7 of the National Housing Act, or an extension of his duty as a board director to bring potentially lucrative projects to the institution as stated in 571.9 of the Act. In the letter, Lewis was clearly hoping Deardorff would agree with the board's final decision that Symington could, and should, remain involved.

19. Burke, Hansen & Homan, Inc.'s December 1, 1985, MAI Appraisal placed the value of the rezoned land at between $57 million and $70 million, Folder 1989–1991, Symington Papers.

20. Fife Symington, "Symington for the record," *Arizona Republic*, September 29, 1991.

21. "Missteps, miscues of Arizona Politics," *Los Angeles Times*, March 15, 1992. The *Times* story details Symington missteps from the year before, most notably his handling of issues surrounding staffer Annette Alvarez.

22. David J. Bodney, "The Price of Arrogance," *Phoenix New Times*, October 30, 1991; see also David J. Bodney, "I.O.U One, Governor," *Phoenix New Times*, September 25, 1991. Bodney has an unusual resume among newsweekly editors. Beyond *New Times*, Bodney, a Yale graduate who received his law degree from the University of Virginia, practiced media and constitutional law as a partner in the Phoenix office of Steptoe & Johnson LLP and has served as adjunct faculty at ASU's College of Law.

23. "Symington aide called unqualified," *Tucson Citizen*, October 23, 1991. This piece depended wholly on quotes from a *New Times* story earlier in the week.

24. William F. Rawson, "Travel log heavy for governor: Symington has made more than a dozen out-of-state trips," Associated Press, September 3, 1991.

25. Doug Cole, in discussion with Robert Nelson, December 5, 2018, author's files.

26. Fife Symington, in discussion with Jack L. August Jr., April 20, 2016, author's files; Symington, discussion with Nelson, June 4, 2019, author's files; Cole, discussion with Nelson, December 5, 2018, author's files.

27. Mark Shaffer, "Bush Meets War Pal," *Arizona Republic*, September 19, 1991; Robert Pear, "Bush Hikes in the Grand Canyon, Mixing Politics and Governance," *New York Times*, September 19, 1991.

28. Mark Shaffer, "Gulf queries pursue Bush at Canyon," *Arizona Republic*, September 19, 1991. Shaffer wrote: "George Bush's loafers were coated with dust. Sweat drenched the back of his shirt and poured from his brow. The president had just rapidly ascended almost 1,000 feet of steep switchbacks on the Grand Canyon's South Kaibab Trail, leaving many of his entourage to eat his dust." At one point in the hike, Shaffer wrote that Manual Lujan gasped, "I'll make it," to a passer-by as Lujan was "clutching a canyon wall."

29. Symington, discussion with Nelson, February 16, 2018, author's files.

## CHAPTER 19: A TALE OF TWO 1992S

1. Michael F. McNally, "It's time for the rest of us to recall Gov. Symington," *Arizona Republic*, March 27, 1992. McNally lists some of his complaints against the governor. "Maybe it's time for the rest of us to get our chance," he wrote.

2. Mary Jo Pitzl, "Symington recall drive runs down," *Arizona Republic*, July 18, 1992. McNally, Pitzl said, "has declined to show his petitions to outside parties so they could verify his count."

3. Mary K. Reinhart, "Aide repays Symington for trip to New York," *Arizona Daily Star*, March 27, 1992. Pollster Bruce Merrill said Symington's growing collection of troubles were beginning to cause the troubles Mecham faced as governor: "The tragedy for the state is that Fife is making the

same darn errors as Evan Mecham," Merrill said. "Mecham never had a chance to govern because he was putting out brush fire after brush fire." Symington brushed aside polls. In a January 20, 1992, interview with the *Tucson Citizen*, Symington responded to bad numbers in a KAET-TV poll by saying, "I don't read all their numbers. That's a Bruce Merrill poll, too. If you go back and check Bruce Merrill's numbers, he had me losing by 10 points when I was winning by 5 against Terry Goddard in the governor's race."

4. "Symington approval rating sinks below 36 percent," *Arizona Daily Star*, April 2, 1992. According to the story, Press Secretary Doug Cole said "it has proved difficult to convince the public that the charges leveled by the federal Resolution Trust Corp. are untrue."

5. Doug Cole, in discussion with Robert Nelson, December 5, 2018, author's files; Peter Hayes, in discussion with Robert Nelson, July 25, 2018, author's files; Jay Heiler, in discussion with Jack L. August Jr., February 2, 2014, author's files; Fife Symington, in discussion with Robert Nelson, September 12, 2017, author's files.

6. Mary K. Reinhart, "Aide repays Symington for trip to New York," *Arizona Daily Star*, March 27, 1992; David J. Bodney, "Why Fife's History," *Phoenix New Times*, April 1, 1992. Bodney's essay explores the history of questionable dealings surrounding Annette Alvarez and other issues while making this prediction: "If Symington's administration crumbles, it will be due to something small. Like a lie. Whether it's a white lie or The Big Lie doesn't really matter. What's gotten this governor a recall petition in record time and cost him the public confidence is the cover-up. Like I said, it's an old story."

7. "Leckie Controversies," *Arizona Republic*, May 22, 1992.

8. Symington, discussion with Nelson, May 9, 2019; Cole, discussion with Nelson, December 5, 2018; Fife Symington, in discussion with Jack L. August Jr., October 13, 2016, all author's files.

9. "Spotlight glares on Symington aide," *Arizona Republic*, May 22, 1992. "The governor has remained loyal to Leckie, whom he met a decade ago," the story read, to which the state Rep. Lisa Graham responded: "If this is loyalty, in the public arena it's been loyalty to a fault." As for Leckie, Graham suggested this: "When you're creating that kind of havoc for the person you're supposed to help, you leave."

10. David Bodney, "The Price of Arrogance," *Phoenix New Times*, October 30, 1991. In his piece about a number of complaints regarding Alvarez's qualification for the international trade job and her job performance, Bodney referred back to his reporting on the Alvarez campaign-era letter the week prior: "Does it matter whether Symington shared a bed with Alvarez? Should anyone care—apart from the participants themselves and the families caught in the crossfire—whether the intimacy was consummated? Not really. But people must ask related questions. Like, if Annette Alvarez lacked both the education and expertise to assume responsibility for the state's international trade . . . why would Symington appoint such a person?" Symington continued to deny this longstanding, underlying assumption that Alvarez was ill prepared for the job: "She did a tremendous job," Symington said in an early 2020 interview. "The press avoided reporting all the things she accomplished. That didn't fit their story. Her record speaks for itself."

11. Mary Jo Pitzl, in discussion with Jack L. August Jr., February 22, 2014, author's files.

12. "Leckie resigns," *Arizona Daily Star*, May 29, 1992. "George Leckie becomes the ninth member of Gov. Fife Symington's administration to resign, bowing to a string of controversies," according to the *Daily Star*.

13. Hayes, discussion with Nelson, July 25, 2018; Cole, discussion with Nelson, December 5, 2018; Symington, discussion with Nelson, March 13, 2021, all author's files.

14. Mary Jo Pitzl, "Symington aide Annette Alvarez calls it quits," *Arizona Republic*, March 31, 1992.

15. "Governor's aides: the good leaves, the bad stays," editorial, *Tucson Citizen*, May 23, 1992; Pitzl, discussion with August, February 22, 2014, author's files; Cole, discussion with Nelson, December 5, 2018, author's files; Hayes, discussion with Nelson, July 25, 2018, author's files. "Despite

OLD MONEY, NEW WEST

the smiling faces and positive words upon his departure," the *Citizen* editorial read, "we suspect Herstam feared there was no opportunity with Gov. Fife Symington."

16. Mary Jo Pitzl, "'Stabilizer' coming aboard: Top Symington aide regarded as nice guy and politics junkie," *Arizona Republic*, June 7, 1992. Pitzl wrote "Hayes' crazy-quilt of job experience crosses government and private-business lines, a mix that was pleasing to Symington"; Symington, discussion with Nelson, February 16, 2018, author's files; Hayes, discussion with Nelson, July 25, 2018, author's files; Cole, discussion with Nelson, December 5, 2019, author's files.

17. Heiler, discussion with August, February 2, 2014, author's files; Symington, discussion with Nelson, May 9, 2019, author's files.

18. Jay Heiler, in discussion with Robert Nelson, June 4, 2018, author's files.

19. Keven Willey, "Governor denies Quayle lobbied him," *Arizona Republic*, June 4, 1992. After Willey explored rumors that Vice President Dan Quayle had lobbied him to sign a controversial private-property-rights bill—a proposal that even Symington's father-in-law, John Pritzlaff, called "anti-environment"—Willey mentions the hiring of Heiler and the resignation of Herstam, writing, "speculation is rampant that the Symington administration is veering sharply to the right."

20. Keven Willey, "Symington at ease in RTC combat," *Arizona Republic*, February 25, 1992.

21. "Relationship of Arizona Governor J. Fife Symington III with Southwest Savings and Loan Association: Hearing Before the Subcommittee on General Oversight and Investigations of the Committee on Banking, Finance and Urban Affairs, House of Representatives, One Hundred Second Congress, Second Session, February 20, 1992" (Washington, DC: US Government Printing Office, 1992); see https://www.c-span.org/video/?24555-1/failed-savings-loan-investigation. In this five-hour hearing, the major complaints of both the RTC and Symington are aired before the US House subcommittee tasked with overseeing the FDIC and RTC investigation.

22. Mary K. Reinhart, "'Cooling off' compromise ends 8-hour standoff," *Arizona Daily Star*, May 13, 1992. "Protesters jeered the Republican governor as he arrived at the entrance to the parking lot," Reinhart noted.

23. George Garties, "FBI raids five reservation casinos," Associated Press, May 12, 1992.

24. Cole, discussion with Nelson, June 18, 2020, author's files. In the interview, Cole described how the governor received news of the standoff from newspaper reporter Mark Flatten. "So I get a call," Cole said. "It's Flatten. He's just about breathless. He says, 'You have a big friggin' problem'— but he doesn't say friggin—'you have a big problem on your hands. I'm out here. There are federal agents out here. This is a ticking time bomb. What are you going to do?' I said, 'That's news to us.' 'We're in a staff meeting,' I told him, 'I'll go get the governor.' So I go into the staff meeting and whisper in Fife's ear and he says 'They did what?'" Cole said that Chief of Staff Wes Gullett then called his ex-wife, who worked in the US Attorney's office. "Then Linda Akers (then US Attorney for the District of Arizona) jumps on the phone and we get the whole story told to us," Cole said. "And then we ran out to the DPS hangar at Sky Harbor and hopped in the helicopter and off we went."

25. Cole, discussion with Nelson, December 5, 2018, author's files; Symington, discussion with Nelson, February 16, 2018, author's files.

26. See "Indian Gaming Rights," a collection of documents and photos related to the gaming debate in Arizona through the 1980s and 1990s, Arizona State Library, Archives, & Public Records; see also *Indian Gaming: The Next 25 Years*, Committee on Indian Affairs, United State Senate (Washington, DC, Government Printing Office, 2015); Heidi McNeil Staudenmaier, "The State of Indian Gaming in Arizona," *Indian Gaming Lawyer*, Spring 2018. McNeil Staudenmaier is the Partner Coordinator of Native American Law & Gaming Law Services for Snell & Wilmer in Phoenix.

27. Jonathan Sidener and Carol Sowers, "Tribal gaming ruled 'inevitable': But judge is silent on legality," *Arizona Republic*, May 29, 1992. The *Republic* story two weeks after the raid ran next to a photo of bulldozers moving concrete barricades into position around the FBI's Mayflower trailers. "Members of the Fort McDowell Indian community braced themselves for another such

raid," Sidener and Sowers wrote. "However, the federal agents did not return, despite an apparent deadline of noon for surrender of the machines."

28. See Jonathan Sidener, "State offers tribe compromise: Would return gaming gear, put issue on November ballot," *Arizona Republic*, May 21, 1992. Sidener's story over a week later was accompanied by photos of an Indian-gaming march and rally that drew an estimated one thousand pro-gaming protesters to the state capitol.

29. See "Indian Gaming Rights," Arizona State Library, Archives & Records. The collection includes several releases from Woods's and Symington's offices regarding the standoff. The State Library archives also include a master's thesis written in 2011 by Louise Alflen regarding the issues "surrounding Arizona Indian Gaming and the standoff at the (Fort McDowell) casino."

30. Grant Woods, in discussion with Jack L. August Jr., March 19, 2014, author's files.

31. Enric Volante, "Symington to pursue compact with Indians: Symington, Woods disagree over their negotiation roles," *Arizona Daily Star*, May 22, 1992.

32. Mary Jo Pitzl, "Symington, Woods swap brusque letters: Each claims to speak for state in Indian gaming," *Arizona Republic*, May 22, 1992. Pitzl wrote: "Who launched the first salvo in the battle to be known as 'The great compromiser' is a matter of debate. Thursday's dispute, conducted via dueling letters and interviews, illuminated the rivalry between the two stubborn politicians. Woods has been mentioned as a possible gubernatorial candidate in 1994."

33. Carol Sowers and Jonathan Sidener, "Fort McDowell rejects Symington gaming proposal: Other raided tribes agree to study plan," *Arizona Republic*, May 23, 1992. According to the story: "Backing off his hardline opposition to casino-style gambling on the reservations, Symington proposed a compact Thursday. He asked for Fort McDowell's release of the machines as a gesture of good faith while he and the tribes hammer out an agreement." The Fort McDowell council members still argued that the proposal, as one council member said, could, as worded, still be "used as subterfuge for imposing state jurisdiction on tribal lands."

34. See Jennifer A. Alewelt, *Indian gaming in Arizona: A resolution of conflict*, dissertation, ASU Library High Density Collection; see also Heidi McNeil, "Indian gaming in Arizona: The great casino controversy continues," *Arizona Attorney*, January 1998.

35. "Betting on the governor," *Arizona Republic*, May 24, 1992. The editorial began: "Fife Symington's handling of the three-way confrontation over casino-style gambling on the state's Indian reservations has been encouraging." The editorial's author seemed to side with Symington in his spat with Woods: "Such dust-ups are inevitable between officials who are elected in their own right. Yet it does appear that Mr. Woods went off on his own hook to negotiate over Mr. Symington's head."

36. "Symington denies critics' charges of drift to the right," *Arizona Republic*, July 19, 1992. A month later, Merrill suggested in a *Republic* story that Symington's support for the increasingly popular King holiday could hurt him with former Mecham voters, which, Merrill claimed, were primarily made up of "Mormons" and "the over-65 group."

37. Hayes, discussion with Nelson, July 25, 2018.

38. Keven Willey, "Symington may be facing final chance," *Arizona Republic*, May 31, 1992. Regarding Hayes replacing Herstam, Willey wrote: "Hayes would start out without people like Leckie and ex-aide Annette Alvarez to worry about. Even the governor's die-hard defenders have to admit that 80 percent of his non-Resolution Trust Corp. public-relations problems have revolved around Leckie and Alvarez."

39. Symington, discussion with Nelson, February 16, 2018, author's files.

40. Cole, discussion with Nelson, December 5, 2018; see John Kolbe, "Symington 'surrounded by yes men, very quiet no men,'" *Phoenix Gazette*, May 3, 1992. The well-respected Kolbe interviewed numerous political figures to get a read on Symington's leadership style and abilities. One unnamed state agency head said this of Symington: "When he doesn't know the subject, he's a good listener and a very quick study. But when he knows a little something about it, save your breath. He's already decided."

CHAPTER 20: BIG BUDGET FEUD

1. See Scott Horsley, "From a Napkin to a White House Medal—The Path of a Controversial Economic Idea," npr.org, June 19, 2019; see Federico N. Fernandez, "Arthur Laffer: 2016 Hayek Lifetime Achievement Award Recipient," *Medium*, December 6, 2016.

2. Jim Chappelow, "What is the Laffer Curve?" *Investopedia*, May 1, 2020; "Trump awards Presidential Medal of Freedom to economist Arthur Laffer," *Washington Post*, June 19, 2019; "Dick Cheney, Donald Rumsfeld and Arthur Laffer on the Dinner Napkin that Changed the Economy," Bloomberg News, December 3, 2014. See also Arthur Laffer, Stephen Moore, Rex A. Sinquefield, and Travis H. Brown, *Wealth of States: More Ways to Enhance Freedom, Opportunity, and Growth* (Saint Louis, Missouri: Pelopidas LLC, 2017).

3. Joel Nilsson, "Oh to be wrong, but it looks like a budget war is coming," *Arizona Republic*, January 18, 1992.

4. Wes Gullett, in discussion with Jack L. August Jr., February 14, 2014, author's files.

5. Mary Jo Pitzl, "Beyond the hope, a Hobson's choice," *Arizona Republic*, January 12, 1992. Pitzl began her piece on Symington's upcoming State of the State with this lead: "Gov. Fife Symington must find a way to make a silk purse out of what is almost universally regarded as a sow's ear when he makes his first State of the State address Monday."

6. Mary K. Reinhart, "Symington budget plan targets indigent care," *Arizona Daily Star*, January 8, 1992. According to the story, "State lawmakers and Pima County officials were stunned by the proposal and pointed out that the costs would be passed on to the counties."

7. Fife Symington, in discussion with Robert Nelson, June 26, 2017.

8. Jane Erikson, "Spend more on health care, 88 percent in poll say," *Arizona Daily Star*, January 14, 1992.

9. Symington, discussion with Nelson, February 16, 2018; Jay Heiler, in discussion with Jack L. August Jr., February 2, 2014; see Joe Nathan, *Charter Public Schools: A Brief History and Preliminary Lessons* (Minneapolis: University of Minnesota, Center for School Change, 1995).

10. Jon Schroeder, *Ripples of Innovation: Chartering Schooling in Minnesota, the Nation's First Charter School State* (Washington, DC: Progressive Policy Institute, April 2004).

11. Bill Scheel, "Education report offers ideas that could make a difference," *Arizona Republic*, January 15, 1992; see Robert Maranto, Scott Milliman, April Gresham, and Frederick Hess, *School Choice in the Real World: Lessons from Arizona Charter Schools* (United States: Avalon Publishing, 1999).

12. Mary K. Reinhart, "'Get back to basics,' urges Symington in State of the State speech," *Arizona Daily Star*, January 14, 1992.

13. "Symington has good news for state taxpayers," *Tucson Citizen*, January 14, 1992.

14. See "Elected officials don't rate well," *Arizona Daily Sun*, April 19, 1992. Northern Arizona University's "Northern Arizona Poll" showed that Symington was just beginning to struggle with voters in the predominantly rural northern region of the state. He wasn't alone, though, the regular poll showed. Symington was one of many state political figures who were losing ground with voters as the economy struggled.

15. "David Pittman, "Governor: No budget, no government," *Tucson Citizen*, May 8, 1992; see "Hull to Senate: Get to work," *Arizona Republic*, April 22, 1992; "Plan to soften blow of state layoffs is unveiled," *Arizona Republic*, April 28, 1992.

16. David Pittman, "Governor's budget hits 'like rock,'" *Tucson Citizen*, June 17, 1992.

17. Steve Yozwiak, "Lawmaker's collapse mars session end," *Arizona Republic*, July 2, 1992. Yozwiak's story was accompanied by a photo of paramedics assisting Rep. Ruth Solomon after she collapsed in the House chamber. Solomon, who was released from a hospital a few hours later, had suffered, according to the photo's cutline, "a bout of high blood pressure" after she had "delivered a futile plea for money to help homeless children."

18. John Kolbe, "Symington's victory is sweeter thanks to court ruling," *Phoenix Gazette*, July 12,

1992. Kolbe revisited Symington's legislative wins and losses—including a favorable court ruling regarding a governor's line-item veto powers.

19. "Lawmakers never took so long to do so little," *Tucson Citizen*, July 2, 1992. The *Citizen's* editors concluded that too many important pieces of legislation had died or been watered down: "After introducing 1,225 pieces of legislation, after five special sessions to consider even more bills, (the state legislature) had relatively little to show for its efforts."

## Chapter 21: Back in the Black

1. John Pacenti, "Holiday heals state's wounds," Associated Press, November 5, 1992; Mary K. Reinhart, "Arizona voters OK 9 of 14 measures on ballot," *Arizona Daily Star*, November 5, 1992. In Reinhart's story, King's widow, Coretta Scott King, was quoted as saying, "We are pleased to have Arizona join with… other states in carrying out this mandate."

2. "Arizona restores King day, image," *News-Journal*, November 5, 1992. The Mansfield, Ohio, newspaper story quoted Steve Roman, co-chairman of the Victory Together Alliance in Arizona, as saying the push for the measure "brought together a coalition of business, religious and civil rights leaders who often are on opposite sides." "These people are now talking," Roman said in the story. "They are friends. They can call each other up and work together, instead of having to hold a news conference to say what's on their mind."

3. Mary K. Reinhart, "Arizona voters OK 9 of 14 measures on ballot," *Arizona Daily Star*, November 5, 1992.

4. "Ballot measures: Some contradictory outcomes, and one big trend," *Arizona Daily Star*, November 7, 1992.

5. Jay Heiler, in discussion with Jack L. August Jr., February 2, 2014; Doug Cole, in discussion with Robert Nelson, December 5, 2018; Fife Symington, in discussion with Robert Nelson, June 26, 2017.

6. "Arizonans escape serious injury," Associated Press, January 10, 1993.

7. Mary K. Reinhart, "Symington plan offers tax cuts of $33.8 million," *Arizona Daily Star*, January 12, 1993; Fife Symington's State of the State Address 1993, Folder 1992–1994, Symington Papers.

8. Howard Fischer, "Symington tax plan is generating debate," Capitol Media Services, January 17, 1993.

9. "UA cuts may harm teaching," *Tucson Citizen*, January 15, 1993. The president of the state's board of regents, Andrew Hurwitz, had this to say about Symington's proposal to cut more than $20 million from university budgets: "We must not destroy the institutions that we have spent over a century building," he argued. "The education, research and public service provided by the three state universities are absolutely indispensable to Arizona's future well-being."

10. John Kolbe, "Gov. Symington's business ills will haunt him in his next campaign," *Phoenix Gazette*, February 7, 1993. "The fact that (Symington), like dozens of other developers, is going down the drain in an economic spiral that began with the 1986 federal income tax law shouldn't matter in measuring his competence as governor," Kolbe argued. "After all, Harry Truman is revered today, and no one seems to remember (or care) that he was an unsuccessful haberdasher before going to Washington."

11. Keven Willey, "Things looking Grimm for governor," *Arizona Republic*, February 4, 1993. When asked how he could pay for his continued defense, Symington said, "Well, I've always believed in Rumpelstiltskin, so I'll call him." Willey retold the story of the magical imp who spins gold to save a maiden (and the dire consequences that follow), then tried to make sense of Symington's cryptic reference. "The message here seems to be that the governor is an optimist. In his line of work, you have to be." But considering how the story ends, "the question, then, is whether Symington will be as clever, or lucky, as the queen was in her dance with the devil. And, if he is not, at what cost to him, his family and his subjects?"

12. Symington, discussion with Nelson, September 12, 2017, author's files.

13. Karin Schill, "AHCCCS cuts have human costs," *Arizona Daily Sun*, January 30, 1993.

14. Mark Thomas Swenson, "Governor: Overhaul child support," *Tucson Citizen*, February 18, 1993. Detailing the plan, Symington also claimed that "the plan would reduce the amount of time it takes to collect child support to one or two months, compared to eight to 14 months it takes now."

15. See Kathleen Ingley, "Squeezing deadbeat dads, moms," *Arizona Republic*, June 3, 1993.

16. Mary Jo Pitzl, "Western governors to discuss trade pact, region's resources," *Arizona Republic*, June 20, 1993. As chairman of the seventeen-state association, Symington was able to steer the annual meeting to Tucson. Besides extensively discussing the North American Free Trade Agreement, other agenda items, Pitzl wrote, "include discussion of new approaches to environmental protection, which is the theme Symington selected for the association during his past year as chairman."

17. John Kolbe, "Gov. Symington's business ills will haunt him in his next campaign," *Phoenix Gazette*, February 7, 1993.

18. "Symington's approval rating climbs," *Arizona Republic*, February 24, 1993. Symington's "favorable" rating climbed to 38 percent from 24 percent, according to the Valley Monitor Poll. According to the poll of six hundred Valley residents, Grant Woods was viewed favorably by 49 percent of those polled while Phoenix Mayor Paul Johnson received a 67 percent favorable rating.

CHAPTER 22: A RIGHT TURN?

1. Jay Heiler, in discussion with Jack L. August Jr., February 2, 2014, author's files.

2. See Jose Cerda III and Al From, "Why American Politicians Don't Talk About Crime Anymore," *Politico Magazine*, November 21, 2013. This fascinating look back at the build-up to the 1994 federal crime bill details how Democrats nationally worked to fight the "soft-on-crime" label Republicans had given them.

3. Edward L. Cook, "Despite applause, some see lack of concern in Symington's plans," *Arizona Daily Star*, January 12, 1993. Cook noted that during Symington's 1993 State of the State, "the governor was interrupted at least 19 times by applause as he spoke in the crowded House chamber yesterday." Symington, according to a *Republic* reporter, only received six standing ovations in his speech the year before; see also Edward L. Cook and Joe Salkowski, "House panel Oks main elements to overhaul criminal code," *Arizona Daily Star*, March 24, 1993. The story on the legislative vote was accompanied by a second Salkowski piece on an Arizona serial rapist who, although given a life term, would be "eligible for parole in three years."

4. See Fife Symington, "1992: Good year for state," *Arizona Daily Sun*, January 3, 1993. In this guest column, Symington gives his take on his first full year in office. Near the end, Symington wrote, "And, perhaps most notably, we now have a basketball team sitting on top of the NBA, led by the indomitable spirit and intensity of Sir Charles Barkley."

5. "Symington names parole board member as successor to panel's ousted chairman," Associated Press, September 3, 1993.

6. Pamela Manson, "Victims must follow rules to get rights," *Arizona Republic*, July 29, 1993; see Lauren-Brooke Eisen, "The Complex History of the Controversial 1994 Crime Bill," Brennan Center for Justice, April 14, 2016. Much of the bill presented in Arizona in 1993 showed up in the sweeping federal crime bill passed a year later.

7. See Katherine J. Rosich and Kamala Mallik Kane, "Truth in Sentencing and State Sentencing Practices," National Institute of Justice, July 1, 2005.

8. David Pittman, "Child crimes get more violent," *Tucson Citizen*, April 12, 1993. "Violent crime committed by adolescents is reaching epidemic proportions in Tucson, Pima County and Arizona," the story began. "Statistics tell much of the story. More youths are entering the juvenile justice system than ever before. Last year, 15,783 were admitted to detention in Arizona, 2,365 more than in 1991 and 4,472 more than in 1987"; see also, "Symington urges war on state's youth crime," *Arizona Republic*, November 3, 1993. According to the story, "Symington said he recently asked Maj. Gen. Donald Owens of the National Guard to draw up a plan to mobilize troops, if necessary." Demo-

cratic State Rep. Cathy Eden called Symington's proposal to call out the National Guard "absolutely irresponsible."

9. Kelly Pearce, "Sheriff to use posse to fight violent crime," *Arizona Republic*, November 2 1993. "Arpaio's plan," Pearce wrote, "derived from frontier days, when a posse was called to chase the bad guys, would include placing almost 400 volunteers with law-enforcement capabilities on the streets to help combat gangs and drug traffickers." Arpaio's posse plan and other tough-on-crime measures were drawing him national headlines just a year after his election as Maricopa County Sheriff.

10. Steve Wilson, "Governor's anti-crime plan has more than just a fist: a heart," *Arizona Republic*, November 7, 1993. "The governor's plan is far preferable to the $22 billion crime bill passed last week by the U.S. Senate," Wilson wrote in support of Symington's $31.7 million plan. The federal bill "would stiffen sentences, pay for 100,000 more police officers and build more prisons. It would treat symptoms, not causes."

11. E. J. Montini, "Sincere, committed, opportunistic," *Arizona Republic*, September 1, 1993. Arizona Department of Corrections statistics, Montini argued, showed that Symington, while "talking tough," had actually been either very lenient or, more often, just disinterested, in early releases of violent criminals.

12. Melissa Healy, "Big Hike in Federal Grazing Fees Proposed by Babbitt," *Los Angeles Times*, August 10, 1993; see Kiana Scott, "Ranchers as Regulators: The Fight over America's Public Lands through *Public Lands Council v. Babbitt*," Evans School Review, Spring 2012.

13. Richard Ducote, "Thousands attend rally against mining legislation," *Arizona Daily Star*, August 29, 1993. A Gila County sheriff's deputy estimated the crowd at between three thousand and five thousand people, but the numbers, according to several media outlets, were probably closer to two thousand. According to Ducote's story, "Symington said the mining reform issue reminds him of the proposed increase of grazing fees on federal lands. Such fees would raise 'a paltry sum of money' for the government but would be of 'dire significance' to ranchers."; "Globe protest of mining bill draws 2,000," *Arizona Republic*, August 29, 1993.

14. Andrew Faught, "Reed: Transsexualism course likely to stay," *Arizona Daily Sun*, December 16, 1993. Faught's story quoted a statement by Kooros Mahmoudi, chairman of NAU's Sociology and Social Work Department, explaining that the class involved no use of state tax dollars. "A graduate student is teaching the class for free," Mahmoudi was quoted as saying; see Mary Jo Pitzl and Charles Kelly, "Symington backs down on NAU transsexuality class," *Arizona Republic*, December 17, 1993. Jay Heiler was quoted as saying, "Whether they cancel the class is up to them. The governor has no power, nor does he wish to exert any."

15. Keven Willey, "Gov. Symington is pretty good at manipulating the media," *Arizona Republic*, December 17, 1993.

16. Fife Symington, in discussion with Robert Nelson, February 16, 2018, author's files.

17. "Johnson, Symington—ever heard of 'em?" *Arizona Republic*, December 12, 1993. The poll of eight hundred Arizonans was conducted by a business and trade association called United for Arizona.

18. Keven Willey, "Self-centered Dems underestimating opponents," *Arizona Republic*, October 17, 1993.

## CHAPTER 23: THE MERCADO

1. See Jon Talton, "Phoenix 101: History," accessible at https://www.roguecolumnist.com/rogue_columnist/phoenix-101/. Talton's Rogue Columnist website has an ever-expanding collection of the award-winning author's pieces on Valley history; see also Andrew Ross, *Bird on Fire: Lessons from the World's Least Sustainable City* (New York, New York: Oxford University Press, 2011); see also Grady Gammage, Jr. *Phoenix in Perspective* (Tempe, Arizona: Herberger Center for Design, 2003); Andrew Ross, in discussion with Robert Nelson, October 12, 2018, author's files.

2. Deborah Laake, "The Mercado," *Phoenix New Times*, April 19, 1989. Laake, who four years

later would have a *New York Times* bestseller *Secret Ceremonies: A Mormon Woman's Intimate Diary of Marriage and Beyond*, was enchanted by the Mercado. But she ended her 1989 piece with a warning: "We know that, in the end, shopping centers do not live or die by the collective imaginations of their planners; their survival is guaranteed only by the sweet sounds of their cash registers. We know it's impossible to predict whether Phoenicians will finally support a downtown project in the numbers it will take to make the Mercado a success. But we also know that it's not ever going to happen without a few mind-bending reasons for it to happen. Perhaps the Mercado will be the first reason."

3. Barbara Rose, "Mercado work ready to begin," *Arizona Republic*, May 27, 1988. Symington told Rose, "It's meant to be not only a strong statement for the Hispanic community in Arizona, but also a very popular spot for the community at large and for tourists. We're hoping that the buses, instead of heading out northeast to Scottsdale, will now stop at the Mercado."

4. Neal Peirce, *Citistates: How Urban America Can Prosper in a Competitive World* (Washington, DC: Seven Locks Press, 1993). Phoenix was the first of several US cities Peirce studied for his book.

5. "One billion invested in downtown Phoenix," *Arizona Republic*, October 2, 1988. The builders of the twenty-six-story One Renaissance Square were blunt when asked if they would have built downtown without tens of millions of dollars in incentives. "No!" A Trammell Crow executive emphatically told the reporter.

6. "Council Oks street work for downtown Mercado," *Arizona Republic*, March 26, 1986. "The Phoenix City Council agreed Tuesday to spend $1.3 million on beautifying streets around the Mercado and to make its 'best efforts' to build a $9 million parking garage nearby within five years."

7. Randy Todd, in discussion with Robert Nelson, September 25, 2017; Fife Symington in discussion with Robert Nelson, September 27, 2017.

8. See "U.S. injects $2.7 million into Phoenix's Mercado project," *Arizona Republic*, February 2, 1988. As part of the Mercado deal, the story said, "City officials are subsidizing part of the cost of the project by not assessing property taxes against developers for eight years and by leasing the project's city-owned land to developers at a low rate. In return, developers have agreed to provide low-cost leased space to minority businesses as well as turn over a percentage of the project's profits to the city."

9. Fife Symington, in discussion with Jack L. August Jr., April 20, 2016; Symington, discussion with Nelson, September 12, 2018; Todd, discussion with Nelson, September 25, 2018; Jean Novotny, "Magic unfolds inside with characters of Mercado," *Arizona Republic*, September 14, 1989. Novotny retold the story of Symington and Todd traveling Mexico in search of inspiration for the Mercado.

10. Symington, discussion with Nelson, May 9, 2019; Todd, discussion with Nelson, November 2, 2018.

11. Kerry Fehr, "Mercado shops facing hard times," *Arizona Republic*, June 22, 1988. Fehr's story described the collapse of many of the fixed-markets in northern Mexico. The story ran the same month ground was being broken on the Mercado project in downtown Phoenix; "History of markets in Mexico," *Sistema de Información Cultual*, March 25, 2011.

12. See Bradford Luckingham, *Phoenix, The History of a Southwestern Metropolis* (Tucson, Arizona: University of Arizona Press, 1989).

13. Deborah Shanahan, "Enthusiastic council Oks $1.3 million for street work on Phoenix Mercado," *Arizona Republic*, March 26, 1986. Near the bottom of Shanahan's story, she mentions something that would come back to haunt developers. The city, she wrote, also agreed to submit "an application for about $2 million in federal Urban Development Action Grant money to create a fund for loans to the project's tenants. The city would also make such an application for the Square One project, so the two proposals will be competing for grant funds." Meaning, the Mercado still had direct competition.

14. Barbara Rose, "Mercado project loses corporate backing," *Arizona Republic*, December 31, 1986. "Recent setbacks for the project include the loss of a retail partner, Evans Development Co. of Baltimore, and a decision by Ramada Inc. not to participate."

15. See Jason Hackworth, *The Neoliberal City: Governance, Ideology, and Development in American Urbanism* (Ithaca, New York: Cornell University Press, 2006).

16. "Financing is obtained for Mercado," *Arizona Republic*, October 20, 1987. "Permanent financing for the Mercado ... has been secured," the story read. "The Arizona Laborers, Teamsters and Cement Masons Local 395 Pension Trust will provide a loan of $10 million for the project." The story noted that, "Failure to begin construction on time could cause the developers to forfeit an agreement with Phoenix to lease the two-block parcel for 60 years."

17. Jean Novotny, "Magic unfolds inside with characters of Mercado," *Arizona Republic*, September 14, 1989.

18. Terry McDonnell, "Tug of war launched for control of Mercado," *Arizona Republic*, December 24, 1991.

19. See Terry Greene Sterling, "The Indomitable Dougherty," *Phoenix New Times*, September 11, 1997. In this piece, Greene Sterling celebrates the work of fellow *New Times* reporter John Dougherty, who, Greene Sterling noted, had been the most dogged investigator of Symington's personal financial world since Dougherty came from the *Dayton Daily News* to the *Mesa Tribune* in August 1991. The column offers fascinating details of the rolling battle between attorney John Dowd and Dougherty that stretched back to Dougherty's groundbreaking 1989 stories for the Dayton paper that arguably prompted the Keating Five investigation. "John Dowd had reason to hate Dougherty" before either arrived in Arizona, Greene Sterling wrote, since Dowd represented Sen. John McCain during the investigation. Of course, Symington, Dowd, and other Symington supporters strongly dispute the portrait of Dougherty as painted by Greene Sterling, now a writer-in-residence at the Walter Cronkite School of Journalism at ASU. There's no doubt, though, that it was Dougherty who first brought to public light many of the financial dealings surrounding the Mercado and the Esplanade that Symington and Dowd clearly hoped would not reach the public.

## Chapter 24: The Bully Pulpit

1. See Mary Jo Pitzl, "Symington lists ambitious Arizona agenda," *Arizona Republic*, January 11, 1994. "Symington had few secrets to unveil Monday," Pitzl wrote, referring to the fact Symington had been announcing major policy initiatives, especially related to crime fighting, throughout the previous year. Democrats, Pitzl wrote, praised the quality of the speech, not its content. "The governor's speech was fabulous," Senate Minority Leader Cindy Resnick quipped. "A wonderful campaign speech, written by truly incredible, intelligent consultants from out of state." (Democrats also credited much of the quality of Symington's presentation to the fact he used a TelePrompTer. It was the first time an Arizona governor, as one Republican legislator put it, "appeared to be looking out at his audience instead of down at his speech.")

2. "*Déjà vu* all over again," *Arizona Daily Star*, January 12, 1994. The ferocious editorial seemed as much a shot at Jay Smith and Art Laffer as it was a shot at Symington: "And he piled on such discredited bits of old-time conservative sloganeering as a James Watt-style call to resist a federal tyranny that proposes only that Arizona not destroy its environment; a Ron Reagan-like ascent of the mountain to affirm blithe optimism; a Peggy Noonan-mode paean to a city below 'full of people doing their best.'" The editorial suggested a different approach: "Elsewhere in America, a new pragmatism has replaced partisan sniping and feel-good rhetoric with a gathering spirit of post-ideological partnership and realistic problem-solving for the good of the community."

3. Jay Heiler, in discussion with Jack L. August Jr., February 2, 2014; Maria Baier, in discussion with Jack L. August Jr., February 25, 2014, author's files. Baier, who had worked with Heiler at ASU's college newspaper and again at the state attorney general's office, described the speech-writing process in her oral interview: "But then for the State of the State there was a team effort and certainly Jay took the lead." Baier served as a member of the executive staff in the governor's office through 2002. Baier later was elected to the Phoenix City Council, from which she stepped down to become state land commissioner under Gov. Jan Brewer in 2009.

4. Fife Symington, in discussion with Robert Nelson, May 9, 2019.

5. Ed Foster, "Symington budget for '95 tops $4 billion: Boosts for schools, zero for rainy days," *Arizona Republic*, January 12, 1994. Foster noted that Symington's budget proposal assumed the state would have $4.264 billion in revenues to begin the next fiscal year.

6. Keven Willey, "Governor says little, says it with feeling, and looks good saying it," *Arizona Republic*, January 11, 1994. "It was Republican Gov. Fife Symington's best State of the State address," Willey wrote. "Too short on specifics and too long on lofty rhetoric, but all in all, it was carefully drawn and well-delivered." She continued: "This judgment may be damning with faint praise. In 1992, a rigid Symington barely glanced at his audience as he delivered his prepared text. It had all the snap and crackle of milk-soaked Rice Krispies. And he was only marginally better last year."

7. Kelly Pearce, "Sheriff to put posses back to mall work," *Arizona Republic*, February 1, 1994. Arpaio predicted the posse would grow to two thousand members by the middle of February of 1994. Pearce wrote: "Arpaio said he wants to send a clear message to tourists that they are safe in Arizona despite a survey by Morgan Quitno Press, a publisher of statistical annuals. Arizona was ranked ninth (among US states) based on 16 crime factors."

8. Symington, discussion with Nelson, February 16, 2018; Tommy Caplan, in discussion with Jack L. August Jr., June 2, 2013; Helen Clay Chace, in discussion with Jack L. August Jr., October 9, 2016, author's files.

9. See Toni McClory, *Understanding the Arizona Constitution* (Tucson, Arizona: University of Arizona Press, 2010); see also David R. Berman, *Arizona Politics & Government: The Quest for Autonomy, Democracy, and Development* (Lincoln, Nebraska: University of Nebraska Press).

10. Barry Burkhart, "Legislature targeting environmental funds," *Arizona Republic*, February 6, 1994. Burkhart's column began: "Here we go again. More skullduggery in the Legislature. More attempted raids on funds dedicated elsewhere."

11. Symington, discussion with Nelson, June 26, 2017; Doug Cole, in discussion with Robert Nelson, December 5, 2018; Maria Baier, in discussion with Jack L. August Jr., February 25, 2014, author's files.

## CHAPTER 25: THE PROBLEM WITH POLLS

1. Stephen Tuttle, "'94 to bring election-year amusement," *Arizona Republic*, January 2, 1994.

2. Doug Cole, in discussion with Robert Nelson, April 30, 2020.

3. Mary Jo Pitzl, "Fellow Republican hopes to unseat Symington," *Arizona Republic*, February 23, 1994.

4. Barrett had grown up poor on a farm in western Pennsylvania. After her father died when she was thirteen, Barrett and her oldest brother managed the family farm while she earned money guiding tourists on horseback rides into the forests surrounding their land. Her father left her a calf as a college endowment. She successfully raised the heifer and made money selling its offspring. She kept her earnings in a Prince Albert tobacco can and used the money to fly to Phoenix after she was awarded a full-ride scholarship to Arizona State University. As she worked her way toward a law degree, she lived in a boardinghouse of a Scottsdale ranch where she fed horses and cooked for room and board.

5. Jay Heiler, in discussion with Jack L. August Jr., February 2, 2014; Cole, discussion with Nelson, December 5, 2018; see "U.S. Sen. John McCain letter to Barbara Barrett," Folder 1994–1995, Symington Papers. On August 23, 1994, McCain wrote a stinging letter to Barrett accusing her of breaking promises to not "go negative." "Again," McCain wrote near the end of the letter, "I am seldom surprised when troubled campaigns 'go negative,' but I am annoyed when they espouse the degree of hypocrisy apparent in your decision to abandon your self proclaimed commitment to run a positive, issue-oriented campaign. I had not previously attributed to you that level of cynicism." The Symington Papers collection contains the faxed copy of the letter McCain's sent to Symington office the same day McCain sent the letter to Barrett. The Symington Papers collection also includes a copy of Barrett's "Unanswered Questions From Project Slim Investigation" press

release from July 1994, part of a collection of historical Symington documents donated in 2019 by Doug Cole, chief operating officer of HighGround Public Affairs Consultants.

6. See Becca Rothschild, "A pointless debate for Symington," *Arizona Daily Sun*, July 31, 1994. "In the interest of fairness, of course an incumbent should be willing to meet in open debate, to give people the chance to find out what all the candidates think and how they defend their policies," Rothschild wrote. "But it may not be the politically expedient thing to do."

7. "Poll: Goddard outpacing Johnson," Associated Press, July 22, 1994. The poll by Earl de Berge showed that Barrett had, according to the story, "picked up strength among women voters but still had little support from men." Overall, Symington led 42 percent to 24 percent in the poll of 416 Arizona voters; "Coppersmith leads Dems in survey," *Arizona Republic*, August 18, 1994. The Rocky Mountain Poll in August showed Symington leading by the nearly same percentage as their June and July polls.

8. "Barrett campaign's "Hey Governor, come out and fight like a … person," ad, *Arizona Republic*, August 21, 1994. A print copy of the full-page ad is in Folder 1994–1995, Symington Papers.

9. Steve Wilson, "Random musings on the searing heat, Barkley and politics," *Arizona Republic*, August 5, 1994. "Unless Barbara Barrett knows that Fife Symington is about to get bashed by a federal grand jury, I can think of only one plausible reason for her to pour $750,000 of her money into her campaign for governor: She's been out in the sun too long," Wilson wrote. Wilson also suggested Grant Woods wouldn't pursue the George Leckie/Project SLIM case, saying "Conventional wisdom says he won't because it would be bad politics. Republicans don't want Leckie in the news at election time."

10. "William F. Rawson, "Symington, Barrett clash over state of state," Associated Press, August 25, 1994. According to Rawson's story detailing the candidates' meeting with *Tribune* writers and editors, Barrett claimed Symington's "administration has been guilty of 'criminal and ethical violations and cronyism,' although she did not provide any specifics." Rawson continued: "Symington bristled at the charge. He noted that the lawsuit was settled without him having to pay any money or admit any wrongdoing. But Barrett noted that Symington's business dealings still are being scrutinized by federal investigators and a grand jury. 'You settled the civil suit but not the criminal side,' Barrett said. 'You would like to convince people that's all over but it isn't.'"

11. Steve Meissner, "Coppersmith is Senate nominee; Symington wins, Demo fight rages," *Arizona Daily Star*, September 14, 1994; Francie Noyes, "Goddard, Basha running neck and neck with about 90 percent of precincts reporting," *Arizona Daily Star*, September 14, 1994; "Capsule comments: A new business: campaigns," *Tucson Citizen*, September 17, 1994. The story noted that "Barbara Barrett invested about $1 million of her money—more than $10 for every vote she received."

12. John Kolbe, "Republicans have plenty to cheer about," *Arizona Republic*, September 18, 1994. "While Gov. Fife Symington handily beat back a well-financed challenge by neophyte Barbara Barrett," Kolbe wrote, "her 32 percent showing is a sign of some discontent in party ranks."

13. David Pittman, "Goddard early leader among Demos in gubernatorial poll," *Tucson Citizen*, January 28, 1994. Bruce Merrill's poll showed, though, that 52 percent of Democratic voters were undecided. "Whether or not he can maintain that lead remains to be seen," Merrill told Pittman; see also https://ballotpedia.org/Terry_Goddard.

14. Keven Willey, "Goddard's star eclipsed by Johnson's," *Arizona Republic*, January 13, 1994. Willey told the story of how Goddard allegedly fell from the national party's good graces. Willey quoted a "high-ranking party source in Washington" as telling her, "Terry Goddard has been playing the card that he's closest to the Clinton administration. Well, that's not true, not any more." Willey's sources suggest Goddard's alleged fall from grace may have just been a case of Goddard missing a few phone calls from party officials regarding a fundraising visit to Phoenix by Vice President Al Gore. "We called everybody to ask for help," the DNC's finance chairman told Willey. "Goddard never returned the calls," Willey added.

15. "Goddard platform: What else besides crime?" *Arizona Republic*, February 19, 1994. "For

all intents and purposes," the *Republic* editorial argued, "the former mayor of Phoenix delivered a single-issue speech intended to capitalize upon—what else?—crime, the hot-button issue of campaign '94."

16. David Pittman, "Phoenix major runs for governor," *Tucson Citizen*, March 17, 1994; Steve Meissner, "Johnson is 3rd Democrat to join race for governor," *Arizona Daily Star*, March 18, 1994.

17. Steve Meissner, "Symington's job rating up, but voter approval lags," *Arizona Daily Star*, January 29, 1994. In Merrill's January KAET-TV poll, Johnson had an astonishing 85 percent approval rating. All the Democratic candidates were well liked, in fact. Goddard had a 75 percent approval rating, compared to 74 percent for Eddie Basha.

18. George Will, "Paul Johnson, somebody worth watching," *Washington Post*, March 25, 1994.

19. Victoria Harker, "Governor called 'deadbeat dad': Basha, fellow Dems assail Symington on kids' aid," *Arizona Republic*, April 14, 1994. According to the story, Basha said, "Where our children need a dollar, Fife Symington gives them 50 cents and says they're lucky to get that." Basha was citing a report from the Children's Action Alliance that said state funding for programs such as education, child-abuse investigations, child care, and treatment for delinquent youths had declined or stayed the same since Symington came into office. According to Harker, "Symington and GOP leaders have disputed that analysis, saying it did not take into account millions of new federal dollars that have poured into Arizona in the past five years." Jay Heiler told Harker that he believed the report was a "political ploy to hurt the governor and help Basha"; see David Hurst, Alexandra Tan, Anne Meek, and Jason Sellers, *Overview and Inventory of State Education Reforms: 1990 to 2000*, US Department of Education, National Center for Education Statistics (Washington, DC: Government Printing Office, 2003).

20. Heiler, discussion with August, February 2, 2014; Cole, discussion with Nelson, December 5, 2018; see John Kolbe, "Rhetoric carries the day at the Capitol," *Arizona Republic*, January 30, 1994. Kolbe, while questioning the motives and logic of a teacher's march at the capitol at which Basha spoke, wrote that at such protests, "Homemade signs must be mounted on sticks to wave when speakers hurl harsh invective at elected officials (especially Gov. Fife Symington, who 'robs' schools) and when the high-school-style chants get going ('What do we want?' *More money!* 'When do we want it?' '*Now!*')." Kolbe continued his lambasting of such events: "Candidates who say things such as 'vouchers are a hoax, a sham, a serious dismantlement of public education,' as Democratic gubernatorial hopeful Eddie Basha did, must be cheered wildly."

21. William F. Rawson, "Democratic primary races too close," Associated Press, September 7, 1994. Rawson wrote, "Basha has released his own polls in recent weeks showing him at or near the lead. Campaign Manager Rick DeGraw said the new poll showing a slight slide for Basha isn't a reason to panic, but 'we're always concerned when we see polls that show things are changing.'"

22. See Steve Wilson, "How Basha overcame bad polls to win the one that counted," *Arizona Republic*, September 15, 1994. "Even in this age of sophisticated number crunching," Wilson wrote, "political polling remains an inexact science. Just how inexact, we saw early Wednesday morning. That's when the Eddie Basha votes poured in from outstate precincts, vaulting him ahead of Terry Goddard and into the general election against Fife Symington." "The final polls," Wilson joked, "were not only wrong, they were spectacularly wrong."

23. See "KAET poll puts Basha in front by 16 points in governor's race," Associated Press, October 6, 1994. In Bruce Merrill's poll of 440 registered voters, he found a surprising number of Republicans—28 percent—saying they would vote across party lines. That compared to only 14 percent of Democrats who said they would back Symington. Merrill predicted, though, that as the general election neared, Republicans would begin to migrate back toward their party's candidate.

## CHAPTER 26: THE BIG SWING

1. See Julia Angwin, "Casino bill threatens tribal sovereignty, Indians say," States News Service, July 18, 1994; see Steven Andrew Light and Kathryn R. L. Rand, *Indian Gaming & Tribal Sovereignty: The Casino Compromise* (Lawrence, Kansas: University Press of Kansas, 2005). Light and

Rand's book arguably is the most comprehensive look at the gaming issue as it has impacted states and tribes across the country over the last several decades; see also W. Dale Mason, *Indian Gaming: Tribal Sovereignty and American Politics* (Norman, Oklahoma: University of Oklahoma Press, 2000); The Indian Gaming Rights collection of the Arizona State Library, Archives, & Public Records can be accessed at the State of Arizona Research Library at the Polly Rosenbaum Archives and History Building at 1901 W. Madison St., Phoenix, Arizona, 85009.

2. "Yaqui blackjack tables could become political tangle for Symington," Associated Press, September 8, 1994; Jonathan Sidener, "Hit me: Tribe deals blackjack," *Arizona Republic*, September 7, 1994. "Last summer," the Sidener argued, "when Symington began signing compacts with tribes, he said he saved Arizona from problems that might be associated with 'full-blown casino gaming' by keeping blackjack and roulette out of the state. If he does nothing about the blackjack, he risks looking like has backed down from a showdown."

3. Jay Heiler, in discussion with Jack L. August Jr., February 2, 2014; Fife Symington, in discussion with Robert Nelson, June 26, 2017; Doug Cole, in discussion with Robert Nelson, December 5, 2018, author's files. Heiler, Symington, and Cole served as the key sources in describing Symington's strategy against Basha in the 1994 general election.

4. Eric Miller and Mary Jo Pitzl, "Election night thrillers," *Arizona Republic*, September 14, 1994.

5. Mary Jo Pitzl, "Symington opens 'book' on Eddie Basha: Paints rival as liberal soft on crime; foe condemns portrayal," *Arizona Republic*, September 16, 1994. Basha's campaign manager Rick DeGraw didn't find the "book" amusing, accusing Symington's staff of distorting Basha's common description of himself as a "bleeding-heart capitalist." DeGraw argued Symington twisted Basha's words to incorrectly present Basha as a "bleeding-heart liberal"; Cole, discussion with Nelson, December 5, 2018.

6. Jonathan Sidener, "Candidates clash to add chapters in 'book wars'," *Arizona Republic*, September 17, 1994. "On Friday," Sidener explained, "Republican incumbent Fife Symington put out the second chapter in his 'book' on Democratic rival Eddie Basha." "Before the day was over, Basha's campaign had fired off four chapters of their 'book' on Symington."

7. Francie Noyes, "Governor's race gets nasty; debates ahead," *Arizona Daily Star*, October 17, 1994.

8. Francie Noyes, "Campaign is 'a labor of love' for Libertarian John Buttrick," *Arizona Daily Star*, October 23, 1994. Noyes wrote a lengthy compare-and-contrast piece on the three candidates that appeared the day of the pivotal debate.

9. "Talk, talk, talk," *Arizona Daily Star*, September 24, 1994; Francie Noyes, "Fiscal policy, schools drive gubernatorial debate," *Arizona Daily Star*, October 24, 1994. Noyes provided an extensive blow-by-blow from the televised gubernatorial debate; David Pittman "Symington takes the offensive," *Tucson Citizen*, October 24, 1994. The debate was aired statewide from the studios of KVOA-TV in Tucson.

10. Symington, discussion with Nelson, March 16, 2019.

11. "Strong, weak points emerge in poll on governor hopefuls," *Arizona Republic*, September 27, 1994. Besides suggesting that Symington was having success branding Basha as a "tax-and-spend liberal," pollster Merrill made an interesting comparison regarding Symington: "In a way, he's kind of like Bill Clinton. Fife's approval ratings have run at best 50 percent positive, 50 percent negative. If I were running an incumbent candidate for office, I'd want at least a 2-to-1 approval rating."

12. See William F. Rawson, "Basha loses ground, Kyl pulls away: poll," Associated Press, November 2, 1994.

13. Wes Gullett, oral history interview by Jack L. August Jr., Folder 1993–1994, Symington Papers. Gullett, who was Symington's chief of staff during the election, provided a colorful take on the Symington team's tough-love strategy against Basha: "After the primary we're like, 'what do we do now? We have the happy grocer. Everybody loves Eddie Basha.' We were looking at each other. We had no polling on the guy; we had no op research on the guy. So we had to figure it out and quickly. What we did know about Eddie Basha was that in his heart he was a liberal. He had been

for the ACE initiative, the billion-dollar education package. We also knew that Eddie believed that he was a big-hearted liberal so we knew that anything he could do to make government bigger and help people he would do that. So we decided we're not going to attack him on his personality. We're going to love him. Everybody loves Eddie Basha. We just argued he was bad for Arizona because he was too liberal."

14. Francie Noyes, "Social issues steal spotlight in governor's race," *Arizona Daily Star*, November 2, 1994; Cole, discussion with Nelson, December 5, 2018; Symington, discussion with Nelson, May 9, 2019.

15. "Gay marriages? Candidates disagree," Associated Press, November 4, 1994. The AP story ran in dozens of newspapers nationwide.

16. Francie Noyes, "Social issues steal spotlight in governor's race," *Arizona Daily Star*, November 2, 1994. "One week from Election Day," Noyes wrote, "the gubernatorial campaign has shifted from high-minded issues like tax policy to the perennial hot button of gay rights and abortion."

17. See Paul Davenport, "Board of Regents appointee's remarks on gays stir controversy in Senate," *Arizona Capitol Times*, February 8, 2012. Heiler's past comments regarding homosexuals returned as an issue in 2012 after he was appointed to the Arizona Board of Regents. According to the story: "The comments included referring to homosexuality as an 'aberration' in an early 1980s article while (Heiler) was a university student. He called gays 'queers' while talking with news reporters in 1994 while a gubernatorial aide." The story continued: "Heiler has said he would not make the remarks today and that he has grown since he made them and now believes all Arizonans need to live in harmony together"; Cole, discussion with Nelson, December 5, 2018; Gullett, interview by August, February 19, 2014, author's files. Besides Cole and Heiler, Wes Gullett offered significant detail regarding the machinations and controversies of the 1994 campaign. In his oral history interview with August, Gullett described a conversation with Symington just before becoming Symington's chief of staff: "Fife called me in and said … so why do you want to (take the chief of staff job)? I said it would be a great opportunity and I think that there is a lot of potential and you're a great guy and he said, 'Well do you think I can win in '94' … and I said, 'I think you can win, absolutely.' And (Symington) said 'you're the only guy that has said that to me in the last three months.'"

18. "Gay activists demand Symington rebuke or fire aide," Associated Press, November 18, 1994. Although Heiler's comments didn't seem to impact the gubernatorial vote, activists continued to call for Symington to punish Heiler after the election. "We need to send a strong message that this kind of gay bashing will not be tolerated," Jeff Ofstedahl wrote in *Echo*, a Valley magazine focused on gay and lesbian issues. The AP story also noted that the leader of the Arizona Human Rights Fund, a gay and lesbian rights group, was seeking a meeting with Symington to protest Heiler's remarks; In her 2014 oral history interview with August, *Republic* reporter Mary Jo Pitzl related what she remembered regarding's Heiler's comments to reporters: "I was down in the press room … and there's Jay Heiler and he's in there making a joke and … sort of putting on these gay airs and I wrote about it." "Jay's comments just seemed a little off-color and we wrote about it and I think he felt very, very chaste about it (afterward)."

19. "Symington, Basha conciliatory," *Tucson Citizen*, November 9, 1994. In the story, Symington was quoted as calling the election results a "miracle" and a "revolution." He continued: "Barry Goldwater and Ronald Reagan started all this and God bless them."

20. Tom Beal, "In Arizona, it's business as usual," *Arizona Daily Star*, November 10, 1994. Beal pointed out that Symington's win was part of a much larger Republican statewide win. "Arizona certainly did its part to alter the political landscape in Washington, D.C. Before the election, Arizona's congressional delegation was evenly split. In January (of 1995), Arizona will be represented by two Republican senators, five Republican congressmen and a lone Democrat, Rep. Ed Pastor." A headline on a national story in the *Daily Star* the same day suggested a national political shift played a role, too: "Pro-GOP wave costs Demos governorships." "Republicans captured at least six

governorships held by Democrats yesterday and appeared set to control a majority of statehouses for the first time since 1970," the story reported.

21. William Rawson, "Symington leads GOP sweep: Republicans take 5 of 6 seats in Arizona's U.S. House races," Associated Press, November 9, 1994. Rawson offered extensive detail regarding the massive exit poll the AP had helped conduct. One clear takeaway from the exit poll: "Symington capitalized on voter dissatisfaction with the politics of the Clinton administration, labeling Basha a 'Clinton tax-and-spend liberal.'"

## Chapter 27: Contract with Arizona

1. Wes Gullett, oral history interview by Jack L. August Jr., February 19, 2014, author's files. Gullett described his approach to being chief of staff in the wake of his eight years working for John McCain. "See we came up with messages and things that stayed on point," Gullett said. "We got (Symington) comfortable in his own skin and I had come from a military background. Not personally but working for McCain for eight years it was a staff model and he was the boss. You could argue, you could do things, but when he made a decision that was it, go march. So what we tried to do was use some of that model to impose discipline and order to a staff that had been reckless at times."

2. See Grant Woods, oral history interview by Jack L. August Jr., March 19, 2014, Oral History Interview Folder, Symington Papers. Woods, speaking of Symington's staff by 1995, said, "I thought Fife surrounded himself with a lot of really good people. I didn't necessarily agree with them on the direction they took him but some of them were my people. Some of them were my people that I was very close to and I can't think of any I don't like today." Wood's interview provides fascinating insight into the tough-on-crime mania that dominated the political discussion in 1994 and into 1995. Woods related a story, which began with him being asked a question by a Tucson television reporter. The reporter, Woods said, asked, "I'm just wondering what's your reaction to the governor saying you're soft on crime." Woods told August: "Well, we had just executed a bunch of people and there had been no death penalty in Arizona for twenty-nine years. Here we're executing people and I'm soft on crime." After explaining the particular case Symington was referring to, Woods continued that he felt Symington had started "using the same playbook as Arpaio," which Woods described this way: "It wasn't necessarily coordinated but Arpaio did the same thing over the years. Arpaio found out you could beat up on the prisoners as much as you wanted to. Do or say anything and no one would rise to their defense. The guy had a remarkable imagination in how many ways he could dream up to abuse prisoners and people would be, 'great, screw those prisoners' and it was just emblematic of the times. There was (no issue) in the world of crime where you could be too tough."

3. "Ralph Siegel, "Whitman shines in GOP response: Says 'revolution' started with the states,'" Associated Press, January 25, 1995.

4. See Keven Willey, "GOP Legislature will aid governor—to a point," *Arizona Republic*, January 19, 1995.

5. Steve Tuttle, "Predictions: Newt's greed, Bill's deeds, Buddy's needs," *Arizona Republic*, January 1, 1995. Next to Tuttle's column ran a similar piece aimed at the national stage by the *Washington Post*'s David Broder. The fight between Gingrich and Democrats had become unusually ugly the year before. "Nothing would make 1995 a better year in America than a strengthening of civic life and the return of civility in our public discourse."

6. "Symington's agenda," *Arizona Republic*, January 10, 1995.

7. See Mark Flatten, "U.S. levels charges in SLIM case: Symington associates indicted," *Mesa Tribune*, March 15, 1996. Flatten's story offers a clear picture of the events of 1995 that led to the federal indictment of Leckie and Yeoman a year later. Flatten himself had done significant investigative reporting on the case in previous years which appeared to expose documents that clearly showed Leckie—then a Symington executive staffer—telling Yeoman how to circumvent the state's contract

bid system to improperly win a $1.5 million state contract for Yeoman's accounting firm, Coopers
& Lybrand. In an oral history interview with August in 2014, Symington Chief of Staff Wes Gullett
singled out Flatten's reporting and its impact on the administration: "The media was as strong then
as it has ever been," Gullett told August. "There were very, very good reporters at the *Republic* and
at the *Gazette* and Tucson guys were fairly aggressive. So the culture was really combative. Flatten
was out at the *Tribune* and he is one of the best investigative reporters in the country so there was
a lot of tension. We convinced Fife that it was a good thing because it was hard but we also had a
thing that by the time I got there it was like, 'What are they going to do? Write a bad story?' We'd
had all the bad stories you could imagine."

8. "Wild talk," *Arizona Daily Star*, January 10, 1995. After quoting Symington as saying, "a little
rebellion is a good thing," the editorial argued, "Now, this is wild talk, even dangerous talk. Leave
aside that it evades discussion of constructive, real-world solutions to Arizona's pressing social
problems. And ignore the fact that a recent *conservative* study has declared the American economy
already to be one of the freest in the world. Instead, such an oppositional stance—if taken to its full
implications—amounts to an urging of anarchy."

9. Mark Kimble, "State issues take back seat to Civil War II launch," *Tucson Citizen*, January 12,
1995.

10. Norm Parish, "Arizona GOP backs off on state's own welfare package," *Arizona Republic*,
March 24, 1995.

11. William F. Rawson, "Symington's day to back up pledges," Associated Press, January 9, 1995;
Rhonda Bodfield, "Fight expected over tax cut," *Tucson Citizen*, January 9, 1995.

12. Barry Burkhart, "Symington starring as wildlife monster in 'horror show'," *Arizona Republic*,
January 15, 1995; Barry Burkhart, "Residents see Symington's power play for what it is," *Arizona
Republic*, February 15, 1995; see also Barry Burkhart, "Symington lets Game and Fish off hook:
Governor promises its political freedom," *Arizona Republic*, May 23, 1995; see also Joel Nilsson, "Fife
Symington's tea party: Throw the Clean Air Act overboard," *Arizona Republic*, January 14, 1995.
Nilsson's reference to "Symington's tea party" came long before the creation of the Tea Party move-
ment that later echoed much of Symington's anti-federal rhetoric.

13. Herb Whitney, "Outer Loop lot decision delayed until Feb. 15," *Arizona Republic*, January 6,
1995.

14. "Symington's siege at the gates of Rome," *Arizona Republic*, January 22, 1995; Mary Jo Pitzl,
in discussion with Jack L. August Jr., February 22, 2014, author's files. In describing her time covering Symington, Pitzl detailed how journalistic coverage of government had changed between the
mid-1990s and 2014: "Frankly, there was sort of a template the way the *Republic* and the *Gazette*
covered the Mecham governorship. They covered, they were aggressive, they were there all the time.
So when I got assigned I thought well that's how you do it." "A lot of that (ability to cover multiple
aspects of a public figure) is a function of staff sizing and we just can't do that now." Covering
Symington specifically, Pitzl, besides joking about trying to keep pace with the governor's growing
vocabulary, described his demeanor under pointed questioning: "It did irritate him but…he's very
well-bred. He's a very polite man and he would disagree and stand up for himself but often the response to me was, 'Well, Mary Jo, you just don't understand.' 'Well, then, explain to me.' You know.
It was a little patronizing." Pitzl said she told Symington, "'So, well, if you think I'm ignorant, well,
then enlighten me.' And (it seemed like) he was not in any rush to enlighten me."

15. Keven Willey, "Income-tax duel looming at Capitol," *Arizona Republic*, January 12, 1995.
"Symington is up against a wall," Willey wrote. "It's called the Senate Republican caucus—which at
this point seems to like Spitzer's plan a lot more than Symington's. Few Senate Republicans want
to increase the progressivity of the tax code. They fear that making the tax code more progressive
would result in a political backlash from the upper and middle classes against the poor. They argue
that a far more effective way to help the poor is to create more jobs by cutting taxes for everybody,
reforming welfare and reshaping education."

16. See "The wrong debate," *Arizona Daily Star*, January 15, 1995. "About the best thing you can say about Symington's budget," *Daily Star* editors wrote, "is that it is much more generous than the legislative proposal, but it is unnecessarily stingy in critical areas."

17. Andrew Glass, "This Day in Politics: Clinton bails out Mexico, Jan. 31, 1995," *Politico*, January 31, 2019; Fife Symington, in discussion with Robert Nelson, May 18, 2020, author's files; Doug Cole, in discussion with Robert Nelson, May 19, 2020.

18. See "Trade Flow Between the United States and Mexico: NAFTA and the Border Region," *Articulo: Journal of Urban Research*, October 2014.

19. "GOP governors scuttle welfare reform of Democrats, prefer block-grant plan," Associated Press, January 30, 1995.

20. Symington, discussion with Nelson, May 20, 2020, author's files. Cole, discussion with Nelson, May 22, 2020; Wes Gullett, oral history interview by Jack L. August Jr., February 19, 2014. Regarding the bailout of Mexico, Gullett said: "The Mexican currency collapsed in 1995 and the Republicans didn't know what to do because it was the beginning of our xenophobia and so they were reluctant to help the Mexicans. So Fife went to explain how important it was and at the time Fife was talking to the Mexicans at the highest level." Gullett added later in his interview: "When Fife was helping in the Mexican deal it made a big difference to Clinton. Fife was close to Gingrich. And I think Fife vouched for Clinton with Gingrich. Of course they knew each other but just having somebody else say 'you guys can make this work' was helpful to the deal."

21. Ernesto Zedillo, "The Right Track: Political and Economic Reform in Mexico," *Harvard International Review* 19, no. 1 (1996).

22. "Gov. Bush Eyes Mexican Aid Support," Associated Press, January 30, 1995. After their meetings with Gingrich and Clinton, Bush and Symington also lobbied fellow governors to pass a resolution announcing the National Governors' Association's support for a $40 billion aid package. The need for a resolution became moot when Clinton announced on the second day of the three-day conference that he would release money to Mexico using an executive order.

23. "Today's markets," Associated Press, January 31, 1995. "The president offered the new plan after becoming convinced that Congress wasn't apt to approve his original proposal," the AP story explained.

24. Nora Lustig, "Mexico in Crisis, the U.S. to the Rescue. The Financial Assistance Packages of 1982 and 1995," Brookings Institution, January 1, 1997.

25. Symington, discussion with Nelson, May 21, 2020.

26. See "Symington's plan better for Arizona's needs," *Tucson Citizen*, January 13, 1995. After lambasting the anti-federal government rhetoric in Symington's State of the State address, the *Citizen*'s editorial board supported Symington's budget compared to the legislature's version, saying, "Symington, who in the past has been branded a foe of social programs, would be far more generous to the neediest residents of Arizona than the Legislature wants to be."

27. "Symington's rating hits 47 percent, highest since he took office," *Arizona Republic*, January 25, 1995.

28. Bill Muller, "Poll: Voters like Symington but say keep Woods' power," *Arizona Republic*, April 1, 1995. After noting Symington's record-high approval numbers, the story continued: "The Legislature is debating whether to allow Symington and the Department of Environmental Quality to have independent lawyers. The measure is a watered-down version of a bill that would have closed Woods' civil division and placed its lawyers under a general counsel appointed by Symington."

29. Anthony Sommer, "Cities ask for revenue guarantees," *Phoenix Gazette*, March 6, 1995. Sommer's story detailed the successes and failures of Symington's proposal in the first half of the legislative session.

30. Cole, discussion with Nelson, July 14, 2000. Cole explained the genesis of the idea of an early Arizona Republican primary. "McCain contacted us and just said, 'I want this done for my friend Phil Gramm.' It was about as simple as that. McCain strong-armed Fife into promoting the idea."

31. "Symington's veto right on," *Arizona Republic*, April 22, 1995.

32. Bill Muller and Norm Parish, "$431 million tax cut OK'd by governor: $4.5 billion budget signed, too," *Arizona Republic*, March 16, 1995.

33. Keven Willey, "2 Vetoes do not put Symington in 'green' column," *Arizona Republic*, May 4, 1995.

## CHAPTER 28: A BAD FALL

1. "Valley of the Sun lives up to its name: Hits temp of 121 degrees," *Arizona Republic*, July 29, 1995. The blistering heatwave in Arizona was a national story. A story in *The Independent-Record* in Helena, Montana, said that temperatures "knocked out air conditioning in city buses and over-heated their motors. Phoenix transit workers were forced to hose down buses to cool them."

2. Fife Symington, in discussion with Robert Nelson, September 26, 2017; Doug Cole, in discussion with Robert Nelson, December 5, 2018. Cole, Baier, Gullett, and Heiler all commented on Symington's ability to focus on the work at hand during his tenure, even when he was spending part of his day away from the office in court.

3. "Governor's discuss tourism," *Arizona Daily Star*, June 5, 1995.

4. See Tim Giago, "Arizona gaming conflict bodes ill for Indian nationals," the *Courier*, May 29, 1995. Giago, long an influential voice for Native American rights as editor-in-chief and publisher of *Indian Country Today*, argued that Symington was targeting Arizona's tribes in retribution for voting heavily in favor of Eddie Basha in the 1994 election. "Now the Indian people of Arizona are beginning to experience fallout for supporting his opponent," Giago wrote. "In an unprecedented move last week, Symington said, 'No more slot machines.' Symington has started the process of limiting and eventually stopping Indian gaming in Arizona."

5. Keven Willey, "Gramm presidency: Playing 'what if'," *Arizona Republic*, March 2, 1995. Willey described a potential scenario in which McCain took a federal post, and then Symington resigned as governor having made a deal with his successor, who would be Secretary of State Jane Hull, to appoint him to McCain's vacated US Senate seat. "If Symington is content to stay put as governor," Willey prognosticated, "the whole situation takes on a different light. Symington could play kingmaker. Message to the rest of us: Watch for just about every other Senate-hungry Republican to get in the ring-kissing line. Given all this," Willey concluded, "it really isn't any wonder McCain is chairing Gramm's national campaign and that Symington is chairing his state campaign."

6. Anthony Sommer, "Sierra Club praises Dems, rips GOP," *Arizona Republic*, July 5, 1995. "Overall, Democrats received far higher grades than Republicans," Sommer wrote, "except for Gov. Fife Symington, who received high marks for vetoing several bills the Sierra Club considered harmful." State Sierra Club lobbyist Raena Honan, though, Sommer wrote, "was less charitable about Symington's staff."

7. Keven Willey, "Grenade-lobbing Legislature scores sad hit," *Arizona Republic*, July 26, 1995. As he announced his resignation as state DEQ director, Ed Fox described the harsh rhetoric of the 1995 legislature as "Fingernails on a chalkboard."

8. Symington, discussion with Nelson, September 12, 2017; Cole, discussion with Nelson, December 5, 2018; Terry Lynam, in discussion with Robert Nelson, April 3, 2019.

9. See "Council Oks street work for downtown Mercado," *Arizona Republic*, March 26, 1986. The story details some of the early promises made by Phoenix City Council members. The city promised "best efforts" to build a $9 million parking garage in that part of downtown Phoenix," the story noted, while explaining that voters actually would make the final decision on any aid projects that were financed by bonds.

10. Jonathan Sidener and Adrianne Flynn, "Symington levied $8 million; Governor, wife ordered to pay over Mercado," *Arizona Republic*, July 27, 1995. "The governor and his wife signed personal guarantees on the Mercado loan unlike other failed projects of Symington's unsuccessful development company," the story explained, "making this the first case in which the couple have been held liable for repayments"; "Symington under $8.8 million repayment order," Associated

Press, July 27, 1995; see also Jonathan Sidener, "Interest sought from Symingtons: $2.7 million more due, suit victors say," *Arizona Republic*, August 5, 1995. Sidener wrote that "neither the governor, who was vacationing in France, nor his attorney, Lonnie J. Williams Jr., could be reached for comment." Symington's France vacation in August would become a major public-relations issue a month later; see also "Symington offers 25 percent of salary to pay $8.8 million Mercado debt," Associated Press, September 8, 1995.

11. "Gov. Fife Symington of Arizona goes bankrupt," Associated Press, September 20, 1995. The AP story on Symington's bankruptcy made headlines in dozens of papers across the country; Francie Noyes, "Symington personally bankrupt," *Arizona Daily Star*, September 21, 1995. Noyes's story was accompanied by a detailed graphic called "Why Fife is broke" that detailed Symington's assets ($61,000), his debts ($24 million), his monthly income (wages, $4,618; trusts, dividends, and interest, $2,260), a listing of his monthly living expenses, and the unusually short list of his remaining personal property and the estimated value of each item.

12. "Bankruptcy Chronology," *Arizona Daily Star*, September 21, 1995; Mary Jo Pitzl, "Behind the Bankruptcy: Phoenix acted slowly on Mercado debt," *Arizona Republic*, September 21, 1995. Related specifically to the $2.7 million loan from the city, Pitzl wrote, "Documents released with (Symington's) bankruptcy statement show that he was offering to repay the city $64,000 for its $2.7 million loan." David Krietor, the city's director of economic development, explained the impact of the unpaid loan: "He said the lack of repayment makes that much less money available for economic-development purposes"; see "El Mercado," *Arizona Daily Star*, September 24, 1995. While Symington and Pete Garcia, president of Chicanos por la Causa, blamed the Mercado failure on bad timing and broken promises from the city (they both pointed to the city allowing the 940,000-square-foot Arizona Center to be built close to the 126,000-square foot Mercado), others suggested the blame fell more on Symington and Garcia. Real estate analyst Robert Kammrath argued the developers spent far too much on the project (The $100 per square foot price tag to build the Mercado, he argued, doomed the project). "The average Safeway shopping center, for example, costs half that," he said. "High costs for the developer meant high rent for the tenants," Kammrath said. "Add those to lack of parking and no anchor and the result was bankruptcy and foreclosure."

13. Willam F. Rawson, "Arizona governor $24 million in debt," Associated Press, September 21, 1995.

14. Bill Muller, "Governor might have to bank on voter's dim memories," *Arizona Republic*, September 21, 1995. Bruce Merrill, Jay Smith, and Democratic House Minority Leader Art Hamilton all suggested Symington could recover from the bankruptcy if, as Muller phrased it, he "has political aspirations in 1998."

15. Francie Noyes and Ann-Eve Pedersen, "Demos attack as GOP defends," *Arizona Daily Star*, September 21, 1995. The story began: "Gov. Fife Symington's personal bankruptcy rocked political circles as fellow Republicans rushed to defend him and Democrats called him a fraud and an embarrassment to the state." According to the story, Democratic Senate Minority Leader Peter Goudinoff had a different reaction to the announcement than many in his party. "I don't find any cause to celebrate," he said. "I know some Democrats are whooping it up. I don't think it does anybody any good. The voters knew he had these financial problems and they went ahead and re-elected him. If anybody is at fault, it's the voters of the state."

16. "Symington looks for money to fund a tax cut," Associated Press, September 5, 1995. The AP story noted that Symington made his request of state agency directors just as "legislative budget analysts (are) predicting a possible recession next year and a subsequent $106 million state budget deficit." Symington's staff countered that assessment with numbers showing the state ended its fiscal year (on June 30, 1995) with a $270 million surplus—$102 million higher than expected.

17. Michael Smith, "Ticket with a grain of salt," *Phoenix New Times*, October 26, 1995. Soon after *New Times*' owners bought Symington's ASU tickets, *New Times* published a letter from Smith in which he sarcastically argued the newspaper's owners would act no differently than Symington if faced with a financial catastrophe. "Congratulations to New Times, Inc., on the acquisition of

# 430 OLD MONEY, NEW WEST

newspapers in Texas, California and Florida!" Smith wrote. "The company won't expect to make a profit on those businesses, will it? And if something terrible happened, and those papers failed, I am confident that the fine people at New Times would pay every single vendor, large and small, out of their personal bank accounts, and would certainly never consider filing bankruptcy!"

18. Eric Miller, "Symington names 'meth czar': Former DEA agent to organize war on drugs," *Arizona Republic*, October 5, 1995. Federal law-enforcement officials argued that Symington was creating a state job for work that was already being done by federal authorities.

19. "Demos model Symington shirt," Associated Press, October 14, 1995. "In the week following his bankruptcy filing," the story noted, "Symington outlined plans to revamp the juvenile justice and education systems in the state and appointed Lt. Col. Alex Mahon of the Arizona National Guard to head the state's anti-drug efforts." The story about the "Symington Diversion Tour: 1995" T-shirts ran in the *Arizona Daily Star* next to a piece by Howard Fischer of Capitol Media Services about *New Times* co-owner and executive editor Mike Lacey buying Symington's ASU tickets and giving them to charity.

20. Francie Noyes, "Financial documents may have broken law," *Arizona Daily Star*, November 9, 1995.

21. Francie Noyes, "Ex-aide says Symington campaign records falsified," *Arizona Daily Star*, November 10, 1995. Marjorie Jane Kendall, a former secretary during Symington's first gubernatorial campaign, told state investigators that she believed campaign documents were "doctored" to, according to Noyes's story, "mislead the public and the press." Kendall's comments from a January 1995 deposition were made public by Arizona Common Cause, Arizona Citizen Action, and United We Stand Arizona, which were all asking Attorney General Grant Woods to revisit the matter. Symington responded by saying, "Those allegations were made a long time ago. The attorney general reviewed that, our attorneys reviewed that and nothing like that ever happened. It's time we end all these nonsensical allegations," Symington was quoted as saying.

22. "Voters' trust shaken: A poll shows lowered confidence in Gov. Symington since he declared bankruptcy," Associated Press, October 2, 1995.

23. Michael Murphy, "Approval rating falls to 37 percent for governor," *Arizona Republic*, October 25, 1995.

24. Victoria Harker, "Grand Canyon closes: Federal impasse claims new victim," *Arizona Republic*, November 16, 1995. Harker's story began: "Grand Canyon National Park will close this morning for the first time in its 76-year-history, a victim of the budget impasse between President Clinton and the Republican Congress." As of that Thursday morning, the park's front gates were closed at 8 a.m. to new visitors. People already in the park had until the next afternoon to leave. Park officials were as angry as many visitors, the story suggested. "It's disappointing, it's frustrating," said Maureen Oltrogge, a spokeswoman for the park. "We know at least 40 percent of our visitors are international and coming from thousands of miles to find the gates closed at Grand Canyon National Park. According to the story, park officials received the orders to close Wednesday afternoon (the day before the story appeared in the morning *Republic*). "With such short notice, there was no way to notify visitors who have lodging and camping reservations in the coming days," Oltrogge said in the story.

25. Fife Symington, in discussion with Jack L. August Jr., April 20, 2016; Symington, discussion with Nelson, June 26, 2017.

26. Wes Gullett, oral history interview by Jack L. August Jr., February 19, 2014, author's files; Cole, discussion with Nelson, December 5, 2018, author's files.

27. Beth Silver, "It's Fife to the rescue: Gov offers help to Canyon," Associated Press (headline from the *Arizona Daily Sun* in Flagstaff, Arizona), November 17, 1995. This AP story, which ran the following day, started: "A contingent of unarmed National Guard troops was ordered to the Grand Canyon today in hopes the federal government accepts Gov. Fife Symington's offer to help keep the park open through the federal budget shutdown." The story continued: "Symington spokes-

man Doug Cole noted the troops were unarmed. He said they, along with workers from other state departments, were preparing to help empty garbage, clean facilities and do other support chores. There was no intention to move into the park without permission from the National Park Service," Cole was quoted as saying.

28. Steve Yozwiak, "South Rim is open, and entry is free: But river runs, mule rides, hiking are out," *Arizona Republic*, December 19, 1995.

29. See Julia Rosen, "November 10, 1934: Arizona declares war against California at Parker Dam," *Earth*, November 2013. Symington's Grand Canyon standoff echoed a move sixty-one years earlier by another Arizona governor. In 1934, the long-simmering feud between California and Arizona regarding Colorado River water came to a head. When the Bureau of Reclamation began construction of the controversial Parker Dam, Arizona Gov. Benjamin Moeur moved to stop construction by declaring martial law and sending 100 Arizona National Guard troops to the dam site. Gov. Moeur succeeded at getting the project postponed, but after Arizona's legal arguments against the dam were revisited by federal officials, the project was reapproved. Construction began again the next year.

30. Symington, discussion with Nelson, June 4, 2019.

31. Doug Kreutz, "Symington's bid to reopen Canyon fails," *Arizona Daily Star*, November 18, 1995. In his press conference following the meeting with federal officials, Symington explained that the mass gathering wasn't intended as a show of force, but rather a show of resources. "We came with the resources to open the park, the human resources, but the offer was rejected by the Interior Department," Symington was quoted as saying. "So we send the Guard home, and we will send the (state) Parks Department personnel home. It's a great disappointment to us. We really wanted to open the park right away."

32. Beth Silver, "Attempt to reopen Grand Canyon fails," Associated Press, November 18, 1995; see Mark Shaffer, Steve Yozwiak, and Bob Golfen, "Grand disappointment: Tourists arrive to find Canyon National Park closed," *Arizona Republic*, November 17, 1995; see Kurt Repanshek, "Grand Canyon 'State' Park? A Look Back at the 1995 Government Shutdown and the Battle over the Grand Canyon," *National Parks Traveler*, March 14, 2011; see also Paul Rogers, "Government shutdown: Closing national parks could spark public outcry similar to 1995," *San Jose Mercury News*, September 30, 2013. The story of the 1995 showdown at the Grand Canyon gets retold whenever a federal government shutdown looms.

33. "Move to reopen Grand Canyon fails," Press Democrat news services, the *Press Democrat* (Santa Rosa, California), November 18, 1995. The Grand Canyon and Yosemite stories were sidebars to news that the federal shutdown likely wouldn't last much longer. The national wire story explained the reason for the impasse and why it appeared nearly solved: "President Clinton has abandoned his opposition to a seven-year route to a balanced budget and Friday began intense negotiations with Congress over the last principal sticking point preventing the reopening of the government: How to predict the future impact of budget cuts on the economy."

34. See "Readers' opinions differ regarding canyon closure," *Arizona Republic*, November 19, 1995. Reader Michael Depowers argued: "I think that Governor Symington's efforts are really childish. He knew from the beginning that he couldn't possibly do that." Rosemary Thompson disagreed: "I think that it is a good idea for the governor to send the National Guard to get the Grand Canyon open. This good old boy outfit in Washington is ridiculous."

35. William Rawson, "Visitors trickle back to Canyon," Associated Press, November 21, 1995.

36. Steve Yozwiak, "Cash gives Canyon a 1-day reprieve," *Arizona Republic*, December 30, 1995.

37. Bonnie Henry and Roderick Gary, "Governor still pushes drastic school reform," *Arizona Daily Star*, November 19, 1995. This story about criticism of Symington's school-reform ideas was the newspaper's lead story. A story on the ongoing closure of the Grand Canyon and Symington's standoff was placed in the bottom right side of the front page.

CHAPTER 29: BLOOD IN THE WATER

1. Rhonda Bodfield, "New Funds will keep canyon open," *Tucson Citizen*, January 3, 1996; Steve Yozwiak, "Canyon funding renewed: Park can stay open through Super Bowl," *Arizona Republic*, January 3, 1996.

2. "Watchdogs hit Fife's defense fund," Associated Press, January 1, 1996; Mary Jo Pitzl, "Defense fund assailed," *Arizona Republic*, January 1, 1996. Pitzl's story began, "The law may permit it, but Gov. Fife Symington's resurrected legal-defense fund still raises ethical and moral questions, two government watchdog groups say." Tim Hogan, director of the Arizona Center for Law in the Public Interest, and Mike Evans, director of Arizona Common Cause, both chastised Symington for allowing the fund to exist. "What do all other Americans do when they're in a jam paying their lawyers?" Hogan, an attorney himself, asked rhetorically. "They get a public defender, or they go to Community Legal Services, or they go without, as is usually the case."

3. "Top Ten Blues," *Arizona Daily Star*, January 2, 1996. In second place in the state AP's top stories list—between the Oklahoma City bombing connection and Symington's bankruptcy—was a now mostly forgotten story. An Amtrak train derailment in Hyder, Arizona, the previous fall that had killed one crew member and injured seventy-eight passengers appeared to be an act of sabotage by right-wing domestic terrorists. The attack, as *Daily Star* editors noted, "seemed to share anti-government motives with the Oklahoma City disaster."

4. Jerry Kammer, Pat Flannery, and Mary Jo Pitzl, "Ex-partner accuses governor of fraud: Lawsuit's claim 'absurd,' Symington's lawyer says," *Arizona Republic*, January 10, 1996. Hirsch's lawsuit, according to the story, "claims that the governor hid the money by giving it to unidentified 'affiliates and family members.'" Hirsch was hoping to stop Symington from having his $1.8 million debt to Hirsch's company discharged by the US Bankruptcy Court. Symington's bankruptcy attorney, Robert Shull, called the allegations "absurd, ridiculous, and patently untrue."

5. Jerry Kammer, "Symington firm owes back taxes: State, IRS seeking $2.2 million," *Arizona Republic*, January 26, 1996. The tax liens filed by both the IRS and State Department of Revenue "add to the financial woes of the governor, who in September filed for Chapter 7 bankruptcy to erase debts of $25 million." Kammer noted that the "documents were unearthed Thursday during research into the governor's bankruptcy."

6. Doug Cole, in discussion with Robert Nelson, December 5, 2018.

7. Steve Wilson, "Curbs on smoking, a brainteaser and SLIM public trust," *Arizona Republic*, March 20, 1996. The columnist wrote in his "Memo to Fife Symington": "Your decision to stiff newspaper reporters is a bush-league and cowardly way of ducking accountability. Speaking only to TV reporters, who won't ask the hard questions, is a transparent dodge."

8. Kris Mayes and Michael Murphy, "Democrats urge 'review': Want panel to probe governor's conduct," *Arizona Republic*, January 26, 1996. Senate President John Greene, himself a tax attorney, argued that Democrats were using the tax-lien story as "a big political football." Greene said Symington's financial problems were far from unique to Symington. The "financial downturn in the mid-1980s hurt a lot of people," Greene was quoted as saying.

9. Steve Wilson, "People are mighty tired of governor's arrogant attitude," *Arizona Republic*, January 31, 1996. Wilson argued that Symington's slipping poll numbers weren't just a product of the onslaught of revelations regarding his personal finances, but also Symington's reaction to questions about those problems. After quoting the O'Neil Associates poll showing Symington's new approval ratings, Wilson quoted pollster Mike O'Neil, who gave a similar opinion on why Symington's rural numbers were dropping: "To ordinary folks in small towns," O'Neil said, "I think it comes across as unseemly the way he has handled himself and tried to walk away from his debts."

10. Martin Van Der Werf, "Symington asks deeper income-tax cut: Wants state to run Grand Canyon," *Arizona Republic*, January 9, 1996. Republican leadership seemed cool to Symington's idea to make more cuts to the state income tax. His idea to have the State of Arizona take over management of the Grand Canyon, environmentalists and critics suggested, was patently absurd. "They say

that Arizona should fund its own parks before it considers taking over any federal parks," wrote the *Republic*'s Steve Yozwiak after interviewing state environmental group leaders.

11. Steve Yozwiak, "Symington wants state to run Grand Canyon, but nature groups don't," *Arizona Republic*, January 9, 1996.

12. Rhonda Bodfield, "School, tax reform top agenda," *Tucson Citizen*, January 8, 1996. Bodfield explained: "Although the state Supreme Court ruled 18 months ago that Arizona's school finance formula was unconstitutional, legislative leaders have been unable to reach a solution because of a dispute about whether to increase funding for fast-growing districts." In his speech, Symington said: "Before this session ends in April, we must devise a responsible means of increasing access to capital funding for low-wealth school districts."

13. "Symington's wishful thinking," *Arizona Daily Star*, January 9, 1996. The newspaper's editorial page editors argued that Symington's 1996 address showed a disconnect between the governor and the majority of Arizonans: "He misunderstands the criticism of his first five years. He doesn't seem to realize that even those who support a declining role for government in their lives also support full funding of government's basic responsibilities. He doesn't understand that most Arizonans would choose better schools over symbolic tax cuts."

14. Eun-Kyung Kim, "Symington's tax plan met with skepticism: Positive response to school funding," Associated Press, January 9, 1996.

15. "Strong opening for Symington," *Arizona Republic*, January 10, 1996; Graciela Sevilla, "Arizona, Sonora meet, edge closer to joint venture," *Arizona Republic*, May 5, 1996.

16. Alisa Wabnik, "Charges of waste sting universities in budget quest," *Arizona Daily Star*, February 2, 1996; see "Protest at ASU," *Arizona Republic*, January 25, 1996. "Sun Devil Stadium becomes the rallying point for 500 Arizona State University students, faculty and staff members, angry over budget cuts proposed by Gov. Fife Symington," a brief in the paper stated.

17. Charles Kelly, "Powerful business body backs universities: Opposes cuts by Symington," *Arizona Republic*, February 22, 1996. The group supported the request by university officials for a $78 million boost in funding for the state's three universities, which equated to about a 10 percent increase in state funding for the schools. Symington had suggested a $5 million increase, while the Joint Legislative Budget Committee recommended a $15 million hike.

18. Jonathan Sidener, Jerry Kammer, and Pat Flannery, "Former Symington aides indicted," *Arizona Republic*, March 15. The news story was accompanied by a detailed timeline of the complex series of events that led to the 1996 indictments regarding the actions of Leckie and Yeoman early in Symington's tenure. Included in the timeline was this nod to the paper's own work under the March 13, 1994, entry: "*Arizona Republic* reporter Jonathan Sidener makes the first revelation of the Leckie-Yeoman contracts." The *Mesa Tribune* and *Phoenix New Times* both similarly trumpeted their own scoops throughout Symington's tenure; see also Howard Fischer, "2 associates of Symington are indicted: Face charges of wire fraud," Capitol Media Services, March 15, 1996.

19. "Symington signs bill on bid-rigging," Associated Press, March 24, 1996.

20. Fife Symington, in discussion with Robert Nelson, May 9, 2019.

21. Keven Willey, "How pal's death affects Symington case," *Arizona Republic*, April 10, 1996. Willey wrote: "The tragic death of John Yeoman, one of two confidants of Gov. Fife Symington indicted last month on federal bid-rigging charges, seems more like a plot line of a mystery novel than the bizarre accident of circumstance that investigators say it is. But this is Arizona. Weird things happen. Especially in politics." Willey suggested Yeoman's death might help Leckie because "he no longer has to worry about his version of private meetings and conversations with Yeoman conflicting with Yeoman's version." She noted too, though, that, "It may not be as significant as it initially seemed. Federal prosecutors have done absolutely nothing since Yeoman's death to lower expectations of additional indictments, which could be interpreted as an indication that those indictments remain on track."

22. Mary K. Reinhart and Chris Limberis, "Grand jury probes his role, if any, in alleged bid-rigging," *Arizona Daily Star*, March 31, 1996.

23. "Local News: Governor's aide quits," *Arizona Republic*, April 13, 1996. In several interviews, Symington consistently denied suggestions that Heiler orchestrated a politically motivated ideological shift during Symington's second term. In his oral history interview with August, Wes Gullett said, "My wife has a great line: 'You take the King's shilling, you do the King's bidding.' That's where we were and that's where we wanted to go. Fife was the boss." "We'd argue it out and no one was ever not allowed to give their opinion and Fife needed to hear it all but at the end of the day when he made his decision, we all supported it." Gullett said he left the job on good terms with Symington. He just needed a change, he said. "I stayed until '96. And the reason I stayed was because it was fun. It was the greatest job I ever had and Fife was really fun. We were doing really interesting things." Gullett did admit that the job, especially under the "growing cloud," "was very challenging and very stressful" for him, as it was for Symington. Symington, Gullett said, often told him to keep his focus on his job, not on Symington's personal issues. "Look, you help me run the government, I'll deal with this," Gullett said Symington told him. Symington continued: "I don't want you to worry about this other stuff. I love your help but I don't want you encumbered by this and I've got a team of the best and brightest who are doing the legal stuff."

24. Howard Fischer, "U.S. judge's logging ban will add to fire woes, Symington says," Capitol Media Services, May 1, 1996. As blazes raged through Four Peaks Wilderness and on Mount Graham near Tucson, Symington suggested that a judge's order halting all logging in Arizona and New Mexico to protect the Mexican spotted owl and the northern goshawk would increase the intensity of future fires. "His order contributes to the fuel loading in the forest, the debris and all the things that you can't go in and can't take care of business because of his ruling."

25. See Graciela Sevilla, "Mexico Journal: Friends of Fife now include Zedillo," *Arizona Republic*, May 29, 1996. Sevilla related details of a private dinner in May at the presidential residence in Mexico City: "In the same week that he was being grilled at home by attorneys in depositions," Sevilla wrote, "Symington was feted as the guest of honor by President Ernesto Zedillo at a private lunch." Sevilla noted that "South of the border, Symington enjoys a reputation among the business and political elite as a 'friend of Mexico.' He's remembered kindly for lobbying in favor of an emergency loan for Mexico after the December 1994 peso devaluation and for opposing the kind of anti-immigrant legislation Gov. Pete Wilson fostered in California." Sevilla noted that Symington was accompanied by his son, Fife IV, who was involved with a Mexican export partnership at the time. Symington, Sevilla said, referred to Fife IV as "my NAFTA son."

26. "Politics traps air pollution," *Arizona Daily Star*, May 10, 1996. The *Daily Star* editorial noted that all clean air proposals in the regular legislative session were nixed by Republicans. "Lawmakers and elected officials can whine all they want about big bad Washington coming in with its rules and regulation, but the truth is it's still better than states and local jurisdictions which don't protect us from air pollution. Political will and public courage to demand true protection of air quality just don't exist yet."

27. R. H. Melton, "Arizona Gov. Symington Indicted," *Washington Post*, June 14 1996; Chris Limberis, "Symington: a riches to bankruptcy saga," *Arizona Daily Star*, June, 14, 1996; "Indictments possible today: Symington won't quit if federal charges are filed," Associated Press, June 13, 1996; Howard Fischer, "Symington indictment could harm bankruptcy defense," Capitol Media Services, June 14, 1996; Steve Wilson, "Symington should resign, but don't count on it," *Arizona Republic*, June 14, 1996; "Text of grand jury's indictment," *Arizona Republic*, June 14, 1996; Pat Flannery, Jerry Kammer, and Charles Kelly, "Symington Indicted: 'Complex system of fraud' alleged by U.S. prosecutor," *Arizona Republic*, June 13, 1996; "Governor's response," *Arizona Republic*, June 14, 1996; Stacy J. Willis and Chris Limberis, "Grand jury indicts Symington: governor says he's innocent," *Arizona Daily Star*, June 14, 1996; see "Symington indictment: Understanding the Charges," *Arizona Republic*, June 15, 1996.

28. "The governor should resign," *Arizona Daily Star*, June 14, 1996. The editorial argued that "you can presume that Gov. Fife Symington is innocent and still conclude that yesterday's 23-count

grand jury indictment, combined with his other troubles, leaves him incapable of governing the state."

29. Michael Murphy, "Poll: 58 percent want Symington out," *Arizona Republic*, June 15, 1996.

30. "Dems want resignation, not impeachment," Associated Press, June 14, 1996; "GOP rallies around Symington: Arizona governor indicted in fraud case," Associated Press, June 14, 1996; Michael Murphy, GOP leaders shocked; none favors resignation," *Arizona Republic*, June 14, 1996.

31. Martin Van Der Werf, "Indictments likely to fuel Symington's intensity," *Arizona Republic*, June 16, 1996.

32. Symington, in discussion with Nelson, May 9, 2019.

33. Martin Van Der Werf, "State Republicans gather, tell Symington they're behind him," *Arizona Republic*, June 21, 1996.

34. Jay Heiler, in discussion with Jack L. August Jr., February 2, 2014, author's files; Cole, discussion with Nelson, December 5, 2018, author's files.

## CHAPTER 30: TOUGH GUY

1. "Arpaio plays role of GOP kingmaker," *Arizona Republic*, September 6, 1996. State Rep. Robin Shaw of northeast Phoenix said she asked Symington for help in getting Arpaio's endorsement. Wes Gullett, who became a political consultant after leaving Symington's office, told the *Republic* that he believed the press was responsible for the reduced interest in a Symington endorsement: "The way you guys (news media) have been beating the hell out of him (Symington), it wouldn't take a rocket scientist to figure that out. The poor guy's so radioactive, he glows in the dark." After leaving state government, Doug Cole would join Gullett in the public affairs consulting firm, High-Ground, of which Cole would become chief operating officer. Former Symington Deputy Chief of Staff Chuck Coughlin is CEO of HighGround.

2. Pamela Manson, "Ex-governors oppose Symington's Prop. 102," *Arizona Republic*, October 29, 1996. Manson's story included a photo by Rob Schumacher that included former governors Jack Williams, Rose Mofford, Sam Goddard, Raul Castro, and Evan Mecham; "Governor rebukes judges: Symington accuses them of ethics abuse in their campaign against Prop. 102," Associated Press, August 23, 1996; Norm Parish, "Prop. 102 unfair to blacks, critics say," *Arizona Republic*, August 18, 1996; Martin Van Der Werf, "Prop. 102 denounced by clerics: Youths would be sent to adult court," *Arizona Republic*, October 9, 1996.

3. "Governor attacks at town hall," Associated Press, October 30, 1996.

4. E.J. Montini, "J. Fife Paranoia at the helm," *Arizona Republic*, October 31, 1996. Accusing Symington of blaming others for problems he caused, Montini asked readers: "If faced with constant media exposure while simultaneously trying to welch on a $25 million debt and weasel out of a 23-count indictment, who would *you* blame for your troubles? Yourself? Or, maybe, the press. The courts. Even the universities?"

5. Fife Symington, "Federalism and Judicial Mandates," *Arizona State Law Journal* vol. 28, no. 17. In Symington's speech at the Goldwater Institute event in 1995, reprinted in the *Law Journal*, he said that federal judges "today bring the full weight of huge fines, power to incarcerate, and deployment of federal marshals to coerce compliance with their whims." "Much of our national life today," he argued, "is predicated not on the Constitution, but on a series of spectacular judicial contortions purporting to reveal what the Constitution really means."

6. Fife Symington, in discussion with Robert Nelson, June 4, 2019.

7. Martin Van Der Werf, "Governor is urged again to step down: 2nd GOP official in weeks joins call," *Arizona Republic*, October 25, 1996. According to the story, "Maricopa County Attorney Rick Romley said Thursday that he and others who are considering calling for the governor to step down are documenting specific instances in which Symington is not doing his job."

8. Doug Cole, in discussion with Robert Nelson, July 14, 2020. Regarding Symington's comments that he might try to veto the results of statewide referendums, Cole said, "Symington was

throwing out the prospect that he had veto power on this. A lot of people were pretty appalled that he would say that."

9. Keven Willey, "Governor may be losing it," *Arizona Republic*, November 6, 1996. "It's easy to understand Gov. Fife Symington's frustration. At least three of the ballot propositions he took a position on went the other way last night. To most people, that might indicate that the governor is out of step with the electorate. That it might be a good idea to try to get back *in* step with the electorate. But not Symington. True to form, when the rules of the game don't fit his purpose, Symington simply changes the rules."

CHAPTER 31: "WHO IS THIS GUY?"

1. "Symington's mother dies; it won't affect bankruptcy," Associated Press, November 28, 1996. According to the story, "Martha Frick Symington, granddaughter of U.S. Steel founder Henry Clay Frick, died Tuesday night at Scottsdale Memorial Hospital-Osborn of complications from pneumonia. She was 79."

2. Lukas Velush, "Day of condor finally arrives," *Arizona Daily Sun*, December 12, 1996; Jerry Nachtigal, "Condors to take historic flight," Associated Press, December 12, 1996; see Scottie Andrew and Brian Ries, "The 1,000th California condor has hatched in a victory for the species that nearly went extinct," cnn.com, July 22, 2019.

3. See "Up, up and away," *Arizona Republic*, December 18, 1996. The writer of a *Republic* editorial described the condor release: "For those hundreds of hearty souls who made the trek to see history in the making, the six young California condors did not disappoint. On the majestic Vermilion Cliffs overlooking the Grand Canyon on a chilly morning last week, the fledgling condors spread their wings, caught the wind and soared off into the azure skies. The significance of the moment was palpable, punctuated by a chorus of oohs and aahs as the young birds, born in captivity, experienced their freedom for the first time." The writer noted that, "Even Arizona Gov. Fife Symington, an ardent opponent of the (Endangered Species Act) and who once advocated its appeal, was moved by the moment."

4. John Kolbe, "Governor shifts rhetoric to match time," *Arizona Republic*, January 19, 1997. Kolbe suggested: "Future historians tracking the political evolution of Gov. Fife Symington and Arizona during the 1990s would do well to study his annual State of the State messages." Kolbe concluded: "So, which is the *real* Fife Symington? They all are. He hasn't won four elections against big odds without skillfully adapting to his times and surroundings. But that skill has never been tested like it will be in the coming months. He has a big climb ahead."

5. "State's economy robust through '98," *Arizona Republic*, March 28, 1997.

6. Catherine Reagor, "Esplanade sells for $87 million," *Arizona Republic*, March 19, 1997. According to the story, the Esplanade was purchased by the Oregon Public Employees Retirement Fund for $174 a square foot, making it, according to Reagor, "one of the most expensive office deals since Arizona's real estate bust of the late 1980s."

7. "Ariz. Exports increase 18 percent to $9.9 billion," Associated Press, March 28, 1997.

8. See Sam Dillon and Craig Pyes, "Mexican governors tied to drug dealers," *New York Times*, February 22, 1997. Beltrones had his own problems in early 1997 after this *Times* story, based on a four-month investigation of intelligence documents and numerous interviews, suggested that Beltrones and other Mexican officials had strong ties to Mexican drug traffickers, a charge Beltrones denied. In particular, Beltrones disputed US law-enforcement officials assertions that Amado Carrillo Fuentes, one of Mexico's most wanted drug kingpins, was operating with impunity in his state of Sonora. Beltrones pointed to evidence he said showed he was fighting the cartels and said the reports were "fabricated by political rivals." Symington defended Beltrones, telling the *Republic*, "I know the man, I respect him, and I think what's happening to him is terribly unfair."

9. Martin Van Der Werf and Graciella Sevilla, "Symington stands behind Sonora chief: Discounts tales of counterpart's drug-world ties," *Arizona Republic*, February 24, 1997. The story detailed the trade deals made between Beltrones and Symington as it described their close working

relationship since both came into office within months of each other. "Both men came to power in 1991," the *Republic* story pointed out, "and each has served under a cloud ever since." An accompanying story by Sevilla detailing Beltrones responses to the allegations was headlined, "Beltrones may sue 'Times.'" According to a *Times* story by Azam Ahmed in 2018, Beltrones survived that scandal to become head of Mexico's Institutional Revolutionary Party in the year's after the PRI lost its first election in seventy years in 2000. (The PRI's Ernesto Zedillo, who had called Symington for help six years earlier with the Mexican currency crisis, lost that race, but was widely celebrated for ensuring the 2000 election was fair enough for the opposing party to win. A *Los Angeles Times* writer described Zedillo as the man who "may be remembered as the president who won by losing.") The lead to Ahmed's story on Beltrones, though, explained that scandal continued to follow Beltrones well into the twenty-first century: "For decades, Manlio Fabio Beltrones has presided over Mexican politics with an assured hand, wielding enormous power, amassing a personal fortune and skating past scandals that might have dragged down a less capable operator. But a sweeping corruption case is threatening his legal and political future." Beltrones allegedly directed a plan to siphon millions of dollars in public money to fund his party's campaigns in 2016. In 2003, Arizona journalist Keith Rosenblum suggested in his book *No Accuser, Nor Crime, But You're Guilty* that the 1997 *Times* story on Beltrones, as a reviewer of Rosenblum's book in *The Latin News* said, "had no firsthand evidence linking Beltrones to the drug trade."

10. "Schools first, tax cuts later," *Arizona Republic*, January 16, 1997.

11. Hal Mattern, "Education message is heard: Pressure results in loosening of school-funding purse strings," *Arizona Republic*, April 20, 1997.

12. Paul Davenport, "In the end, action on schools, welfare," Associated Press, April 22, 1997.

13. Shaun McKinnon, "Governor 'did darn well' on his legislative agenda," *Arizona Daily Star*, April 20, 1997.

14. "Symington does right thing," *Arizona Republic*, May 1, 1997. "The two issues have nothing in common—cracking down on hate crimes and barring insurance companies from using genetic testing to deny coverage—except the fact that Gov. Fife Symington this week signed them both into law," the paper's editorial page read. "They were both bold and prudent moves. We applaud the governor on both counts."

15. "A troubling session," The *Daily Star* editorial writers were less supportive of Symington's work in another editorial, saying sarcastically, "Gov. Fife Symington had reason to feel good about himself because the Republicans often marched in lock step with him to cut taxes, pass the inadequate school finance measure, put in the welfare reforms and make far stricter laws for juvenile justice than the voters ever approved in another miscarried proposition."

16. Tom Beal, "Promoters now exploit our heat," *Arizona Daily Star*, May 11, 1997. Amid a column on the news of the previous week, Beal retold the story of Symington's comments at the May Arizona Town Hall with this segue suggesting Symington's high-speed transit ideas were farfetched: "He won't be copping an insanity plea" in the federal criminal case, Beal wrote, "which is the case he seemed to be building last week."

CHAPTER 32: SPACE INVADERS

1. See MJ Banias, "Lights Are Still Unexplained," vice.com, March 13, 2020. "23 years ago today, the people of Arizona witnessed one of the most infamous UFO incidents in history." The story was focused on a new documentary series called "Phoenix Lights: On the Trail of UFOs." Breedlove gave his explanation for the continuing fascination with the sightings: "As an event, the Phoenix Lights is important simply because it gained so much media attention, was witnessed by so many people, and today, can still not be precisely explained away." "Every year more witnesses come forward; from airline pilots to military personnel to ordinary people living from places as far removed as downtown Phoenix to Las Vegas."

2. Kris Mayes, "Defiant governor to run again: Symington 'charging forward' despite troubles," *Arizona Republic*, March 14, 1997.

3. Susie Steckner, "Object seen over state a puzzle—was it UFO?" *Arizona Republic*, March 18, 1997.

4. "Panel for 23rd anniversary of the Phoenix Lights to be held March 15," fox10phoenix.com, March 8, 2020. Dr. Lynne Kitei, who has researched the Phoenix Lights since she witnessed lights in the sky over Phoenix in 1997, was planned to lead the event, which was later postponed due to Covid-19 restrictions. Kitei has published several books on the subject as well as producing a documentary. Former longtime KTAR radio host Preston Westmoreland, who was also scheduled to be part of the panel, said that he came to believe the dozens of people who called into his afternoon radio show describing a giant V-shaped craft; see Tony Ortega, "The Great UFO Coverup," *Phoenix New Times*, June 26, 1997. Ortega presented the story of an amateur astronomer who saw a formation of lights that he quickly and easily identified through his telescope as a group of airplanes. Ortega's story began with a description of eyewitness accounts by two fellow *New Times* reporters. "David Holthouse and Michael Kiefer were in separate parts of the Valley that night, but their reports are remarkably consistent: Each saw a V-shape of five lights moving slowly from north to south. The lights were bright and yellow-white, and seemed very high in the sky. No sound accompanied them. Holthouse says he perceived that something connected the lights in a boomerang shape; Kiefer disagrees, saying they didn't seem connected." Ortega continued to report on the Phoenix Lights and, in time, arguably became the leading skeptic against claims that the event had extraterrestrial origins. On the twentieth anniversary of the "Phoenix Lights," Ortega wrote this on his website, tonyortega.com. "Count on media outlets once again to fail in their most basic responsibility: To explain that there were TWO, very distinct incidents that happened that night. An earlier 'vee' of lights traversed nearly the entire state, and was identified as a group of planes flying in formation by an astronomer in Phoenix using a powerful telescope. Later, a drop of flares was seen over a military range southwest of the city. Because news outlets never make this clear, people who saw the planes argue that flares can't explain what they saw, and the people who saw the flares know that they didn't see planes." Ortega argued that his *New Times* story one year after the event, "The Hack and the Quack," fully explained away any UFO claims.

5. Richard Price, "Arizonans say the truth about UFO is out there," *USA Today*, June 18, 1997. Price wrote that the Phoenix sightings "come at a time when interest in UFOs borders on a national obsession, saturating the move industry, television and literature." He referenced a Gallup poll a year before that found 72 percent of Americans "think there is life on others planets," while "71 percent said they think the U.S. government knows more about UFO's than it's telling."

6. "National media spotlight UFO sighting in Phoenix," *Arizona Republic*, June 20, 1997; "Tapping UFO Flap to Bait the Hook, Ariz. Governor Reels in Reporters," Associated Press, June 20, 1997.

7. Howard Fischer, "The X-Fife: Governor pokes fun at brouhaha over UFOs," Capitol Media Services, June 20, 1997.

8. Fife Symington, in discussion with Robert Nelson, May 9, 2019; see Lynne Kitei, *The Phoenix Lights: A Skeptics Discovery that We are Not Alone* (Charlottesville, Virginia: Hampton Roads Publishing Company, Inc., 2000).

9. Susie Steckner and Chris Fiscus, "X-File is opened into Phoenix 'UFO': Barwood asks staff to investigate lights," *Arizona Republic*, May 10, 1997.

10. Marc Martinez, "Two decades later, 'Phoenix Lights' remains a mystery," fox10phoenix.com, March 13, 2017.

11. Steve Cheseborough, "On a political note: Young composer receives raves in setting 'Guv' sequel to music," *Arizona Republic*, September 20, 1996; "Fife stands in for Ev in new comedy revue," *Arizona Republic*, September 4, 1996. See Dolores Tropiano, "Governors to get 3rd round of lampooning," *Arizona Republic*, October 5, 2005.

12. Kris Mayes, "State politics on hold as case against governor unfolds," *Arizona Republic*, May 14, 1997.

Chapter 33: Pre-Trial Diversions

1. "Trust Me: Charles Keating and the Missing Billions," *Publishers Weekly*, June 1993. In the review of Bowden and Binstein's book, the reviewer wrote, "They follow Mike Manning, Keatings' righteous government tracker who creates a new lexicon of financial terms—'upstreaming cash,' 'straw buyers,' etc.—to argue a big case"; see Emma Lathen, "The Great American Bank Robbery," *New York Times*, November 21, 1993.

2. Charles Kelly, "Lawyer goes for the green on golf course, in court," *Arizona Republic*, December 15, 1996. Kelly quoted friends and opponents of Manning in his extensive profile of the controversial Phoenix attorney. Kelly quoted one Phoenix attorney, who wished not to be identified in the story, describing Manning as both a "shameless self-promoter" and "a very able guy." Steve Pizzo, author of the S&L crisis book *Inside Job*, said, "Mike is one of the invisible heroes of that period of history." Kelly ended his piece with a reference to an exchange between Symington and Manning during a deposition in 1995: "'You laugh,'" Symington told Manning at one point, 'but hindsight's worth a lot, isn't it?' 'So is honesty, Governor,' Manning snapped back. To Manning's critics, that was a noxious bit of piety. To his admirers, it was a nugget of wisdom."

3. Fife Symington, in discussion with Robert Nelson, May 9, 2019; "No louts, please," *Arizona Republic*, May 10, 1996; "Creditors to begin months of confrontations with Symington," *Arizona Republic*, October 29, 1995; Rhonda Bodfield, "Symington documents not public," *Tucson Citizen*, December 22, 1995; Howard Fischer, "Symington funds reach $2M deal," Capitol Media Services, September 14, 2001.

4. See John Kolbe, "Paper chase may benefit Symington," *Arizona Republic*, May 23, 1997.

5. Lisa Bowman, "Schindler heads toward life post-Mitnick," zdnet.com, October 3, 1999. Bowman wrote this profile as Schindler was stepping down as an assistant US attorney to go into private practice. "This month, Schindler, 37, is leaving his life as a prosecutor and settling into a swank new workplace as partner at the law firm of Latham & Watkins. Behind him, he leaves a legacy that includes not only bringing down a governor, but also locking up the most high-profile hackers yet to hit the computer industry."

6. Charles Kelly, "Government's point man is studious and LA cool," *Arizona Republic*, May 11, 1997. Kelly, arguably the *Republic*'s lead feature and profile writer at the time, was tasked with profiling all the major characters in the Symington trial. He described Schindler as "dark-haired and dark-eyed, with the olive skin of a Mediterranean beachcomber." Kelly added that, "Schindler is thoughtful, subtly funny and self-effacing."

7. George S. Cardona, "Faculty Profiles," law.ucla.edu. Cardona became a law professor at UCLA three years after the Symington trial. Cardona was awarded the Attorney General's Award for Distinguished Service in 1998 for his work in the Symington case.

8. John Dowd, in discussion with Robert Nelson, March 2, 2017; Pat Flannery and Charles Kelly, "Symington's advocate a bear for his clients," *Arizona Republic*, May 11, 1997. Flannery and Kelly described Dowd as, "Tall, heavyset, jowly and double-chinned, an ex-Marine with an upturned Irish nose, Dowd can be bearishly charming or bluntly overbearing."

9. Charles Kelly, "Seasoned pair part of 'a good team,'" *Arizona Republic*, May 11, 1997. Lynam, according to attorney Tom Buchanan, was "very thorough, very bright, very careful. He's not going to miss anything." Mejia's friend, DC attorney Patrick Mitchell, suggested Mejia wasn't a typical inside-the-beltway attorney: "I would consider him a lot more thoughtful and well-balanced than a lot of folks back here," Mitchell told Kelly.

10. Terry Lynam, in discussion with Robert Nelson, April 3, 2019.

11. Dowd, discussion with Nelson, March 2, 2017.

12. "Project SLIM could be called Project SLIME," *Tucson Citizen*, July 14, 1995.

13. Martin Van Der Werf, "CPA firm off criminal hook: Symington's ex-accountants agree to $2.2 million settlement," *Arizona Republic*, September 21, 1996. Van Der Werf's story began: "Gov.

Fife Symington's accounting firm has dodged criminal charges by admitting a pattern of deceit and saying the governor himself deserves much of the blame"; Chris Limberis, "Accounting firm agrees to fine in Leckie case," *Arizona Daily Star*, September 21, 1996. "The settlement," Limberis wrote, "gives federal prosecutors a big victory in their pursuit of criminal charges against Symington and his former top aide, George Leckie."

14. "Fife settlement," Associated Press, February 5, 1997. "The agreement knocks Symington's debt down to about $15 million," according to the story.

15. Howard Fischer, "Creditor agrees to settlement with Symington," Capitol Media Services, February 15, 1997.

16. Jerry Kammer, "Symington deposition turns touchy: Lawyers ask judge to step in," *Arizona Republic*, April 29, 1997.

17. David Madrid, "1 claim settled, governor faces 2 more cases," *Tucson Citizen*, January 7, 1997.

18. "Supreme Court ruling a setback to Symington," *Arizona Republic*, February 27, 1997.

19. Paul Davenport, "Symington 'looking forward' to facing additional counts," Associated Press, January 10, 1997.

20. Shaun McKinnon, "Symington jury panelists may be queried on voting," *Arizona Daily Star*, April 17, 1997.

21. Steve Wilson, "Symington judge's temperament will be tested," *Arizona Republic*, May 4, 1997. Wilson interviewed several attorneys and judges familiar with Strand. Wilson said one judge he interviewed suggested Strand, "a Republican appointed to the bench by Ronald Reagan," might have been a lucky draw for Symington. "By virtue of his Republican, Ivy League, country-club background, he probably has some social and political affinity for Symington," the unnamed judge told Wilson. Another judge suggested Strand would be impartial. "I don't think Roger Strand has a defense bent," another judge told Wilson. "He came on the bench from private practice as a civil lawyer. He won't lean one way or the other. He's a diligent, honorable and fair man."

22. Howard Fischer, "Symington lawyers seek disclosure of federal prosecutors' information," Capitol Media Services, March 6, 1997.

23. See "Symington trial timeline," *Arizona Daily Star*, September 5, 1997.

24. Shaun McKinnon, "Opening arguments due in Symington trial," *Arizona Daily Star*, May 16, 1997.

## CHAPTER 34: "ARIZONA'S TRIAL OF THE CENTURY"

1. Sheila McLaughlin, "Courtroom linking up to computers: Terminals could eliminate the need for reams of legal documents," *Cincinnati Enquirer*, January 30, 1992. Five years before the Symington trial, Strand made national news with his work to modernize courtrooms. "It will be just a lifesaver," Strand told the *Enquirer* in 1992. At the time, Strand was helping federal judges based in Cincinnati update their systems.

2. "Courtroom clicks on computers for Symington's fraud trial," *Arizona Republic*, May 7, 1997. "A true marvel," according to the story, "is the court reporter's transcripts of the proceedings, which print, line by line, across a screen at the defense and prosecution tables as courtroom activity progresses."

3. Eric Miller, "Many national media outlets sitting out trial," *Arizona Republic*, May 14, 1997. Miller suggested there was an even bigger trial drawing the country's attention: "Maybe it's the competition from the Oklahoma City bombing trial," he theorized. He listed two other potential dampeners on interest: "The complex nature of the criminal charges" and maybe even "Arizona's reputation for skullduggery."

4. E. J. Montini, "Ignore trial, don't have hopes sunk," *Arizona Republic*, May 11, 1997. Montini argued that "every other well-informed, socially conscious and civic-minded citizen of Arizona" should not "give a damn" to avoid disappointment when Symington is inevitably found not guilty. He suggested the only two satisfying parts of the trial for those who believed Symington was guilty

would be "during opening arguments, when prosecutors get to call Symington a crook" and "during closing arguments, when prosecutors get to call Symington a crook."

5. "Courtroom seating," *Arizona Republic*, May 14, 1997. *Republic* graphic artists offered readers a detailed layout of the courtroom after the first day of the trial, even noting the exact seating of all the main characters and all of Symington's guests. The *Republic*'s coverage included a sketch portrait of Symington by Marlene Linderman.

6. "The Court Observer: Family day in court for both sides," *Arizona Republic*, May 17, 1997. "It could have been a family holiday in the courtroom," the writer of the short piece quipped.

7. See *Arizona Republic*, May 17, 1997. The *Republic*'s coverage included more than a dozen secondary stories and graphics along with the main front-page news story. Besides exceptionally detailed graphics that showed readers key lines from critical Symington financial documents, the coverage included lighter bits. Under the subhead "Legal excitations" in "The Court Observer," for example, the reporter described this scene: "As tension accumulated in the courtroom just before Friday's opening statements, a deputy U.S. marshal unwittingly lightened the mood when he announced to spectators that they should keep their pagers from beeping—and interrupting the proceedings—by setting them in silent mode. 'Ladies and gentlemen, make sure your vibrators are on—er, that your pagers are on vibrate,' he said. The courtroom roared with laughter."

8. The case files of *United States v. John Fife Symington III*, CR-96-250-PHX-RGS, can be obtained by contacting the clerk's office of the United States district court in Phoenix or the National Archives repository in Perris, California. The original court files are stored at the National Archives in Perris in section L021-07-1026, Box 35-41. Federal court case files were not digitized until 2005. Therefore, the full Symington criminal case file is only available in print form. The cost to have the seven boxes of the Symington case made available at the Phoenix federal district court building is $298 ($64 for the first box, $39 for each additional box). The *Arizona Republic* published much of the evidence and testimony from each day's arguments between May and September of 1997. Full access to the newspaper's archives can be obtained for $7.95 a month or $29.95 for six months. The *Republic*'s coverage of the Symington trial can also be accessed with a subscription to Newspapers.com for $19.90 a month, or $74.90 for six months; see Jerry Kammer, "Understanding the Charges: Details of the Counts," *Arizona Republic*, May 17, 1997.

9. Jerry Nachtigal, "Arizona governor called crafty liar," Associated Press, May 17, 1997.

10. David Madrid, "Governor 'abused' position, jury told," *Tucson Citizen*, May 16, 1997.

11. Steve Wilson, "Figuring out what really matters in Symington case," *Arizona Republic*, May 18, 1997. Wilson honed in on the issue of the "materiality" of the prosecution's evidence, nothing that Judge Strand had clearly stated that "prosecuting attorneys need to show that the statements were material to lending decisions, but they don't need to prove the banks relied on them when loans were made to Symington." "This may seem to be a subtle difference," Wilson rightly pointed out, "but it's significant. It's one thing to convince a jury that the statements contained false information that was relevant to loan decisions. It would be harder to prove that the banks actually relied on the information."

12. "Governor 'too optimistic,' defense concedes," *Arizona Republic*, May 17, 1997.

13. Steve Wilson, "Leckie, Symington trials are no cousins of the court," *Arizona Republic*, May 16, 1997. Wilson suggested that even though Leckie's acquittal came on indictments from the same grand jury used in the Symington case, the cases were too dissimilar to believe the Leckie acquittal boded well for Symington. "Symington's fate will not hinge, as Leckie's did, on whether the government can prove what was said in a phone conversation. It will not be hamstrung by a judge's ruling to disallow what might have been the most compelling piece of testimony." "One other key difference in the trials," Wilson suggested after interviews with several legal analysts, was that "Leckie's jury felt more compassion toward him than Symington's will. Weakened by cancer, Leckie was a sympathetic figure. Symington has his health, his family's substantial wealth, and the powers of the state's highest office. Jurors will have a harder time feeling sorry for him."

14. "The Court Observer," *Arizona Republic*, May 30, 1997.

15. See "Last Week's Highlights," *Arizona Republic*, May 19, 1997.

16. Jerry Kammer, "'Feeling great,' he tells listeners of radio show," *Arizona Republic*, May 20, 1997. Symington's bi-weekly KFYI show was moved from its normal Wednesday slot to Monday for the duration of his trial because the court did not convene on Mondays.

17. Shaun McKinnon, "Statements were 'private,' secretary says," *Arizona Daily Star*, May 21, 1997; Jerry Kammer, Pat Flannery, and Charles Kelly, "Reluctant 1st Witness: Confirms Symington secretive about finances," *Arizona Republic*, May 21, 1997.

18. Keven Willey, "Symington's former secretary is reluctant star of 3-ring circus," *Arizona Republic*, May 21, 1997. As Willey described it, one of the dramas playing out was, "Schindler—patiently, politely, unrelentingly—trying to extract damning information from Riebel about her boss." Then, "Riebel wanting to shield the governor as much as possible without perjuring herself."

19. Shaun McKinnon, "Riebel assailed over loyalty to governor," *Arizona Daily Star*, May 24, 1997. McKinnon replayed several testy exchanges between Schindler and Riebel.

20. "Symington's Secretary Testifies About Finances," Associated Press, May 21, 1997.

21. Shaun McKinnon, "27 government witnesses testify over 29 days," *Arizona Daily Star*, July 6, 1997.

22. "The Court Observer: 'Overflow' room lures the media," *Arizona Republic*, May 22, 1997.

23. "Esplanade drained thrift, ex-president testifies," *Arizona Republic*, June 4, 1997.

24. Shaun McKinnon, "Former thrift head tells of Esplanade project gone sour," *Arizona Daily Star*, June 4, 1997. McKinnon's story started: "Southwest Savings and Loan smelled big-time profits when developer Fife Symington proposed in 1983 to build a high-end office and retail complex on the region's most south-after piece of real estate," McKinnon wrote. "Within four years, the former president of the savings and loan testified, the still-unbuilt Camelback Esplanade was stinking up Southwest's books so bad that officials loaned Symington nearly $1 million just to get out of the deal." The document was important to prosecutors because they argued it showed Symington had little remaining interest in the property at the same time he was telling others that his ownership position was more substantial.

25. Shaun McKinnon, "27 government witnesses testify over 29 days," *Arizona Daily Star*, July 6, 1997.

26. "Symington's conflicting claims of value," *Arizona Republic*, June 7, 1997. The *Republic*'s graphics staff worked overtime providing detailed copies of key case documents with critical numbers highlighted and explained. In one document to a business partner, Symington clearly explained why he wanted to sell his remaining interest in two properties during the collapse of his real estate portfolio: "My reason for doing this, Peter, is to gain a little liquidity because I have an enormous payment to make to Jerry Hirsch in early January. I really don't want to sell my interest in Missouri Court but I feel it is the best thing to do at this time and I am trying to make it as attractive an investment as possible for you without totally raping my interest."

27. "The Court Observer: Well, LA Fitness was full . . .," *Arizona Republic*, June 4, 1997. Reynolds became a star of the *Republic*'s daily collection of peripheral news and feature bits related to the trial. "One observer who appeared taken aback by the performance was former Symington aide George Leckie," the story noted.

## Chapter 35: Dog Days and End Times

1. Keven Willey, "Casting call: 'The Trial' needs help," *Arizona Republic*, June 15, 1997. In her inspired effort to bring levity into dreary days, Willey also had Francis McDormand playing Ann Symington, suggesting that besides a good fit, casting McDormand "might get the Coen brothers to direct." Mary Dell Pritzlaff would be played by actress Nancy Marchand: "Remember Mrs. Pynchon in the old Lou Grant TV series? They could be sisters." Willey had Salma Hayek appearing as Annette Alvarez, who Willey admitted hadn't even attended the trial. "Hayek in any role in this movie will guarantee the requisite male attendance."

2. Pat Flannery, "Prosecutors revisit issue of 'materiality,'" *Arizona Republic*, June 28, 1997; "Defense focuses on accounting," *Arizona Republic*, June 28, 1997.

3. Jerry Kammer, "Symington cashed in on mom's bailout: $2,000 investment returned $500,000," *Arizona Republic*, June 21, 1997.

4. "Lender confirms data missing from statements," *Arizona Republic*, June 21, 1997.

5. Shaun McKinnon, "Bank officer raised risk of bankruptcy over indebtedness," *Arizona Daily Star*, June 21, 1997.

6. Steve Wilson, "Newspapers' coverage suggests 2 Symington trials," *Arizona Republic*, July 2, 1997. Wilson pointed out that the *Republic*'s story was headlined, "Bankers feared governor." "It led with testimony from Citicorp executive David Feingold that his company didn't foreclose on a $10 million loan to Symington partly because it was concerned about possible repercussions," Wilson pointed out. "The *Tribune*'s story was headlined, 'Official: Governor disclosed finances to lender.' The story was also based on what Feingold said, but on a totally different piece of testimony, which was favorable to Symington. Feingold's comments about fearing the governor weren't even included in the *Tribune* story." Wilson surmised that, "If reporters can evaluate the testimony so differently, so can jurors. It will not come as a shock if this jury deliberates long and hard and ultimately fails to reach a unanimous verdict."

7. See Howard Fischer, "Symington lawyers accused of 'fishing expedition,'" Capitol Media Services, May 21, 1997; David Madrid, "Pension funds ordered to produce employee files," *Tucson Citizen*, May 24, 1997; John Dowd, in discussion with Robert Nelson, March 2, 2017; Terry Lynam, in discussion with Robert Nelson, April 3, 2019; David Schindler, in discussion with Robert Nelson, March 18, 2017.

8. Shaun McKinnon, "Defense charges witness had personal vendetta," *Arizona Daily Star*, July 12, 1997.

9. Pat Flannery, "Lender: Governor tried to use clout," *Arizona Republic*, July 12, 1997.

10. Pat Flannery, Jerry Kammer, and Charles Kelly, "1989 report was basis for loan, jurors told: Financial statement is key, advisor says," *Arizona Republic*, July 11, 1997. According to the story, "Donald Eaton, a former vice president at McMorgan & Co., which managed the pension funds that made the Mercado loan, told the jury in Symington's federal bank-fraud case that he had never before had anyone 'misrepresent' their net worth on a financial statement."

11. Jerry Nachtigal, "Pension funds believed development was sound," Associated Press, July 11, 1997; see "The Court Observer: Dynamic Duo Dowd, Dougherty at it again," *Arizona Republic*, July 11, 1997. It was during the noon break prior to Eaton's appearance that the feud between Dowd and *New Times* reporter John Dougherty reached new heights. "The Court Observer" described the scene, still famous in media circles to this day, this way: "On Thursday, the sometimes bearishly charming barrister was simply bearish. The only spin he applied was to a reporter's tape recorder, which he swatted into the intersection of First Avenue and Monroe Street. In a foul mood after his lackluster cross-examination of former banker Jane Proctor, Dowd refused to answer questions, twice suggesting that reporters answer each others' questions." The story continued: "Dowd rushed through the huddle and stalked down the sidewalk toward the office rented by the Symington defense team." Dougherty followed Dowd, repeatedly asking him to comment on a legal issue. "Dowd refused to respond, hurling an insult that did not shake the pony-tailed reporter, who has long written critically of Symington's financial dealings. Dougherty held his tape recorder up to Dowd's face, pressing for an answer. Finally as the two crossed the street, Dowd snapped. He smacked at Dougherty's tape recorder with a sweeping backhand that also caught the reporter on the shoulder."

12. Dowd, discussion with Nelson, March 2, 2017; Lynam, discussion with Nelson, April 3, 2019.

13. "The Symington trial: Now, the governor's side," *Arizona Republic*, July 17, 1997. The editors ranked Eaton as the weakest of the government's witnesses. James Cockerham, Jean Wong, Noel Thompson, David Feingold, Paul Meyer, and Katherine Wrigley were deemed "effective as prosecution witnesses."

14. Dowd, discussion with Nelson, March 2, 2017.

15. Jerry Kammer, Pat Flannery, and Charles Kelly, "Prosecution's final witness: Symington detail-oriented," *Arizona Republic*, July 17, 1997.

16. Russ Wiles, "State jobless rate at 13-year low," *Arizona Republic*, July 19, 1997.

17. Steve Wilson, "Symington duplicity at least is helping society," *Arizona Republic*, May 17, 1997. Wilson began his column suggesting Symington was pushing for the CPS money to soften his image with juror with this shot: "You can say this much for Fife Symington, he's consistent. Ever since becoming governor, he has consistently used his office in almost any imaginable way for his personal benefit. We saw it two years ago when he took a pre-bankruptcy European vacation and brought along a three-man security detail, costing taxpayers $14,000. Now, as the day approaches when 12 jurors will decide his guilt or innocence, he's exploiting his position to try to persuade them he's a decent guy."

18. See Martin Van Der Werf, "Clinton, Symington fare differently in poll: President popular in state, governor isn't," *Arizona Republic*, February 1, 1997. Clinton had a 62 percent approval rate while Symington's stood at 33 percent. Symington's approval ratings would stay low throughout the remainder of his tenure.

19. Dowd, discussion with Nelson, March 2, 2017; Lynam, discussion with Nelson, April 3, 2019.

20. Randy Todd, in discussion with Robert Nelson, September 25, 2017.

21. "Symington on Trial: Mercado defended by witness," *Arizona Republic*, July 19, 1997. The *Republic*'s coverage included a letter from Todd and other former Symington employees to his Snell & Wilmer attorneys detailing the Mercado leases McMorgan officials refused to accept. The letter referenced a meeting in late 1989 in which Todd and others claimed Don Eaton talked about how he had "inherited" the loan and that "he was not thrilled with this inheritance." Eaton, Todd, and those who met with Eaton claimed that Eaton, who lived in California, "indicated that he thought Arizona developers were one of the lowest life forms."

22. Shaun McKinnon, "Firm to blame for statements, CPA testifies," *Arizona Daily Star*, July 23, 1997. "Errors in Gov. Fife Symington's financial statements could have been corrected had his accountants used all the available information," McKinnon wrote in the lead of his story.

23. Pat Flannery, Charles Kelly, and Jerry Kammer, "Prosecution grills key defense expert: Major points are given up by accountant," *Arizona Republic*, July 24, 1997. According to the story, "Schindler curtly suggested that Field's desire to get more state work was part of his motive for testifying. 'You know if you scratch Mr. Symington's back, he'll scratch yours, right?' the prosecutor asked. 'No sir,' Field replied, 'I don't know that at all.'" The *Republic*'s coverage included the news that Symington would be taking the stand the following day. "The governor's cheering section in the court will be expanded today, as he takes the stand in his own defense," "The Court Observer" noted. "The seats reserved for the media behind the defense have been cleared out to make way for more supporters of the governor." The announcement the media was being moved in the court-room came the same day that Pritzlaff gave Lew Ruggiero "two major elbow shots in the back and *Arizona Republic* photographer Michael Chow also absorbed a whack." According to "The Court Observer," Symington's son Scott, "tried to laugh off the situation by saying to Pritzlaff, "'Oh, let it go.'"

24. Hal Mattern, "Media circus packs its tent," *Arizona Republic*, July 25, 1997. Mattern's story ran next to the Michael Chow photo of Mary Dell Pritzlaff elbowing Channel 12 reporter Lew Ruggiero; "From the Observer," *Arizona Republic*, September 4, 1997. "Mary Dell Pritzlaff, Gov. Fife Symington's mother-in-law, showed Wednesday that the governor isn't the only fighter in the family," the short piece began. "She waded into news photographers and reporters outside the courthouse after Wednesday's session and dealt them a few body checks to get them away from the governor's elderly father, John Fife Symington Jr., who had flown in from Maryland to attend the trial for the first time." Another *Republic* writer suggested Pritzlaff's hockey-style body-checking acumen should get her name "engraved on the Stanley Cup."

25. Dowd, discussion with Nelson, March 2, 2017; Fife Symington, in discussion with Robert Nelson, May 9, 2019; Lynam, discussion with Nelson, April 3, 2019.

26. Keven Willey, "Symington, the 'little guy,' has eyes, ears of jurors," *Arizona Republic*, July 25, 1997; "Governor takes stand, denies all fraud counts," *Arizona Republic*, July 25, 1997.

27. Shaun McKinnon, "Lender knew his financial plight, governor testifies," *Arizona Daily Star*, July 26, 1997. McKinnon referred to the five hours of questioning as "unexpectedly methodical testimony." "Schindler's confrontation with Symington has been long anticipated," McKinnon continued. "But the prosecutor surprised many with a low-key scattershot approach that touched on Symington's background, his record-keeping and the money he collected as a developer."

28. Shaun McKinnon, "Prosecution misled jurors, defense says," *Arizona Daily Star*, July 30, 1997. At one point, Dowd asked for a mistrial after Schindler mentioned evidence related to a charge that had been dropped. "The government gratuitously injected the non-payment of taxes into this trial," Dowd told Strand. "Nothing offends people more than not paying taxes"; Shaun McKinnon, "Feds methodically chip away at defense case," *Arizona Daily Star*, July 31, 1997. McKinnon concluded in his lead that: "Federal prosecutors chiseled away chunks of two key defense arguments in Gov. Fife Symington's bank fraud trial yesterday, forcing Symington to backtrack on earlier testimony."

29. Shaun McKinnon, "Cross-examination grueling to governor," *Arizona Daily Star*, August 2, 1997. McKinnon described a tense exchange between Symington and Schindler on Symington's fourth day of testifying. "Symington sat ramrod straight, his face rigid and his eyes narrow during the 20-minute exchange with Schindler," McKinnon wrote, "but he was clearly shaken when U.S. District Judge Roger Strand called for a break. After leaving the stand, Symington walked over to the defense table and commented to Ann, who was sitting nearby: 'That was outrageous. Absolutely outrageous'"; "Feds methodically chip away at defense case," *Arizona Daily Star*, July 31, 1997; Paul Davenport, "Lawyer: Elections played role in financial dealings," Associated Press, July 31, 1997. Davenport led his story on Symington's fourth day of testimony with: "The lead prosecutor in Gov. Fife Symington's bank-fraud trial has suggested the pre-election timing of some of the former developer's financial maneuvers is something the jury should note."

30. "Symington testifies in his own defense—Day Four," *Arizona Daily Star*, July 31, 1997. The *Daily Star* ran the full transcript of the telling day-four exchange between Symington and Schindler regarding loan guarantees.

31. See Jerry Kammer and Charles Kelly, "Prosecution didn't prove case, defense tells court," *Arizona Republic*, August 5, 1997. According to the story, in a hearing before Strand separate from Symington's testimony, Lynam and Dowd argued that prosecutors didn't offer evidence that their client took "a substantial step" to follow up on his alleged attempt in 1990 to extort concessions from the lender on his Mercado project. Dowd and Lynam's attack on the extortion charge was part of their ongoing broader attempt to have Strand dismiss all twenty-two counts.

32. "Symington judge drops 1 count, defense rests," *Arizona Republic*, August 6, 1997; "Symington Trial Highlights," *Arizona Republic*, August 6, 1997.

33. Shaun McKinnon, "Closing arguments seen as crucial in complex trial," *Arizona Daily Star*, August 6, 1997.

34. "Don't be deceived, Symington's jury is told," *Arizona Republic*, August 7, 1997; Shaun McKinnon, "Schindler revisits opening plea: 'It's time for lies to stop,'" *Arizona Daily Star*, August 8, 1997; see Terry Greene Sterling, "The Fifester, the Wifester, the Mother and the Prosecutor," *Phoenix New Times*, August 14, 1997. Greene Sterling explored Schindler's use of class conflict. "Schindler is smart. He played on the aversion most middle-class working people have for the elitist rich. Over and over again, he mentioned Symington's pedigree and education as though they were character flaws. Even privileged Harvard graduates, he said, aren't allowed to defraud banks and get away with it." Greene Sterling continued: "The young prosecutor even offered the jury a pathetic, but likely, motivation for the governor's need to be seen as a successful guy—he wanted to be like his great-grandfather, steel robber baron Henry Clay Frick."

35. "Dowd at end of 'painful journey,'" *Arizona Daily Star*, August 8, 1997. The *Daily Star* ran large portions of Dowd's final argument. "I'm sure you're as glad as I am to come to the end of this three-month audit," Dowd said. "That's what this trial has been about."

36. See Pat Flannery, "Jury retires, work is just starting: 4 picked as alternates; shelves of papers follow 12 on panel," *Arizona Republic*, August 9, 1997.

37. Steve Wilson, "Jury likely to find Symington guilty on at least 1 count," *Arizona Republic*, July 30, 1997. One of the federal judges Wilson spoke with suggested that if the jury was hung, there would be no retrial: "You don't put a sitting governor through this again, unless the vote is 11–1 for conviction and one nut is the only holdout," the judge told Wilson.

38. Joe Burchell, "Predictions lean toward conviction," *Arizona Daily Star*, August 10, 1997.

Chapter 36: Hard Times

1. Jay Heiler, in discussion with Jack L. August Jr., February 2, 2014; Doug Cole, in discussion with Robert Nelson, December 5, 2018; Fife Symington, in discussion with Robert Nelson, May 9, 2019.

2. David Pittman, "Boyd on list for Hull job: If a conviction forces Symington to step down, the secretary of state post would open up," *Tucson Citizen*, June 16, 1997; "Hull ready to take reins," *Arizona Republic*, September 2, 1997; see Howard Fischer, "Joe Arpaio has the edge in '98 governor's race," Capitol Media Services, June 27, 1997. As reporters explored the potential implications of a conviction, polls conducted by Michael O'Neil suggested Arpaio was the most popular official in the state. "Speculation about Arpaio's political future has been rampant since he started polling approval ratings far higher than any other elected official," Fischer wrote. Symington had a 37 percent approval rating in O'Neil's poll.

3. Keven Willey, "Gutsy schools idea may prove fatal," *Arizona Republic*, August 10, 1997. Referring to her "Klan" comment, Graham Keegan said: "Some will say that's hyperbole, but I'm not sure I understand the difference." In the same column, Willey noted details from May surveys of the eventual twelve jurors in the Symington case: "There are five Republicans, five Democrats, one registered Independent and one non-voter on the jury. Seven jurors say they voted for Symington in 1994, one voted for Basha and four didn't vote at all." Willey also noted that, "Only three jurors have college degrees; nine own their own homes. One juror lost money he'd invested with a real estate company that went bankrupt. Another—a 23-year-old former Taco Bell shift manager who lives with his parents—said his father lost his real estate business in a market downturn."

4. Matt Kelley, "Ozone in red zone: EPA calls it 'serious' in Phoenix, at least for now," Associated Press, August 27, 1997; see Mary Jo Pitzl, "Women sue EPA over Valley air: Complaint seeks ruling on ozone in Phoenix," *Arizona Republic*, July 9, 1997.

5. Maureen West, "Panel to consider state guidelines for doctors," *Arizona Republic*, August 11, 1997. West wrote that, "The governor formed the group in the wake of a U.S. Supreme Court decision in June giving states authority to regulate physician-assisted suicide."

6. Matt Kelley, "Officials order tribes to stop offering card games," Associated Press, August 13, 1997.

7. Pat Flannery, "Stirrings fruitless in Symington case," *Arizona Republic*, August 16, 1997.

8. See Shaun McKinnon, "False alarm breaks lull; jurors work for a 4th day," *Arizona Daily Star*, August 15, 1997. Things were so slow that McKinnon led his daily trial story with this: "No news is no news at the federal courthouse where seven men and five women are deliberating the fate of Gov. Fife Symington."

9. Shaun McKinnon, "Juror is dismissed; reason kept secret," *Arizona Daily Star*, August 20, 1997; David Madrid, "Off-limits tax issue plagues defense, prosecution, jurors," *Tucson Citizen*, August 21, 1997. "Judge Dismisses Juror in Arizona Governor's Fraud Trial," *Los Angeles Times*, August 20, 1997.

10. Pat Flannery, Jerry Kammer, and Charles Kelly, "Symington juror dismissed: Deliberations to continue with remaining panelists," *Arizona Republic*, August 20, 1997.

11. Mark Flatten, "Ousted juror says she was 'obstruction': Pro-acquittal panelist refused to bargain, take straw votes," *Mesa Tribune*, August 20, 1997; Pat Flannery, Charles Kelly, and Jerry Kammer, "Former juror called confused: Symington deliberations sent back to Square 1," *Arizona Republic*, August 21, 1997. The *Republic*'s coverage included extensive excerpts from transcripts of closed-door hearings related to Cotey's competence as a juror.

12. See Steve Wilson, "'Symington defense' doesn't work for former juror," *Arizona Republic*, August 22, 1997. Wilson wasn't alone in suggesting Dowd was reaching by painting Cotey as a competent juror who made enemies by standing her ground on Symington's innocence. "A woman so befuddled she couldn't recall what she had just voted on and couldn't fill out her lunch card, this is a juror Dowd insists is lucid and coherent," Wilson wrote sarcastically.

13. Symington, discussion with Nelson, May 9, 2019.

14. Pat Flannery and Jerry Kammer, "Symington lawyer files 3rd motion for mistrial," *Arizona Republic*, August 22, 1997.

15. Maria Baier, in discussion with Jack L. August Jr., February 25, 2014. Baier, a speechwriter for Symington at the time, said in her interview with August: "He just did not let (the legal issues) interfere with his obligations. He just didn't. And even when he was in trial, and I thought this was one of the most amazing things, you're in federal court every day on trial and the guy would come in every day after court and he would have a meeting with his senior staff and he would ask questions that were so detailed and like perfect recollections of what the discussion had been the day before." "How could you sit in court all day and then come to meet with your staff and remember in great detail what's going on in the office." "I was always shocked by it."

16. Richard Ruelas, "Arena football already a big deal in Iowa," *Arizona Republic*, August 25, 1997.

17. See Steve Yozwiak, "Volatile politics the norm: Symington trial continues tradition of strange events," *Arizona Republic*, September 2, 1997. In the lull of jury deliberations, the *Republic* explored the "bizarre history" of Arizona's governors. Yozwiak's story began with the story of John Addison Gurley, who was appointed the state's first territorial governor in 1863 but died before ever seeing the territory; Kathleen Ingley, "Goddard was right in long run: Governor's image as success refuted," *Arizona Republic*, September 4, 1997. Ingley began her story: "The one thing Terry Goddard will never say is, 'I told you so.' And yet he did."

18. Howard Fischer, "Conviction wouldn't halt governor's pension," Capitol Media Services, August 31, 1997.

19. Catherine Reagor, "Many developers cooked books in '80s," *Arizona Republic*, September 4, 1997. Reagor's sources were unusually frank in describing the real estate development landscape in Phoenix in the 1980s. Where there wasn't intentional number manipulation, there was nearly always over-optimism, she suggested. Reagor quoted Jay Butler, director of the Arizona State University Center for Real Estate, as saying, "Many developers made the mistake of living on hope instead of paying attention to the cycle of real-estate ups and downs." "All developers who lost properties, like Symington, believed their projects would be viable when the economy rebounded, as it did a few years ago," Reagor wrote. Reagor noted, though, that the recent sale of the Camelback Esplanade for $87 million wasn't necessarily confirmation that the Esplanade was a winner. "But even at that price," Reagor wrote, "during a peak in the market, the project wouldn't have been viable with its original $120 million loan, real-estate analysts say."

20. John Dowd, in discussion with Robert Nelson, March 2, 2017; Symington, discussion with Nelson, May 9, 2019; Terry Lynam, in discussion with Robert Nelson, April 3, 2019.

21. Mark Flatten, "Guilty and Gone," *Mesa Tribune*, September 4, 1997; Jerry Nachtigal, "Guilty Arizona governor resigns," Associated Press, September 4, 1997; Rhonda Bodfield and David Madrid, "Symington convicted: He's found guilty on seven counts," *Tucson Citizen*, September 3, 1997. Paul Davenport, "Jane Hull ready to lead Arizona," Associated Press, September 4, 1997; Todd S. Purdum, "Arizona Governor Convicted of Fraud and Will Step Down," September 4, 1997.

22. Symington, discussion with Nelson, May 9, 2019; Dowd, discussion with Nelson, March 2, 2017.

23. Fife Symington, in discussion with Jack L. August Jr., April 20, 2016; Symington, discussion with Nelson, September 12, 2017.

24. See "Symington shows he still puts state first," *Tucson Citizen*, September 4, 1997. The editorial page editors commended Symington for stepping down immediately. "Although the resignation was required, there had been concerns that Symington would delay his departure, citing ambiguous legal wording about whether he was actually 'convicted' when the jury returned its verdict or when he is sentenced two months hence. But he didn't want any part of such a constitutional crisis, and the state is much better because of his statesmanlike decision." Considering how the following months and years played out, it is feasible that Symington could have remained until his term ended more than a year later.

25. Dave Walker, "Media winners, losers: Broadcasters out in force for Symington's big day," *Arizona Republic*, September 4, 1997.

26. See David Leibowitz, "Ousted juror could have saved him," *Arizona Republic*, September 4, 1997. Leibowitz watched the coverage of the jury's decision with Mary Jane Cotey, the juror who had been ousted ten days earlier. After two hour with Cotey, he wrote: "The question was lucidity, and though Cotey seems exactly that as you share chicken sandwiches, who can say better than the 11 others plus a judge who spent 15 weeks with her? Two hours with her does not a psychological exam make." Leibowitz, a rising young star in print, radio, and television in Phoenix at the time, continued: "But you do believe her about one thing. She never would have buckled, she confides, she would have held fast." "I would have," she told Leibowitz. "But the anger in the room was getting very high. I'd rather walk out than deal with that, all their whining."

27. Hal Mattern and Chris Moeser, "GOP stoic after verdict: Both parties say they'll back Hull during the transition," *Arizona Republic*, September 4, 1997; see John Kolbe, "Too many fights for a man who'd 'rather fight than eat,'" *Arizona Republic*, September 4, 1997. In his post-conviction column, Kolbe focused on Symington's fierce competitiveness and how that trait, in Kolbe's opinion, both made him and broke him. Kolbe revisited a conversation with a state lobbyist who had told him that Symington "would rather fight than eat." "But he may have picked one fight too many." Kolbe, whose work appeared in both the *Republic* and the afternoon paper at which he spent most of his career, the *Phoenix Gazette*, finished his column with another comment to future historians: "Never able to marshal public affection or media sympathy, he commanded—by sheer dint of intellect, hard work and maniacal persistence—a grudging respect and admiration in political precincts. Amid the wreckage of the reputation of Fife Symington, the man and developer, that record may not give him much solace. But the guess here is that history, the kind written long after newspapers have turned to dust, will be somewhat kinder to Fife Symington, the governor." Kolbe, often labeled "the dean of Arizona political writers," died two years later of colon cancer. Since his death, the Arizona Press Club has yearly awarded the state's top political reporter with the John Kolbe Politics and Government Reporting Award.

28. Howard Fischer, "GOP spin is friendly to Symington; Demos' less so," Capitol Media Services, September 4, 1997.

29. Symington, discussion with Nelson, June 26, 2017 and June 4, 2019.

30. Arthur H. Rotstein, "Governor's time in prison won't be easy, former inmates say," Associated Press, October 15, 1997.

31. Martin Van Der Werf, "State GOP losing conservative edge," *Arizona Republic*, September 9, 1997. "The conservatives who control the party at the grass roots," Van Der Werf wrote, "are not happy" about Hull replacing Symington. Also, "They don't much favor on Attorney General Grant Woods or Superintendent of Public Instruction Lisa Graham Keegan." "The right wing," Van Der Werf suggested, "is likely to lay out a number of litmus tests for Hull, starting with a tax cut that could be as large as $350 million, and see how she does."

Chapter 37: The Waiting Game

1. Jerry Nachtigal, "Symington penalties debated in documents: Stiff punishment vs. probation," Associated Press, December 16, 1997; Howard Fischer, "Both sides seek to delay Symington sentencing until Feb. 2," Capitol Media Services, September 25, 1997.

2. "Pensions sue firm for $10 million payment: The union funds are going after Symington's accountants in an attempt to collect," Associated Press, December 4, 1997. Manning accused Symington's accounting firm of conspiring with Symington to defraud lenders in the Mercado project.

3. Steve Wilson, "Symington's crime-fighting words prove true in the end," *Arizona Republic*, September 4, 1997.

4. Steve Tuttle, "Symington got what he deserved," *Arizona Republic*, September 28, 1997; David Leibowitz, "Symington backers reek of hypocrisy," *Arizona Republic*, September 10, 1997; David L. Teibel, "Symington's future: searches, cells," *Tucson Citizen*, September 8, 1997; "Symington assistants beginning to pack it in," Associated Press, September 10, 1997. Heiler resigned within days of Symington's conviction, which, the AP story noted, was greeted as a positive step by Democrats and moderate Republicans who "often blamed Heiler for killing programs they favored." Assistant Senate Minority Leader Ruth Solomon, a Democrat from Tucson, said: "I think (Heiler's) advice to former Governor Symington was the reason he moved the government and the policies of the state way out of the mainstream." With Heiler gone, she speculated, "we'll move more back to the way mainstream Arizonans feel."

5. Jerry Kammer, "Symington disputes 'lavish' life claim: Says he's a victim of 'financial bigotry,'" *Arizona Republic*, January 8, 1998. Schindler argued that a report of Symington's personal expenses from 1986 to 1991 supporting their call for a ten-year sentence. According to Kammer's story, government accountants "reported that Symington spent more than $50,000 on ski trips, $280,000 for travel, $55,000 for club dues and expenses, $100,000 on household employees, and $200,000 on school and travel for his two oldest children over the six-year period."

6. Jerry Kammer, "Banker asks for leniency for Symington: Letter sent to judge despite loss on loan," *Arizona Republic*, January 15, 1998. Kammer wrote that "the letter also raises the question of whether the bank is giving Symington special treatment." Kammer quoted banking expert Bert Ely as saying, "As a general rule, banks are pretty hard-nosed about collecting money, and you'd expect a publicly held bank to be particularly sensitive about appearing to do favors for anyone."

7. "Arthur B. Laffer letter to Judge Roger G. Strand," January 12, 1998, Symington Papers, Folder 1995–1997.

8. Arthur Rotstein, "Symington face 'humbling' experience inside U.S. prison," Associated Press, October 12, 1997; Tom Beal, "Fife gets good advice from pragmatic, experienced convicts," *Arizona Daily Star*, February 1, 1998.

9. Terry Lynam, in discussion with Robert Nelson, April 3, 2019.

10. See Howard Fischer, "U.S. sought to jinx Symington re-election, defense says," Capitol Media Services, January 8, 1998. Fischer wrote that while Dowd argued prosecutors went after "Fife Symington to overturn the 1994 gubernatorial election and thwart the will of Arizona voters," Schindler suggested that Symington "should take his own advice that criminals should be held accountable for their actions."

11. Howard Fischer, "Rejection of blame may hurt Symington: Report advises against leniency," Capitol Media Services, January 27, 1998. Fischer wrote that, "Mark Nebgen, a senior federal probation officer, said in a report released yesterday that the former governor doesn't deserve leniency because he won't accept blame for the fact that those who lent him money lost millions of dollars." According to Fischer, "Nebgen said federal law gives consideration to those who accept responsibility for their actions. Dowd said that isn't possible here, as Symington contested the charges."

12. "Judge throws out one Symington conviction," Associated Press, January 21, 1998.

13. Ann Symington, in discussion with Robert Nelson, April 18, 2018; Fife Symington, in discussion with Robert Nelson, June 4, 2019.

14. "Primer on Symington sentencing," *Arizona Republic,* February 2, 1998.

15. Pat Flannery, Jerry Kammer, and Charles Kelly, "Symington sentenced for Fraud: Down for the counts," *Arizona Republic,* February 3, 1998. The *Republic* dedicated four pages to Symington's sentencing beyond four front-page stories; Jerry Kammer, "Restitution to end in 2nd court," *Arizona Republic,* February 3, 1998. Kammer detailed Stand's decision to refer the issue of restitution to the US Bankruptcy Court, a move defense attorney Mike Black called "extremely unusual." According to Kammer's story, Black "said he had never heard of a federal court judge leaving the matter of restitution up to a Bankruptcy Court." At the same time, though, Black admitted that, "On the other hand, I don't know how many other fraud defendants had a bankruptcy pending at the same time."

16. Jerry Nachtigal, "My non-violent offenses 'different,' Symington says," Associated Press, February 4, 1998.

17. David Madrid, "Next stop may be Nev. Prison," *Tucson Citizen,* February 3, 1998.

18. Symington, discussion with Nelson, May 9, 2019; Ann Symington, discussion with Nelson, April 18, 2018; Whitney Morgan, in discussion with Jack L. August Jr., December 11, 2015.

19. "Symington gets 30 months, fine," *Arizona Republic,* February 3, 1998; see "Sentence fit crime, jury says: But some expected more jail time, fines." *Republic* reporters interviewed several jurors in the case. The jurors, the *Republic* story suggested, "agreed generally that the punishment fit the crime." "None of the jurors," according to the story, "seemed surprised by Symington's refusal to accept responsibility for the crimes" since, as one juror said, "He probably feels that he didn't do anything wrong, and he has no reason to show remorse."

20. See Jerry Kammer, "Symington is likely to avoid prison during appeal: Has a good chance to be granted bail, Phoenix lawyers say," *Arizona Republic,* February 4, 1998.

CHAPTER 38: NEW HOPE AND $8.25 AN HOUR

1. Pat Flannery and Jerry Kammer, "Symington fate still in limbo: Judge says he'll rule on request to remain free 'with dispatch,'" *Arizona Republic,* March 10, 1998. In the story, Symington was quoted as saying he was using his free time to "work hard to make sure we abolish the state income tax." See James D. Karis, "Just favors the rich," *Tucson Citizen,* February 25, 1998. Karis was not alone in believing Symington had received a lighter sentence than the average citizen: "I am an inmate at the Arizona State Prison at Florence. There are a lot of men here who disagree with the sentence handed out to Fife Symington. It really shows that we have a real double standard. We have had two very large white-collar crimes take place here in Arizona: Symington and Keating, and in both cases, the defendants got off with just a small slap on the wrist. In retrospect a man such as James Hamm—who received a second-degree murder conviction for killing a drug dealer, served 17 years for his crime and became a model inmate—is now being denied a license to practice law because he was in prison. I have never in all my 75 years on this earth seen such unfairness. Our justice system has really developed a double standard and it's in favor of the rich."

2. Jerry Kammer and Pat Flannery, "Symington ordered to jail: Loses in effort to stay free pending appeal," *Arizona Republic,* March 11, 1998.

3. Fife Symington, in discussion with Robert Nelson, May 9, 2019.

4. Terry Lynam, in discussion with Robert Nelson, April 3, 2019; John Dowd, in discussion with Robert Nelson, March 2, 2017; Symington, discussion with Nelson, May 9, 2019.

5. "United States v Symington III," United States Court of Appeals, Ninth Circuit, https://case-law.findlaw.com/us-9th-circuit/1437257.html.

6. Michelle Rushlo, "Fife not going to prison yet," Associated Press, March 14, 1998.

7. Mike McCloy, "Talk shows, tax plan resurrect Symington," *Arizona Republic,* March 27, 1998. "Buoyed by a federal appeals-court ruling that keeps him out of prison while he challenges his bank and wire fraud convictions," McCloy wrote, "the former governor on Thursday was back in the limelight, granting media interviews and appearing on radio talk shows." Symington was even

talking about another political campaign: "I'd make a good candidate," he told David Leibowitz.

8. Michael Murphy, "Drive to repeal income tax dies: Lack of time, circulators citied," *Arizona Republic*, June 15, 1998.

9. Howard Fischer, "Symington cooks up tasty boredom-beater," Capitol Media Services, August 29, 1998; Symington, discussion with Nelson, June 4, 2019; Robert Wilson, in discussion with Robert Nelson, July 26, 2019.

10. Fife Symington, "Headmaster of the old school," *Arizona Republic*, February 9, 1999. Symington and Kolbe were neighbors in the Arcadia neighborhood.

11. Rhonda Bodfield, "Symington's fate in hands of those he often criticized," *Arizona Daily Star*, November 5, 1998; "Former Arizona governor seeking federal appeal," *Baltimore Sun*, November 5, 1998; Jerry Kammer, "Court hears Symington appeal: Dismissal of juror is key in bid to toss fraud counts," *Arizona Republic*, November 5, 1998.

12. Symington, discussion with Nelson, May 9, 2019; Ann Symington, in discussion with Robert Nelson, April 18, 2018; Lynam, discussion with Nelson, April 3, 2019.

13. Dowd, discussion with Nelson, March 2, 2017; Lynam, discussion with Nelson, April 3, 2019; "United States v Symington III, Ninth Circuit," FindLaw, https://caselaw.findlaw.com/us-9th-circuit/1437257.html.

14. "Symington verdicts overturned: Court: Juror wrongly dismissed," Associated Press, June 22, 1999.

15. Symington, discussion with Nelson, May 9, 2019; Ann Symington, discussion with Nelson, April 18, 2018.

16. Howard Fischer, "'Bankrupt' Symington may have ready cash," Capitol Media Services, June 23, 1999. Fischer wrote that "Fife Symington still says he's bankrupt—or at least that he was broke four years ago. But that hasn't stopped him from spending more than $3 million on legal fees, mostly in his effort to stay out of prison." "Facing a possible new trial after yesterday's appellate court ruling," Fischer continued, "he sidestepped questions about whether he's prepared for the costs of going back to court." Dowd wouldn't tell Fischer exactly how much Symington had already spent in legal bills, only calling it "a king's ransom."

17. See Julie Amparano, "Court's decision met with dismay," *Arizona Republic*, June 23, 1999. Amparano interviewed a random Arizonans to get their thoughts on the case. The majority of those interviewed suggested Symington was receiving favoritism that the average Arizonan wouldn't get: "This shows that Arizona has two sets of laws," Marina Della said. "One for the rich and powerful and one for us."

18. Jerry Kammer, "Lawyers weigh next move: Dowd reacts cautiously, Schindler emphasizes solidness of case," *Arizona Republic*, June 23, 1999; "New Day for Symington: Symington conviction void," *Arizona Republic*, June 23, 1999. The *Republic*'s June 23 coverage included the full opinions of the three judges in the case; see Michael Janofsky, "A Technicality Becomes a Get-Out-of-Jail-Free Card," *New York Times*, March 28, 2002.

19. Pat Flannery, "Symington reversal likely to hold fast," *Arizona Republic*, June 24, 1999.

20. Lisa M. Bowman, "Q&A with David Schindler," zdnet.com, July 28, 2000.

21. Symington, discussion with Nelson, May 9, 2019; Lynam, discussion with Nelson, April 3, 2019.

22. Pat Flannery, "Symington prosecutor to join LA law firm," *Arizona Republic*, August 18, 1999. Schindler told Flannery, though, that he might return as a "temporary special prosecutor" if the Symington case was to be retried.

23. "Fife free and clear: Appeals court upholds decision to overturn his conviction," Associated Press, March 27, 2000.

24. Howard Fischer, "$11M judgment vs. Symington void: Court rules he didn't get a fair hearing on Mercado debt," Capitol Media Services, January 7, 2000.

25. Franco Fazzuoli, in discussion with Robert Nelson, June 4, 2019; Symington, discussion with

Nelson, June 4, 2019; Jerry Kammer, "Symington: Standing calmly in the eye of the storm," *Arizona Republic*, April 16, 2000. Kammer, one of the lead writers throughout Symington legal tribulations, wrote a lengthy profile of the Symington in his new life as a rookie chef.

CHAPTER 39: THE REMAINING LEGAL ISSUES

1. Pat Flannery, "Symington's finances prompt new court battle," *Arizona Republic*, March 11, 2000.

2. "Feds postpone decision on Symington retrial for 6 months: Former governor's attorney lobbying against prosecution," Associated Press, May 25, 2000.

3. Patrick Graham, "Symington confident he'll beat lawsuit," Associated Press, March 15, 2000.

4. Jerry Kammer, "Fife returns to court: Pension funds press for loan repayment," *Arizona Republic*, March 16, 2000.

5. Steve Wilson, "Symington has some nerve, chastising lenders," *Arizona Republic*, April 6, 2000.

6. Patrick Graham, "Former CFO testifies: Symington misled pension funds," Associated Press, March 18, 2000; "Symington finances described at trial," *Arizona Republic*, March 21, 2000.

7. Jerry Kammer, "Unruffled Symington takes stand: Defends bid to obtain loan," *Arizona Republic*, April 1, 2000.

8. Jerry Kammer, "Symington: Standing calmly in the eye of the storm," *Arizona Republic*, April 16, 2000. Symington explained that his back pain, Kammer said, "was the lingering effect of tumbling into a street as he fought off a knife-wielding mugger during a trip to Spain last year with his wife." He had taken that trip soon after he was given back his passport after the federal appeals court ruling in his criminal case. Manning brought up Symington's Spain vacation, which was paid for by Ann, as one of the examples of Symington's alleged lavish lifestyle as he claimed poverty, a claim Symington denied while on the stand in the case.

9. Jerry Kammer, "Bankruptcy judge quizzes Symington: Key issues surface in court's queries," *Arizona Republic*, May 26, 2000.

10. Penelope Overton, "Judge leaning toward Symington," Associated Press, July 22, 2000.

11. Jerry Kammer, "Symington's fraud trial is expected to end today," *Arizona Republic*, August 30, 2000; Jerry Kammer, "Ex-banker bolsters Symington claim," *Arizona Republic*, September 2, 2000.

12. John Dowd, in discussion with Robert Nelson, March 2, 2017; Terry Lynam, in discussion with Robert Nelson, April 3, 2019; Fife Symington, in discussion with Robert Nelson, May 9, 2019.

13. Howard Fischer, "Retrial decision deadline extended: End of January is latest date in Symington case," Capitol Media Services, December 29, 2000.

14. See Rick Barrs, "Criminal with an Asterisk," *Phoenix New Times*, May 15, 2003. Amid a biting column focused on Dowd's attacks on writers who forgot to note that Symington's convictions were overturned, the *New Times* editor wrote that "one source claims Fife went so far as to actually sign a plea agreement" on one count, "but Dowd declared, 'We never signed anything.' 'The correct way to say it is, we were in discussions about a plea agreement ... but we hadn't accepted the (government's) offer.'"

15. Symington, discussion with Nelson, June 4, 2019.

16. David Johnston, "The Nation; Pardons: Having to Say You're Sorry," *New York Times*, September 12, 1999.

17. Symington, discussion with Nelson, May 9, 2019.

18. Ann Symington, in discussion with Robert Nelson, April 18, 2018.

19. Tommy Caplan, in discussion with Jack L. August Jr., June 2, 2013.

20. Dowd, discussion with Nelson, March 2, 2017.

21. Lynam, discussion with Nelson, April 3, 2019.

22. John Solomon, "Clinton pardons 140 Americans, including brother," Associated Press,

January 21, 2001. In Solomon's piece, Symington got fourth billing behind Roger Clinton, ex-CIA director John Deutch, and Cisneros.

23. David Schindler, in discussion with Robert Nelson, March 18, 2017.

24. Howard Fischer, "Symington says he may have saved Clinton from sea," Capitol Media Services, January 21, 2001. In a press conference following the pardon news, Symington, speaking of the 1960s swimming incident, said he believed Clinton "probably would have survived, but I certainly lent him a helping hand." He downplayed the idea that Clinton pardoned him because of the near-drowning experience. "I think he probably had good feelings about me, as would I for somebody pulling me out of the drink if I was in trouble." But he added, "I think the issue was a little more profound than that."

25. "Admission of wrongdoing now lost: Pardon of Symington error on Clinton's part," *Arizona Republic*, January 21, 2001; see Pat Flannery, "Symington pardon a bolt from the blue," *Arizona Republic*, January 21, 2001. In this short piece, Flannery described from a personal perspective what it had been like covering the Symington trial and the events that followed. "This wasn't the way anyone expected it to end—including Fife Symington." Flannery said "there had been rumors recently of a plea agreement being offered by prosecutors. Newspaper reporters started digging through old files, updating telephone numbers, trying to prepare for what they expected to be an announcement ending the case. A plea deal made sense, after all. There were new prosecutors on the case, and nobody seemed to relish the idea of another long, costly trial." What nobody in the media knew "was this: Three weeks ago, an emissary arrived in Symington's legal camp saying President Clinton would entertain a presidential pardon." At the *Republic*, he wrote, "an editor heard it first on National Public radio shortly after 9 a.m. Saturday." "A call went out for all hands on deck. Pagers and cell phones started making noise. Extra editors were brought in. That's the nature of news. It happens when and where it wants, and often it is surprising. In this case, it was fitting. Like Symington himself, it was unpredictable to the end but never a dull moment."

26. See Robbie Sherwood, "Why a pardon? Symington saved Clinton's life, story goes," *Arizona Republic*, January 21, 2001. After interviewing several people familiar with the story of Symington rescuing Clinton at the 1960s party, Sherwood wrote: "No one is daring to say the rescue played any part in Clinton's decision to grant a pardon, but most agree on this: It couldn't have hurt."

27. Howard Fischer, "Symington can't evade debt: Former governor defrauded pension funds, judge rules," Capitol Media Services, February 17, 2001; "Judge: Fife gave false info to get $10M loan," Associated Press, February 17, 2001.

28. Joel Eskovitz, "Pensioners declare hollow victory in Symington bankruptcy case," Associated Press, February 18, 2001.

29. Howard Fischer, "Bank told to pay $12M for part in Fife Scandal," Capitol Media Services, February 17, 2005. A jury determined that Wells Fargo Bank (formerly First Interstate Bank) owed the pension funds the money for not doing enough to investigate Symington's finances. First Interstate had provided interim financing for the construction of the Mercado, which was then to be replaced with permanent financing provided by the pension funds. The jury concluded that Wells Fargo owed $4.1 million related to the 1990 deal. Including interest over fifteen years and $1.9 million in attorneys fees, the number would hit $12 million.

30. Howard Fischer, "Symington faces questioning on source of money," Capitol Media Services, February 22, 2001.

31. Howard Fischer, "Symington, funds reach $2M deal," Capitol Media Services, September 14, 2001. Fischer wrote that, "Facing a threat by Fife Symington to 'disinherit' himself, union pension funds have agreed to accept a $2 million payment from the former governor to satisfy their $17.4 million-bankruptcy judgment against him. But they may have to wait awhile to get their money— at least until one of Symington's relatives dies." Fischer noted another key reason for pension funds to agree to a settlement: "Under the deal, Symington would drop his appeal of the February ruling by" Nielsen.

32. "Symington may cook up bid for Az. House," Associated Press, July 30, 2001. While many scoffed at Symington's plan, Jim Weiers, the Republican who would end his term as house speaker in 2002, said Symington, "would make a great speaker." "The man does know the issues incredibly well, but I am remaining neutral about the speaker's race," Weiers said. But another house Republican, Rep. Steve May, argued that Symington "knows nothing about the beast he hopes to run."

33. Jonathan Marshall, "Simple solution to stadium maze," *Arizona Republic*, August 4, 2001.

CHAPTER 40: THE FOODIE

1. Fife Symington, in discussion with Robert Nelson, June 4, 2019; Ann Symington, in discussion with Robert Nelson, April 18, 2018; Robert Wilson, in discussion with Robert Nelson, July 26, 2019.

2. Howard Fischer, "Symington cooks up tasty boredom-beater," Capitol Media Services, August 29, 1998.

3. Wilson, discussion with Nelson, July 26, 2019; Symington, discussion with Nelson, June 4, 2019.

4. Symington, discussion with Nelson, May 9, 2019.

5. David Leibowitz, "You know best, here's the worst," *Arizona Republic*, September 5, 1998. In his "best and worst" list, he called Symington's entry into culinary school "Worst Comeback by a Disgraced Political Hack." "The Fifester has his eyes on the restaurant biz, but I'm thinking, why not a cooking show: 'The Defrauding Gourmet.' How about 'Cooking With Conviction'?"

6. Dolores Tropiano, "Scottsdale to boast culinary competitors," *Arizona Republic*, November 10, 2001.

7. Franco Fazzuoli, in discussion with Robert Nelson, June 4, 2019; "Symington stirring up dishes, talk on radio," *Arizona Republic*, November 5, 1999. Soon after becoming Fazzuoli's "apprentice chef," Symington and Fazzuoli began appearing every other Thursday afternoon on Tony Femino's show on KTAR-AM. A *Republic* piece described the occasional show, called "Cooking with Fife." "Symington cooks up special recipes with chef Franco Fazzuoli while chewing the fat with Femino about everything from cooking to politics to sports to pop culture."

8. Dolores Tropiano, "Symington cooking up a brand new career in Scottsdale," *Arizona Republic*, August 27, 1999.

9. Randy Todd, in discussion with Robert Nelson, September 25, 2017.

10. Charles Kelly, "Meet Glendale's go-to guy: Jerry Moyes gets the job done, and he isn't in it for the glory," *Arizona Republic*, September 1, 2002. Besides owning Swift, valued at over $1.5 billion at the time, Moyes was part owner of the Phoenix Coyotes and, as Kelly noted, "the primary investor in the Arizona Culinary Institute in Scottsdale, of which former Gov. Fife Symington's wife, Ann, is a co-owner."

11. David Schwartz, "Comeback Kid," *Phoenix Magazine*, September 2007; Nikki Buchanan, "Franco Fazzuoli is Back in Town," *Phoenix New Times*, October 9, 2012.

12. Howard Seftel, "Franco's (and Fife) moves to Esplanade," *Arizona Republic*, October 30, 2002; Michelle Rushlo, "Former Arizona governor reinvents himself—as chef," Associated Press, March 31, 2003.

13. See "Ball in Trump's court as his team decides on next move in Biltmore plan," *Arizona Republic*, May 29, 2005. According to the story, "Trump, the superstar New York developer who projects a street-savvy image, and partner Bayrock Group want to put up a high-rise building on a prime parcel east of 24th Street and Camelback Road, the hub of the ritzy Camelback Corridor. Despite signing up a roster of top lobbying muscle, the developers appear to have been out-muscled by nearby residents, who have scored big wins against Trump."

14. Mark Kimble, "'The Governor' definitely gets my vote—as dessert," *Tucson Citizen*, February 24, 2004; Camilla Strongin, in discussion with Robert Nelson, June 15, 2019.

15. Doug Cole, in discussion with Robert Nelson, December 5, 2018.

16. C. J. Karamargin, "Symington may make new run for governor," *Arizona Daily Star*, Febru-

ary 5, 2005; Robbie Sherwood, "State sizes up a Symington run," *Arizona Republic*, February 5, 2005. Jim Pederson, chairman of the state Democratic Party, said Symington could be a "formidable" candidate. Democratic consultant Bob Grossfeld disagreed, telling Sherwood: "He would have to spend his entire campaign explaining away a felony conviction for ripping off pension funds and engaging in other fraudulent activities, and trying to explain why his conviction was overturned. Lord knows, our side has a history of taking blessings like this and still losing. But even we couldn't screw this one up."

17. "Solemn State of the State: Hull delivers challenge," *Arizona Republic*, January 15, 2002. The lead editorial began: "Let's forgive the Arizona Legislature for barely raising a blip on the applause meter during Gov. Jane Hull's final State of the State address Monday. She didn't bring them a lot of clap-generating good news."

18. Robert Robb, "Hull's ideological vacuum a disappointment," *Arizona Republic*, January 18, 2002. Gannett Company Inc. bought Central Newspapers, owner of the *Republic*, in 2000, which brought it under common ownership with the *Tucson Citizen*. The newspapers began sharing content in the 2000s. For example, Robb's column on Hull's State of the State also appeared in the *Tucson Citizen*.

19. Robert Robb, "Who leads, who follows, and where to?" *Arizona Republic*, March 1, 2002.

20. Chip Scutari, "Symington 'just a happy chef,'" *Arizona Republic*, June 14, 2001.

## CHAPTER 41: "YOU COULDN'T MAKE THIS STUFF UP"

1. "Republic poll says 83 percent of voters confident in governor's abilities," *Arizona Republic*, January 1, 2006. The Arizona poll showed that 39 percent of those polled felt "very confident" in Napolitano's ability to govern, while another 44 percent felt "somewhat confident."

2. Doug MacEachern, "Fife is back," *Arizona Republic*, February 13, 2005.

3. Mike Manning, *Arizona Republic*, February 13, 2005.

4. See Jeff Smith, "Symington's comeback hinges on dark miracles," *Tucson Citizen*, February 9, 2005. Smith argued that Symington wouldn't have the freedom to run for governor if he wasn't a wealthy, connected blue blood. If Symington's name was "Chuy Pesquira and his curriculum vitae comprised a G.E.D. and a career at Vance Goodman's Tires, do you think he could have prevailed against his felony convictions to become ... a pastry chef?" Smith argued. "Hell, he'd have been getting his mail forwarded to (the prison) in Florence. But when your name is preceded by an initial and followed by Roman numerals, your diploma reads "Harvard" and the blood in your veins runs so blue your skin and hair are practically translucent, well, things are different for you."

5. "GOP: Who will face Napolitano," *Arizona Republic*, April 22, 2005. As of late April, the field of Republicans yet to officially step out of the race included Symington, former Second Lady of the United States Marilyn Quayle, US Surgeon General Richard Carmona, Senate President Ken Bennett, Secretary of State Jan Brewer, and financial advisor Keith DeGreen. By November, the only Republicans running were Jan Smith Florez, former State Senate President John Greene, and Don Goldwater, nephew of Barry Goldwater.

6. "Symington to sit out '06 vote," Associated Press, May 6, 2005. "I just don't have the enthusiasm that I had when I was there and I ran my two races," Symington told the Associated Press. Symington said he did not think he would run for governor again, but didn't close the door on running for some other office.

7. Luci Scott, "Covance enlists PR assistance: Firm responding to pressure from animal activists," *Arizona Republic*, September 24, 2005. Strongin, a longtime public relations expert who served as the media spokeswoman for the Republican Party during the 2004 campaign season, told Scott, "the benefit of having a firm like ours is that we can only take on things that we believe in. We're not going to represent a company or issue we don't all agree is the right thing." A separate story noted that becoming a foe of the left-leaning members of PETA probably wouldn't damage Symington's reputation much with Republican voters if he chose to run for office in the future.

8. Christina Leonard, "Tent City joins list of biometrics users: Sheriff wants to combat terror-

ism," *Arizona Republic*, September 20, 2002. Leonard quoted "Daniel Biondi" in her story about Arpaio's push to improve the department's ability to do background checks on inmates. Biondi, identified as "a retired Army major general assigned to the National Security Agency," told Leonard, "The key to the kingdom is getting access to the larger databases. We need someone nationally respected and who has credibility on a national basis, and the sheriff has that." Hummingbird Defense Systems had donated a $350,000 facial-recognition system to the Maricopa County Sheriff's Office. Although the Hummingbird system could successfully "perform fingerprint and retinal or iris scans and the capability to search several databases at once," it was never used to track down the true identity of "General Biondi" himself.

9. Fife Symington, in discussion with Robert Nelson, June 4, 2019. Symington said his company worked with "General Biondi" for six months before Arpaio identified the man as a fraud. "He had been recommended to us by a software developer who didn't know his real identity either. We wanted a military guy on board to help us as we went looking for defense industry contract," Symington said in a 2019 interview. "The guy had fabricated his story brilliantly. He never broke his façade. He even showed us his scrapbook." "He wanted a $250,000 salary, we couldn't afford that so we offered him stock in the company." Symington continued: "Arpaio called up and said, 'Governor, your General Biondi isn't a general. He's a con artist.' I told (the con artist) I would sick the FBI on him if he wasn't gone immediately. He just disappeared." "We never heard another word about him," Symington said.

10. See Mary Jo Pitzl, "Symington: 10 Years Later," *Arizona Republic*, September 3, 2007. Pitzl, who had written extensively about the governor during his tenure, revisited him for an extensive profile on the tenth anniversary of his resignation.

11. Symington, discussion with Nelson, May 9, 2019.

12. *Out of the Blue*, James Fox, Sci Fi Channel, June 24, 2003. Peter Coyote narrated the documentary, which was distributed on DVD by Hannover House. Fox's sequel, *I Know What I Saw*, aired on the History Channel in 2009. Symington, discussion with Nelson, June 4, 2019; John Hook, "Fife Symington Reflects on his Time as Governor," Fox 10 News, May 8, 2014. Hook's fascinating television interview with Symington regarding his alleged sighting can be seen at https://www.youtube.com/watch?v=v1Fhog5wJ7A.

13. Howard Fischer, "The X-Fife: Governor pokes fun at brouhaha over UFOs," Capitol Media Services, June 20, 1997. Fischer's lede noted that prior to the Heiler-as-alien stunt, "Gov. Fife Symington perked up a few ears earlier this week when he told radio listeners he thinks Earth already may have been visited by extraterrestrial beings."

14. Fox's videotaped interview with Symington is available through OpenMindsTV at https://www.youtube.com/watch?v=y2ZW96F_UWs.

15. See "UFO: Leslie Kean, Nick Pope, Fife Symington, and James Fox" on HLN's "The Joy Behar Show," August 24, 2011, Part 2 of 2, https://www.youtube.com/watch?v=y2ZW96F_UWs. Don Lemon, sitting in for Joy Behar, guided the ten-minute panel discussion with three UFO researchers and Symington.

16. Symington, discussion with Nelson, October 12, 2019. Symington's retelling of the story in the 2019 interview and several other interviews hasn't varied from the story he first told to Fox.

17. Leslie Kean, "Symington confirms he saw UFO 10 years ago," *Daily Courier*, March 19, 2007.

18. Anderson Cooper, "Anderson Cooper 360" blog, cnn.com, March 21, 2007. "It's not every day a former governor tells you he witnessed a UFO that he believes came from another world," Cooper wrote in his blog. "Ok, that's an understatement. I don't believe a person who has served as governor has ever uttered such words on camera. But that's what Fife Symington, who served as governor of Arizona for six years in the 1990s, just did." Cooper struggled to make sense of Symington's admission: "What was it? Frankly, I have no idea and wouldn't hazard a guess. But Symington's revelation a decade later only adds to the mystery surrounding this event."

19. A video of the November 12, 2007, panel discussion at the National Press Club, is available at https://www.youtube.com/watch?v=y2ZW96F_UWs.

20. "Larry King Live," CNN, November 9, 2007. A transcript of the panel discussion can be found on CNN's website at http://transcripts.cnn.com/TRANSCRIPTS/0711/09/lkl.01.html.

21. See Dolores Tropiano, "Symington promotes new cooking school in Scottsdale," *Arizona Republic*, June 22, 2001. "Construction is underway on the $2 million school, which will incorporate a restaurant," Tropiano wrote. "The facility will cater initially to 100 students and eventually to about 300. Tuition is set at $15,000 for the nine-month course." "We will be teaching the traditional classic French method of cooking," Symington told Tropiano. "Leite will be president and chief executive officer of the Arizona Culinary Institute," Tropiano continued, "partnering with Symington's wife, Ann, in her company, Fleur de LLC. Fife Symington will serve as an assistant and advisor in the project."

22. Robert Wilson, in discussion with Robert Nelson, July 26, 2019; Symington, discussion with Nelson, June 4, 2019; Randy Todd, in discussion with Robert Nelson, September 25, 2017.

23. See Peter Corbett, "Valley has ingredients: More chefs in kitchen," *Arizona Republic*, May 10, 2002. Corbett described the difficult and seemingly saturated market in which ACI was operating. At the same time there were numerous schooling options for budding chefs, Corbett argued, there also seemed to be a booming market for well-trained chefs. "The dot.com bomb," Corbett wrote, "sent thousands of workers searching for a stable career and others, fed up with their jobs, switching to something they have a passion for, such as cooking."

24. Wilson, discussion with Nelson, July 26, 2019; Symington, discussion with Nelson, June 4, 2019.

25. "Culinary school leader found dead in his home," *Arizona Republic*, July 14, 2005.

26. Arizona Culinary Institute, "Accreditation and Licensure," http://azculinary.edu/accreditation-licensure/.

27. Todd, discussion with Nelson, September 25, 2017. Todd provided most of the details of the difficult negotiations with FirstBank Holding Co.; Symington, discussion with Nelson, June 4, 2019.

Chapter 42: Reefer Sensibleness

1. Rhonda Bodfield, "Symington, voters don't see eye to eye," *Arizona Republic*, November 6, 1996.

2. Keven Willey, "Governor may be losing it," *Arizona Republic*, November 6, 1996.

3. "Ballot propositions," *Arizona Republic*, November 1, 1998.

4. Barbara Bruce, "Snowflake tomato plant to close," *White Mountain Independent*, September 20, 2015.

5. Doug Cole, in discussion with Robert Nelson, March 3, 2021; Five Symington IV, in discussion with Robert Nelson, March 9, 2021.

6. Naomi Hatch, "Snowflake Town Council reaffirms votes on marijuana grow facilities," *Tribune*, August 17, 2016.

7. Fife Symington III, in discussion with Robert Nelson, March 12, 2021.

8. "Copperstate Farms Announces Plans to Expand Cannabis Cultivation," *GlobeNewswire*, March 4, 2021.

# INDEX

FS = Fife Symington III
Page numbers in *italics* indicate images

5080 Building (Phoenix, Arizona), 65

abortion: Arizonans reject restrictive law on,
    199; FS on, 272; as issue in 1990 Arizona
    gubernatorial election, 122, 125, 132, 139
Adams, Howard, 222; on Camelback
    Esplanade, 74
Aetna, 61–62
Agnew, Spiro, 249; FS and, 36, 60–61
Air Force: FS in, 44, 48, 49–52
air quality regulations, 196
Akin Gump, 166, 293, 347
Alaric: quoted by FS, 251
Alaska: fishing trips to, 387, 392
Albo, Joe, 2, *207*
Albuquerque, New Mexico: Phoenix compared
    to, 54
Aleshire, Peter: on similarities between
    candidates in 1990 Arizona gubernatorial
    election, 132
Ally (alligator), 27–28
Alvarez, Annette: controversies surrounding,
    177, 179–80; as international relations aide
    to FS, 157, 161, 172; resignation of, 180;
    romantic relationship with FS conjectured,
    179–80
America West: bailout of, 159–61; flights to
    Mexico City by, 161
American Continental: bankruptcy of, 108
American Museum of Natural History: Childs
    Frick's contributions to, 16
Anti-Drug Abuse Act (1988), 117
ArenaBowl XI (1997), 330
Arizona Biltmore Hotel, 59, 60
Arizona Business Leadership for Education
    (ABLE), 159
Arizona Center (Phoenix, Arizona), 216, 429n12
Arizona Citizens for Education (ACE):
    Proposition 103 and, 133–34, 138
Arizona Court of Appeals: FS's case before, 349

Arizona Culinary Institute (ACI), 376–79,
    390; expansion considered, 391; financing
    and construction of, 363; growth of, 366;
    opening of, 364; preliminary discussions
    about, 361–62
Arizona House of Representatives: Evan
    Mecham impeached by, 87, 97; FS considers
    run for, 358-59
Arizona Military Institute, 252
Arizona State University (ASU): Barbara
    Barrett at, 420n4; budget cuts for, 154; Jay
    Heiler at, 182; Mercado space rented by, 315;
    renewable energy at, 373; Super Bowl XXX
    on campus of, 198
Arizona Town Hall, 217, 279, 284
Arpaio, Joe, *211*, 373; anti-crime stance of,
    210, 228; as Republican golden boy, 278;
    satirized, 288
art: FS and, 46–47; Henry Clay Frick's
    collection, 13
assisted suicide, 327–28
athletics: FS and, 36–38
Atwater, Lee, 115
AzScam, 176

Babbitt, Bruce, 204, 281; on FS as governor,
    148–49; Grand Canyon's closure (1995) and,
    264, 265; Martin Luther King Jr. holiday
    established in Arizona by, 84; on mining
    royalties, 212; retirement, 83
Badertscher, Bunny, 178; in 1990 Arizona
    gubernatorial election, 119
Baier, Maria, *207*, 226; on FS's focus during
    legal proceedings, 447n15; on FS's speech-
    writing process, 419n3
Baltimore, Maryland: Symingtons in, 20–21;
    World War II's effect on, 34
Bans, Larry, 363–64
Baring Brothers Merchant Bank (London): FS's
    internship at, 47

Barker, Leslie. *See* Symington, Leslie Barker
    (first wife of FS)
Barkley, Charles: FS on, 416n4; satirized, 288
Barnes, Bob: in 1990 Arizona gubernatorial
    election, 116, 120
Barr, Burton: in 1986 Arizona gubernatorial
    election, 83
Barrett, Barbara: in 1994 Arizona gubernatorial
    election, 232–34, 241; John McCain's letter
    to, 235; as potential candidate in 1994
    Arizona gubernatorial election, 214
Barrett, Craig, 233
Bartlett, David: on FS's legislative tactics, 193
Barwood, Frances: on Phoenix Lights, 287
Basha, Eddie: in 1994 Arizona gubernatorial
    election, 238–39, 241–47; calls for FS to take
    a leave of absence, 276
Bassett, R. Steven: on Mercado project, 222
Bayless, Betsey, 346–47
Beal, Tom: on 1994 Arizona gubernatorial
    election, 246–47; on FS, 284
Beltrones, Manlio Fabio, 258, 259, 283
Bennett, Ken: as potential candidate in 2006
    Arizona gubernatorial election, 455n5
Bennett, William, 117
Berkman, Alexander, 12–13
Biden, Joe, 390
Bidwill, Bill, *160*
Biondi, Daniel, 373
Black, Charles: on FS's nomination as Arizona
    governor in 1990, 126
Blacky (steer), 28
Blim, Warren, 361
Bodney, David, 172
Bono: on Evan Mecham, 85
*Book on Basha: Chronicles of a Liberal, The. See
    Chronicles of a Liberal* (campaign book)
Boyce, Timothy: testimony at FS's criminal trial
    of, 308–9
Brewer, Jan, *371*; on FS, 277; as potential
    candidate in 2006 Arizona gubernatorial
    election, 455n5
Bronze Star: won by FS, 52, 304, 321
Brooklyn Bridge: closed by escaped bear, 25
Brooklyn Zoo, 25
Bruce, Robert the, 19
Buchanan, Pat: on US government's bailout of
    Mexico (1995), 253
Buck, Ed: Evan Mecham recall movement led
    by, 86–88
budget policy: of FS, 150, 152–54, 184, 189, 191,
    193–97, 226, 251–52, 254, 271
Bundgaard, Scott, 278; on Arizona legislative

calendar, 289
Burgess, Ken, *206*
Burke, Edmund: FS on, 43
Bush, George H. W., *174*, 190, 199, 201; in 1990
    Arizona gubernatorial election, 144; on FS
    as governor, 148; Grand Canyon hike of
    (1991), 173–75; on supply-side economics,
    195
Bush, George W.: in 1996 US presidential
    election, 258; inauguration of (2001), 2–3,
    9, 356; US federal government's bailout of
    Mexico (1995) and, 253–54
Butcher, Preston, 61
Buttrick, John: in 1994 Arizona gubernatorial
    election, 244–45, 246
Byrne, Alfred, 166

California condor: reintroduction into wild
    of, 281
Calvert School (Baltimore, Maryland): FS at,
    32–34
Camelback East Village Planning Committee:
    Camelback Esplanade and, 74, 78
Camelback Esplanade (Phoenix, Arizona),
    3, 57, 83, 217; development of, 66–80;
    financing of, 93–96, 163, 167; materials for,
    92–93; sale of, 282–83, 310; tenets for, 92,
    167, 365; as white elephant, 168
Camelback High Neighborhood Association:
    on Camelback Esplanade, 74
Camelback Mountain preserve, 1
cannabis: Arizona's growth and, 386. *See also*
    marijuana
Cantelme, Patrick Emmett, 88–89
Caplan, Tommy, 7–9; FS and, 7, 38; FS's
    presumptive pardon and, 8–9, 355–56
Cardona, George: as prosecutor in FS's criminal
    trial, 292, 318, 325, 340, 344, 345–46, 349
Career Education Corporation: Scottsdale
    Culinary Institute purchased by, 361
Carmona, Richard: as potential candidate in
    2006 Arizona gubernatorial election, 455n5
Carnegie, Andrew, 10, 11; Homestead Steel
    Strike (1892) and, 12; philanthropy of, 13
Carnegie Museum of Natural History: Childs
    Frick's contributions to, 14
Carter, Jimmy: draft dodgers pardoned by, 2
Castle Point (Bermuda) estate, 47, 48
Castro, Raul, *371*
cattle: Arizona's growth and, 53, 386
Chanel No. 5 (skunk), 28
Charles Schwab & Co.: job growth at, 262–63
Charter Government Committee (Phoenix,

Arizona), 56
charter schools, 119, 191–93, 196, 202, 229, 367;
    as issue in the 1994 Arizona gubernatorial
    election, 245
Cheuvront, Ken, 263, 289
Chicanos por la Causa, 215; Mercado project
    and, 217, 222
child support collections, 201, 204–5
Children's Rehabilitative Services (Arizona):
    budget cuts for, 153
Childs, Adelaide Howard. See Frick, Adelaide
    Howard Childs (wife of Henry Clay Frick)
Chow, Michael, 319–20
Chronicles of a Liberal (campaign book), 242–43
Citicorp, 314; verdict about FS's dealings with,
    332
citrus fruits: Arizona's growth and, 53, 386
Civil War: FS's states' rights approach
    compared to Confederacy in, 250; William
    Stuart Symington in, 20–21
Civilian Military Training Program: Childs
    Frick in, 15
Clay, David, 161
Clayton mansion (Roslyn Harbor, New York),
    16–17
Clean Air Act (1963), 250
clean air initiatives, 118, 173, 250, 282
climate: Arizona's growth and, 53, 386
Clinton, Bill, 203; 1994 midterms and, 242,
    247; 1995 State of the Union address, 248;
    elected president, 199; FS presumptively
    pardoned by, 355–57; FS's relationship with,
    4–5, 6; Grand Canyon's closure (1995) and,
    265; life saved by FS of, 8; pardons of, 356,
    357; Tommy Caplan and, 7, 8; US federal
    government's bailout of Mexico (1995) and,
    253–54, 385
Clinton, Hillary, 203
Coalition for Effective State Leadership, 87
Cockerham, James: testimony at FS's
    bankruptcy proceedings of, 352; testimony
    at FS's criminal trial of, 310–11, 317
Colangelo, Jerry, 200; as Thaifoon investor, 364
Cole, Doug, 185, 188, 380; on 1991, 172–73; in
    1994 Arizona gubernatorial election, 233; on
    decision-making while FS was governor,
    188; effectiveness of, 204; fishing trips of,
    387; on FS during criminal trial, 278, 327;
    FS's criminal indictment and, 277; on FS's
    debt, 263; on FS's polling numbers, 208,
    270; on FS's privacy, 335; on FS's travel, 172;
    Grand Canyon's closure (1995) and, 264,
    265; as lobbyist, 383–84; on Resolution

Trust Corporation (RTC)'s investigation's
    effect on FS, 173; Steve Tuttle on, 249
commercial lease tax: proposed, 201–2
Communism: Barry Goldwater and Fife
    Symington Jr. on, 34; FS on, 43
Considine, Terry: on Porcellian Club, 46; on
    similarities between candidates in 1990
    Arizona gubernatorial election, 132
Consolidated Gas Company, 21
Constitutional Defense Council, 230, 249
Contract with America, 248; effect on Arizona
    of, 255
Cooper, Anderson, 376
Coopers & Lybrand, 178, 272–73, 336; blame for
    FS's legal issues asserted, 305–6, 310, 311, 314,
    319; settlement by, 273, 293–94
copper: Arizona's growth and, 53, 386
Copperstate Farms, 380–86
Cotey, Mary Jane (juror 161): legality of
    dismissal questioned, 328–29, 330, 338, 342,
    343–44, 345–46, 347
cotton, 245; Arizona's growth and, 53, 386
Coughlin, Chuck, 341; 1994 Arizona
    gubernatorial election, 232, 233, 244; fishing
    trips of, 387; on FS's candidacy in 2006
    Arizona gubernatorial election, 369; as
    lobbyist, 383; on Proposition 400, 371–72;
    on tax policy, 257
Covance: public relations campaign for, 372–73
Covid-19, 387, 390
Cox, Roderick H.: on FS's maturity, 30–31
Cranston, Alan: in Keating S&L scandal, 143
criminal justice policy: of FS, 119, 202, 209–11,
    212, 228–29, 256, 278, 283; of Paul Johnson,
    237
Cunningham, George, 269; on FS's resignation,
    334

Dai-Ichi Kangyo Bank (DKB): Camelback
    Esplanade financing and, 94–96; FS accused
    of defrauding, 276, 311, 324, 343; verdict
    about FS's dealings with, 332
Daily, Sam: on Mike Manning, 290
de Berge, Earl, 73, 83, 238–39, 256
Deardorff, Charles, 170
death penalty: FS on, 210; Grant Woods on,
    425n2
DeBolske, Jack, 131
debt-service moratoriums, 61–62
DeConcini, Dennis: in Keating S&L scandal,
    108, 142; poll numbers of, 176
DeGraw, Rick, 422n21, 423n5; on 1990 Arizona
    gubernatorial election, 141

DeGreen, Keith: as potential candidate in 2006 Arizona gubernatorial election, 455n5

Del E. Webb Construction Company: Camelback Esplanade and, 92, 93; Grand Canyon's closure (1995) and, 265; Phoenix's growth and, 53–54, 55

Democratic Party (Arizona): FS and, 150, 152, 156, 177; on FS as governor, 149–50, 153; FS's bankruptcy and, 262, 276

Depository Institutions Deregulation and Monetary Control Act (1980), 105–6

desegregation: in Baltimore, 34

Desert Island Restaurants, 364

Deutch, John: pardon of, 453n22

Dixon, Frances Shoemaker ("Dixie"), *17*; inheritance of, 16; marriage of, 15

Dole, Bob, *137*, 147; in 1990 Arizona gubernatorial election, 144; on S&L investigations, 145

Donofrio, Robert: on school choice, 159

Dowd, John: in 1990 Arizona gubernatorial election, 144; on Coopers & Lybrand, 294; cost for legal services of, 203, 268; as FS's criminal attorney, 3–4, 291, 292–93, 294, 296–98, 301, 302–3, 304, 305, 306, 307, 309, 310, 311, 315, 316, 317, 318, 319, 320, 321, 322, 323, 325–26, 328, 330, 331–32, 336, 337, 338, 341, 342–44, 345–46, 347; FS's presumptive pardon and, 2–3, 4–5, 6, 9, 356; on John Yeoman's death, 274; in Keating S&L scandal, 108; on Resolution Trust Corporation investigation of Southwest Savings and Loan, 165–66, 168–69, 170

drug cartels, 283

drug policy: of FS, 117, 118, 263, 280

Ducey, Doug: Copperstate Farms and, 385

Dukakis, Michael, 134

Eagle Rock cottage, 15, 45, 47

Eaton, Donald: testimony at FS's bankruptcy proceedings of, 352; testimony at FS's criminal trial of, 315–16

Eaton Centre (Toronto, Ontario), 71

Echo Canyon Trail, 1

economic policy: of FS, 118–19, 189–91 (*see also* supply-side economics)

education policy: of FS, 119, 158–59, 191, 202, 204, 229, 250, 263, 271, 271–72, 327. *See also* school choice; school funding

Eisenhower, Dwight, *35*, 45

Eisenhower, Milton: in 1964 US presidential election, 34

El Paso, Texas: Phoenix compared to, 54

elections: 1960 US presidential, 38; 1964 US presidential, 34, 41, 45; 1982 US midterms, 81–82; 1986 Arizona gubernatorial, 83–84; 1986 Arizona Senate, 82–83; 1990 Arizona gubernatorial, 98–103, 110–47; 1994 Arizona gubernatorial, 208, 214, 232–47; 1994 US midterms, 242; 1996 US federal, 278; 1996 US presidential, 258–59; 2002 Arizona gubernatorial, 369; 2006 Arizona gubernatorial, 366, 368, 369–71, 372; 2020 Arizona Senate, 391; 2020 US presidential, 390

Employing and Moving People Off Welfare and Encouraging Responsibility (EMPOWER), 251

Endangered Species Act (1973), 241, 257; FS on, 260, 281

"English Only" movement, 88–90, 128, 129

ENSCO, 153, 155, 157

environmental policy: of FS, 118, 119, 152, 196, 202, 230, 250, 257, 260, 276, 282, 318; as issue in the 1994 Arizona gubernatorial election, 241, 243

Episcopalianism: FS and, 1

Espinoza, Tommy: Mercado project and, 217

euthanasia. *See* assisted suicide

Evans, Mike: on FS's attorney's fees, 264

Fazzuoli, Franco, 390–91; on FS, 362; FS hired as pastry chef by, 365; FS's externship with, 349–50, 362, 364

Federal Home Loan Bank Board: capital rules of, 106; on Southwest Savings and Loan, 165, 169

federal overreach: FS on, 212, 229–30, 250, 264, 279

Federal Savings and Loan Insurance Corporation (FSLIC): insolvency and dissolution of, 107

Feingold, David: testimony at FS's criminal trial of, 314–15, 317

Field, Lawrence: testimony at FS's criminal trial of, 319

Fife, Earl of, 19

Fife, Margaret Leith, 19

Figge, Fred: on Mike Manning, 290

Finney, Redmond ("Reddy"), 36; as coach, 37–38

First Interstate Bank: FS accused of defrauding, 276, 304, 323–24; Mercado project and, 220; verdict about FS's dealings with, 332

FirstBank Holding Co.: Arizona Culinary Institute (ACI) and, 378, 379

Fischer, Howard, 117, 330–31; on FS's legal problems, 297

Fitzgerald, James, 346, 347

Fitzpatrick, Tom: on Camelback Esplanade, 75–76; on FS, 57, 67, 72–73, 75–76, 122; on Sam Steiger's candidacy in 1990 Arizona gubernatorial race, 122

Flatten, Mark, 185, 425n7

Fletcher, Betty, 346, 347

football: FS and, 32, 36, 37–38, 39; FS's Arizona State University (ASU) season tickets to, 261, 263. *See also* ArenaBowl XI (1997); National Football League (NFL); Super Bowl XXVII (1993); Super Bowl XXX (1996)

Fort McDowell Indian Gaming Center: raid on (1992), 184–86

Fort McHenry (Baltimore, Maryland): British attack on (1814), 20

Fox, Ed, 257; resignation of, 260

Fox, James, 374–76

foxhunting: Fife Symington Jr. and, 21, 29, 36

Franco's Italian Caffe (Phoenix, Arizona), 365, 390

Franco's Trattoria (North Scottsdale, Arizona), 349, 350, 365

Franke, Bill: America West bailout and, 160–61

freeway construction, 251, 372

Frick, Adelaide (daughter of Childs Frick), 17

Frick, Adelaide Howard Childs (wife of Henry Clay Frick), 14

Frick, Childs, 17; birth, 14; inheritance of, 16; on Marsie's pregnancy, 24; professional life of, 14, 16, 28; Rupert River canoeing expedition and, 40; in World War I, 15

Frick, Frances (daughter of Childs Frick), 17

Frick, Helen Clay ("Grauntie"), 1; social consciousness of, 14–15; trust fund established by, 295

Frick, Henry Clay, 1–2, 10–14, 24; art collection of, 13; attempted assassination of, 12–13; death and estate of, 16; family life of, 14; Iron Rail and, 15; philanthropy of, 13; portrait of, 13–14, 113

Frick, Henry Clay, II: estate of, 358

Frick, Martha Howard ("Marsie"; mother of subject), 17, 18, 26; alcoholism of, 31; animals and, 25, 28–29; birth, 15; childhood of, 25; children of, 24; death, 281; engagement and marriage, 16–17; FS's inheritance from, 295; knowledge of FS's financial troubles of, 314; as mother, 31; New York move to, 25; Valley National Bank and, 295

Frick family, 10–17

Friedman, David, 69

Friedman Family Trust, 169, 171

Friedman parcel (Phoenix, Arizona), 69, 71, 73, 167, 171. *See also* Camelback Esplanade (Phoenix, Arizona)

Fromm, Freddie: rescue of, 51–52

Gaia, Jeff: on Mike Manning, 290

gambling: on Native American reservations, 184–87, 240, 258, 280, 328

gang violence, 119, 123, 154, 202, 228; FS on, 209, 210

Garcia, Pete: Mercado project and, 215, 217, 429n12

Gardiner, Jim, 73

Georgetown University, 7

Getchell, Will: on FS's culinary skills, 347

Gettysburg, Battle of (1863), 20–21

Gilman School (Baltimore, Maryland): football team (1962), 37; FS at, 7, 34, 36, 37–39

Gingrich, Newt: US federal government's bailout of Mexico (1995) and, 253–54, 385

Gingrich Revolution, 247

Glenn, John: in Keating S&L scandal, 142

Goddard, Samuel Pearson, Jr., 132

Goddard, Terry: in 1990 Arizona gubernatorial election, 103, 121, 124–25, 126–27, 130, 131–35, 138–40, 145–47; in 1994 Arizona gubernatorial election, 236, 239; Camelback Esplanade and, 73, 78, 80; financial allegations against, 145–46; FS compared to, 131–33; political ideals of, 132; as potential candidate in 1994 Arizona gubernatorial election, 208, 214

Goldwater, Barry: in 1990 Arizona gubernatorial election, 102, 112, 115, 123, 134; Camelback Mountain preserve and, 1; Evan Mecham's recall and, 86; FS and, 90–91, 99; on FS as governor, 148; FS's support for, 7, 34, 38, 41, 45; Phoenix municipal reform and, 56; on Republican Party's future in Arizona, 98–99; retirement, 82; Richard Nixon's resignation and, 82

Goldwater, Don: in 2006 Arizona gubernatorial election, 455n5

Gordon, Frank X., Jr.: in 1990 Arizona gubernatorial election, 103

government waste: FS on (*see* Project SLIM)

Governor's Task Force on Educational Reform, 158–59

Gramm, Phil, 256, 258

Grand Canyon: Arizona's control over

considered, 270; closure of (1995), 264–67; closure of (1996), 268; George H. W. Bush hike of (1991), 173–75

Gray, Edwin J., 143

Great Salt River Cleanup (1993), *200*, 201

Greater Phoenix Leadership, 272

Greene, John: in 2006 Arizona gubernatorial election, 455n5; on FS's legislative tactics, 193–94

Grogan, Cindy, *206*

Guanajuato, Guanajuato: as model for Mercado project, 218

Gullett, Wes, *206*; in 1994 Arizona gubernatorial election, 233; as governor's chief of staff, 204, 274; Grand Canyon's closure (1995) and, 264; on supply-side economics, 190–91

gun control: Paul Johnson on, 237; Sam Steiger on, 122; of teens, FS on, 202

Gutierrez, Alfredo: on FS's candidacy in 2006 Arizona gubernatorial election, 370

Gutierrez, Jaime: on budget cuts, 194; on FS's budget policy, 150, 152, 153

*Guv: The Emperor Strikes Back*, 288–89

*Guv: The Musical*, 287–89

H. C. Frick Coke Company, 11

Hambleton, John, 21, 23

Hamilton, Alexander: quoted by FS, 279

Hamilton, Art, 263; on FS's resignation, 334

Harvard University: FS at, 7, 8, 32, 39, 41–48, 49; Terry Goddard at, 132–33

Harvard Young Republicans Club, 45

hate-crime laws, 282

Hawes, Douglas: testimony at FS's criminal trial of, 314

Hawkins, Max: in 1990 Arizona gubernatorial election, 139

Hayden, Carl: Phoenix's growth and, 55

Hayek, Friedrich: classical liberalism of, 43, 190; influence on FS of, 41–42, 90

Hayes, Peter, *181*; in 1990 Arizona gubernatorial election, 102, 111; as governor's chief of staff, 180–81, 183, 187, 204

Hayworth, J. D.: in 2006 Arizona gubernatorial election, 369, 372

hazardous waste, 119, 154, 155. *See also* ENSCO

Head Start Programs, 119

healthcare policy: of FS, 119, 196, 284; for indigent people, 191, 201, 204, 226–27, 251, 252, 280

Heiler, Jay, *183*, 336; in 1994 Arizona gubernatorial election, 233, 241; effectiveness of, 204; FS's criminal

indictment and, 277; FS's criminal justice policy and, 202, 209, 210–11; on FS's reelection chances, 209; as governor's chief of staff, 274; as governor's special assistant for policy development, 182–83, 204; on keeping FS on point, 226; at Phoenix Lights press conference, 287, 374; on same-sex marriage, 246; on tax policy, 257; on transsexual studies course at Northern Arizona University (NAU), 213

Hellon, Michael: on bid-rigging scandal, 273

Helm, Dave, 357

Hensley, Jim, 81

Heritage Fund, 230–31

Herstam, Chris, 178; resignation of, 180

HighGround: Copperstate Farms hired by, 383

Hirsch, Jerome: Camelback Esplanade and, 71, 269; FS sued by, 294–95

Homestead Steel Strike (1892), 10, 12–13

Honan, Raena: on FS's wildlife conservation policy, 259

Hook, John, 376

horse racing: Fife Symington Jr. and, 36; FS and, 36–37

Houston's (restaurant): Camelback Esplanade and, 92

Howard, Jim: on 1990 Arizona gubernatorial election, 141, 146

Huck, Lew, 59

Hughes, Mary: Mercado project and, 217–18

Hull, Jane, 150, *151*, *190*, 333, *371*, 428n5; as governor, 335, 346–47, 366–67; popular support for, 367; readiness to assume governorship of, 327

Hummingbird Defense Systems, 373

Hunt, Robert: testimony at FS's criminal trial of, 310

income tax: FS on, 201, 227–28, 244, 249, 252, 255, 270–71, 283; Matt Salmon's repeal initiative for, 342, 344–45; supply-side economics and, 189–90

indigent people: healthcare for, 191, 201, 204, 226–27, 251, 252, 280

Inverness (company), 62, 63

Iron Rail, the, 15

Japan: Arizona's trade with, 161, 162–64

Japanese: Arizona business community and, 84, 89–90; Camelback Esplanade financing and, 94; on FS's potential run for governor, 101–2

Japanese External Trade Organization:

representative in Arizona considered, 172
Jewett, Jack: on FS's candidacy in 2006 Arizona
     gubernatorial election, 369–70
Jirov, Rebecca, 389, 389–90
job training programs, 202, 251
joblessness. See unemployment
Johnson, Lydon Baines: Harvard students'
     support for, 41
Johnson, Paul, 194, 237; in 1994 Arizona
     gubernatorial election, 236–38, 239; as
     potential candidate in 1994 Arizona
     gubernatorial election, 205–6, 214
Johnson, William, 92
Johnstown Flood (1889), 10, 11–12
Jones, Elizabeth ("Betty"), 46
judicial abuse: FS on, 279
juror 161. See Cotey, Mary Jane (juror 161)
juvenile crime, 209, 210, 278

Kadomoto, Tom, 172
Kean, Leslie, 375, 376
Keating, Charles: S&L scandal of, 2, 104, 108–9,
     134, 142–43, 144, 176, 290, 292, 293
Keegan, Lisa Graham, 347; conservatives and,
     448n31; on FS's resignation, 334; school
     funding plan of, 327
Keewaydin Camp (Ontario, Canada), 47
Kemp, Jack, 147
Kendall, Margaret, 430n21; on bid-rigging
     scandal, 273
Kennedy, John F., 7, 8, 38
Kennedy, Joseph P.: Porcellian Club and, 45
Kennedy, Sandra: on FS's bankruptcy, 262
Kent State University: shootings at (1970), 56
Killian, Mark: on Grand Canyon's closure
     (1995), 266
Kimball, Richard, 83
Kimble, Mark: on FS's states' right approach,
     250
Kleindienst, Richard, 132
Kolbe, Jim: in 1990 Arizona gubernatorial
     election, 103, 110, 115, 115–16, 119
Kolbe, John: on David Schindler, 291; death,
     345; on FS's legislative record, 197; on FS's
     post-indictment transformation, 282; on
     FS's staff effectiveness, 204
Koory, Fred: in 1990 Arizona gubernatorial
     election, 103, 110, 110–11, 118, 120, 121, 122,
     124
Korrick, Ed, 69; Camelback Esplanade and, 71,
     72–73, 75–76, 80
Kunasek, Andy: fishing trips of, 387
Kyl, Jon: in 1990 Arizona gubernatorial

election, 110, 115

lacrosse: FS and, 8, 36, 37, 39, 41, 353
Laffer, Art: curve of, 189–91; on FS's sentencing,
     337
Landers, Jack, 144
Larry King Live, 376
Latinos: FS and, 88, 156, 161, 218; in Phoenix,
     56. See also Mercado project (Phoenix,
     Arizona)
Latter-day Saints (LDS) community: Evan
     Mecham's candidacy and, 121; on marijuana
     cultivation, 382, 384; Snowflake, Arizona,
     temple of, 383
law: considered as career for FS, 52, 58
Le Cordon Bleu College of Culinary Arts-
     Scottsdale, 361, 362; Arizona Culinary
     Institute (ACI) compared to, 376. See also
     Scottsdale Culinary Institute (SCI)
League of Cities and Towns debate (1990),
     130–31
lease-back plan. See Purchase and Lease-Back
     Plan
Leckie, George: acquittal of, 302; bid-
     rigging scandal of, 249, 272–73, 293, 302;
     controversies surrounding, 177–79, 195, 234,
     243; at FS's criminal trial, 302; resignation
     of, 180
legal defense fund: for FS, 203–4, 268
Leishman, Alexander, 13
Leite, Darren: Arizona Culinary Institute (ACI)
     and, 362, 363, 377–78; death, 378; Scottsdale
     Culinary Institute and, 360, 361
Leite, Elizabeth: Scottsdale Culinary Institute
     and, 360, 361
Levine, Bill, 63
Lewis, Donald, 94, 170; testimony at FS's
     criminal trial of, 309–10, 311
Lewis and Roca, 293
libertarianism: in Arizona, 129; John Buttrick
     and, 244, 245; Sam Steiger and, 121–22
Lincoln Property Company, 59, 60; FS at, 61–62
Lincoln Savings and Loan: dissolution of,
     108–9, 143
line-item veto: FS accused of abusing, 177
London, United Kingdom: FS in, 47
Long, John F.: Grand Canyon's closure (1995)
     and, 265
lottery policy, 160, 178, 180, 196, 230
Ludwig, Daniel K., 66, 106, 166; Camelback
     Esplanade and, 69, 71
Lujan, Manuel, 174; during George H. W.
     Bush's Grand Canyon hike (1991), 173–75

Luke Air Force Base (Phoenix, Arizona): FS
  stationed at, 49–50, 56; Phoenix Lights seen
  from, 286, 375; Phoenix's growth and, 55
Lulu (spider monkey), 25, 27, 28, 30
Lustberg, Arch, 76–77
Lynam, Terry: as FS's criminal attorney, 293,
  297, 304, 305, 307, 310, 311, 314, 316, 318, 319,
  321, 328, 331–32, 337, 338, 340, 341, 342–44,
  345–46, 347; FS's presumptive pardon and,
  2, 4, 5, 6, 9, 356; intelligence of, 439n9

MacDonald, Tim: on Phoenix Lights, 286
MacEachern, Doug: on FS's candidacy in 2006
  Arizona gubernatorial election, 369
Madison, Danny, 62, 63
Mallery, Richard, 60, 62, 64, *160*; America West
  bailout and, 160; on FS, 218
Manning, Mike: as attorney in FS's bankruptcy
  case, 275, 290, 295, 336, 351, 352–54, 357–58,
  364; on FS's candidacy in 2006 Arizona
  gubernatorial election, 369; on FS's wealth,
  295; on John Yeoman's death, 274; in
  Keating S&L scandal, 109; perception of,
  290
Maricopa County Superior Court, 388; FS's
  case before, 349
marijuana: criminal penalties for expanded,
  209; Fife Symington IV as grower of,
  380–86; legalization of, opposed by FS, 283,
  380; medical, 280, 380, 382; recreational,
  385. *See also* Proposition 200
Marsh, Jim: Charles Schwab & Co. job growth
  and, 262–63
Martin, Steve, 365
Martin Luther King Jr. Day (MLK Day)
  holiday: in Arizona, debate surrounding,
  84–85, 147, 155, 187, 193, 194–95, 198, 232, 268
mass-transit projects, 251, 282, 284. *See also*
  Proposition 400
Mayorkas, Alejandro: on refiling charges
  against FS, 3, 348–49, 351, 355
McCain, Cindy, 81; at FS's criminal trial, 301
McCain, John: in 1994 Arizona gubernatorial
  election, 234, *235*; in 1996 US presidential
  election, 256, 258; 2020 election to fill
  vacated Senate seat of, 391; at California
  condor release ceremony, 281; Donald
  Trump and, 390; early political career
  of, 81–83, 102, 232; FS and, 82–83; on FS's
  candidacy for governor in 1990, 110; at FS's
  criminal trial, 301; in Keating S&L scandal,
  2, 108, 142, 143, 144, 292, 293; moving up
  Arizona's presidential primary and, 256;

Phoenix Lights and, 287; poll numbers of,
  176; as Republican Party golden boy, 82, 278
McFarland, Ernest: Phoenix's growth and, 55
McInturff, Bill: in 1990 Arizona gubernatorial
  election, 135
McMorgan & Co., 315–16, 318, 351–52, 357
McNally, Michael: recall of FS initiated by, 176
McVeigh, Timothy, 301
Mead, Lake: lowering of, 303
Mecham, Evan, *85*, 149, 277; in 1986 Arizona
  gubernatorial election, 83–84; in 1990
  Arizona gubernatorial election, 110, 111,
  115, 117, 118, 120, 121, 122, 123–26, 130, 131; FS
  on, 125; as governor, 84–88; impeachment
  and removal of, 87, 97, 276; legacy of, 91,
  98, 128–29, 153, 156, 176; political base of,
  122, 176, 282; on Proposition 102, 278; recall
  movement against, 86–88; satirized, 288–89
medically needy, medically indigent (MNMI)
  program, 191
Mejia, Luis: as FS's criminal attorney, 293;
  thoughtfulness of, 439n9
Mellon, Thomas, 11
Mellon Bank, 306
mental illness policy: of FS, 153, 191, 196
MeraBank, 146
Mercado project (Phoenix, Arizona), 89, 164,
  215–33; financing of, 109, 260–61, 275, 304,
  314–16, 318, 349, 350, 351, 352, 357, 358
Mercantile Bank, 295–96
Merrill, Bruce: on 1994 Arizona gubernatorial
  election, 244; on crime, 228; on FS's
  political pragmatism, 187; on FS's poll
  numbers, 155, 176, 177
Metzenbaum, Howard, 143–46
Mexico: Arizona's trade with, 155, 159, 161–62,
  163, 202, 271, 283; Childs Frick's scientific
  expedition to, 16; drug traffic from, 117; FS's
  greenhouses in, 374, 381; independence day
  of, celebrated at Mercado, 222; Mercado
  modeled on cities in, 215, 218; US federal
  government bailout of (1995), 252–54, 385
Mexico City: Arizona trade office established
  in, 161
Meyer, Paul: testimony at FS's criminal trial
  of, 317
Middle Income Tax Reduction Act (1994), 227
Milhon, Kendall: testimony at FS's criminal
  trial of, 314
military: Phoenix's growth and, 54–55; FS in,
  44–45, 49–52, 58. *See also* Air Force; *specific
  conflicts*
Miller, Eric: on media coverage of FS's criminal

trial, 299–300
Miller, Herb, 62
mining policy, 229
mining royalties, 212
Minnesota: as model for Arizona's charter
    school program, 192
Mirage Crossings (North Scottsdale, Arizona),
    363
Mistassini, Lake, 39
Mofford, Rose, 89, 371; in 1990 Arizona
    gubernatorial election, 115, 121; as governor,
    87–88, 97–98, 102–3, 111
Montini, E. J.: on FS, 112, 279; on FS's criminal
    trial, 300; on FS's record on crime, 211; on
    similarities between candidates in 1990
    Arizona gubernatorial election, 132; on tax
    cuts (1995), 255
Morris, Robert, 19
Moyes, Jerry: Arizona Culinary Institute (ACI)
    financed by, 363

Napolitano, Janet, 293, 347; in 2002 Arizona
    gubernatorial election, 369; FS on, as
    governor, 370–71; Grand Canyon's closure
    (1995) and, 265; public support for, 370
Nassau County Museum of Art, 16
National Football League (NFL): in Martin
    Luther King Jr. Day controversy, 85–86, 147,
    187, 195, 198
National Governors' Association: 1995 meeting
    of, 253, 427n22
Native Americans: gambling on reservations of,
    184–87, 240, 258, 280, 328
NatureSweet: greenhouses of, 382, 383
Neddie (horse), 36–37
Nellis Prison Camp (Nevada), 335; FS
    sentenced to be incarcerated at, 340;
    prisoner experience at, 337–38
Nelson, Jerry, 62, 64
New Democrat: Paul Johnson as, 237
news media: FS on, 277, 279, 345
Nielsen, George: on Ann Symington's
    liability for FS's debt, 294; as judge in FS's
    bankruptcy trial, 291, 294, 336, 351, 353–55,
    357, 358
Ninth Circuit Court of Appeals: FS's conviction
    appealed to, 3, 5, 342–44, 345–47, 348, 349
Nissan, 163
Nixon, Richard: in 1964 US presidential
    election, 34; presumptive pardon of, 2;
    resignation of, 82
NoOn400 campaign, 371–72
North American Free Trade Agreement

(NAFTA), 162, 253; Arizona's benefits from,
    163, 202, 271, 275; FS on, 202, 205, 283
Northern Arizona University (NAU):
    transsexual studies class at, 212–13
Norton, John, 63, 121
Novak, Robert, 115
Novotny, Jean: on Mercado project, 220, 222

O'Connor, Sandra Day, 346
Oklahoma City bombing (1995), 268, 301
Olin, Franklin, 64
Olin, Spencer Truman, 64
Olin Corporation, 64
One Renaissance Square (Phoenix, Arizona),
    216
O'Neil, Mike: on FS's polling numbers, 270
Ontario, Canada: FS in, 30–31
Organization of American States (OAS): FS
    given award by, 254
Organization of Arab Petroleum Exporting
    Countries (OAPEC): embargo of (1973), 61
Out of the Blue (documentary), 374–76

Pan American World Airways, 2, 16, 21, 23–24
Parents Advocating Choice in Education
    (PACE), 159
Pattea, Clinton, 185
Patterson, Tom, 276–77; on FS's resignation, 334
Peace Corps, 38
Pearson, Rita, 157
Peirce, Neal: on Phoenix's downtown, 216
People for the Ethical Treatment of Animals
    (PETA), 373
Phoenix, Arizona: Cold War growth of, 53–56,
    68; counterculture in, 56; downtown
    revitalization of, 215–33; economic
    inequality in, 56–57; extreme heat in, 258;
    municipal reform in, 56; pollution in, 56;
    racial division in, 56; urban sprawl in, 56;
    vice in, 55–56
Phoenix Lights (1997), 285–87, 374–76
Phoenix Suns: twenty-fifth anniversary
    celebration, 200
Pickett, George E., 20
Pittsburgh, Pennsylvania: economic
    importance of, 11
Pitzl, Mary Jo: on 1990 Arizona gubernatorial
    election, 146; on Annette Alvarez, 179–80;
    on FS as governor, 155, 156; on FS's legal
    defense fund, 268
Pogue, Mack, 61
poor people. See indigent people
Porcellian Club (Harvard University), 45–46

Poscharsky, Tom, 383, 384
Price, Richard: on Phoenix Lights, 286
Princeton University: Childs Frick at, 14;
    FS consider attending, 38–39; John Fife
    Symington Jr. at, 21, 23, 64; John Pritzlaff
    at, 64
prison reform policy: of FS, 119, 152, 158, 228
Pritzlaff, Ann. *See* Symington, Ann Pritzlaff
    (second wife of FS)
Pritzlaff, John, 64, 72; at FS's criminal trial, 300,
    321, 340
Pritzlaff, Mary Dell, 64, *320*; at FS's criminal
    trial, 300, 307, 319–20, 321, 340
private property rights: FS on, 123
Project SLIM, 153–54, 178, 226, 293; bid-rigging
    of contracts of, 272–73, 274; George Leckie
    credited for revitalizing, 180; as issue in
    1994 Arizona gubernatorial election, 234;
    public reaction to, 195; tax cuts and, 191,
    193, 196
property taxes, 201, 271, 276,327
Proposition 102, 278–80
Proposition 103, 133–34, 138
Proposition 105, 128–30; FS on, 129–30
Proposition 106, 90, 128. *See also* "English
    Only" movement
Proposition 200, 380
Proposition 400, 371–72
Public Enemy: on Evan Mecham, 85
public speaking: FS and, 45
Pulitzer, Michael, 64
Pulliam, Eugene, 56
Purchase and Lease-Back Plan, 119, 123–24, 153;
    Democrats on, 157–58

Quayle, Dan, *136*, 147, 412n19
Quayle, Marilyn: as potential candidate in 2006
    Arizona gubernatorial election, 455n5

racial tensions: in Arizona, 194–95
Ragan, John: Covance public relations
    campaign and, 372–73
Rahall, Nick, 212
Ralston, Joanne, 76
Ramada Inc.: Mercado project and, 220
Rand, Frank, 59
Rawson, William F.: on FS's bankruptcy, 262
Reagan, Ronald, *136*, 141; supply-side
    economics and, 189–90
Reagor, Catherine, 331
real estate: FS as professional in, 58–80
"Red Light Row" (Phoenix, Arizona), 55
Red Mountain Freeway, 251

Reilly, William K., *174*
Reinhart, Mary K., 193
Remuda Oil, 63
Renzi, Rick: in 2006 Arizona gubernatorial
    election, 372
Republican National Committee (RNC): in
    1990 Arizona gubernatorial election, 114–15
Republican Party (Arizona): FS and, 81
Republican Party (Maryland): Symingtons and,
    34, 36
Reserve Officer Training Corps (ROTC), 15; FS
    in, 44–45, 49
Resolution Trust Corporation (RTC), 107–8;
    below-market sales by, 305, 308; Southwest
    Savings and Loan investigation of, 165–72,
    184, 202–3
Reynolds, Quinny: at FS's criminal trial, 306–7,
    311, 312, 313, 321
Rhodes, John, 81–82, 88, 98, 180; in 1990
    Arizona gubernatorial election, 130; on FS
    as governor, 148
Richards, Brian, 383; on Copperstate Farms, 385
Riebel, Joyce, *206*; testimony at FS's criminal
    trial of, 303–6, 310, 314, 323
Riegle, Don: in Keating S&L scandal, 142
Rigby, Suzanne, 165
Rios, Pete, *190*; on FS's vacation timing, 194
Ritz-Carlton Hotel: at Camelback Esplanade, 3,
    78, 92, 167, 353
Robb, Robert: on 1990 Arizona gubernatorial
    election, 141–42; on Jane Hull as governor,
    367
Rockefeller, John D.: wealth of, 10, 13
Rockefeller, Larry, 59
Romley, Rick: in 2006 Arizona gubernatorial
    election, 369, 372; on FS, 279; satirized, 288
Roosevelt, Franklin Delano: Porcellian Club
    and, 45
Roosevelt, Theodore: Porcellian Club and, 45
Rose, Pete, 2, 292, 293
Rosenzweig, Harry, 60
Rouse Company, 216
Ruggiero, Lew, 334; assault upon, 319–20
Rupert River: canoe trip down, 39–40

Salinas de Gotari, Carlos, 161, *162*
Salmon, Matt: in 2002 Arizona gubernatorial
    election, 369; income tax repeal initiative
    of, 342, 344–45
Salomon Brothers: Camelback Esplanade
    financing and, 94
Salt River: Phoenix's growth and, 53; pollution
    in, 118. *See also* Great Salt River Cleanup

(1993)

Salt River Project, 53, 111, 180

Salt River Reservation: gambling on, 280

same-sex marriage: as issue in the 1994 Arizona gubernatorial election, 245–46, 247

Santan Freeway, 251

savings and loan (S&L) industry: crash of (late 1980s), 104–9; in Phoenix, 54; scandals of, FS on, 117. See also specific S&Ls

Schindler, David, 291; on FS's presumptive pardon, 356-57; as prosecutor in FS's criminal trial, 5–6, 291–92, 296–98, 301–2, 304, 305–6, 307, 310, 315, 317, 322–25, 328, 329, 331–32, 336, 340, 343, 344, 346, 348, 349

Schloeder, Nick, 36

Schoch, Randy: on FS's culinary career, 364

school choice, 158–59, 229; as issue in the 1994 Arizona gubernatorial election, 244, 245. See also charter schools

school funding: FS on, 153, 191, 196; as issue in 1990 Arizona gubernatorial election, 123, 133–34; Lisa Graham Keegan's plan for, 327

school vouchers, 250, 252; Eddie Basha on, 245; FS on, 158, 159, 191, 245, 250, 270, 271, 281, 284

Schulz, Bill: in 1986 Arizona gubernatorial election, 83–84

Schwarzenegger, Arnold, 137, 156

Scotland: Symington family origins in, 17, 19

Scott, Hugh, 82

Scottsdale, Arizona: Arizona Culinary Institute (ACI) located in, 362; Franco's Trattoria in, 349, 365; greenhouses in, 382; Symington home in, 49; Thaifoon restaurant placed in, 364

Scottsdale Centre, 308–9

Scottsdale Culinary Institute (SCI), 339, 344, 345, 346; FS as student at, 360–62. See also Le Cordon Bleu College of Culinary Arts-Scottsdale

Scottsdale Sunrise Rotary Club, 82

Scranton, William, 34

Seville Center (Scottsdale, Arizona), 71

Shady Side Academy (Pittsburgh, Pennsylvania): Childs Frick at, 14

Shanahan, Deborah: on Camelback Esplanade's publicity campaign, 73; on Mercado project, 219

Shapiro, Ellie, 58–59, 60

Shark Tank: Symington Group working environment compared to, 373

Shimizu Land Corp.: Camelback Esplanade financing and, 94–96, 283; on FS's potential

run for governor, 101–2

Shore, Bill, 166, 168

Shull, Robert: as FS's bankruptcy attorney, 290–91, 295, 336, 350, 351–52, 353, 354, 357–58

Sierra Club: on FS's wildlife conservation policy, 154, 259

Skipworth, Lelia Wayles, 21

Slive, Seymour, 46

Smith, Jay, 82; in 1990 Arizona gubernatorial election, 102, 110, 111, 115, 116, 119, 124, 125, 130, 131, 135, 142, 144, 145; Peter Hayes recommended as governor's chief of staff by, 180; on Resolution Trust Corporation investigation of Southwest Savings and Loan, 165, 166

Smith Florez, Jan: in 2006 Arizona gubernatorial election, 455n5

Snell, Frank, 56

Snell & Wilmer, 95, 260

Snowball (dog), 30, 30

Sorensen, Ted, 38

Soto, Olga, 221

South Fork Fishing and Hunting Club, 11–12

Southwest Savings and Loan Association, 141; Camelback Esplanade and, 69; FS and, 54, 60; insolvency of, 104; as issue in 1990 Arizona gubernatorial election, 143–45; Resolution Trust Corporation (RTC) investigation of, 165–72, 184, 202–3

Soviet Union: Barry Goldwater and Fife Symington Jr. on, 34

Springer, Carol, 347

Square One development (Phoenix, Arizona), 215, 216–17

St. Jacques Miles, Candice, 287–89; on FS, 289

Star (horse), 28

Starr, Hale: on FS's criminal trial, 326

State Lake Improvement Fund (SLIF), 230–31

State Long-Term Improved Management Plan. See Project SLIM

State of the State addresses: of 1991, 189–90, 193; of 1993, 201–2; of 1994, 224–31; of 1995, 249; of 1996, 268, 270–71; of 1997, 281; of 2002, 367

state workers: pay for, 251, 252, 271, 282

states' rights: FS on, 123, 213, 229–30, 241, 249, 252, 256, 260, 270. See also federal overreach

Steckner, Susie: on Phoenix Lights, 286

Steele, Carol, 222

Steiger, Sam: in 1990 Arizona gubernatorial election, 116, 118, 120, 121–22, 123–25; political ideals of, 122

Steinbrenner, George, 292

Stillman Farm, 15

Stone, Roger, 115

Strand, Roger: as judge in FS's criminal trial, 296–98, 299, 301, 315, 319, 325, 328, 329, 330, 331–32, 335, 337, 338, 339, 340, 341, 343, 345, 347; on merit of FS's appeal, 342

Strongin, Camilla, 366; Covance public relations campaign and, 372–73; on Proposition 400, 371; on Symington Group work environment, 373

Stuart, William, 20

Success by Six initiative, 229, 237

Sun Devil Stadium (Tempe, Arizona), 85; Super Bowl XXX awarded to, 198

Super Bowl XXVII (1993): move of, 85–86, 147, 198. *See also* National Football League (NFL)

Super Bowl XXX (1996), 258, 268; awarded to Sun Devil Stadium, 198

supply-side economics, 189–91; 1995 tax cuts and, 255

swimming: FS and, 8

Symington, Angeline Stuart, 20

Symington, Ann Pritzlaff (second wife of FS), 89, 135, 137, 264, 355, 356; in 1990 Arizona gubernatorial election, 116–17, 134, 139, 143–44; Arizona Culinary Institute (ACI) and, 363; bankruptcy deposition of, 275; church work of, 348; courtship and marriage of, 64–65; divorce of, 387–89; on FS's criminal indictment, 277; at FS's criminal trial, 300, 321, 332, 339, 341, 346; on FS's potential run for governor, 101; FS's resignation and, 334; in Great Salt River Cleanup (1993), 201; inherited wealth of, 261; liability for FS's debt of, 294; Phoenix Lights event and, 375, 376; public relations training of, 76–77; in Resolution Trust Corporation investigation, 171–72; as restaurateur, 347; satirized, 288; as Scottsdale Culinary Institute student, 360; as Thaifoon investor, 364

Symington, Arabella (sister of FS), 21, 26, 32; FS and, 31–32

Symington, Evelyn, 21

Symington, Harry, 21

Symington, Helen Clay (sister of FS), 26, 32; birth, 24; FS and, 32; at FS's criminal trial, 340

Symington, Fife, III (FS; subject of biography): animals and, 25–29; appendicitis of, 25; bankruptcy of, 261, 268–69; bankruptcy proceedings against, 336, 351–55, 357–58;

Bill Clinton's life saved by, 8; birth, 24; cancers of, 363–64, 389; childhood of, 25–32; conflict-of-interest allegations against, 169–70; considered for Arizona governor, 99–103; criminal trial of (1997), 3–4, 276–77, 299–326, 328–35; divorces, 60, 387–89; fishing trips of, 387; on governor's power, 256; inauguration of, 148; Marsie and, 31; military service of, 44–45, 49–52; outreach by, 155–56; personal finances of, 260–62, 269–70, 272; pictured, 26, 27, 28, 29, 30, 42, 44, 50, 51, 70, 89, 113, 114, 135, 136, 137, 149, 151, 162, 174, 181, 190, 200, 206, 207, 211, 221, 225, 227, 237, 259, 288, 333, 371, 377, 381, 388; as pilot, 45, 374; political ideals of, 34, 36, 41–42, 111, 114, 117–19, 132 (*see also* Symington Plan); presumptive pardon for, 2–3, 4–5, 6, 8–9, 355–57; public support for, 154–55, 164, 165, 175, 176, 187, 188, 191, 199, 213–14, 227, 239, 255–56, 257, 264, 270, 276, 318; resignation of, 333–34; sentencing of, 339–41; siblings and, 31–32; staffing by, 157, 177–83, 187–88, 204, 205, 208, 248; as student, 32–34, 36–48; testimony at own bankruptcy proceedings of, 352–54; testimony at own criminal trial of, 320–25; travel of, 381; weddings of, 48, 65

Symington, Fife, IV ("Fifie"; son of FS), 50, 58, 135, 374, 381; at FS's criminal trial, 332, 340, 341

Symington, James, 19

Symington, John ("Jack"; grandfather of FS), 21

Symington, John Fife, Jr. (father of FS), 2, 21–24; engagement and marriage, 16–17; as father, 31, 36–37; on FS, 31; at FS's criminal trial, 321; New York move to, 25; pictured, 18, 22, 23, 28, 35, 381; temperament of, 31

Symington, Leslie Barker (first wife of FS), 47–48; divorce, 60

Symington, Martie (brother of FS), 26; FS and, 31

Symington, Richard (son of FS), 135

Symington, Scott (son of FS), 58; at FS's criminal trial, 332

Symington, Stuart (US senator from Missouri; cousin of FS), 45; FS's Air Force career and, 49, 50

Symington, Thomas Alexander, 19–20

Symington, Thomas of, 17, 19

Symington, Tom (son of FS), 135; at FS's criminal trial, 339, 341

Symington, Whitney (daughter of FS), 135; at FS's criminal trial, 339; on FS's potential run

for governor, 101
Symington, William Stuart ("Stuart"), 20–21
*Symington: Four Short Tragic Stories* (campaign
    book), 243
Symington Company, 63–64, 65–66, 168;
    Camelback Esplanade and, 69, 72; Mercado
    project and, 219, 222
Symington family, 17–24
Symington Group: capital fundraising by,
    373; Covance public relations campaign
    fashioned by, 372–73; founding of, 365; FS's
    focus on, 372; work environment at, 373
Symington Plan, 117–19, 184, 189, 202, 226, 250,
    252, 270, 370; Jaime Gutierrez on, 153–54;
    Jane Hull and, 367; Project SLIM and, 195;
    public perception of, 127
Symington Private Equity Group, 373; founding
    of, 365

T. H. Symington Company, 21
Tagliabue, Paul, 198
Talley Industries, 59–60
Tashima, A. Wallace, 346, 347
tax policy: of FS, 191, 196, 201–2, 227–28, 250,
    254–55, 257, 270–71, 276, 283. *See also specific
    types of tax*
Tax Reform Act (1986), 106, 117
Teen Democrats of Maryland, 7, 38
Teets, John: America West bailout and, 160
Thaifoon (Scottsdale restaurant), 364
Thailand: FS in, 50–52, 58, 321
Thatcher, Margaret, 190
Theodore Roosevelt Dam: Phoenix's growth
    and, 53
Thompson, Dave: on Proposition 400, 371
Thompson, Noel: testimony at FS's criminal
    trial of, 307, 317
Thunderbird Field (Glendale, Arizona):
    Phoenix's growth and, 54–55
timber use policy, 229
Todd, Randy, 168, 317; 5080 Building and, 65;
    Arizona Culinary Institute (ACI) and, 363,
    378–79; Camelback Esplanade and, 66, 69,
    79, 80, 92, 95, 101, 102; on FS's focus on
    Camelback Esplanade project, 71; Mercado
    project and, 217–18, 219, 220; testimony at
    FS's criminal trial of, 318
Tomey, Dick: as Thaifoon investor, 364
tourism policy: of FS, 152, 154, 161, 258, 283
Toyota, 163
trade policy: of FS, 155, 161–63, 283
Trammell Crow Company, 59, 60
transexual studies: Northern Arizona

University (NAU) class about, 212–13
transportation policy, 151, 282, 284
travel: FS criticized for excessive, 164, 172
Travelers Insurance Co., 308–9
trickle-down economics. *See* supply-side
    economics
Trippe, Juan Terry, 21, 23
Tropiano, Dolores, 362
Trump, Donald: FS on, 390
truth in sentencing, 202, 209, 210, 228
Tucson, Arizona, 64; FS's support in, 103;
    Phoenix compared to, 54
Turner, William Cochrane: Camelback
    Esplanade financing and, 94
Tusk & Trunk Club (Phoenix, Arizona), 60, 81
Tuttle, Steve, 232; on FS's political power,
    248–49
Tyndall Air Force Base (Florida): FS stationed
    at, 48, 49

Udorn Air Force Base (Thailand): FS at, 50–52,
    58, 82
unclaimed property, 224
unemployment, 194, 228, 251, 317; in Navajo
    County, Arizona, Copperstate Farms and,
    384
Union Memorial Hospital (Baltimore,
    Maryland), 37
*United States v. Brown,* 343
*United States v. John Fife Symington III,* 3–4,
    276–77, 299–326, 328–35
*United States v. Ross,* 343
Urban Village Concept, 68; Camelback
    Esplanade and, 69, 74, 78
Usdane, Bob, 86

Valley National Bank: FS accused of defrauding,
    276, 295, 297, 304–5, 314, 324, 338; Martha
    Howard Frick Symington and, 295; verdict
    about FS's dealings with, 332
Van Der Werf, Martin: on FS's criminal
    indictment, 276–77
Vega Petroleum: FS at, 62–63, 64, 381
Vietnam War: FS in, 49–52, 58; FS on, 43;
    Harvard students' reactions to, 43–44,
    45–46
Voter Protection Act (1998), 280, 380, 382

Waddell, Paul, *207*
Wadsworth, James S., 21
Wald, Jonathan: on Phoenix Lights, 286
Walker, Dave: on media coverage of FS's
    criminal trial, 334

Wallace, George, 34

War of 1812, 20

Warner, Carolyn: in 1986 Arizona gubernatorial election, 83–84

Waters, John, 33–34

Webb, Del. *See* Del E. Webb Construction Company

Weinberger, Casper: presumptive pardon of, 2

Welborn, Michael, 337

welfare policy: discussed at National Governors' Association meeting (1995), 253; of FS, 153, 251

Western Governors' Association: FS as chairman of, 205

Whitman, Christine Todd: on FS, 248

Wilcox, Mary Rose, 79

wildfires (1996), 274–75, 276

wildlife: conservation, 251, 259, 271, 282; habitats, funding for, 196. *See also* Endangered Species Act (1973)

Wilkinson, Bud: on Camelback Esplanade planning hearings, 79

Will, George: on Paul Johnson's candidacy in the 1994 Arizona gubernatorial election, 237–38

Willey, Keven, 228; on Ed Fox's resignation, 260; on Eddie Basha's chances in the 1994 Arizona gubernatorial election, 241; on FS's budget, 152–53; on FS's criminal trial, 313; on FS's handling of the transsexual studies course at NAU, 213; on FS's hypocrisy, 380; on FS's legal defense fund controversy, 203–4; on FS's mental state, 280; on FS's promise keeping, 214; on FS's staff effectiveness, 204; on FS's tax policy, 257; on FS's veto of Environmental Species Act implementation bill, 257; on Terry Goddard's chances in the 1994 Arizona gubernatorial election, 236

Williams, Frank, 1

Williams, Kimberly, 185

Williams Field (Mesa, Arizona): Phoenix's growth and, 55

Wilson, Robert: Arizona Culinary Institute (ACI) and, 361, 362, 363, 377–79, 390, 391; as culinary instructor, 361

Wilson, Steve: on Eddie Basha's chances in the 1994 Arizona gubernatorial election, 239; on FS's bankruptcy proceedings, 352; on FS's criminal trial, 315, 326; on FS's "liberal fever," 210

Wonder, Stevie: on Evan Mecham, 85

Wong, Jean: Randy Todd on, 318; testimony at FS's criminal trial of, 316–17

Woods, Grant, 82, 168; in 1994 Arizona gubernatorial election, 234; in 2006 Arizona gubernatorial election, 372; conservatives and, 448n31; FS and, 256; on FS's political future, 348; on FS's resignation, 334; on Native American casinos, 185, 186; as potential candidate in 1994 Arizona gubernatorial election, 214; satirized, 288

World War I: Childs Frick in, 15

World War II: effect on Arizona of, 53, 54, 104–5; effect on Baltimore of, 34

Wrigley, Katherine: testimony at FS's criminal trial of, 313–14, 317

Wrigley family: Friedman parcel (Phoenix, Arizona) owned by, 59–60

Yeoman, John: bid-rigging scandal of, 249, 272–73; blamed for FS's financial transgressions, 293, 319; death, 273–74, 319; FS on, 274; FS's financial statements coded by, 313–14; knowledge of FS's accounts of, 317

Youth to Youth Pilot Project, 7, 38

Zedillo, Ernesto, 253

Zeidler, Eberhard: Camelback Esplanade and, 71–72, 73, 74, 77, 79

Zemlyn Porches, 25, 29; Barry Goldwater fundraising events at, 34